Lecture Notes in Computer Science 8565

Commenced Publication in 1973
Founding and Former Series Editors:
Gerhard Goos, Juris Hartmanis, and Jan van Leeuwen

More information about this series at http://www.springer.com/series/7410

Hyang-Sook Lee · Dong-Guk Han (Eds.)

Information Security and Cryptology – ICISC 2013

16th International Conference
Seoul, Korea, November 27–29, 2013
Revised Selected Papers

 Springer

Editors
Hyang-Sook Lee
EWHA Womans University
Seoul
Korea, Republic of (South Korea)

Dong-Guk Han
Kookmin University
Seoul
Korea, Republic of (South Korea)

ISSN 0302-9743   ISSN 1611-3349   (electronic)
ISBN 978-3-319-12159-8   ISBN 978-3-319-12160-4   (eBook)
DOI 10.1007/978-3-319-12160-4

Library of Congress Control Number: 2014953265

LNCS Sublibrary: SL4 – Security and Cryptology

Springer Cham Heidelberg New York Dordrecht London

Printed on acid-free paper

Springer is part of Springer Science+Business Media (www.springer.com)

Preface

ICISC 2013, the 16th International Conference on Information Security and Cryptology, was held in Seoul, Korea, during November 27–29, 2013. This year's conference was hosted by the KIISC (Korea Institute of Information Security and Cryptology) jointly with the NSRI (National Security Research Institute), in cooperation with the Ministry of Science, ICT and Future Planning (MSIP).

The aim of this conference is to provide an international forum for the latest results of research, development, and applications in the field of information security and cryptology. This year we received 126 submissions from more than 20 countries and were able to accept 31 papers from 14 countries, with an acceptance rate of 24.6 %. The review and selection processes were carried out by the Program Committee (PC) members, 86 prominent experts worldwide, via the IACR review system. Submissions by Program Committee members received at least five reviews. The review process was double-blind, and conflicts of interest were handled carefully.

The conference featured two invited talks: "Making NTRUEncrypt and NTRUSign as Secure as Worst-Case Problems over Ideal Lattices" by Damien Stehlé and "Introduction to Quantum Cryptography and Its Technology Trends" by Jeong Woon Choi. We thank the invited speakers for their kind acceptance and nice presentations.

We would like to thank all authors who submitted their papers to ICISC 2013 and all of the 86 PC members. It was a truly great experience to work with such talented and hard-working researchers. We also appreciate the external reviewers for assisting the PC members in their particular areas of expertise. Finally, we would like to thank all attendees for their active participation and the organizing team who nicely managed this conference. We look forward to seeing you again at next year's ICISC.

August 2014

Hyang-Sook Lee
Dong-Guk Han

The 16th International Conference on Information Security and Cryptology ICISC 2013

November 27–29, 2013
New Millennium Hall, Konkuk University, Seoul, Korea

Hosted by
Korea Institute of Information Security and Cryptology (KIISC)
National Security Research Institute (NSRI)

Supported by
Ministry of Science, ICT and Future Planning (MSIP)
Electronics and Telecommunications Research Institute (ETRI)
Korea Internet & Security Agency (KISA)

Organization

General Chairs

Sukwoo Kim — Hansei University, Korea
Seok-Yeol Kang — NSRI, Korea

Program Co-chairs

Hyang-Sook Lee — Ewha Womans University, Korea
Dong-Guk Han — Kookmin University, Korea

Program Committee

Gail-Joon Ahn	Arizona State University, USA
Joonsang Baek	Khalifa University, UAE
Yoo-Jin Baek	Woosuk University, Korea
Alex Biryukov	University of Luxembourg, Luxembourg
Andrey Bogdanov	Technical University of Denmark, Denmark
Zhenfu Cao	Shanghai Jiao Tong University, China
Aldar Chan	Institute for Infocomm Research (I2R), A*STAR, Singapore
Kefei Chen	Hangzhou Normal University, China
Dooho Choi	ETRI, Korea
Yongwha Chung	Korea University, Korea
Nora Cuppens	TELECOM Bretagne, France
Paolo D'Arco	Università degli Studi di Salerno, Italy
Rafael Dowsley	Karlsruhe Institute of Technology, Germany
Shaojing Fu	National University of Defence Technology, China
Matthew D. Green	Johns Hopkins University, USA
Johann Großschädl	University of Bristol, UK
JaeCheol Ha	Hoseo University, Korea
Martin Hell	Lund University, Swede
Swee-Huay Heng	Multimedia University, Malaysia
Dowon Hong	Kongju National University, Korea
Jin Hong	Seoul National University, Korea
Jiankun Hu	University of New South Wales, Australia
Jung Yeon Hwang	ETRI, Korea
Eul Gyu Im	Hanyang University, Korea
David Jao	University of Waterloo, Canada
Chong Hee Kim	Brightsight, The Netherlands
Dong Kyue Kim	Hanyang University, Korea

Jorge L. Villar	Universitat Politecnica de Catalunya, Spain
Hongxia Wang	Southwest Jiaotong University, China
Yongzhuang Wei	Guilin University of Electronic Technology, China
Wenling Wu	Institute of Software Chinese Academy of Sciences, China
Toshihiro Yamauchi	Okayama University, Japan
Wei-Chuen Yau	Multimedia University, Malaysia
Ching-Hung Yeh	Far East University, Taiwan
Sung-Ming Yen	National Central University, Taiwan
Yongjin Yeom	Kookmin University, Korea
Jeong Hyun Yi	Soongsil University, Korea
Kazuki Yoneyama	NTT Secure Platform Laboratories, Japan
Myungkeun Yoon	Kookmin University, Korea
Dae Hyun Yum	Myongji University, Korea
Aaram Yun	Ulsan National Institute of Science and Technology, Korea
Fangguo Zhang	Sun Yat-sen University, China

Organization Chair

| Changho Seo | Kongju National University, Korea |

Organizing Committee

Daesung Kwon	NSRI, Korea
Daeyoub Kim	Soowon University, Korea
Keecheon Kim	Konkuk University, Korea
Kihyo Nam	Umlogics, Korea
Heuisu Ryu	Gyeongin National University of Education, Korea
Howon Kim	Pusan National University, Korea
Junbeom Hur	Chung Ang University, Korea
Okyeon Yi	Kookmin University, Korea
Seokwon Jeong	Mokpo National University, Korea
Sungbeom Pan	Chosun University, Korea
Young-Ho Park	Sejong Cyber University, Korea
Sanguk Shin	Pukyong National University, Korea

Contents

Security Protocol

Cyber Security

Public Key Cryptography

Secure Multiparty Computation

Privacy Assurances in Multiple Data-Aggregation Transactions

Kim Le[1(✉)], Parmesh Ramanathan[2], and Kewal K. Saluja[2]

[1] University of Canberra, Canberra, Australia
kim.le@canberra.edu.au
[2] University of Wisconsin-Madison, Madison, USA
{parmesh, saluja}@ece.wisc.edu

Abstract. In this paper, we propose a privacy-preserving algorithm for aggregating data in multiple transactions from a large number of users at a third-party application. The aggregation is performed using the most commonly used weighted sum function. The new algorithm has several novel features. First, we propose a method to generate a privacy-assurance certificate that can be easily verified by all users without significant computation effort. In particular, the computational complexity of verification does not grow with the number of users. Second, the proposed approach has a very desirable feature that users do not have to directly communicate with each other. Instead, they only communicate with the application. These features distinguish our approach from the existing research in literature.

Keywords: Secure multiparty computation · Third-party application · Privacy data assurance · Multiple data-aggregation transactions · Cryptosystems · Social network security

1 Introduction

With the growing popularity of mobile and social networking applications, there is commensurate growth in the number of third-party applications (TPA) whose services are based on the collection and aggregation of data from a large number of users. Traditionally, the data collected by these applications were often considered so sensitive that no user would have voluntarily shared them with anyone else. However, this perception has changed dramatically over the past years. Present day users are increasingly willing to share their sensitive information with TPA under the assurance that their data will be kept private. The focus of this paper is on privacy-assured data aggregation in third-party applications in multiple transactions.

This paper proposes algorithms for data aggregation through weighted sum (WSUM), which is a key step in many interesting computations. In the WSUM function, a third-party application A computes a weighted sum of users' private data without violating the following two privacy constraints: (i) each user's data is not revealed to either A or to other users, and (ii) the result and the weights used in the computation are proprietary to A.

H.-S. Lee and D.-G. Han (Eds.): ICISC 2013, LNCS 8565, pp. 3–19, 2014.
DOI: 10.1007/978-3-319-12160-4_1

At the first glance, it appears that the WSUM function can be implemented using secure multi-party computations (SMC) [1, 6, 17]. In SMC, a group of users collaboratively compute a pre-agreed function of users' private data without exposing their data to each other. For example, in the pioneering work by Yao [18], two users collaboratively determine whose data is larger without revealing their data to the other user. Since then, SMC algorithms have been developed for a variety of functions and problems such as multi-party auctions, electronic voting, insurance applications, wireless sensor network, and secure queries on medical databases [2, 4, 7, 9, 10, 12, 16]. There is explosive growth in SMC research, especially after the recent seminal work by Craig Gentry on fully-homomorphic encryption [5].

However, there are several key differences between SMC and the TPA scenario considered in this paper. First, in SMC, the users are in a collaborative environment and hence, they are willing to directly exchange messages with each other. In contrast, in the TPA scenario, the identity of the users participating in data aggregations is proprietary to the application and hence, the users are unable and/or unwilling to communicate directly with other users. Second, in the TPA scenario, the number of users involved in data aggregations may be very large, e.g., could be in tens of thousands. In contrast, SMC algorithms are typically designed for tens to hundreds of users and they usually do not scale well with the number of users. Third, unlike in SMC, there is no requirement for users in the TPA scenario to take on significant computation or communication burden; in particular in TPA scenario, the per-user computation and communication burden should not increase with the number of users. Finally, in the TPA scenario, the application may request a user to participate in multiple data aggregation transactions. Privacy assurances in such multiple transaction settings are typically not considered in SMC. Due to these salient differences, the conventional SMC algorithms are not well-suited for use in the TPA scenario. Hence, in this paper, we propose a new algorithm for the aggregation of multiple WSUM function transactions tailored for use in the TPA scenario.

More specifically, we focus on privacy assurances in settings where a user participates in multiple WSUM function transactions. When users participate in multiple data aggregations, a particular user's privacy can be compromised by transactions in which the user is not even a participant. To provide privacy assurances to all users in this setting, we rely on a novel certification-based approach, in which an application A generates a new verifiable certificate prior to the start of each transaction. A user performs simple computations on information contained in the certificate to satisfy himself/herself that the newly initiated transaction will not compromise his/her private data. If a user detects that his/her data will be compromised, he/she raises an alarm to stop other users from participating in the transaction. A key feature of this approach is that the computational effort to generate a certificate rests with A and not on individual users.

The rest of this paper is organized as follows. In Sect. 2, we first introduce a simple motivation example, and then formulate the problem addressed in this paper. Section 3 describes the proposed solutions for WSUM computations. Related research is discussed in Sect. 4. The paper concludes with Sect. 5.

2 Motivation and Problem Formulation

2.1 Motivation

Statistical surveys to determine shopping habits, political opinions, E-election results, etc. are becoming very prevalent. The following scenario explains how an insurance company may use the results of a survey on its clients' driving experience, and describes the characteristics of the survey.

Scenario: An insurance company wants to collect driving statistics on its clients to set premiums for its insurance policies, as well as to advise road authorities on optimal traffic settings. For example, the company wants to calculate the average distance from a traffic light at which drivers will start braking to stop their cars when the traffic light turns amber. A client is asked to send to the application the minimum distance at which he/she will decide to stop his/her car when he/she sees the traffic light turning amber; otherwise he/she will continues to drive the car through the traffic light.

Characteristics: There are several interesting characteristics in this survey:

- *Incentive to participate:* The company is willing to give some discount to the clients who participate in the survey. The utilitarian value of the survey results enables the company to set its competitive policies.
- *Limited computational burden:* The amount of computation and communication performed by any client does not increase with the number of involved clients.
- *Privacy requirement:* Clients do not want to unveil their private data. The application considers its clients' data differently with various weights based on the information like ages, driving experience, etc. These weights are the company's proprietary, and are not exposed to the clients.
- *Multiple transactions:* The survey may be repeated with different weight sets.

2.2 Problem Formulation

Let U be a set of all users, and A be a third-party application that wants to initiate a series of transactions T_i, $i = 1, 2, \ldots k$. In each transaction, A and all users cooperate in computations of a WSUM function on the data x_j of all users $j \in U$.

2.2.1 Security Model

We assume that the application A and all users are *honest* (not malicious) i.e., they will all faithfully and correctly follow the proposed protocols.

- Users: All users are honest. However, there are at most *m* users who are *honest-but-curious*.

    - Honest users are not willing to collaborate with each other to create a common/shared encryption key not known to A.
    - Honest users will only send messages to A and not to any other user.
    - Honest-but-curious users may collude with each other and with A to collectively deduce the data of any honest user. As part of this collusion, honest-but-curious

users may share with A their data as well as any information they have gathered during the transactions.

- Application: The application A is honest-but-curious, i.e., although A is honest but it may legally try to derive the private data of any honest user.

2.2.2 Problems

At the time instant of interest, assume that A has already completed $(k - 1)$ WSUM transactions T_i, $i = 1, 2, \ldots, (k - 1)$. We then propose solutions for the following three problems:

Table 1. Notations used in the paper

Notation	Explanation	Notation	Explanation
U	Set of all n users j, $j \in [1, n]$. Note: j (and other letters g, q, z, etc....) is used to note a user; wherever j appears as an index or superscript of a parameter, it shows the association of the parameter to that user, e.g., x_j is private datum of User j	$W = [w_{ij}]$	A $(k \times n)$ matrix of weights with w_{ij} is the obfuscated weight sent to User j in Transaction T_i, $i = 1, 2, .., k$
		$*$	A wild cart for indexes; it implies the repeat of all possible indexes
$X = [x_j]^T$	A $(n \times 1)$ column vector where Element x_j, $j \in [1, n]$ is the datum of User j, and T is the matrix transpose operator	w_{*j}	A column of Matrix W, i.e., a column vector of obfuscated weights sent to User j in all k transactions
X^P	A sub-matrix of X with the elements x_j of the users $j \in P \subset U$	W^P or M^P	A sub-matrix of W (or M) that is composed of columns corresponding to all users $j \in P \subset U$
$Q^{U_z} = [q_j]$	A $(1 \times n)$ row vector $[q_1 \quad q_2 \cdots \quad q_j \cdots \quad q_n]$ with $q_j = 1$ if $j = z$, otherwise $q_j = 0$	w_{i*}	A row of W, which is composed of obfuscated weights sent to all users in the ith transaction T_i

- **Certification Challenge:** At the start of the transaction T_k, A must provide every user a privacy-assurance certificate that allows the user to verify the security of its datum even when all the honest-but-curious users share with A any information available to them through the transactions T_i, $i = 1, 2, \ldots, k$; i.e., even when Transaction T_k has completed.
- **Function Computation:** The problem here is to devise a scheme to compute the WSUM function of users' data in k transactions such that: (i) the results are known only to A, (ii) the data of each honest user remains private, (iii) A does not reveal the weights it selects for the honest users.

- **Constrains:** Since honest users do not collaborate with each other and since the number of users may be large, the devised scheme must satisfy the following constraint: Users are not required to perform a significant amount of computation and communication. In particular, the amount of computation and communication performed by a user should not increase with the total number of users.

2.3 Notations

Table 1 is a summary of notations used in the paper.

3 Proposed Solution for WSUM

3.1 Certification Challenge

Example 1: Suppose that A has obtained $(k-1)$ sums s_i, $i = 1, 2, \ldots, (k-1)$, and is interested in having another WSUM transaction $s_k = \sum_j w_{kj} x_j$. For example, the application already has two weighted sums of six users: $s_1 = x_1 + x_2 + x_3 + x_4 + x_5 + x_6$ and $s_2 = 2x_1 + 0x_2 + x_3 + 2x_4 + 3x_5 + 4x_6$.

Now the application wants another sum with a new weight set of 3, 4, 3, 2, 1, 0.

The weight matrix for the three transactions is $W = \left[w_{ij} \right] = \begin{bmatrix} 1 & 1 & 1 & 1 & 1 & 1 \\ 2 & 0 & 1 & 2 & 3 & 4 \\ 3 & 4 & 3 & 2 & 1 & 0 \end{bmatrix}$.

Since the rank of W is 3, these transactions are linearly independent of each other. With a secure single WSUM transaction protocol, in each of these transactions, when they are considered separately, no user's private datum is compromised. Furthermore, no user's datum is exposed to the application at the end of the first two transactions. However, if the users go ahead with the third transaction, a curious application can derive the private datum x_1, $x_1 = s_3 + s_2 - 4s_1$, thus the privacy of the first user's datum is violated. To avoid such privacy violations, at the start of a new WSUM transaction, all honest users should verify that A cannot derive their private data from the results of all WSUM transactions, including that of the current transaction, i.e., $s_3 = 3x_1 + 4x_2 + 3x_3 + 2x_4 + x_5 + 0x_6$.

At the first glance, this problem appears similar to the sum query auditing problem addressed in the database community [3], in which it was shown that when A knows the weights of all users, the application can deduce a user's data if and only if the following Theorem 1 is satisfied.

Theorem 1: When the application A knows the sums $S = \begin{bmatrix} s_1 & s_2 \ldots & s_i \ldots & s_k \end{bmatrix}^T$ after k transactions, A can deduce the private datum of the user j if and only if there exists k constants $\alpha_i, i = 1, 2, \ldots, k$, such that $\sum_{i=1}^{k} \alpha_i w_{i*} = Q^{Uj}$, where $Q^{Uj} = \begin{bmatrix} q_1 & q_2 \ldots & q_r \ldots & q_n \end{bmatrix}$, a row vector with $q_r = 1$ if $r = j$, otherwise $q_r = 0$.

Proof: Given in [3]   **Q.E.D.**

3.2   Single WSUM Transaction Protocol

Consider the transaction T_i in which the application A wants to have the weighted sum $s_i = \sum_j w'_{ij} x_j$, where x_j is the private data of the user j, and w'_{ij} is the weight the application assigns to the user. (Note that we reserve symbol w_{ij} for obfuscated weights). Let us also consider that there is a small set of p users, each equipped with a different additive cryptosystem. An additive cryptosystem has the property: $E(x) \otimes E(y) = E(x + y)$, where $E(x)$ is an encrypt function on the variable x, and $\otimes$ is a math operator, e.g., in Paillier's cryptosystem system [13], $E(x) \times E(y) = E(x + y)$. Solutions for the SUM and other data aggregations were proposed in literature [7, 9, 16]. The following algorithm, which is similar to that of [16], will assure the security of honest users' private data if $p > m$, where m is the maximal number of colluding users.

Algorithm 1

(1) Application A sends to each user $j \in U$, where U is the set of all users,

   (a) An obfuscated weight $w_{ij} = \rho_i w'_{ij}$, where w'_{ij} is the weight assigned to User j, which is blurred by multiplying it with a common random factor $\rho_i > 0$. A must assure that there are at least $(m + 2)$ users with the weights $w_{ij} \neq 0$.
   (b) The public keys of all users $g \in G \subset U$; $|G| = p$.

(2) Each user $j \in U$, i.e., including the users in G, does the following:

   (a) Computes the product $w_{ij} x_j$.
   (b) Divides the result product into p parts x_j^{Ug}, so that $\sum_{g \in G} x_j^{Ug} = w_{ij} x_j$.
   (c) Encrypts each x_j^{Ug} with the public key of the user $\in G$. Let $y_j^{Ug} = E^{Ug}\left(x_j^{Ug}\right)$.
   (d) Sends all y_j^{Ug} to the application.

(3) Application does the following:

   (a) Computes p encrypted partial sums (using the $\otimes$ operator).
   (b) Sends each encrypted partial sum $E^{Ug}\left(s_i^{Ug}\right)$ to the associate user $g \in G$ for decryption.
   (c) Receives p decrypted partial sums s_i^{Ug} from the users $g \in G$.
   (d) Computes the total weighted sum $s_i = \frac{1}{\rho_i} \sum_{g \in G} s_i^{Ug} = \sum_j w'_{ij} x_j$.

Note that, there is at least one honest user in the group G because $p > m$; hence with Algorithm 1 the private data of all honest users are secure.

Example 2: Consider an application A with four users $j, j = 1, 2, 3$ and 4. Suppose that the users' private data are $x_1 = 10, x_2 = 20, x_3 = 30$, and $x_4 = 40$. Further, let us assume that the number of colluding users $m = 2$. In the 1st transaction T_1, A wants to compute the weighted sum $s_1 = 2x_1 + 4x_2 + 3x_3 + 2x_4 = 270$. The algorithm is performed as follows.

(1) **A** chooses the obfuscating factor $\rho_1 = 10$ and sends to each user:

    (a) Obfuscated weights: $w_{11} = 20, w_{12} = 40, w_{13} = 30,$ and $w_{14} = 20$.

    (b) The public keys of 3 users in $G = \{2, 3, 4\}$. Note that we have $p = 3 > m = 2$.

(2) Each user $j \in U$ does the following:

    (a) Computes the product $w_{ij}x_j$: $(w_{11}x_1 = 20 \times 10 = 200)$; $(w_{12}x_2 = 40 \times 20 = 800)$; $(w_{13}x_3 = 30 \times 30 = 900)$; $(w_{14}x_4 = 20 \times 40 = 800)$.

    (b) Divides the result product into 3 parts: $\left(x_1^{U2} = 50, x_1^{U3} = 70, x_1^{U4} = 80\right)$; $\left(x_2^{U2} = 500, x_2^{U3} = 100, x_2^{U4} = 200\right)$; $\left(x_3^{U2} = 100, x_3^{U3} = 700, x_3^{U4} = 100\right)$; $\left(x_4^{U2} = 400, x_4^{U3} = 100, x_4^{U4} = 300\right)$.

    (c) Encrypts $y_j^{Ug} = E^{Ug}\left(x_j^{Ug}\right)$: $\left(y_1^{U2} = E^{U2}(50), y_1^{U3} = E^{U3}(70), y_1^{U4} = E^{U4}(80)\right)$; $\left(y_2^{U2} = E^{U2}(500), y_2^{U3} = E^{U3}(100), y_2^{U4} = E^{U4}(200)\right)$; $\left(y_3^{U2} = E^{U2}(100), y_3^{U3} = E^{U3}(700), y_3^{U4} = E^{U4}(100)\right)$; $\left(y_4^{U2} = E^{U2}(400), y_4^{U3} = E^{U3}(100), y_4^{U4} = E^{U4}(300)\right)$.

    (d) Sends all y_j^{Ug} to the application.

(3) Application does the following:

    (a) Computes encrypted partial sums $E^{Ug}\left(s_i^{Ug}\right) = \prod_{j \in U} y_j^{Ug}$:
$E^{U2}\left(s_1^{U2}\right) = y_1^{U2}y_2^{U2}y_3^{U2}y_4^{U2} = E^{U2}\left(x_1^{U2} + x_2^{U2} + x_3^{U2} + x_4^{U2}\right) = E^{U2}(1050)$
Similarly, $E^{U3}\left(s_1^{U3}\right) = E^{U3}(970)$ and $E^{U4}\left(s_1^{U4}\right) = E^{U4}(680)$.

    (b) Sends each $E^{Ug}\left(s_i^{Ug}\right)$ to User $g \in G$ for decryption.

    (c) Receives decrypted partial sums s_i^{Ug} from the associated users $g \in G : s_1^{U2} = 1050, s_1^{U3} = 970, s_1^{U4} = 680$.

    (d) Computes sum:
$$s_i = \sum_j w_{ij}'x_j = \frac{1}{\rho_i}\sum_{g \in G} s_i^{Ug} = \frac{1}{10}(1050 + 970 + 680) = 270.$$

3.3 WSUM Privacy Assurance Certificate

For simplicity of presentation, in the rest of this paper, we assume that the obfuscating factor $\rho_i = 1$, i.e., $w_{ij} = w_{ij}'$. Suppose that the application has obtained $(k - 1)$ sums s_i, and is interested in having another transaction $s_k = \sum_j w_{kj}x_j$. We can present the problem in a matrix form $WX = S$. Without loss of generality, we assume that all transactions are linearly independent of each other, i.e., the rank of W equals k. Our problem is how to ensure that the application A cannot derive the value of any private datum x_z.

Definition
The datum of User z remains private at the end of k WSUM transactions if the application A cannot uniquely determine its value from the WSUM results $S = \begin{bmatrix} s_1 & s_2 \ldots & s_i \ldots & s_k \end{bmatrix}^T$. That is there are at least two $(n \times 1)$ vectors X and Y such that $WX = S$, $WY = S$ and $x_z \neq y_z$, where x_z and y_z are the elements in the zth row of X and Y, respectively; and W is the $(k \times n)$ weight matrix.

3.3.1 Certification When Only a Is Honest-But-Curious

Consider the case in which all users are honest and only A is honest-but-curious. For this special case we first prove the following theorem.

Theorem 2: The datum x_Z of the user z remains private after k WSUM transactions if and only if $rank(W^N) = k$, where $N = U - \{z\}$, and W^N is a sub-matrix of W, which is composed of the columns corresponding to all users $j \in N \subset U$.

Proof: *(Only If part)* We prove this by contradiction. Suppose the datum of User z remains private but $rank(W^N) < k$. Then, there are constants α_i, $i = 1, 2, \ldots, k$, such that $\sum_{i=1}^{k} \alpha_i w_{i*}^N = \vec{o}$, where w_{i*}^N denotes the ith row of W^N, i.e., the row vector w_{i*} of W without the element w_{iz}, and $\vec{o}$ is a $(1 \times (n-1))$ row vector with all components equal to zero. Since W has one additional column as compared to W^N, it follows that $\sum_{i=1}^{k} \alpha_i w_{i*} = \beta Q^{Uz}$, where Q^{Uz} is a $(1 \times n)$ row vector $[q_1 q_2 \ldots q_j \ldots q_n]$ with $q_j = 1$ if $j = z$, otherwise $q_j = 0$. Furthermore, due to $rank(W) = k$ as assumed, we have $\beta = \sum_{i=1}^{k} \alpha_i w_{iz} \neq 0$. This implies that the application A can uniquely compute the private datum $x_z = \frac{\sum_i \alpha_i s_i}{\beta}$, i.e., the datum of User z does not remain private: this contradicts the hypothesis; hence: $rank(W^N) = k$.

(If part): Since the rank of the matrix W^N is k, it must have a $(k \times k)$ sub-matrix C with $rank(C) = k$. Let V be the set of the users that correspond to the k columns of C. Let $W_{1 \leftrightarrow z}$ is the matrix derived from W by swapping its two columns w_{*1} and w_{*z}. Let E_z is the reduced row echelon form (RREF) of $W_{1 \leftrightarrow z}$: $E_z = rref(W_{1 \leftrightarrow z})$. If $\exists i : w_{iz} \neq 0$, we have $E_z(1, 1) = 1$. In this RREF transform, C becomes C_E. Due to $rank(C) = k$, every row of C_E must have at least one non-zero element. Let $\gamma_q \neq 0$ be one of such elements of the 1st row of C_E, which corresponds to the user q. We can derive $x_z = -\gamma_q x_q + f$ (x_j, s_i), where $j \neq z$ and $j \neq q$. Hence A cannot derive a unique value for User z's data. We say the secure of x_z relies on x_q.   **Q.E.D.**

From Theorem 2 we can devise a certification approach as follows. At the start of the kth WSUM transaction, the application A supplies each user z an assurance certificate $C \subset W$ in the form of a $(k \times k)$ matrix with rank k. All elements of C are the obfuscated weights of the users j of a set V that does not contain the user z, i.e., $C = W^V$, $z \notin V$. The certificate C is called the *individual assurance certificate* for the user z. The certificate can also be used for any other user not belonging to V. Another certificate is needed for the users belonging to V. Two such certificates can be combined to make a *universal assurance certificate*, i.e., a common certificate for all users. This observation leads us to the following theorem.

Theorem 3: The data of all users remains private at the end of k transactions if and only if there is a subset of users $V \subseteq U$ such that: (i) $k + 1 < |V| \leq 2k$, and (ii) $\forall j \in V$, we have $rank(W^N) = k$ where $N = V - \{j\}$. The matrix $C = W^N$, a sub-matrix of W, is composed of the weights of all users $j \in V$. It is a universal assurance certificate.

Proof: *(only if part)* Since $rank(W) = k$ as assumed, we can perform row and column operations to transform W into E, a reduced row echelon form (RREF) matrix, such that $E = rref(W) = [I_{k \times k} R_{k \times (n-k)}]$, where $I_{k \times k}$ is an identity matrix of dimensions

$(k \times k)$, and R is the remaining sub-matrix. Let V_1 denote the set of users corresponding to the first k columns of E, i.e., the columns of the identity matrix. Note that each row of R has at least one non-zero element; otherwise, there exists a row vector Q^{Uj} (a vector with all zero elements except one at Column j) in E. From Theorem 1, we know that this is not possible because the hypothesis states that the data of all users remains private. Therefore, there must exist a subset of users $V_2 \subseteq U - V_1$ such that every row in E^{V_2}, a sub-matrix of R relating to all user $j \in V_2$, has at least one non-zero element, and we have $1 \leq |V_2| \leq k$.

We argue below that $V = V_1 \cup V_2$ satisfies the two conditions in the theorem.

(i) We have $|V_1| = k$, $1 \leq |V_2| \leq k$ and $V_1 \cap V_2 = \emptyset$, hence $k + 1 < |V| \leq 2k$

(ii) For each user $j \in V_2$, let $N = V - \{j\}$, we have $N \supseteq V_1$. However, $rank(W^{V_1}) = k$; therefore $rank(W^N) = k$. Now consider each user $j \in V_1$. With the RREF transform, the column corresponding to the user j in the identity matrix $I_{k \times k}$ of E has exactly one element equal to 1, and all other elements equal to 0. Suppose that the non-zero element is in the ith row. Then the ith row of E^{V_2} must have at least one non-zero element. Let $z \in V_2$ be the user corresponding to that non-zero element, and $W_{j \leftrightarrow z}$ be the matrix obtained by swapping the two columns corresponding to the two users j and z of W. Let $E_{j \leftrightarrow z} = rref(W_{j \leftrightarrow z})$, we have $E_{j \leftrightarrow z} = \left[I_{k \times k} R'_{k \times (n-k)} \right]$. Let V'_1 be the set of the users corresponding to the columns of the new identity matrix in $E_{j \leftrightarrow z}$, we have $V'_1 = (V_1 - \{j\}) \cup \{z\}$, $V'_2 = (V_2 - \{z\}) \cup \{j\}$, $V = V_1 \cup V_2 = V'_1 \cup V'_2$ and $N = V - \{j\} \supseteq V'_1$. Due to $rank(V'_1) = k$, we have $rank(W^N) = k$.

Finally, $rank(W^N) = k, \forall j \in V$.

Therefore, V satisfies both conditions in the theorem.

(if part): The 2nd condition $rank(W^N) = k$ is sufficient to assure the privacy of any user's data based on Theorem 2. **Q.E.D.**

From Theorem 3, it is possible to have an universal assurance certificate $C_{k \times h}$ with $k + 1 < h \leq 2k$. A user verifies its privacy assurance as follows. For any user $j \notin V$, the user needs to check the rank of the certificate C. For any user $j \in V$, the user needs to check the rank of the matrix C^N, where $N = V - \{j\}$. Since the size of an assurance certificate C does not depend on the total number of users, a user's computational burden to verify its privacy assurance does not increase with the number of users.

Example 3: We now illustrate this certification approach for Example 1 given in Sect. 3.1, with six users j, $j = 1, 2, \ldots, 6$, each with a private datum x_j. The obfuscated weight matrix is $W = [w_{ij}] = \begin{bmatrix} 1 & 1 & 1 & 1 & 1 & 1 \\ 2 & 0 & 1 & 2 & 3 & 4 \\ 3 & 4 & 3 & 2 & 1 & 0 \end{bmatrix}$. In this example, $n = 6$ and $k = 3$; we consider the privacy of the users **1** and **6**. Suppose that at the start of the 3rd transaction, A supplies all users a universal assurance certificate $C = W^V = \begin{bmatrix} 1 & 1 & 1 & 1 & 1 \\ 2 & 0 & 1 & 2 & 3 \\ 3 & 4 & 3 & 2 & 1 \end{bmatrix}$, with $V = U - \{6\}$. We have $|V| = 5 < 2k$. For User $6 \notin V$, we have $rank(C) = 3 = k$: The privacy of User **6** is assured. For any user j belonging to V, e.g., $j = 1$, by removing the column w_{*1} from C, we have $C^{V-\{1\}} = \begin{bmatrix} 1 & 1 & 1 & 1 \\ 0 & 1 & 2 & 3 \\ 4 & 3 & 2 & 1 \end{bmatrix}$ and $rank(C^{V-\{1\}}) = 2$. The privacy of User **1** would be compromised, as shown in Sect. 3.1, if the 3rd transaction does happen.

Certificate generation: For simplicity as well as to reduce the computation complexity of users in assurance certificate verification, an application A will supply each user an individual assurance certificate in the form of a square matrix $C_{k \times k}$.

Certificate verification – Algorithm 2: When a user receives an individual assurance certificate C at the start of the kth WSUM transaction, it will verify the validity of the certificate as follows:

(1) Check the size ($k \times k$) of the certificate.
(2) Check that it is not a member of the set V of the users that correspond to the weights in the certificate. If necessary, confirm with the users in V the correctness of the weights in the certificate.
(3) Check that $rank(C) = k$.

We will illustrate the algorithm with the following example.

Example 4: We reuse the data in Example 3, and let us consider the condition in which the user **6** is supplied an individual certificate containing the weights of the users **1, 2** and **3:** $C_6 = [\, w_{*1} \quad w_{*2} \quad w_{*3}\,] = \begin{bmatrix} 1 & 1 & 1 \\ 2 & 0 & 1 \\ 3 & 4 & 3 \end{bmatrix}$. We have $rank(C_6) = 3$: Certificate C_6 successfully passes all the three steps of the algorithm: The certificate is valid for User **6**.

Quality of an individual privacy-assurance certificate: We will illustrate how to evaluate the quality of an individual assurance certificate with the data in Example 4. Let $B_6 = [\, w_{*6} C_6\,] = \begin{bmatrix} 1 & 1 & 1 & 1 \\ 4 & 2 & 0 & 1 \\ 0 & 3 & 4 & 3 \end{bmatrix}$. We have $E_6 = rref(B_6) = \begin{bmatrix} 1 & 0 & 0 & 0.25 \\ 0 & 1 & 0 & 0 \\ 0 & 0 & 1 & 0.75 \end{bmatrix}$. Hence, A can derive $x_6 = Cst\_3 - 0.25 x_3$, where Cst_3 does not depend on the value of x_3. Let $rel(x_6/x_3) = \left| \frac{\partial x_6}{\partial x_3} \right|$, we have $rel(x_6/x_3) = 0.25$. Similarly by swapping the columns w_{*1} or w_{*2} with the column w_{*3}, we have two more matrixes B_6' and B_6'' with: $B_6' = [\, w_{*6} \quad w_{*3} \quad w_{*2} \quad w_{*1}\,] = \begin{bmatrix} 1 & 1 & 1 & 1 \\ 4 & 1 & 0 & 2 \\ 0 & 3 & 4 & 3 \end{bmatrix}$ and $\quad B_6'' = [\, w_{*6} \quad w_{*1}$

$w_{*3} w_{*2}\,] = \begin{bmatrix} 1 & 1 & 1 & 1 \\ 4 & 2 & 1 & 0 \\ 0 & 3 & 3 & 4 \end{bmatrix}$.

However from both B'_6 and B''_6 matrixes, we can derive only one more expression for x_6: $x_6 = Cst\_2 + 0.33x_2$, where Cst_2 does not depend on the value of x_2.

Let us define the _reliance degree_ of x_z in the assurance certificate C as follows: $rel(x_z) = min_{j \in V}\left(rel(x_z/x_j), 1\right)$. We have $rel(x_6) = 0.25$. The reliance degree is a measure for the quality of an individual privacy-assurance certificate: a higher reliance degree implies a more reliable certificate. For example, if the application A knows that the range of users' data, e.g., $x_j \in [0, 100]$, then with $x_6 = Cst\_3 - 0.25x_3$, A can derive that $x_6 \in [a, b]$, with $b - a = 25$, i.e., the guess range for a user's data is narrower when its reliance degree is smaller. For example if $x_1 = 10$, $x_2 = 20$, $x_3 = 30$, $x_4 = 40$, $x_5 = 50$ and $x_6 = 60$, we have $s_1 = 12$, $s_2 = 29$, $s_3 = 30$ and $Cst\_3 = 67.5$. Hence the application can derive that $x_6 \in [42.5, 67.5]$. It is to be noted that this reliance degree is over-pessimistic because the value of Cst_3 in the solution for x_6 may also depend on the values of other users' data, e.g., x_4 and x_5.

3.3.2   Certification When A and m Users are Honest-But-Curious

We now extend our certification approach to the case there are m honest-but-curious users.

Theorem 4: If A and at most m users are honest-but-curious, then all honest users' data remain private after k WSUM transactions if $rank(W^N) = k$, where $N = U - J$, for all $J \subseteq U$ such that $|J| = m + 1$.

Proof: Let D be the set of m honest-but-curious users and U^H be the set of all honest users, we have $U^H = U - D$ and $|U^H| = n - m = n_H$. Consider any honest user $j \in U^H$. Let $J = D \cup \{j\} \subseteq U$, a special set that satisfies the condition $|J| = m + 1$. We have: $N = U - J = U - (D \cup \{j\}) = U^H - \{j\}$. Hence $N \subseteq U^H$. Let W^H be a sub-matrix of W, which relates to all honest users $j \in U^H$. We have: $(W^H)^N = W^N$. Therefore, _rank_ $((W^H)^N) = rank(W^N) = k$. Hence from Theorem 2, the data of all honest users $j \in U^H$ remain private. **Q.E.D.**

Certificate generation: Similar to the case with all honest users, by using Theorem 4 we can devise an assurance certification approach for the case with colluding users as follows. At the start of the kth WSUM transaction, the application A supplies each user z an individual assurance certificate $C \subset W$ in the form of a $(k \times (k + m))$ matrix of rank k. All elements of $C_{k \times (k+m)}$ are the obfuscated weights of all users j of a set V, with $z \notin V$. Similarly, A provides another assurance certificate for the users belonging to V.

Certificate verification – Algorithm 3: When a user receives an individual assurance certificate C at the start of the kth WSUM transaction, the user will verify the validity of the certificate as follows:

(a)   Check the size $(k \times (k + m))$ of the certificate.
(b)   Check that it is not a member of the set V associated with the certificate.
(c)   Extract all $\frac{(k+m)!}{k!m!}$ possible square sub-matrixes C^E from C, each sub-matrix corresponding to k users selected from the $(k + m)$ users of V.
(d)   For each matrix C^E, check that $rank(C^E) = k$; if this condition is not satisfied: Certificate is not valid. Exit.

We will illustrate the algorithm with the following example.

Example 5: We reuse the data in Example 3, but with the assumption that there are at most two users collude with the application, i.e., $m = 2$. Suppose that User **6** is supplied with the individual certificate $C_6^{\&m}$ containing the weights of the other users:

$C_6^{\&m} = \begin{bmatrix} 1 & 1 & 1 & 1 & 1 \\ 2 & 0 & 1 & 2 & 3 \\ 3 & 4 & 3 & 2 & 1 \end{bmatrix}$. Because $\frac{(k+m)!}{k!m!} = 10$, there are ten possible square sub-

matrixes, including the following square matrix: $C_{6a}^{\&m} = [w_{*3}w_{*4}w_{*5}] = \begin{bmatrix} 1 & 1 & 1 \\ 1 & 2 & 3 \\ 3 & 2 & 1 \end{bmatrix}$,

We have $rank(C_{6a}^{\&m}) = 2$: Certificate $C_6^{\&m}$ is not valid.

Note that the certificate $C_{k \times (k+m)}$ is of minimal size ($k \times (k + m)$); however, users need more computational time to check the ranks of all possible square sub-matrixes. We will investigate another certification approach that generates a larger assurance certificate but needs smaller computation effort for verification.

Theorem 5: When the application A and at most m users are honest-but-curious, the datum x_z of the honest user z remains private at the end of k transactions if there are $(m + 1)$ sub-sets $V_r \subset U$, $r = 1, 2, \ldots, m + 1$, such that, $\forall r$: (i) $j \notin V_r$; (ii) $rank(W^{V_r}) = k$; (iii) $\forall t \in \{1, 2, \ldots, m + 1\}$ and $t \neq r : V_r \cap V_t = \emptyset$.

Proof: Let $V = V_1 \cup V_2 \cup \ldots \cup V_r \cup \ldots \cup V_{m+1}$, and $C = [C_1 \quad C_2 \ldots \ C_r \ldots C_{m+1}]$, where $C_r = W^{V_r}$. We have $C = W^V$. Let $B = [w_{*z}C]$ and $E = rref(B)$. If $\exists i, w_{iz} \neq 0$ then E will have the form: $E = [C_0^M \quad C_1^M \quad C_2^M \ldots \ C_r^M \ldots \ C_{m+1}^M]$, where $C_0^M = [1 \quad 0 \quad 0 \ldots \quad 0]^T$, a column vector with all zero elements except the first one, and all $C_{r \neq 0}^M$ are square matrixes, each with at least one non-zero element in every row because $\forall r$, $rank(C_r) = k$. Therefore, we can derive an expression for x_z as follows: $x_z = Cst - \sum_{r=1}^{m+1} \left(\sum_{t=1}^{k} \beta_{r,t} x_{r,t}^M \right)$, where Cst does not depend on x_z and any $x_{j \in V}$; and $\forall r, \exists \beta_{r,t} \neq 0$ and $x_{r,t}^M$ is the datum of the user corresponding to the tth column of C_r^M. Therefore x_z depends on the data of at least $(m + 1)$ other users, each belonging to a set V_r, $r = 1, 2, \ldots, m + 1$. In other words, there is at least one honest user whom User z can rely on to keep the security of its private datum. **Q.E.D.**

Corollary 1: When the application A and at most m users are honest-but-curious, the datum x_z of the honest user z remains private at the end of k transactions if there are $(m + 2)$ sub-sets $V_r \subset U$, $r = 1, 2, \ldots, m + 2$, such that, $\forall r$: (a) $rank(W^{V_r}) = k$; (b) $\forall t \in \{1, 2, \ldots, m + 2\}$ and $t \neq r : V_t \cap V_r = \emptyset$.

Proof: User z will belong to at most one set V_r because $\forall t \in \{1, 2, \ldots, m + 2\}$ and $t \neq r : V_t \cap V_r = \emptyset$. If there is such a V_r, by excluding that V_r from the hypothesis, we return to Theorem 5. **Q.E.D.**

The matrix $C = W^V$, where $V = \bigcup_{r=1}^{m+2} V_r$, is a universal assurance certificate.

Certificate generation: By using Theorem 5 we can devise an assurance certification approach for the case with colluding users as follows. The application A supplies each user z an individual assurance certificate $C = \begin{bmatrix} C_1^F & C_2^F \ldots & C_r^F \ldots & C_{m+1}^F \end{bmatrix} \subset W$, where C_r^F, $r = 1, 2, .., (m+1)$ are square matrixes, with: $\forall r$, (i) $z \notin V_r$, (ii) $rank(C_r^F) = k$ and (iii) $\forall t \neq r, V_t \cap V_r = \emptyset$; where V_r and V_t are the sets of users corresponding to the obfuscated weights in C_r^F and C_t^F. The certificate C with elements being the obfuscated weights of all users $j \in V = \bigcup_r (V_r)$ is a matrix with $size(C) = (k \times (m+1)k) \geq (k \times (k+m))$; however users need less time to verify C.

Certificate verification – Algorithm 4: When a user receives an individual assurance certificate C at the start of the kth WSUM transaction, it will verify the validity of the certificate as follows:

(a) Check the size $(k \times (m + 1)k)$ of the certificate.
(b) Check that it is not a member of the set V associated with the certificate.
(c) Partition the certificate into $(m + 1)$ square sub-matrixes C_r^F, $r = 1, 2, .., m+1$, i.e., $C = \begin{bmatrix} C_1^F & C_2^F \ldots & C_r^F \ldots & C_{m+1}^F \end{bmatrix}$.
(d) For each matrix C_r^F,

     i. Check that $rank(C_r^F) = k$.
     ii. If the condition is not satisfied, i.e., the certificate is not valid, Exit.

It is to be noted that, in Step (c) a user needs to extract a smaller number of square matrixes than that in Algorithm 3 because $m + 1 \leq \frac{(k+m)!}{k!m!}$.

We will illustrate the algorithm with the following example.

Example 6: Consider an application A and seven users j, $j = 1, 2, \ldots 7$. Suppose that the number of colluding users $m = 1$, and at the start of the 3rd WSUM transaction, A supplies the individual assurance certificate $C =$

$$\begin{bmatrix} w_{*2} & w_{*3} & w_{*4} & w_{*5} & w_{*6} & w_{*7} \end{bmatrix} = \begin{bmatrix} 1 & 2 & 3 & 4 & 3 & 2 \\ 1 & 3 & 4 & 2 & 3 & 1 \\ 2 & 4 & 5 & 8 & 3 & 0 \end{bmatrix}$$ to User 1. User 1

extracts two square sub-matrixes $C_1^F = \begin{bmatrix} 1 & 2 & 3 \\ 1 & 3 & 4 \\ 2 & 4 & 5 \end{bmatrix}$ and $C_2^F = \begin{bmatrix} 4 & 3 & 2 \\ 2 & 3 & 1 \\ 8 & 3 & 0 \end{bmatrix}$. The

ranks of these two sub-matrixes are both equal to 3, therefore the certificate is valid.

Quality of the certificate: We will compute the reliance degree for each of the two sub-matrixes. Suppose that the column weight vector of user 1 is $w_{*1} = \begin{bmatrix} 3 & 4 & 5 \end{bmatrix}^T$.

Let $B_1 = \begin{bmatrix} w_{*1} & C_1^F \end{bmatrix}$. We have $B_1 = \begin{bmatrix} 3 & 1 & 2 & 3 \\ 4 & 1 & 3 & 4 \\ 5 & 2 & 4 & 5 \end{bmatrix}$ and $E_1 =$

$rref(B_1) = \begin{bmatrix} 1 & 0 & 0 & 1 \\ 0 & 1 & 0 & 0 \\ 0 & 0 & 1 & 0 \end{bmatrix}$, and then $x_1 = Cst\_4 - x_4$, where Cst_4 does not depend

on x_4. The reliance degree of x_1 on x_4 equals 1. With the 2nd extract matrix C_2^f, by putting either w_{*5}, w_{*6} or w_{*7} in the last column, we can have three different matrixes and their RREF matrixes:

$$B_2^{U5} = [\, w_{*1} \quad w_{*6} \quad w_{*7} \quad w_{*5} \,] = \begin{bmatrix} 3 & 3 & 2 & 4 \\ 4 & 3 & 1 & 2 \\ 5 & 3 & 0 & 8 \end{bmatrix},$$

$$E_2^{U5} = rref\left(B_2^{U5}\right) = \begin{bmatrix} 1 & 0 & -1 & 0 \\ 0 & 1 & 1.7 & 0 \\ 0 & 0 & 0 & 1 \end{bmatrix};$$

$$B_2^{U6} = [\, w_{*1} \quad w_{*5} \quad w_{*7} \quad w_{*6} \,] = \begin{bmatrix} 3 & 4 & 2 & 3 \\ 4 & 2 & 1 & 3 \\ 5 & 8 & 0 & 3 \end{bmatrix},$$

$$E_2^{U6} = rref\left(B_2^{U6}\right) = \begin{bmatrix} 1 & 0 & 0 & 0.6 \\ 0 & 1 & 0 & 0 \\ 0 & 0 & 1 & 0.6 \end{bmatrix};$$

$$B_2^{U7} = [\, w_{*1} \quad w_{*5} \quad w_{*6} \quad w_{*7} \,] = \begin{bmatrix} 3 & 4 & 3 & 2 \\ 4 & 2 & 3 & 1 \\ 5 & 8 & 3 & 0 \end{bmatrix},$$

$$E_2^{U7} = rref\left(B_2^{U7}\right) = \begin{bmatrix} 1 & 0 & 0 & -1 \\ 0 & 1 & 0 & 0 \\ 0 & 0 & 1 & 1.7 \end{bmatrix}.$$

From E_2^{U5} and E_2^{U7} we derive $x_1 = Cst\_7 + x_7$, and $\left|\frac{\partial x_1}{\partial x_7}\right| = 1$. From E_2^{U6} we have $x_1 = Cst\_6 - 0.6x_6 \rightarrow \left|\frac{\partial x_1}{\partial x_6}\right| = 0.6$: Hence $rel(x_1) = min(1, 0.6) = 0.6$.

3.3.3 Certification in General Case

We will consider the case in which a user receives an individual assurance certificate with the size $(k \times h)$, where $k \leq h \leq (m + 1)k$. Suppose we have an application and numerous users that are going to be involved in the kth WSUM transaction, and we are especially interested in the security of x_z, the private datum of User z, when it receives the individual assurance certificate $C_{k \times h}$ composed of the weights of a set V of h users. Let P_r is a set of $(k - 1)$ users selected from V; we have $N_s = \frac{h!}{(k-1)!(h-k+1)!}$ possible selections. For each P_r, $r = \{1, 2, \ldots, N_s\}$, we find another subset $Q_r = V - P_r$, i.e., $P_r \cup Q_r = V$ and $P_r \cap Q_r = \emptyset$, and then try to find the solution for the variable x_z of the following system of k linear equations $WX = S$, where $W_{k \times (h+1)} = [\, w_{*z} \quad C \,]$ with

$$C = \left[\, \left[w_{*j}^{P_r} \right] \quad \left[w_{*j}^{Q_r} \right] \,\right], X = \left[\, x_z \quad \left[x_j^{P_r} \right] \quad \left[x_j^{Q_r} \right] \,\right]^T \text{ and } S = [\, s_1 \quad s_2 \ldots \quad s_i \ldots \quad s_k \,]^T.$$

From the last $(k - 1)$ equations of $WX = S$, we can find $(k - 1)$ expressions, f_i^r, $i = 2, \ldots, k$, each being the relationship from x_p, the datum of a user $p \in P_r$, to x_z and the data of all users $q \in Q_r$. By substituting these $(k - 1)$ expressions f_i^r into the first equation of $WX = S$ we can derive an expression f_r showing the relationship from x_z to the data x_q of all users $q \in Q_r$. Let $rel(x_z/x_q)_r = \left|\frac{\partial f_z}{\partial x_q}\right|$. Similarly, we can define a *reliance degree* of x_z on $x_{q \in Q_r}$ as follows: $rel(x_z/x_q) = min_r\left(rel(x_z/x_q)_r, 1\right)$.

Example 7: We will reuse the data in Example 6. Consider the system $WX = S$ with, when $r = 1$, we have $P_1 = \{2, 3\}$, $Q_1 = \{4, 5, 6, 7\}$, $C = \left[\left[w_j^{P_r}\right] \quad \left[w_j^{Q_r}\right]\right]$ and $S = [s_1 \quad s_2 \quad s_3]^T$. We have: $W_{3\times7} = [w_{*z} \quad w_{*2} \quad w_{*3} \quad w_{*4} \quad w_{*5} \quad w_{*6} \quad w_{*7}]$, $X = [x_z \quad x_2 \quad x_3 \quad x_4 \quad x_5 \quad x_6 \quad x_7]^T$ and $V = \{2, 3, 4, 5, 6, 7\}$. Suppose that $w_{*z} = [3 \quad 4 \quad 5]^T$, we have: $C = \begin{bmatrix} 1 & 2 & 3 & 4 & 3 & 2 \\ 1 & 3 & 4 & 2 & 3 & 1 \\ 2 & 4 & 5 & 8 & 3 & 0 \end{bmatrix}$, $W = $

$\begin{bmatrix} 3 & 1 & 2 & 3 & 4 & 3 & 2 \\ 4 & 1 & 3 & 4 & 2 & 3 & 1 \\ 5 & 2 & 4 & 5 & 8 & 3 & 0 \end{bmatrix}$ and $E = rref(W) = \begin{bmatrix} 1 & 0 & 0 & 1 & 0 & 3 & 4 \\ 0 & 1 & 0 & 0 & 8 & 0 & 0 \\ 0 & 0 & 1 & 0 & -2 & -3 & -5 \end{bmatrix}$.

Therefore $x_z = Cst - (x_4 + 0x_5 + 3x_6 + 4x_7)$, where Cst does not depend on any $x_{j \in V}$. Hence $rel(x_z/x_4)_{r=1} = \left|\frac{\partial x_z}{\partial x_4}\right| = 1$, $rel(x_z/x_5)_{r=1} = \left|\frac{\partial x_z}{\partial x_5}\right| = 0$, $rel(x_z/x_6)_{r=1} = min\left(\left|\frac{\partial x_z}{\partial x_6}\right|, 1\right) = 1$ and $rel(x_z/x_7)_{r=1} = min\left(\left|\frac{\partial x_z}{\partial x_7}\right|, 1\right) = 1$. With $h = 6$, $N_s = 15$. Hence we have 15 different sets P_r. However, with the RREF transform applied on W corresponding to these P_r, we have only 4 more different expressions for x_z. Finally, we derive reliance degrees of x_z in Table 2. We see that the value of x_z depends on the values of at least 3 other variables (when $r = 1$). If there are at most two users colluding with the application, i.e., $m = 2$, the datum of User z is still secure when it receives the assurance certificate C. However, its reliance degree is only equal to 0.6, the minimum of the 3rd greatest values (when $r = 5$).

Table 2. Reliance Degree of User z's Data

r	Expression for x_z for different values of r	$\left|\frac{\partial x_z}{\partial x_2}\right|$	$\left|\frac{\partial x_z}{\partial x_3}\right|$	$\left|\frac{\partial x_z}{\partial x_4}\right|$	$\left|\frac{\partial x_z}{\partial x_5}\right|$	$\left|\frac{\partial x_z}{\partial x_6}\right|$	$\left|\frac{\partial x_z}{\partial x_7}\right|$
1	$Cst\_1 - (x_4 + 0x_5 + 3x_6 + 4x_7)$			1	0	3	4
2	$Cst\_2 - (x_3 + x_4 - 2x_5 - x_7)$		1	1	2		1
3	$Cst\_3 - (0.8x_3 + x_4 - 1.6x_5 + 0.6x_6)$		0.8	1	1.6	0.6	
4	$Cst\_4 - (0.25x_2 + x_3 + x_4 - x_7)$	0.25	1	1			1
5	$Cst\_5 - (0.2x_2 + 0.8x_3 + x_4 + 0.6x_6)$	0.2	0.8	1		0.6	
	Reliance degree $rel(x_z/x_q)$	0.2	0.8	1	0	0.6	1

4 Related Research

There are some differences between traditional SMC and the TPA problem considered in this paper. For instance, most works in SMC assume that all involved parties have similar computational capabilities. With increasing popularity of cloud computing, there is a growing interest in performing secure computations on confidential data on more powerful "cloud" computers. In [10], a solution to address data confidentiality-privacy is proposed in the context of cloud computing. In this solution, users cooperatively generate a multi-user multi-key which they use to perform fully-homomorphic encryptions [11]. Similar to our approach, the solution in [10] does not require much computation from users. However, the computational effort involved in the generation of the keys is proportional to the number of users, which may be very large.

Another related work in the SMC area is designed for function computations on the Web [8], with the goal to eliminate the need for synchronous communication between the parties during SMC. However, the solution in [8] is still based on the traditional SMC assumption that all users involved in the computations are aware of each other, and collaborate with each other; each user is also required to encrypt using the public keys of all participating users. Therefore, the amount of computation increases with number of users.

There are several specialized approaches for evaluating a specific function like SUM [14, 15]. The approaches differ in the security threat model. One major disadvantage of the algorithms in [14, 15] is that it arranges the communication among all users as a cycle. If cyclic arrangement is specified by A, then the scheme is vulnerable to collusion between A and some users. In particular, A can arrange to have a honest-but-curious user just before and immediately after some honest users in the cycle. By colluding with these honest-but-curious users, A can determine the private data values of some honest users. An alternative is for users to organize themselves into a cycle, but this approach requires users to know each other. Although the papers [14, 15] do not discuss weighted sum, one can extend them to weighted sum. Some other approaches for SUM and other data aggregation are given in [7, 9, 16]. However they are used for single transaction.

5   Conclusions

In this paper, we proposed algorithms for computing the weighted sum function on users' private data values. These algorithms are tailored for the scenario where a third-party application is interested in aggregating data from a large number of users in multiple transactions. Unlike most work in privacy-assured function computations, the users in our scenario are not collaborating with each other. In fact, a user often does not even know the identity of other users. This novel aspect distinguishes our work from other schemes in literature. A key feature of our solution is a new certification-based method for providing privacy assurance to each user. Such a method reduces the computational burden on users to ensure that their private data will not be compromised. The end result is a solution in which the computation and communication burden for a user does not increase with the number of users. This is a significant advantage of the solution proposed in this paper.

References

1. Ben-David, A., Nisan, N., Pinkas, B.: FairplayMP: A system for secure multi-party computation. In: Proceedings of the ACM Conference on Computer and Communications Security, pp. 257–266. ACM, New York (2008)
2. Bogetoft, P., Christensen, D.L., Damgård, I., Geisler, M., Jakobsen, T., Krøigaard, M., Nielsen, J.D., Nielsen, J.B., Nielsen, K., Pagter, J., Schwartzbach, M., Toft, T.: Secure multiparty computation goes live. In: Dingledine, R., Golle, P. (eds.) FC 2009. LNCS, vol. 5628, pp. 325–343. Springer, Heidelberg (2009)
3. Chin, F.: Security problems in inference control for SUM, MAX, and MIN queries. J. ACM 33(3), 451–464 (1986)
4. Choi, S.G., Hwang, K.-W., Katz, J., Malkin, T., Rubenstein, D.: Secure multi-party computation of boolean circuits with applications to privacy in on-line marketplaces. In: Dunkelman, O. (ed.) CT-RSA 2012. LNCS, vol. 7178, pp. 416–432. Springer, Heidelberg (2012)
5. Gentry, C.: A fully homomorphic encryption scheme. Ph.D. Thesis, Stanford University (2009)
6. Goldreich, O.: Foundations of Cryptography: Basic Applications, vol. 2. Cambridge University Press, New York (2004)
7. Groat, M.M., He, W., Foreest, S.: KIPDA: k-Indistinguishable privacy-preserving data aggregation in wireless sensor networks. In: 2010 Proceedings IEEE on INFOCOM, pp. 2024–2032. IEEE (2011)
8. Halevi, S., Lindell, Y., Pinkas, B.: Secure Computation on the Web: Computing without Simultaneous Interaction. In: Rogaway, P. (ed.) CRYPTO 2011. LNCS, vol. 6841, pp. 132–150. Springer, Heidelberg (2011)
9. He, W., et al.: PDA: Privacy-preserving data aggregation in wireless sensor networks. In: INFOCOM 2007, 26th IEEE International Conference on Computer Communications, pp. 2045–2053. IEEE (2007)
10. Kentapadi, K.: Models and algorithms for data privacy, Ph.D. Thesis, Stanford University (2006)
11. L'opez-Alt, A., Tromer, E., Vaikuntanathan, V.: On-the-fly multiparty computation on the cloud via multikey fully homomorphic encryption. In: Proceedings of the Symposium on Theory of Computing (STOC), pp. 1219–1234 (2012)
12. Naor, M., Pinkas, B., Sumner, R.: Privacy preserving auctions and mechanism design. In: Proceedings of ACM Conference on Electronic Commerce, pp. 129–139 (1999)
13. Paillier, P.: Public-Key cryptosystems based on composite degree residuosity classes. In: Stern, J. (ed.) EUROCRYPT 1999. LNCS, vol. 1592, pp. 223–238. Springer, Heidelberg (1999)
14. Sheikh, R., Kumar, B., Mishra, D.K.: Privacy preserving k-secure sum protocol. Int. J. Comput. Sci. Inf. Secur. 6(2), 68–72 (2009)
15. Sheikh, R., Kumar, B., Mishra, D.K.: A modified k-secure sum protocol for multi-party computation. Int. J. Comput. 2(2), 62–66 (2010)
16. Shi, J., et al.: Prisense: privacy-preserving data aggregation in people-centric urban sensing systems. In: 2010 Proceedings IEEE on INFOCOM. IEEE (2010)
17. Toft, T.: Primitives and applications of secure multi-party computation. Ph.D. Thesis, University of Aarhus, Denmark (2007)
18. Yao, A.C.-C.: How to generate and exchange secrets. In: Proceedings of Foundations of Computer Science (FOCS), pp. 162–167, October 1986

A Secure Priority Queue; Or: On Secure Datastructures from Multiparty Computation

Tomas Toft[✉]

Department of CS, Aarhus University, Aarhus, Denmark
ttoft@cs.au.dk

Abstract. Secure multiparty computation (MPC) – computation on distributed, private inputs – has been studied for thirty years. This includes "one shot" applications as well as reactive tasks, where the exact computation is not known in advance. We extend this line of work by exploring efficient datastructures based on MPC primitives. The oblivious RAM (ORAM) provides a completeness theorem. However, implementing the ORAM-CPU using MPC-primitives is costly; current IT-secure constructions incur a poly-log overhead on computation and memory, while computationally secure constructions require MPC-evaluation of one-way functions, which introduces considerable overhead. Using ideas radically different from those in ORAM's, we propose a secure priority queue. Data accesses are *deterministic*, whereas ORAM's hide the access pattern through *randomization*. n priority queue operations – insertion and deletion of the minimal element – require $O(n \log^2 n)$ invocations of the cryptographic primitives in $O(n)$ rounds. The amortized cost of each operation is low, thus demonstrating feasibility.

Keywords: MPC · Reactive functionalities · Datastructures

1 Introduction

Secure function evaluation considers the problem of evaluating a function f on data held by N parties in a distributed manner. The goal is *privacy*: The parties learn $f(x_1, \ldots, x_N)$, but do so without revealing additional information about the x_i. This problem has been rigorously studied in the cryptographic community since it was proposed by Yao more than thirty years ago, [Yao82]. The notion can be extended to secure multiparty computation (MPC), which considers reactive tasks: An MPC protocol may consist of multiple sequential function evaluations, where each one depends on – and potentially updates – a secret state.

Different notions of security have been proposed, e.g., protocols can provide passive or active security. In the former, all parties follow the protocol, but may

---

Supported by the Danish Council for Independent Research via DFF Starting Grant 10-081612. Additional support from the Danish National Research Foundation and The National Science Foundation of China (under grant 61061130540) for the Sino-Danish Center for the Theory of Interactive Computation.

H.-S. Lee and D.-G. Han (Eds.): ICISC 2013, LNCS 8565, pp. 20–33, 2014.
DOI: 10.1007/978-3-319-12160-4_2

collude in an attempt to break the privacy of others. For active security, an adversary controls all corrupt parties who not only pool information, but can misbehave arbitrarily in a coordinated manner. Classic results demonstrate that any function can be computed with active security and polynomial overhead given a fully connected, synchronous network with authenticated channels (authenticated and secure channels when the adversary is computationally unbounded, i.e., the information theoretic (IT) case) [GMW87, BGW88, CCD88].

Many specialized protocols for specific, well-motivated problems have also been proposed – auctions and data mining are two popular examples. Utilizing domain specific knowledge and focusing solely on the task at hand may allow considerable efficiency gains. Though solutions may be reactive, this is rarely the case for the tasks themselves. Put differently: the topic of explicit datastructures based on MPC primitives has received surprisingly little attention.

Contribution. With the exception of realizations of the oblivious RAM (ORAM; see related work below), to our knowledge, we consider the first datastructure based on MPC. We construct an efficient priority queue (PQ) based on protocols providing secure storage and arithmetic over a ring, $\mathbb{Z}_M$, and inherit their security guarantees. Formally, protocols will be presented in a hybrid model providing secure black-box arithmetic; this can, e.g., be based on secret sharing.

Our PQ is inspired by the bucket heap of Brodal et al. [BFMZ04] and allows two operations: INSERT(p, x) which inserts a secret element, x, into the queue with secret priority p; and GETMIN() which deletes and returns (in secret form) the element with minimal priority. Each operations use $O(\log^2 n)$ primitive operations – arithmetic and comparisons – in $O(1)$ rounds (both amortized).

The overall approach taken in this paper is to construct a datastructure where the actions performed are completely independent of the inputs. From there it is merely a matter of implementing the operations using MPC primitives. This strategy presents an immediate path to the present goal, however, it is not at all clear that it is the only one, or indeed the best one.

Related Work. We find three areas of related work: *incremental cryptography (IC)* of Bellare et al. [BGG94, BGG95]; *history independent (HI) datastructures* introduced by Naor and Teague building on Micciancio's oblivious datastructures [NT01, Mic97]; and the *Oblivious RAM* due to Goldreich and Ostrovky [GO96].

IC considers evaluating some cryptographic function – e.g. a digital signature – on *known*, changing data *without* recomputing that function from scratch every time. HI datastructures on the other hand focus the problem of eliminating unintentional information leakages when datastructures containing *known* data are passed on to other parties. E.g., the shape of the structure itself may reveal information on the operations performed. Both consider security and structuring data, but are fundamentally different as the data is known to some party.

The closest related concept is the ORAM, where a CPU (with $O(1)$ private memory) runs a program residing in main memory. An adversary observes the memory access pattern (but not the data/instructions retrieved) and attempts to extract information. Damgård et al. observed (as hinted by Goldreich and

Ostrovky) that implementing the CPU using MPC primitives provides a secure RAM, i.e., allows arbitrary datastructures to be used in MPC.

Oblivious RAMs hide the access pattern by randomizing it. [GO96] achieved this using a random oracle instantiated by a one-way function. In a recent result (with security issues fixed in subsequent papers), Pinkas and Reinman brought the computational overhead down to $O(\log^2 n)$ and the memory overhead down to $O(1)$ [PR10]; this was further reduced to $O(\log^2 n / \log\log n)$ by Kushilevitz et al. [KLO12]. The approach used has two drawbacks when considering datastructures in MPC: The use of one-way functions implies that the solution cannot be IT-secure. Moreover, the one-way function must be evaluated using MPC; this can be done but will most likely be costly in terms of secure computation. Independently, Ajtai [Ajt10], and Damgård et al. [DMN10] have proposed information theoretic ORAM's. Though the solutions are different, both have poly-logarithmic overhead on both (secure) computation and memory usage. Recently Lu and Ostrovsky have proposed a much more efficient ORAM solution for the two party setting [LO11]. Combining their ideas with a heap matches the theoretic complexity of the present solution. However, recent advances by Damgård et al. allow *highly efficient* IT-secure two-party arithmetic, given a preprocessing phase [DPSZ12]. These are among the fastest MPC protocols presently known, and it is unclear how to implement the shuffles needed for the ORAM in that setting without using super-linear preprocessing or online communication, i.e., without incurring an overhead.

Where the ORAM provides a completeness theorem, the present work focuses on whether different strategies may provide more efficient means of reaching specific goals. Indeed, the present approach is radically different than those used when constructing ORAM's: in stark contrast to the above, the access pattern of the PQ solution presented is *completely deterministic*, whereas *any* IT secure realization of the ORAM require at least $\log n$ bits of randomness per operation, where n is the overall size of the memory, [DMN10]. This is possible since the overall "program" is known: Actions may depend on the task at hand.

Despite the common ground, ORAM's do not provide all answers regarding MPC datastructures, at least not presently. In addition to the above, using MPC to implement present ORAM solutions (other than [LO11]) incurs at least an overhead of $O(\log^2 n)$ on every read/write operation – this *equals* the cost of our PQ operations. The sequential nature of the ORAM also implies that it cannot provide round-efficient solutions. Further, both IT secure ORAM's have a poly-logarithmic overhead on memory usage, whereas the present construction does not, thus, to our knowledge the present work contains the first IT secure datastructure with constant memory overhead. Finally, there are no obvious reasons why the secure PQ could not be improved, while an IT secure ORAM with constant overhead seems less plausible.

2   The Basic Model of Secure Computation

We consider a setting where N parties, $P_1, \ldots, P_N$, are pairwise connected by authenticated channels in a synchronous network, and focus on MPC protocols based on linear primitives over a ring $\mathbb{Z}_M$. Secure storage and arithmetic is modeled using an ideal functionality – the arithmetic black-box (ABB), $\mathcal{F}_{ABB}$ – and protocols are constructed in the $\mathcal{F}_{ABB}$-hybrid model. This functionality was introduced by Damgård and Nielsen [DN03]; the benefits include abstracting away irrelevant low-level details as well as simplifying security proofs: The underlying primitives provides security for any the application, thus privacy can only be lost if we *explicitly* output a value.

2.1   The Arithmetic Black-Box

Reference [DN03] presents $\mathcal{F}_{ABB}$ in the UC framework of Canetti [Can00] and realizes it efficiently based on Paillier encryption [Pai99]. The protocols are shown secure against an active, adaptive adversary corrupting a minority of the parties. For simplicity, we present a modified $\mathcal{F}_{ABB}$ focusing on passive corruption only:

- **Input:** If party P_i sends "$P_i : x \leftarrow v$" and all other send "$P_i : x \leftarrow ?$", $\mathcal{F}_{ABB}$ stores v under the variable name x,[1] and sends "$P_i : x \leftarrow ?$" to everyone.
- **Output:** If all parties send "$\text{output}(x)$", then assuming that value v was stored under x, $\mathcal{F}_{ABB}$ sends "$x = v$" to everyone as well as the adversary.
- **Arithmetic:** Upon receiving "$x \leftarrow y + z$" from all parties, $\mathcal{F}_{ABB}$ computes the sum of the values stored under y and z and stores the result as x. Similarly, upon receiving "$x \leftarrow y \cdot z$" from all parties, the product is stored under x.

Input/output can be though of as secret sharing/reconstruction, in which case linear primitives implies that addition of shares is addition of secrets; multiplication then requires interaction. Shamir sharing along with the protocols of Ben-Or et al. fit this description [Sha79, BGW88], see Appendix A, though we can equally well instantiate $\mathcal{F}_{ABB}$ using homomorphic encryption, e.g., [Pai99, CDN01].

  In case of active adversaries, minor alterations must be made to $\mathcal{F}_{ABB}$ to ensure that it exactly captures the possible behavior. It is stressed that such change do not invalidate our construction below. Consider, e.g., the case of honest majority and guaranteed termination: Adversarial parties are allowed to abort, hence $\mathcal{F}_{ABB}$ should only receive $\lfloor (N + 1)/2 \rfloor$ output messages before sending "$x = v$". In a similar vein, when fairness is not ensured, the adversary receives "$x = v$" first, and can decide if the honest parties should receive it as well.

2.2   Complexity

As abstract primitives are used, one can merely count the number of operations performed by $\mathcal{F}_{ABB}$. These correspond directly to the computation and communication of the underlying primitives. We focus on communication complexity of such operations; since linear primitives are assumed, this implies that addition (and multiplication by public values) is costless. We will not distinguish between the complexities of the remaining operations, but remark that multiplication is generally both the most used and the most costly one.

---

[1] For simplicity, consider these distinct, i.e., variables are never overwritten.

Regarding instantiations of $\mathcal{F}_{ABB}$, the basic operations are typically reasonably cheap. For passive adversaries, typically only $O(1)$ ring elements are communicated per player or pair of players. E.g., performing a passively secure multiplication of Shamir shared values can be done by having each party reshare the product of its shares (plus local computation), i.e., two field elements per pair. The dominating term of the Paillier based protocols of [DN03] – and in other actively secure constructions – is $O(N)$ *Byzantine agreements* on ring elements (e.g., encryptions) per (non-costless) operation, i.e., $O(1)$ Byzantine agreements per player. Unless a broadcast channel is assumed, such an overhead is required to guarantee robustness against actively malicious adversaries.

A second measure of complexity of protocols is the number of rounds required (the number of message exchanges). For clarity this was left out of the presentation above, however, it is easily incorporated: Assume that all operations take the same, constant number of rounds. Now, rather than receiving *one* instruction from each party, parties send *lists of independent instructions* to be performed by the functionality. Each invocation of $\mathcal{F}_{ABB}$ then refers to one round of operations, which in turn translates to one or more rounds of communication.

The straightline program notation used below improves readability, but has a drawback: The description of the protocols is detached from the actual execution in the $\mathcal{F}_{ABB}$ hybrid model. Hence, complexity analysis becomes slightly more complicated, as the description does not explicitly state which operations can be performed in parallel. Clearer descriptions easily makes up for this, though.

3   Extending the Arithmetic Black-Box

The secure priority queue is not constructed directly based on $\mathcal{F}_{ABB}$. We extend that functionality with additional operations. These are realized using nothing more than the basic operations of $\mathcal{F}_{ABB}$. This section can be viewed as containing preliminaries in the sense that it introduces a number of known constructions.

3.1   Secure Comparison

Having priorities implies some notion of order with respect to the stored elements. Further, $\mathcal{F}_{ABB}$ must allow us to compare priorities to determine which is larger. Extending the functionality with such an operation is straightforward:

– **Comparison:** Upon receiving "$x \leftarrow y >^? z$" from all parties, $\mathcal{F}_{ABB}$ determines if y is larger than z, and stores the result as x; 1 for true and 0 for false.

As an example, consider the "integer ordering" of $\mathbb{Z}_M$-elements. For prime M, this can be implemented using $O(\log M)$ non-costless operations in $O(1)$ rounds, e.g. [NO07]. When M is an RSA modulus – e.g., a public Paillier key – complexity is increased to $O(N \log M)$ due to more expensive sub-protocols. In specific settings other solutions may be preferable, e.g., [Tof11,LT13]. It is stressed that these are merely options; *any* secure computation and *any* ordering works.

For simplicity of the analysis, we assume that the comparison requires only a constant number of rounds, and count the number of comparison invocations separately from the basic operations due to its (in general) much higher cost. Given a specific protocol one can determine the actual cost.

3.2   Secure Conditional Swap

Based on the ability to compare, it is possible to perform conditional swaps: Given two values, swap them if the latter is larger than the former. This can be viewed as sorting lists of length two, and is easily constructed within the ABB by simply computing the maximal and minimal of the two.

$$max \leftarrow \left(a >^? b\right)(a - b) + b; \quad min \leftarrow a + b - max$$

These expressions easily translate to messages from parties to $\mathcal{F}_{ABB}$; work is constant – $O(1)$ basic operations and a single comparison – and multiple swaps may be executed in parallel. The swap computation can be generalized to multi-element values, say pairs consisting of a priority and a data element. It is simply a question of having a well-defined comparison operator and using its output to choose between the two candidates on a single element basis.

3.3   Secure Merging

The main, large-scale primitive is the ability to merge sorted lists of length ℓ stored within $\mathcal{F}_{ABB}$. This is written MERGE (X, Y), where X and Y refer to lists of stored values. A solution is obtained from sorting networks – sorting algorithms created directly based on conditional swaps. No branching is performed, hence they are deterministic and oblivious to the inputs, except the problem size, ℓ.

Any sorting network can be utilized to merge, by simply viewing the whole input as a single unsorted list. However, for efficiency, we take the inner workings of Batcher's odd-even mergesort [Bat68]. The whole sorting network requires $O(\ell \log^2 \ell)$ conditional swaps, but merging alone requires only $O(\ell \log \ell)$ conditional swaps in $O(\log \ell)$ rounds, and constants are low.

A primitive for merging lists of *differing* lengths, $\ell \neq \ell'$, is also required. The shorter list is simply padded – assume that some element, e_∞, which is greater than all others is reserved for this – such that they become of equal length. Now merge the lists using the above solution and remove the padding; since these elements are greater than any valid ones, all such elements are pushed to one side. The size of the padding is known, so those elements can be removed by truncating the list. Complexity is $O(\max(\ell \log \ell; \ell' \log \ell'))$ operations in $O(\max(\log \ell, \log \ell'))$ rounds. We overload MERGE $(\cdot, \cdot)$ to avoid introducing additional notation.

We present a final, needed primitive which is highly related to merging: *merge-split*. This operation, denoted MERGESPLIT (X, Y), takes two lists as input as above. As the name suggests, the goal is to merge two lists into one, which is then split (cut into two parts whose concatenation is the sorted list). The only requirement is that lengths of the new lists must equal the lengths of the old ones.

The effect of a merge-split is that the most significant elements end up in one of the lists, while the least significant ones end up in the other. Naturally, both new lists are still sorted. Clearly this operation is equivalent to a merge, as the split merely renames variables. Hence, its complexity is the same as merging.

4 The Goal: A Secure Priority Queue

We are now ready to present the desired goal, an ideal functionality for a priority queue, $\mathcal{F}_{PQ}$. However, the data of a datastructure is not separated from the rest of the world in general and inputs to the datastructure may not originate from some party, but could be the result of previous computation. Thus, the goal is to *further extend* the arithmetic black-box with a priority queue. As with the introduction of a comparison operator, we simply list all operations needed. I.e., $\mathcal{F}_{PQ}$ contains the operations of the extended $\mathcal{F}_{ABB}$ in addition to the following:

– INSERT(p, x):[2] Upon receiving "PQinsert(p, x)" from all parties, where p and x are variables, $\mathcal{F}_{PQ}$ stores the values associated with the pair (p, x) in an internal, initially empty list, L. All parties then receive "PQinsert(p, x)".
– GETMIN(): Upon receiving "$y \leftarrow$PQgetmin()" from all parties, $\mathcal{F}_{PQ}$ determines and deletes from L the pair with the lowest p-value. The corresponding x-value is stored as y, and all parties receive "$y \leftarrow$PQgetmin()" from $\mathcal{F}_{PQ}$.

Naturally, parties engaging in a protocol may interleave these two operations arbitrarily with other computation. This could even contain operations for other priority queues. Note, however, that $\mathcal{F}_{PQ}$ must treat the operations on a given PQ as atomic with respect to each other. There is a small issue with the above description: The behavior of $\mathcal{F}_{PQ}$ is not specified if GETMIN() is executed on an empty queue. In this case, $\mathcal{F}_{PQ}$ may simply discard the operation. All parties always know the exact number of elements in the queue, as they are notified whenever operations occur, hence this has no consequences.

5 The Secure Bucket Heap

A standard binary heap is not directly implementable using MPC primitives as one cannot traverse a tree from root to leaf by a path depending on secret data. The realization of $\mathcal{F}_{PQ}$ is instead based off of the bucket heap of Brodal et al. [BFMZ04], though a few significant changes are made. Jumping ahead, the original solution merges sorted lists using linear scans – we must employ Batcher's solution from Sect. 3.3. Secondly, we impose a rigid structure (with respect to the priorities) of the elements of each bucket. This actually causes the name *bucket heap* to be slightly misleading. Finally, we consider a simple problem than [BFMZ04] – the decrease-key operation has been eliminated, which implies that the actual content can be ignored.

---

[2] This is referred to as INSERT(p) below; x, is left implicit to avoid clutter.

5.1   The Intuition of the Secure Bucket Heap

We stress that this section is *not*, strictly speaking, correct. However, it explains the core ideas nicely: Store a list, D, containing all the data in sorted order. Doing so naively makes inserts too costly, as a newly inserted element can end up anywhere. Thus, rather than inserting directly into that list, elements are placed in buffers until sufficiently many have arrived to pay for the combined cost of all insertions. More formally, the data is split into sub-lists (buckets), $D_0, D_1, D_2, \ldots$, where the elements of D_i are less than those of D_{i+1}. The size of the D_i double with each step (or level) – $|D_i| = 2^i$. In addition to this, at each level, i, there is a buffer, B_i, of the same length as the data; see Fig. 1.

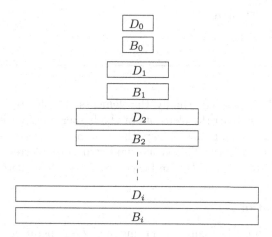

Fig. 1. The structure of the bucket heap

Inserting new data means placing it in the uppermost buffer, B_0, the intuition being, that whenever a buffer B_i is full, its contents are processed. The elements that "belong at this level" are moved to D_i, while the rest are pushed down to B_{i+1}. The D_i can be viewed as a sorted list of "buckets" of elements, where elements increase with each step. Thus, "belong at" means that an element is smaller than some $p \in D_i$. The minimal is obtained by returning the contents of D_0. Subsequent GETMIN()'s will find, D_0 empty, but the desired element is found in the top-most, non-empty bucket. The remainder of the content of its bucket is then placed in the buckets above.

5.2   Invariants

Data is stored as specified above, but with a few additional requirements. Bucket D_i is either completely full or completely empty, $|D_i| \in \{0, 2^i\}$. Buffers are slightly different as the B_i must contain strictly less than 2^i elements. They may temporarily exceed this limit – denoted that the buffer is full – at which point

---

Protocol 1. FLUSH(i) – flushing buffer B_i at level i

Require: Full buffer, B_i, at level i.

Operation: Flush B_i, moving the elements contained into data or subsequent buffers.

    if $|D_i| = 0$ and i is the lowest level **then**

        $D_i \leftarrow B_i(1..2^i)$

        $B_i \leftarrow B_i((2^i + 1)..|B_i|)$

        if $|B_i| \geq 2^i$ **then**

5:            FLUSH(i)

        end if

    else

        $(D_i, B_i) \leftarrow$ MERGESPLIT (D_i, B_i)

        $B_{i+1} \leftarrow$ MERGE (B_i, B_{i+1})

10:     Set B_i empty

        if $|B_{i+1}| \geq 2^{i+1}$ **then**

            FLUSH($i + 1$)

        end if

    end if

---

the contents will be processed. Finally, the elements of buffer B_i are greater than (have higher priority than) the elements of the higher-lying buckets, D_j, $j < i$. In difference to the original bucket heap, the contents of the buckets and buffers are stored sorted by priority. This is the rigid structure referred to above. Note that the concatenation of the D_i can be viewed as one long, sorted list.

5.3 The Operations

The datastructure must be maintained using only $\mathcal{F}_{\text{ABB}}$-operations. The two operations needed are the insertion of a new value and the extraction of the present minimal. The main parts of these operations are seen as Protocols 1 and 2.

The insert operation, INSERT(p), is performed by placing p in the top buffer, B_0. This fills it and it must be flushed using Protocol 1. The GETMIN() operation is realized by the (attempted) extraction the element stored in the top-level bucket. This is done by executing DELMIN (0); the details are seen as Protocol 2.

5.4 Correctness

To show correctness, it suffices to show that the invariants hold and that these imply the desired behavior. It is clear that for the starting position – an empty priority queue – all invariants hold. All buckets are empty which is acceptable; further, there are no elements so the required ordering between elements of different buckets and buffers as well as the internal ordering are clearly satisfied.

An INSERT(p) operation places p in B_0. Note that all invariants holds except that B_0 is full – no relationship to other elements is required of the sole element in B_0. After this, the buffer is flushed. There are two possible states, as seen from the "outer" if-statement of Protocol 1: either this is the lowest level and D_i is empty; *or* there is data here or below. At the bottom we simply move the

---

Protocol 2. DELMIN(i) – return the 2^i smallest elements from level i and below (or everything if there are fewer than 2^i elements)

Require: Non-empty bucket heap; all levels above the i'th are completely empty.
Operation: DELMIN(i) – determine and return the 2^i minimal elements

    if $|D_i| = 2^i$ **then**
        $(D_i, B_i) \leftarrow$ MERGESPLIT (D_i, B_i)
        Return D_i and set it empty
    else if i is the lowest level **then**
5:      Return B_i and set it empty
    else
        $B_{i+1} \leftarrow$ MERGE (B_i, B_{i+1})
        Set B_i empty
        if $|B_{i+1}| \geq 2^{i+1}$ **then**
10:     FLUSH($i + 1$)
        end if
        $\tilde{D} \leftarrow$ DELMIN $(i + 1)$
        if $|\tilde{D}| = 2^{i+1}$ **then**
            $D_i \leftarrow \tilde{D}(2^i + 1..2^{i+1})$
15:     Return $\tilde{D}(1..2^i))$
        else if $|\tilde{D}| > 2^i$ **then**
            $B_i \leftarrow \tilde{D}(2^i + 1..|\tilde{D}|)$
            Return $\tilde{D}(1..2^i))$
        else
20:     Return $\tilde{D}$
        end if
    end if

2^i smallest elements into the bucket (buffers are only flushed when they contain 2^i elements). As *all* the elements in the buffer are bigger than the elements in the buckets above, then the new relationship with all buckets hold.

Alternatively, there is data in the present bucket, D_i, or below. By the invariant, all elements are greater than the elements of the buckets above. Thus, performing the merge-split, line 8, does not violate invariants. This step ensures that the smallest elements of the level end in D_i; these are at most as big as the previous largest element of D_i, and must therefore be smaller than the elements of the levels below. Additionally, it is guaranteed that the elements of D_i are smaller than those of B_i, so the latter can be pushed into the buffer below. All invariant still hold, except that B_{i+1} may now have become full; if so, flush it.

The minimal element is obtained using DELMIN(0). The intuition behind Protocol 2 is that the minimal element must come from a bucket. Only when *no* such elements exist will a buffer-element be taken, line 5. The invariant implies that the minimal element will be in the top-most, non-empty bucket *or* in a buffer above. Starting with B_0, buffers are flushed until a non-empty bucket is found, lines 7 and 12. Note that these buffer merges do not affect the invariant.

Once a non-empty bucket is found, it is merge-split with its buffer to ensure that it contains the 2^i smallest elements, not only at this level, but *overall*:

buckets and buffers above are empty, and any element in the bucket is less significant than any at a level below. The bucket is then emptied into the buckets above, filling them and leaving one element to be returned – this task is trivial as all buckets (and their concatenation) are sorted. It is easily verified that the invariants hold at this point.

If all buckets are empty, then all buffers are merged until only a single non-empty one exists (at the lowest level, i). Viewing B_i as a sorted list, its contents may be distributed to the top buckets above, exactly as with the emptying of a bucket above, *except* that there may be "excess elements." For $|B_i| = 2^j + k$, with $k < 2^j$, the minimal element can be returned and the j top-most buckets filled. This leaves the k largest elements; these are placed in the buffer B_{j+1}. The elements of B_i are easily distributed such that the invariant holds.

5.5 Complexity

Complexity of both INSERT(p) and DELMIN(0) is $O(\log^2 n)$ amortized, where n is the overall number of operations. This follows from a coin argument, where each coin pays for a conditional swap.

When inserting an element into B_0, $\Theta(\log^2 n)$ coins are placed on it. The invariant is that every element in B_i has $\Theta(((\log n) - i)\log n)$ coins, which is clearly satisfied for both the initial (empty) datastructure and for the newly inserted element. These coins pay for the flushes caused by full buffers, Protocol 1.

Moving elements from the buffer to the empty bucket at the lowest level is costless. In the other case, the buffer B_i is merged with bucket, D_i, (in the merge-split) and with buffer B_{i+1} below. Both merges require $O(2^i \log 2^i)$ conditional swaps – the lists are at most a constant factor longer than 2^i. This cost is paid using $\Theta(2^i \log n)$ coins from the elements of B_i. The merge-split potentially moves elements between the buffer and bucket, however, the number of elements in the buffer remains the same. The second merge moves the contents to the level below. As B_i was full, it contained at least 2^i elements; thus, it suffices if each one moved pays $\Theta(\log n)$ coins. As the entire contents of the buffer is pushed one level down, the elements only require $\Theta(((\log n) - (i + 1))\log n)$ to ensure that the invariant holds. Hence, the invariant holds after each element has paid the coins needed for the flush. This implies the stated complexity for INSERT(p).

A similar argument is needed for deletion, DELMIN(0). However, rather than placing coins on the elements themselves, the deletion coins are placed on the buffers. Each operation places $\Theta(\log n)$ coins on each of the buffers, B_i; this requires $\Theta(\log^2 n)$ coins overall. The invariant is, that B_i has $\Omega(k \log n)$ coins, where k is the combined size of the empty buckets above, i.e. $k = \sum_{j=0; |D_j|=0}^{i-1} 2^j$. Whenever DELMIN($i$) is called, it implies that the buckets of all levels $j < i$ above are empty. Hence, the buffer B_i has $\Omega((2^i - 1)\log n)$ coins allowing it to pay for a merge at level i, either with the contents of bucket D_i or the buffer below.

Either way, all buckets above are filled,[3] implying that B_i no longer needs coins to satisfy the invariant. Thus, earlier delete operations pay for the required merge.

Regarding round complexity, the operations require at most a constant number of merges per level, so worst-case complexity is $O(\log^2 n)$. Amortized complexity is only constant, though. Lower levels are rarely processed ($\Omega(2^i)$) operations occur between the ones "touching" level i) and upper levels are cheap (only $O(i)$ rounds are required to merge at level i); for n operations, $\sum_{i=0}^{\log n} \frac{n}{2^i} i^2$ rounds are needed overall implying $O(1)$ rounds on average.

5.6 Security

Intuitively, security of the bucket heap follows directly from the security of $\mathcal{F}_{\mathsf{ABB}}$: An adversary, $\mathcal{A}$, can only learn information when the ideal functionality outputs a value, i.e., when the underlying primitives explicitly reveal information. However, at no point in the present computation is an output command given by any of the honest parties. Hence, as $\mathcal{A}$ does not control what amounts to a qualified set, it cannot make $\mathcal{F}_{\mathsf{ABB}}$ perform an output operation. By similar reasoning, it can be seen that no adversary – i.e., set of parties behaving incorrectly – can influence the computation resulting in incorrect values stored in $\mathcal{F}_{\mathsf{ABB}}$.

The above is of course only the intuitive explanation. Formally, the view of $\mathcal{A}$ must be simulated in the $\mathcal{F}_{\mathsf{ABB}}$-hybrid model. The required simulator, however, is trivial. It simply "executes" the realizing PQ computation, except that for every operation that the basic $\mathcal{F}_{\mathsf{ABB}}$ should be instructed to perform, the simulator will simply play the role of $\mathcal{F}_{\mathsf{ABB}}$ towards the corrupt players. It will receive their commands and send the messages (acknowledgments) to the corrupt players that they expect to receive. This is clearly indistinguishable from the point of view of any adversary. For each PQ operation, it simply sees a fixed set of messages, namely the ones corresponding to the secure computation implementing the operation, which it "knows" is being executed.

5.7 Hiding Whether an Operation Is Performed

A simple variation consists of conditional operations, i.e., operations based on secret bit, b. To achieve this, we add an additional key, $e_{-\infty}$, smaller than any real key and implement conditional INSERT(p) as INSERT $(b \cdot (p - e_\infty) + e_\infty)$ – this inserts p or e_∞ depending on b. Similarly, we can implement a conditional GETMIN() as INSERT $(b \cdot (e_\infty - e_{-\infty}) + e_{-\infty})$; GETMIN (). If $b = 0$ $e_{-\infty}$ is inserted and immediately removed. Otherwise e_∞ is inserted and the minimal removed.

Note that we no longer know the number of real keys in the PQ. This is unavoidable – a conditional GETMIN() cannot decrease the number of elements stored, while INSERT($\cdot$) must always add an element. If desired, one can keep count of the actual size, adding (subtracting) b for every INSERT($\cdot$) (GETMIN()).

---

[3] The only possible exception occurs when all buckets are empty and the buffers contain too few elements to fill them all. In this case a "completely full" structure is constructed from scratch so no coins are needed.

A   An ABB Realization

Consider a *passive* adversary and Shamir's secret sharing scheme over $\mathbb{Z}_M = \mathbb{F}_M$ for prime M, [Sha79]. Secret sharing allows one party to store a value privately and robustly among multiple others. If *and only if* sufficiently many agree, the value will be revealed. Input (respectively output) simply refers to secret sharing a value (respectively reconstructing a secret shared value). To implement arithmetic, note that Shamir's scheme is linear, so addition is simply addition of shares, while secure multiplication can be obtained through the protocols of Ben-Or et al. when less than $N/2$ parties are corrupt [BGW88]. It can be shown (given secure communication between all pairs of players, and assuming that all parties agree on the secure computation being performed) that these protocols realize $\mathcal{F}_{ABB}$ with perfect security in the presence of passive adversaries. Further, the protocols of [BGW88] even realize (a variation of) the presented $\mathcal{F}_{ABB}$ in the presence of active adversaries if the corruption threshold is reduced to $N/3$ – this solution guarantees termination.

References

[Ajt10] Ajtai, M.: Oblivious rams without cryptogrpahic assumptions. In: 42nd Annual ACM Symposium on Theory of Computing, pp. 181–190. ACM Press (2010)

[Bat68] Batcher, K.E.: Sorting networks and their applications. In: AFIPS Spring Joint Computing Conference, pp. 307–314 (1968)

[BFMZ04] Brodal, G.S., Fagerberg, R., Meyer, U., Zeh, N.: Cache-oblivious data structures and algorithms for undirected breadth-first search and shortest paths. In: Hagerup, T., Katajainen, J. (eds.) SWAT 2004. LNCS, vol. 3111, pp. 480–492. Springer, Heidelberg (2004)

[BGG94] Bellare, M., Goldreich, O., Goldwasser, S.: Incremental cryptography: the case of hashing and signing. In: Desmedt, Y.G. (ed.) CRYPTO 1994. LNCS, vol. 839, pp. 216–233. Springer, Heidelberg (1994)

[BGG95] Bellare, M., Goldreich, O., Goldwasser, S.: Incremental cryptography and application to virus protection. In: 27th Annual ACM Symposium on Theory of Computing, pp. 45–56. ACM Press (1995)

[BGW88] Ben-Or, M., Goldwasser, S., Wigderson, A.: Completeness theorems for noncryptographic fault-tolerant distributed computations. In: 20th Annual ACM Symposium on Theory of Computing, pp. 1–10. ACM Press (1988)

[Can00] Canetti, R.: Universally composable security: a new paradigm for cryptographic protocols. Cryptology ePrint Archive, Report 2000/067 (2000). http://eprint.iacr.org/

[CCD88] Chaum, D., Crépeau, C., Damgård, I.: Multiparty unconditionally secure protocols. In: 20th Annual ACM Symposium on Theory of Computing, pp. 11–19. ACM Press (1988)

[CDN01] Cramer, R., Damgård, I.B., Nielsen, J.B.: Multiparty computation from threshold homomorphic encryption. In: Pfitzmann, B. (ed.) EUROCRYPT 2001. LNCS, vol. 2045, pp. 280–300. Springer, Heidelberg (2001)

[DMN10] Damgård, I., Meldgaard, S., Nielsen, J.B.: Perfectly secure oblivious ram without random oracles. Cryptology ePrint Archive, Report 2010/108 (2010). http://eprint.iacr.org/. (conference version to appear at TCC 2011)

[DN03] Damgård, I.B., Nielsen, J.B.: Universally composable efficient multiparty computation from threshold homomorphic encryption. In: Boneh, D. (ed.) CRYPTO 2003. LNCS, vol. 2729, pp. 247–264. Springer, Heidelberg (2003)

[DPSZ12] Damgård, I., Pastro, V., Smart, N., Zakarias, S.: Multiparty computation from somewhat homomorphic encryption. In: Safavi-Naini, R., Canetti, R. (eds.) CRYPTO 2012. LNCS, vol. 7417, pp. 643–662. Springer, Heidelberg (2012)

[GMW87] Goldreich, O., Micali, S., Wigderson, A.: How to play any mental game. In: STOC '87: Proceedings of the Nineteenth Annual ACM Conference on Theory of Computing, pp. 218–229. ACM Press, New York (1987)

[GO96] Goldreich, O., Ostrovsky, R.: Software protection and simulation on oblivious rams. J. ACM 43(3), 431–473 (1996)

[KLO12] Kushilevitz, E., Lu, S., Ostrovsky, R.: On the (in)security of hash-based oblivious ram and a new balancing scheme. In: Rabani, Y. (ed.) SODA, pp. 143–156. SIAM (2012)

[LO11] Lu, S., Ostrovsky, R.: Distributed oblivious ram for secure two-party computation. Cryptology ePrint Archive, Report 2011/384 (2011). http://eprint.iacr.org/

[LT13] Lipmaa, H., Toft, T.: Secure equality and greater-than tests with sublinear online complexity. In: Fomin, F.V., Freivalds, R., Kwiatkowska, M., Peleg, D. (eds.) ICALP 2013, Part II. LNCS, vol. 7966, pp. 645–656. Springer, Heidelberg (2013)

[Mic97] Micciancio, D.: Oblivious data structures: applications to cryptography. In: STOC, pp. 456–464 (1997)

[NO07] Nishide, T., Ohta, K.: Multiparty computation for interval, equality, and comparison without bit-decomposition protocol. In: Okamoto, T., Wang, X. (eds.) PKC 2007. LNCS, vol. 4450, pp. 343–360. Springer, Heidelberg (2007)

[NT01] Naor, M., Teague, V.: Anti-persistence: history independent data structures. In: STOC, pp. 492–501 (2001)

[Pai99] Paillier, P.: Public-Key cryptosystems based on composite degree residuosity classes. In: Stern, J. (ed.) EUROCRYPT 1999. LNCS, vol. 1592, p. 223. Springer, Heidelberg (1999)

[PR10] Pinkas, B., Reinman, T.: Oblivious RAM revisited. In: Rabin, T. (ed.) CRYPTO 2010. LNCS, vol. 6223, pp. 502–519. Springer, Heidelberg (2010)

[Sha79] Shamir, A.: How to share a secret. Commun. ACM 22(11), 612–613 (1979)

[Tof11] Toft, T.: Sub-linear, secure comparison with two non-colluding parties. In: Catalano, D., Fazio, N., Gennaro, R., Nicolosi, A. (eds.) PKC 2011. LNCS, vol. 6571, pp. 174–191. Springer, Heidelberg (2011)

[Yao82] Yao, A.: Protocols for secure computations (extended abstract). In: 23th Annual Symposium on Foundations of Computer Science (FOCS '82), pp. 160–164. IEEE Computer Society Press (1982)

Towards Secure Two-Party Computation
from the Wire-Tap Channel

Hervé Chabanne[1,2,3]($^{(⊠)}$), Gérard Cohen[2,3], and Alain Patey[1,2,3]

[1] Morpho, Issy les Moulineaux, Paris, France
[2] Télécom ParisTech, Paris, France
{herve.chabanne,gerard.cohen,alain.patey}@telecom-paristech.fr
[3] Identity and Security Alliance (The Morpho and Télécom ParisTech
Research Center), Paris, France

Abstract. We introduce a new tentative protocol for secure two-party computation of linear functions in the semi-honest model, based on coding techniques. We first establish a parallel between the second version of the wire-tap channel model and secure two-party computation. This leads us to our protocol, that combines linear coset coding and oblivious transfer techniques. Our construction requires the use of binary intersecting codes or q-ary minimal codes, which are also studied in this paper.

Keywords: Secure Two-Party Computation · Secure Function Evaluation · Wire-Tap Channel · Oblivious transfer · Coset coding · Intersecting codes · Minimal codewords · Minimal linear codes

1 Introduction

Secure Multi-party Computation has been introduced in the late eighties by Yao [25] and has been subject to a lot of studies to demonstrate its feasibility and completeness in several adversarial settings. Recently, a lot of work has been done to make these techniques practical. We refer the reader to [9,12,14] for overviews on the state of the art in Secure Multi-Party Computation. We here focus on the two-party setting. In this setting, two parties P_1 and P_2, holding respective inputs X and Y, wish to securely compute a function f on their inputs. At the end of the protocol, one party (or both) learns $f(X, Y)$, but gains no more information about the other party's input than what can be deduced from this output. The seminal example given by [25] is the millionaire's problem: two millionaires wish to know which one of them is the richer, without revealing their respective wealths. We here focus on the semi-honest adversarial model, where both parties are supposed to follow the protocol but where they try to infer more information than they should from all data exchanges. Yao [25] gives a construction fulfilling these requirements [15], applicable to any function expressed as binary circuit. This technique is based on garbled circuits and oblivious transfer.

© Springer International Publishing Switzerland 2014
H.-S. Lee and D.-G. Han (Eds.): ICISC 2013, LNCS 8565, pp. 34–46, 2014.
DOI: 10.1007/978-3-319-12160-4_3

Oblivious transfer, originally introduced by Rabin [18] in a slightly different version, enables one receiver $\mathcal{R}$ to get one out of N secrets $X_1, \ldots, X_N$ held by a sender $\mathcal{S}$. The receiver chooses an index $c \in \{1, \ldots, N\}$, gets X_c and learns nothing about the X_j's, for $j \neq c$. Symmetrically, the sender $\mathcal{S}$ learns nothing about c. This is also known as *Symmetric Private Information Retrieval* (SPIR). Many protocols and implementations exist for oblivious transfer, some pointers can be found in [16].

The Wire-Tap Channel model has been introduced by Wyner [24] and later extended by Ozarow and Wyner [17] to a second version considering an erasure channel for the eavesdropper. We here consider the Wire-Tap Channel II (WTC2) [17] to establish a parallel with Secure Two-Party Computation. The model for WTC2 is described in Fig. 1. Alice sends an encoded message to Bob. Eve is allowed to access a bounded number of coordinates of the codeword, and she moreover controls the erasure positions. In the original model, Eve is not supposed to learn any information about the original message, even knowing the coding and decoding algorithms. Later [7,23], the information gained by Eve if she learns more than the original bound was studied. In particular, using coset coding techniques, there exists a sequence (d_i) of bounds such that Alice gains less than i information bits about the original message if she has access to less than d_i coordinates of the message.

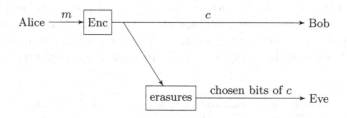

Fig. 1. The Wire-Tap Channel II

This is where we establish the parallel with Secure Two-Party Computation. We see the two parties performing the secure computation as Alice and Eve in the WTC2 model. The message that is encoded by Alice would be the input X of Alice. We want the bits of information that Eve gets about X to be the actual bits of $f(X, Y)$. We will explain in this paper how to do this using linear coset coding techniques and some classes of linear functions. The last thing we need to achieve the parallel is a modeling of the erasure channel. This will be done using oblivious transfers. We illustrate this parallel in Fig. 2.

In Sect. 2, we recall some results about Wire-Tap Channel II and linear coset coding. We infer a protocol for secure two-party computation in Sect. 3. This raises the problem of finding minimal linear codes, that we study in Sect. 4. Finally, we conclude in Sect. 5.

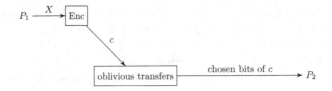

Fig. 2. From WTC2 to Secure Two-Party Computation

2   Wire-Tap Channel II and Linear Coset Coding

In the following, an $[n, k, d]$ *linear code* denotes a subspace of dimension k of $\mathbb{F}_q^n$ with minimum Hamming distance d, where $q = p^k$, for p prime and $k \in \mathbb{N}$. We denote by $C^\perp$ the dual code of C. The support of $c \in C$ is $supp(c) = \{i \in \{1, \ldots, n\} | c_i \neq 0\}$. We might use *bit*, by abuse of language, even if $q \neq 2$, to denote a coordinate of a message or of a codeword.

2.1   Linear Coset Coding

Coset coding is a random encoding used for both models of Wire-Tap Channel [17,24]. This type of encoding uses an $[n, k, d]$ linear code C with a parity-check matrix H. Let $r = n - k$. To encode a message $m \in \mathbb{F}_q^r$, one randomly chooses an element among all $x \in \mathbb{F}_q^n$ such that $m = H \cdot x^T$. To decode a codeword x, one just applies the parity-check matrix H and obtains the syndrome of x for the code C, which is the message m. This procedure is summed up in Fig. 3.

Given: C an $[n, n - r, d]$ linear code with a $r \times n$ parity-check matrix H
Encode: $m \in \mathbb{F}_2^r \mapsto_R x \in \mathbb{F}_2^n$ s.t. $H \cdot x^T = m$
Decode: $x \in \mathbb{F}_2^n \mapsto m = H \cdot x^T$

Fig. 3. Linear coset-coding

2.2   The Wire-Tap Channel I

The Wire-Tap Channel was introduced by Wyner [24]. In this model, a sender Alice sends messages over a potentially noisy channel to a receiver Bob. An adversary Eve listens to an auxiliary channel, the Wire-Tap channel, which is a noisier version of the main channel. It was shown that, with an appropriate coding scheme, the secret message can be conveyed in such a way that Bob has complete knowledge of the secret and Eve does not learn anything. In the special case where the main channel is noiseless, the secrecy capacity can be achieved through a linear coset coding scheme.

2.3   The Wire-Tap Channel II

Ten years later, Ozarow and Wyner introduced a second version of the WT Channel [17]. In this model, both main and Wire-Tap channels are noiseless. This time, the disadvantage for Eve is that she can only see messages with erasures: she has only access to a limited number of bits per codeword. She is however allowed to choose which bits she can learn. We summarize the Wire-Tap Channel II in Fig. 1.

The encoding used in this model is again a coset coding based on a linear code C, as in the Wire Tap Channel I with a noiseless main channel. Let $d^\perp$ denote the minimum distance of the dual $C^\perp$ of C. One can prove (see [23] for instance) that, if Eve can access less than $d^\perp$ bits of a codeword, then she gains no information at all on the associated message.

2.4   Generalized Hamming Distances

Generalized Hamming distances (or generalized Hamming weights) have first been considered by Wei [23]. The ith generalized Hamming distance, denoted by $d_i(C)$ or d_i is the minimum size of the union of the supports of i linearly independent codewords in C. We have $1 \leq d = d_1 \leq \ldots \leq d_k \leq n$.

Using generalized Hamming distances, we get a more precise evaluation of the information gained by Eve in the WTC2, depending on the linear code used for coset coding. For $i = 1, \ldots, r$, let $d_i^\perp$ denote the ith generalized Hamming distance of $C^\perp$, the dual code of C. We have the following result [23]:

Theorem 1 (WTC2 and Generalized Hamming Distances). *If Eve gets less than $d_i^\perp$ bits of the codeword c, she gains at most $i-1$ information bits about the original message m.*

3   Our Protocol for Secure Two-Party Computation

3.1   The Setting

We describe our setting in Fig. 4. Notice that we can also give the result to P_1: since we work in the semi-honest model, where both parties follow the protocol, we can let P_2 send $f(X, Y)$ to P_1, once he has computed it.

We consider the secure evaluation of functions of the form

$$f : \mathbb{F}_q^r \times S \to \mathbb{F}_q$$

$$(X, Y) \mapsto f(X, Y) = \sum_{i=1}^{r} f_i(Y) \cdot x_i$$

where S is a given set, and $f_i : S \to \mathbb{F}_q$, for $i = 1, \ldots, r$. This class covers all linear functions of X and Y with range $\mathbb{F}_q$ (*i.e.* giving one "bit of information" about X to P_2).

For instance, if $Y \in \mathbb{F}_q^r$ and $f_i(Y) = y_i$, f is the scalar product over $\mathbb{F}_q^r$.

Inputs:
- Party P_1 inputs $X \in \mathbb{F}_q^r$
- Party P_2 inputs $Y \in S$
- Both parties know a description of $f : \mathbb{F}_q^r \times S \to \mathbb{F}_q$

Outputs:
- P_1 learns nothing about Y
- P_2 obtains $f(X, Y)$ but learns nothing more about X than what can be inferred from $f(X, Y)$.

Fig. 4. Our Secure Two-Party Computation setting

Squared Euclidean distance can also be computed this way. In addition to X, P_1 also inputs $x_{r+1} = \sum_{i=1}^{r} x_i^2$ and $f_i(Y) = -2y_i$, for $i = 1, \ldots, r$, $f_{r+1}(Y) = 1$.

Thus, P_2 obtains $\sum_{i=1}^{r} x_i^2 - 2x_i y_i$, which is equivalent (for P_2) to the knowledge of $d(X, Y) = \sum_{i=1}^{r} (x_i - y_i)^2$: it gives no additional information.

If $q = p > \log(r)$ and inputs are binary vectors seen in $\mathbb{F}_q$, it is also possible to compute Hamming distance (take $f_i(Y) = 1 - 2y_i$).

Securely computing these functions has applications in the signal processing and cryptographic domains, especially for privacy-preserving biometric recognition [4,19].

Privacy. We consider the usual definition of privacy in the two-party and semi-honest setting, we refer the reader to [14] for a complete definition. In a few words, privacy is proven if the view of party P_i during an execution of the protocol can be simulated, given the input and the output of P_i only (but not the input of P_{3-i}). In particular, we consider the OT-hybrid model, where, in the simulations, parties have access to a trusted party that computes oblivious transfers for them.

3.2 From the Wire-Tap Channel to Secure Two-Party Computation

As discussed in the introduction and illustrated in Fig. 2, we transpose the WTC2 model to the Secure Two-party Computation setting, by assigning the role of Alice to P_1, the role of Eve to P_2 and modelling the erasure channel by oblivious transfers. We will use the notation OT_t^n to denote the t-out-of-n functionality described in Fig. 5. This can be implemented either using t OT_1^n's or more specific constructions, see [16].

3.3 Choosing the Code

Let us first see how P_2 can choose the coordinates of the codeword that he gets through oblivious transfer, in order to obtain $f(X, Y)$. Let us consider the $r \times n$

Inputs:
- Sender S inputs n elements $X_1, \ldots, X_n \in \mathbb{F}_q$
- Receiver R inputs t indices $i_1, \ldots, i_t \in \{1, \ldots, n\}$

Outputs:
- S learns nothing about $i_1, \ldots, i_t$
- R obtains $X_{i_1}, \ldots, X_{i_t}$ but learns nothing about $(X_i)_{i \notin \{i_1, \ldots, i_t\}}$

Fig. 5. The OT_t^n functionality

matrix H that is the parity-check matrix of the code C used for coset coding, or, equivalently, the generator matrix of its dual code $C^\perp$. We denote by H_i the ith row of H. Let Z be an encoding of X, i.e. such that $X = H \cdot Z^T = \sum H_i z_i$. We consequently have $x_i = H_i \cdot Z^T$ and $f(X, Y) = \sum f_i(Y) \cdot x_i = \sum f_i(Y) \cdot H_i \cdot Z^T = (\sum f_i(Y) \cdot H_i) \cdot Z^T$.

Thus, P_2 only needs the coordinates of Z at the positions where $\sum f_i(Y) \cdot H_i$ is nonzero, i.e. at the positions belonging to the support of $V = \sum f_i(Y) \cdot H_i$. This will ensure correctness. Let $i_1, \ldots, i_t = supp(V)$.

Now we need to ensure privacy of P_1's data. We assume that P_2 only gets $z_{i_1}, \ldots, z_{i_t}$. If there exists another vector $W \in C^\perp$, such that V and W are linearly independent and $supp(W) \subset supp(V)$, then P_2 learns at least another bit of information $(W \cdot Z^T)$ about Z. To ensure P_2 only learns $f(X, Y)$, we need to enforce that V is minimal in $C^\perp$, i.e. that its support does not contain the support of another linearly independent codeword $W \in C^\perp$. Since we wish to ensure a notion of completeness, i.e. to make our protocol usable with any f and Y fitting our setting, we require every codeword of $C^\perp$ to be minimal, i.e. we require $C^\perp$ to be a minimal linear code (see Sect. 4).

Now let us fix some $V \in C^\perp$, let $t = |supp(V)|$ and let us consider the linear application $\phi : C^\perp \to \mathbb{F}_q^{n-t}; c \mapsto (c_i)_{i \notin supp(V)}$. Due to the definition of minimality, only the λV's, for $\lambda \in \mathbb{F}_q$, have a support included in $supp(V)$, thus $Ker\phi = \mathbb{F}_q.V$ and $rank(\phi) = dim(C^\perp) - 1 = r - 1$. Thus, if we let P_2 learn the t coordinates of Z corresponding to $supp(V)$, the remaining coordinates lie in a space of dimension $r - 1$ and P_2 only learns one bit of information about X.

Consequently, using a minimal codeword ensures privacy of P_1 against P_2.

3.4   Our Protocol

We put together our studies of the last paragraphs and get the protocol described in Fig. 6. Privacy against P_2 is ensured thanks to the remarks of Sect. 3.3 and privacy against P_1 is ensured by the use of oblivious transfer, which is the only data exchange from P_2 to P_1. Correctness is also discussed in Sect. 3.3.

Some details still need to be considered. The size t of $supp(V)$ can reveal information about Y to P_1. Thus, either we need an oblivious transfer protocol that hides from the sender the number of transferred items, or we require P_2 to perform $w_{max} - t$ dummy requests, where w_{max} is the maximal weight of a codeword of $C^\perp$. Since we work in the semi-honest model, this will not break

Inputs:
- Party P_1 inputs $X = (x_1, \ldots, x_r) \in \mathbb{F}_q^r$
- Party P_2 inputs Y
- An $[n, r]$ minimal linear code C with generator $r \times n$ matrix H. Let H_i be the ith row of H.
- A function f such that $f(X, Y) = \sum\limits_{i=1}^{r} f_i(Y) \cdot x_i$, where $f_i(Y) \in \mathbb{F}_q$.

Protocol:
- P_1 uniformly randomly picks an element $Z = (z_1, \ldots, z_n) \in \mathbb{F}_q^n$ such that $X = H \cdot Z^T$
- P_2 computes $V = \sum\limits_{i=1}^{r} f_i(Y) \cdot H_i \in \mathbb{F}_q^n$
- Let $(i_1, \ldots, i_t) = supp(V)$, P_1 and P_2 perform an OT_t^n on Z and $(i_1, \ldots, i_t)$. P_2 gets $z_{i_1}, \ldots, z_{i_t}$.
- P_2 outputs $f(X, Y) = \bar{V} \cdot \bar{Z}$, where $\bar{V} = (v_{i_1}, \ldots, v_{i_t})$ and $\bar{Z} = (z_{i_1}, \ldots, z_{i_t})$

Fig. 6. Our protocol for Secure Two-Party Computation

the security properties (of course, a malicious (active) adversary would use real requests instead, but that setting is out of the scope of this paper).

We would like to point out that this protocol might not only have theoretical interest. For instance, the protocol of [4] uses coding-like techniques and oblivious transfer only, and is one of the most efficient protocols for securely computing functions such as Hamming distances on binary vectors, outperforming protocols based on additively homomorphic cryptosystems or on garbled circuits. In the case of the protocol of this paper, performance will highly rely on the rate of the underlying code. As we explain in Sect. 4, we are lacking results in the q-ary case.

3.5   Privacy

Theorem 2 (Privacy of our Protocol). *The protocol described in Fig. 6 achieves privacy in the semi-honest setting, in the OT-hybrid model.*

Proof. As explained before, we prove privacy by simulating the view of party P_i during an execution of the protocol, given the input and output of P_i only.

Since P_1 only receives oblivious transfer requests, we are guaranteed by the OT-hybrid model that the protocol is private against P_1.

Now we study the case of a corrupted P_2. We are given the input Y of P_2 and the output *out* computed by P_2 at the end of the protocol. We simulate the view of P_2 as follows:

- We compute $V = \sum\limits_{i=1}^{r} f_i(Y) \cdot H_i \in \mathbb{F}_q^n$ as in Fig. 6.
- We answer to P_2's OT requests with $\tilde{Z} = \tilde{z}_{i_1}, \ldots, \tilde{z}_{i_t}$, uniformly randomly among all t-tuples such that $\sum\limits_{i=i_1, \ldots, i_t} z_i \cdot v_i = out$. (For instance, take $\tilde{z}_{i_1}, \ldots, \tilde{z}_{i_{t-1}}$

uniformly randomly from $\mathbb{F}_q^{t-1}$ and compute $\tilde{z}_{i_t} = v_{i_t}^{-1}(out - \sum_{i=i_1,\ldots,i_{t-1}} \tilde{z}_i \cdot v_i)$.

Note that v_{i_t} is invertible because $i_t \in supp(V))$.

Thus, the result of P_2 is indeed out. It remains to prove that the view of P_2 during the simulation and during a real execution of the protocol are indistinguishable. Therefore, we prove that, if V is minimal, all the t-tuples $\tilde{Z}$ satisfying the output condition appear the same number of times in the possible random coset encodings of any X such that $f(X,Y) = out$.

To see this, let us consider the dual $[n, n-r]$ code $C^\perp$ of C. The encoding of the input X of P_1 is chosen uniformly in $z + C^\perp$, where z is such that $H \cdot z = X$. We consider the linear application $\phi_V : C^\perp \to \mathbb{F}_q^{t-1}; c \mapsto c_{i_1}, \ldots, c_{i_{t-1}}$. If ϕ_V is not of full rank, then there exists $(\lambda_1, \ldots, \lambda_{t-1}) \in \mathbb{F}_q^{t-1} \backslash \{0^{t-1}\}$ such that, for all $c \in C^\perp$, $\sum_{j=1}^{t-1} \lambda_j c_{i_j} = 0$, thus we define a nonzero codeword with a support strictly included in the support of V, which contradicts the minimality of V. Consequently, ϕ_V has full rank and all possible $t - 1$-tuples appear at positions $supp(V) \backslash \{i_t\}$ in the codewords of $C^\perp$, and they do so the same number of times, thanks to linearity. By translation, they also appear (the same number of times) in all possible encodings of a given input X of P_1. Then, $\tilde{z}_{i_t}$ is fully determined by the output condition. This uniform repartition confirms that the view of P_2 in our simulation is indistinguishable from his view in a real execution of the protocol and our protocol achieves privacy. $\qquad\square$

3.6   Examples

We consider as an illustration the secure evaluation of scalar product over $\mathbb{F}_q^r$, i.e. $f(X,Y) = \sum_{i=1}^{r} x_i \cdot y_i$. One can deduce how to proceed for any function encompassed by our protocol, by replacing y_i by $f_i(Y)$.

Simplex and Hamming Codes. One can easily be convinced that one-weight codes are minimal, in the binary or the q-ary case. Indeed, if c and c' are two nonzero codewords of a one-weight code C such that $supp(c) \subset supp(c')$, then $supp(c) = supp(c')$, by cardinality. Consider $i \in supp(c)$ and define $\lambda_i = c_i/c_i'$, then $c - \lambda_i c'$ is a codeword of C, with support $\subsetneq supp(c)$. Since C is one-weight, $c - \lambda_i c' = 0$ then c and c' are linearly dependent. Thus, C is minimal. Since we use linear codes, one-weight codes are simplex codes (or equivalent), duals of Hamming codes [2]. Let $q = 2, r = 3, n = 7$. The 3×7 matrix H can for example be written as follows:

$$H = \begin{pmatrix} 0 & 0 & 0 & 1 & 1 & 1 & 1 \\ 0 & 1 & 1 & 0 & 0 & 1 & 1 \\ 1 & 0 & 1 & 0 & 1 & 0 & 1 \end{pmatrix}$$

Let $X = (101)$ and $Y = (110)$. P_1 can for instance encode X with $Z = (0000100)$. Y computes $V = H_1 + H_2 = (0111100)$ and requests, using oblivious transfers, the bits z_2, z_3, z_4, z_5. P_2 thus gets $\bar{Z} = (0001)$. By dot-product with $\bar{V}$, P_2 gets the result $f(X, Y) = \sum x_i \cdot y_i = 1$.

Notice that, since the code is one-weight, P_2 always requests 4 bits, we thus do not need to hide the number of requested bits. Unfortunately, this nice property is only enjoyed by simplex codes, that have a very bad rate, n growing exponentially with r, the rates being even worse in the q-ary case.

A More Efficient Binary Example. In the binary case, we can easily obtain minimal codes with better rates than simplex codes (see Sect. 4). For instance, let $r = 4$, we can have $n = 9$ (optimal [21]), for instance using

$$
H = \begin{pmatrix}
1 & 0 & 1 & 0 & 0 & 0 & 1 & 0 & 1 \\
0 & 1 & 1 & 0 & 0 & 0 & 0 & 1 & 1 \\
0 & 0 & 0 & 1 & 0 & 1 & 1 & 0 & 1 \\
0 & 0 & 0 & 0 & 1 & 1 & 0 & 1 & 1
\end{pmatrix}
$$

Using this code, P_2 will request either 4 or 6 coordinates of Z, to obtain $f(X, Y)$, depending on Y. For instance if $Y = (1000)$ or $Y = (0011)$, P_2 will only request 4 coordinates, but if $Y = (0110)$, P_2 will need 6 coordinates.

Comparison to Yao's Protocol. Let us consider secure evaluation of scalar product over $\mathbb{F}_2^r$ using Yao's protocol [14, 20, 25]. The binary circuit contains r AND gates, we do not count XOR gates (see [20] and references therein for known optimizations on garbled circuits). Let k be a security parameter (e.g. 80 or 128). Party P_1 has to compute r garbled gates ($4r$ hash function evaluations). Party P_2 has to evaluate r garbled gates (r hash function evaluations). They perform k OT_1^2's on k-bit inputs (P_2's input wire labels). Furthermore, P_1 also needs to send r k-bit keys (P_1's input wire labels) and r garbled gates ($3rk$ bits).

Now let us consider our protocol using an $[n, r]$ minimal code with maximum codeword Hamming weight equal to w_{max}. Our protocol requires linear algebra operations and a $OT_{w_{max}}^n$, with 1-bit inputs. For instance, the $OT_{w_{max}}^n$ operation can be realized using $w_{max} OT_1^{n-w_{max}+1}$, still with 1-bit inputs, but there might be more efficient procedures. Using for instance the construction of [8] to build minimal binary codes, one can have $n \approx 6.4r$, for any r. This comparison in the binary case is summed up in Table 1.

4   Intersecting Codes and Minimal Codes

In our protocol, we need linear codes where all codewords are *minimal*. Let C be a linear code of length n. A codeword c is said to be *minimal* if $\forall c' \in C, (supp(c') \subset supp(c)) \implies$ (c and c' are linearly dependent). We say that a linear code C is *minimal* if every nonzero codeword of C is minimal. This notion is closely related to the notion of intersecting codes [6]. The notions are identical in the binary case but no more in the q-ary case (a minimal code is intersecting,

Table 1. Comparison with Yao's protocol, in the binary case

Protocol	OT (computation + data exchanges)	Add. data exchanges	Add. computation (P_1)	Add. computation (P_2)
Yao	$r \times OT_1^2$ (k-bit inputs)	$4rk$ bits	$4r$ hash function evaluations	r hash function evaluations
Our protocol	$1 \times OT_{w_{max}}^n$ (1-bit inputs)	$\emptyset$	Linear algebra	Linear algebra

but the inverse is not always true). We recall that an *intersecting code C* is such that for all nonzero $c, c' \in C, supp(c) \cap supp(c') \neq \emptyset$.

Interestingly, use of intersecting codes or minimal codewords has been suggested for oblivious transfer [3] and for secret sharing [1,10,22], which is a tool widely used for Secure Multi-Party Computation [9].

A very recent work [5] deepens our study on minimal linear codes.

4.1   The Binary Case

Due to the coincidence with the notion of intersecting codes, binary minimal codes have received a lot of attention [3,6,8,11,21]. For instance, [6] gives definitions, some generic constructions and non-constructive bounds on rates; [21] gives explicit constructions for small dimensions and summarizes bounds on minimum distance; [8] gives an explicit constructive sequence of intersecting codes with high rate, and so on. We do not here detail these results. We only sum up what is important for us: there exist explicit constructions of minimal binary linear codes with good rates. Thus, our protocol of Sect. 3 can be constructed in the binary case using codewords whose size grows linearly with the size of the inputs.

4.2   The q-Ary Case

Finding minimal q-ary codes has received little attention [10,13,22] in the domain of secret sharing. Reference [22] details some properties of minimal linear codes, in particular some sufficient conditions for a code to be minimal are given. References [10,22] exhibit constructions of minimal codes using irreducible cyclic codes, which unfortunately do not achieve good rates. As said before, simplex codes are minimal, they however suffer from a very bad rate. Indeed, a simplex code of dimension k has length $(q^k - 1)/(q - 1)$. This gives us an existential and constructive result about q-ary minimal linear codes, but we still need better rates.

We exhibit two bounds on the rates of minimal codes.

Theorem 3 (Maximal Bound). *Let C a minimal linear $[n, k, d]$ q-ary code, then $R \leq \log_q(2)$.*

Proof. This bound is even true for non-linear minimal codes. Let us consider the family F of the supports of the vectors of C. Due to the definition of minimal codes, this is a Sperner family. It is known that $|F| \leq \binom{n}{n/2}$. Thus, $|C| = q^k \leq 1 + (q-1)\binom{n}{n/2}$ then $R = k/n \leq \log_q(2)$.   □

Theorem 4 (Minimal Bound). *For any R, $0 \leq R = k/n \leq \frac{1}{2}\log_q(\frac{q^2}{q^2-q+1})$, there exists an infinite sequence of $[n,k]$ minimal linear codes.*

Proof. The proof is similar to the one of [6] in the binary case. Let us fix n and k. For $a \in \mathbb{F}_q^n$, such that $|supp(a)| = i$, there are $q^i - q$ linearly independent vectors b such that $supp(b) \subset supp(a)$. The pair (a,b) belongs to $\begin{bmatrix} n-2 \\ k-2 \end{bmatrix}$ linear $[n,k]$ codes, where $\begin{bmatrix} x \\ k \end{bmatrix}$ denotes the q-ary Gaussian binomial coefficient.

There are less than $\sum_{i=0}^{n} \binom{n}{i}(q-1)^i(q^i-q) = (1+(q-1)q)^n - q^{n+1} \leq (q^2-q+1)^n$ such ordered "bad" (a,b) pairs. At least $\begin{bmatrix} n \\ k \end{bmatrix} - \begin{bmatrix} n-2 \\ k-2 \end{bmatrix}(q^2-q+1)^n$ linear $[n,k]$ codes thus contain no "bad" pairs, *i.e.* are minimal. For $k/n \leq \frac{1}{2}\log_q(\frac{q^2}{q^2-q+1})$, this quantity is positive.   □

Notice that the minimal bound exposed in Theorem 4 meets the $\frac{1}{2}\log_2(\frac{4}{3})$ bound in the binary case exhibited in [6]. We can however not use the same techniques as in the binary case (e.g. [6,8]) to obtain explicit constructions with high rates, which remains an open issue.

5   Conclusion

We present a theoretical protocol for performing secure two-party computation of linear functions based on linear codes and oblivious transfer only, using a parallel with the Wire-Tap Channel II model. Due to the efficiency of linear algebra and current constructions of oblivious transfer, this could be a basis for efficient protocols for secure evaluation of some classes of functions.

Several leads for future research are:

- Constructions of good q-ary minimal linear codes;
- Other encoding techniques than linear coset coding;
- Techniques to encompass secure computation of non-linear functions;
- Techniques to deal with malicious adversaries.

Acknowledgements. This work has been partially funded by the ANR SecuLar project.

References

1. Ashikhmin, A.E., Barg, A.: Minimal vectors in linear codes. IEEE Trans. Inf. Theory **44**(5), 2010–2017 (1998)
2. Bonisoli, A.: Every equidistant linear code is a sequence of dual hamming codes. Ars Comb. **18**, 181–186 (1984)
3. Brassard, G., Crépeau, C., Santha, M.: Oblivious transfers and intersecting codes. IEEE Trans. Inf. Theory **42**(6), 1769–1780 (1996)
4. Bringer, J., Chabanne, H., Patey, A.: SHADE: Secure HAmming DistancE computation from oblivious transfer. In: Workshop on Applied Homomorphic Cryptography (WAHC) (2013)
5. Cohen, G.D., Mesnager, S., Patey, A.: On minimal and quasi-minimal linear codes. In: Stam, M. (ed.) IMACC 2013. LNCS, vol. 8308, pp. 85–98. Springer, Heidelberg (2013)
6. Cohen, G.D., Lempel, A.: Linear intersecting codes. Discret. Math. **56**(1), 35–43 (1985)
7. Cohen, G.D., Litsyn, S., Zémor, G.: Upper bounds on generalized distances. IEEE Trans. Inf. Theory **40**(6), 2090–2092 (1994)
8. Cohen, G.D., Zémor, G.: Intersecting codes and independent families. IEEE Trans. Inf. Theory **40**(6), 1872–1881 (1994)
9. Cramer, R., Damgard, I., Nielsen, J.B.: Secure multiparty computation and secret sharing - an information theoretic approach, Book Draft (2012)
10. Ding, C., Yuan, J.: Covering and secret sharing with linear codes. In: Calude, C.S., Dinneen, M.J., Vajnovszki, V. (eds.) DMTCS 2003. LNCS, vol. 2731, pp. 11–25. Springer, Heidelberg (2003)
11. Encheva, S.B., Cohen, G.D.: Constructions of intersecting codes. IEEE Trans. Inf. Theory **45**(4), 1234–1237 (1999)
12. Goldreich, O.: The Foundations of Cryptography - vol. 2, Basic Applications. Cambridge University Press, Cambridge (2004)
13. Guo, Y., Li, Z., Lai, H.: A novel dynamic and verifiable secret sharing scheme based on linear codes. J. Shaanxi Normal Univ. (Nat. Sci. Ed.), **4**, 013 (2010)
14. Hazay, C., Lindell, Y.: Efficient Secure Two-Party Protocols. Springer, Heidelberg (2010)
15. Lindell, Y., Pinkas, B.: A proof of security of Yao's protocol for two-party computation. J. Cryptol. **22**(2), 161–188 (2009)
16. Lipmaa, H.: Oblivious transfer or private information retrieval. http://www.cs.ut.ee/~lipmaa/crypto/link/protocols/oblivious.php
17. Ozarow, L.H., Wyner, A.D.: Wire-tap channel II. In: Beth, T., Cot, N., Ingemarsson, I. (eds.) EUROCRYPT 1984. LNCS, vol. 209, pp. 33–50. Springer, Heidelberg (1985)
18. Rabin, M.O.: How to exchange secrets with oblivious transfer. Technical report TR-81, Aiken Computation Lab, Harvard University (1981)
19. Sadeghi, A.-R., Schneider, T., Wehrenberg, I.: Efficient privacy-preserving face recognition. In: Lee, D., Hong, S. (eds.) ICISC 2009. LNCS, vol. 5984, pp. 229–244. Springer, Heidelberg (2010)
20. Schneider, T.: Engineering Secure Two-Party Computation Protocols - Design, Optimization, and Applications of Efficient Secure Function Evaluation. Springer, Heidelberg (2012)
21. Sloane, N.J.A.: Covering arrays and intersecting codes. J. Comb. Des. **1**, 51–63 (1993)

22. Song, Y., Li, Z.: Secret sharing with a class of minimal linear codes. CoRR, abs/1202.4058 (2012)
23. Wei, V.K.-W.: Generalized hamming weights for linear codes. IEEE Trans. Inf. Theory **37**(5), 1412–1418 (1991)
24. Wyner, A.D.: The wire-tap channel. Bell Syst. Tech. J. **54**(8), 1355–1387 (1975)
25. Yao, A.C.-C.: How to generate and exchange secrets (extended abstract). In: FOCS, pp. 162–167. IEEE Computer Society (1986)

Proxy Re-encryption

Combined Proxy Re-encryption

Sébastien Canard[1]([✉]) and Julien Devigne[1,2]

[1] Orange Labs, Applied Crypto Group, Caen, France
sebastien.canard@orange.com
[2] UCBN, GREYC, Caen, France

Abstract. Among the variants of public key encryption schemes, the proxy re-encryption primitive (PRE) allows a user, say Alice, to decide that a delegate, say Bob, will be able to read her private messages. This is made possible thanks to a third party, the proxy, which is given a re-encryption key to transform a ciphertext intended to Alice into one intended to Bob. Different properties on PRE schemes exist. Some of them are *unidirectional* and allow the proxy to translate a ciphertext only from Alice to Bob. The other case is called *bidirectional* and permits the proxy, with only one re-encryption key, to translate from Alice to Bob but also from Bob to Alice. Most of the time, a bidirectional scheme is *multi-hop*, meaning that a ciphertext can be forwarded several times, and a unidirectional scheme is *single-hop*, meaning that a ciphertext can be transformed just once. We here investigate the way to design a combined (single/multi hop) PRE scheme which permits both unidirectional single-hop and bidirectional multi-hop. We formalize this concept, give several generic results and finally propose a practical construction. We argue that this case is very interesting in practice to the design of a secure and privacy-preserving cloud storage system, such as defined by Ateniese *et al.* in 2006, and particularly when the device of a user is lost.

Keywords: Proxy re-encryption · Uni and bidirectional · Cloud storage

1 Introduction

CLOUD STORAGE. With the advent of cloud computing and mobile devices, it is very functional to use the cloud to run all applications which can be used in any user's devices, as users want to have their favorite applications available anywhere at anytime and not only from their home computer. The problem is that some applications need user's data to be run. There are then two possible solutions. In the first one, each user needs to have all of his data with him at every time, which might not be practical, even if a lot of progress has already been done in storage devices. The other way is to consider that users/devices are in constant connection with the Internet via all wireless networks and to store all data on a dedicated server: we then talk of cloud storage. Cloud storage is a secure storage system which stores users' data in a "secure way", with as purpose those users to be able to access their data anywhere, at anytime, from

© Springer International Publishing Switzerland 2014
H.-S. Lee and D.-G. Han (Eds.): ICISC 2013, LNCS 8565, pp. 49–66, 2014.
DOI: 10.1007/978-3-319-12160-4_4

any authorized devices, and only them. The most interesting case is when the cloud storage is dynamic since it permits to control the access to the data by adding/deleting devices/users. The idea behind cloud storage is that data are stored as if they were in a safe, where the cloud storage plays the role of an access control to this safe. In reality, the data are encrypted and, most of the time, the cloud server has the decryption key and manages the rights to each user to access or not the data. In [2], Ateniese *et al.* have proposed a privacy-preserving architecture for distributed storage which makes use of a so-called PRE scheme. A similar system has then been proposed in the case of cloud storage in [12]. With such a system, where the cloud plays the role of the proxy, the access to a plaintext is only permitted to authorized users, while the cloud cannot derive the plaintext from the stored ciphertext. A data can *e.g.* be stored on a dedicated cloud storage using Alice's public key. If Bob can access this document, the proxy/cloud makes use of a re-encryption from Alice to Bob. Similarly, if Alice owns several devices, one document encrypted with the key on one of them can be re-encrypted for another one (without needing them to share the same secret decryption key).

PROXY RE-ENCRYPTION SCHEMES. Proxy re-encryption (PRE) [3] allows a user to delegate its decryption capability in case of unavailability. To do so, this user, Alice, computes a *re-encryption key* $R_{A \to B}$ which is given to a proxy. $R_{A \to B}$ allows the proxy to transform a ciphertext intended to Alice into one intended to Bob. While doing this, the proxy cannot learn *any* information on the plaintexts nor any secret key. The cloud storage system of Ateniese *et al.* [2] makes use of a *unidirectional* and *single-hop* scheme, which means (1) that with a re-encryption key $R_{A \to B}$, a proxy cannot translate Bob's ciphertexts into ciphertexts intended to Alice and (2) that once a message has been moved into a ciphertext intended to Bob, no more transformation on the new ciphertext intended to Bob is possible. It also exists in the literature several PRE schemes which are *bidirectional*, meaning that they allow a symmetrical transformation, and *multi-hop*, meaning that several "consecutive" translations of ciphertexts are possible.

RELATED WORK. Numerous papers on PRE schemes exist. Some of them are unidirectional and single-hop [1,2,4,6,9,11,13] (UPRE for short) and some others are bidirectional and multi-hop [3,5,10] (BPRE for short). Thus, even if this is theoretically possible, both couples (unidirectional, single-hop) and (bidirectional, multi-hop) seem to be indissociable in practical constructions. This can be partially explained by the way re-encryption keys are computed. Indeed, a bidirectional re-encryption key from Alice to Bob is a link between their secret keys. The bidirectional re-encryption process works as if it is possible to replace in the ciphertext each occurrence of Alice's secret key with an occurrence of Bob's secret key, such that the re-encrypted ciphertext has always the same form than the first one and can be re-encrypted again: a BPRE is most of the time multi-hop. Regarding UPRE, the re-encryption key from Alice to Bob is a link between Alice's secret key and Bob's public key and does not allow replacing occurrences of Alice's secret key in a ciphertext with occurrences of Bob's secret key without modifying the form of the ciphertext. A re-encrypted cipher-text does not have the same form than a non-re-encrypted ciphertext and can thus not be re-encrypted with the same process: a UPRE is most of the time single-hop. Yet, in [8], Weng *et al.* propose a secure bidirectional single-hop PRE. But, as far as we know, the other possibility – design of a secure unidirectional multi-hop PRE – does not exist in practice, while corresponding to our need.

A MATTER OF TRUST. In fact, using a bidirectional (and thus most of the time multi-hop) PRE in the case of cloud storage is not really a good thing regarding security. In fact, in the above example, Alice trusts Bob so that this latter can access Alice's confidential documents, but this does not necessarily mean that Bob trusts Alice. Similarly, if Alice trusts Bob and Bob trusts Carol, it does not necessarily mean that Alice trusts Carol: trust is thus not transitive and a multi-hop scheme is not necessarily a good choice for such system.

However, in some cases, a multi-hop (and thus most of the time bidirectional) scheme can be really useful, and in particular when *e.g.* Alice loses one of her device: the corresponding decryption secret key is compromised and cannot be used anymore. Thus, if a data is encrypted with the corresponding public key, this can be a problem[1]. But the power of a PRE scheme (even unidirectional) is such that the proxy can re-encrypt the ciphertext – and then delete the old one – so that another key can be used to decrypt the ciphertext. However, the result could not be re-encrypted anymore if a single-hop PRE scheme is used. One possibility consists in asking the owner of the secret key related to the new encrypting public key to decrypt and then encrypt again the data, which leads to a very unpractical system. The second possibility is to make use of a bidirectional multi-hop scheme but this implies the above problem regarding trust between people. Another solution one can see is to use a unidirectional multi-hop PRE scheme but, as said above, no practical construction exists in the literature. Finally, one may think about a simple combination of a UPRE and a BPRE but this implies to multiply the number of ciphertext, one for each type of PRE.

COMBINED PRE. In this paper, we investigate a new approach which consists in designing a combined (single/multi hop) scheme which can be either unidirec-tional and single-hop *or* bidirectional and multi-hop (see Fig. 1). If Alice owns several different devices, the trust she has in all her devices is similar and thus, we can use a bidirectional and multi-hop PRE. Regarding one Alice's device and one Bob's device, there is (*a priori*) no mutual and transitive trust and we use a unidirectional and single-hop PRE. We thus introduce the new notion of *combined PRE*. In the following, we formally introduce the concept in Sect. 2 and then give in Sect. 3 several generic results. We finally propose in Sect. 4 a practical Combined-PRE scheme which can directly be implemented to manage

---

[1] In fact, in [2], the system makes use of a single public key for the encryption, and the corresponding secret key is only used to compute re-encryption keys. But if the device containing this secret key is lost, the problem is similar.

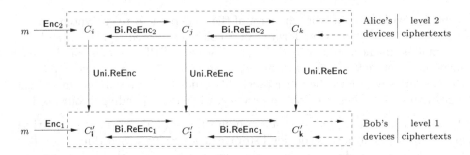

Fig. 1. General scheme for combined PRE

the lost of devices in a privacy-preserving cloud storage system. Some details on such system are given in Sect. 5.

2   Combined Proxy Re-encryption

In this section, we formally introduce the concept of combined proxy re-encryption schemes by giving the different procedures and the expected security properties.

2.1   Syntactic Definition

Definition 1 (Combined-PRE). *Let κ be an integer. A Combined Proxy Re-Encryption scheme consists of the twelve algorithms defined as follows.*

- Setup(κ) $\rightarrow \mathcal{P}$: *this setup algorithm takes a security parameter κ as input and produces a set of public parameters $\mathcal{P}$ shared by all parties.*
- KeyGen($\mathcal{P}$) $\rightarrow (sk, pk)$: *this algorithm, executed by each user, whose input is $\mathcal{P}$, outputs a pair of secret and public keys (sk, pk).*
- Uni.ReKG($\mathcal{P}, sk_i, pk_i$) $\rightarrow R_{i \rightarrow i}$: *given the public parameters, the secret key of the user i, the public key of the user i, this algorithm produces a unidirectional re-encryption key $R_{i \rightarrow i}$ which allows to transform second level ciphertexts intended to i into first level ciphertexts for i.*
- Bi.ReKG$_1$($\mathcal{P}, sk_i, sk_j$) $\rightarrow R_{i \leftrightarrow j,1}$ *(resp.* Bi.ReKG$_2$($\mathcal{P}, sk_i, sk_j$) $\rightarrow R_{i \leftrightarrow j,2}$*): given $\mathcal{P}$, the secret key of the user i (resp i), the secret key of the user j (resp. j), this algorithm produces a re-encryption key $R_{i \leftrightarrow j,1}$ (resp. $R_{i \leftrightarrow j,2}$) which allows to transform first (resp. second) level ciphertexts intended to i (resp. i) into first level ciphertexts for j (resp. j), and inversely.*
- Enc$_1$($\mathcal{P}, pk, m$) $\rightarrow C'$ *(resp.* Enc$_2$($\mathcal{P}, pk, m$) $\rightarrow C$*): this first (resp. second) level encryption algorithm takes as inputs $\mathcal{P}$, a public key and a message. It outputs a first (resp. second) level ciphertext C' (resp. C) that cannot be unidirectionally re-encrypted.*
- Uni.ReEnc($\mathcal{P}, R_{i \rightarrow i}, C_i$) $\rightarrow C'_i / \perp$: *this algorithm takes as inputs $\mathcal{P}$, a re-encryption key $R_{i \rightarrow i}$ and a level 2 ciphertext intended to user i. The output is a level 1 ciphertext C'_i re-encrypted for user i or an invalid message $\perp$.*

- $\mathsf{Bi.ReEnc_1}(\mathcal{P}, R_{i\leftrightarrow j,1}, C_i') \to C_j'/\bot$ *(resp.* $\mathsf{Bi.ReEnc_2}(\mathcal{P}, R_{i\leftrightarrow j,2}, C_i) \to C_j/\bot)$*: this algorithm takes as inputs* $\mathcal{P}$*, a re-encryption key* $R_{i\leftrightarrow j,1}$ *(resp.* $R_{i\leftrightarrow j,2}$*) and a first (resp. second) level ciphertext intended to user i (resp. i). The output is a first (resp. second) level ciphertext* C_j' *(resp.* C_j*) re-encrypted for user j (resp. j) or an invalid message* $\bot$*.*
- $\mathsf{Dec_1}(\mathcal{P}, sk, C) \to m/\bot$ *(resp.* $\mathsf{Dec_2}(\mathcal{P}, sk, C) \to m/\bot)$*: this first (resp. second) level decryption algorithm takes as inputs* $\mathcal{P}$*, a secret key and a first (resp. second) level ciphertext and outputs a plaintext m or an error* $\bot$*.*

2.2 Security

A Combined-PRE is considered as RCCA secure (for Replayable CCA as defined in [5]) if it verifies the IND-RCCA security of $\mathsf{Enc_1}$, $\mathsf{Enc_2}$ and $\mathsf{Uni.ReEnc}$.

ORACLES AND NOTATION. In the following experiments, we have neglected all public parameters $\mathcal{P}$ on inputs to the algorithms for simplicity.

In the following, each experiment begins with the execution of PGen which works as follows. It first executes $\mathcal{P} \leftarrow \mathsf{Setup}(\kappa)$ and then, for all $i \in [1, n]$, where n is a parameter of the experiment, $(sk_i, pk_i) \leftarrow \mathsf{KeyGen}(\mathcal{P})$. The variable $\mathcal{PK}$ then contains the set $\{pk_i\}_{i=1..n}$ of all user public key, while the corresponding secret keys are kept secret by oracles. The procedure PGen then outputs $\mathcal{PP} = (\mathcal{P}, \mathcal{PK})$. All oracles used in our security model are defined as follows:

- OSecKey: when queried on pk, OSecKey answers with sk the secret key associated to pk. The key pk becomes corrupted.
- OUni.ReKG: when queried on (pk_i, pk_i) for a unidirectional re-encryption key from user i to user i, OUni.ReKG answers with $R_{i\to i} \leftarrow \mathsf{Uni.ReKG}(sk_i, pk_i)$.
- OBi.ReKG$_1$: when queried on (pk_i, pk_j) for a bidirectional re-encryption key for first level from user i to user j, OBi.ReKG$_1$ answers with $R_{i\leftrightarrow j,1} \leftarrow \mathsf{Bi.ReKG_1}(sk_i, sk_j)$. In all the experiments, re-encryption key generation queries between a corrupted key and an uncorrupted key are not allowed, which is classical for BPRE schemes.
- OBi.ReKG$_2$: when queried on (pk_i, pk_j) for a bidirectional re-encryption key for second level from user i to user j, OBi.ReKG$_2$ answers with $R_{i\leftrightarrow j,2} \leftarrow \mathsf{Bi.ReKG_2}(sk_i, sk_j)$. Re-encryption key generation queries between a corrupted key and an uncorrupted key are not allowed in all the experiments.
- ODec$_1$ (resp. ODec$_2$): when queried on (pk, C') (resp. (pk, C)), a first level ciphertext C' (resp. second level ciphertext C) intended to $pk \in \mathcal{PK}$, this oracle answers with $m \leftarrow \mathsf{Dec_1}(sk, C')$ (resp. $m \leftarrow \mathsf{Dec_2}(sk, C)$).
- OUni.ReEnc: on input (pk_i, pk_i, C_i) where C_i is a second level ciphertext intended to pk_i, this oracle answers with $C_i' \leftarrow \mathsf{Uni.ReEnc}(R_{i\to i}, C_i)$.
- OBi.ReEnc$_1$: on input (pk_i, pk_j, C_i') where C_i' is a first level ciphertext intended to pk_i, this oracle answers with $C_j' \leftarrow \mathsf{Bi.ReEnc_1}(R_{i\leftrightarrow j,1}, C_i')$.
- OBi.ReEnc$_2$: on input (pk_i, pk_j, C_i) where C_i is a second level ciphertext intended to pk_i, this oracle answers with $C_j \leftarrow \mathsf{Bi.ReEnc_2}(R_{i\leftrightarrow j,2}, C_i)$.

An adversary is then divided into two different phases. During the choose phase, denoted $\mathcal{A}_f$, the adversary has access to a subset $\mathcal{O}$ of the above oracles defined by the experiment. During the guess phase, denoted $\mathcal{A}_g$, the adversary has access to the same oracles but with some restrictions that are given by the experiment. During this phase, the set of oracles is denoted $\widetilde{\mathcal{O}}$. These restrictions are related to both the impossibility for the adversary to decrypt itself the challenge ciphertext and the impossibility to ask for a decryption of the challenge ciphertext. We now distinguish the three above cases.

SECURITY RELATED TO Enc_1. We define the IND-RCCA of Enc_1 for a Combined-PRE by describing a two-stage adversary $\mathcal{A} = (\mathcal{A}_f, \mathcal{A}_g)$ having access to different oracles $\mathcal{O}_1 = \{\mathsf{ODec}_1, \mathsf{ODec}_2, \mathsf{OUni.ReKG}, \mathsf{OBi.ReKG}_1, \mathsf{OBi.ReKG}_2, \mathsf{OBi.ReEnc}_1, \mathsf{OBi.ReEnc}_2, \mathsf{OSecKey}\}$. The condition cond_1 in this experiment states that the key pk_{i_ℓ} should be a key of an uncorrupted user (meaning that pk_{i_ℓ} has not been queried on input of $\mathsf{OSecKey}$). Figure 2 (left part) gives the formal description of the related experiment. The restrictions regarding $\widetilde{\mathcal{O}}_1$ are as follows.

- $\mathcal{A}_g$ should not query pk_{i_ℓ} to $\mathsf{OSecKey}$.
- There should not exist a path of re-encryption keys coming from $\mathsf{OBi.ReKG}_1$ from pk_{i_ℓ} to a corrupted pk^*. It implies restrictions regarding both the $\mathsf{OSecKey}$ and the $\mathsf{OBi.ReKG}_1$ oracles.
- $\mathcal{A}_g$ should not query a decryption of the challenge ciphertext C'_ℓ using ODec_1.[2]
- $\mathcal{A}_g$ is not allowed to query to ODec_1 a ciphertext C' for an honest entity – with associated secret key sk – such that $\mathsf{Dec}_1(\mathsf{sk}, C') \in \{m_0, m_1\}$

Definition 2 (IND-RCCA security of Enc_1). *Let κ and n be integers. Let $\mathcal{A} = (\mathcal{A}_f, \mathcal{A}_g)$ be an adversary against the IND-RCCA of Enc_1. Let $\mathsf{Adv}^{ind\text{-}rcca}_{\mathsf{Enc}_1, \mathcal{A}}(\kappa, n) := 2 \cdot \Pr\left[\mathsf{Exp}^{ind\text{-}rcca}_{\mathsf{Enc}_1, \mathcal{A}}(\kappa, n) \to true\right] - 1$, with $\mathsf{Exp}^{ind\text{-}rcca}_{\mathsf{Enc}_1, \mathcal{A}}$ as defined in Fig. 2. We say that PRE has IND-RCCA security of Enc_1 if for every p.p.t. adversary $\mathcal{A} = (\mathcal{A}_f, \mathcal{A}_g)$, the advantage $\mathsf{Adv}^{ind\text{-}rcca}_{\mathsf{Enc}_1, \mathcal{A}}(\kappa, n)$ is negligible in κ.*

$\mathbf{Exp}^{ind\text{-}rcca}_{\mathsf{Enc}_1, \mathcal{A}}(\kappa, n); \ \delta \xleftarrow{\$} \{0, 1\}$;

$\overline{\mathcal{PP} \leftarrow \mathsf{PGen}(\kappa, n)}$;
$(m_0, m_1, \{pk_{i_j}\}_{j=1..\ell}, st) \leftarrow \mathcal{A}_f^{\mathcal{O}_1}(\mathcal{PP})$;
if cond_1, return $\bot$;
$C'_1 \leftarrow \mathsf{Enc}_1(pk_{i_1}, m_\delta)$;
$\forall j \in [2, \ell], \ C'_j \leftarrow \mathsf{Bi.ReEnc}_1(R_{i_{j-1} \leftrightarrow i_j, 1}, C'_{j-1})$;
$\delta' \leftarrow \mathcal{A}_g^{\widetilde{\mathcal{O}}_1}(st, C'_\ell)$;
return $(\delta' = \delta)$

$\mathbf{Exp}^{ind\text{-}rcca}_{\mathsf{Enc}_2, \mathcal{A}}(\kappa, n)$

$\overline{\mathcal{PP} \leftarrow \mathsf{PGen}(\kappa, n)} \ ; \ \delta \xleftarrow{\$} \{0, 1\}$;
$(m_0, m_1, \{pk_{i_j}\}_{j=1..\ell}, st) \leftarrow \mathcal{A}_f^{\mathcal{O}_2}(\mathcal{PP})$;
if cond_2, return $\bot$;
$C_1 \leftarrow \mathsf{Enc}_2(pk_{i_1}, m_\delta)$;
$\forall j \in [2, \ell], \ C_j \leftarrow \mathsf{Bi.ReEnc}_2(R_{i_{j-1} \leftrightarrow i_j, 2}, C_{j-1})$;
$\delta' \leftarrow \mathcal{A}_g^{\widetilde{\mathcal{O}}_2}(st, C_\ell)$
Return $(\delta' = \delta)$

Fig. 2. IND-RCCA for Enc_1 and Enc_2

---

[2] This restriction can be incorporated into the next one, but we prefer to keep this separation as this first restriction is inherent for all CCA proxy re-encryption schemes whereas the next one is inherent only for RCCA ones.

SECURITY RELATED TO Enc_2. We define the IND-RCCA of Enc_2 for a Combined-PRE scheme by describing a two-stage adversary $\mathcal{A} = (\mathcal{A}_f, \mathcal{A}_g)$ having access to different oracles $\mathcal{O}_2 = \{\mathsf{ODec}_1, \mathsf{ODec}_2, \mathsf{OUni.ReKG}, \mathsf{OBi.ReKG}_1, \mathsf{OBi.ReKG}_2,$ $\mathsf{OUni.ReEnc}, \mathsf{OBi.ReEnc}_1, \mathsf{OBi.ReEnc}_2, \mathsf{OSecKey}\}$. The condition cond_2 in this experiment states that the key pk_{i_ℓ} should be a key of an uncorrupted user (meaning that pk_{i_ℓ} has not been queried on input of $\mathsf{OSecKey}$). Figure 2 (right part) gives the related experiment. The restrictions regarding $\widetilde{\mathcal{O}}_2$ are as follows.

- $\mathcal{A}_g$ should not query pk_{i_ℓ} to $\mathsf{OSecKey}$.
- There should not exist a path of re-encryption keys coming from $\mathsf{OBi.ReKG}_2$, $\mathsf{OBi.ReKG}_1$ and/or $\mathsf{OUni.ReKG}$ from pk_{i_ℓ} to a corrupted pk^*. It implies restrictions on the $\mathsf{OSecKey}$, $\mathsf{OBi.ReKg}_2$, $\mathsf{OBi.ReKG}_1$ and $\mathsf{OUni.ReKG}$ oracles.
- $\mathcal{A}_g$ should not query a decryption of the challenge ciphertext C_ℓ using ODec_2.
- $\mathcal{A}_g$ is not allowed to query to ODec_1 a ciphertext C' for an honest entity – with associated secret key sk – such that $\mathsf{Dec}_1(\mathsf{sk}, C') \in \{m_0, m_1\}$

Definition 3 (IND-RCCA security of Enc_2). *Let κ and n be integers. Let $\mathcal{A} = (\mathcal{A}_f, \mathcal{A}_g)$ be an adversary against the IND-RCCA of Enc_2. Let $\mathsf{Adv}_{\mathsf{Enc}_2, \mathcal{A}}^{ind\text{-}rcca}(\kappa, n) := 2 \cdot \Pr\left[\mathsf{Exp}_{\mathsf{Enc}_2, \mathcal{A}}^{ind\text{-}rcca}(\kappa, n) \to true\right] - 1$, with $\mathsf{Exp}_{\mathsf{Enc}_2, \mathcal{A}}^{ind\text{-}rcca}$ as defined in Fig. 2. We say that PRE has IND-RCCA security of Enc_2 if for every p.p.t. adversary $\mathcal{A} = (\mathcal{A}_f, \mathcal{A}_g)$, the advantage $\mathsf{Adv}_{\mathsf{Enc}_2, \mathcal{A}}^{ind\text{-}rcca}(\kappa, n)$ is negligible in κ.*

SECURITY RELATED TO ReEnc. We define the IND-RCCA of ReEnc for a Combined-PRE scheme by describing a two-stage adversary $\mathcal{A} = (\mathcal{A}_f, \mathcal{A}_g)$ having access to different oracles $\mathcal{O}_R = \{\mathsf{ODec}_1, \mathsf{ODec}_2, \mathsf{OUni.ReKG}, \mathsf{OBi.ReKG}_1, \mathsf{OBi.ReKG}_2,$ $\mathsf{OSecKey}\}$. The condition cond_R states that the key $pk_{i_{\ell+\ell'+1}}$ should be a key of an uncorrupted user (meaning that $pk_{i_{\ell+\ell'+1}}$ has not been queried on input of $\mathsf{OSecKey}$). Figure 3 gives the related experiment. The restrictions regarding the restricted version $\widetilde{\mathcal{O}}_R$ are here similar to the case of the IND-RCCA security of $\mathsf{Enc}1$.

Definition 4 (IND-RCCA security of ReEnc). *Let κ and n be integers. Let $\mathcal{A} = (\mathcal{A}_f, \mathcal{A}_g)$ be an adversary against the IND-RCCA of ReEnc. Let $\mathsf{Adv}_{\mathsf{ReEnc}, \mathcal{A}}^{ind\text{-}rcca}(\kappa, n) := 2 \cdot \Pr\left[\mathsf{Exp}_{\mathsf{ReEnc}, \mathcal{A}}^{ind\text{-}rcca}(\kappa, n) \to true\right] - 1$, with $\mathsf{Exp}_{\mathsf{ReEnc}, \mathcal{A}}^{ind\text{-}rcca}$ as defined in Fig. 3. We say that PRE has IND-RCCA security of ReEnc if for every p.p.t. adversary $\mathcal{A} = (\mathcal{A}_f, \mathcal{A}_g)$, the advantage $\mathsf{Adv}_{\mathsf{ReEnc}, \mathcal{A}}^{ind\text{-}rcca}(\kappa, n)$ is negligible in κ.*

3   Generic Results on Combined-PRE

In this section, we show the link between CPRE and other existing concepts. The definition of a bidirectional PRE is given in Appendix B.

$$\mathbf{Exp}_{\mathsf{PRE.ReEncrypt},\mathcal{A}}^{\text{ind-rcca}}(\kappa, n)$$

$\mathcal{PP} \leftarrow \mathsf{PGen}(\kappa, n)$; $\delta \xleftarrow{\$} \{0,1\}$;

$(m_0, m_1, \ell, \ell', \{pk_{i_j}\}_{j=1..\ell+\ell'+1}, st) \leftarrow \mathcal{A}_f^{\mathcal{O}_R}(\mathcal{PP})$;

if cond_R, return $\perp$;

$C_1 \leftarrow \mathsf{Enc}_2(pk_{i_1}, m_\delta)$;

$\forall j \in [2, \ell]$, $C_j \leftarrow \mathsf{Bi.ReEnc}_2(R_{i_{j-1} \leftrightarrow i_j, 2}, C_{j-1})$;

$C'_{\ell+1} \leftarrow \mathsf{Uni.ReEnc}(rk_{i_\ell \to i_{\ell+1}}, C_\ell)$;

$\forall j \in [\ell+2, \ell+\ell'+1]$, $C'_j \leftarrow \mathsf{Bi.ReEnc}_1(R_{i_{j-1} \leftrightarrow i_j, 1}, C'_{j-1})$;

$\delta' \leftarrow \mathcal{A}_g^{\tilde{\mathcal{O}}_R}(st, C'_{\ell+\ell'+1})$

Return $(\delta' = \delta)$

Fig. 3. IND-RCCA for ReEnc

3.1   Combined-PRE $\Longrightarrow$ BPRE + UPRE

The following states that the existence of a secure Combined-PRE necessarily implies the existence of both a secure UPRE and two (possibly similar) secure BPRE. Let $\mathcal{C} = \{\mathsf{Setup}, \mathsf{KeyGen}, \mathsf{Uni.ReKG}, \mathsf{Bi.ReKG}_1, \mathsf{Bi.ReKG}_2, \mathsf{Enc}_1, \mathsf{Enc}_2, \mathsf{Uni.ReEnc}, \mathsf{Bi.ReEnc}_1, \mathsf{Bi.ReEnc}_2, \mathsf{Dec}_1, \mathsf{Dec}_2\}$ be a secure Combined-PRE as defined by Definition 1.

We first define the single-hop unidirectional PRE $\mathcal{U} = \{\mathsf{Setup}, \mathsf{KeyGen}, \mathsf{Uni.ReKG}, \mathsf{Enc}_1, \mathsf{Enc}_2, \mathsf{Uni.ReEnc}, \mathsf{Dec}_1, \mathsf{Dec}_2\}$.

We then define two different multi-hop bidirectional PRE as $\mathcal{B}_1 = \{\mathsf{Setup}, \mathsf{KeyGen}, \mathsf{Bi.ReKG}_1, \mathsf{Enc}_1, \mathsf{Bi.ReEnc}_1, \mathsf{Dec}_1\}$ and $\mathcal{B}_2 = \{\mathsf{Setup}, \mathsf{KeyGen}, \mathsf{Bi.ReKG}_2, \mathsf{Enc}_2, \mathsf{Bi.ReEnc}_2, \mathsf{Dec}_2\}$. We obtain the following result (the proof is given in Appendix A).

Lemma 1. *If $\mathcal{C}$ is a secure combined Combined-PRE scheme, then $\mathcal{U}$ is a secure unidirectional PRE and both $\mathcal{B}_1$ and $\mathcal{B}_2$ are secure bidirectional PRE.*

3.2   BPRE + encrypted token $\Longrightarrow$ Combined-PRE

We present here a generic construction of a Combined-PRE from a BPRE. In fact, we need three BPRE that can be three different instantiations of the same BPRE, under some restrictions given below[3].

The main point to create a Combined-PRE is that we need two BPRE and one UPRE such that the message and key spaces and the different procedures are compatible one with each other. Our idea is then to use only BPRE and to construct the UPRE from it. For this purpose, we generalize an idea given by Chow *et al.* [6] and refined in [4]. Thus, for each delegate, a random token is chosen by the delegator during the generation of the re-encryption key, which token will play the role of the "secret key" of the delegate in the BPRE. Then, the delegate (and only him) is allowed by the delegator to recover this

---

[3] Using the result above, we obtain that it is possible to obtain a secure UPRE from any secure BPRE, which is not very surprising.

token by adding to the re-encryption key an encryption of this token under the real public key of the delegate. Moreover, during the re-encryption process, the re-encrypted ciphertext - intended now for the random token mentioned previously - is encrypted under the public key of the delegate. To obtain a bidirectional re-encryption at first level, we then make use for both encryption - the encryption of the re-encrypted ciphertext and the encryption of the random token - of two encryptions of BPRE to allow it to be bidirectionally re-encrypted later.

We give the formal description of the Combined-PRE scheme in Appendix B.

4   Practical Construction

We now present a practical Combined-PRE scheme, which one can be directly used in the cloud storage context. Our construction is based on the Libert-Vergnaud's UPRE scheme [9] (LV for short). In fact, we show that, contrary to what one can believe in first, this is possible to design a Combined-PRE scheme with the same level of efficiency as a unidirectional one. We thus obtain a much more efficient scheme than the one described in the previous section which complexity was similar to the one of three BPRE.

4.1   General Intuition

The LV scheme works on a bilinear group, where p is a prime number, $\mathbb{G}$ and $\mathbb{G}_t$ are two groups of prime order p and there exists a bilinear pairing $e : \mathbb{G} \times \mathbb{G} \longrightarrow \mathbb{G}_T$. It mainly corresponds to an adaptation of the bilinear variant of the ElGamal encryption scheme and the use of a one-time signature scheme $\mathcal{S}$ to obtain a RCCA security (see [9] for more details).

A second level ciphertext corresponds to the tuple $C_1 = svk$, $C_2 = X_i^r$, $C_3 = e(g,g)^r \cdot m$, $C_4 = (u^{svk} \cdot v)^r$ and $\sigma = \mathcal{S}.\text{SIGN}(ssk, C_3 \| C_4)$ where (svk, ssk) is a key pair for the one-time signature scheme and g, u, v are public generators of $\mathbb{G}$. A first level ciphertext[4] then corresponds to $C_1 = svk$, $D_2 = g^t$, $E_2 = X_i^{1/t}$, $F_2 = g^{rt}$, $C_3 = e(g,g)^r \cdot m$, $C_4 = (u^{svk} \cdot v)^r$ and $\sigma = \mathcal{S}.\text{SIGN}(ssk, C_3 \| C_4)$.

In particular, a secret key x_i is related to a public key $X_i = g^{x_i}$. A re-encryption key from i to j is obtained by computing $R_{i \to j} = X_j^{1/x_i} = g^{x_j/x_i}$. Under the discrete logarithm assumption, this is not feasible to compute the key $R_{j \to i}$ from this key, and the LV scheme is clearly unidirectional. However, we remark that the knowledge of x_i/x_j, and thus x_j/x_i for obvious reasons, permits to compute both $R_{i \to j}$ and $R_{j \to i}$, which is a condition to obtain a bidirectional system, which obviously works for the second level ciphertexts. In fact, regarding a level 1 or a level 2 ciphertext, the secret key of the user who can decrypt it only appears with the form g^{x_i}, which makes it easy to transform to a similar form with g^{x_j} instead, for the one who knows x_j/x_i. We have thus all the ingredient to obtain our Combined-PRE scheme.

---

[4] As explained in [9], a first level ciphertext can be publicly re-randomized and also we use a re-randomized version of the first level encryption given in [9] for a better understanding of our bidirectional re-encryption at first level.

4.2   Our Combined PRE

SETUP AND KEY GENERATION. We consider a (symmetric) bilinear environment which corresponds to a prime p and two groups $\mathbb{G}$ and $\mathbb{G}_t$ of prime order p such that there exists a pairing $e : \mathbb{G} \times \mathbb{G} \longrightarrow \mathbb{G}_T$. This map is bilinear ($\forall g, h \in \mathbb{G}$ and $a, b \in \mathbb{Z}_p$, $e(g^a, h^b) = e(g, h)^{ab} = e(g^b, h^a)$) and non-degenerated ($\forall g \in \mathbb{G} \setminus \{1\}$, $e(g, g) \neq \mathbf{1}_T$). Let g, u, v be three generators of $\mathbb{G}$ and $\mathcal{S} = (\text{KEYGEN}, \text{SIGN}, \text{VERIF})$ be a strongly unforgeable one-time signature scheme such that verification keys are in $\mathbb{Z}_p^*$ (see [9] for more details). The global parameters output by Setup are $\mathcal{P} = (p, \mathbb{G}, \mathbb{G}_T, e, g, u, v, \mathcal{S})$. Then, using KeyGen, each user is able to generate her own private key sk as $x \xleftarrow{\$} \mathbb{Z}_p^*$ and the corresponding public key pk as $X = g^x$.

As said above, the unidirectional re-encryption key $R_{i \to i}$ (using Uni.ReKG) is computed as $R_{i \to i} = X_i^{1/x_i}$. Then, both bidirectional re-encryption keys (coming from Bi.ReKG$_1$ and Bi.ReKG$_2$) are similar[5] (and thus, $R_{*,1} = R_{*,2} = R_*$). More precisely, the re-encryption key is computed as $R_{i \leftrightarrow j} = sk_j/sk_i$ and we obtain $R_{j \leftrightarrow i} = 1/R_{i \leftrightarrow j} = x_i/x_j$.

ENCRYPTION PHASES. The description of the (re-)encryption procedures (Enc$_1$ and Enc$_2$, Uni.ReEnc, Bi.ReEnc$_1$ and Bi.ReEnc$_2$) are all given[6] in Fig. 4. We only need to detail the validity checks which are executed as follows. For a level 1, it checks if $e(D_{i,2}, E_{i,2}) = e(X_i, g)$, if $e(F_{i,2}, u^{C_1} \cdot v) = e(D_{i,2}, C_4)$ and if $\mathcal{S}.\text{VERIF}(C_1, \sigma, C_3 \| C_4) = 1$. For a level 2, it checks if $e(C_2, u^{C_1} \cdot v) = e(X_i, C_4)$ and if $\mathcal{S}.\text{VERIF}(C_1, \sigma, C_3 \| C_4) = 1$. Then, regarding decryption, they both begin by a validity check as described above. The message m is obtained by $m = C_3/e(E_{i,2}, F_{i,2})^{1/x_i}$ for level 1 and by $m = C_3/e(C_{i,2}, g)^{1/x_i}$ for level 2.

We then have Theorem 1 below (its proof is given in Appendix C), which states that our scheme has IND-RCCA security under the 3-QDBDH assumption [9] in the standard model. This assumption is a variant of the Decision Bilinear Diffie-Hellman assumption, and can be defined as follows.

Definition 5 (modified 3-QDBDH). *The modified[7] 3-Quotient Decision Bilinear Diffie-Hellman assumption (3-QDBDH) posits the hardness of distinguishing* $e(g, g)^{b/a^2}$ *from random, given* $(g, g^a, g^{a^2}, g^{a^3}, g^b)$.

Theorem 1. *The scheme has* IND-RCCA *security of* Enc$_1$, Enc$_2$ *and* ReEnc *under the* 3-QDBDH *assumption in the standard model.*

---

[5] We could consider a stronger security model where an entity could be partially corrupted – at level 1 but not at level 2. In this case, we should consider different secret keys for each level and each entity.

[6] One can remark that when $\ell = i$, $D_{\ell,2} \neq D_{i,2}$, $E_{\ell,2} \neq E_{i,2}$ and $F_{\ell,2} \neq F_{i,2}$. In other words, a re-encrypted level 2 ciphertext is different from a directly computed level 1 ciphertext. This specificity comes from the basic scheme from [9].

[7] Equivalent to the one with $e(g, g)^{b/a}$, see [9].

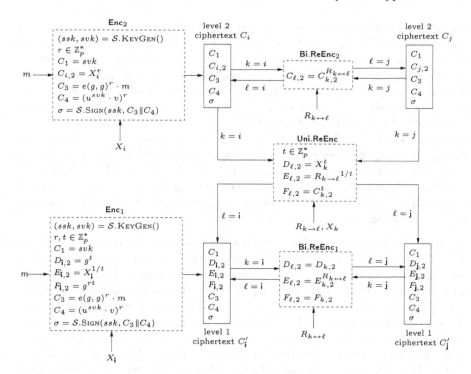

Fig. 4. Our construction

5   Details on the Application to Cloud Storage

We now present an example of a distributed secure storage system based on our practical solution of Sect. 4 between two users, A which has devices A_1, A_2, A_3 and A_4 and a B which has devices B_1, B_2 and B_3.

KEYS GENERATION. A computes some bidirectional re-encryption keys between her devices such that all bidirectional re-encryption keys from any A's device to any other A's device can be computed, for example[8]: $R_{A_1 \leftrightarrow A_2}$, $R_{A_1 \leftrightarrow A_3}$ and $R_{A_2 \leftrightarrow A_4}$. The user B does the same for her devices. To finish, A computes at least one unidirectional re-encryption key from one of her devices to one of B's devices, for example $R_{A_3 \to B_2}$. All re-encryption keys are given to the proxy. With such configuration, there are enough re-encryption keys for A's devices. For example with $R_{A_1 \leftrightarrow A_2}$ and $R_{A_1 \leftrightarrow A_3}$, one can compute $R_{A_2 \leftrightarrow A_3} = R_{A_1 \leftrightarrow A_3} / R_{A_1 \leftrightarrow A_2}$. Similarly, we can easily compute all re-encryptions keys from any A's devices to any B's devices. Indeed $R_{A_1 \leftrightarrow B_2} = R_{A_3 \leftrightarrow B_1}^{R_{A_1 \leftrightarrow A_3} \cdot R_{B_1 \leftrightarrow B_2}}$.

DISTRIBUTED SECURE STORAGE. Suppose A wants to store a message m in her cloud, so that B can access it. She selects one of her devices, *e.g.* A_3, and

---

[8] In practice, when a user adds a new device to the cloud, she computes a bidirectional re-encryption key between her new device and one of her already existing devices.

encrypts the data m under the corresponding public key (with the second level encryption algorithm), she obtains $C_{A_3} = \mathsf{Enc}_2(m, pk_{A_3})$ and sends it to the cloud. A can recover her data from any of her devices as follows. If she wants to recover it from her device A_3, the proxy sends her C_{A_3} and A can easily decrypt it with the device A_3. If she wants to recover it from another device, $e.g.$ A_1, the proxy can obtain from all available bidirectional re-encryption keys, the re-encryption key from A_3 to A_1. With this latter, the proxy can then compute the ciphertext $C_{A_1} = \mathsf{Bi.ReEnc}_1(C_{A_3}, R_{A_3 \leftrightarrow A_1})$ intended to A_1. A_1 can finally decrypt it, using the level 2 decryption procedure of the BPRE. Suppose that B wants to recover the message m from any of her devices (let $i \in [1, 4]$). As already explained, the proxy can compute the re-encryption key from A_3 to B_i (related to the UPRE): $R_{A_3 \to B_i}$. It can also re-encrypts C_{A_3} into a level 1 ciphertext $C'_{B_i} = \mathsf{Uni.ReEnc}(C_{A_3}, R_{A_3 \to B_i})$ intended to B_i and related to the UPRE.

CASE OF A LOST DEVICE. Our Combined-PRE permits to easily manage the lost of a device. If A has still at least one device, then the proxy re-encrypts all ciphertexts intended to the lost device, say A_2, into ciphertexts intended to a remaining device of A. This is possible as the proxy can compute all re-encryptions keys between A's devices. Then it stores all new ciphertexts and deletes ciphertexts intended for this lost device. Moreover, to prevent the lost device to access to data via a re-encryption, the proxy also deletes all unidirectional and bidirectional re-encryption keys involving the key of the lost device. Before doing this, the proxy has to be careful since it is necessary for it to keep a set of minimum re-encryption keys to recover all re-encryption keys between remaining devices. For example if the only link to compute the re-encryption key between A_1 and A_3 is $R_{A_1 \leftrightarrow A_2}$ and $R_{A_2 \leftrightarrow A_3}$, then the proxy has first to compute $R_{A_1 \leftrightarrow A_3}$ and to store it before deleting $R_{A_1 \leftrightarrow A_2}$ and $R_{A_2 \leftrightarrow A_3}$. Otherwise, if A has no more device, the proxy does as described previously, except that the target device is one device of B. Then, the proxy can delete all re-encryption keys involving the lost device, as they are not useful anymore. The advantage of this solution is that it is not necessary to ask the user to use one of his devices in order to decrypt a ciphertext, so as to encrypt it for another key. It is however important to motivate users to have more than one device in such system.

6   Conclusion and Acknowledgments

This paper introduces the concept of combined proxy re-encryption, which can be very useful to secure a cloud storage service. We have also provided evidence that our concept can be efficiently implemented and that it can directly be embedded into existing systems.

We are grateful to Fabien Laguillaumie for helpful discussions and to anonymous referees for their valuable comments.

A   Proof of Lemma 1

We recall that Lemma 1 states that if $\mathcal{C}$ is a secure combined Combined-PRE scheme, then $\mathcal{U}$ is a secure unidirectional PRE and both $\mathcal{B}_1$ and $\mathcal{B}_2$ are secure BPRE.

It is obvious that if $\mathcal{C}$ verifies the IND-CCA security of Enc_1, Enc_2 and ReEnc, then the underlying PRE scheme $\mathcal{U}$ (resp. $\mathcal{B}_1$ and $\mathcal{B}_2$) is also secure. An adversary against $\mathcal{U}$ (resp. $\mathcal{B}_1$ and $\mathcal{B}_2$) can be used to design an adversary against $\mathcal{C}$. In a nutshell, this is done by simply forwarding the parameters, requests and answers to oracles between the adverary against $\mathcal{U}$ (resp. $\mathcal{B}_1$ and $\mathcal{B}_2$) and the challenger related to $\mathcal{C}$. We have the following associations: (i) IND-CCA of $\mathcal{U}$ related to Enc_1 (resp. Enc_2) $\longrightarrow$ IND-CCA of $\mathcal{C}$ related to Enc_1 (resp. Enc_2) with $\ell = 0$ (resp. $\ell' = 0$); (ii) IND-CCA of $\mathcal{U}$ related to ReEnc $\longrightarrow$ IND-CCA of $\mathcal{C}$ related to ReEnc with $\ell = \ell' = 0$; and (iii) IND-CCA of $\mathcal{B}_1$ (resp. $\mathcal{B}_2$) $\longrightarrow$ IND-CCA of $\mathcal{C}$ related to Enc_1 (resp. Enc_2) with $\ell \neq 0$ (resp. $\ell' \neq 0$).   □

B   Generic Results on Combined-PRE

B.1   Definition of a BPRE

DEFINITION OF A BPRE. A BPRE scheme consists of the algorithms (Setup, KeyGen, ReKeyGen, Enc, ReEnc, Decrypt) defined as in Sect. 2. The IND-RCCA experiment is given as follows, where $\mathcal{O}_B = \{\mathsf{ODec}, \mathsf{OReKG}, \mathsf{OReEnc}, \mathsf{OSecKey}\}$ (with the "Obi" oracles as defined in Sect. 2.2) and cond_B states that the key pk_{i_ℓ} should be a key of an uncorrupted user (meaning that pk_{i_ℓ} has not been queried on input of $\mathsf{OSecKey}$). First, execute $\mathcal{PP} \leftarrow \mathsf{PGen}(\kappa, n)$ and states $\delta \xleftarrow{\$} \{0,1\}$. Then, $(m_0, m_1, \{pk_{i_j}\}_{j=1..\ell}, st) \leftarrow \mathcal{A}_f^{\mathcal{O}_B}(\mathcal{PP})$. If cond_B, return $\perp$. Else, $C_1 \leftarrow \mathsf{Enc}(pk_{i_1}, m_\delta)$ and $\forall j \in [2, \ell]$, $C_j \leftarrow \mathsf{ReEnc}(R_{i_{j-1} \leftrightarrow i_j}, C_{j-1})$. Finally, we have $\delta' \leftarrow \mathcal{A}_g^{\widetilde{\mathcal{O}}_B}(st, C_\ell)$ and the experiment returns $(\delta' = \delta)$. The version $\widetilde{\mathcal{O}}_B$ is defined such that (i) $\mathcal{A}_g$ should not query pk_{i_ℓ} to $\mathsf{OSecKey}$, (ii) there is no path of re-encryption keys coming from OReKG from pk_{i_ℓ} to a corrupted pk^*, (iii) $\mathcal{A}_g$ should not query a decryption of the challenge ciphertext C_ℓ using ODec and (iv) $\mathcal{A}_g$ is not allowed to query to ODec a ciphertext C' for an honest entity such that $\mathsf{Dec}(\mathsf{sk}, C') \in \{m_0, m_1\}$.

B.2   BPRE + UPRE $\not\Rightarrow$ Combined-PRE?

We point out the reasons why the reciprocity seems to be wrong in general. Consider a UPRE $\mathcal{U} = \{\mathsf{Setup}, \mathsf{KeyGen}, \mathsf{Uni.ReKG}, \mathsf{Enc}_1, \mathsf{Enc}_2, \mathsf{Uni.ReEnc}, \mathsf{Dec}_1, \mathsf{Dec}_2\}$ and two BPRE $\mathcal{B}_1 = \{\mathsf{Setup}, \mathsf{KeyGen}, \mathsf{Bi.ReKG}_1, \mathsf{Enc}_1, \mathsf{Bi.ReEnc}_1, \mathsf{Dec}_1\}$ and $\mathcal{B}_2 = \{\mathsf{Setup}, \mathsf{KeyGen}, \mathsf{Bi.ReKG}_2, \mathsf{Enc}_2, \mathsf{Bi.ReEnc}_2, \mathsf{Dec}_2\}$.

It is first obvious that the combination of the three above schemes does not necessarily give a correct Combined-PRE scheme since there may be some non compatible transitions. More precisely, ciphertexts would not necessarily be compatible in the sense that the ciphertext formats corresponding to the two BPRE would not be compatible to level 1 ciphertext and level 2 ciphertext (respectively) of the UPRE.

Then, regarding security, we suppose having a black-box adversary against the Combined-PRE and we try to use it to break *e.g.* the IND-CCA security of the BPRE scheme. For this purpose, we need to simulate all the oracles of the adversary against the Combined-PRE, including the generation of re-encryption keys. However, in some cases (mainly the case of a re-encryption key from an uncorrupted to a corrupted user), we will not be able to create such key that will be coherent with the unknown keys related to the BPRE scheme (we need for the above example the secret key of an uncorrupted user). One may think of decreasing the power of the adversary by giving it only some "relevant" keys instead of all possible ones (such as defined in Sect. 2). But this leads to a less powerful adversary that will not necessarily be relevant in most practical cases. However, we show below that it exists an alternative way to design a secure Combined-PRE using one BPRE, but with some additional work.

B.3   BPRE + encrypted token $\Longrightarrow$ Combined-PRE

OUR GENERIC SCHEME. Let κ be a security parameter. Suppose we have three secure BPRE schemes Bi_f, Bi_s and Bi_r with the following algorithms: (Setup, KeyGen, ReKeyGen, Enc, ReEnc, Decrypt) (see Appendix B.1). We moreover ask that (i) the space of secret key of Bi_s is included in the space of plaintext of Bi_r and (ii) the space of ciphertext of Bi_s is included in the space of plaintext of Bi_f.

- Setup(κ): run Bi_f.Setup(κ), Bi_s.Setup(κ) and Bi_r.Setup(κ) to create $\mathcal{P} = (\mathcal{P}_f, \mathcal{P}_s, \mathcal{P}_r)$.
- KeyGen($\mathcal{P}$): this algorithm first runs Bi_s.KeyGen($\mathcal{P}_s$) (for the second level ciphertexts), then Bi_f.KeyGen($\mathcal{P}_f$) and finally Bi_r.KeyGen($\mathcal{P}_r$) to obtain the secret key $sk = (sk_f, sk_s, sk_r)$ and the public one $pk = (pk_f, pk_s, pk_r)$.
- Uni.ReKG($\mathcal{P}, sk_i, pk_i$): on input i's private key sk_i and i's public key pk_i, this algorithm generates the unidirectional re-encryption key $R_{i \to i}$ as follows. It creates a new virtual entity "ii" and run Bi_s.KeyGen(κ) to obtain (sk_{ii}, pk_{ii}) and computes $R_{i \leftrightarrow ii,s} = \mathsf{Bi}_s$.ReKG($\mathcal{P}_s, sk_{i,s}, sk_{ii}$). It runs $R_{i,i} = \mathsf{Bi}_r$.Enc($\mathcal{P}_r, pk_{i,r}, sk_{ii}$) as the encryption of sk_{ii} and the unidirectional re-encryption key is $R_{i \to i} = (R_{i \leftrightarrow ii,s}, R_{i,i}, pk_{i,f})$.
- Bi.ReKG$_1$($\mathcal{P}, sk_i, sk_j$): on input i's secret key sk_i and j's secret key sk_j, this algorithm runs Bi_f.ReKG($\mathcal{P}_f, sk_{i,f}, sk_{j,f}$) and Bi_r.ReKG($\mathcal{P}, sk_{i,r}, sk_{j,r}$) to obtain respectively $R_{i \leftrightarrow j,f}$ and $R_{i \leftrightarrow j,r}$. Then it outputs $R_{i \leftrightarrow j,1} = (R_{i \leftrightarrow j,f}, R_{i \leftrightarrow j,r})$.
- Bi.ReKG$_2$($\mathcal{P}, sk_i, sk_j$): on input i's secret key sk_i and j's secret key sk_j, this algorithm runs Bi_s.ReKG($\mathcal{P}_s, sk_{i,s}, sk_{j,s}$) to compute and output $R_{i \leftrightarrow j,2}$.
- Enc$_1$($\mathcal{P}, pk, m$): on input a user public key pk and a plaintext m belonging to the space of plaintext of the Bi_f scheme, this algorithm generates a first level ciphertext of m as follows. It creates a new virtual entity tmp and run $(sk_{\mathsf{tmp}}, pk_{\mathsf{tmp}}) = \mathsf{Bi}_s$.KeyGen($\kappa$) and then encrypts (i) m with the virtual public key as $T = \mathsf{Bi}_s$.Enc($\mathcal{P}_s, pk_{\mathsf{tmp}}, m$), (ii) the above resulting ciphertext with the user's public key as Bi_f.Enc($\mathcal{P}_f, pk_r, T$) to obtain C_1' and (iii) the virtual

secret key as $R' = \mathsf{Bi_r}.\mathsf{Enc}(\mathcal{P}_r, pk_r, sk_{\mathsf{tmp}})$. It outputs the first level ciphertext $C' = (C'_1, R')$.

- $\mathsf{Enc_2}(\mathcal{P}, pk, m)$: on input a user public key pk and a plaintext m belonging to the space of plaintext of the $\mathsf{Bi_s}$ scheme, this algorithm simply runs $\mathsf{Bi_s}.\mathsf{Enc}(\mathcal{P}_s, pk_s, m)$ to obtain C and outputs it as a second level ciphertext of m intended to pk.

- $\mathsf{Uni}.\mathsf{ReEnc}(\mathcal{P}, R_{i\rightarrow i}, C_i)$: on input a unidirectional re-encryption key $R_{i\rightarrow i} = (R_{i\leftrightarrow ii,s}, R_{i,i}, pk_{i,f})$ and a second level ciphertext C_i, it works as follows. It first re-encrypts C_i to obtain a ciphertext $w.r.t.$ $\mathcal{P}_s$ and the virtual public key contained in $R_{i\rightarrow i}$ as $T = \mathsf{Bi_s}.\mathsf{ReEnc}(\mathcal{P}_s, R_{i\leftrightarrow ii,s}, C_i)$. It then encrypts T (to obtain a security without non-natural restrictions) as for the $\mathsf{Enc_1}$ procedure, as $C'_1 = \mathsf{Bi_f}.\mathsf{Enc}(\mathcal{P}_f, pk_{i,f}, T)$ and retrieves the encrypted virtual secret key from the re-encryption key $(R' = R_{i,i})$ and output the first level ciphertext $C' = (C'_1, R')$.

- $\mathsf{Bi}.\mathsf{ReEnc_1}(\mathcal{P}, R_{i\leftrightarrow j,1}, C'_i)$: on input a bidirectional re-encryption key $R_{i\leftrightarrow j,1}$ and a first level ciphertext $C'_i = (C'_{i,1}, R'_i)$, it works as follows. It computes $C'_{j,1} = \mathsf{Bi_f}.\mathsf{ReEnc}(\mathcal{P}_f, R_{i\leftrightarrow j,f}, C'_{i,1})$ and $R'_j = \mathsf{Bi_r}.\mathsf{ReEnc}(\mathcal{P}_r, R_{i\leftrightarrow j,r}, R'_i)$ and outputs the first level ciphertext $C'_j = (C'_{j,1}, R'_j)$.

- $\mathsf{Bi}.\mathsf{ReEnc_2}(\mathcal{P}, R_{i\leftrightarrow j,2}, C_i)$: on input a bidirectional re-encryption key $R_{i\leftrightarrow j,2}$ and a second level ciphertext C_i, it executes $\mathsf{Bi_s}.\mathsf{ReEnc}(\mathcal{P}_s, R_{i\leftrightarrow j,2}, C_i)$ to obtain the second level ciphertext C_j.

- $\mathsf{Dec_1}(\mathcal{P}, sk, C')$: On input $\mathcal{P} = (\mathcal{P}_f, \mathcal{P}_s, \mathcal{P}_r)$ and $sk = (sk_f, sk_s, sk_r)$ and a first level ciphertext $C' = (C'_1, R')$, it works as follows. It retrieves $T = \mathsf{Bi_f}.\mathsf{Dec}(\mathcal{P}_f, sk_f, C'_1)$, computes $sk_{\mathsf{tmp}} = \mathsf{Bi_r}.\mathsf{Dec}(\mathcal{P}_r, sk_r, R')$ and obtains $m = \mathsf{Bi_s}.\mathsf{Dec}(\mathcal{P}_s, sk_{\mathsf{tmp}}, T)$.

- $\mathsf{Dec_2}(\mathcal{P}, sk, C)$: on input the user secret key sk and a second level ciphertext C, this algorithm runs $\mathsf{Bi_s}.\mathsf{Dec}(\mathcal{P}_s, sk_s, C)$ to retrieve m.

Remark 1. As explained in their paper, Chow *et al.* [6] make use, for the secret key of the second level encryption, of a random sum of two secret keys $sk_1 + \mathcal{H}_4(pk_2).sk_2$, where $\mathcal{H}_4$ is a hash function. As sk_1 is only used in this second level encryption, we have decided in our generic construction to replace this sum by a single secret key which will be used only for the second level encryption.

The two following theorems give the security of this construction.

Theorem 2. *The scheme achieves the IND-RCCA security of $\mathsf{Enc_1}$ and $\mathsf{Uni}.\mathsf{ReEnc}$.*

Theorem 3. *The scheme achieves the IND-RCCA security of $\mathsf{Enc_2}$.*

B.4   Proof of Theorem 2

In fact, a level 1 ciphertext can be seen as two ciphertexts: one related to a random token h and the other related to the message and encrypted with the h. Therefore both $\mathsf{Enc_1}$ and $\mathsf{Uni}.\mathsf{ReEnc}$ securities depend on the security of those two encryptions, which are supposed to be secure – with RCCA restrictions and not CCA ones due to this concatenation.   □

B.5   Proof of Theorem 3

Let $\mathcal{A}$ an adversary against the Enc_2 security, $\mathcal{B}$ the algorithm to break the security of one of the two BPRE Bi_s and Bi_r. Due to limited space, we only give the idea of the proof and we will provide a complete proof in the full version. Let q_{sk}, q_u, q_{bf} and q_{bs} be the number of queries to the secret key generation oracle, to the unidirectional re-encryption key generation oracle, to the bidirectional re-encryption key for first level oracle and to the bidirectional re-encryption key for second level oracle. We separate entities in two sets by using the Coron's technique [7]: for an entity, c (for an entity i, c is noted c_i) is a bit set to h with probability $\frac{1}{1+q_{sk}+q_u+q_{bf}+q_{bs}}$ and to $\perp$ otherwise. h is chosen to designate entities considered as honest by $\mathcal{B}$ during all the simulation. Those entities are potential challenge entities. If the adversary queries for some requests involving such an entity - details of those queries are given in the simulation -, then $\mathcal{B}$ aborts. The probability mentioned before minimizes the event "$\mathcal{B}$ aborts" during different oracle's queries. Then we separate the set of entities with $c_i = \perp$ into two different sets ($c_i = k$ and $c_i = r$) depending on different oracles' queries. Definition of k and r are linked and defined as follows:

- if the adversary queries for a request to obtain the secret key of an entity i, not considered as honest by $\mathcal{B}$ and such that the adversary has not already obtained a unidirectional re-encryption key from an honest entity i to this entity i, then $\mathcal{B}$ returns the secret key and sets c_i to k. k is helpful for $\mathcal{B}$ to remember that i can not be involved in a unidirectional re-encryption key from an entity i as this last one is potentially the challenge entity.
- if the adversary queries for a request to obtain the unidirectional re-encryption key from an honest entity i to an entity i not considered as honest by $\mathcal{B}$ and not already corrupted by the adversary, then $\mathcal{B}$ sets c_i to r. r is helpful for $\mathcal{B}$ to remember that i can not be corrupted as the entity i involved in this re-encryption key is potentially the challenge entity.

The Coron's trick and its different values h, r and k help $\mathcal{B}$ to manage the adaptive corruption model. $\mathcal{B}$ maintains four lists: $\mathcal{K}^{\mathsf{list}}$, $\mathcal{R}^{\mathsf{list}}_{\mathsf{Uni}}$, $\mathcal{R}^{\mathsf{list}}_{\mathsf{Bi1}}$ and $\mathcal{R}^{\mathsf{list}}_{\mathsf{Bi2}}$ which are initially set as empty and which will store respectively public/secret keys, unidirectional and (level 1 and 2) bidirectional re-encryption keys. The oracle are defined as follows.

- KeyGen(κ): if $c = h$, then $\mathcal{B}$ queries for $\mathsf{OBi}_s.\mathsf{Keygen}(\kappa)$ for an honest entity and obtains pk_s. It runs $\mathsf{Bi}_f.\mathsf{KeyGen}(\kappa)$ and $\mathsf{Bi}_r.\mathsf{KeyGen}(\kappa)$ to obtain (sk_f, pk_f) and (sk_r, pk_r). Then it defines $pk = (pk_f, pk_s, pk_r)$ and $sk = (sk_f, \perp, sk_r)$ and adds (pk, sk, c) to $\mathcal{K}^{\mathsf{list}}$. If $c = \perp$, $\mathcal{B}$ queries for $\mathsf{OBi}_s.\mathsf{Keygen}(\kappa)$ for a corrupted entity and obtains (sk_s, pk_s). It runs $\mathsf{Bi}_f.\mathsf{KeyGen}(\kappa)$ and $\mathsf{Bi}_r.\mathsf{KeyGen}(\kappa)$ to obtain (sk_f, pk_f) and (sk_r, pk_r). Then it defines $pk = (pk_f, pk_s, pk_r)$ and $sk = (sk_f, sk_s, sk_r)$ and adds (pk, sk, c) to $\mathcal{K}^{\mathsf{list}}$.
- OSecKey(pk): $\mathcal{B}$ recovers (pk, sk, c) from $\mathcal{K}^{\mathsf{list}}$. If $c = h$ or r, $\mathcal{B}$ aborts. If $c = \perp$, it returns sk to $\mathcal{A}$, redefines $c = k$ and updates it in $\mathcal{K}^{\mathsf{list}}$.

- OUni.ReKG(pk_i, pk_i): recover both entries (pk_i, sk_i, c_i) and $(pk_\mathsf{i}, sk_\mathsf{i}, c_\mathsf{i})$ from $\mathcal{K}^{\mathsf{list}}$. Then $\mathcal{B}$ proceeds as follows. If $c_i = h$ and $c_\mathsf{i} = \perp$, it redefines $c_\mathsf{i} = r$ and updates it in $\mathcal{K}^{\mathsf{list}}$. Create a new virtual entity ii and run $\mathsf{Bi_s.KeyGen}(\kappa)$ to obtain pk_{ii}, query $\mathsf{OBi_s.ReKeygen}(pk_{i,s}, pk_{ii})$ to obtain $R_{i \leftrightarrow ii,s}$. Create a new virtual entity ii' and run $\mathsf{Bi_s.KeyGen}(\kappa)$ to obtain $(sk_{ii'}, pk_{ii'})$ and run $R_{i,\mathsf{i}} = \mathsf{Bi_r.Enc}(sk_{ii'}, pk_{\mathsf{i},r})$. Return the unidirectional re-encryption key $R_{i \to \mathsf{i}} = (R_{i \leftrightarrow ii,s},$
  $R_{i,\mathsf{i}})$. $\mathcal{B}$ adds the tuple $(pk_i, pk_\mathsf{i}, pk_{ii}, sk_{ii'}, \perp, R_{i \leftrightarrow ii,s}, R_{i,\mathsf{i}})$ to $\mathcal{R}^{\mathsf{list}}_{\mathsf{Uni}}$. If $c_i = h$ and $c_\mathsf{i} = k$, then $\mathcal{B}$ aborts and outputs "failure".
- OBi.ReKG$_2$(pk_i, pk_j): recover both entries (pk_i, sk_i, c_i) and (pk_j, sk_j, c_j) from $\mathcal{K}^{\mathsf{list}}$. If $c_i = c_j = h$ then query $\mathsf{OBi_s.ReKeygen}(pk_{i,s}, pk_{j,s})$ to obtain $R_{i \leftrightarrow j,s}$ and output it as the bidirectional re-encryption key at second level. Then add the tuple $(pk_i, pk_j, R_{i \leftrightarrow j,s})$ to $\mathcal{R}^{\mathsf{list}}_{\mathsf{Bi2}}$.
- OBi.ReKG$_1$(pk,i, pk_j): recover both entries (pk_i, sk_i, c_i) and (pk_j, sk_j, c_j) from $\mathcal{K}^{\mathsf{list}}$. If $c_i = h$ and $c_j \neq h$ or if $c_j = h$ and $c_i \neq h$, then $\mathcal{B}$ aborts and outputs "failure". $\mathcal{B}$ proceeds as in the scheme in the other cases.
- OUni.ReEnc(pk_i, pk_i, C_i) with $c_i = h$, $c_\mathsf{i} = k$ and C a ciphertext different from the challenge - this last condition is unnecessary during the first phase: $\mathcal{B}$ recovers $sk_i = (sk_{i,f}, sk_{i,s}, sk_{i,r})$ and $pk_\mathsf{i} = (pk_{\mathsf{i},f}, pk_{\mathsf{i},s}, pk_{\mathsf{i},r})$ from $\mathcal{K}^{\mathsf{list}}$ and proceeds as follows. If there is an entry $(pk_i, pk_\mathsf{i}, \perp, sk_{ii'}, pk_{ii'}, \perp, R_{i,\mathsf{i}})$ in $\mathcal{R}^{\mathsf{list}}_{\mathsf{Uni}}$, then it queries $\mathsf{OBi_s.Decrypt}(pk_{i,s}, C)$ to obtain m, run $\mathsf{Bi_f.Enc}(pk_{\mathsf{i},r}, \mathsf{Bi_s.Enc}$ $(pk_{ii'}, m))$ to obtain $C'_{i,1}$ and then outputs the first level ciphertext $C'_\mathsf{i} = (C'_{i,1}, R'_{i,\mathsf{i}})$. If there is no such entry in $\mathcal{R}^{\mathsf{list}}_{\mathsf{Uni}}$, then it creates a new virtual entity ii' and run $\mathsf{Bi_s.KeyGen}(\kappa)$ to obtain $sk_{ii'}$ and $pk_{ii'}$. It runs $\mathsf{Bi_r.Enc}(pk_{i,r}, sk_{ii'})$ and add $(pk_i, pk_\mathsf{i}, \perp, sk_{ii'}, pk_{ii'}, \perp, R_{i,\mathsf{i}})$ in $\mathcal{R}^{\mathsf{list}}_{\mathsf{Uni}}$ and then proceeds as in the first case.
- OBi.ReEnc$_2$(pk_i, pk_j, C_i) with $c_i = c_j = h$: $\mathcal{B}$ queries $\mathsf{OBi_s.ReEncrypt}(pk_i, pk_j, C_i)$ to obtain C_j and outputs it to $\mathcal{A}$.
- OBi.ReEnc$_1$(pk_i, pk_j, C_i): $\mathcal{B}$ proceeds as in the scheme.
- ODec$_1$(pk, C') with pk honest - $c \neq k$: on input a first level ciphertext $C' = (C'_1, R')$. Recover $sk = (sk_f, sk_s, sk_r)$ from $\mathcal{K}^{\mathsf{list}}$. Compute $T = \mathsf{Bi_f.Dec}(sk_f, C'_1)$ and $sk_{\mathsf{tmp}} = \mathsf{Bi_r.Dec}(sk_r, R')$. If there is an entry $(pk_i, pk_\mathsf{i}, sk_{ii}, sk_{\mathsf{tmp}}, \perp, R_{i \leftrightarrow ii,s}, R_{i,\mathsf{i}})$ in $\mathcal{R}^{\mathsf{list}}_{\mathsf{Uni}}$, then return $m = \mathsf{Bi_s.Dec}(sk_{ii}, T)$ or $\perp$ if one decryption algorithm returns $\perp$. If there are any such entry, proceed as in the scheme.

Regarding the challenge phase, $\mathcal{A}$ outputs $\{pk_{i_j}\}_{j=1..\ell'}$ and two messages m_0 and m_1. If the Coron's trick c_{i_ℓ} associated to pk_{i_ℓ} – entity outputted by $\mathcal{A}$ during the challenge – is different from h, then $\mathcal{B}$ aborts. $\mathcal{B}$ recovers different re-encryption keys needed in the following execution or defined it as in different re-encryption key generation oracles. Then, $\mathcal{B}$ outputs $(m_0, m_1, \{pk_{i_j,s}\}_{j=1..l'}, st)$, receives the challenge C^*_ℓ and gives it to $\mathcal{A}$. $\qquad \square$

C   Security Proofs for Our Practical Construction

Regarding the security related to Enc_2, the proof is the same as the one the scheme [9] with some adaptations to include bidirectional re-encryption keys.

The idea is to use the Coron's trick [7] on uncorrupted keys: a public uncorrupted key pk with a trick $c = 0$ (resp. $c = 1$) is computed as $pk = (g^{(a^2)})^x$ (resp. $pk = (g^a)^x$). If the two keys pk_i and pk_j, output by the adversary, have the same Coron's trick (so of the form $a^2.x$ or $a.x$), it is possible to compute the bidirectional re-encryption key corresponding as x_i/x_j (which one can be computed). One can choose the distribution related to $c = 0$ or 1, so that this is almost always the case. The value $T = e(g, g)^{b/a^2}$ is used in $C_3 = m_\delta \cdot T$ which is given to the adversary.

Regarding the security related to Enc_1 and ReEnc, the proof is also the same and the above adaptations can be similarely applied, except that we do not use Coron's trick. Indeed, all uncorrupted keys have the same form: $(g^a)^x$.   □

References

1. Ateniese, G., Benson, K., Hohenberger, S.: Key-private proxy re-encryption. In: Fischlin, M. (ed.) CT-RSA 2009. LNCS, vol. 5473, pp. 279–294. Springer, Heidelberg (2009)
2. Ateniese, G., Fu, K., Green, M., Hohenberger, S.: Improved proxy re-encryption schemes with applications to secure distributed storage. ACM Trans. Inf. Syst. Secur. **9**(1), 1–30 (2006)
3. Blaze, M., Bleumer, G., Strauss, M.J.: Divertible protocols and atomic proxy cryptography. In: Nyberg, K. (ed.) EUROCRYPT 1998. LNCS, vol. 1403, pp. 127–144. Springer, Heidelberg (1998)
4. Canard, S., Devigne, J., Laguillaumie, F.: Improving the security of an efficient unidirectional proxy re-encryption scheme. J. Internet Serv. Inf. Secur. **1**(2/3), 140–160 (2011)
5. Canetti, R., Hohenberger, S.: Chosen-ciphertext secure proxy re-encryption. In: ACM CCS'07, pp. 185–194. ACM (2007)
6. Chow, S.S.M., Weng, J., Yang, Y., Deng, R.H.: Efficient unidirectional proxy re-encryption. In: Bernstein, D.J., Lange, T. (eds.) AFRICACRYPT 2010. LNCS, vol. 6055, pp. 316–332. Springer, Heidelberg (2010)
7. Coron, J.-S.: On the exact security of full domain hash. In: Bellare, M. (ed.) CRYPTO 2000. LNCS, vol. 1880, pp. 229–235. Springer, Heidelberg (2000)
8. Deng, R.H., Weng, J., Liu, S., Chen, K.: Chosen-ciphertext secure proxy re-encryption without pairings. In: Franklin, M.K., Hui, L.C.K., Wong, D.S. (eds.) CANS 2008. LNCS, vol. 5339, pp. 1–17. Springer, Heidelberg (2008)
9. Libert, B., Vergnaud, D.: Unidirectional chosen-ciphertext secure proxy re-encryption. In: Cramer, R. (ed.) PKC 2008. LNCS, vol. 4939, pp. 360–379. Springer, Heidelberg (2008)
10. Matsuda, T., Nishimaki, R., Tanaka, K.: CCA proxy re-encryption without bilinear maps in the standard model. In: Nguyen, P.Q., Pointcheval, D. (eds.) PKC 2010. LNCS, vol. 6056, pp. 261–278. Springer, Heidelberg (2010)
11. Shao, J., Cao, Z.: CCA-secure proxy re-encryption without pairings. In: Jarecki, S., Tsudik, G. (eds.) PKC 2009. LNCS, vol. 5443, pp. 357–376. Springer, Heidelberg (2009)
12. Tysowski, P.K., Hasan, M.A.: Re-encryption-based key management towards secure and scalable mobile applications in clouds. IACR ePrint 2011, 668 (2011)
13. Weng, J., Chen, M., Yang, Y.J., Deng, R., Chen, K.F., Bao, F.: Cca-secure unidirectional proxy re-encryption in the adaptive corruption model without random oracles. Sci. China Inf. Sci. **53**, 593–606 (2010)

Certificateless Proxy Re-Encryption Without Pairings

Kang Yang$^{(\boxtimes)}$, Jing Xu, and Zhenfeng Zhang

Laboratory of Trusted Computing and Information Assurance,
Institute of Software, Chinese Academy of Sciences, Beijing, China
{yangkang,xujing,zfzhang}@tca.iscas.ac.cn

Abstract. Proxy re-encryption (PRE) allows a proxy with re-encryption keys to transform a ciphertext under a given public key into a ciphertext of the same message under a different public key, and can not learn anything about the encrypted message. Due to its transformation property, PRE has many practical applications such as cloud storage, confidential email, and digital right management, and so on. Certificateless proxy re-encryption (CLPRE) provides not only the transformation property of PRE but also the advantage of identity-based cryptography without suffering from its inherent key escrow. Unfortunately, construction of CLPRE schemes has so far depended on the costly bilinear pairings. In this paper, we propose the first construction of CLPRE schemes without the bilinear pairings whose security is based on the standard computational Diffie-Hellman (CDH) assumption in the random oracle model. We first present a chosen-plaintext (CPA) secure CLPRE scheme, and then convert it into a chosen-ciphertext (CCA) secure CLPRE scheme. Compared with other CLPRE schemes, our CLPRE schemes provide the shortest re-encryption key and do not require any pairing operation and map-to-point hash operation, which are more efficient and more suitable for low-power devices.

Keywords: Certificateless public key cryptography · Unidirectional proxy re-encryption · Provable security

1 Introduction

Proxy re-encryption (PRE) was first introduced by Blaze et al. [6] and has received much attention in recent years. In a PRE scheme, a semi-trusted proxy with re-encryption keys can transform ciphertexts under the public key of Alice (the delegator) into other ciphertexts for Bob (the delegatee) without seeing the underlying plaintext. PRE schemes have many practical applications in digital rights management (DRM) [27], encrypted email forwarding [6], cloud storage [30], distributed file systems [1], law enforcement [18], and outsourced filtering of encrypted spam [1]. According to the direction of transformation, PRE can be categorized into bidirectional PRE [6,11], in which the proxy can transform

© Springer International Publishing Switzerland 2014
H.-S. Lee and D.-G. Han (Eds.): ICISC 2013, LNCS 8565, pp. 67–88, 2014.
DOI: 10.1007/978-3-319-12160-4_5

ciphertexts from Alice to Bob and vice versa, and unidirectional PRE [1,22], in which the proxy cannot transform ciphertexts in the opposite direction. According to the times of transformation, PRE can also be categorized into single-hop PRE [1], in which the ciphertexts can only be transformed once, and multi-hop PRE [6,11], in which the ciphertexts can be transformed from Alice to Bob and then to Charlie and so on. In this paper, we address the problem of obtaining single-hop unidirectional PRE schemes.

In 1998, Blaze et al. [6] proposed the first bidirectional PRE scheme based on a simple modification of the ElGamal encryption scheme [14]. In 2005, Ateniese et al. [1] proposed the unidirectional PRE schemes based on bilinear pairings with the collusion-"safe" property in which the proxy cannot collude with the delegatees in order to recover the delegator's secret key. However, these PRE schemes only achieve security against chosen plaintext attacks (CPA), which may not be sufficient to guarantee security for some complex network environments. In 2007, Canetti and Hohenberger [11] formalized definitions of security against chosen ciphertext attacks (CCA) for PRE schemes and proposed the first CCA secure bidirectional multi-hop PRE scheme in the standard model. Simultaneously with their work, Green and Ateniese [16] proposed the first identity-based PRE (IBPRE) schemes in the random oracle model, and the first scheme is multi-hop unidirectional against chosen plaintext attacks (CPA) and the other scheme is single-hop unidirectional against chosen ciphertext attacks (CCA). In 2008, Libert and Vergnaud [22] proposed the first single-hop unidirectional PRE scheme against replayable chosen-ciphertext attacks (RCCA) in the standard model. In the same year, Deng et al. [13] proposed a bidirectional CCA secure PRE scheme without the bilinear pairings. In 2012, Hanaoka et al. [17] proposed a generic construction of CCA secure PRE scheme. Later, Isshiki et al. [19] proposed a CCA secure PRE scheme. Both of their schemes are single-hop unidirectional and CCA secure in the standard model.

Above all these PRE schemes are constructed based on either traditional public key cryptography (PKC) or identity-based cryptography (IBC). However, it is well recognized that PKC suffers from the issues associated with certificate management such as revocation and IBC has inherent key escrow problem for which the private key generator (PKG) knows every user's private key. To alleviate the aforementioned problems, the concept of certificateless public key cryptography (CLPKC) was introduced by Al-Riyami and Paterson [2], which combines the best aspects of PKC and of IBC. They considered two types of adversary. A Type I adversary can replace public keys of arbitrary identities with other valid public keys of its choice, but it does not have access to master key. In contrast, a Type II adversary is equipped with master-key but is not allowed to replace public keys of entities. In 2005, Baek et al. [9] proposed an efficient certificateless public key encryption (CLPKE) scheme that does not rely on the bilinear parings. The main difference between them is that Baek et al.'s scheme requires a user must authenticate himself/herself to the Key Generation Center (KGC) and obtain an appropriate partial public key to create a public key, while the original CLPKE [2] does not require a user to contact the KGC to set up his/her public keys. In addition, the security proof of Baek et al.'s scheme only holds for a weaker security model in which the Type I adversary is not allowed to replace the public key associated with the challenge identity nor allowed to extract the partial private key of the challenge identity.

Compared with traditional PRE and IBPRE, certificateless proxy re-encryption (CLPRE) provides the advantage of CLPKC (i.e., keeps the implicit certification property of IBC without suffering from its inherent key escrow problem). In 2010, Sur et al. [26] introduced the notion of CLPRE and proposed a CCA secure CLPRE scheme based on the Libert and Quisquater's CLPKE [21] scheme in the random oracle model. In 2012, Xu et al. [30] proposed a CLPRE scheme based on the original CLPKE scheme [2], which is claimed to be CPA secure in the random oracle model. It should be emphasized that so far all existing CLPRE schemes are constructed based on the costly bilinear pairings. Although the recent advances in implementation technique, the pairing computation is still considered as expensive compared with "standard" operation such as modular exponentiations in finite fields. According to the current jPBC library [10] implementation, a "Type a" pairing operation in [10] takes 14.65 ms when preprocessing was used, whereas a 1024-bit prime modular exponentiation operation takes 1.18 ms. Hence, what is clearly desirable but has not been proposed until now, is a more efficient CLPRE scheme without the costly bilinear pairings.

1.1 Technical Contributions

Our work is aimed at filling this void. We first show that Xu et al.'s scheme [30] can not provide the ciphertext confidentiality. The vulnerability allows a Type I adversary to reveal any message shared between the legal users by replacing the receiver's public key. Then we present a simple patch which fixes the security problem. However, possible fix further degrade efficiency for encryption and re-encryption key generation.

As the main goal of this paper, we propose the first construction of CLPRE schemes without the bilinear pairings. We first propose a CPA secure CLPRE scheme, and then convert it into a CCA secure CLPRE scheme. Our CLPRE schemes are single-hop unidirectional and gain high efficiency. Compared with Xu et al.'s scheme [30] and Sur et al.'s CLPRE scheme [26], our schemes much more efficient and more suitable for low-power devices. To support our claim of efficiency, we evaluate these schemes following the benchmark data provided by the jPBC project [10]. As outlined in Table 2, our schemes have the least average running time. Moreover, the bit-length of a re-encryption key in our schemes is extremely short which is only 160 bits and the ciphertext size in our CCA secure scheme decrease with re-encryption. Additionally, in terms of complexity assumption, both of our schemes are proven secure under standard Computational Diffie-Hellman (CDH) assumption, while Xu et al.'s scheme [30] is based on the Decisional Bilinear Diffie-Hellman (DBDH) assumption [5] and Sur et al.'s scheme [26] is based on the p-Bilinear Diffie-Hellman Inversion (p-BDHI) assumption [5].

1.2 Organization

The rest of this paper is organized as follows. Section 2 gives necessary notations and security model for CLPRE schemes. Section 3 reviews and analyzes Xu et al.'s CLPRE scheme. We then present the first construction of CLPRE schemes without the bilinear pairings in Sect. 4, where security analysis and performance evaluation are also included. Section 5 concludes the paper.

2 Preliminaries

2.1 Notations

For a finite set S, $x \xleftarrow{\$} S$ denotes sampling an element x from S according to the uniform distribution. Let $\mathbb{G}^*$ denotes $\mathbb{G}\backslash\{1\}$ where $\mathbb{G}$ is a multiplicative group of prime order q. Except for specially illustrating, let user A denotes the delegator and user B denotes the delegatee.

2.2 Security Model for Single-Hop Unidirectional CLPRE

The precise definition (Definition 1) of single-hop unidirectional CLPRE schemes can be found in Appendix A. We formalize the security model of single-hop unidirectional CLPRE schemes by taking into account both certificateless public key encryption (CLPKE) security notion [2,9] and proxy re-encryption (PRE) security notion [11,22]. As defined in [2,9], we consider two types of adversaries, named Type I adversary $\mathcal{A}_I$ and Type II adversary $\mathcal{A}_{II}$ which represent an eavesdropping third party (i.e., an honest-but-curious KGC). $\mathcal{A}_I$ does not have access to the master key **msk**, but $\mathcal{A}_I$ may replace public keys with values of its choice. In contrast, $\mathcal{A}_{II}$ is equipped with master-key **msk**, but is not allowed to replace public keys of entities. We also provide the re-encryption key extraction oracle and re-encryption oracle for both $\mathcal{A}_I$ and $\mathcal{A}_{II}$. In order to prove the second level ciphertext security for our CLPRE schemes, we need to make an additional restriction for $\mathcal{A}_I$ which is not allowed to replace the public key of the challenge identity ID^*. This restriction is not necessary, but we do not know how to prove the second level ciphertext security for our CLPRE schemes without the restriction. Indeed, it is a mild security model since the additional restriction, but our CLPRE schemes are highly efficient under the mild security model. Moreover, our CLPRE schemes does not rely on the bilinear pairings. The mild security model is enough for many practical applications such as secure data sharing with public cloud [30]. The details of the security model can be found in Appendix B.

3 Analysis of Xu et al.'s CLPRE Scheme

3.1 Review of Xu et al.'s Scheme

Xu et al.'s CLPRE scheme [30] is reviewed as follows:

- **Setup(1^λ):** Let G_1, G_2 be two groups of prime order q, g be a random generator of G_1, and $e : G_1 \times G_1 \rightarrow G_2$ be a bilinear map. The message space $\mathcal{M}$ is G_2. $H_1 : \{0,1\}^* \rightarrow G_1$ and $H_2 : G_2 \rightarrow G_1$ are two map-to-point hash functions. Pick a random $s \in \mathbb{Z}_q^*$ and compute $g_1 = g^s$. The public parameters **params** $= (q, G_1, G_2, e, g, g_1, H_1, H_2)$ and the master-key **msk** $= s$.
- **PartialPrivateKeyExtract:** On input **params** and user A's identifier ID_A, this algorithm returns A's partial private key $D_A = g_A^s$ where $g_A = H_1(ID_A)$.
- **SetSecretValue:** On input **params** and ID_A, this algorithm picks $x_A, t_A \in \mathbb{Z}_q^*$ at random and returns (x_A, t_A).
- **SetPrivateKey:** On input **params**, user A's partial private key D_A and A's secret value (x_A, t_A), this algorithm computes $sk_A = D_A^{x_A} = g_A^{sx_A}$ and returns A's private key $SK_A = (sk_A, t_A)$.
- **SetPublicKey:** On input **params** and user A's secret value (x_A, t_A), this algorithm returns A's public key $PK_A = (g_A = H_1(ID_A), g_1^{x_A} = g^{sx_A}, g^{t_A})$.
- **Encrypt:** On input **params**, a message $m \in G_2$ and the A's public key PK_A, this algorithm does as follows:
  - To obtain a ciphertext can only be decrypted by user A, this algorithm randomly chooses $r \in \mathbb{Z}_q^*$ and returns

$$Enc_A(m) = (g^r, m \cdot e(g_A^r, g^{sx_A})).$$

  - For decryption delegation, this algorithm randomly chooses $r \in \mathbb{Z}_q^*$ and returns a second level ciphertext

$$C_A = Enc_A'(m) = (g^{t_A r}, g^r, m \cdot e(g_A^r, g^{sx_A})).$$

- **SetReEncKey:** On input **params**, user A's private key $SK_A = (g_A^{sx_A}, t_A)$ and user B's public key PK_B, this algorithm randomly chooses $X \in G_2$ and returns a re-encryption key from user A to user B:

$$RK_{A \rightarrow B} = (g_A^{-sx_A} \cdot H_2^{t_A}(X), Enc_B(X))$$

- **ReEncrypt:** On input **params**, a re-encryption key $RK_{A \rightarrow B}$ and a second level ciphertext $C_A = (g^{t_A r}, g^r, m \cdot e(g_A^r, g^{sx_A}))$, this algorithm computes

$$c = m \cdot e(g_A^r, g^{sx_A}) \cdot e(g_A^{-sx_A} \cdot H_2^{t_A}(X), g^r) = m \cdot e(H_2^{t_A}(X), g^r)$$

and returns a first level ciphertext $C_B' = (g^{t_A r}, c, Enc_B(X))$.
- **Decrypt$_1$:** On input **params**, user B's private key SK_B and a first level ciphertext C_B', this algorithm decrypts $Enc_B(X)$ with SK_B to obtain the X by running the decryption algorithm **Decrypt$_2$**, and returns

$$c/e(H_2(X), g^{t_A r}) = m \cdot e(H_2^{t_A}(X), g^r)/e(H_2(X), g^{t_A r}) = m.$$

- **Decrypt$_2$:** On input **params**, user A's private key $SK_A = (sk_A, t_A)$, a ciphertext $Enc_A(m) = (u, v)$ or a second level ciphertext $C_A = (w, u, v)$, this algorithm returns

$$v/e(sk_A, u) = m \cdot e(g_A^r, g^{sx_A})/e(g_A^{sx_A}, g^r) = m.$$

3.2 Attack Against Confidentiality

In this subsection, we present a realistic attack against Xu et al.'s CLPRE scheme [30]. In our attack, a Type I adversary $\mathcal{A}_I$ can decrypt any re-encrypted ciphertext by replacing the delegatee's public key. A more detailed description of the attack is as follows:

(1) If $\mathcal{A}_I$ wants to reveal the message m sent to the legal user B, $\mathcal{A}_I$ chooses $\alpha \in \mathbb{Z}_q^*$ randomly and replaces the user B's public key $PK_B = (g_B, g^{sx_B}, g^{t_B})$ with $\check{PK}_B' = (g_B, g^\alpha, g^{t_B})$.

(2) The delegator A randomly chooses $X \in G_2$ and generates a re-encryption key from A to B

$$RK_{A \to B}' = \left(g_A^{-sx_A} \cdot H_2^{t_A}(X), Enc_{PK_B'}(X) = (g^{r'}, X \cdot e(g_B^{r'}, g^\alpha)) \right)$$

using its private key $SK_A = (g_A^{sx_A}, t_A)$ and the replaced B's public key PK_B', and then sends $RK_{A \to B}'$ to the proxy server in the public cloud.

(3) The adversary $\mathcal{A}_I$ issues an access request for delegator A's sharing data by impersonating the legal user B. Then the proxy server generates a re-encrypted ciphertext

$$C_B' = (g^{t_A r}, c = m \cdot e(H_2^{t_A}(X), g^r), Enc_{PK_B'}(X)).$$

(4) The adversary $\mathcal{A}_I$ intercepts the ciphertext C_B' from the proxy server to B, decrypts $Enc_{PK_B'}(X) = (u', v')$ with the stored α

$$v'/e(g_B^\alpha, u') = X \cdot e(g_B^{r'}, g^\alpha)/e(g_B^\alpha, g^{r'}) = X$$

to obtain X, and then recovers the message $m = c/e(H_2(X), g^{t_A r})$.

Clearly, the Type I adversary $\mathcal{A}_I$ can reveal any message shared between the legal users by replacing the delegatee's public key. Thus, Xu et al.'s CLPRE scheme can not provide the ciphertext confidentiality. Alternatively, it is easy to see that the above attack is a legal attack under our mild security model, namely their scheme is not secure under our mild security model. Xu et al. prove that their scheme is CPA-secure in the random oracle model. However, their security proof ignores the case that $\mathcal{A}_I$ can replace the user's public key with any public key of its choice. That is why they do not discover the above attack. The weakness of Xu et al.'s CLPRE scheme root in the fact that there is no way to check whether the receiver's public key is correctly-formed. A simple improvement is to change the user's public key $PK = (H_1(ID), g^{sx}, g^t)$ into $PK = (g^x, g^{sx}, g^t)$ and check whether the equality $e(g^x, g^s) = e(g^{sx}, g)$ holds before using each user's public key. This modification effectively fixes the flaw mentioned above. However, the modified scheme still requires expensive bilinear pairing operations and map-to-point hash operations, further degrades the encryption and re-encryption key generation efficiency.

4 Our Single-Hop Unidirectional CLPRE Schemes

Certificateless proxy re-encryption (CLPRE) has very appealing features, namely both preserves the implicit certification advantage of identity based cryptography without suffering from its inherent key escrow problem and realizes delegation of decryption rights. Unfortunately, construction of CLPRE schemes so far depends on the costly bilinear pairings. In this paper, we focus on constructing CLPRE schemes that do not depend on the bilinear pairings. In this way, our CLPRE schemes are more efficient and more suitable for low-power devices when compare with other CLPRE schemes [26,30]. Our CLPRE schemes are motivated by the construction of Baek et al.'s CLPKE scheme [9]. However, we apply their scheme non-trivially to construct our CLPRE schemes. In particular, we use the technique of the static Diffie-Hellman sharing keys between delegator and delegatee to delegate the decryption rights. We add a public key ϕ to build the suitable static Diffie-Hellman sharing keys in order to resist possible attacks (cf. Appendix B). In order to be able to re-encrypt a second level ciphertext with the suitable re-encryption key, we non-trivially combine γ^r and μ^r in [9] into $\gamma^{H_4(\mu)r}\mu^r$. We first present a CPA secure CLPRE scheme, and then convert it into a CCA secure CLPRE scheme by known technique. The detailed construction of our CLPRE schemes as follows.

4.1 A Chosen Plaintext Secure Scheme (CLPRE1)

- **Setup(1^λ)**: Taking a security parameter 1^λ, the algorithm works as below:
  1. Generate a λ-bit prime q and a group $\mathbb{G}$ of order q. Pick a random generator $g \in \mathbb{G}$.
  2. Randomly pick $x \in \mathbb{Z}_q^*$ and compute $y = g^x$.
  3. Choose cryptographic hash functions $H_1 : \{0,1\}^* \times \mathbb{G} \to \mathbb{Z}_q^*$, $H_2 : \mathbb{G} \to \{0,1\}^n$ for some $n \in \mathbb{N}$, $H_3 : \{0,1\}^* \to \mathbb{Z}_q^*$ and $H_4 : \mathbb{G} \to \mathbb{Z}_q^*$.
  The public parameters are **params** $= (\mathbb{G}, q, g, y, n, H_1, H_2, H_3, H_4)$ and the master key is **msk** $= x$. The message space is $\mathcal{M} = \{0,1\}^n$.
- **PartialKeyExtract(params,msk,ID_A)**: Pick a random $s_A \in \mathbb{Z}_q^*$ and compute $\omega_A = g^{s_A}$ and $t_A = s_A + xH_1(ID_A, \omega_A) \bmod q$. Return $(P_A, D_A) = (\omega_A, t_A)$.
- **SetSecretValue(params,ID_A)**: Pick $z_A, v_A \in \mathbb{Z}_q^*$ at random and return $S_A = (z_A, v_A)$.
- **SetPrivateKey(params,D_A,S_A)**: Return $SK_A = (D_A, S_A) = (t_A, z_A, v_A)$.
- **SetPublicKey(params,P_A,S_A)**: Let $P_A = \omega_A$ and $S_A = (z_A, v_A)$. Compute $\mu_A = g^{z_A}$ and $\phi_A = g^{v_A}$. Return $PK_A = (\omega_A, \mu_A, \phi_A)$.

- **SetReEncKey(params,SK_A,ID_A,PK_A,ID_B,PK_B):** Parse PK_A as $(\omega_A, \mu_A, \phi_A)$, SK_A as (t_A, z_A, v_A) and PK_B as $(\omega_B, \mu_B, \phi_B)$, then compute $\gamma_B = \omega_B y^{H_1(ID_B, \omega_B)}$ and $X_{AB} = H_3(\gamma_B^{v_A}, \phi_B^{v_A}, ID_A, PK_A, ID_B, PK_B)$. Return $RK_{A \to B} = (t_A H_4(\mu_A) + z_A) \cdot X_{AB} \bmod q$.
- **Encrypt(params,ID_A,PK_A,m):** Parse PK_A as $(\omega_A, \mu_A, \phi_A)$. Then, compute $\gamma_A = \omega_A y^{H_1(ID_A, \omega_A)}$ and $Y_A = \gamma_A^{H_4(\mu_A)} \mu_A$. Pick a random $r \in \mathbb{Z}_q^*$ and compute

$$c_1 = g^r, \quad c_2 = m \oplus H_2(Y_A^r).$$

Return $C_A = (c_1, c_2)$.
- **ReEncrypt(params,$RK_{A \to B}$,C_A):** Parse C_A as (c_1, c_2), compute $c_1' = c_1^{RK_{A \to B}}$ and set $c_2' = c_2$. Return $C_B' = (c_1', c_2')$.[1]
- **Decrypt$_1$(params,SK_B,C_B'):** Parse C_B' as (c_1', c_2'), PK_A as $(\omega_A, \mu_A, \phi_A)$ and SK_B as (t_B, z_B, v_B). Compute

$$m = c_2' \oplus H_2 \left(c_1'^{1/X_{AB}} \right)$$

where $X_{AB} = H_3(\phi_A^{t_B}, \phi_A^{v_B}, ID_A, PK_A, ID_B, PK_B)$ and return m.
- **Decrypt$_2$(params,SK_A,C_A):** Parse C_A as (c_1, c_2), PK_A as $(\omega_A, \mu_A, \phi_A)$ and SK_A as (t_A, z_A, v_A). Compute

$$m = c_2 \oplus H_2 \left(c_1^{(t_A H_4(\mu_A) + z_A)} \right)$$

and return m.

It is not hard to check the correctness of CLPRE1 scheme, we omit it here.

- **Remark 1.** $H_4(\mu_A)$ is necessary for resisting the following public key replacement attacks. If remove the $H_4(\mu_A)$ from our scheme, a Type I adversary $\mathcal{A}_I$ can replace $PK_A = (\omega_A, \mu_A, \phi_A)$ with $PK_A' = (\omega_A', \mu_A' = g^{z_A'} \omega_A'^{-1} y^{-H_1(ID_A, \omega_A')}, \phi_A')$. Then any other user encrypts a message m with the user A's public key $(\omega_A', \mu_A', \phi_A')$ and gets a second level ciphertext $C_A = (g^r, m \oplus H_2(Y_A'^r))$ where $Y_A'^r = \omega_A'^r y^{H_1(ID_A, \omega_A')r} \mu_A'^r = g^{z_A' r}$. Thereby, $\mathcal{A}_I$ can recover the message m with z_A'. Analogously, $\mathcal{A}_I$ can also replace PK_A with $PK_A' = (g^{s_A}, g^{z_A} y^{-H_1(ID_A, g^{s_A})}, \phi_A')$. Since H_4 is collision free hash function, the technique of $\gamma_A^{H_4(\mu_A)} \mu_A$ well resists the above attack.
- **Remark 2.** Even though proxy collude with delegatees, they can only recover the $t_A H_4(\mu_A) + z_A$ for delegator A, but not the concrete value of t_A or z_A. Moreover, v_A is kept secret. This gives an intuition why our scheme achieves master secret security.
- **Remark 3.** $\gamma_B^{v_A} = g^{t_B v_A}$ and $\phi_B^{v_A} = g^{v_B v_A}$ are the static Diffie-Hellman sharing keys between delegator A and delegatee B.

---

[1] In the application background such as secure data sharing with public cloud [30], ID_A is omitted.

Theorem 1. The proposed CLPRE1 scheme is CLPRE-CPA secure in the random oracle model, if the CDH[2] assumption holds in $\mathbb{G}$ and the Schnorr[3] signature is EUF-CMA secure.

The security proof of this theorem is provided in Appendix C.

4.2 A Chosen Ciphertext Secure Scheme (CLPRE2)

In some complex network environments such as cloud computing, CPA security may not be sufficient to guarantee security. Therefore, certificateless proxy re-encryption scheme with strong security (CCA) is desirable. We use a well known technique due to Fujisaki-Okamoto transformation [15] to convert CPA secure scheme into CCA secure scheme. The Fujisaki-Okamoto transformation [15] is not enough to achieve CCA security. The proxy must be able to check validity of second level ciphertexts (i.e., the validity of second level ciphertexts must be public verifiable). We achieve the goal by resorting to the Schnorr signature [25] technique given in [13]. We do not specify the full details of CLPRE2 scheme and only present the different algorithm.

- We redefine $H_2 : \mathbb{G} \rightarrow \{0,1\}^{n+n'}$, where n and n' denote the bit-length of a message and a randomness respectively. In addition, we add two hash functions $H_5 : \{0,1\}^* \rightarrow \mathbb{Z}_q^*$ and $H_6 : \{0,1\}^* \rightarrow \mathbb{Z}_q^*$.
- **Encrypt(params,ID_A,PK_A,m):** Parse PK_A as $(\omega_A, \mu_A, \phi_A)$. Then, compute $\gamma_A = \omega_A y^{H_1(ID_A, \omega_A)}$ and $Y_A = \gamma_A^{H_4(\mu_A)} \mu_A$. Pick a random $\sigma \in \{0,1\}^{n'}$ and compute $r = H_5(m, \sigma, ID_A, PK_A)$. Pick a random $\hat{r} \in \mathbb{Z}_q^*$ and compute $C_A = (c_1, c_2, c_3, c_4)$ such that

$$c_1 = g^{\hat{r}}, \quad c_2 = g^r, \quad c_3 = (m \| \sigma) \oplus H_2(Y_A^r), \quad c_4 = \hat{r} + r H_6(c_1, c_2, c_3) \bmod q.$$

  Return C_A.
- **ReEncrypt(params,$RK_{A \rightarrow B}$,C_A):** Parse C_A as (c_1, c_2, c_3, c_4) and check whether $g^{c_4} = c_1 \cdot c_2^{H_6(c_1, c_2, c_3)}$ holds. If not, return $\perp$. Otherwise, compute $c_2' = c_2^{RK_{A \rightarrow B}}$ and set $c_3' = c_3$. Return $C_B' = (c_2', c_3')^4$.
- **Decrypt$_1$(params,SK_B,C_B'):** Parse C_B' as (c_2', c_3'), PK_A as $(\omega_A, \mu_A, \phi_A)$ and SK_B as (t_B, z_B, v_B). Then compute as follows:
  1. Compute $X_{AB} = H_3(\phi_A^{t_B}, \phi_A^{v_B}, ID_A, PK_A, ID_B, PK_B)$.
  2. Compute $m \| \sigma = c_3' \oplus H_2\left(c_2'^{1/X_{AB}}\right)$.
  3. Compute $r' = H_5(m, \sigma, ID_A, PK_A)$ and $Y_A = \gamma_A^{H_4(\mu_A)} \mu_A$ where $\gamma_A = \omega_A y^{H_1(ID_A, \omega_A)}$.

---

[2] Informally, we say that the CDH assumption holds for $\mathbb{G}$ if it is infeasible to compute g^{ab} when is given a tuple $(g, g^a, g^b) \in \mathbb{G}^3$ where $a, b \xleftarrow{\$} \mathbb{Z}_q^*$.

[3] The well known Schnorr signature [25] is existential unforgeable against chosen message attack (EUF-CMA) under the discrete logarithm (DL) assumption [24] in the random oracle model.

[4] In the application background such as secure data sharing with public cloud [30], ID_A is omitted.

4. If $Y_A^{X_{AB}r'} = c_2'$ holds, return m. Otherwise, return $\perp$.
- **Decrypt$_2$(params,SK_A,C_A):** Parse C_A as (c_1, c_2, c_3, c_4), PK_A as $(\omega_A, \mu_A, \phi_A)$ and SK_A as (t_A, z_A, v_A). Then compute as follows:
   1. If $g^{c_4} = c_1 \cdot c_2^{H_6(c_1, c_2, c_3)}$ does not hold, return $\perp$.
   2. Otherwise, compute $m \| \sigma = c_3 \oplus H_2 \left(c_2^{(t_A H_4(\mu_A) + z_A)} \right)$.
   3. If $c_2 = g^{H_5(m, \sigma, ID_A, PK_A)}$ holds, return m. Otherwise, return $\perp$.

It is not hard to check the correctness of CLPRE2 scheme, we omit it here.

Theorem 2. The proposed CLPRE2 scheme is CLPRE-CCA secure in the random oracle model, if the CDH assumption holds in $\mathbb{G}$ and the Schnorr signature is EUF-CMA secure.

Proof. The idea of the proof is analogous to that of Theorem 1. In addition, the challenger $\mathcal{B}$ needs to respond re-encryption queries and decryption queries. Due to the space limit, the proof of this theorem will be given in the full paper.

4.3 Comparisons

In this subsection, we compare our schemes with modified Xu et al.'s scheme [30] and Sur et al.'s scheme [26] in terms of computational cost, ciphertext size and security level. Firstly, we consider the number of "bignum" operations that CLPRE schemes need to perform. We then estimate the running time of these schemes on an Intel(R) Core(TM) 2 Quad 2.40 GHz CPU desktop PC with 3 GB RAM powered by Ubuntu 10.04, by using some benchmark results in the Java Pairing Based Cryptography Library (jPBC) [10], which is a Java port of the PBC library [20] written in C. In our comparisons, the complexity of highly efficient operations such as multiplication or addition in group, conventional hash function evaluation and XOR operation is omitted, since the computational cost of these operations is far less than that of exponentiations or pairings.

In Table 1 we summarize the comparison results. For all schemes, fast algorithms for multi-exponentiation can be used in order to improve the performance. By using simultaneous multiple exponentiation algorithm [23], the two modular exponentiations and the three modular exponentiations can be computed at a cost of about 1.17 exponentiations and 1.25 exponentiations respectively. By using Avanzi's algorithm [4] based on a sliding windows method for the joint sparse form [28], for the ECC setting, where the group inverse comes for free, the two exponentiations in G_1 can be computed at a cost of about 1.08 exponentiations. Alternatively, both Xu et al.'s scheme [30] and Sur et al.'s scheme [26] require a special hash function called map-to-point[5] hash function for mapping $\{0,1\}^*$ into a point on the underlying elliptic curve. Since the computation time of one admissible encoding function **MapToPoint** is more expensive than one exponentiation in G_1, a map-to-point hash operation is also time consuming and cannot be treated as conventional hash operation.

---

[5] The special map-to-point hash function is also called "hash-and-encode" function [16] and can be constructed by a conventional hash function and an admissible encoding function **MapToPoint** [7].

Table 1. Comparison of CLPRE schemes

Schemes	Modified [30]	[26]	Our CLPRE1	Our CLPRE2
Encrypt	$t_p + 3t_e$	$5.08t_e$	$2.25t_e$	$3.25t_e$
SetReEncKey	$3t_p + 3t_e$	$4.08t_e$	$2.17t_e$	$2.17t_e$
ReEncrypt	t_p	$6t_p$	t_e	$2.17t_e$
Decrypt$_2(C_A)$	t_p	$2t_p + 3.08t_e$	t_e	$3.17t_e$
Decrypt$_1(C'_B)$	$2t_p$	$t_p + 4t_e$	$3t_e$	$4.25t_e$
$|C_A|$	$2|G_1| + |G_2|$	$3|G_1| + |m| + |\sigma|$	$|G| + |m|$	$2|G| + |\mathbb{Z}_q| + |m| + |\sigma|$
$|RK_{A\to B}|$	$2|G_1| + |G_2|$	$3|G_1|$	$|\mathbb{Z}_q|$	$|\mathbb{Z}_q|$
$|C'_B|$	$2|G_1| + 2|G_2|$	$|G_1| + 2|G_2| + |m| + |\sigma|$	$|G| + |m|$	$|G| + |m| + |\sigma|$
Pairing-Free	×	×	✓	✓
map-to-point-Free	×	×	✓	✓
Assumption	DBDH	p-BDHI	CDH	CDH
Security	CPA	CCA	CPA	CCA

The notations in Table 1 is illustrated as follows: C_A, $RK_{A\to B}$ and C'_B denote a second level ciphertext, a re-encryption key from A to B and a first level ciphertext respectively. $\mathbb{G}$ denotes the group used in our schemes, while G_1 and G_2 denote the bilinear groups used in [26,30] (i.e., the bilinear pairing is $e : G_1 \times G_1 \to G_2$). t_p and t_e denote the computational cost of a bilinear pairing and an exponentiation respectively. $|C_A|$, $|RK_{A\to B}|$ and $|C'_B|$ denote the bit-length of C_A, $RK_{A\to B}$ and C'_B respectively. $|X|$, $|m|$ and $|\sigma|$ denote the bit-length of an element in group X, a message m and a randomness σ respectively.

Next, in order to make our comparison more clear, we evaluate concrete running time and communication cost in Table 2. We consider the case that both modified Xu et al.'s scheme [30] and Sur et al.'s scheme [26] are implemented on an elliptic curve defined on 512 bits prime field with a generator of order 160 bits (i.e., "Type a" in [10]), and our schemes are implemented on 1024-bit prime finite field with a generator of order 160 bits (i.e., $\mathbb{G} = G_T$ of "Type e" in [10]). We also assume that the bit-length of $|m|$ and $|\sigma|$ is 1024 bits and 160 bits respectively. Note that the computation time in Table 2 is not precise since we only consider the computational costs of "bignum" operations. In addition, we also ignore the computation time of map-to-point hash operations in the schemes [26,30].

From Tables 1 and 2, we can see that both of our schemes are much more computation efficient than modified Xu et al.'s scheme [30] and Sur et al.'s scheme [26] across all phases (i.e., Encrypt, SetReEncKey, ReEncrypt and Decrypt) of CLPRE schemes. It's worth pointing out that the bit-length of a re-encryption key in our schemes is only $|\mathbb{Z}_q|$ (160 bits) which is the shortest among the CLPRE schemes. Moreover, the ciphertext size in our CLPRE2 scheme decreases with re-encryption, while that in [30] increases with re-encryption and that in [26] remains unchanged. In particular, our CCA secure CLPRE2 scheme is even more efficient than CPA secure scheme such as [30].

Table 2. Concrete value comparison

Schemes	Modified [30]	[26]	Our CLPRE1	Our CLPRE2
Encrypt	14.97 ms	25.12 ms	0.74 ms	1.07 ms
SetReEncKey	52.67 ms	24.74 ms	2.57 ms	2.57 ms
ReEncrypt	7.23 ms	58.24 ms	1.18 ms	2.57 ms
$Decrypt_2(C_A)$	7.23 ms	22.43 ms	1.18 ms	2.90 ms
$Decrypt_1(C'_B)$	21.89 ms	14.16 ms	3.55 ms	5.03 ms
$\|C_A\|$	3072 bits	4256 bits	2048 bits	3392 bits
$\|RK_{A \to B}\|$	3072 bits	3072 bits	160 bits	160 bits
$\|C'_B\|$	4096 bits	4256 bits	2048 bits	2208 bits

5 Conclusions

In this paper, we showed that Xu et al.'s scheme [30] is vulnerable to the confidentiality attack, and then proposed the first construction of CLPRE schemes without the costly bilinear pairings. We also prove security of our CLPRE schemes under the CDH assumption in the random oracle model. The comparison results show that our schemes significantly outperform Xu et al.'s scheme [30] and Sur et al.'s scheme [26] in terms of computational and communicational efficiency. Even though our CLPRE schemes are highly efficient, they are proven secure under our mild security model. Thereby, we leave an interesting open problem to devise a pairing-free efficient CLPRE scheme in a stronger security model.

Acknowledgements. This work was supported by the National Basic Research 973 Program of China under Grant No. 2013CB338003, the National Natural Science Foundation of China under Grant No. 61170279, the 863 project under Grant No. 2012AA01A403 and the National Natural Science Foundation of China under Grant No. 61170278. The authors would like to thanks the anonymous reviewers for their helpful comments.

A Single-Hop Unidirectional CLPRE

Definition 1 (CLPRE). A single-hop unidirectional CLPRE scheme consists of the following algorithms:

- **Setup(1^λ):** Taking security parameter 1^λ as input, the Key Generation Center (KGC) runs the algorithm to generate the public parameters **params** and a master key **msk**. The **params** includes the description of message space $\mathcal{M}$. We assume throughout that **params** are publicly and authentically available.
- **PartialKeyExtract(params,msk,ID_A):** Taking **params**, **msk** and a user A's identifier ID_A as inputs, the KGC runs the algorithm to generate a partial public key P_A and a partial private key D_A. P_A and D_A are transported to the user A over a secure channel by KGC.

- **SetSecretValue(params,ID_A):** Taking **params** and user A's identifier ID_A as inputs, this algorithm returns a randomly chosen secret value S_A. This algorithm and the next two are performed by the user A himself.
- **SetPrivateKey(params,D_A,S_A):** Taking **params**, D_A and S_A as inputs, user A runs the algorithm to generate a private key SK_A.
- **SetPublicKey(params,P_A,S_A):** Taking **params**, P_A and S_A as inputs, this algorithm returns a public key PK_A.
- **SetReEncKey(params,SK_A,ID_A,PK_A,ID_B,PK_B):** Taking **params**, user A's identifier ID_A and a public/private key pair (PK_A,SK_A), user B's identifier ID_B and public key PK_B as inputs, this algorithm returns a re-encryption key $RK_{A \to B}$ that allows converting second level ciphertexts for ID_A into first level ciphertexts for ID_B.
- **Encrypt(params,ID_A,PK_A,m):** Taking **params**, user A's identifier ID_A and public key PK_A, a message $m \in \mathcal{M}$ as inputs, this algorithm returns a second level ciphertext C_A that can be re-encrypted into a first level one (intended for a possibly different receiver) using the suitable re-encryption key. A ciphertext is called first level ciphertext if it cannot be re-encrypted for another party. In our schemes, first level ciphertexts are re-encrypted ciphertexts.
- **ReEncrypt(params,$RK_{A \to B}$,C_A):** Taking **params**, a re-encryption key $RK_{A \to B}$ from user A to user B and a second level ciphertext C_A for user A as inputs, this algorithm returns a first level ciphertext C'_B for user B or $\bot$.
- **Decrypt$_1$(params,SK_B,C'_B):** Taking **params**, a user B's private key SK_B and a first level ciphertext C'_B as inputs, this algorithm returns either a message m or $\bot$.
- **Decrypt$_2$(params,SK_A,C_A):** Taking **params**, a user A's private key SK_A and a second level ciphertext C_A as inputs, this algorithm returns either a message m or $\bot$.

Correctness. For all $m \in \mathcal{M}$ and all pair (PK_A,SK_A), (PK_B,SK_B), these algorithm should satisfy the following conditions of correctness:

- **Decrypt$_2$(params, SK_A, Encrypt(params, ID_A, PK_A, m))** $= m$.
- **Decrypt$_1$(params, SK_B, ReEncrypt(params, $RK_{A \to B}, C_A$))** $= m$.

where C_A = **Encrypt(params,ID_A, PK_A, m)**, $RK_{A \to B}$ = **SetReEncKey (params,$SK_A, ID_A, PK_A, ID_B, PK_B$)**.

B Security Model

Definition 2. Security of Second Level Ciphertexts (2nd-IND-CLPRE-ATK). Let $ATK \in \{CPA, CCA\}$, security of second level ciphertexts is defined according to the following two games "Game I" and "Game II". The challenger $\mathcal{B}$ maintains a public key list $Publickey^{List}$ which is set of (ID, PK_{ID}, st). Let PK_{ID} denotes the current public key for ID, $st = 0$ denotes the PK_{ID} is generated honestly by $\mathcal{B}$, $st = 1$ denotes $\mathcal{B}$ embed the hard problem into the PK_{ID} and $st = \bot$ denotes the public key for ID has already replaced by $\mathcal{A}_I$.

"Game I": This is a game between $\mathcal{A}_I$ and the challenger $\mathcal{B}$.

Setup: The challenger $\mathcal{B}$ takes a security parameter 1^λ and runs the **Setup**(1^λ) algorithm to generate the system parameter **params** and a master key **msk**. The challenger gives **params** to $\mathcal{A}_I$ while keeping **msk** secret.

Phase 1: $\mathcal{A}_I$ issues queries $q_1, \cdots, q_m$ adaptively where query q_i is one of the following:

- Partial key extraction queries: On input ID by $\mathcal{A}_I$, the challenger $\mathcal{B}$ responds by running algorithm **PartialKeyExtract** to generate the partial key (P_{ID}, D_{ID}) for entity ID.

- Public key request queries: On input ID by $\mathcal{A}_I$, the challenger $\mathcal{B}$ searches whether exists a tuple $(ID, PK_{ID}, st) \in Publickey^{List}$. If exists, $\mathcal{B}$ returns PK_{ID} to $\mathcal{A}_I$. Otherwise, $\mathcal{B}$ runs algorithm **SetPublicKey** to generate the public key PK_{ID} for ID. $\mathcal{B}$ adds (ID, PK_{ID}, st) to the $Publickey^{List}$ where the value of st is decided by the $\mathcal{B}$'s strategy and return PK_{ID} to $\mathcal{A}_I$.

- Private key extraction queries: On input ID by $\mathcal{A}_I$, $\mathcal{B}$ searches a tuple $(ID, PK_{ID}, st) \in Publickey^{List}$. If $st \neq \perp$, $\mathcal{B}$ responds by running algorithm **SetPrivateKey** to generate the private key SK_{ID} for entity ID. However, it is unreasonable to expect $\mathcal{B}$ to be able to respond to such a query if $\mathcal{A}_I$ has already replaced ID's public key and $\mathcal{B}$ returns "Reject" for this case $st = \perp$.

- Replace public key queries: $\mathcal{A}_I$ can repeatedly replace the public key PK_{ID} for any entity ID with any valid public key PK'_{ID} of its choice. PK'_{ID} is called a valid public key if $PK'_{ID} \in G^* \times G^* \times G^*$ in our CLPRE schemes. If does not exist a tuple $(ID, PK_{ID}, st) \in Publickey^{List}$, $\mathcal{B}$ adds $(ID, PK'_{ID}, st = \perp)$ to $Publickey^{List}$. Otherwise, $\mathcal{B}$ renews (ID, PK_{ID}, st) with $(ID, PK'_{ID}, st = \perp)$.

- Re-encryption key extraction queries: On input (ID_1, ID_2) by $\mathcal{A}_I$, $\mathcal{B}$ searches a tuple $(ID_1, PK_{ID_1}, st_1) \in Publickey^{List}$. if $st_1 \neq \perp$, $\mathcal{B}$ responds by running algorithm **SetReEncKey** to generate the re-encryption key $RK_{ID_1 \rightarrow ID_2}$. Otherwise, return "Reject". It is unreasonable to expect $\mathcal{B}$ to be able to respond to such a query if $\mathcal{A}_I$ has already replaced ID_1's public key.

- Re-encryption queries: On input (ID_1, ID_2, C_{ID_1}) by $\mathcal{A}_I$,
  1. If $ATK = CCA$, $\mathcal{B}$ searches a tuple $(ID_1, PK_{ID_1}, st_1) \in Publickey^{List}$. if $st_1 \neq \perp$, $\mathcal{B}$ responds by running algorithm **ReEncrypt** to convert the second level ciphertext C_{ID_1} into a first level C'_{ID_2} with the suitable re-encryption key $RK_{ID_1 \rightarrow ID_2}$. Otherwise, return "Reject". It is also unreasonable to expect $\mathcal{B}$ to be able to respond to such a query if $\mathcal{A}_I$ has already replaced ID_1's public key.
  2. If $ATK = CPA$, return $\perp$ to $\mathcal{A}_I$.

- Decryption queries for first level ciphertext: On input (ID, C) by $\mathcal{A}_I$,
  1. $ATK = CCA$: If C is a first level ciphertext, $\mathcal{B}$ runs the algorithm **Decrypt$_1$** using the related private key to decrypt the C and returns the result to $\mathcal{A}_I$. Otherwise, return "Reject".
  2. $ATK = CPA$: return $\perp$ to $\mathcal{A}_I$.

- Decryption queries for second level ciphertext: On input (ID,C) by $\mathcal{A}_I$,
  1. $ATK = CCA$: If C is a second level ciphertext, $\mathcal{B}$ runs the algorithm **Decrypt**$_2$ using the related private key to decrypt the C and returns the result to $\mathcal{A}_I$. Otherwise, return "Reject".
  2. $ATK = CPA$: return $\perp$ to $\mathcal{A}_I$.

Challenge: Once the adversary $\mathcal{A}_I$ decides that Phase 1 is over it outputs the challenge identity ID^* and two equal length plaintexts $m_0, m_1 \in \mathcal{M}$. In particular, ID^* can not be corrupted[6]. Moreover, $\mathcal{A}_I$ is restricted to choose a challenge identity ID^* such that trivial decryption is not possible (i.e., It does not happen both $\mathcal{A}_I$ has extracted the re-encryption key $RK_{ID^* \to ID}$ and ID has been corrupted by $\mathcal{A}_I$). $\mathcal{B}$ searches a tuple $(ID^*, PK_{ID^*}, st^*) \in Publickey^{List}$. $\mathcal{B}$ then picks a random bit $\beta \in \{0,1\}$ and computes the challenge ciphertext $C^* = \textbf{Encrypt}(\textbf{params},ID^*,PK_{ID^*}, m_\beta)$. The challenger returns C^* to $\mathcal{A}_I$.

Phase 2: Almost the same as that in Phase 1, but with the following restrictions.

- Partial key extraction queries: On input ID by $\mathcal{A}_I$, if $\mathcal{A}_I$ has already replaced the public key for ID and exists a pair (ID, C) is a derivative of (ID^*, C^*), the challenger $\mathcal{B}$ returns $\perp$. Derivatives of (ID^*, C^*) [12] is defined as follows:
  1. Reflexivity: (ID^*, C^*) is a derivative of itself.
  2. Derivation by re-encryption: If the adversary has issued a re-encryption query on input (ID^*, ID, C^*) and obtained the resulting re-encryption ciphertext C, then (ID, C) is a derivative of (ID^*, C^*).
  3. Derivation by re-encryption key: If the adversary has issued a re-encryption key extract query on input (ID^*, ID) and obtained the re-encryption key $RK_{ID^* \to ID}$, then (ID, C) is a derivative of (ID^*, C^*) where $C = \textbf{ReEncrypt}(\textbf{params}, RK_{ID^* \to ID}, C^*)$.
- Private key extraction queries: On input ID by $\mathcal{A}_I$ if exists a pair (ID, C) is a derivative of (ID^*, C^*) or $ID = ID^*$, $\mathcal{B}$ returns $\perp$.
- Re-encryption key extraction queries: On input (ID_1, ID_2) by $\mathcal{A}_I$, if $ID_1 = ID^*$ and the entity ID_2 has been corrupted by $\mathcal{A}_I$, $\mathcal{B}$ returns $\perp$.
- Re-encryption queries: On input (ID_1, ID_2, C_{ID_1}) by $\mathcal{A}_I$, if (ID_1, C_{ID_1}) is a derivative of (ID^*, C^*) and ID_2 has been corrupted by $\mathcal{A}_I$, $\mathcal{B}$ returns $\perp$.
- Decryption queries for first level ciphertext: On input (ID,C) by $\mathcal{A}_I$, if (ID, C) is a derivative of (ID^*, C^*), the challenger returns $\perp$.
- Decryption queries for second level ciphertext: On input (ID,C) by $\mathcal{A}_I$, if $(ID, C) = (ID^*, C^*)$, the challenger returns $\perp$.

Guess: Finally, the adversary $\mathcal{A}_I$ outputs a guess $\beta' \in \{0,1\}$ and wins the game if $\beta' = \beta$.

"Game II": This is a game between $\mathcal{A}_{II}$ and the challenger $\mathcal{B}$. We merely describe the difference between "Game I" and "Game II" as follows:

---

[6] In "Game I", an entity ID is called corrupted if $\mathcal{A}_I$ has extracted the private key for ID, or $\mathcal{A}_I$ has both replaced the public key for ID and extracted the partial private key for ID.

- $\mathcal{A}_{II}$ knows the master-key but is disallowed to replace public keys during the "Game II". Hence, $\mathcal{A}_{II}$ does not need partial key extraction oracle and is not provided the public key replacement oracle.
- In "Game II", an entity ID is called corrupted if $\mathcal{A}_{II}$ has already extracted the private key for ID.
- For public key request queries issued by $\mathcal{A}_{II}$, $\mathcal{B}$ additionally needs to return a randomness s_{ID} with respect to the partial public key P_{ID} such that $\mathcal{A}_{II}$ can compute the partial private key by itself.

We define $\mathcal{A}_i$'s advantage in "Game i" at level 2 where $i \in \{I, II\}$ as

$$Adv_{Game\ i,\ \mathcal{A}_i}^{2nd-IND-CLPRE-ATK}(\lambda) = |Pr[\beta' = \beta] - \frac{1}{2}|$$

A single-hop unidirectional CLPRE scheme is said to be (t, ϵ)-2nd-IND-CLPRE-ATK secure if for any t-time 2nd-IND-CLPRE-ATK adversary $\mathcal{A}_i$ we have $Adv_{Game\ i,\ \mathcal{A}_i}^{2nd-IND-CLPRE-ATK}(\lambda) < \epsilon$ for both $i = I$ and $i = II$. We simply say that a single-hop unidirectional CLPRE scheme is 2nd-IND-CLPRE-ATK secure if t is polynomial with respect to security parameter λ and ϵ is negligible.

Definition 3. Security of First Level Ciphertexts (1st-IND-CLPRE-ATK). We merely describe the difference between Definitions 2 and 3 as follows:

- Since first level ciphertexts cannot be re-encrypted, $\mathcal{A}_i$ ($i \in \{I, II\}$) is granted access to all re-encryption keys. The re-encryption oracle becomes useless since all re-encryption keys are available to $\mathcal{A}_i$.
- Derivatives of the challenge ciphertext are simply defined as (ID^*, C^*) is a derivative of itself.
- For challenge query issued by $\mathcal{A}_i$, $\mathcal{A}_i$ is required to provide the delegator $\widetilde{ID}$, the delegatee ID^* and two equal length plaintexts $m_0, m_1 \in \mathcal{M}$. The challenge ciphertext is then generated by the re-encryption process. Specifically, $C^* = $ **ReEncrypt**$(\textbf{params}, RK_{\widetilde{ID} \to ID^*}, \textbf{Encrypt}(\textbf{params}, \widetilde{ID}, \widetilde{PK}, m_\beta))$ where $\beta \xleftarrow{\$} \{0, 1\}$. Note that Type I adversary $\mathcal{A}_I$ disallows replace the public key of $\widetilde{ID}$ before the challenge phase, otherwise the challenge ciphertext C^* can not be generated correctly. We also require that $\mathcal{A}_i$ for both $i = I$ and $i = II$ cannot issue the private key extract query for $\widetilde{ID}$. Since the construction of our CLPRE schemes (cf. Sect. 4) has the original access [1] property, the restriction is necessary. Obviously, ID^* is uncorrupted.

A single-hop unidirectional CLPRE scheme is said to be (t, ϵ)-1st-IND-CLPRE-ATK secure if for any t-time 1st-IND-CLPRE-ATK adversary $\mathcal{A}_i$ we have $Adv_{Game\ i,\ \mathcal{A}_i}^{1st-IND-CLPRE-ATK}(\lambda) = |Pr[\beta' = \beta] - \frac{1}{2}| < \epsilon$ for both $i = I$ and $i = II$.

Definition 4 (CLPRE-ATK Security). We say a CLPRE scheme is CLPRE-ATK secure where $ATK \in \{CPA, CCA\}$ if the scheme is 1st-IND-CLPRE-ATK secure and 2nd-IND-CLPRE-ATK secure.

C   Security Proof of Theorem 1

We shall accomplish our proof with two following lemmas. Lemmas 1 and 2 show that the proposed CLPRE1 scheme is 2nd-IND-CLPRE-CPA secure and 1st-IND-CLPRE-CPA secure respectively.

Lemma 1. The proposed CLPRE1 scheme is 2nd-IND-CLPRE-CPA secure in the random oracle model, if the CDH assumption holds in $\mathbb{G}$ and the Schnorr signature is EUF-CMA secure.

Firstly, we prove that the proposed CLPRE1 scheme is 2nd-IND-CLPRE-CPA secure against Type I adversary $\mathcal{A}_I$ in the random oracle model. In particular, if there exists a 2nd-IND-CLPRE-CPA Type I adversary $\mathcal{A}_I$ against our CLPRE1 scheme with advantage ϵ when running in time t, making q_{pk} public key request queries, q_{pak} partial key extract queries, q_{prk} private key extract queries, q_{pr} public key replacement queries, q_{rk} re-encryption key extract queries and q_{H_i} random oracle queries to H_i ($1 \leqslant i \leqslant 4$). Then, for any $0 < v < \epsilon$, there exists

– either an algorithm $\mathcal{B}$ to solve the (t', ϵ')-CDH problem in $\mathbb{G}$ with

$$t' \leq t + (q_{H_1} + q_{H_2} + q_{H_3} + q_{H_4} + q_{pk} + q_{pak} + q_{prk} + q_{pr} + q_{rk})O(1)$$
$$+ (2q_{pk} + q_{pak} + 2q_{prk} + 3q_{rk})t_e$$

$$\epsilon' \geq \frac{1}{q_{H_2}} \left(\frac{2(\epsilon - v)}{e(1 + q_{prk} + q_{rk})} - \tau \right)$$

where t_e denotes the running time of an exponentiation in group $\mathbb{G}$, e denotes the base of the natural logarithm and τ denotes the advantage that $\mathcal{A}_I$ can distinguish the incorrectly-formed re-encryption keys in our simulation from all correctly-formed re-encryption keys in a "real world" interaction.

– or an attacker who breaks the EUF-CMA security of the Schnorr signature with advantage v within time t'.

Proof. Without loss of generality, we assume that the Schnorr signature is (t', v)-EUF-CMA secure. Suppose there exists a t-time 2nd-IND-CLPRE-CPA Type I adversary $\mathcal{A}_I$ who can break the 2nd-IND-CLPRE-CPA security of our CLPRE1 scheme with advantage $\epsilon - v$. Then we show how to construct an algorithm $\mathcal{B}$ which can solve the (t', ϵ')-CDH problem in group $\mathbb{G}$.

Suppose $\mathcal{B}$ is given a CDH challenge tuple $(g, g^a, g^b) \in \mathbb{G}^3$ with unknown $a, b \xleftarrow{\$} \mathbb{Z}_q^*$ as input. The goal of $\mathcal{B}$ is to compute the g^{ab}. $\mathcal{B}$ can act as the challenger and play the 2nd-IND-CLPRE-CPA "Game I" with $\mathcal{A}_I$ as follows.

Setup. $\mathcal{B}$ computes $y = g^x$ where $x \xleftarrow{\$} \mathbb{Z}_q^*$ and gives $(\mathbb{G}, q, g, y, n, H_1, H_2, H_3, H_4)$ to $\mathcal{A}_I$ as **params**, where H_1, H_2, H_3, H_4 are random oracles controlled by $\mathcal{B}$.

Random Oracle Queries. Algorithm $\mathcal{B}$ maintains four hash lists H_1^{List}, H_2^{List}, H_3^{List} and H_4^{List} which are initially empty, and responds as follows:

- H_1 queries: On receiving a query (ID, ω) to H_1:
  1. If $\langle (ID, \omega), e \rangle$ has appeared in the H_1^{List}, return e as answer.
  2. Otherwise, pick a random $e \in \mathbb{Z}_q^*$, add $\langle (ID, \omega), e \rangle$ to H_1^{List} and return e as answer.
- H_2 queries: On receiving a query K to H_2:
  1. If $\langle K, R \rangle$ has appeared in the H_2^{List}, return R as answer.
  2. Otherwise, pick a random $R \in \{0, 1\}^n$, add $\langle K, R \rangle$ to H_2^{List} and return R as answer.
- H_3 queries: On receiving a query $(k_1, k_2, ID_1, PK_1, ID_2, PK_2)$ to H_3:
  1. If $\langle (k_1, k_2, ID_1, PK_1, ID_2, PK_2), X \rangle$ has appeared in the H_3^{List}, return X as answer.
  2. Otherwise, pick a random $X \in \mathbb{Z}_q^*$, add $\langle (k_1, k_2, ID_1, PK_1, ID_2, PK_2), X \rangle$ to H_3^{List} and return X as answer.
- H_4 queries: On receiving a query μ to H_4:
  1. If $\langle \mu, \delta \rangle$ has appeared in the H_4^{List}, return δ as answer.
  2. Otherwise, pick a random $\delta \in \mathbb{Z}_q^*$, add $\langle \mu, \delta \rangle$ to H_4^{List} and return δ as answer.

Phase 1: $\mathcal{B}$ responds a series of $\mathcal{A}_I$'s queries as follows:

- Partial key extraction queries: On input ID by $\mathcal{A}_I$, the challenger $\mathcal{B}$ responds as below:
  1. If $\langle ID, (\omega, t), s \rangle$ has appeared in $Partialkey^{List}$, return (ω, t) as answer.
  2. Otherwise, pick a random $s \in \mathbb{Z}_q^*$ and compute $\omega = g^s$. Run the random oracle query (ID, ω) to H_1 and obtain $\langle (ID, \omega), e \rangle \in H_1^{List}$. Compute $t = s + ex \bmod q$, add $\langle ID, (\omega, t), s \rangle$ to $Partialkey^{List}$ and return (ω, t) as answer.
- Public key request queries: On input ID by $\mathcal{A}_I$, the challenger $\mathcal{B}$ responds as below:
  1. If $\langle ID, (\omega, \mu, \phi), coin \rangle$ has appeared in $Publickey^{List}$, return $PK_{ID} = (\omega, \mu, \phi)$ as answer.
  2. Otherwise, pick a $coin \in \{0, 1\}$ such that $Pr[coin = 0] = \theta$ (θ will be determined later).
  3. The challenger $\mathcal{B}$ runs the above simulation algorithm for partial key extraction taking ID as input to get a partial key (ω, t).
  4. If $coin = 0$, pick $z, v \in \mathbb{Z}_q^*$ at random and compute $\mu = g^z$ and $\phi = g^v$. Add $\langle ID, (t, z, v) \rangle$ to $Privatekey^{List}$ and $\langle ID, (\omega, \mu, \phi), coin \rangle$ to $Publickey^{List}$. Return $PK_{ID} = (\omega, \mu, \phi)$ as answer.
  5. Otherwise, pick $z, v \in \mathbb{Z}_q^*$ at random and compute $\mu = (g^a)^z$ and $\phi = g^v$. Add $\langle ID, (t, ?, v), z \rangle$ to $Privatekey^{List}$ and $\langle ID, (\omega, \mu, \phi), coin \rangle$ to $Publickey^{List}$. Return $PK_{ID} = (\omega, \mu, \phi)$ as answer.
- Private key extraction queries: On input ID by $\mathcal{A}_I$, the challenger $\mathcal{B}$ can respond as below:
  1. The challenger $\mathcal{B}$ runs the above simulation algorithm for public key request taking ID as input to get a tuple $\langle ID, (\omega, \mu, \phi), coin \rangle \in Publickey^{List}$.
  2. If $coin = 0$, search $Privatekey^{List}$ for a tuple $\langle ID, (t, z, v) \rangle$ and return $SK_{ID} = (t, z, v)$ as answer.

3. If $coin = \bot$, $\mathcal{B}$ returns "Reject". By $coin = \bot$ we denote the case that the public key for ID has been replaced by $\mathcal{A}_I$.
4. Otherwise, $\mathcal{B}$ aborts the simulation.

– Replace public key queries: $\mathcal{A}_I$ can repeatedly replace the public key $PK_{ID} = (\omega, \mu, \phi)$ for any ID with any valid public key $PK'_{ID} = (\omega', \mu', \phi')$ of its choice. On input (ID, PK'_{ID}), $\mathcal{B}$ checks whether $(\omega', \mu', \phi') \in \mathbb{G}^* \times \mathbb{G}^* \times \mathbb{G}^*$. If not, return "Reject". Otherwise $\mathcal{B}$ searches $Publickey^{List}$ for a tuple $\langle ID, (\omega, \mu, \phi), coin \rangle$. If the tuple exists, $\mathcal{B}$ sets $(\omega, \mu, \phi) = (\omega', \mu', \phi')$ and $coin = \bot$. Otherwise, add $\langle ID, (\omega', \mu', \phi'), coin = \bot \rangle$ to $Publickey^{List}$.

– Re-encryption key extraction queries: On input (ID_1, ID_2) by $\mathcal{A}_I$, $\mathcal{B}$ runs the above simulation algorithm for public key request taking ID_1 as input to get a tuple $\langle ID_1, (\omega_1, \mu_1, \phi_1), coin_1 \rangle \in Publickey^{List}$.
1. If $coin_1 = \bot$, return "Reject".
2. If $coin_1 = 0$, $\mathcal{B}$ searches $Privatekey^{List}$ for a tuple $\langle ID_1, (t_1, z_1, v_1) \rangle$ and runs the above simulation algorithm for public key request taking ID_2 as input to get a public key $(\omega_2, \mu_2, \phi_2)$. $\mathcal{B}$ computes $\gamma_2 = \omega_2 y^{H_1(ID_2, \omega_2)}$ and $X_{12} = H_3(\gamma_2^{v_1}, \phi_2^{v_1}, ID_1, PK_1, ID_2, PK_2)$. Return $RK_{ID_1 \rightarrow ID_2} = (t_1 H_4(\mu_1) + z_1) \cdot X_{12} \bmod q$.
3. Otherwise, return $RK_{ID_1 \rightarrow ID_2} \xleftarrow{\$} \mathbb{Z}_q^*$.

Challenge: On receiving a challenge query $(ID^*, (m_0, m_1))$, $\mathcal{B}$ responds $\mathcal{A}_I$'s query as follows:

1. The challenger $\mathcal{B}$ runs the above simulation algorithm for public key request taking ID^* as input to get a tuple $\langle ID^*, (\omega^*, \mu^*, \phi^*), coin^* \rangle \in Publickey^{List}$.
2. If $coin^* = 0$, $\mathcal{B}$ aborts the simulation.
3. Otherwise (i.e., $coin^* = 1$ since the additional restriction for $\mathcal{A}_I$), $\omega^* = g^{s^*}, \mu^* = (g^a)^{z^*}$, $\mathcal{B}$ does as follows:
   (a) Compute $\gamma^* = \omega^* y^{e^*} = g^{s^* + xe^*}$ where $e^* = H_1(ID^*, \omega^*)$ and $Y^* = \gamma^{*H_4(\mu^*)} \mu^*$.
   (b) Set $c_1^* = g^b$, pick $c_2^* \in \{0, 1\}^n$ and $\beta \in \{0, 1\}$ at random.
   (c) Implicitly define $H_2(Y^{*b}) = H_2((g^b)^{(s^* + xe^*)H_4(\mu^*)} \cdot (g^{ab})^{z^*}) = c_2^* \oplus m_\beta$
4. Return $C^* = (c_1^*, c_2^*)$ as the challenge ciphertext.

Phase 2: Adversary $\mathcal{A}_I$ continues to issue the rest of queries with the restrictions described in the 2nd-IND-CLPRE-CPA "Game I". $\mathcal{B}$ responds $\mathcal{A}_I$'s queries as in Phase 1.

Guess: Finally, $\mathcal{A}_I$ outputs a guess $\beta' \in \{0, 1\}$. Algorithm $\mathcal{B}$ randomly picks a tuple (K, R) from the list H_2^{List}. Since we make an additional restriction that $\mathcal{A}_I$ cannot replace the public key for ID^*, $\mathcal{B}$ knows s^* and z^* with respect to PK_{ID^*}. Thereby, $\mathcal{B}$ can compute $K' = \left(\frac{K}{(g^b)^{(s^* + xe^*)H_4(\mu^*)}} \right)^{1/z^*}$ and outputs K' as the solution to the given CDH instance.

[**Analysis**] The main idea of the analysis is borrowed from [9]. Firstly, we evaluate the simulations of the random oracles given above. From the construction of H_1, H_3 and H_4, it's clear that the simulations of H_1, H_3 and H_4 are perfect.

As long as $\mathcal{A}_I$ does not query Y^{*b} to H_2, the simulation of H_2 is perfect. By $AskH_2^*$ we denote the event that Y^{*b} has been queried to H_2.
Next, we analyse the conditions for abort as follows:

1. The value $coin^*$ corresponding to ID^* is 1.
2. For each of $\mathcal{A}_I$'s private key extraction queries on input $ID \neq ID^*$, the $coin$ corresponding to ID is 0.
3. For each of $\mathcal{A}_I$'s re-encryption key extraction queries on input (ID_1, ID_2), if $ID_1 \neq ID^*$, the $coin_1$ corresponding to ID_1 is 0.

If any of the above conditions are false, $\mathcal{B}$ aborts the simulation. Let $Abort$ denotes the event that $\mathcal{B}$ aborts during the simulation. Then $Pr[\neg Abort] \geq (1-\theta) \cdot \theta^{q_{prk}} \cdot \theta^{q_{rk}} = (1-\theta)\theta^{q_{prk}+q_{rk}}$ which is maximized at $\theta = \frac{q_{prk}+q_{rk}}{1+q_{prk}+q_{rk}}$. Hence, $Pr[\neg Abort] \geq \frac{1}{e(1+q_{prk}+q_{rk})}$ where e denotes the base of the natural logarithm.

Next, one can notice that the simulated challenge ciphertext is identically distributed as the real one from the construction. The simulation of re-encryption key extraction queries is perfect other than these re-encryption keys $RK_{ID^*\rightarrow ID}$ where ID is uncorrupted. By F we denote the event that there exists a probabilistic polynomial time (p.p.t.) 2nd-IND-CLPRE-CPA Type I adversary $\mathcal{A}_I'$ which can distinguish the incorrectly-formed re-encryption keys in our simulation from all correctly-formed re-encryption keys in a "real world" interaction. By τ denotes the probability that the event F occurs. We make a separate argument if $Pr[F] = \tau$ is non-negligible, then we can construct an algorithm $\mathcal{B}'$ who can solve the CDH problem in $\mathbb{G}$ with a non-negligible probability. Due to the space limit, the separate argument will be given in the full paper. By the separate argument, we can obtain that $Pr[F] = \tau$ is negligible under the CDH assumption.

Now we define an event E to be $(AskH_2^* \vee F)|\neg Abort$. If E does not happen, it is clear that $\mathcal{A}_I$ does not gain any advantage in guessing β due to the randomness of the output of the random oracle H_2. Namely, we have $Pr[\beta' = \beta|\neg E] = \frac{1}{2}$. Hence, by splitting $Pr[\beta' = \beta]$, we have $Pr[\beta' = \beta] = Pr[\beta' = \beta|\neg E]Pr[\neg E] + Pr[\beta' = \beta|E]Pr[E] \leq \frac{1}{2}Pr[\neg E] + Pr[E] = \frac{1}{2} + \frac{1}{2}Pr[E]$ and $Pr[\beta' = \beta] \geq Pr[\beta' = \beta|\neg E]Pr[\neg E] = \frac{1}{2} - \frac{1}{2}Pr[E]$.

By the definition of advantage $(\epsilon - \upsilon)$ for the 2nd-IND-CLPRE-CPA Type I adversary $\mathcal{A}_I$, we have $\epsilon - \upsilon = |Pr[\beta' = \beta] - \frac{1}{2}| \leq \frac{1}{2}Pr[E] = \frac{1}{2}Pr[(AskH_2^* \vee F)|\neg Abort] \leq \frac{1}{2Pr[\neg Abort]}(Pr[AskH_2^*] + Pr[F])$.

Since $Pr[\neg Abort] \geq \frac{1}{e(1+q_{prk}+q_{rk})}$ and $Pr[F] = \tau$, we obtain $Pr[AskH_2^*] \geq \frac{2(\epsilon-\upsilon)}{e(1+q_{prk}+q_{rk})} - \tau$.

If $AskH_2^*$ happens then $\mathcal{B}$ will be able to solve the CDH instance.

Hence, we obtain $\epsilon' \geq \frac{1}{q_{H_2}}\left(\frac{2(\epsilon-\upsilon)}{e(1+q_{prk}+q_{rk})} - \tau\right)$. $\qquad\square$

The security proof against Type II adversary $\mathcal{A}_{II}$ is analogous. Due to the space limit, we omit the details. The probability loss of the reduction is the same as the security proof against $\mathcal{A}_I$. Note that the Type II adversary $\mathcal{A}_{II}$ has the master-key and can not replace public keys of entities.

Lemma 2. The proposed CLPRE1 scheme is 1st-IND-CLPRE-CPA secure in the random oracle model, if the CDH assumption holds in $\mathbb{G}$ and the Schnorr signature is EUF-CMA secure.

Due to lack of space, the proof of this lemma will be given in the full paper. We re-write $C'_B = \langle g^{X_{AB}\tilde{r}}, m \oplus H_2(g^{\tilde{r}}) \rangle$ where $\tilde{r} = (t_A H_4(\mu_A) + z_A)r \bmod q$. Then, 1st-IND-CLPRE-CPA security of the proposed CLPRE1 scheme is following the fact that the first level ciphertext C'_B is indeed a "hashed" CPA-secure ElGamal encryption where the associated secret key X_{AB} can merely be computed by the delegator A or delegatee B.

References

1. Ateniese, G., Fu, K., Green, M., Hohenberger, S.: Improved proxy re-encryption schemes with applications to secure distributed storage. ACM Trans. Inf. Syst. Secur. (TISSEC) **9**(1), 1–30 (2006)
2. Al-Riyami, S.S., Paterson, K.G.: Certificateless public key cryptography. In: Laih, C.-S. (ed.) ASIACRYPT 2003. LNCS, vol. 2894, pp. 452–473. Springer, Heidelberg (2003)
3. Al-Riyami, S.S., Paterson, K.G.: CBE from CL-PKE: a generic construction and efficient schemes. In: Vaudenay, S. (ed.) PKC 2005. LNCS, vol. 3386, pp. 398–415. Springer, Heidelberg (2005)
4. Avanzi, R.M.: The complexity of certain multi-exponentiation techniques in cryptography. J. Cryptology **18**(4), 357–373 (2005)
5. Boneh, D., Boyen, X.: Efficient selective-ID secure identity-based encryption without random oracles. In: Cachin, C., Camenisch, J.L. (eds.) EUROCRYPT 2004. LNCS, vol. 3027, pp. 223–238. Springer, Heidelberg (2004)
6. Blaze, M., Bleumer, G., Strauss, M.J.: Divertible protocols and atomic proxy cryptography. In: Nyberg, K. (ed.) EUROCRYPT 1998. LNCS, vol. 1403, pp. 127–144. Springer, Heidelberg (1998)
7. Boneh, D., Franklin, M.: Identity-based encryption from the weil pairing. SIAM J. Comput. **32**(3), 586–615 (2003)
8. Bellare, M., Rogaway, P.: Random oracles are practical: a paradigm for designing efficient protocols. Proc. ACM CCS **1993**, 62–73 (1993)
9. Baek, J., Safavi-Naini, R., Susilo, W.: Certificateless public key encryption without pairing. In: Zhou, J., López, J., Deng, R.H., Bao, F. (eds.) ISC 2005. LNCS, vol. 3650, pp. 134–148. Springer, Heidelberg (2005)
10. De Caro, A.: jPBC Library - The Java Pairing Based Cryptography Library (2013). http://gas.dia.unisa.it/projects/jpbc/. Accessed May 2013
11. Canetti, R., Hohenberger, S.: Chosen-ciphertext secure proxy re-encryption. Proc. ACM CCS **2007**, 185–194 (2007)
12. Chow, S.S.M., Weng, J., Yang, Y., Deng, R.H.: Efficient unidirectional proxy re-encryption. In: Bernstein, D.J., Lange, T. (eds.) AFRICACRYPT 2010. LNCS, vol. 6055, pp. 316–332. Springer, Heidelberg (2010)
13. Deng, R.H., Weng, J., Liu, S., Chen, K.: Chosen-ciphertext secure proxy re-encryption without pairings. In: Franklin, M.K., Hui, L.C.K., Wong, D.S. (eds.) CANS 2008. LNCS, vol. 5339, pp. 1–17. Springer, Heidelberg (2008)
14. El Gamal, T.: A public key cryptosystem and a signature scheme based on discrete logarithms. In: Blakely, G.R., Chaum, D. (eds.) CRYPTO 1984. LNCS, vol. 196, pp. 10–18. Springer, Heidelberg (1985)

15. Fujisaki, E., Okamoto, T.: Secure integration of asymmetric and symmetric encryption schemes. In: Wiener, M. (ed.) CRYPTO 1999. LNCS, vol. 1666, pp. 537–554. Springer, Heidelberg (1999)
16. Green, M., Ateniese, G.: Identity-based proxy re-encryption. In: Katz, J., Yung, M. (eds.) ACNS 2007. LNCS, vol. 4521, pp. 288–306. Springer, Heidelberg (2007)
17. Hanaoka, G., Kawai, Y., Kunihiro, N., Matsuda, T., Weng, J., Zhang, R., Zhao, Y.: Generic construction of chosen ciphertext secure proxy re-encryption. In: Dunkelman, O. (ed.) CT-RSA 2012. LNCS, vol. 7178, pp. 349–364. Springer, Heidelberg (2012)
18. Ivan, A., Dodis, Y.: Proxy cryptography revisited. In: Proceedings of NDSS'03. The Internet Society (2003)
19. Isshiki, T., Nguyen, M.H., Tanaka, K.: Proxy re-encryption in a stronger security model extended from CT-RSA2012. In: Dawson, E. (ed.) CT-RSA 2013. LNCS, vol. 7779, pp. 277–292. Springer, Heidelberg (2013)
20. Lynn, B.: PBC Library - The Pairing-Based Cryptography Library (2013). http://crypto.stanford.edu/pbc/. Accessed May 2013
21. Libert, B., Quisquater, J.-J.: On constructing certificateless cryptosystems from identity based encryption. In: Yung, M., Dodis, Y., Kiayias, A., Malkin, T. (eds.) PKC 2006. LNCS, vol. 3958, pp. 474–490. Springer, Heidelberg (2006)
22. Libert, B., Vergnaud, D.: Unidirectional chosen-ciphertext secure proxy re-encryption. IEEE Trans. Inf. Theory 57(3), 1786–1802 (2011)
23. Menezes, A., van Oorschot, P.C., Vanstone, S.: Handbook of Applied Cryptography, 1st edn. CRC Press, Boca Raton (1997)
24. Pointcheval, D., Stern, J.: Security arguments for digital signatures and blind signatures. J. Cryptology 13(3), 361–396 (2000)
25. Schnorr, C.-P.: Efficient signature generation by smart cards. J. Cryptology 4(3), 161–174 (1991)
26. Sur, C., Jung, C.D., Park, Y., Rhee, K.H.: Chosen-ciphertext secure certificateless proxy re-encryption. In: De Decker, B., Schaumüller-Bichl, I. (eds.) CMS 2010. LNCS, vol. 6109, pp. 214–232. Springer, Heidelberg (2010)
27. Smith, T.: DVD jon: Buy DRM-less tracks from Apple iTunes, January 2005. http://www.theregister.co.uk/2005/03/18/itunes_pymusique
28. Solinas, J.: Low-weight binary representations for pairs of integers. Technical report CORR 2001–41 (2001). http://cacr.uwaterloo.ca/techreports/2001/corr2001-41.ps
29. Sun, Y., Zhang, F.T., Baek, J.: Strongly secure certificateless public key encryption without pairing. In: Bao, F., Ling, S., Okamoto, T., Wang, H., Xing, C. (eds.) CANS 2007. LNCS, vol. 4856, pp. 194–208. Springer, Heidelberg (2007)
30. Xu, L., Wu, X., Zhang, X.: CL-PRE: a certificateless proxy re-encryption scheme for secure data sharing with public cloud. In: Proceedings of the 7th ACM Symposium on Information, Computer and Communications Security, pp. 1–10 (2012)

Side Channel Analysis
and Its Countermeasures

Enabling 3-Share Threshold Implementations for all 4-Bit S-Boxes

Sebastian Kutzner[1,2], Phuong Ha Nguyen[1,2(✉)], and Axel Poschmann[1,2]

[1] PACE Temasek Laboratories, Nanyang Technological University,
Singapore, Singapore
[2] Division of Mathematical Sciences, SPMS, Nanyang Technological University,
Singapore, Singapore
{skutzner,aposchmann}@ntu.edu.sg, phuongha.ntu@gmail.com

Abstract. Threshold Implementation (TI) is an elegant and promising lightweight countermeasure for hardware implementations to resist first order Differential Power Analysis (DPA) in the presence of glitches. Unfortunately, in its most efficient version with only three shares, it can only be applied to 50 % of all 4-bit S-boxes so far. In this paper, we introduce a new approach, called *factorization*, that enables us to protect *all* 4-bit S-boxes with a 3-share TI. This allows—for the first time—to protect numerous important ciphers to which the 3-share TI countermeasure was previously not applicable, such as CLEFIA, DES, DESL, GOST, HUMMINGBIRD1, HUMMINGBIRD2, LUCIFER, mCrypton, SERPENT, TWINE, TWOFISH among others. We verify the security and correctness with experiments on simulations and real world power traces and finally provide exemplary decompositions of all those S-boxes.

1 Introduction

In 1996, Paul Kocher [13] showed that although a cryptographic algorithm is theoretically secure, when implemented on ordinary digital circuits, the physical side-effect observed during the processing of the algorithm, such as the timing, power [14], or electromagnetic emanation [10], could potentially leak information if properly analyzed. Though the existence of these so-called *side-channels* have been known since 1943 [23], Kocher's work marks the beginning of the (public) research in the field of side-channel analysis, and powerful attacks, such as Simple Power Analysis (SPA) [14], Differential Power Analysis (DPA) [14], Correlation Power Analysis (CPA) [6], and Mutual Information Analysis (MIA) [11] have been developed since. At the same time ever more sophisticated countermeasures have been proposed. Most countermeasures aim at decreasing the *signal-to-noise ratio* (SNR) [17] by balancing the leakage, that is *hiding* the information processed [27] and/or breaking the link between the processed data and the secret, which is called *masking* [7]. However, in [18,19] it was shown that masking is still vulnerable to DPA due to the presence of glitches in hardware

© Springer International Publishing Switzerland 2014
H.-S. Lee and D.-G. Han (Eds.): ICISC 2013, LNCS 8565, pp. 91–108, 2014.
DOI: 10.1007/978-3-319-12160-4_6

implementations. For that reason, a secret-sharing based countermeasure called *Threshold Implementation* (TI) [24] was proposed in 2006, that is provably secure against first-order DPA even in the presence of glitches. A few follow-up papers have discussed mostly applications to 4-bit S-boxes [5,24–26] and implementations of TI have been reported for PRESENT [28], AES [20] and KECCAK [2,3].

In its most resource-efficient form the TI countermeasure needs only 3 shares, which implies the function that is to be shared can have at most an algebraic degree of 2. In order to apply a 3-share TI to a function with a larger degree (4-bit S-boxes typically have a degree of 3), this function, for minimal area requirements,[1] should be represented as a composition of quadratic functions [28]. According to [25,28] there are two stages in applying the 3-share TI: the *decomposition stage*, during which a given S-box is decomposed into quadratic permutations, and the *sharing stage*, during which all those quadratic permutations are shared into 3 shares in a way that we obtain 12-bit permutations. According to [5], all 4-bit S-boxes that can be protected by a 3-share TI using the *sequential structure*, belong to the alternating group A_{16} of the symmetric group S_{16}. This result implies that we cannot apply a 3-share TI to those 50 % of all 4-bit S-boxes which do not belong to A_{16}.

Our main contribution is the introduction of the *factorization structure* which is an extension of the sequential structure. This idea allows to decompose any 4-bit S-box into quadratic vectorial Boolean functions and, hence, enables to *protect any given 4-bit S-box with the TI countermeasure using only 3 shares*.

To support our claims we show how to apply the 3-share TI to SERPENT and many other 4-bit S-boxes, what, up to now, was believed to be not possible.

The remainder of this article is organized as follows. In Sect. 2, we recall the basics of the Threshold Implementation countermeasure. Then we will discuss how to decompose any 4-bit S-box into quadratic decompositions, i.e., studying the decomposition stage in Sect. 3. Subsequently, we show how to share each quadratic decomposition in a way that the uniformity property is fulfilled, i.e., being a 12-bit permutation, in Sect. 4. We verify our claims by successfully applying the 3-share TI countermeasure to the S-box S_5 of SERPENT, which does not belong to A_{16}. Our experimental results, provided in Sect. 5, verify that the protected S_5 implementation is secure against first-order DPA attacks. The paper is concluded in Sect. 6 and in the appendix we list 3-share TIs for S-boxes and important permutations which are not in A_{16}, and thus, previously could not have been protected by 3-share TIs.

2   Threshold Implementation

In this section we recall the preliminaries of the Threshold Implementation countermeasure and the results of [28] describing a 3-share TI of PRESENT.

---

[1] See Sect. 5 for our detailed line of argumentation.

2.1   Threshold Implementation Countermeasure

In [24], the Threshold Implementation (TI) was introduced as a side-channel analysis countermeasure. It is based on secret sharing and multi-party computation and provably secure against first order DPA, even in the presence of glitches. Let denote by small characters x, y, ... stochastic variables and by capitals X, Y, ... samples of these variables. The probability that x takes the value X is denoted by $Pr(x = X)$. The variable x is divided into s shares x_i, $1 \leq i \leq s$, such that $x = \bigoplus_{i=1}^{s} x_i$. Denote $\bar{x} = (x_1, \ldots, x_{i-1}, x_i, x_{i+1}, \ldots, x_s)$, $\bar{x}_i = (x_1, \ldots, x_{i-1}, x_{i+1}, \ldots, x_s)$ (or the vector $\bar{x}_i$ does not contain the share x_i) and denote by $Pr(\bar{x} = \bar{X} | x = X)$ the conditional probability of an event that $\bar{x} = \bar{X}$ under condition $x = X$. The method can be described as follows. Let $F(x, y, z, \ldots)$ be a vectorial Boolean function which needs to be shared. A sharing of F is a set of s functions F_i which it must fulfill the following properties:

1. **Non-completeness:** All functions F_i must be independent of at least one share of the input variables x, y, z, ... This can be translated to F_i should be independent of x_i, y_i, z_i, ..., i.e., the inputs of F_i does not have x_i, y_i, z_i, ... or $F_i = F_i(\bar{x}_i, \bar{y}_i, \bar{z}_i, \ldots)$.
2. **Correctness:** $F(x, y, z, \ldots) = \bigoplus_{i=1}^{s} F_i(\bar{x}_i, \bar{y}_i, \bar{z}_i, \ldots)$.

According to Theorems 2 and 3 of [24–26], if the inputs satisfy the following condition

$$Pr(\bar{x} = \bar{X}, \bar{y} = \bar{Y}, \ldots) = q \times Pr(x = \bigoplus_{i}^{s} X_i, y = \bigoplus_{i}^{s} Y_i, \ldots), \qquad (1)$$

where q is a constant or $Pr(\bar{x} = \bar{X}, \bar{y} = \bar{Y}, \ldots | x = \bigoplus_{i}^{s} X_i, y = \bigoplus_{i}^{s} Y_i, \ldots)$ is a constant, then the sharing of F can resist first order DPA even in the presence of glitches.

In general, F is a round function (or a nonlinear function) and its output is the input of next round (or of next nonlinear function). Hence, the following property for the output of F is required in order to make the cipher resistant against first order DPA in the presence of glitches. Assume that $(u, v, \ldots, w) = F(x, y, \ldots, z)$ and $u = \bigoplus_{i=1}^{s} u_i$, $\bar{u} = (u_1, u_2, \ldots, u_s)$, ..., $w = \bigoplus_{i=1}^{s} w_i$, $\bar{w} = (w_1, w_2, \ldots, w_s)$, then the third property is defined as follows:

3. **Uniformity:** A shared version of $(u, v, \ldots, w) = F(x, y, \ldots, z)$ is uniform, if $Pr(\bar{u} = \bar{U}, \ldots, \bar{w} = \bar{W}) = q \times Pr(u = \bigoplus_{i}^{s} U_i, \ldots, w = \bigoplus_{i}^{s} W_i)$ where q is a constant or $Pr(\bar{u} = \bar{U}, \ldots, \bar{w} = \bar{W} | u = \bigoplus_{i}^{s} U_i, \ldots, w = \bigoplus_{i}^{s} W_i)$ is a constant.

If the function $u = F(x)$ is invertible, then every vector $\bar{u}$ is reached for exactly one input vector $\bar{x}$. In this paper, the function F is a 4-bit S-box which is a 4-bit permutation. Hence, its 3-share TI is required to be 12-bit permutation.

All 4-bit permutations constitute the *symmetric group* S_{16} [12]. The identity permutation is an even permutation. An *even permutation* can be obtained as the composition of an even number and only an even number of exchanges (called transpositions) of two elements, while an *odd permutation* can be obtained by (only) an odd number of transpositions [12]. All 4-bit even permutations in S_{16} constitute a subgroup which is called the *alternating group* A_{16}. Let B_{16} be the set of all 4-bit odd permutations or $B_{16} = S_{16} \backslash A_{16}$.

Assume that the degree of F is d, then the number of shares s required is computed as follows:

Theorem 1. *[25] The minimum number of shares required to implement a product of d variables satisfying Properties 1 and 2 is given by*

$$s \geq 1 + d.$$

Since the minimum degree of a nonlinear vectorial Boolean function is 2, the number of shares s is at least 3. The more shares are needed, the bigger the hardware implementation. Therefore, a 3-share TI is the most efficient—and thus, most desirably–case.

2.2   3-Share TI for Cubic 4-Bit S-Boxes

In this section we revisit the results of [28] describing a 3-share TI of PRESENT. Since the PRESENT S-box $S(\cdot)$ is a cubic 4-bit permutation, the minimum number of shares is 4 [25]. To apply 3-share TI, the S-box is decomposed into two quadratic permutations $S(\cdot) = F(G(\cdot))$ as shown in Fig. 1, i.e., transforming it into a *sequential structure*.

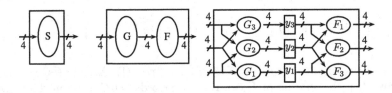

Fig. 1. Composition of the PRESENT S-box [28].

According to [25, 28] there are two stages in applying 3-share TI to a 4-bit S-box when using a sequential structure:

1. **Decomposition:** Finding the decompositions of a given S-box, which are required to be quadratic permutations.
2. **Sharing:** Constructing the 3-share TIs for those quadratic permutations. Their shared versions should fulfill all three requirements, most importantly uniformity, i.e., the shared versions must be 12-bit permutations.

Note 1. In the sharing stage, constructing a 3-share TI satisfying non-completeness property and correctness property to any 4-bit at most quadratic permutation is not difficult. Unfortunately it does not guarantee that its 3-share TI is a 12-bit permutation, i.e., it is not guaranteed that the uniformity property is satisfied. For that purpose, the so-called *remasking* technique [25] may be applied, which remasks the input(s) of next round or the input(s) of the next function with fresh (and uniformly distributed) random bits.

In this paper, we discuss how to decompose an arbitrary 4-bit S-box first (decomposition stage), before we show how to obtain its 3-share TIs of decompositions which are 12-bit permutations. It means that these 3-share TIs satisfy the uniformity without using the remasking method, which is a significant advantage, as the generation of random bits suitable for cryptographic masking can be very expensive on embedded devices.

Note 2. In order to apply 3-share TI to any arbitrary 4-bit S-box, we have to extend the decomposition and the sharing stages. Those extensions yield the *factorization structure*, our main contribution in this article. We will detail these extensions in Sect. 3.2.

3   The Decomposition Stage

In this section we investigate the decomposability of 4-bit S-boxes. In Sect. 3.1, we will recall the results from [5]. If a 4-bit S-box can be decomposed in a sequential structure then it must belong to the alternating group A_{16}. In order to apply a 3-share TI to the remaining 50 % of 4-bit S-boxes which are in B_{16}, we extend the sequential structure by using our new idea: *Factorization*, which yields the *factorization structure*. Our contribution allows to decompose any 4-bit S-box.

3.1   Decomposition of 4-Bit S-Boxes Using a Sequential Structure

Assume that $S(\cdot) = F(\ldots \ G(H(\cdot)))$ and if S is a permutation then all its decompositions $H, G, \ldots, F$ have to be permutations as well. Hence, if S is a 4-bit permutation then $H, G, \ldots, F$ are also 4-bit permutations. We recall the following important result about permutations in S_{16}.

Theorem 2. *[5] If a permutation $F(\cdot)$ is a composition of quadratic permutations, then $F(\cdot)$ is in A_{16}.*

However, 50 % of all 4-bit S-boxes are not decomposable using a sequential structure, i.e., all those S-boxes belong to B_{16}. Hence, there is no method known so far on how to apply 3-share TIs to those S-boxes. We now introduce a new methodology to solve this open problem.

3.2   Decomposition of 4-Bit S-Boxes Using a Factorization Structure

We start with a very simple example, i.e., decomposing a cubic term. The *Algebraic Normal Form* (ANF) of a cubic 4-bit S-box contains at least one cubic term. Without loss of generality, we first assume that the ANF contains only one cubic term $T(w, z, y, x) = (d, c, b, a) = (xyz, 0, 0, 0)$. The input bits of T are x, y, z, w and the output bits of T are a, b, c, d. The left most bit represents the most significant bit and the right most bit represents the least significant bit, respectively. The ANF of T is:

$$d = xyz$$
$$c = 0$$
$$b = 0$$
$$a = 0.$$

We can also write T as follows:

$$T(\cdot) = F(G(\cdot)) \oplus V(\cdot),$$

where F, G and V are the following quadratic vectorial Boolean functions:

$$
G : \quad
\begin{aligned}
d &= xy \oplus w \\
c &= z \\
b &= y \\
a &= x.
\end{aligned}
\qquad
F : \quad
\begin{aligned}
d &= zw \\
c &= 0 \\
b &= 0 \\
a &= 0.
\end{aligned}
\qquad
V : \quad
\begin{aligned}
d &= zw \\
c &= 0 \\
b &= 0 \\
a &= 0.
\end{aligned}
$$

As one can see, using this approach, it is possible to represent a cubic term of an ANF by a set of quadratic vectorial Boolean functions. By applying this approach term-by-term, it is possible to decompose any cubic vectorial Boolean function, *including odd permutations*. This observation results in the following theorem.

Theorem 3. *For any given 4-bit S-box S we can always find a set of quadratic vectorial Boolean functions F_i, G_i, $1 \le i \le n$, and V such that:*

$$S(\cdot) = \bigoplus_{i=1}^{n} F_i(G_i(\cdot)) \oplus V(\cdot).$$

We call the format above *factorization structure* and we summarize the idea for the decomposition stage in Fig. 2.

In order to make our idea clear, we provide another example, the 4-bit odd permutation $M = [0, 1, 2, 3, 4, 5, 6, 15, 8, 9, 10, 11, 12, 13, 14, 7]$. Its ANF is:

$$d = w \oplus xyz$$
$$c = z$$
$$b = y$$
$$a = x.$$

Please note that the example above is only *one* out of many choices for M. We chose M for its simplicity and implementation efficiency. The permutation M can be factorized as follows:

$$M(\cdot) = M_2(M_1(\cdot)) \oplus M_3(\cdot).$$

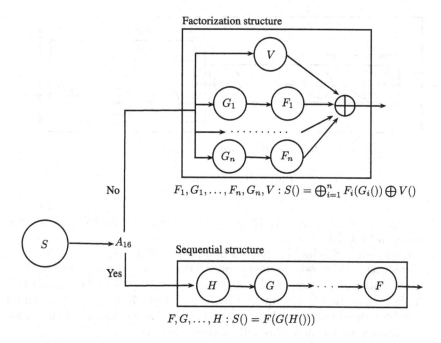

Fig. 2. Flowchart of the decomposition stage for a given 4-bit S-box.

Where the ANFs of M_1, M_2, and M_3 are:

$$M_1 : \begin{aligned} d &= xy \oplus w \\ c &= z \\ b &= y \\ a &= x. \end{aligned} \qquad M_2 : \begin{aligned} d &= zw \\ c &= 0 \\ b &= 0 \\ a &= 0. \end{aligned} \qquad M_3 : \begin{aligned} d &= zw \oplus w \\ c &= z \\ b &= y \\ a &= x. \end{aligned}$$

3.3 Decomposition of 4-Bit S-Boxes Using a Hybrid Structure

We will discuss the sharing stage in Sect. 4 where we ensure that the 3-share TI of a 4-bit S-box is a 12-bit permutation, i.e., the 3-share TI fulfills the uniformity property. Please note that the sharing stage for sequential structures is not complicated, and we will show how to solve this problem in Sect. 4.1.

Sharing a factorization structure, however, without using the remasking method to fulfill the uniformity is a challenge, and it is extremely difficult for 4-bit S-boxes which have many cubic terms. In order to make the workload in the sharing stage easier, we propose the following approach:

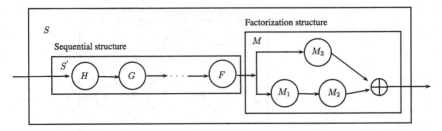

$$F, G, \ldots, H, M : S() = M(S'()) = M(F(\ldots G(H())))$$

Fig. 3. Hybrid structure.

1. If a given S-box S is in A_{16} (S is an even permutation) then we use the method in Sect. 4.1.
2. If a given S-box S is in B_{16} (S is an odd permutation) then:
    (a) Construct a 4-bit odd permutation M that can be shared into a 12-bit permutation, for example $M = [0, 1, 2, 3, 4, 5, 6, 15, 8, 9, 10, 11, 12, 13, 14, 7]$. This permutation is decomposed by using a factorization structure and it can be ensured that its 3-share TI is a 12-bit permutation, i.e., permutation M satisfies uniformity. This will be shown in Sect. 4.2.
    (b) Since M and S are odd permutations, the permutation S' such that $S(\cdot) = M(S'(\cdot))$ is an even permutation, i.e., S' is in A_{16} [12]. Then we apply the result in Sect. 4.1 to share the decompositions of S'.

Actually, the method above is a *hybrid structure* between a sequential structure and a factorization structure. This hybrid structure is very useful, because it can help us to fulfill the uniformity property without using remasking, thus we will work with the hybrid structure instead of a plain factorization structure. Figure 3 depicts the hybrid structure.

So far, we already presented how to decompose a given 4-bit S-box. If the given S-box is in A_{16} we use a sequential structure, otherwise we use a hybrid structure which is a mixture of a sequential and a factorization structure.

Now that the decomposition stage is done, we can move on to the sharing stage, which will be treated in the next section. It is interesting to see how to construct the 3-share TIs of these decompositions such that they are 12-bit permutations, i.e., they fulfill the uniformity property without using the remasking method.

3.4   Application to Important S-Boxes in B_{16}

In the appendix we list decompositions of S-boxes in B_{16}, that are used by the following algorithms: CLEFIA [32], DES [22], DESL [15], GOST [35], HUMMINGBIRD1 [9], HUMMINGBIRD2 [8], LUCIFER [33], mCrypton [16], SERPENT [4], TWINE [34], TWOFISH [31], and the Inversion (x^{-1}) function in $GF(2^4)$ which is used in mCrypton [16] or in [20]. Previously, all of these algorithms could not have been protected by a 3-share TI.

4 The Sharing Stage

In this section, we discuss how to make 3-share TIs of decompositions of a given 4-bit S-box being 12-bit permutations. Since the given S-box can belong to A_{16} or B_{16}, we have two structures: a sequential structure, which is treated in Sect. 4.1, and a hybrid structure, which is composed of a sequential structure and a factorization structure. Consequently, in Sect. 4.2 we will treat the factorization structure, and we will also discuss its security, i.e., why it resists first order DPA in the presence of glitches and why it satisfies uniformity.

4.1 Sharing Stage Using a Sequential Structure

In this subsection, we discuss how to share the decompositions of a given S-box S in A_{16}. We adopt the sharing in [24, 25, 28]. For a given function $F(w, z, y, x)$ and inputs x, y, z, w, they are split into 3 shares F_1, F_2, F_3, x_1, ..., w_3. For monomials involving two indices, it is obvious which F_i to place them in. For example, we must place monomials $y_1 w_2$ and $z_2 w_1$ in F_3. For monomials involving just one index, e.g., x_1 or $y_2 w_2$, we adopt the convention that terms with index 1 (resp. 2, 3) are placed in F_3 (resp. F_1, F_2). The constant term is placed in F_1. In [5], this approach is called *direct sharing*. For example a given Boolean function $f = xy \oplus z \oplus 1$ then the 3-share TI by using the direct sharing is as follows:

$$f_1 = z_2 \oplus x_2 y_2 \oplus x_2 y_3 \oplus x_3 y_2 \oplus 1$$
$$f_2 = z_3 \oplus x_3 y_3 \oplus x_1 y_3 \oplus x_3 y_1$$
$$f_3 = z_1 \oplus x_1 y_1 \oplus x_1 y_2 \oplus x_2 y_1$$

According to [5], all 4-bit permutations in A_{16} can be decomposed by using a sequential structure and their 3-share TIs satisfy uniformity by simply using direct sharing.

4.2 Sharing Stage Using a Factorization Structure

The sharing stage for S-boxes in B_{16} is detailed here. As we have already pointed out, it is better to use a hybrid structure to decompose an S-box in B_{16}. In the previous section, based on [5], we already saw that all 3-share TIs of 4-bit permutations in A_{16} can be made being 12-bit permutations by using direct sharing. Hence, we only focus on the 3-share TI of M, i.e., the 3-share TIs of the quadratic vectorial Boolean functions M_1, M_2, M_3. Let denote M_s, M_{s_1}, M_{s_2}, M_{s_3} as 3-share TIs of M, M_1, M_2, M_3, respectively.

The ANF of the 12-bit M_{s_1} of M_1 is:

$$d_1 = w_2 \oplus y_2 x_2 \oplus y_2 x_3 \oplus y_3 x_2$$
$$d_2 = w_3 \oplus y_3 x_3 \oplus y_1 x_3 \oplus y_3 x_1$$
$$d_3 = w_1 \oplus y_1 x_1 \oplus y_1 x_2 \oplus y_2 x_1$$

$$c_1 = z_2$$
$$c_2 = z_3$$
$$c_3 = z_1$$
$$b_1 = y_2$$
$$b_2 = y_3$$
$$b_3 = y_1$$
$$a_1 = x_2$$
$$a_2 = x_3$$
$$a_3 = x_1.$$

The ANF of the 12-bit M_{s_2} of M_2 is:

$$d_1 = z_2w_2 \oplus z_2w_3 \oplus z_3w_2$$
$$d_2 = z_3w_3 \oplus z_1w_3 \oplus z_3w_1$$
$$d_3 = z_1w_1 \oplus z_1w_2 \oplus z_2w_1$$
$$c_1 = 0$$
$$c_2 = 0$$
$$c_3 = 0$$
$$b_1 = 0$$
$$b_2 = 0$$
$$b_3 = 0$$
$$a_1 = 0$$
$$a_2 = 0$$
$$a_3 = 0.$$

The ANF of the 12-bit M_{s_3} of M_3 is:

$$d_1 = w_2 \oplus z_3w_3 \oplus z_2w_3 \oplus z_3w_2$$
$$d_2 = w_3 \oplus z_1w_1 \oplus z_1w_3 \oplus z_3w_1$$
$$d_3 = w_1 \oplus z_2w_2 \oplus z_1w_2 \oplus z_2w_1$$
$$c_1 = z_2$$
$$c_2 = z_3$$
$$c_3 = z_1$$
$$b_1 = y_2$$
$$b_2 = y_3$$
$$b_3 = y_1$$
$$a_1 = x_2$$
$$a_2 = x_3$$
$$a_3 = x_1.$$

Then $M_s = M_{s_2}(M_{s_1}(\cdot)) \oplus M_{s_3}(\cdot)$ is a 12-bit permutation and thus M fulfills uniformity. Note that all the sharings of all decompositions of M are found by hand due to the simplicity of their ANF.

Note 3. Studying Fig. 3 allows to observe the following:

1. Among three quadratic vectorial Boolean functions M_1, M_2, M_3, only M_1 is a 4-bit permutation and M_{s_1} is a 12-bit permutation. Hence, M_1 satisfies the uniformity property.
2. It is obvious that M_{s_2} and M_{s_3} do not fulfill the uniformity property. However, both functions are *not required to satisfy uniformity*, only their XOR sum has to (as this will potentially be the input to a subsequently shared function). Instead both functions M_{s_2} and M_{s_3} only need to satisfy non-completeness and correctness, and their inputs need to fulfill Eq. 1, in order to resist first order DPA in the presence of glitches (Theorems 2 and 3 in [24–26]).
3. The output of M_s is the result of XORing the outputs of M_{s_2} and M_{s_3}. Since an XOR is a linear operation (i.e., having degree 1), only outputs from the same share are combined together. This means, this operation is first order DPA resistant in the presence of glitches, as potential leakage will only depend on a single share, but information of all three shares are required for a successful DPA.
4. Since M is in B_{16} and M_s is a 12-bit permutation, the 3-share TI of M satisfies uniformity. It means our proposed hybrid structure is secure.
5. We will present experimental results for supporting our theoretical arguments about the security of our proposed structure in the next section.

5   Experiments

To verify the correctness and security of our new scheme we decomposed and shared the SERPENT S-box S_5 as described in the previous sections. The decomposition formulas for all stages can be found in the Appendix. We ensured that every stage of the shared S-box fulfills all requirements given in [24], especially the uniformity property. It should also be noted that a register has to be inserted in between every decomposition stage. Figure 5 shows a schematic of the hardware implementation.

First, several attacks were mounted on noise-free simulated power traces (assuming a HW leakage), i.e., CPA attacks on all (intermediate) registers. Neither of the attacks revealed the correct key hypothesis, hence supporting our claims. For testing purposes we also attacked a non-uniform implementation of S_5, i.e., M_3 was varied such that the XOR-output is not uniform. Here, a CPA attack on the output register was successful, proving (again) the importance of the uniformity property.

Next, we implemented the (uniform) shared S-box as shown in Fig. 5 on an FPGA, i.e., a SASEBO-GII. To synthesize the design we used Xilinx ISE Webpack 13.3. The FPGA hosting the S-box ran at 2 MHz derived from the 24 MHz on-board oscillator. 20,000,000 measurements were taken at 1.25 GS/s

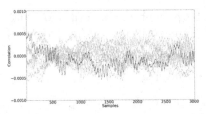
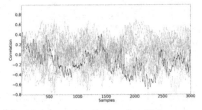

(a) CPA results attacking the SERPENT   (b) Correlation-enhanced collision attack
S-box S_5.

Fig. 4. Attack Results

(625 samples per clock cycle) and a CPA was performed, using the Hamming distance between the outputs of two consecutive S-box lookups as the attack model. Furthermore, we mounted a correlation-enhanced collision attack [21] to test the resistance against glitches, as failing attacks on registers do not necessarily prove the security of a scheme [19]. Figure 4 shows the results of both attacks. The first clock edge is at sample 125. One S-box computation takes four clock cycles, thus the computation is finished at sample 2625. As we can see, in neither of both attacks does the correct hypothesis yield the highest correlation.

Efficiency of 3-share TI for 4-bit Sboxes based on hybrid structure: One of important factors in masking countermeasure is randomness. Generating a random number used for cryptographic purpose is very expensive in terms of time and power consumption because at least one full encryption of a cipher should be processed (hash function, block cipher, ...) [1,30]. Therefore, the number of random numbers used should be as small as possible in crypto system. In lightweight crypto designs the serialized implementation and 4-bit S-boxes are preferred due to their hardware compactness. Reference [5] has provided 3-share TIs of all 4-bit S-boxes in A_{16} and 4- and 5-share TIs for the other in B_{16}. Some of the 4- and 5-share TIs require less area than the corresponding 3-share TI with hybrid structure. Thus, the authors concluded that a 3-share realization may not be the optimal case in terms of hardware. However, it should be noted that all shares need to be maintained (i.e. stored) throughout the whole encryption process. In a lightweight setting, i.e. serialized implementation, the S-box layer contributes only 15 % to the whole area [28], while the registers take the lion's share. Thus any reduction of the number of shares will reduce the overall gate count significantly at the potential cost of a slightly larger S-box. Hence, in all cases (with or without using remasking method) a 3-share TI is much more efficient than 4- and 5-share TI in terms of hardware and randomness (or time and power consumption).

It is well-known that the number of shares can be reduced to 2 for the linear layer to reduce the storage overhead for the shares. However, this approach requires extensive use of fresh randomness which is an expensive resource especially in embedded systems for the remasking step. The more shares are used in the non-linear part, the more randomness is required. Thus this approach nullifies the elegance of TI as a lightweight DPA countermeasure (only needing randomness once in the beginning), and consequently it is convinced the 3-share case is the most optimal in all aspects.

6 Conclusion

Threshold Implementation (TI) [24] is an elegant and promising lightweight countermeasure for hardware implementations to resist first order Differential Power Analysis (DPA) in the presence of glitches. The most challenging part in applying TI to ciphers are the non-linear functions, e.g., the S-boxes for block ciphers. To implement TI in its most efficient version, namely with only three shares, the functions to be shared have to have a degree smaller than three. For 50 % of all S-boxes this requirement can be fulfilled by decomposing an S-box of degree three to several functions with a smaller degree [5,28]. After decomposition, the quadratic and linear functions can now be split into three shares.

Unfortunately, for the other 50 % of the S-boxes, said method can not be applied. Therefore, we introduced the *factorization structure* which enables us to decompose those functions of degree three, which previously were deemed to be not decomposable, to several quadratic and linear functions. It should be noted that the shared version of a function has to fulfill certain properties to be secure, namely correctness, non-completeness and uniformity. Using the *factorization structure* exacerbates fulfilling those requirements; especially the uniformity property is a very challenging task. Therefore, we introduced the *hybrid structure* combining the previous method and our *factorization structure*, enabling us to decompose cubic functions into quadratic and linear functions which subsequently can be easily shared and simultaneously fulfill all requirements of TI.

A   Appendix: 3-Share TIs of S-Boxes in B_{16}

In this section, we present the 3-share TIs of some S-boxes or important permutations which are in B_{16} by using a hybrid structure. All examples use the odd permutation $M = [0, 1, 2, 3, 4, 5, 6, 15, 8, 9, 10, 11, 12, 13, 14, 7]$ which is also used in previous sections. Recall, that M can be any odd permutation of which the shared version is a 12-bit permutation, i.e., satisfying the uniformity property without using remasking.

For the sake of convenience, a given permutation is described in hexadecimal representation. For example, if a permutation $F = [15, 5, 6, 14, 13, 7, 2, 10, 8, 0, 11, 1, 12, 4, 9, b]$, then F is written as follows: F = f56ed72a80b1c493. All S-boxes in this section can be found in [5,29] or from their respective specifications.

All S-boxes below belong to B_{16} and they can be decomposed in two different ways (see Fig. 5):

– **type 1:** $S(\cdot) = M(F(G(G(\cdot))))$
– **type 2:** $S(\cdot) = M(F(G(\cdot)))$

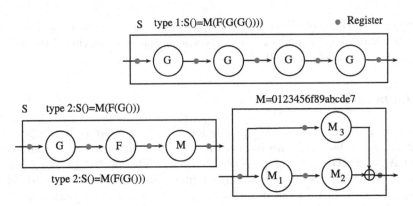

Fig. 5. Decompositions of S-boxes.

In fact nearly all S-boxes belong to type 1 and only two S-boxes (iS_4 of HUMMINGBIRD2 and S_5 of SERPENT) belong to type 2. The 3-share TIs of all F and G by using direct sharing are 12-bit permutations.

CLEFIA [32]

1. SS_0: F = e6ca89d24b10537f, G = 021346fda89bce57;
2. SS_1: F = 6f29a5e3781cd4b0, G = 053f8db72694ae1c;
3. SS_2: F = b56e7302da981cf4, G = 094c187f2b6e3a5d;
4. SS_3: F = a6d295c37bf048e1, G = 02319b8a57ec46df;

DES [22]. Actually, the i-th DES S-box ($DESi$) contains a set of four 4-bit S-boxes. Notation $DESi_j$ means the j-th row (i.e., 4-bit S-box) of the i-th DES S-box.

1. $DES2_0$: F = f986bda42c710e35, G = 4c28a0f7d539b16e;
2. $DES2_1$: F = acd1265b97403fe8, G = 1c593a7f0d482b6e;
3. $DES2_2$: F = d3f0c481b596a2e7, G = 9d26a78503cf4e1b;
4. $DES2_3$: F = dc8b37421f6a5e09, G = 0b1a46579382decf;
5. $DES3_0$: F = d69e75a410f2b3c8, G = 168c079d24be35af;
6. $DES3_1$: F = 803a46ed952f17bc, G = 17069a8b5243dfce;
7. $DES3_2$: F = df47ae50b921c836, G = 0d861c972ea53fb4;
8. $DES3_3$: F = 9716fac0b8e4d532, G = fb647ec318a59d02;
9. $DES4_0$: F = fd3402cb75168ae9, G = 419b03c8de62fa57;
10. $DES4_1$: F = 3edf68ba70c41592, G = 125ac68e9bd34f07;
11. $DES4_2$: F = abc4fd928375e610, G = 094b6a285d1f3e7c;
12. $DES4_3$: F = 36dea581b2f047c9, G = 02d64f135e8a9bc7;
13. $DES5_0$: F = 28fc1b569a7d304e, G = 0e1f869725bcad34;
14. $DES6_0$: F = 792bd3c54a81e06f, G = 4e396f18a0d7c5b2;
15. $DES6_3$: F = 48ac537b2e9f601d, G = 0a7c1e68295f3d4b;

16. $DES7_0$: F = 6b3d719c2e5a8f40, G = 21e74da903c56f8b;
17. $DES7_1$: F = 68f143bc970ead52, G = be364f290c1d57a8;
18. $DES7_2$: F = abd4c93e671805f2, G = 1a084e5c293b7d6f;
19. $DES8_0$: F = d572c908143be6af, G = 0eb4962c1da7853f;
20. $DES8_1$: F = fd963b2745c01ae8, G = 1c0d3a2b59487f6e;
21. $DES8_2$: F = fa41e5830b6d72c9, G = 048c9d152f6b3e7a;

DESL [15]

1. Row_0: F = e6a3d4197f2b5c80, G = 091d7f6b5c482a3e;
2. Row_1: F = 51ebc9378d6204af, G = 02cf1b5e93d68a47;
3. Row_2: F = 15dbef74c2a63809, G = 17ad358f269c04be;
4. Row_3: F = dae51379f80b64c2, G = af53269e8d7104bc;

GOST [35]

1. k_3: F = 52840cadb79e613f, G = 063d1f24acb5978e;
2. k_4: F = f93457dec1a62b08, G = 0e7d1b4a2c5f3968;
3. k_7: F = d7954f6b2c08e1a3, G = 0a6f384c1b7e295d;
4. k_8: F = 5b79d3f104ae62c8, G = 179fda52e46cb038;

HUMMINGBIRD1 [9]

1. S_0: F = 82f7e639c40ab1d5, G = 0f1e9687bd24ac35;
2. S_1: F = 063b7f42d1eca895, G = 0f861e97ad24bc35;
3. S_2: F = 21430895dbeca76f, G = 0ad7b16c92e54f38;
4. S_3: F = 0f2e7d5c4a6b3819, G = 0a7f295c6e1b4d38;

HUMMINGBIRD2 [8]

1. S_1: F = f56ed72a80b1c493, G = 0a5bd38217ce469f;
2. S_2: F = a8034ce7b61d52f9, G = 14860d9fae3cb725;
3. S_3: F = 2f6e5d1c4a380b79, G = 0f5bc78293d64a1e;
4. S_4: F = 0819ae37c4d562fb, G = 853b29a47ed1f06c;

The inverse S-boxes of HUMMINGBIRD2:

1. iS_1: F = 0d42ca8597eb631f, G = 3c4b21de56a9780f;
2. iS_2: F = de8c94b162305f7a, G = 14a69d2fcbe05378;
3. iS_3: F = c36740b18e5d2fa9, G = 0c6f2a583b491d7e;
4. iS_4: F = f5ac403b16927ed8, G = 209a8b3164fced75; (type 2)

Inversion (x^{-1}) in $GF(2^4)$. The function x^{-1} = 019edb76f2c5a438 which is defined over $GF(2)/(x^4 \oplus x \oplus 1)$.
F = 843dae67f25bc91 and G = 059dbf278e3416ac.

LUCIFER [33]

1. S_0: F = a2fde8b7906534c1, G = 1e482c6b0f593d7a;
2. S_1: F = f21deb047c93658a, G = 068f9e174bd3c25a;

mCrypton [16]

1. S_0: F = 4af0827c3516b9de, G = 0a7c5e28396d4f1b;
2. S_1: F = 19df3b647580cea2, G = 06d71fce8a5b9342;
3. S_2: F = 31078f46ec25ad9b, G = 2b5f097d4e186c3a;
4. S_3: F = b420af918c7e3d65, G = 041d3f26ac97b58e;

SERPENT [4]

1. S_3: F = 072e351c9db4af86, G = 0c792f5a3e4b1d68;
2. S_4: F = 53bd19f708e6ca24, G = ea5d69cf0873214b;
3. S_5: F = 7c4b259a3e6f01d8, G = 05432761c89feabd; (type 2)
4. S_7: F = 18679d3f5acb024e, G = 0d87961c3fa4b52e;

The inverse S-boxes of S_3, S_4, S_5, S_7:

1. iS_3: F = 09dacef3b1624578, G = 0c483e7a6f2b195d;
2. iS_4: F = 98b7406fac5e21d3, G = 1a0bc2d34e5f8796;
3. iS_5: F = 87f6dc43b915e2a0, G = 0eb63c95842da71f;
4. iS_7: F = 35f921edc60a874b, G = 0c489d5173bfa6e2;

TWINE [34]

1. S: F = d2305ebc7a98f614, G = bda5e92c0687431f;

TWOFISH [31]

1. $q1, t1$: F = a0f2d785c139b64e, G = 0c483e7a6f2b195d;
2. $q1, t0$: F = 2847ba6e1c9d350f, G = 069c8d1734aebf25;
3. $q0, t0$: F = 50d87b3fa6e29c14, G = b4ace16058732f9d;
4. $q0, t2$: F = 456f09ba23e781dc, G = 0d841cb73e952fa6;

References

1. NIST Special Publication 800-90A.: Recommendation for random number generation using deterministic random bit generators. Technical report (2012). http://csrc.nist.gov/publications/nistpubs/800-90A/SP800-90A.pdf
2. Bertoni, G., Daemen, J., Debande, N., Le, T.-H., Peeters, M., Van Assche, G.: Power analysis of hardware implementations protected with secret sharing. Cryptology ePrint Archive, Report 2013/067 (2013). http://eprint.iacr.org/

3. Bertoni, G., Daemen, J., Peeters, M., Van Assche, G.: Building power analysis resistant implementations of KECCAK. In: Second SHA-3 Candidate Conference (2010)
4. Biham, E., Anderson, R., Knudsen, L.R.: SERPENT: a new block cipher proposal. In: Vaudenay, S. (ed.) FSE 1998. LNCS, vol. 1372, pp. 222–238. Springer, Heidelberg (1998)
5. Bilgin, B., Nikova, S., Nikov, V., Rijmen, V., Stütz, G.: Threshold implementations of all 3×3 and 4×4 s-boxes. In: Prouff, E., Schaumont, P. (eds.) CHES 2012. LNCS, vol. 7428, pp. 76–91. Springer, Heidelberg (2012)
6. Brier, E., Clavier, C., Olivier, F.: Correlation power analysis with a leakage model. In: Joye, M., Quisquater, J.-J. (eds.) CHES 2004. LNCS, vol. 3156, pp. 16–29. Springer, Heidelberg (2004)
7. Coron, J.-S., Goubin, L.: On Boolean and arithmetic masking against differential power analysis. In: Koç, Ç.K., Paar, C., et al. (eds.) CHES 2000. LNCS, vol. 1965, pp. 231–237. Springer, Heidelberg (2000)
8. Engels, D., Saarinen, M.-J.O., Schweitzer, P., Smith, E.M.: The HUMMINGBIRD-2 lightweight authenticated encryption algorithm. In: Juels, A., Paar, C. (eds.) RFIDSec 2011. LNCS, vol. 7055, pp. 19–31. Springer, Heidelberg (2012)
9. Fan, X., Hu, H., Gong, G., Smith, E.M., Engels, D.: Lightweight implementation of HUMMINGBIRD cryptographic algorithm on 4-bit microcontroller. In: ICITST 2009 (2009)
10. Gandolfi, K., Mourtel, C., Olivier, F.: Electromagnetic analysis: concrete results. In: Koç, Ç.K., Naccache, D., Paar, C. (eds.) CHES 2001. LNCS, vol. 2162, pp. 251–261. Springer, Heidelberg (2001)
11. Gierlichs, B., Batina, L., Tuyls, P., Preneel, B.: Mutual information analysis. In: Oswald, E., Rohatgi, P. (eds.) CHES 2008. LNCS, vol. 5154, pp. 426–442. Springer, Heidelberg (2008)
12. Jacobson, N.: Basic Algebra, vol. 1, 2nd edn. Dover, Mineola (2009). ISBN 978-0-486-47189-1
13. Kocher, P.C.: Timing attacks on implementations of Diffie-Hellman, RSA, DSS, and other systems. In: Koblitz, N. (ed.) CRYPTO 1996. LNCS, vol. 1109, pp. 104–113. Springer, Heidelberg (1996)
14. Kocher, P.C., Jaffe, J., Jun, B.: Differential power analysis. In: Wiener, M. (ed.) CRYPTO 1999. LNCS, vol. 1666, pp. 388–397. Springer, Heidelberg (1999)
15. Leander, G., Paar, C., Poschmann, A., Schramm, K.: New lightweight DES variants. In: Biryukov, A. (ed.) FSE 2007. LNCS, vol. 4593, pp. 196–210. Springer, Heidelberg (2007)
16. Lim, C.H., Korkishko, T.: mCrypton – a lightweight block cipher for security of low-cost RFID tags and sensors. In: Song, J.-S., Kwon, T., Yung, M. (eds.) WISA 2005. LNCS, vol. 3786, pp. 243–258. Springer, Heidelberg (2006)
17. Mangard, S., Oswald, E., Popp, T.: Power Analysis Attacks: Revealing the Secrets of Smart Cards. Advances in Information Security. Springer, New York (2007)
18. Mangard, S., Popp, T., Gammel, B.M.: Side-channel leakage of masked CMOS gates. In: Menezes, A. (ed.) CT-RSA 2005. LNCS, vol. 3376, pp. 351–365. Springer, Heidelberg (2005)
19. Mangard, S., Pramstaller, N., Oswald, E.: Successfully attacking masked AES hardware implementations. In: Rao, J.R., Sunar, B. (eds.) CHES 2005. LNCS, vol. 3659, pp. 157–171. Springer, Heidelberg (2005)
20. Moradi, A., Poschmann, A., Ling, S., Paar, C., Wang, H.: Pushing the limits: a very compact and a threshold implementation of AES. In: Paterson, K.G. (ed.) EUROCRYPT 2011. LNCS, vol. 6632, pp. 69–88. Springer, Heidelberg (2011)

21. Moradi, A., Mischke, O., Paar, C., Li, Y., Ohta, K., Sakiyama, K.: On the power of fault sensitivity analysis and collision side-channel attacks in a combined setting. In: Preneel, B., Takagi, T. (eds.) CHES 2011. LNCS, vol. 6917, pp. 292–311. Springer, Heidelberg (2011)

22. U.S. Department of Commerce National Bureau of Standards.: Data encryption standard. Technical report (1977). http://csrc.nist.gov/publications/fips/fips46-3/fips46-3.pdf

23. National Security Agency.: TEMPEST: a signal problem. Cryptologic Spectrum, vol. 2(3) (1972) (declassified 2007)

24. Nikova, S., Rechberger, C., Rijmen, V.: Threshold implementations against side-channel attacks and glitches. In: Ning, P., Qing, S., Li, N. (eds.) ICICS 2006. LNCS, vol. 4307, pp. 529–545. Springer, Heidelberg (2006)

25. Nikova, S., Rijmen, V., Schläffer, M.: Secure hardware implementation of nonlinear functions in the presence of glitches. J. Cryptol. 24(2), 292–321 (2011)

26. Nikova, S., Rijmen, V., Schläffer, M.: Secure hardware implementation of nonlinear functions in the presence of glitches. In: Lee, P.J., Cheon, J.H. (eds.) ICISC 2008. LNCS, vol. 5461, pp. 218–234. Springer, Heidelberg (2009)

27. Popp, T., Mangard, S.: Masked dual-rail pre-charge logic: DPA-resistance without routing constraints. In: Rao, J.R., Sunar, B. (eds.) CHES 2005. LNCS, vol. 3659, pp. 172–186. Springer, Heidelberg (2005)

28. Poschmann, A., Moradi, A., Khoo, K., Lim, C., Wee, C., Wang, H., Ling, S.: Side-channel resistant crypto for less than 2,300 GE. J. Cryptol. 24(2), 322–345 (2011)

29. Saarinen, M.-J.O.: Cryptographic analysis of all 4×4-bit s-boxes. In: Miri, A., Vaudenay, S. (eds.) SAC 2011. LNCS, vol. 7118, pp. 118–133. Springer, Heidelberg (2012)

30. Schindler, W.: Random number generators for cryptographic applications. In: Koç, Ç.K. (ed.) Cryptographic Engineering. Springer, New York (2009)

31. Schneier, B., Kelsey, J., Whiting, D., Wagner, D., Hall, C., Ferguson, N.: The TWOFISH encryption algorithm. Technical report (1998)

32. Shirai, T., Shibutani, K., Akishita, T., Moriai, S., Iwata, T.: The 128-bit blockcipher CLEFIA (extended abstract). In: Biryukov, A. (ed.) FSE 2007. LNCS, vol. 4593, pp. 181–195. Springer, Heidelberg (2007)

33. Sorkin, A.: LUCIFER, a cryptographic algorithm. Cryptologia 8(1), 22–41 (1984)

34. Suzaki, T., Minematsu, K., Morioka, S., Kobayashi, E.: TWINE: a lightweight block cipher for multiple platforms. In: Knudsen, L.R., Wu, H. (eds.) SAC 2012. LNCS, vol. 7707, pp. 339–354. Springer, Heidelberg (2013)

35. Zabotin, I.A., Glazkov, G.P., Isaeva, V.B.: Cryptographic protection for information processing systems, Government Standard of the USSR, GOST 28147-89. Government Committee of the USSR for Standards. Technical report (1989)

Using Principal Component Analysis for Practical Biasing of Power Traces to Improve Power Analysis Attacks

Yongdae Kim[✉] and Haengseok Ko

The Attached Institute of Electronics and Telecommunications Research Institute,
P.O.Box 1, Yuseong, Daejeon 305-600, Korea
{kimyd,hsko}@ensec.re.kr

Abstract. Researchers have focused significant attention on side-channel attacks since the first power analysis attack was introduced. To date, several ideas have been introduced to efficiently analyze cryptographic modules. A power trace selection method for improving attack efficiency was recently presented; however, applying it involves many restrictions. Therefore, we propose a new selection method to improve power analysis attacks using principal component analysis. Our method is a practical one for biasing power traces. Our experimental results show that the proposed method improves attack efficiency in terms of the number of traces used for finding the secret key.

Keywords: Power analysis attack · Principal component analysis · Correlation power analysis · AES · DES

1 Introduction

In the past, cryptanalysis aimed at defeating cryptographic techniques had been focused on mathematical or algorithmic weaknesses. In 1999, however, P. Kocher et al. introduced a new class of attacks involving cryptographic modules [1]. They demonstrated that secret information, such as secret keys, can be retrieved by analyzing of the physical information leakages, including power consumption and electromagnetic emanation, from cryptographic modules as they processed encryption/decryption tasks. Because side-channel attacks are more accessible to the general public, these types of techniques have become the focus of many researchers. As a results, cryptographic modules are now scrutinized much more thoroughly, using an increasing array of methods for identifying physical vulnerabilities.

Side-channel attacks are classified by what side-channel information they exploit. For example, power analysis attacks and timing attacks exploit power consumption and timing information, respectively. Among these attacks, power analysis attacks have received considerable attention because they are very effective and can be conducted with relative ease and low cost with basic tools, such

© Springer International Publishing Switzerland 2014
H.-S. Lee and D.-G. Han (Eds.): ICISC 2013, LNCS 8565, pp. 109–120, 2014.
DOI: 10.1007/978-3-319-12160-4_7

as a PC and a digital oscilloscope [1]. Moreover, this attack does not leave evidence that an attack was performed on the cryptographic module.

In a power analysis attack, the adversary analyzes power consumption, which is directly measured from the target cryptographic module while it performs encryption (or decryption) computations. Several statistical distinguishers have been reported to analyze the leakages since the first difference-of-means distinguisher was proposed by P. Kocher et al. [1]. F.-X. Standaert et al. proposed a developed distinguisher using the variance test [2], and E. Brier et al. introduced a distinguisher that uses the Pearson correlation coefficient [3], to examine a linear relationship between the power consumption and a given power model. The correct key can be retrieved by finding the highest correlation peaks. Based on the assumption that an adversary can utilize a reference cryptographic module that has identical physical properties as the target module, S. Chari et al. proposed template attacks that utilize a multivariate model created from reference cryptographic modules [4]. This type of attacks is referred to as a profiling attack; several profiling attack techniques have been published [5].

Many researchers in this area are focusing on finding a more efficient distinguisher. This approach is based on the assumption that acquired power consumptions has distinguishable statistical distributions with respect to the power model. However, Y. Kim et al. proposed the novel idea of changing the distributions of power traces to improve conventional distinguishers [6]. They suggested that the Pearson correlation coefficient can be improved by biasing power traces. However, the specific point should be determined before the method is applied. They assert that the point can be heuristically determined, such as with simple power analysis or using a reference module; however, that is under a strong assumption.

To address the above issues, we propose a new method for selecting power traces, based on principal component analysis (PCA). Though similar in intent to the method described by [6], our method is also meant to provide a practical and systematic technique for making biasing power traces using PCA. To apply our method with this technique, an adversary does not have to determine the specific point in the measured power traces; only an approximate range of multiple points where the target computation is processed would need to be identified. Even data-independent points are included, our proposed method has less impact on performance; however, if an adversary finds wrong single specific point in traces when applying the conventional method [6], it is not able to improve the power analysis attack. We demonstrate this characteristic in our experimental results using the FPGA implementation of the Advanced Encryption Standard (AES) and the ASIC implementation of the Data Encryption Standard (DES).

2   Principal Component Analysis

This section describes the theoretical basis of principal component analysis (PCA) and introduces several related works that use PCA for side-channel attacks.

2.1   Theoretical Basis of PCA

Principal component analysis is a statistical technique for analyzing high-dimensional data. It is possible to reduce the data dimensionality by finding a new set of variables that retain most of the original information. The variables (i.e., principal components) are ordered by the fraction of the total information that each retains. For example, given a p-dimensional data set, $\boldsymbol{x}$, and the new set of variables, $\boldsymbol{z}$ is represented by

$$\boldsymbol{z} = \boldsymbol{A}\boldsymbol{x}, \tag{1}$$

where $\boldsymbol{A}$ is standard linear combination matrix consisting of the eigenvectors as $\boldsymbol{A} = (\boldsymbol{e}_1, \boldsymbol{e}_2, \cdots, \boldsymbol{e}_m)^T$. For example, the first principal component is calculated using the first eigenvector as

$$z_1 = \boldsymbol{e}_1^T \boldsymbol{x}^T. \tag{2}$$

$z_i (1 \leq i \leq m)$ is the i-th principal component containing as much of the variability in the data as possible in descending order. The variance of the i-th component corresponds to the i-th eigenvalue denoted by λ_i. Therefore, the eigenvalues can measure the proportional amount, R_{λ_i}, of variance of each components as

$$R_{\lambda_i} = \frac{\lambda_i}{\sum_{k=1}^{p} \lambda_k}, \tag{3}$$

where p is the number of eigenvalues.

2.2   Side-Channel Attacks Using PCA

Principal component analysis has been adapted in many fields, including image processing, facial recognition, economic trend analysis, and many others. In addition, PCA can be applied in side-channel attacks as pre-processing methods, distinguishers, etc.

Profiling attacks, such as the template attack, are based on multivariate normal distribution [4,5]. Therefore, it needs data-dependent points (known as *interesting points*) to create templates using a reference device. However, it contains an extremely large number of variables (time instants) to be considered. Therefore, profiling attacks are able to employ PCA to reduce the number of data dimensions in the profiling phase [7,8].

In 2010, Y. Souissi et al. suggested a new distinguisher using PCA [9]. In their approach, the measured traces are classified into several groups based on the corresponding power model, such as the Hamming distance value, after which PCA is applied to the mean (or variance) of each group. The eigenvalue is higher than others when the key candidate is correct.

PCA has also been used in a pre-processing technique for non-profiling attacks. Proposed by L. Batina et al., the technique improves the results of DPA by first using PCA to reduce noise [10]. In addition, they proposed a new distinguisher by calculating the absolute average value of the correlation on the PCA transformed traces.

As another approach to the side-channel attack, we deploy PCA as a pre-processing technique to increase the correlation coefficient. Details are provided in the next section.

3   Power Traces Selection Method

3.1   Conventional Method

To measure the performance of a power analysis attack, most researchers count the minimum number of power traces required to find a key [5,11]. Known as MTD (measurements to disclosure), this number also forms the basis of our comparative evaluation. The biasing traces technique enhances CPA in terms of MTD [6]. This is not a pre-processing technique like the others. Rather than considering noise reduction from power traces, its main idea is biasing statistical distributions by selecting a set of power traces. This is the first approach used to enhance CPA by selecting power traces.

Note that in order to apply this technique, an adversary must determine the most data-dependent point in the power trace. The point is typically acquired by calculating the correlation coefficient. This approach is the same as an attack by CPA on the target module. It is possible to obtain the point only if the adversary can employ a reference module. The authors argue that an adversary can determine the point by observing one trace; that is, by using simple power analysis (SPA). The author's assumption is feasible if there is only one sample point per clock cycle. However, the traces are typically captured from the target module at a higher sampling rate than the running frequency of the device. This means that there are several sample points per clock cycle. Furthermore, if the signal-to-noise ratio is extremely low in the captured traces, trace patterns will tend to be very similar, so it will be difficult to choose among the multiple sample points in practice.

Clearly, what is needed is a more practical means of selecting the traces. We propose a practical selection method for biasing traces using PCA. Our contribution is not based on a heuristic approach, such as SPA; rather, it is a systematic method. We demonstrate that PCA can also be utilized to bias the distribution of traces.

3.2   Proposed Method

We denote the number of traces and sample points per trace as n and p, respectively. The measured trace (denoted by $t_{ij}(1 \leq i \leq n, 1 \leq j \leq p)$) is centered by subtracting the means across all time instants, and expressed as

$$X = \begin{bmatrix} (t_{1,1} - \bar{t}_1) & \cdots & (t_{1,p} - \bar{t}_p) \\ \vdots & \ddots & \vdots \\ (t_{n,1} - \bar{t}_1) & \cdots & (t_{n,p} - \bar{t}_p) \end{bmatrix}, \tag{4}$$

where $\bar{t}_j$ is the mean value, which is calculated by

$$\bar{t}_j = \frac{1}{n} \sum_{i=1}^{n} t_{ij}. \tag{5}$$

We then, calculate the covariance matrix, C with p dimensions of the mean centered data, X. Eigenvalues and eigenvectors are calculated for the covariance. Finally, the first component is derived by selecting the eigenvector that is the largest eigenvalue of the eigenvector (the first one). The computed components for each of the traces (total n traces with p sample points) are represented as follows:

$$z_1 = e_1^T X^T, \tag{6}$$

where $z_1 = (z_{11}, z_{21}, \cdots, z_{n1})$.

We assume that biasing the first component is equivalent to carrying out the original data for each of the time instants, because each principal component is calculated by a linear transformation, and the coefficients (i.e., eigenvectors) are fixed. In other words, if we choose a subset from traces to increase the component variance, the variance of the original data is also increased by the subset. This is the main concept of our proposed method.

We have PCA transformed data with one dimension since we selected only one principal component. In [7], they assumed that the transformed data follows a Gaussian noise model. However, we do not use this assumption; therefore, we cannot use the conventional method as described in [6], even though the data has only one dimension. Instead, we sort the data by alternately choosing as the maximum and minimum values of the component. For example, if we have $z_1 = (z_{11}, z_{21}, z_{31}, z_{41}, z_{51}, z_{61}) = (4, 5, 9, 8, 1, 2)$, then we have the new order is $(9, 1, 8, 2, 5, 4)$, and the corresponding trace number order changes to $(z_{31}, z_{51}, z_{41}, z_{61}, z_{21}, z_{11})$ from $(z_{11}, z_{21}, z_{31}, z_{41}, z_{51}, z_{61})$. The adversary then select corresponding $n'(n' < n)$ traces from the first one in the new order. In the example, if the adversary choose 3 out of 6, then $3, 5, 4$-th traces are selected for analysis. This method can also create a truncated distribution if the component distribution follows the same normal distribution as the one proposed in [6].

The advantage of this approach is that an adversary does not have to choose a single time index that is the most relevant to the processed data. Instead, multiple time instants (sample points) can be employed to bias the power trace from the first principal component. Therefore, the subset of traces is more systematically determined by our method. We will show our experimental results in the next section.

4   Experimental Results

In this section, we present our experimental results using two different cryptographic algorithms and platforms. The first one is DES on an ASIC implementation provided by the DPA Contest 2008/2009 [12]; the second one is AES on an FPGA implementation. We used a SASEBO-GII platform for the second experiment [13].

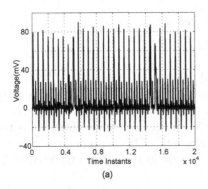 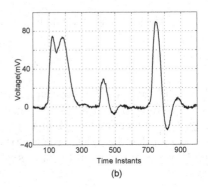

(a)   (b)

Fig. 1. Power consumption on the DES implementation (a) All rounds, and (b) The first round (our target trace)

4.1   DES Implementation Result

We applied our proposed method on power consumption traces from the DES implementation. The traces are available in the DPA Contest 2008/2009. Each trace had a very high signal-to-noise ratio (because an averaging technique was used to reduce the noise). In addition, DES was implemented on ASIC without any countermeasures [12].

We selected a subset of 200 traces from a set of 30,000 measured traces.[1] In addition, the total number of sample points in a trace is 20,000. Our target round was the first round; therefore, we designated a range of points 5,001 to 6,000 during which the first round encryption was processed. This rage was easily identified by observing the measured trace and counting the 16 distinct patterns (corresponding to the 16 rounds of DES). The first pattern corresponded to the first round of DES encryption. Figure 1 (a) and (b) show the DES power consumption trace for all rounds and the first round of encryption, respectively. Using the traces, we selected 200 traces by our proposed method. For comparison, we also randomly chose 200 out of the 30,000 traces. Without having selected this method, the power analysis attack would have used random traces because traces are typically captured using random plaintext (or ciphertext).

For our distinguisher, we employed the Pearson correlation coefficient [3]. Figure 2 (a) and (b) show the first DES S-Box key retrieving result using randomly selected traces and our proposed method, respectively. The y-axis represents the maximum absolute value of the correlation coefficient, and the x-axis indicates the number of traces for calculating the correlation coefficient. As shown in the figures, we successfully improved the correlation coefficient with our proposed method.

---

[1] Originally, the number of entire provided traces was 80,000. However, we downloaded 30,000 traces out of it for computational and storage space reasons.

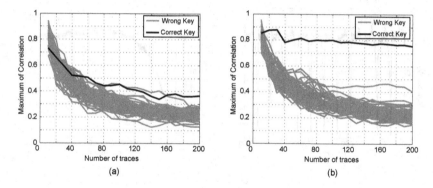

Fig. 2. DES key retrieving result using CPA: (a) Random traces, and (b) Proposed method

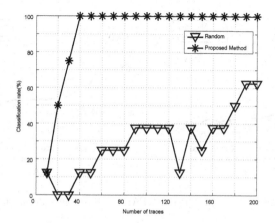

Fig. 3. Classification rate of the DES implementation

We define a classification rate, R_i as follows:

$$R_i(\%) = \frac{N_i^{ck}}{S_{keys}} \times 100, \qquad (7)$$

where N_i^{ck}, S_{keys} denote the number of correctly estimated keys using i traces, and all keys, respectively. For DES, $S_{keys} = 8$. Figure 3 indicates the classification rate using two different subsets of traces. The measurements to disclosure for all keys are significantly improved as shown in Fig. 3. We could obtain all S-Boxes keys at 40 traces if we employed our proposed method. In this experiment, we demonstrated only CPA as a distinguisher; however, other distinguishers, such as difference-of-means, can also be improved using our method. Most distinguishers are essentially based on finding different statistical distributions between power model and captured traces. Our method modifies the distribution of captured traces to easily find the statistical differences.

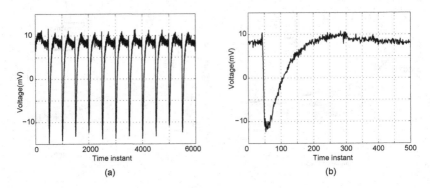

Fig. 4. Power consumption on the AES implementation (a) All rounds, and (b) The last round (our target trace)

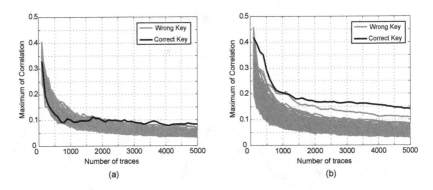

Fig. 5. AES key retrieving result using CPA: (a) Random traces, and (b) Proposed method

4.2   AES Implementation Result

We utilized the SASEBO-GII platform for our experiment on the AES hardware implementation [13]. For cryptographic operation, Xilinx Virtex-5 LX30 is embedded in the SASEBO-GII. We implemented straightforward AES with a 128-bit key length on the device. Countermeasures were not supported.

During encryption of randomly generated plaintext, we captured 100,000 power consumption traces from the SASEBO-GII board, without the aid of filters or amplifiers (see Fig. 4 (a)). Our target round was the last round in AES, so we pulled all sample points from the range of points 5401 to 5900, during which the last round of encryption operated. The truncated traces are shown in Fig. 4 (b).

Figure 5 (a) and (b) indicate results of the first S-Box key retrieving using random traces and biased traces selected by our proposed method. As with the DES implementation, the correlation could also be improved using our selected power traces. By increasing the correlation, CPA could easily discriminate the correct key candidates among other wrong keys using approximately 1,500 traces.

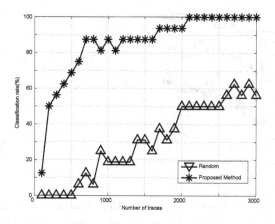

Fig. 6. Classification rate of the AES implementation

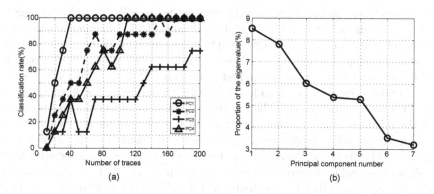

Fig. 7. Results using DES Implementation (a) Classification rate using the 1st (PC1) to 4th (PC4) components, and (b) The proportion of corresponding eigenvalues

Figure 6 represents the classification rate used both subsets of traces. Note that, in terms of MTD, the attack efficiency appears to improve under the proposed method, though the margin of improvement is lower than that of the DES implementation, likely due to the lower SNR in the AES power traces. In some cases, it is difficult to describe original data using only one component. Therefore, we then must focus on other principal components rather than on only the first component. In this case, it is assumed that other principal components could explain more of the data. The classification rate using other principal components is described in the next section.

4.3 Utilize Different Principal Components

To investigate the influence of the each principal component on the attack performance, we conducted our proposed method using four different principal

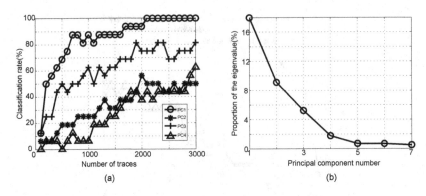

Fig. 8. Results using AES Implementation (a) Classification rate using the 1st (PC1) to 4th (PC4) components, and (b) The proportion of corresponding eigenvalues

components from the first to the fourth component in order of associated eigenvalue. The result is shown in Fig. 7 (a). In addition, Fig. 7 (b) represents the proportion of variance of the corresponding eigenvalues. From the results, we confirmed that the highest variance in the measured trace was observed in the PCA transformed data with the first eigenvector. However, the classification rate using the third component is lower than that when using the fourth component. This result indicates that the fourth component retained more information than the third one, but less than the first and second components, as expected.

Even in the AES implementation, we have the same result, as shown in Fig. 8 (a). The MTD is decreased by taking the eigenvector associated with the higher eigenvalue. Figure 8 (b) indicates the proportion of variance in order of decreasing eigenvalue. Interestingly, in the AES implementation, the third component shows a higher the classification rate than the second component. We found that, except for the first component, the proportion of the eigenvalue is not sufficient to determine the influence of the partial principal components. This phenomenon was also observed by [10], who found that their noise reduction by PCA did not always perform better by removing up to the higher eigenvalue. The principal component to be removed is variable according to the implementation.

4.4 Variance of the Measured Trace

In this section, we examine the variance of the subset of measured traces using our proposed method. Figure 9 (a) shows the first S-Box CPA results on the DES implementation using the biased traces by the first principal component. The figure is trimmed for legibility to include the highest absolute value of the correlation. The variance of all traces, and each subset of measured traces using the corresponding principal components, is represented in Fig. 9 (b). Although we did not determine one specific sample point, we could obtain biased traces using our proposed method. The same observation can be found in the result of the AES implementation (see, Fig. 10). Contrary to the DES results, the variance

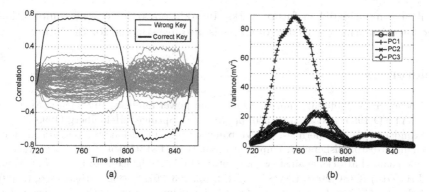

Fig. 9. Results of the DES Implementation (a) CPA Result using the biased traces by PC1, and (b) The variance of the subsets of traces

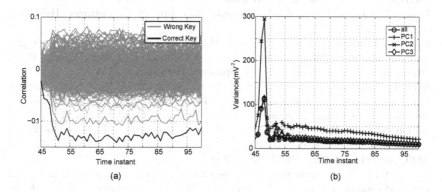

Fig. 10. Results of the AES Implementation (a) CPA Result using the biased traces by PC1, and (b) The variance of the subsets of traces

of traces using the first component is not always higher than the others. As illustrated in Fig. 10 (b), the variance of traces using the second component is the highest value at approximately the 48th sample point. However, around the point has a lower correlation than other points as shown in Fig. 10 (a). Therefore, it does not affect its performance.

5   Conclusion

In this paper, we proposed a new method for selecting biased power traces to improve the performance of power analysis attacks using principal component analysis. Unlike conventional biasing methods, the proposed method can be used without prior knowledge of the targeted module. Experimental results, using two different platforms and cryptographic algorithms, demonstrate that our approach is more systematic and practical. Other target modules and algorithms should be investigated in future works. In addition, reducing the computation time for calculating covariance of traces is also investigated for the future.

References

1. Kocher, P.C., Jaffe, J., Jun, B.: Differential power analysis. In: Wiener, M. (ed.) CRYPTO 1999. LNCS, vol. 1666, pp. 388–397. Springer, Heidelberg (1999)
2. Standaert, F.-X., Gierlichs, B., Verbauwhede, I.: Partition *vs.* comparison side-channel distinguishers: an empirical evaluation of statistical tests for univariate side-channel attacks against two unprotected CMOS devices. In: Lee, P.J., Cheon, J.H. (eds.) ICISC 2008. LNCS, vol. 5461, pp. 253–267. Springer, Heidelberg (2009)
3. Brier, E., Clavier, C., Olivier, F.: Correlation power analysis with a leakage model. In: Joye, M., Quisquater, J.-J. (eds.) CHES 2004. LNCS, vol. 3156, pp. 16–29. Springer, Heidelberg (2004)
4. Chari, S., Rao, J., Rohatgi, P.: Template attacks. In: Kaliski Jr, B.S., Koç, Ç.K., Paar, C. (eds.) CHES 2002. LNCS, vol. 2523, pp. 13–28. Springer, Heidelberg (2003)
5. Kim, Y., Homma, N., Aoki, T., Choi, H.: Security evaluation of cryptographic modules against profiling attacks. In: Kwon, T., Lee, M.-K., Kwon, D. (eds.) ICISC 2012. LNCS, vol. 7839, pp. 383–394. Springer, Heidelberg (2013)
6. Kim, Y., Sugawara, T., Homma, N., Aoki, T., Satoh, A.: Biasing power traces to improve correlation in power analysis attacks. In: International Workshop on Constructive Side-Channel Analysis and Secure Design (COSADE), pp. 77–80 (2012)
7. Archambeau, C., Peeters, E., Standaert, F.-X., Quisquater, J.-J.: Template attacks in principal subspaces. In: Goubin, L., Matsui, M. (eds.) CHES 2006. LNCS, vol. 4249, pp. 1–14. Springer, Heidelberg (2006)
8. Standaert, F.-X., Archambeau, C.: Using subspace-based template attacks to compare and combine power and electromagnetic information leakages. In: Oswald, E., Rohatgi, P. (eds.) CHES 2008. LNCS, vol. 5154, pp. 411–425. Springer, Heidelberg (2008)
9. Souissi, Y., Nassar, M., Guilley, S., Danger, J.-L., Flament, F.: First principal components analysis: a new side channel distinguisher. In: Rhee, K.-H., Nyang, D.H. (eds.) ICISC 2010. LNCS, vol. 6829, pp. 407–419. Springer, Heidelberg (2011)
10. Batina, L., Hogenboom, J., van Woudenberg, J.G.J.: Getting more from PCA: first results of using principal component analysis for extensive power analysis. In: Dunkelman, O. (ed.) CT-RSA 2012. LNCS, vol. 7178, pp. 383–397. Springer, Heidelberg (2012)
11. Peeters, E., Standaert, F.-X., Quisquater, J.-J.: Power and electromagnetic analysis: improved model, consequences and comparisons. J. Integr. VLSI J. (Special Issue: Embedded Cryptographic Hardware) **40**, 52–60 (2007)
12. DPA Contest (2008/2009). http://www.dpacontest.org
13. Research Center for Information Security: Side-channel Attack Standard Evaluation BOard (SASEBO). http://www.rcis.aist.go.jp/special/SASEBO

Cryptanalysis 1

Impossible Differential Attack
on Reduced-Round TWINE

Xuexin Zheng[1] and Keting Jia[2]([✉])

[1] Key Laboratory of Cryptologic Technology and Information Security,
Ministry of Education, School of Mathematics, Shandong University, Jinan, China
zhxuexin@mail.sdu.edu.cn
[2] Department of Computer Science and Technology, Tsinghua University,
Beijing, China
ktjia@mail.tsinghua.edu.cn

Abstract. TWINE, proposed at the ECRYPT Workshop on Lightweight Cryptography in 2011, is a 64-bit lightweight block cipher consisting of 36 rounds with 80-bit or 128-bit keys. In this paper, we give impossible differential attacks on both versions of the cipher, which is an improvement over what the designers claimed to be the best possible. Although our results are not the best considering different cryptanalysis methods, our algorithm which can filter wrong subkeys that have more than 80 bits and 128 bits for TWINE-80 and TWINE-128 respectively shows some novelty. Besides, some observations which may be used to mount other types of attacks are given. Overall, making use of some complicated subkey relations and time-memory tradeoff trick, the time, data and memory complexity of attacking 23-round TWINE-80 are $2^{79.09}$ 23-round encryptions, $2^{57.85}$ chosen plaintexts and $2^{78.04}$ blocks respectively. Besides, the impossible differential attack on 24-round TWINE-128 needs $2^{58.1}$ chosen plaintexts, $2^{126.78}$ 24-round encryptions and $2^{125.61}$ blocks of memory.

Keywords: TWINE · Lightweight block cipher · Impossible differential attack

1 Introduction

Impossible differential attack is a powerful cryptanalysis method introduced by Biham et al. [2] and Knudsen [10] independently. It is often used in cryptanalyzing block ciphers with (generalized) Feistel structures and SPN structures. The main trick of this method is to find an impossible differential path as long as possible and then extend two truncated differentials from it. Then any candidate subkey involved in both truncated differentials, which can lead to the impossible differential path is a wrong key and should be discarded. So long as enough

This work is partially supported by the National 973 Program of China (Grant No. 2013CB834205), and the National Natural Science Foundation of China (Grant No. 61133013).

H.-S. Lee and D.-G. Han (Eds.): ICISC 2013, LNCS 8565, pp. 123–143, 2014.
DOI: 10.1007/978-3-319-12160-4_8

Table 1. Summary of attacks on TWINE

Key (bits)	Number of rounds	Data (block)	Time (encryption)	Memory (block)	Attack	Source
80	22	2^{62}	$2^{68.43}$	2^{67}	Saturation attack	[15]
	23	$2^{57.85}$	$2^{79.09}$	$2^{78.04}$	Impossible differential attack	Section 4
	36	2^{60}	$2^{79.10}$	2^{8}	Biclique attack	[6]
128	23	$2^{62.81}$	$2^{106.14}$	2^{103}	Saturation attack	[15]
	24	$2^{58.1}$	$2^{126.78}$	$2^{125.61}$	Impossible differential attack	Section 5
	25	2^{48}	2^{122}	2^{125}	MITM	[3]
	27	$2^{62.95}$	$2^{119.5}$	2^{60}	Key-difference invariant bias attack	[1]
	36	2^{60}	$2^{126.82}$	2^{8}	Biclique attack	[6]

plaintext-ciphertext pairs are collected, an attacker can eliminate all wrong keys and recover the right key.

Due to the requirement of lightweight encryption algorithms which are used in tiny computing devices, such as RFID and sensor network nodes, many lightweight block ciphers have been proposed, for example PRESENT, KATAN, KTANTAN, KLEIN, LED, HIGHT, LBlock, TWINE [4,5,7–9,11–16], and much more. TWINE is a 64-bit lightweight block cipher designed by Suzaki, Minematsu, Morioka and Kobayashi in [15], which has two versions supporting 80-bit and 128-bit keys respectively. Consisting of 36 rounds, TWINE employs Type-2 generalized Feistel structure with 16 nibbles. When TWINE was proposed, the designers presented security evaluation including impossible differential attacks on 23-round TWINE-80 and 24-round TWINE-128 which were the most powerful attacks given by the designers. Unfortunately, the time complexity of their impossible differential attacks may have a flaw and may lead to a complexity of more than exhaustive key search. Besides the designers' security analysis, Çoban et al. gave an biclique analysis of full round TWINE [6], Boztaş et al. gave an multidimensional meet-in-the-middle attack on reduced-round TWINE-128 [3], Bogdanov et al. gave an key-difference invariant bias attack on reduced-round TWINE-128 [1]. All the results are summarized in Table 1. Note that although our results are not the best considering different cryptanalysis methods, our algorithm which can filter wrong subkeys that have more than 80 bits and 128 bits for TWINE-80 and TWINE-128 respectively shows some novelty. Besides, some observations which may be used to mount other types of attacks are given.

Our Contribution. This paper focuses on the security of TWINE against impossible differential attack. The novelty includes the following aspects:

– Propose an algorithm to filter wrong subkeys which exceeds the master key size;

- Several observations on key relations and optimization of our algorithm are given;
- Several tables are precomputed to decrease the time complexity.

This paper is organized as follows. In Sect. 2, we present the necessary notations and a simple description of the TWINE encryption algorithm and the key schedule. Section 3 gives useful observations and the reason for our choice of the impossible differential paths. Section 4 first explains the flaw of attacks in [15], and then shows the impossible differential attack against 23-round TWINE-80. The result of attacking 24-round TWINE-128 is showed in Sect. 5. Section 6 concludes the paper.

2 Preliminaries

Some notations used in this paper and a simple description of the TWINE algorithm are given in this section.

2.1 Notations

$\tilde{0}^m$: the concatenation of m 4-bit 0s. $\quad C_L^r, C_H^r$: constants used in the Key Schedule of TWINE.

$x\|y$: the concatenation of x and y. $\quad k(i,j)$: $k_i \oplus s[k_j]$, where s stands for 4-bit sbox.

$A_{[i_1,...,i_m]}$: $A_{i_1}\|...\|A_{i_m}$. $\quad RK_{[0,...,7]}^r$: the 32-bit round subkey of round r.

α_{i+1}: one possible value for output difference of sbox with input difference α_i.

β_{i+1}: one possible value for output difference of sbox with input difference β_i.

$\triangle s[b]$: $\{s[x] \oplus s[x \oplus b]\|x \in \{0,...,f\}\}$ the set of output differences of s with input difference b.

$a \in \triangle s[b]$: a is one of the possible output difference of sbox with input difference b.

$(X_0^r, X_1^r, ..., X_{14}^r, X_{15}^r)$: the 64-bit input value of round r.

$\#RK_p^r$: the number of possible values of RK_p^r for each plaintext-ciphertext pair.

2.2 Description of TWINE

TWINE is a 64-bit block cipher with 80-bit or 128-bit key. The global structure of TWINE is a variant of Type-2 generalized Feistel structure with 16 nibbles. Consisting of 8 4-bit S-boxes and a diffusion permutation π as described in Table 2, the round function of TWINE is showed in Fig. 1. Expressed in a formula form, the round function encrypts an input value of round r to the input value of round $r + 1$ in the following two steps:

$$X_{2j+1}^r \leftarrow s[X_{2j}^r \oplus RK_j^r] \oplus X_{2j+1}^r (j = 0, ..., 7),$$
$$X_{\pi(i)}^{r+1} \leftarrow X_i^r.$$

For both versions of TWINE, the round function is iterated for 36 times and the diffusion permutation is omitted in the last round.

The key schedules of TWINE-80 and TWINE-128 produce 36 32-bit round subkeys $RK_{[0,...,7]}^r$ $(r = 1, ..., 36)$ from the 80-bit master key (denoted as $k_0, ..., k_{19}$) and 128-bit master key (denoted as $k_0, ..., k_{31}$) respectively as described in Algorithm D.1. and Algorithm D.2. (Appendix D).

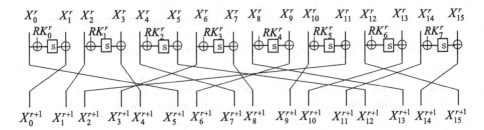

Fig. 1. Round function of TWINE

Table 2. S-box and π permutation

x	0	1	2	3	4	5	6	7	8	9	A	B	C	D	E	F
$s[x]$	C	0	F	A	2	B	9	5	8	3	D	7	1	E	6	4

x	0	1	2	3	4	5	6	7	8	9	10	11	12	13	14	15
$\pi(x)$	5	0	1	4	7	12	3	8	13	6	9	2	15	10	11	14

3   Observations and 14-Round Impossible Differentials of TWINE

This section gives several useful observations and the reason for our choice of the impossible differential path. Observation 1 is used in [15]. For the sake of completeness, we describe it here. Observation 2, 3, 4, 5 are about the subkeys. We give the round subkeys of TWINE-80 from round 1 to round 5 and the round subkeys of TWINE-128 from round 1 to round 7 in Table D.1 and Table D.2 (Appendix D).

Observation 1. *For any input difference $a(\neq 0)$ and output difference $b(\in \triangle s[a])$ of the sbox in TWINE, the average number of pairs that satisfy the differential characteristic $(a \rightarrow b)$ is $\frac{16}{7}$. Given an 8-bit pair (X_{2i}^r, X_{2i+1}^r) and $(X_{2i}^r \oplus a, X_{2i+1}^r \oplus b)$, the probability that RK_i^r leads to the sbox differential characteristic $(a \rightarrow b)$ is 7^{-1}.*

Observation 2. *The round subkeys of TWINE-80 satisfy the following equations among four adjacent rounds.*

$$RK_5^{r+2} = RK_1^r; RK_3^{r+2} = RK_5^r; RK_6^{r+2} = s^{-1}[RK_7^{r+1} \oplus RK_0^r] \oplus C_L^{r+1}, (1 \leq r \leq 34);$$
$$RK_4^{r+3} = RK_3^r; RK_0^{r+3} = RK_4^r; RK_1^{r+3} = RK_6^r \oplus C_H^{r+2}; RK_2^{r+3} = RK_7^r, (1 \leq r \leq 33);$$
$$RK_6^{r+3} = RK_2^r \oplus s[RK_7^r] \oplus C_L^{r+2}, (1 \leq r \leq 33).$$

Observation 3. *The round subkeys of TWINE-80 satisfy the following equations among RK^1, RK^2, RK^{21}, RK^{22} and RK^{23}.*

$$f_1(RK_{[2,7]}^2, RK_2^{22}, RK_1^{23}) = 0; \qquad f_2(RK_1^1, RK_4^2, RK_7^{21}, RK_{[3,4,6]}^{22}, RK_{[0,4]}^{23}) = 0;$$
$$f_3(RK_6^2, RK_{[2,5,6]}^{22}) \quad\;\; = 0; \qquad f_4(RK_{[5,7]}^1, RK_{[4,7]}^{21}, RK_6^{22}, RK_{[0,4]}^{23}) \;\;\, = 0;$$
$$f_6(RK_{[1,6]}^1, RK_{[3,4,5]}^{23}) \quad\; = 0; \qquad f_5(RK_5^1, RK_6^2, RK_4^{21}, RK_{[1,5]}^{22}, RK_3^{23}) \;\; = 0;$$
$$f_7(RK_0^1, RK_7^2, RK_{[2,5,6]}^{23}) = 0; \qquad p$$

The precise expression of functions $f_i(i = 1, ..., 8)$ are shown in Appendix A.

Observation 4. *The round subkeys of TWINE-128 satisfy the following equations among six adjacent rounds.*

$$RK_7^{r+5} = RK_2^{r+1} \oplus s[RK_6^r]; RK_6^{r+5} = RK_4^r \oplus s[RK_2^{r+1} \oplus s[RK_6^r]], (1 \le r \le 31);$$
$$RK_7^{r+4} = RK_2^r \oplus s[RK_2^{r+3}]; RK_3^{r+4} = RK_7^r \oplus C_L^{r+3} \oplus s[RK_1^{r+1}], (1 \le r \le 32);$$
$$RK_4^{r+4} = RK_0^r; RK_5^{r+4} = RK_1^r; RK_0^{r+4} = RK_5^r; RK_2^{r+4} = RK_6^r, (1 \le r \le 32);$$
$$RK_1^{r+3} = RK_3^r \oplus C_H^{r+2}, (1 \le r \le 33).$$

Observation 5. *The round subkeys of TWINE-128 satisfy the following equations among RK^1, RK^2, RK^3, RK^4, RK^{21}, RK^{22}, RK^{23} and RK^{24}.*

$$g_1(RK_1^1, RK_{[2,3]}^{22}, RK_5^{23}) = 0;$$
$$g_2(RK_6^1, RK_2^2, RK_0^{21}, RK_{[6,7]}^{24}) = 0;$$
$$g_3(RK_{[0,1]}^3, RK_0^{21}, RK_2^{22}, RK_{[5,7]}^{23}, RK_2^{24}) = 0;$$
$$g_4(RK_5^1, RK_3^2, RK_1^3, RK_2^{21}, RK_6^{22}, RK_0^{23}, RK_{[2,3]}^{24}) = 0;$$
$$g_5(RK_{[0,1]}^1, RK_5^3, RK_0^4, RK_{[0,2]}^{22}, RK_{[1,2,4]}^{23}, RK_{[5,7]}^{24}) = 0;$$
$$g_6(RK_{[0,7]}^1, RK_{[4,5]}^2, RK_5^3, RK_{[0,2]}^{22}, RK_{[1,2,3,4,7]}^{23}, RK_{[5,7]}^{24}) = 0;$$
$$g_7(RK_{[2,4,6]}^1, RK_{[0,2,3,7]}^2, RK_{[1,3]}^3, RK_2^{21}, RK_2^{22}, RK_{[0,3]}^{23}, RK_{[4,5]}^{24}) = 0;$$
$$g_8(RK_{[2,4,6]}^1, RK_{[0,2,6,7]}^2, RK_{[1,3,5]}^3, RK_0^{22}, RK_{[0,1,2,4]}^{23}, RK_{[4,5,7]}^{24}) = 0;$$
$$g_9(RK_{[2,4,5,6]}^1, RK_{[2,3,7]}^2, RK_{[0,1,3]}^3, RK_{[0,2]}^{21}, RK_6^{22}, RK_{[0,5]}^{23}, RK_{[1,4]}^{24}) = 0.$$

The precise expression of functions $g_i(i = 1, ..., 9)$ are shown in Appendix A.

The 14-Round Impossible Differential Paths. Several 14-round impossible differential paths are given in [15]. This paper uses $(0||\alpha||\tilde{0}^{14}) \xrightarrow{14r} (\tilde{0}^7||\beta||\tilde{0}^8)$ and $(\tilde{0}^5||\alpha||\tilde{0}^{10}) \xrightarrow{14r} (\tilde{0}^{11}||\beta||\tilde{0}^4)$ in attacking TWINE-80 and TWINE-128 respectively. Our choice of the impossible differential paths is determined by the following two reasons. Making use of the relations in Observation 2 and Observation 4, the truncated differential paths involve the least number of round subkeys. What's more, the truncated differential paths involve subkeys that have less complicated equations in Observation 3 and Observation 5. Observation 6 is used in [15]. For the sake of completeness, we give a clear description. Observation 6 and 7 are useful in selecting more accurate plaintext/ciphertext pairs for attacking TWINE-80 and TWINE-128 respectively. Observation 8 is used in key recovery phase of our attacking TWINE-80. Its proof gives a detailed computation and analysis of the number of co responding subkeys that passing the differential path.

Observation 6. *If the impossible differential $(0||\alpha||\tilde{0}^{14}) \xrightarrow{14r} (\tilde{0}^7||\beta||\tilde{0}^8)$ is extended 4 rounds ahead and 5 rounds behind, then the input difference is of the form*

$$(\alpha_3, \alpha_4, 0, \alpha_2, \tilde{0}^6, \alpha_1, \alpha_2'', \alpha_1', \alpha_2', 0, \alpha)$$

where $\alpha \neq 0$, $\alpha_2' \in \Delta s[\alpha_1']$, $\alpha_1' \in \Delta s[\alpha]$, $\alpha_3 \in \Delta s[\alpha_2]$, $\alpha_2'' \in \Delta s[\alpha_1]$, $\alpha_4 \in \Delta s[\alpha_3]$, $\alpha_2 \in \Delta s[\alpha_1]$, $\alpha_1 \in \Delta s[\alpha]$;
and the output difference is of the form

$$(0, \beta_1', 0, \beta_3, \beta_2', \beta_3', \beta, x, \beta_4, \beta_5, \beta_2, \beta_3''', \beta_2'', \beta_3'', \tilde{0}^2)$$

where $\beta \neq 0$, $\beta_3' \in \triangle s[\beta_2']$, $\beta_5 \in \triangle s[\beta_4]$, $\beta_3''' \in \triangle s[\beta_2]$, $\beta_3'' \in \triangle s[\beta_2'']$, $\beta_2' \in \triangle s[\beta_1']$, $\beta_4 \in \triangle s[\beta_3]$, $\beta_3 \in \triangle s[\beta_2]$, $\beta_1' \in \triangle s[\beta]$;
$Pr(\alpha\beta \neq 0$, and all the relations hold$) = (\frac{15}{16})^2 \cdot (\frac{7}{16})^{15} = 2^{-18.08}$.

Observation 7. *If the impossible differential* $(\tilde{0}^5 || \alpha || \tilde{0}^{10}) \overset{14r}{\nrightarrow} (\tilde{0}^{11} || \beta || \tilde{0}^4)$ *is extended 5 rounds on the top and the bottom of it respectively, then the input difference is of the form*

$$(\alpha_4, \alpha_5, 0, \alpha_3, \alpha_2', \alpha_3', \tilde{0}^3, \alpha_1''', \alpha_2, \alpha_3''', \alpha_2'', \alpha_3'', \alpha, y)$$

where $\alpha \neq 0$, $\alpha_5 \in \triangle s[\alpha_4]$, $\alpha_3' \in \triangle s[\alpha_2']$, $\alpha_3''' \in \triangle s[\alpha_2]$, $\alpha_3'' \in \triangle s[\alpha_2'']$, $\alpha_2' \in \triangle s[\alpha_1']$, $\alpha_1' \in \triangle s[\alpha]$, $\alpha_3 \in \triangle s[\alpha_2]$, $\alpha_4 \in \triangle s[\alpha_3]$;
and the output difference is of the form

$$(\beta_2', \beta_3', \beta_4, \beta_5, 0, \beta_1', \beta_2'', \beta_3'', 0, \beta_3, \tilde{0}^2, \beta, x, \beta_2, \beta_3''')$$

where $\beta \neq 0$, $\beta_3' \in \triangle s[\beta_2']$, $\beta_5 \in \triangle s[\beta_4]$, $\beta_3''' \in \triangle s[\beta_2]$, $\beta_3'' \in \triangle s[\beta_2'']$, $\beta_2' \in \triangle s[\beta_1']$, $\beta_4 \in \triangle s[\beta_3]$, $\beta_3 \in \triangle s[\beta_2]$, $\beta_1' \in \triangle s[\beta]$;
$Pr(\alpha\beta \neq 0$, and all the belonging relations holds$) = (\frac{15}{16})^2 \cdot (\frac{7}{16})^{16} = 2^{-19.27}$.

Observation 8. *For a plaintext-ciphertext pair satisfying the input-output difference relations in Observation 6, the following can be deduced according to the differential path in attacking TWINE-80:*

(1) *Given* $RK^1_{[1,6,7]}$, RK^2_6 *that pass the differential path, then* $\frac{16}{7}$ *values of* RK^1_2 *on average can pass the path and be computed;*

(2) *Given* $RK^{23}_{[2,3,4,5]}$ *that pass the differential path, then* $\frac{16}{7}$ *values of* RK^{22}_0 *on average can pass the path and be computed;*

(3) *Given* $RK^{23}_{[3,6]}$ *that pass the differential path, then* $\frac{16}{7}$ *values of* RK^{22}_4 *on average can pass the path and be computed;*

(4) *Given* $RK^{23}_{[1,3,4,5]}$, $RK^{22}_{[0,5]}$ *that pass the differential path, then* $(\frac{16}{7})^2$ *values of* RK^{21}_7 *on average can pass the path and be computed.*

Proof

(1) Compute X^4_2 using $RK^4_1 = RK^1_6 \oplus C^3_H$ and $(\triangle X^4_2, \triangle X^4_3)$, where we get $\#X^4_2 = 16/7$ for every RK^1_6. Besides, $X^3_{11} = X^2_{14}$ is computed using RK^1_7 by partial encryption. Then X^3_{10} is computed using $RK^3_5 = RK^1_1$ by partial decryption, where we get $\#X^3_{10} = 16/7$ for every $RK^1_{[1,6,7]}$. After that, together with the known $X^2_{13} = X^1_8$ and RK^2_6, we get the values of X^2_{12} where $\#X^2_{12} = 16/7$ for every $(RK^1_{[1,6,7]}, RK^2_6)$. Finally, with the knowledge of $X^1_{[4,5]}$, we can compute RK^1_2 with $\#RK^1_2 = 16/7$ for every $(RK^1_{[1,6,7]}, RK^2_6)$.

(2) Compute $X^{21}_3 = X^{20}_6$ using $RK^{20}_3 = RK^{23}_4$ and $(\triangle X^{20}_6, \triangle X^{20}_7)$, where we get $\#X^{21}_3 = 16/7$ for every RK^{23}_4. Besides, X^{22}_4 is computed using RK^{23}_3. Then X^{22}_1 is computed using $RK^{21}_1 = RK^{23}_5$, where we get $\#X^{22}_1 = 16/7$ for

every $RK_{[3,4,5]}^{23}$. What's more, X_0^{22} is computed using RK_2^{23}. Then together with the known $X_0^{22} = X_0^{23}$, we can compute RK_0^{22} with $\#RK_0^{22} = 16/7$ for every $RK_{[2,3,4,5]}^{23}$.

(3) Compute $X_9^{22} = X_{10}^{21}$ using $RK_5^{21} = RK_3^{23}$ and $(\triangle X_{10}^{21}, \triangle X_{11}^{21})$, where we get $\#X_9^{22} = 16/7$ for every RK_3^{23}. Besides, X_8^{22} is computed using RK_6^{23}. Then together with X_6^{23}, we can compute RK_4^{22} with $\#RK_4^{22} = 16/7$ for every $RK_{[3,6]}^{23}$.

(4) As just mentioned, $16/7$ values of X_9^{22} is computed for every RK_3^{23}. Since $X_9^{22} = X_{10}^{21}$, we get $16/7$ values of X_{10}^{21} for every RK_3^{23}. Besides, Compute $X_{13}^{20} = X_8^{19}$ using $RK_4^{19} = RK_0^{22}$ and $(\triangle X_8^{19}, \triangle X_9^{19})$, where we get $\#X_{13}^{20} = 16/7$ for every RK_0^{22}. Then X_{12}^{20} is computed using $RK_6^{20} = RK_1^{23} \oplus C_H^{22}$, where $\#X_{12}^{20} = (16/7)^2$ for every $(RK_{[1,3]}^{23}, RK_0^{22})$. Furthermore, compute X_{14}^{22} using RK_5^{23}, compute X_{10}^{22} using RK_4^{23}, then compute X_{11}^{22} using RK_5^{22}. With the knowledge of X_{12}^{20}, X_{14}^{22} and X_{11}^{22}, we can compute RK_7^{21} with $\#RK_7^{21} = (16/7)^2$ for every $(RK_{[1,3,4,5]}^{23}, RK_{[0,5]}^{22})$. □

4 Impossible Differential Cryptanalysis of 23-Round TWINE-80

4.1 Analysis of Suzaki et al.'s Attack on TWINE-80

In the last paragraph of page 9 in the TWINE-80 attack [15], the authors said that *In the key elimination we need to COMPUTE some other subkeys (64 bits in total), which is uniquely determined by the key of Eq. (5). These keys contain RK_4^{19}, RK_4^{21}, and RK_6^{23} and they can cause a contradiction with other keys.* Therefore, an attacker has to compute these *other subkeys* using the 80-bit $(\mathcal{K}_1, \mathcal{K}_2, \mathcal{K}_3)$, and then check whether there is a contradiction. Unfortunately, it seems that this part is omitted in their time complexity formula $2^{50.11+10} \cdot 2^{20} \cdot 22/(23 \cdot 8) = 2^{77.04}$. Because we notice that $2^{50.11+10}$ means the number of plaintext/ciphertext pairs, 2^{20} stands for the time regarding $\mathcal{K}_1$, and $22/(23 \cdot 8)$ is the time regarding $(\mathcal{K}_2, \mathcal{K}_3)$. If the omitted time is considered, the time complexity is supposed to be bigger than exhaustive key search. Take the computation of $RK_6^{23} = s[RK_2^{23}] \oplus s[RK_1^{21}] \oplus s^{-1}[RK_7^2 \oplus RK_0^1]$ as an example[1], we know that the numbers of RK_2^{23}, RK_1^{21}, RK_7^2, and RK_0^1 that pass the differential path are all $16/7$ for one right plaintext/ciphertext pair. Hence the time for checking whether there is a contradiction regarding RK_6^{23} is $(16/7)^4$. Multiplied by the extra $(16/7)^4$, the time complexity is $2^{77.04} \cdot (16/7)^4 = 2^{81.81}$. It seems that there is a similar problem in the analysis of their attack on TWINE-128.

4.2 Impossible Differential Attack on 23-Round TWINE-80

In this section, we present an impossible differential attack on 23-round TWINE-80 using the impossible differential $(0||\alpha||\tilde{0}^{14}) \xrightarrow{14r} (\tilde{0}^7||\beta||\tilde{0}^8)$. This paper uses

---

[1] Reference [15] ignores some known constants C_H^r, C_L^r in their subkey relations.

the same impossible differential as in [15] for TWINE-80, because it leads to the least number of involved round subkeys. The 14-round impossible differential is extended 4 rounds on the top and 5 rounds on the bottom. The extended truncated differential paths are showed in Fig. 2. Making use of Observation 2, eight equations $RK_3^3 = RK_5^1$, $RK_5^3 = RK_1^1$, $RK_1^4 = RK_1^1 \oplus C_H^3$, $RK_0^{19} = RK_0^{22}$, $RK_3^{20} = RK_4^{23}$, $RK_6^{20} = RK_1^{23}$, $RK_1^{21} = RK_5^{23}$ and $RK_5^{21} = RK_3^{23}$ are discovered. Hence the added 9 rounds involve $44 + 68 = 112$ bits round subkeys (see Tables 3 and 4). Therefore, $112 - 80 = 32$ bits subkey information are redundant, which are described in Observation 3.

The idea of attacking is to discard these $\mathcal{K}_{112}$ which pass the truncated differential paths under the condition that $\mathcal{K}_{112}$ is indeed generated from one 80-bit master key according to the key schedule. Denote $\mathcal{K}_0 = (RK_{[1,7]}^1, RK_{[0,1,7]}^{23})$, $\mathcal{K}_1 = (RK_{[0,2,3,5,6]}^1, RK_{[2,4,6,7]}^2, RK_{[1,3,5]}^{22}, RK_{[2,3,5]}^{23})$, $\mathcal{K}_2 = (RK_{[4,7]}^{21}, RK_{[0,2,4,6]}^{22}, RK_{[4,6]}^{23})$. The main steps of our attack are as follows. Firstly, some tables are computed in the precomputation phase for the sake of time and memory balance. Secondly, for every guess of $\mathcal{K}_0$, combine $(\mathcal{K}_1, \mathcal{K}_2)$ which pass the truncated differentials and all the subkeys equations. And then the $\mathcal{K}_1$ in the combined $(\mathcal{K}_1, \mathcal{K}_2)$ is removed from an initialized subkey table. After all the chosen plaintext-ciphertext pairs are utilized, store $\mathcal{K}_0$ and the finally remained $\mathcal{K}_1$. (Notice that once $(\mathcal{K}_0, \mathcal{K}_1)$ is known, $\mathcal{K}_2$ can be computed uniquely according to the subkey equations.) Finally, do trial encryptions for the remaining keys.

Table 3. Subkeys involved in the extended head path of attacking 23-r TWINE-80

Round r	RK_0^r	RK_1^r	RK_2^r	RK_3^r	RK_4^r	RK_5^r	RK_6^r	RK_7^r
Round 1	k_1	k_3	k_4	k_6		k_{14}	k_{15}	k_{16}
Round 2			k_8		k_{17}		$k_{19} \oplus C_L^1$	$k(1,0)$
Round 3				k_{14}		k_3		
Round 4		$k_{15} \oplus C_H^3$						

Table 4. Subkeys involved in the extended tail path of attacking 23-r TWINE-80

Round r	RK_0^r	RK_1^r	RK_2^r	RK_3^r	RK_4^r	RK_5^r	RK_6^r	RK_7^r
Round 19					$RK_4^{19} = RK_0^{22}$			
Round 20				$RK_3^{20} = RK_4^{23}$			$RK_6^{20} = RK_1^{23} \oplus C_H^{22}$	
Round 21		$RK_1^{21} = RK_5^{23}$			RK_4^{21}	$RK_5^{21} = RK_3^{23}$		RK_7^{21}
Round 22	RK_0^{22}	RK_1^{22}	RK_2^{22}	RK_3^{22}	RK_4^{22}	RK_5^{22}	RK_6^{22}	
Round 23	RK_0^{23}	RK_1^{23}	RK_2^{23}	RK_3^{23}	RK_4^{23}	RK_5^{23}	RK_6^{23}	RK_7^{23}

Table 5. KT_i tables

Table	Index	Content[a]
KT_2	$(RK_1^1, RK_0^{23}, RK_4^{23}, RK_6^{22}, RK_7^{21}, RK_{[3,4]}^{22})$	RK_4^2
KT_3	$RK_{[2,5,6]}^{22}$	RK_6^2
KT_4	$(RK_7^1, RK_0^{23}, RK_4^{23}, RK_5^{22}, RK_5^1, RK_4^{21})$	RK_7^{21}
KT_5	$(RK_3^{23}, RK_6^2, RK_5^{22}, RK_5^1, RK_4^{21})$	RK_1^{22}
KT_8	$(RK_7^1, RK_7^{23}, RK_7^{22}, RK_1^{21}, RK_0^{22})$	RK_2^1

[a]The number of possible values of the subkey stored in content is 1 for each index.

Precomputation. Firstly, two tiny tables are precomputed for sbox. A difference distribution table for sbox is computed to facilitate choosing more accurate plaintext-ciphertext pairs using Observation 6. So that $\alpha_1 \in \Delta s[\alpha]$ can be examined by looking up the table. Besides, another tiny table is needed in computing round subkeys, which stores the input pairs of sbox with input and output difference as index. Take the computation of RK_0^1 as an example, suppose a plaintext pair satisfies $\Delta X_1^1 \in \Delta s[\Delta X_0^1]$, looking up this table with index $(\Delta X_0^1, \Delta X_1^1)$ gives the input pair (In1, In2) for sbox, and then $RK_0^1 = In1 \oplus X_0^1$.

Secondly, in order to decrease time complexity at the cost of a little memory in key recovery phase, five tables KT_i $(i = 2,3,4,5,8)$ are precomputed for functions f_i. Hence the computation of f_i can be replaced by one table looking up. A detailed description of these tables is showed in Table 5.

Data Collection. Choose 2^n structures of plaintexts, and each structure contains plaintexts with the following form $(p_0, p_1, \gamma_0, p_2, \gamma_1, \gamma_2, \gamma_3, \gamma_4, \gamma_5, \gamma_6, p_3, p_4, p_5, p_6, \gamma_7, p_7)$, where $\gamma_i(i = 0, ..., 7)$ are constants in each structure and $p_i(i = 0, ..., 7)$ take all possible values. As a result, there are 2^{32} plaintexts in each structure and we can get 2^{n+63} plaintext pairs.

Ask for encryptions of the plaintexts in each structure and get the corresponding ciphertexts. The ciphertext is denoted as $(C_0, C_1, C_2, C_3, C_4, C_5, C_6, C_7, C_8, C_9, C_{10}, C_{11}, C_{12}, C_{13}, C_{14}, C_{15})$. A hash table with index $C_{[0,2,14,15]}$ is built to choose the pairs that satisfy the condition $\Delta C_{[0,2,14,15]} = 0$. The pairs that do not satisfy the condition are discarded. Hence there are $2^{n+63-16} = 2^{n+47}$ pairs remained.

Furthermore, filter the pairs using the plaintext and ciphertext difference relations listed in Observation 6. Therefore, $2^{n+47-18.08} = 2^{n+28.92}$ pairs are finally obtained.

Key Recovery. A detailed key recovery procedure is showed in the following Algorithm 1. It's main steps are as follows. Firstly, 20-bit $\mathcal{K}_0$ is guessed. And then for each plaintext-ciphertext pair, substeps (1.2.1) to (1.2.10) compute some round subkeys that pass the differential path. And then substep (1.2.11) combines all the subkeys according to f_6, f_7, f_1, f_3, f_5, f_4, f_8 and f_2 in sequence and the differential characteristic to obtain 92-bit round subkeys. After these done, the combined 112-bit $(\mathcal{K}_0, \mathcal{K}_1, \mathcal{K}_2)$ pass the differential path and contains

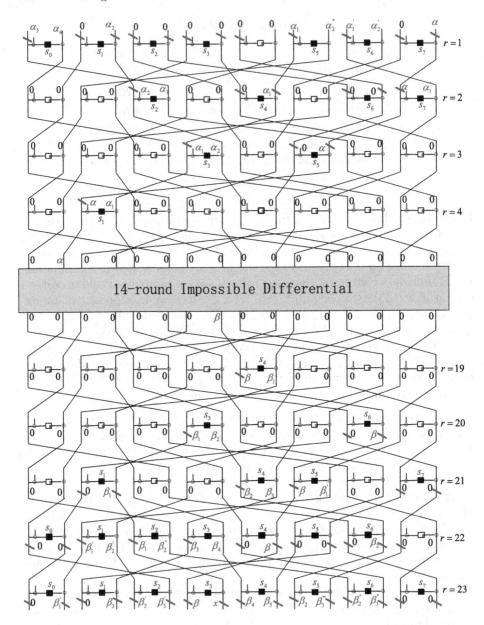

Fig. 2. Attack path for 23-round TWINE-80 (Input (output) values marked with short sloping line and the round subkeys corresponding to black s-box are involved in the attack.)

exactly 80-bit key information which can be expressed by $(\mathcal{K}_0, \mathcal{K}_1)$. Therefore, the obtained $\mathcal{K}_1$ in the combined 92-bit round Sunkeys are wrong keys and then be discarded in substep (1.2.12). After step 1, the right round subkey is in the remained ones. Hence step 2 aims to recover the right key by trial encryptions. After the candidate master key is computed in substeps (2.1.1) and (2.1.2), a trial encryption is done in substep (2.1.3) to find the right master key.

Algorithm 1. TWINE-80 Key Recovery

Input: chosen plaintext-ciphertext pairs, functions f_i ($i = 1,...,8$), differential characteristic

Output: right key used in TWINE-80

1: **For** every possible value of $\mathcal{K}_0 = (RK^1_{[1,7]}, RK^{23}_{[0,1,7]})$, **do**

(1.1):   Initialize a table Γ of 2^{60} all possible values of $\mathcal{K}_1$;

(1.2):   **For** each chosen plaintext-ciphertext pair, **do**

(1.2.1):   Compute $X^2_{[4,14]}$ using $RK^1_{[1,7]}$ by partial encryption of plaintext;

(1.2.2):   Compute $X^{22}_{[2,6,12]}$ using $RK^{23}_{[0,1,7]}$ by partial decryption of ciphertext;

(1.2.3):   Compute $RK^1_{[0,5,6]}$, (RK^{23}_2, X^{22}_0), (RK^{23}_4, X^{22}_{10}), (RK^{23}_5, X^{22}_{14}), (RK^{23}_6, X^{22}_8) using the plaintext-ciphertext pair and differential characteristic;

(1.2.4):   Compute RK^2_7 using X^2_{14} and $(\triangle X^2_{14}, \triangle X^2_{15})$;

(1.2.5):   Compute RK^{22}_3 using X^{22}_6 and $(\triangle X^{22}_6, \triangle X^{23}_8)$;

/* each 4-bit subkey computed above has $\frac{16}{7}$ values */

(1.2.6):   **For** every possible value of RK^{23}_3, **do**   /* 2^4 loops */

Compute X^{22}_4 using partial decryption for the ciphertext pair;

If $\triangle X^{22}_4 \in \triangle s[\triangle X^{23}_6]$, $\triangle X^{23}_{10} \in \triangle s[\triangle X^{22}_4]$ and $\triangle X^{22}_{12} \in \triangle s[\triangle X^{22}_4]$ all holds,   /* $Pr = (\frac{7}{16})^3$ */
then store (RK^{23}_3, X^{22}_4)

(1.2.7):   Compute RK^1_2 using Observation 8, and then store RK^1_2 in Q_0 with index (RK^1_6, RK^2_6);

(1.2.8):   Compute RK^{22}_4 using Observation 8, and then store RK^{22}_4 in Q_1 with index $RK^{23}_{[3,6]}$;

(1.2.9):   Compute RK^{22}_0 using Observation 8, and then store RK^{22}_0 in Q_2 with index $RK^{23}_{[2,3,4,5]}$;

(1.2.10):   Compute RK^{21}_7 using Observation 8, and then store RK^{21}_7 in Q_3 with index $(RK^{23}_{[3,4,5]}, RK^{22}_{[0,5]})$;

(1.2.11):   Combine all the involved subkeys using **Algorithm 2** to obtain $(\mathcal{K}_1, \mathcal{K}_2)$ with known $\mathcal{K}_0$;

(1.2.12):   Remove $\mathcal{K}_1$ in the combined $(\mathcal{K}_1, \mathcal{K}_2)$ from Γ;

(1.3):   Store $\mathcal{K}_0$ and the finally remained $\mathcal{K}_1$ from Γ.

2: After the above steps, suppose there are 2^m $(\mathcal{K}_0, \mathcal{K}_1)$.

(2.1): **For** each value of $(\mathcal{K}_0, \mathcal{K}_1)$, **do**

(2.1.1):   compute the value of $\mathcal{K}_2$ using f_i ($i = 1,...,8$);

(2.1.2):   and then compute the 9 partial master keys $k_2, k_5, k_7, k_9, k_{10}, k_{11}, k_{12}, k_{13}, k_{18}$ using $(\mathcal{K}_0, \mathcal{K}_1, \mathcal{K}_2)$;

/* the other 11 partial master keys are known in $(\mathcal{K}_0, \mathcal{K}_1)$ */

(2.1.3):   And then do a trial encryption. If it is correct, then return the right key and abort the loop.

Complexity Analysis. As can be seen from Fig. 2, there are 36 active sboxes. Among these sboxes, 17 sboxes with zero input difference let the corresponding subkey pass the truncated differential with probability 1. Any of the 15 sboxes whose input and output difference appeared in the plaintext/ciphertext difference make the corresponding subkey pass the truncated differential with probability 7^{-1}. The subkey RK^{23}_3 passes the truncated differential with probability $(\frac{7}{16})^3$ as described in substep (1.2.6). After RK^{23}_3 passing, any of the 3 sboxes who has $\triangle X^{22}_4$ as its input(output) difference and nonzero output(input) difference let the corresponding subkey pass the truncated differential with probability 7^{-1}. Therefore, the proportion of removing wrong subkeys for each pair is $7^{-18} \cdot (\frac{7}{16})^3 = 2^{-54.11}$. Hence the number of remained 80-bit subkey after analyzing all $2^{n+28.92}$ pairs is $\sigma = 2^{80}(1 - 2^{-54.11})^{2^{n+28.92}} = 2^m$.

Algorithm 2. Subkeys Combining Procedure

Input: a plaintext-ciphertext pair, $\mathcal{K}_0 = (RK^1_{[1,7]}, RK^{23}_{[0,1,7]})$, tables $\{KT_j\}(j = 2, 3, 4, 5, 8)$, $\{Q_i\}(i = 0, ..., 3)$,
    and the already computed subkeys $RK^1_{[0,5,6]}$, $RK^{23}_{[2,3,4,5,6]}$, RK^2_7, RK^{22}_3

Output: combined 92-bit subkeys $(\mathcal{K}_1, \mathcal{K}_2)$ which pass the path and all the subkey equations

1: **For** $(RK^1_6, RK^{23}_{[3,4,5]})$ **do:**   /* $l_1 = (\frac{16}{7})^3 \cdot (2^4 \cdot (\frac{7}{16})^3) = 2^4$ loops */
    Compute f_6 with the above subkeys;
    If the result is zero, then store $RK = (RK^1_6, RK^{23}_{[3,4,5]})$;   /* holds with $Pr = 2^{-4}$ */
    otherwise, try next $(RK^1_6, RK^{23}_{[3,4,5]})$;

2: **For** every obtained $(RK^1_0, RK^2_7, RK^{23}_2)$, **do:**   /* $l_2 = (\frac{16}{7})^3$ loops */
    Compute RK^{23}_6 using f_7; and then compute X^{22}_8 using RK^{23}_6 by partial decryption;
    If $\triangle X^{22}_8 = 0$, then add $(RK^1_0, RK^2_7, RK^{23}_{[2,6]})$ to RK;   /* $Pr = \frac{16}{7} \cdot 2^{-4}$ */
    otherwise, try next $(RK^1_0, RK^2_7, RK^{23}_2)$;
    compute RK^{22}_2 using the obtained X^{22}_4 and $(\triangle X^{22}_4, \triangle X^{23}_{12})$;   /* $\frac{16}{7}$ values */

3: **For** every obtained RK^{22}_2, **do:**   /* $l_3 = \frac{16}{7}$ loops */
    Compute RK^2_2 using f_1; and then compute X^3_{12} using RK^2_2 by partial encryption;
    If $\triangle X^3_{12} = 0$, then add (RK^2_2, RK^{22}_2) to RK;   /* $Pr = \frac{16}{7} \cdot 2^{-4}$ */
    otherwise, try next RK^{22}_2;

4: **For** every guessed $RK^{22}_{[5,6]}$, **do:**   /* $l_4 = 2^8$ loops */
    Look up KT_3 to get the value of RK^2_6, then add $(RK^2_6, RK^{22}_{[5,6]})$ to RK;
    Compute X^{21}_8 using RK^{22}_6 and $X^{23}_{[10,15]}$ by partial decryption, and then compute RK^{21}_4;

5:     **For** every obtained (RK^1_5, RK^{21}_4), **do:**   /* $l_5 = (\frac{16}{7})^2$ loops */
    Look up KT_5 to obtain RK^{22}_1, and then compute X^{21}_6 using RK^{22}_1 by partial decryption;
    If $\triangle X^{21}_6 = 0$, then add $(RK^1_5, RK^{21}_4, RK^{22}_1)$ to RK;   /* $Pr = \frac{16}{7} \cdot 2^{-4}$ */
    otherwise, try next (RK^1_5, RK^{21}_4);

6:     Look up KT_4 to get the value for RK^{21}_7;
    For every RK^{22}_0 in Q_2, **do:**   /* $l_6 = \frac{16}{7}$ loops */
    If RK^{21}_7 appears in Q_3 with index $(RK^{23}_{[1,3,4,5]}, RK^{22}_{[0,5]})$,   /* $Pr = (\frac{16}{7})^2 \cdot 2^{-4}$ */
    then add (RK^{21}_7, RK^{22}_0) to RK; otherwise, try next RK^{22}_0;

7:     Look up KT_8 to get the value for RK^1_2;
    If it appears in Q_0 with index (RK^1_6, RK^2_6), then add RK^1_2 to RK;   /* $Pr = \frac{16}{7} \cdot 2^{-4}$ */
    otherwise, try next RK^{22}_0;

8:     **For** every RK^{22}_4 (from Q_1) and RK^{22}_2, **do:**   /* $l_8 = (\frac{16}{7})^2$ loops */
    Look up KT_2 to get the value for RK^2_4;
    compute X^3_6 using $RK^3_3 = RK^1_5$ and $(\triangle X^3_6, \triangle X^3_7)$,
    and then X^2_8 is computed using RK^2_4 by partial decryption, and then RK^1_3 is computed using
    the plaintext pair and X^2_8; and then add $(RK^{22}_{[3,4]}, RK^2_4, RK^1_3)$ to FK.

9: Return the combined $RK = (RK^1_6, RK^{23}_{[3,4,5]}, RK^1_0, RK^2_7, RK^{23}_{[2,6]}, RK^2_2, RK^{22}_2,$
                $RK^2_6, RK^{22}_{[5,6]}, RK^1_5, RK^{21}_4, RK^{22}_1, RK^{21}_7, RK^{22}_0, RK^1_2, RK^{22}_{[3,4]}, RK^2_4, RK^1_3)$.

The time complexity of data collection contains: 2^{n+32} to build the hash table, and $2^{n+47}(\frac{15}{16} \cdot \sum_{i=0}^{7}(\frac{7}{16})^i + (\frac{15}{16})^2 \cdot \sum_{i=8}^{14}(\frac{7}{16})^i) = 2^{n+47.737}$ looking up difference distribution table to choose the pairs with required ciphertext/plaintext difference, which is $2^{n+38.628}$ encryptions.

The time complexity of computing the tables in precomputation phase can be omitted compared to the time in key recovery phase.

Notice that the time for substep (1.2.11) dominates the time of step (1.2). Hence the complexity of step (1.2) is $l_1 \cdot (11 + 2^{-4} \cdot l_2 \cdot (9 + \frac{16}{7} + 1 + 7^{-1} \cdot (1 + \frac{16}{7} + l_3 \cdot (7 + 3 + 1 + 7^{-1} \cdot l_4 \cdot (1 + 3 + \frac{16}{7} + l_5 \cdot (1 + 1 + \frac{16}{7} + 1 + 7^{-1} \cdot (1 + l_6 \cdot (1 + (\frac{16}{7})^2 \cdot 2^{-4} \cdot (2 + 7^{-1} \cdot l_8(2 + \frac{16}{7} \cdot 7)))))))))) = 2^{12.73}$ xor, where the computation of f_6, f_7, f_1 needs 11, 9, 7 xor or looking up sbox respectively. (The computation of values l_i ($i = 1,...,10$) and time estimation for substeps (1.2.7) to (1.2.10) is showed in Appendix B.) Hence the time complexity of step 1 in Key Recovery is $T_1 = 2^{20+n+28.92+12.73} \cdot \frac{1}{23 \cdot 24}$ 23-round encryptions $= 2^{n+52.54}$ encryptions.

The time complexity of step 2 in Key Recovery is $T_2 = 2^m$ encryptions, because the time of computing $\mathcal{K}_2$ and nine partial master key (k_2, k_5, k_7, k_9, k_{10}, k_{11}, k_{12}, k_{13}, k_{18}) is much less than one encryption for each $\mathcal{K}_1$ (see Appendix A). Let $n = 25.85$, $m = 77.72$, then the time complexity of this attack is $T_1 + T_2 = 2^{79.09}$ encryptions. Hence, the data complexity is $2^{57.85}$ blocks and the memory complexity is $2^m \cdot 80/64 + 2^{60}/64 = 2^{78.04}$ blocks.

5   Impossible Differential Attack on 24-Round TWINE-128

Attack on 24-round TWINE-128 uses the impossible differential $(\tilde{0}^5 \| \alpha \| \tilde{0}^{10}) \xrightarrow{14r} (\tilde{0}^{11} \| \beta \| \tilde{0}^4)$, because it involves the least number of round subkeys. What's more, subkeys involved in the truncated differential paths have less complicated equations which are showed in Observation 5. We extend 5 rounds on the top and the bottom of the 14-round impossible differential respectively. Table 6 and Table 7 show that the top 5 rounds involve 80-bit subkey information and the bottom 5 rounds involve 84-bit subkey information respectively. Therefore, $80 + 84 - 128 = 36$ bits subkey information are redundant, which are described in Observation 5.

Attacking TWINE-128 is similar to attack on TWINE-80. Suppose 2^n structures are used in this attack, and each structure contains plaintexts with the form $(p_0, p_1, \gamma_0, p_2, p_3, p_4, \gamma_1, \gamma_2, \gamma_3, p_5, p_6, p_7, p_8, p_9, p_{10}, p_{11})$, where $\gamma_i (i = 0, ..., 3)$

Table 6. Subkeys involved in the extended head path of attacking TWINE-128

Round r	RK_0^r	RK_1^r	RK_2^r	RK_3^r	RK_4^r	RK_5^r	RK_6^r	RK_7^r
Round 1	k_2	k_3	k_{12}	k_{15}	k_{17}	k_{18}	k_{28}	k_{31}
Round 2	k_6		k_{16}	$k_{19} \oplus C_L^1$	k_{21}	k_{22}	$k(1,0)$	k_0
Round 3	k_{10}	$k_{11} \oplus C_H^2$		$k(23,30) \oplus C_L^2$	k_{26}			
Round 4	k_{14}	$k_{15} \oplus C_H^3$						
Round 5	k_{18}							

Table 7. Subkeys involved in the extended tail path of attacking TWINE-128

Round r	RK_0^r	RK_1^r	RK_2^r	RK_3^r	RK_4^r	RK_5^r	RK_6^r	RK_7^r
Round 20		$RK_1^{20} = RK_5^{24}$						
Round 21	RK_0^{21}		RK_2^{21}					
Round 22	RK_0^{22}		RK_2^{22}	RK_3^{22}			RK_6^{22}	
Round 23	RK_0^{23}	RK_1^{23}	RK_2^{23}	RK_3^{23}	RK_4^{23}	RK_5^{23}		RK_7^{23}
Round 24	RK_0^{24}	RK_1^{24}	RK_2^{24}	RK_3^{24}	RK_4^{24}	RK_5^{24}	RK_6^{24}	RK_7^{24}

are constants and $p_i(i = 0, ..., 11)$ take all possible values in each structure. As a result, there are 2^{48} plaintexts in each structure and 2^{n+95} pairs are obtained. And then select the pairs that satisfy Observation 7, $2^{n+95-16-19.27} = 2^{n+59.73}$ pairs are finally obtained. The complexity of data collection is $2^{n+70.6278}$ encryptions.

Let $\mathcal{K}_0 = (RK^1_{[1,4]}, RK^{24}_{[2,4,5]}), \mathcal{K}_1 = (RK^1_{[0,2,3,5,6,7]}, RK^2_{[0,2,3,4,5,6,7]}, RK^3_{[0,1,3,5]}, RK^4_0, RK^{21}_2, RK^{22}_6, RK^{23}_{[0,1,2,4]}, RK^{24}_{[0,6,7]}), \mathcal{K}_2 = (RK^{21}_1, RK^{22}_{[0,2,3]}, RK^{23}_{[3,5,7]}, RK^{24}_{[1,3]})$, Since the main idea of key recovery is similar to that in TWINE-80, we give the detailed description of key recovery algorithm in Appendix C. Combining $(\mathcal{K}_0, \mathcal{K}_1, \mathcal{K}_2)$ that pass the truncated differentials and the equations in Observation 5 can be done in $2^{45.48}$ xor operations according to $g_1, g_2, g_3, g_4, g_9, g_7, g_8, g_5, g_6$ in sequence (see Appendix C).

Therefore, the time for filtering wrong keys is $\mathcal{T}_1 = 2^{20+n+59.73+45.48} \cdot \frac{1}{24 \cdot 24}$ 24-round encryptions = $2^{n+116.04}$ encryptions, followed by $\mathcal{T}_2 = 2^m$ encryptions to do trial encryptions. Since the probability of differential path is Pr= $(7^{-11} \cdot (\frac{7}{16})^3)^2 = 2^{-68.92}$, let $\sigma = 2^{128} \cdot (1 - 2^{-68.92})^{2^{n+59.73}} = 2^m$. Take $n = 10.1$, $m = 125.29$, then the time complexity is $\mathcal{T}_1 + \mathcal{T}_2 = 2^{126.78}$ encryptions. And the memory complexity and data complexity are $2^m \cdot 80/64 + 2^{108}/64 = 2^{125.61}$ blocks and $2^{58.1}$ blocks respectively.

6   Conclusion

This paper gives an impossible differential cryptanalysis of reduced-round TWINE-80 and TWINE-128. In the attacks, we present some key relations, and then an optimal algorithm is proposed to recovery subkeys using these relations, which may be used in other types of attacks. According to the known results, it seems that TWINE currently remains immune to impossible differential attack.

A

The following equations are deduced from the TWINE-80 key schedule.

$$f_1 = RK^2_2 \oplus s[RK^2_7] \oplus RK^{22}_2 \oplus s[RK^{23}_1 \oplus C^{22}_H \oplus C^{19}_L] \oplus C^7_H \oplus C^4_L = 0$$

$$f_2 = RK^{22}_4 \oplus RK^2_4 \oplus C^9_H \oplus C^{11}_L \oplus s[C^9_H \oplus C^6_L \oplus RK^{21}_7 \oplus s[RK^{22}_6 \oplus C^{21}_L]] \oplus s[RK^{22}_3 \oplus C^{17}_H \oplus C^{14}_L]$$
$$\oplus s[RK^{23}_0 \oplus C^{12}_H \oplus C^9_L] \oplus s[RK^1_1 \oplus s[RK^{23}_4 \oplus C^{15}_H \oplus C^{12}_L]] \oplus s[RK^{23}_0 \oplus C^{12}_H \oplus C^9_L]] = 0$$

$$f_3 = RK^2_6 \oplus C^4_H \oplus C^1_L \oplus C^{21}_L \oplus RK^{22}_6 \oplus s[RK^{22}_5 \oplus C^{19}_H \oplus C^{16}_L] \oplus s[RK^{22}_2] = 0$$

$$f_4 = RK^{23}_0 \oplus RK^{23}_4 \oplus C^9_H \oplus C^{12}_L \oplus s[RK^1_5 \oplus s[C^{13}_H \oplus C^{10}_L \oplus RK^{21}_4]] \oplus C^{12}_H \oplus C^9_L$$
$$\oplus s^{-1}[RK^1_7 \oplus C^9_H \oplus C^6_L \oplus RK^{21}_7 \oplus s[RK^{22}_6 \oplus C^{21}_L]] = 0$$

$$f_5 = RK^{23}_2 \oplus RK^1_5 \oplus C^{18}_H \oplus C^{15}_L \oplus s[RK^{21}_4 \oplus C^{13}_H \oplus C^{10}_L]$$
$$\oplus s[RK^{22}_1 \oplus s[RK^2_6 \oplus C^4_H \oplus C^1_L \oplus s[RK^{22}_5 \oplus C^{19}_H \oplus C^{16}_L]] \oplus C^{21}_H \oplus C^{18}_L] = 0$$

$$f_6 = RK^{23}_5 \oplus s[C^{15}_H \oplus C^{12}_L \oplus RK^{23}_4] \oplus C^{20}_H \oplus C^{17}_L \oplus RK^1_1 \oplus s[RK^1_6 \oplus C^3_H \oplus s[C^{18}_H \oplus C^{15}_L \oplus RK^{23}_3]] = 0$$

$$f_7 = RK^{23}_6 \oplus s[C^{20}_H \oplus C^{17}_L \oplus RK^{23}_5] \oplus s[RK^{23}_2] \oplus s^{-1}[RK^2_7 \oplus RK^1_0] \oplus C^5_H \oplus C^2_L \oplus C^{22}_L = 0$$

$$f_8 = s^{-1}[RK^{23}_7 \oplus RK^{22}_0] \oplus s[RK^{21}_1] \oplus s[C^{21}_H \oplus C^{18}_L \oplus RK^{22}_1] \oplus RK^1_2 \oplus C^6_H \oplus C^3_L \oplus s[RK^1_7] = 0$$

As can be seen from the above equations, $\mathcal{K}_2 = (RK^{21}_{[4,7]}, RK^{22}_{[0,2,4,6]}, RK^{23}_{[4,6]})$ can be computed from $(\mathcal{K}_0, \mathcal{K}_1) = (RK^1_{[0,1,2,3,5,6,7]}, RK^2_{[2,4,6,7]}, RK^{22}_{[1,3,5]}, RK^{23}_{[0,1,2,3,5,7]})$ successively according to equations $f_1, f_3, f_5, f_6, f_7, f_4, f_8, f_2$ in $87/(23 \cdot 24)$ Xor $= 2^{-2.67}$ encryptions.

$$k_9 = s^{-1}[RK^1_7 \oplus C^9_H \oplus C^6_L \oplus RK^{21}_7 \oplus s[RK^{22}_6 \oplus C^{21}_L]] \oplus s[RK^2_2 \oplus s[RK^2_7]]$$

$$k_{10} = RK^{22}_3 \oplus C^{17}_H \oplus C^{14}_L \oplus s[RK^{23}_0 \oplus C^{12}_H \oplus C^9_L] \oplus s[RK^1_1 \oplus s[RK^{23}_4 \oplus C^{15}_H \oplus C^{12}_L]]$$

$$k_5 = RK^{22}_0 \oplus C^{11}_H \oplus C^8_L \oplus s[RK^2_2 \oplus s[RK^1_7]] \oplus s[RK^2_4 \oplus s[RK^1_7 \oplus s[k_9 \oplus s[RK^2_2 \oplus s[RK^2_7]]]]]$$

$$k_{11} = RK^{23}_1 \oplus C^2_H \oplus C^{22}_H \oplus C^{19}_L \oplus s[RK^{22}_3 \oplus C^{17}_H \oplus C^{14}_L] \oplus s[s^{-1}[RK^2_7 \oplus RK^1_0]$$
$$\oplus C^5_H \oplus C^2_L \oplus s[RK^{23}_5 \oplus C^{20}_H \oplus C^{17}_L]]$$

$$k_{18} = RK^{22}_5 \oplus C^{19}_H \oplus C^{16}_L \oplus s[RK^{22}_4 \oplus C^{14}_H \oplus C^{11}_L] \oplus s[k_{11} \oplus C^2_H \oplus s[RK^{22}_3 \oplus C^{17}_H \oplus C^{14}_L]]$$

$$k_7 = RK^{22}_1 \oplus C^1_H \oplus C^{21}_H \oplus C^{18}_L \oplus s[RK^1_3 \oplus s[RK^{22}_0 \oplus C^{11}_H \oplus C^8_L] \oplus s[k_{18} \oplus s[RK^{22}_4$$
$$\oplus C^{14}_H \oplus C^{11}_L]]] \oplus s[RK^2_6 \oplus C^4_H \oplus s[RK^{22}_5 \oplus C^{19}_H \oplus C^{16}_L]]$$

$$k_2 = RK^{23}_4 \oplus C^{15}_H \oplus C^{12}_L \oplus s[RK^2_7 \oplus s[RK^{21}_4 \oplus C^{13}_H \oplus C^{10}_L \oplus s[RK^1_3 \oplus s[RK^{22}_0$$
$$\oplus C^{11}_H \oplus C^8_L]]]] \oplus s[RK^1_5 \oplus s[RK^{21}_4 \oplus C^{13}_H \oplus C^{10}_L]]$$

$$k_{12} = RK^{23}_2 \oplus C^8_H \oplus C^5_L \oplus s[k_5 \oplus s[RK^2_2 \oplus s[RK^1_7]]] \oplus s[RK^1_6 \oplus C^3_H \oplus s[RK^{23}_3$$
$$\oplus C^{18}_H \oplus C^{15}_L] \oplus s[RK^1_2 \oplus C^6_H \oplus C^3_L \oplus s[RK^1_7] \oplus s[RK^{22}_1 \oplus C^{21}_H \oplus C^{18}_L]]]$$

$$k_{13} = RK^{21}_4 \oplus C^{13}_H \oplus C^{10}_L \oplus s[k_{12} \oplus s[k_5 \oplus s[RK^2_2 \oplus s[RK^1_7]]]] \oplus s[RK^1_3 \oplus s[RK^{22}_0 \oplus C^{11}_H \oplus C^8_L]]$$

As can be seen from the above equations, the nine partial master key $(k2, k5, k7, k9, k10, k11, k12, k13, k18)$ can be computed in $114/(23 \cdot 24)$ encryptions $= 2^{-2.276}$ encryptions.

The following equations are deduced from the TWINE-128 key schedule.

$$g_1 = RK^{22}_3 \oplus s[RK^{23}_5] \oplus C^{21}_L \oplus s^{-1}[RK^{22}_2 \oplus RK^1_1] = 0$$

$$g_2 = RK^{21}_0 \oplus s[RK^{24}_6 \oplus s[RK^{24}_7]] \oplus C^{12}_L \oplus C^9_L \oplus RK^2_2 \oplus s[RK^1_6] = 0$$

$$g_3 = s^{-1}[RK^3_1 \oplus RK^{24}_2] \oplus s[RK^{23}_7 \oplus s[RK^{22}_2]] \oplus RK^3_0 \oplus s[RK^{23}_5 \oplus C^{18}_H \oplus C^{15}_L \oplus s[RK^{21}_0]] = 0$$

$$g_4 = C^{20}_H \oplus C^{17}_L \oplus s[RK^{23}_0] \oplus s^{-1}[s^{-1}[RK^{24}_2 \oplus RK^3_1] \oplus C^{23}_L \oplus RK^{24}_3] \oplus s^{-1}[RK^1_5 \oplus s^{-1}[RK^{22}_6$$
$$\oplus C^4_H \oplus RK^3_3] \oplus s[RK^{21}_2]] = 0$$

$$g_5 = RK^1_0 \oplus s^{-1}[RK^1_1 \oplus RK^{22}_2] \oplus s[RK^4_0 \oplus s[RK^{24}_6 \oplus C^{19}_H \oplus C^{16}_L \oplus s[RK^{22}_0]]] \oplus s[C^{16}_H \oplus C^{13}_L \oplus s[RK^{23}_4]$$
$$\oplus s^{-1}[RK^{23}_1 \oplus C^{22}_H \oplus C^{19}_L \oplus s^{-1}[RK^{24}_7 \oplus RK^3_5 \oplus s[RK^{23}_2]]]] = 0$$

$$g_6 = RK^2_4 \oplus s[RK^{22}_0 \oplus C^{13}_H \oplus C^{10}_L \oplus s[C^7_H \oplus C^4_L \oplus RK^1_7 \oplus s[RK^{23}_2 \oplus s[RK^{23}_3 \oplus C^{22}_L \oplus s[RK^{24}_5]]]]]$$
$$\oplus s[RK^1_0 \oplus s[C^{16}_H \oplus C^{13}_L \oplus s[RK^{23}_4]] \oplus s^{-1}[RK^{23}_1 \oplus C^{22}_H \oplus C^{19}_L \oplus s^{-1}[RK^{24}_7 \oplus RK^3_5 \oplus s[RK^{23}_2]]]]]$$
$$\oplus s^{-1}[RK^{23}_7 \oplus RK^2_5 \oplus s[RK^{22}_2]] = 0$$

$$g_7 = C^{22}_L \oplus RK^2_0 \oplus RK^{23}_3 \oplus s[RK^{24}_5] \oplus s[s^{-1}[RK^{22}_6 \oplus C^4_H \oplus RK^3_3] \oplus s[RK^{21}_2]] \oplus s[s^{-1}[RK^{23}_0 \oplus C^{14}_H$$
$$\oplus C^{11}_L \oplus s^{-1}[RK^{24}_4 \oplus C^{11}_H \oplus C^8_L \oplus RK^1_2 \oplus s[C^5_H \oplus RK^3_3]] \oplus s[C^8_H \oplus C^5_L \oplus RK^2_7 \oplus s[RK^1_1]]]$$
$$\oplus s[RK^1_4 \oplus s[RK^2_2 \oplus s[RK^1_6]]]] = 0$$

$$g_8 = s^{-1}[RK_5^3 \oplus RK_7^{24} \oplus s[RK_2^{23}]] \oplus s^{-1}[RK_5^{24} \oplus C_H^{19} \oplus C_L^{16} \oplus s^{-1}[RK_6^2 \oplus C_H^{16} \oplus C_L^{13} \oplus s[RK_4^{23}]$$

$$\oplus s^{-1}[RK_1^{23} \oplus C_H^{22} \oplus C_L^{19} \oplus s^{-1}[RK_7^{24} \oplus RK_5^3 \oplus s[RK_2^{23}]]]] \oplus s[RK_0^{22}]] \oplus s[RK_0^2 \oplus s[$$

$$s^{-1}[RK_0^{23} \oplus C_H^{14} \oplus C_L^{11} \oplus s^{-1}[RK_4^{24} \oplus C_H^{11} \oplus C_L^{8} \oplus RK_2^1 \oplus s[C_H^5 \oplus RK_3^3]] \oplus s[C_H^8 \oplus C_L^5$$

$$\oplus RK_7^2 \oplus s[RK_1^3]]] \oplus s[RK_4^1 \oplus s[RK_2^2 \oplus s[RK_6^1]]]]] = 0$$

$$g_9 = s^{-1}[RK_4^1 \oplus s[RK_2^2 \oplus s[RK_6^1]] \oplus s^{-1}[RK_5^1 \oplus s^{-1}[RK_6^{22} \oplus C_H^4 \oplus RK_3^2] \oplus s[RK_2^{21}]]] \oplus s[RK_0^3 \oplus s[$$

$$RK_5^{23} \oplus C_H^{18} \oplus C_L^{15} \oplus s[C_H^{12} \oplus C_L^9 \oplus RK_0^{21} \oplus C_H^{12} \oplus C_L^9]]] \oplus s[C_H^{17} \oplus C_L^{14} \oplus s^{-1}[RK_0^{23} \oplus C_H^{14} \oplus C_L^{11}$$

$$\oplus s^{-1}[RK_4^{24} \oplus C_H^{11} \oplus C_L^8 \oplus RK_2^1 \oplus s[C_H^5 \oplus RK_3^3]] \oplus s[C_H^8 \oplus C_L^5 \oplus RK_7^2 \oplus s[RK_1^3]]]$$

$$\oplus s[RK_4^1 \oplus s[RK_2^2 \oplus s[RK_6^1]]] \oplus s[RK_4^{24}]] \oplus C_H^{23} \oplus C_L^{20} \oplus RK_1^{24} = 0$$

B

It is obvious that the value of $\#RK_0^1, \#RK_5^1, \#RK_6^1, \#RK_2^{23}, \#RK_4^{23}, \#RK_5^{23}, \#RK_6^{23}, \#RK_1^{22}$ are all $\frac{16}{7}$ for each plaintext-ciphertext pair when these subkeys pass the differential path with known RK_3^{23}. Besides, RK_3^{23} passes the truncated differential with probability $(\frac{7}{16})^3$, so $\#RK_3^{23} = 2^4 \cdot (\frac{7}{16})^3$ for each accurate plaintext-ciphertext pair. Furthermore, once RK_7^1 that pass the differential path is known, $\#RK_7^2 = \frac{16}{7}$; once RK_1^1 that pass the differential path is known, $\#RK_2^2 = \frac{16}{7}$; once RK_3^{23} that pass the differential path is known, $\#RK_2^{22} = \frac{16}{7}$; once RK_6^{22} that pass the differential path is known, $\#RK_4^{21} = \frac{16}{7}$ with the known RK_1^{23}; once RK_1^{23} that pass the differential path is known, $\#RK_3^{22} = \frac{16}{7}$.

Therefore, it is easy to compute the value of loops l_i with the above knowledge and Observation 8.

The following is a time estimation for substep (1.2.7) to substep (1.2.10) in key recovery algorithm.

As showed in the proof of Observation 8, the computation of RK_2^1 for each (RK_6^1, RK_6^2) can be done in much less than one encryption. Therefore, $\#RK_6^1 = \frac{16}{7}$ and $\#RK_6^2 = 2^4$ indicate that the time for computing RK_2^1 is less than $\frac{16}{7} \cdot 2^4$ encryptions.

Similarly, since $\#RK_3^{23} = 2^4 \cdot (\frac{7}{16})^3$, $\#RK_6^{23} = \frac{16}{7}$, the time for computing RK_2^{22} is less than $2^4 \cdot (\frac{7}{16})^2$ encryptions. Because $\#RK_2^{23}, \#RK_4^{23}$ and $\#RK_5^{23}$ are all $\frac{16}{7}$, and $\#RK_3^{23} = 2^4 \cdot (\frac{7}{16})^3$, the time for computing RK_0^{22} is less than 2^4 encryptions. Known from Observation 8, the number of values of $RK_{[2,3,4,5]}^{22}$ is $\frac{16}{7}$ for each $RK_{[2,3,4,5]}^{23}$. Hence the time for computing RK_7^{21} is less than $\frac{16}{7} \cdot 2^4$ encryptions.

C

This appendix gives a detailed description of the Key Recovery algorithm for TWINE-128. Before introducing the algorithm, an observation similar to Observation 8 used in attacking TWINE-80 is given, followed by some precomputed tables for g_i functions.

Observation C.1. *For a plaintext-ciphertext pair satisfying the input-output difference relations in Observation 7, the following can be deduced according to the differential path in attacking TWINE-128.*

(1) Given $RK_2^{21}, RK_3^{22}, RK_0^{24}, RK_6^{24}$ that pass the differential path, then $\frac{16}{7}$ values of RK_1^{23} on average can pass the path and be computed;

(2) Given $RK_{[1,5,7]}^{24}, RK_3^{23}, RK_2^{22}, RK_0^{21}$ that pass the differential path, then $(\frac{16}{7})^2$ values of RK_0^{22} on average can pass the path and be computed; and then if RK_3^{24} is also known, then $\frac{16}{7}$ values of RK_2^{23} on average can pass the path and be computed;

(3) Given $RK_0^1, RK_0^2, RK_0^3, RK_5^1, RK_1^3$ that pass the differential path, then $(\frac{16}{7})^2$ values of RK_0^4 on average can pass the path and be computed;

(4) Given RK_1^1, RK_1^3 that pass the differential path, then $\frac{16}{7}$ values of RK_5^2 on average can pass the path and be computed;

(5) Given $RK_2^1, RK_7^1, RK_6^2, RK_5^3$ that pass the differential path, then $\frac{16}{7}$ values of RK_3^1 on average can pass the path and be computed; and then if RK_3^3 is also known, then $(\frac{16}{7})^2$ values of RK_4^2 on average can pass the path and be computed;

Proof. Making use of the differential path and the equations $RK_1^4 = RK_3^1$, $RK_0^5 = RK_1^1$ and $RK_1^{20} = RK_5^{24}$, it is easy to prove the above observation similarly to the proof in Observation 8.

The following tables $KT_i'(i = 3, ..., 9)$ are precomputed for equations g_i respectively.

Table	Index	Content
KT_3'	$(RK_{[0,1]}^3, RK_0^{21}, RK_2^{22}, RK_5^{23}, RK_2^{24})$	RK_7^{23}
KT_4'	$(RK_5^1, RK_3^2, RK_1^3, RK_6^{22}, RK_0^{23}, RK_{[2,3]}^{24})$	RK_2^{21}
KT_5'	$(RK_{[0,1]}^1, RK_5^3, RK_{[0,2]}^{22}, RK_{[1,2,4]}^{23}, RK_{[5,7]}^{24})$	RK_0^4
KT_6'	$(RK_{[0,7]}^1, RK_{[4,5]}^2, RK_5^3, RK_{[0,2]}^{22}, RK_{[1,2,3,4,7]}^{23}, RK_{[5,7]}^{24})$	RK_4^2
KT_7'	$(RK_{[2,4,6]}^1, RK_{[0,2,3,7]}^2, RK_{[1,3]}^3, RK_2^{21}, RK_6^{22}, RK_{[0,3]}^{23}, RK_{[4,5]}^{24})$	RK_3^{23}
KT_8'	$(RK_{[2,4,6]}^1, RK_{[0,2,6,7]}^2, RK_{[1,3,5]}^3, RK_0^{22}, RK_{[0,1,2,4]}^{23}, RK_{[4,5,7]}^{24})$	RK_5^3
KT_9'	$(RK_{[2,4,5,6]}^1, RK_{[2,3,7]}^2, RK_{[0,1,3]}^3, RK_{[0,2]}^{21}, RK_6^{22}, RK_{[0,5]}^{23}, RK_{[1,4]}^{24})$	RK_3^3

As can be seen from Algorithm C.2, the time for combining all the subkeys involved in attacking TWINE-128 is $l_1 \cdot (5 + l_2 \cdot (13 + l_3 \cdot (1 + 3 + 1 + \frac{16}{7} + l_4 \cdot (1 + l_{5.1} \cdot (1 + \frac{16}{7} + l_{5.2} \cdot (1 + l_6 \cdot (1 + 1 + \frac{16}{7} + 1 + l_{7.1} \cdot (1 + l_{7.2} \cdot (1 + l_8 \cdot (2 + (\frac{16}{7})^2 \cdot 2^{-4} \cdot l_9 \cdot 2))))))))) = 2^{45.48}$ xor $= 2^{36.31}$ 24-round encryptions.

Algorithm C.1. TWINE-128 Key Recovery

Input: chosen plaintext-ciphertext pairs, functions g_i $(i = 1, ..., 9)$, differential characteristic

Output: right key used in TWINE-128

1: **For** every possible value of $\mathcal{K}_0 = (RK^1_{[1,4]}, RK^{24}_{[2,4,5]})$, **do**

(1.1):   Initialize a table Γ of 2^{108} all possible values of $\mathcal{K}_1$;

(1.2):   **For** each chosen plaintext-ciphertext pair, **do**

(1.2.1):   Compute $X^2_{[4,6]}$ using $RK^1_{[1,4]}$ by partial encryption of plaintext;

(1.2.2):   Compute $X^{23}_{[0,10,14]}$ using $RK^{24}_{[2,4,5]}$ by partial decryption of ciphertext;

(1.2.3):   Compute (RK^1_0, X^2_0), (RK^1_2, X^2_{12}), (RK^1_5, X^2_2), (RK^1_6, X^2_{10}), (RK^{24}_0, X^{23}_2), (RK^{24}_1, X^{23}_6), (RK^{24}_3, X^{23}_4), (RK^{24}_7, X^{23}_{12}) using the plaintext-ciphertext pair and differential characteristic;

(1.2.4):   Compute RK^2_2 using X^2_4 and $(\triangle X^2_4, \triangle X^2_5)$; Compute RK^2_3 using X^2_6 and $(\triangle X^2_6, \triangle X^2_7)$;

(1.2.5):   Compute RK^{23}_0 using X^{23}_0 and $(\triangle X^{23}_0, \triangle X^{23}_1)$; Compute RK^{23}_5 using X^{23}_{10} and $(\triangle X^{23}_{10}, \triangle X^{23}_{11})$;

/* each 4-bit subkey computed above has $\frac{16}{7}$ values */

(1.2.6):   **For** every possible value of RK^1_7, **do**   /* 2^4 loops */
Compute X^2_{14};
If $\triangle X^2_{15} \in \triangle s[\triangle X^2_{14}]$, $\triangle X^1_{10} \in \triangle s[\triangle X^2_{14}]$ and $\triangle X^1_{14} \in \triangle s[\triangle X^1_{14}]$ all holds,   /* $Pr = (\frac{7}{16})^3$ */
then store (RK^1_7, X^2_{14});

(1.2.7):   **For** every possible value of RK^{24}_6, **do**   /* 2^4 loops */
Compute X^{23}_8;
If $\triangle X^{23}_8 \in \triangle s[\triangle X^{24}_{12}]$, $\triangle X^{24}_6 \in \triangle s[\triangle X^{23}_8]$ and $\triangle X^{24}_{14} \in \triangle s[\triangle X^{23}_8]$ all holds,   /* $Pr = (\frac{7}{16})^3$ */
then store (RK^{24}_6, X^{23}_8);

(1.2.8):   Compute RK^{23}_1 using Observation C.1, and then store it in Q_0 with index $(RK^{21}_2, RK^{22}_3, RK^{24}_0, RK^{24}_6)$;

(1.2.9):   Compute (RK^{22}_0, RK^{23}_2) using Observation C.1, and then store it in Q_1
with index $(RK^{24}_{[1,3,5,7]}, RK^{23}_3, RK^{22}_2, RK^{21}_0)$;

(1.2.10):   Compute RK^4_0 using Observation C.1, and then store it in Q_2 with index $(RK^1_0, RK^2_0, RK^3_0, RK^1_5, RK^3_1)$;

(1.2.11):   Compute RK^2_5 using Observation C.1, and then store it in Q_3 with index (RK^1_6, RK^3_1);

(1.2.12):   Compute (RK^2_4, RK^3_3) using Observation C.1, and then store it in Q_4
with index $(RK^1_2, RK^1_7, RK^2_6, RK^3_{[3,5]})$;

(1.2.13):   Combine all the involved subkeys using **Algorithm C.2** to obtain $(\mathcal{K}_1, \mathcal{K}_2)$ with known $\mathcal{K}_0$;

(1.2.14):   Remove $\mathcal{K}_1$ in the combined $(\mathcal{K}_1, \mathcal{K}_2)$ from Γ;

(1.3):   Store $\mathcal{K}_0$ and the finally remained $\mathcal{K}_1$ from Γ.

2: After the above steps, suppose there are 2^m $(\mathcal{K}_0, \mathcal{K}_1)$.

(2.1): **For** each value of $(\mathcal{K}_0, \mathcal{K}_1)$, **do**

(2.1.1):   compute the value of $\mathcal{K}_2$ using g_i $(i = 1, ..., 9)$;

(2.1.2):   and then compute the 12 partial master keys k_4, k_5, k_7, k_8, k_9, k_{13}, k_{20}, k_{23}, k_{24}, k_{25}, k_{27}, k_{29}
using $(\mathcal{K}_0, \mathcal{K}_1, \mathcal{K}_2)$;   /* the other 20 partial master keys are known in $(\mathcal{K}_0, \mathcal{K}_1)$ */

(2.1.3):   And then do a trial encryption. If it is correct, then return the right key and abort the loop.

Algorithm C.2. Subkeys Combining Procedure for TWINE-128

Input: a plaintext-ciphertext pair, $\mathcal{K}_0 = (RK^1_{[1,4]}, RK^{24}_{[2,4,5]})$, functions g_i $(i = 1, 2)$, tables KT'_i $(i = 3, ..., 9)$, $\{Q_i\}(i = 0, ..., 4)$, and the already computed subkeys $RK^1_{[0,2,5,6,7]}$, $RK^{24}_{[0,1,3,6,7]}$, $RK^2_{[2,3]}$, $RK^{23}_{[0,5]}$

Output: combined 144-bit subkeys $(\mathcal{K}_1, \mathcal{K}_2)$ which pass the path and all the subkey equations

1: **For** every (RK^{23}_5, RK^{22}_2) **do:**   /* $l_1 = \frac{16}{7} \cdot 2^4$ loops */
   Compute RK^{22}_3 using g_1; and then store $RK = (RK^{23}_5, RK^{22}_{[2,3]})$;

2: **For** every $(RK^1_6, RK^2_2, RK^{24}_{[6,7]})$, **do:**   /* $l_2 = (\frac{16}{7})^3 \cdot (2^4 \cdot (\frac{7}{16})^3) = 2^4$ loops */
   Compute RK^{21}_0 using g_2; and then add $(RK^1_6, RK^2_2, RK^{24}_{[6,7]}, RK^{21}_0)$ to RK;

3: **For** every $RK^3_{[0,1]}$, **do:**   /* $l_3 = 2^8$ loops */
   Look up KT'_3 to get the value of RK^{23}_7; and then add $(RK^3_{[0,1]}, RK^{23}_7)$ to RK;
   Compute X^{23}_{15} using RK^{23}_7, and then compute RK^{22}_6 using X^{23}_{15} and $(\triangle X^{23}_{15}, \triangle X^{23}_{10})$;

4: **For** every $(RK^1_5, RK^3_3, RK^{22}_6, RK^{23}_0, RK^{24}_3)$, **do:**   /* $l_4 = (\frac{16}{7})^5$ loops */
   Look up KT'_4 to get the value of RK^{21}_2, then add $(RK^1_5, RK^3_3, RK^{22}_6, RK^{23}_0, RK^{24}_3, RK^{21}_2)$ to RK;

5: **For** every (RK^1_7, X^2_{14}), **do:**   /* $l_{5.1} = 2^4 \cdot (\frac{7}{16})^3$ loops */
   Compute RK^2_7 using X^2_{14} and $(\triangle X^2_{14}, \triangle X^2_{15})$;
   For every $(RK^1_2, RK^2_7, RK^{24}_1)$, **do:**   /* $l_{5.2} = (\frac{16}{7})^3$ loops */
   Look up KT'_9 to obtain RK^3_3, and then add $(RK^1_{[2,7]}, RK^2_7, RK^{24}_1, RK^3_3)$ to RK;

6: **For** every RK^2_0, **do:**   /* $l_6 = 2^4$ loops */
   Look up KT'_7 to get the value for RK^{23}_3; and then add (RK^2_0, RK^{23}_3) to RK;

7: Compute RK^{23}_4 using X^{23}_8 and $(\triangle X^{23}_8, \triangle X^{23}_9)$; Look up Q_1 to obtain (RK^{22}_0, RK^{23}_2);
   For every RK^{24}_0, **do:**   /* $l_{7.1} = \frac{16}{7}$ loops */
   Look up Q_0 to obtain RK^{23}_1;
   For every $(RK^{23}_{[1,2,4]}, RK^{22}_0, RK^2_6)$, **do:**   /* $l_{7.2} = (\frac{16}{7})^5 \cdot 2^4$ loops */
   Look up KT'_8 to get RK^3_5; and then add $(RK^{24}_0, RK^{23}_{[1,2,4]}, RK^{22}_0, RK^2_6, RK^3_5)$ to RK;

8: **For** every RK^1_0, **do:**   /* $l_8 = \frac{16}{7}$ loops */
   Look up KT'_5 to get the value for RK^4_0;
   If it appears in Q_2 with index $(RK^1_0, RK^2_0, RK^3_0, RK^1_5, RK^3_1)$,   /* $Pr = (\frac{16}{7})^2 \cdot 2^{-4}$ */
   then add (RK^2_0, RK^4_0) to RK; otherwise, try next RK^1_0;

9: **For** every RK^2_5 from Q_3, **do:**   /* $l_9 = \frac{16}{7}$ loops */
   Look up KT'_6 to get the value for RK^2_4;
   If it appears in Q_4 with index $(RK^1_2, RK^1_7, RK^2_6, RK^3_5)$,   /* $Pr = (\frac{16}{7})^2 \cdot 2^{-4}$ */
   then add RK^2_5, RK^2_4 together with RK^1_3 (from Q_3) to RK; otherwise, try next RK^2_5;

10: Return the combined $RK = (RK^{23}_5, RK^{22}_{[2,3]}, RK^1_6, RK^2_2, RK^{24}_{[6,7]}, RK^{21}_0, RK^3_{[0,1]}, RK^{23}_7, RK^1_5, RK^3_3, RK^{22}_6, RK^{23}_0,$
$RK^{24}_3, RK^{21}_2, RK^1_{[2,7]}, RK^2_7, RK^{24}_1, RK^3_3, RK^2_0, RK^{23}_3, RK^{24}_0, RK^{23}_{[1,2,4]}, RK^{22}_0, RK^2_6, RK^3_5, RK^1_0, RK^4_0, RK^2_5, RK^2_4, RK^1_3)$.

D

Algorithm   D.1.   Algorithm   2.3:   TWINE.KeySchedule-80$((k_0, ..., k_{19}),$ $RK^r_{[0,...,7]})$ in [15]

1: $(WK_0||WK_1||...||WK_{18}||WK_{19}) \leftarrow (k_0, ..., k_{19})$
2: **for** r $\leftarrow$ 1 to 35 **do**
3: $\quad RK^r_{[0,...,7]} \leftarrow (WK_1||WK_3||WK_4||WK_6||WK_{13}||WK_{14}||WK_{15}||WK_{16})$
4: $\quad WK_1 \leftarrow WK_1 \oplus s[WK_0], WK_4 \leftarrow WK_4 \oplus s[WK_{16}],$
5: $\quad WK_7 \leftarrow WK_7 \oplus C^r_H, WK_{19} \leftarrow WK_{19} \oplus C^r_L,$
6: $\quad (WK_0||WK_1||WK_2||WK_3) \leftarrow (WK_1||WK_2||WK_3||WK_0)$
7: $\quad (WK_0||...||WK_{19}) \leftarrow (WK_4||...||WK_{19}||WK_0||WK_1||WK_2||WK_3)$
8: **end for**
9: $RK^{36}_{[0,...,7]} \leftarrow (WK_1||WK_3||WK_4||WK_6||WK_{13}||WK_{14}||WK_{15}||WK_{16})$

Algorithm   D.2.   Algorithm   A.1:   TWINE.KeySchedule-128$((k_0, ..., k_{31})$, $RK^r_{[0,...,7]})$ in [15]

1: $(WK_0||WK_1||...||WK_{18}||WK_{31}) \leftarrow (k_0, ..., k_{31})$
2: **for** r $\leftarrow$ 1 to 35 **do**
3:    $RK^r_{[0,...,7]} \leftarrow (WK_2||WK_3||WK_{12}||WK_{15}||WK_{17}||WK_{18}||WK_{28}||WK_{31})$
4:    $WK_1 \leftarrow WK_1 \oplus s[WK_0]$, $WK_4 \leftarrow WK_4 \oplus s[WK_{16}]$, $WK_{23} \leftarrow WK_{23} \oplus s[WK_{30}]$,
5:    $WK_7 \leftarrow WK_7 \oplus C^r_H$, $WK_{19} \leftarrow WK_{19} \oplus C^r_L$,
6:    $(WK_0||WK_1||WK_2||WK_3) \leftarrow (WK_1||WK_2||WK_3||WK_0)$
7:    $(WK_0||...||WK_{31}) \leftarrow (WK_4||...||WK_{31}||WK_0||WK_1||WK_2||WK_3)$
8: **end for**
9: $RK^{36}_{[0,...,7]} \leftarrow (WK_2||WK_3||WK_{12}||WK_{15}||WK_{17}||WK_{18}||WK_{28}||WK_{31})$

Table D.1. Subkeys of round 1–5 in TWINE-80

Round r	RK^r_0	RK^r_1	RK^r_2	RK^r_3	RK^r_4	RK^r_5	RK^r_6	RK^r_7
Round 1	k_1	k_3	k_4	k_6	k_{13}	k_{14}	k_{15}	k_{16}
Round 2	k_5	$k_7 \oplus C^1_H$	k_8	k_{10}	k_{17}	k_{18}	$k_{19} \oplus C^1_L$	$k(1,0)$
Round 3	k_9	$k_{11} \oplus C^2_H$	k_{12}	k_{14}	k_2	k_3	$k_0 \oplus C^2_L$	k $(5,(4,16))$
Round 4	k_{13}	$k_{15} \oplus C^3_H$	k_{16}	k_{18}	k_6	$k_7 \oplus C^1_H$	$k(4,16) \oplus C^3_L$	k $(9,(8,(1,0)))$
Round 5	k_{17}	$k_{19} \oplus C^4_H \oplus C^1_L$	$k(1,0)$	k_3	k_{10}	$k_{11} \oplus C^2_H$	$k(8,(1,0)) \oplus C^4_L$	k $(13,(12,(5,(4,16))))$

Table D.2. Subkeys of round 1–7 in TWINE-128

Round r	RK^r_0	RK^r_1	RK^r_2	RK^r_3	RK^r_4	RK^r_5	RK^r_6	RK^r_7
Round 1	k_2	k_3	k_{12}	k_{15}	k_{17}	k_{18}	k_{28}	k_{31}
Round 2	k_6	$k_7 \oplus C^1_H$	k_{16}	$k_{19} \oplus C^1_L$	k_{21}	k_{22}	$k(1,0)$	k_0
Round 3	k_{10}	$k_{11} \oplus C^2_H$	k_{20}	$k(23,30) \oplus C^2_L$	k_{25}	k_{26}	k $(5,(4,16))$	k $(4,16)$
Round 4	k_{14}	$k_{15} \oplus C^3_H$	k_{24}	$k(27,3) \oplus C^3_L$	k_{29}	k_{30}	k $(9,(8,20))$	k $(8,20)$
Round 5	k_{18}	$k_{19} \oplus C^4_H \oplus C^1_L$	k_{28}	$k_{31} \oplus s[k_7 \oplus C^1_H] \oplus C^4_L$	k_2	k_3	k $(13,(12,24))$	k $(12,24)$
Round 6	k_{22}	$k(23,30) \oplus C^2_L \oplus C^5_H$	$k(1,0)$	$k_0 \oplus s[k_{11} \oplus C^2_H] \oplus C^5_L$	k_6	$k_7 \oplus C^1_H$	k $(17,(16,28))$	k $(16,28)$
Round 7	k_{26}	$k(27,3) \oplus C^3_L \oplus C^6_H$	k $(5,(4,16))$	$k(4,16) \oplus s[k_{15} \oplus C^3_H] \oplus C^6_L$	k_{10}	$k_{11} \oplus C^2_H$	k $(21,(20,(1,0)))$	k $(20,(1,0))$

References

1. Bogdanov, A., Boura, C., Rijmen, V., Wang, M., Wen, L., Zhao, J.: Key difference invariant bias in block ciphers. In: Sako, K., Sarkar, P. (eds.) ASIACRYPT 2013, Part I. LNCS, vol. 8269, pp. 357–376. Springer, Heidelberg (2013)
2. Biham, E., Biryukov, A., Shamir, A.: Cryptanalysis of Skipjack reduced to 31 rounds using impossible differentials. In: Stern, J. (ed.) EUROCRYPT 1999. LNCS, vol. 1592, pp. 12–23. Springer, Heidelberg (1999)
3. Boztaş, Ö., Karakoç, F., Çoban, M.: Multidimensional meet-in-the-middle attacks on reduced-round TWINE-128. In: Avoine, G., Kara, O. (eds.) LightSec 2013. LNCS, vol. 8162, pp. 55–67. Springer, Heidelberg (2013)
4. Bogdanov, A.A., Knudsen, L.R., Leander, G., Paar, C., Poschmann, A., Robshaw, M., Seurin, Y., Vikkelsoe, C.: PRESENT: an ultra-lightweight block cipher. In: Paillier, P., Verbauwhede, I. (eds.) CHES 2007. LNCS, vol. 4727, pp. 450–466. Springer, Heidelberg (2007)
5. De Cannière, C., Dunkelman, O., Knežević, M.: KATAN and KTANTAN — a family of small and efficient hardware-oriented block ciphers. In: Clavier, C., Gaj, K. (eds.) CHES 2009. LNCS, vol. 5747, pp. 272–288. Springer, Heidelberg (2009)
6. Çoban, M., Karakoç, F., Boztaş, Ö.: Biclique cryptanalysis of TWINE. In: Pieprzyk, J., Sadeghi, A.-R., Manulis, M. (eds.) CANS 2012. LNCS, vol. 7712, pp. 43–55. Springer, Heidelberg (2012)
7. Gong, Z., Nikova, S., Law, Y.W.: KLEIN: a new family of lightweight block ciphers. In: Juels, A., Paar, C. (eds.) RFIDSec 2011. LNCS, vol. 7055, pp. 1–18. Springer, Heidelberg (2012)
8. Guo, J., Peyrin, T., Poschmann, A., Robshaw, M.: The LED block cipher. In: Preneel, B., Takagi, T. (eds.) CHES 2011. LNCS, vol. 6917, pp. 326–341. Springer, Heidelberg (2011)
9. Hong, D., et al.: HIGHT: a new block cipher suitable for low-resource device. In: Goubin, L., Matsui, M. (eds.) CHES 2006. LNCS, vol. 4249, pp. 46–59. Springer, Heidelberg (2006)
10. Knudsen, L.R.: DEAL - a 128-bit block cipher. Technical report, Department of Informatics, University of Bergen, Norway (1998)
11. Knudsen, L., Leander, G., Poschmann, A., Robshaw, M.J.B.: PRINTCIPHER: a block cipher for IC-printing. In: Mangard, S., Standaert, F.-X. (eds.) CHES 2010. LNCS, vol. 6225, pp. 16–32. Springer, Heidelberg (2010)
12. Leander, G., Paar, C., Poschmann, A., Schramm, K.: New lightweight DES variants. In: Biryukov, A. (ed.) FSE 2007. LNCS, vol. 4593, pp. 196–210. Springer, Heidelberg (2007)
13. Mace, F., Standaert, F.X., Quisquater, J.J.: ASIC implementations of the block cipher SEA for constrained applications. In: Proceedings of the Third International Conference on RFID Security (2007). http://www.rfidsec07.etsit.uma.es/confhome.html
14. Shibutani, K., Isobe, T., Hiwatari, H., Mitsuda, A., Akishita, T., Shirai, T.: *Piccolo*: an ultra-lightweight blockcipher. In: Preneel, B., Takagi, T. (eds.) CHES 2011. LNCS, vol. 6917, pp. 342–357. Springer, Heidelberg (2011)
15. Suzaki, T., Minematsu, K., Morioka, S., Kobayashi, E.: TWINE: a lightweight, versatile block cipher. In: ECRYPT Workshop on Lightweight Cryptography, Louvain-la-Neuve, Belgium, 28–29 November 2011
16. Wu, W., Zhang, L.: LBLOCK: a lightweight block cipher. In: Lopez, J., Tsudik, G. (eds.) ACNS 2011. LNCS, vol. 6715, pp. 327–344. Springer, Heidelberg (2011)

Optimal Storage for Rainbow Tables

Gildas Avoine[1,2] and Xavier Carpent[1(✉)]

[1] Université catholique de Louvain, 1348 Louvain-la-Neuve, Belgium
xavier.carpent@uclouvain.be
[2] INSA de Rennes, IRISA UMR 6074, 35043 Rennes, France

Abstract. Cryptanalytic time-memory trade-offs were introduced by Martin Hellman in 1980, and they have since had a major impact on practical cryptanalysis. Hellman's technique has been studied as well as improved significantly, most notably by Philippe Oechslin who introduced the rainbow tables. As it has been highlighted in various papers, the way the memory is handled is extremely important. In this paper, we analytically describe how rainbow tables are currently stored, and we introduce a new structure that considerably reduces the memory requirement. We mathematically analyze these techniques, provide optimal parameterization, and show that our structure is extremely close to the theoretical lower bound. Using our optimized storage for rainbow tables realizes the equivalent of a speedup of three with respect to the naive approach.

Keywords: Time-memory trade-offs · Implementation · Compression

1 Introduction

Cryptanalytic time-memory trade-offs are a tool to make brute-force attacks on hash functions or ciphers more practical. As their name suggest, they consist in a trade-off between online time and required memory to invert a one-way function. They were first introduced by Hellman in [7], and were later refined and improved. Time-memory trade-offs have been used in many practical attacks such as against A5/1 (used for GSM communications) in 2000 [3], or other stream ciphers like LILI-128 in 2002 [14].

Arguably, the most important of the algorithmic improvements is the rainbow tables, introduced by Oechslin in [11]. Rainbow tables have been illustrated by the very efficient cracking of Windows LM Hash passwords in 2003 [11] or Unix passwords (using FPGA) in 2005 [10].

Algorithmic advances in time-memory trade-offs therefore have an important impact in the field of cryptanalysis. Implementation optimizations are also very valuable: while it is stated in [11] that rainbow tables present a gain of a factor 2 in time with respect to Hellman tables, a gain of 3 can be gained through implementation optimizations, as introduced in this article. Despite some implementation optimizations having been discussed [1–3,9], they have never been the focus of a rigorous analysis and the optimal parameters have consequently

© Springer International Publishing Switzerland 2014
H.-S. Lee and D.-G. Han (Eds.): ICISC 2013, LNCS 8565, pp. 144–157, 2014.
DOI: 10.1007/978-3-319-12160-4_9

never been investigated. Endpoint truncation, such as described in [9] has other implications than simple storage optimizations and is complementary to the techniques described in this paper.

This paper presents a revision of the techniques used to optimize the implementations of time-memory trade-offs and introduces new ones. A rigorous analysis of their behavior is done, using a mathematical approach. In particular, the contributions are the following: a lower bound for endpoints compression (Sect. 3); an analysis and optimal configuration for the already-known *prefix-suffix decomposition* method (Sect. 4); a new way to store the endpoints that we name *compressed delta encoding*, along with optimal parameterization (Sect. 5); evidence that startpoints can not be compressed further than what is known today (Sect. 6); and finally, evidence that compressed delta encoding fares better than the prefix-suffix decomposition, and that it gets very close to the lower bound (Sect. 7).

2   Time-Memory Trade-Offs

Section 2 describes the context and the algorithms of time-memory trade-offs. For a more detailed description, see for instance [2] or [9].

2.1   Context

Let $h : A \rightarrow B$ be a one-way function, with $|A| = N$. Given $y \in B$, the problem consists in finding $x \in A$ such that $h(x) = y$. The common way to solve it is to perform a brute-force: computing $h(x)$ for each possible x until one that matches y is found. The brute-force can be performed for every new instance of the problem. In such a case, it is memory-less but it requires N calculations (worst case) for every instance. The other option consists in carrying out an exhaustive brute force once and storing the N pairs $(x, h(x))$. A lookup in the memory is then enough to solve a problem instance. None of these approaches are satisfying due to the practical computation and memory constraints. Hellman introduced in [7] a trade-off between those two approaches. It is composed of a precomputation phase performed once, and an online phase achieved for every new problem instance.

2.2   Precomputation Phase

In the *precomputation phase*, a series of *chains* of hashes[1] is constructed by alternating the h function, and $r : B \rightarrow A$ a *reduction function*. The purpose of the reduction function is to map a point in B to a point in A in a uniform and efficient way. Typically, it is implemented with a modulo: $r(y) = y \bmod N$. A chain j starts at an arbitrarily chosen startpoint $X_{j,1} \in A$, and it is iteratively

---

[1] The technique works for inverting any one-way function, but we use the vocabulary of hash functions liberally.

built with $X_{j,i+1} = h(r(X_{j,i}))$ until the endpoint $X_{j,t}$, where the length of the chain t is a fixed parameter. Once m chains are computed this way, the startpoint/endpoint pairs are sorted according to their endpoints, and stored in a table[2]. Figure 1 is a representation of the structure of such a table.

$$
\begin{array}{ccccccccc}
\boxed{X_{1,1}} & \xrightarrow{roh} & X_{1,2} & \xrightarrow{roh} & \cdots & \xrightarrow{roh} & X_{1,i} & \xrightarrow{roh} & \cdots & \xrightarrow{roh} & X_{1,t-1} & \xrightarrow{roh} & \boxed{X_{1,t}} \\
X_{2,1} & \xrightarrow{roh} & X_{2,2} & \xrightarrow{roh} & \cdots & \xrightarrow{roh} & X_{2,i} & \xrightarrow{roh} & \cdots & \xrightarrow{roh} & X_{2,t-1} & \xrightarrow{roh} & X_{2,t} \\
\vdots & & \vdots & & \ddots & & \vdots & & \ddots & & \vdots & & \vdots \\
X_{j,1} & \xrightarrow{roh} & X_{j,2} & \xrightarrow{roh} & \cdots & \xrightarrow{roh} & X_{j,i} & \xrightarrow{roh} & \cdots & \xrightarrow{roh} & X_{j,t-1} & \xrightarrow{roh} & X_{j,t} \\
\vdots & & \vdots & & \ddots & & \vdots & & \ddots & & \vdots & & \vdots \\
X_{m,1} & \xrightarrow{roh} & X_{m,2} & \xrightarrow{roh} & \cdots & \xrightarrow{roh} & X_{m,i} & \xrightarrow{roh} & \cdots & \xrightarrow{roh} & X_{m,t-1} & \xrightarrow{roh} & X_{m,t}
\end{array}
$$

Fig. 1. Structure of a Hellman table. The framed columns, respectively the startpoints and the endpoints, are the parts stored in memory.

2.3 Online Phase

Given $y \in B$, the online phase aims to retrieve $x \in A$ such that $y = h(x)$. For that, $r(y)$ is computed and a lookup is performed in the table to check whether it matches a stored endpoint[3]. Assuming it matches $X_{j,t}$ for some $1 \le j \le m$, the chain j is rebuilt from $X_{j,1}$ up to $X_{j,t-1}$. If $h(X_{j,t-1}) = y$, then the problem is solved given that $X_{j,t-1}$ is the expected value. If they are not equal or if no match was found in the first place, the process moves up to the next step by computing $r(h(r(y)))$ and repeating the same procedure. This goes on until a solution is found, or until the table is completely searched through (t steps).

2.4 Rainbow Tables

Rainbow tables [11] are an important improvement over Hellman tables, even though the difference is subtle. Instead of a single reduction function within one table, a different one per column is used. An example of a typical reduction function family is $r_i(y) = r(y+i)$, with r a reduction function such as a modulo. The drawback is that, during the online phase, the chain $r_{t-1}(h(r_{t-2}(h(\ldots))))$ must be recomputed entirely at each step rather than just computing $r \circ h$ of the previous result. However, it is much easier in rainbow tables to build *clean*[4]

---

[2] We actually need to build several tables this way. The reason for this is that the coverage quickly saturates in Hellman tables. See [7]. Also note that with rainbow tables, although 3 or 4 tables are generally required for a good probability of success, the number of Hellman tables required is usually much bigger.

[3] Since the endpoints are sorted, this lookup is inexpensive.

[4] Although the word "perfect" is usually attributed to tables without merges in the literature, we find this terminology more intuitive and more adapted.

tables, which are tables without *merges*. A merge is a situation in which two chains contain an identical point in a given column. The two chains "merge" because the series of values obtained afterwards are the same. A merge appearing in rainbow tables therefore always results in identical endpoints, but it is generally not the case with Hellman tables, in which merges are the cause of a drastic decrease in performances. At the end of the precomputation phase, duplicate endpoints are thus filtered out of rainbow tables. This results in much more efficient tables. In this paper, we focus on rainbow tables for these reasons, although the results are in theory applicable to Hellman tables as well.

2.5   Memory in Time-Memory Trade-Offs

It has been showed [7,11] that the efficiency of both the Hellman tables and rainbow tables follows the rule $T \propto N^2/M^2$, with T the average time during an online search, and M the amount of memory required for the table[5]. This means that optimizing storage has a great impact on the online time. This will be the focus of the discussion in the rest of the paper.

To summarize the notations, we note $N = |A|$ the size of the searching space; m_1 is, in accordance with the literature, the amount of chains generated during the precomputation phase to compute a rainbow table; and m is the amount of chains that remain after the duplicates have been filtered out.

3   Bounds for Endpoint Storage

The memory available for the tables is a very important factor. More memory means faster inversion and/or bigger searching space. It is therefore an interesting objective to reduce the memory required to store the tables. Note that, because of the nature of the search process, an efficient random access to the chains is necessary. This means that one can not simply compress the tables using a regular entropy compression technique (e.g. deflate, lzw).

In the following, we first discuss the storage of endpoints, and then move on to the storage of startpoints. Their analysis may be done separately, as motivated in Sect. 6.

In the naive algorithm, each endpoint is stored on $\lceil \log_2 N \rceil$ bits. Therefore, the total memory for endpoints M_{ep} is:

$$M_{ep}^{orig} = m \lceil \log_2 N \rceil. \tag{1}$$

We first mention here a theoretical lower bound for endpoint storage. A natural assumption that is usually made is that the endpoints are uniformly distributed in A. Indeed, we assume that the output of h is uniformly distributed in B and that therefore the output of $r_i \circ h$ is uniformly distributed in A (i.e., expected to behave like a random oracle). This is the case with cryptographic hash functions which are the focus of time-memory trade-offs such as rainbow

---

[5] As said above, the constant factor greatly favors rainbow tables [11].

tables. Work has been done on more general (but less efficient) time-memory trade-offs for any function [4]. A second point is that, since the endpoints are free of duplicates, the number of possible sets of endpoints is $\binom{N}{m}$ (they are all equiprobable). Therefore, the average minimal number of bits to store one such set of endpoints is:

$$M_{ep}^{opt} = \log_2 \binom{N}{m}. \tag{2}$$

Indeed, if we could index each possible endpoint set by an integer, this would be the size of one such index. In the following, we discuss how to get close to this bound.

4   Decomposition of the Endpoints in Prefix and Suffix

4.1   Description

The technique that is used in current implementations (see e.g. Ophcrack [12]) for storing endpoints efficiently is the *prefix-suffix decomposition* of the endpoints. It is discussed in [1,2]. The technique takes advantage of the fact that endpoints are sorted to store them more efficiently. In the following, it is assumed that $N = 2^n$ for the sake of simplicity, but the technique also works if N is not a power of two (see e.g. [1]).

The endpoints are sorted and divided in two parts: the p most significant bits form the *prefix*, and the $s = n - p$ least significant ones the *suffix* of an endpoint. They are then stored in two separate files: the *prefix file* and the *suffix file*. The suffix file simply contains all the suffixes, in the order of the sorted whole endpoints. The suffix file will also typically contain the startpoints corresponding to each suffix. The prefix file contains a list of indices relating to the suffix file. Each index indicates up to which suffix the corresponding prefix maps to.

Let us illustrate this with an example with $n = 32$, $p = 12$ and $s = 20$. Figure 2 represents a possible list of sorted endpoints in binary format. The first entry of the prefix table is 62, because the prefix 000000000000 is used up to chain 62; the next entry is 198 because prefix 000000000001 is used up to there, and so on. Whenever a prefix actually does not appear in the list of endpoints (this is possible although unlikely if p is adequate), the index put in the prefix table is simply the same as the previous one. If we take our example again, the index related to prefix 000000000010 is also 198 because it does not appear in the list of endpoints.

For the online phase, what needs to be specified is the operation that gives the startpoint corresponding to some point x, or nothing if x is not in the endpoint list. For that we again decompose x in a prefix and suffix (with the same p and s parameters). We look at the prefix of x, let's say 011101011100, and go fetch that entry in the prefix table. We get a number, let's say 11152, and we also look at the value just before this one, let's say 10440 (note: if the entry is the first, then the previous is simply 0). So, by construction, we know that if x appears in the list of endpoints, it must lie between entry 10441 and entry 11152 of the suffix

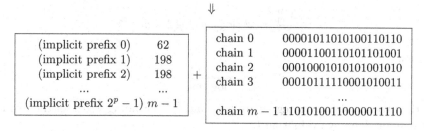

	p	s
chain 0	000000000000	00001011010100110110
chain 1	000000000000	00001100110101101001
chain 2	000000000000	00010001010101001010
chain 3	000000000000	00010111110001010011
	...	...
chain 62	000000000000	10010101010111011100
chain 63	000000000001	00000010110101101001
	...	...
chain 198	000000000001	11010101111101101011
chain 199	000000000011	00000100010011110111
	...	...
chain $m-1$	111111111111	11010100110000011110

⇓

(implicit prefix 0)	62
(implicit prefix 1)	198
(implicit prefix 2)	198
...	...
(implicit prefix $2^p - 1$)	$m - 1$

+

chain 0	00001011010100110110
chain 1	00001100110101101001
chain 2	00010001010101001010
chain 3	00010111110001010011
...	
chain $m-1$	11010100110000011110

Fig. 2. Prefix-suffix decomposition example.

table (included). A simple binary search (or linear for that matter, the range should be very small anyway) in that area of the suffix table is then carried out to find the right entry. The fetching operation is therefore very comparable to the naive approach in terms of speed.

Finally, note that both prefix-suffix decomposition and compressed delta encoding (described in Sect. 5) add negligible overhead in time in the precomputation and online phases. Indeed, the added cost consists in a handful of simple operations (shifts, additions, ...) versus typically thousands of cryptographic hashes to compute a chain.

4.2 Analysis and Optimality

Let us again note p the size in bits of the prefix, and $s = n - p$ the size in bits of the suffix. The total memory used for endpoints is therefore:

$$M_{\text{ep}}^{\text{ps}} = 2^p \lceil \log_2 m \rceil + ms. \tag{3}$$

The first term is for the prefix file, with each possible prefix having an index in the suffix file. Since the latter has m entries, the size of this index is $\lceil \log_2 m \rceil$. The second term is for the suffix file and its size is straightforward.

Theorem 1. *The optimal parameter p^{opt} for the prefix-suffix decomposition is one of $\lfloor p^* \rfloor$ or $\lceil p^* \rceil$, where*

$$p^* = \log_2 \frac{m}{\lceil \log_2 m \rceil \log 2}. \tag{4}$$

Proof. First note that (3) is convex, because:

$$\frac{\partial^2 M_{\mathrm{ep}}^{\mathrm{ps}}}{\partial p^2} = 2^p \lceil \log_2 m \rceil \log^2 2 > 0.$$

A simple way to find the optimal value is thus to find the minimum of the relaxed optimization problem, where p is a real-valued parameter, and test the two neighboring integer values. We have:

$$\frac{\partial M_{\mathrm{ep}}^{\mathrm{ps}}}{\partial p} = 2^p \lceil \log_2 m \rceil \log 2 - m.$$

Therefore,

$$p^* = \log_2 \frac{m}{\lceil \log_2 m \rceil \log 2},$$

and the two neighboring integers are $\lfloor p^* \rfloor$ and $\lceil p^* \rceil$. Finding which of the two is best may be done by evaluating (3).

5   Compressed Delta Encoding of the Endpoints

5.1   Description

We introduce in this paper a new technique to store the endpoints. Given a clean table, the endpoints are stored using a delta encoding. The technique consists in computing the vector of differences between each consecutive endpoint[6], which is then compressed using Rice coding [13] (this choice is argued in Sect. 5.2).

The online phase requires to efficiently perform random accesses on the elements stored in the table. In order to make the encoding efficient, an additional index table is computed and stored. Let us divide the space A into L blocks of the same size. The start of each block is indexed in a dedicated area of the memory, which size should be small compared to the compressed endpoints. The index table contains L pairs of values that each indicate the starting (bit) position of the corresponding block and the number of the chain. The former is used to jump into the right block, and the latter is used to know what startpoint to use in case the point is found.

When the differences are computed during the offline phase, at the start of each i-th block, the first difference is computed with respect to $\lfloor \frac{iN}{L} \rfloor$, and not the last endpoint encoded. The reason is that if the difference was computed with respect to the previous endpoint instead, one would need to decompress all

---

[6] Note that endpoints are unique meaning that a zero difference is not possible. One can therefore also decrease the differences by one.

the endpoints from the beginning. The resulting gain in space due to the smaller differences is negligible.

During the online phase, given x, we find the corresponding block by computing $\lfloor \frac{xL}{N} \rfloor$, go to the address pointed by that block, and start recomputing the sum of the differences with the offset $\lfloor \lfloor \frac{xL}{N} \rfloor \frac{N}{L} \rfloor$ (i.e. the start of the corresponding block). Once the sum is bigger or equal to x, the search is over. On average, $\frac{m}{2L}$ decodings are required for each search (each block contains on average $\frac{m}{L}$ compressed endpoints). Experiences show that a value of about $L = \lfloor \frac{m}{2^8} \rfloor$ is reasonable for practical applications, as we show in Sect. 7.1.

We now describe the technique quantitatively. A complete example of compressed delta encoding is given in Sect. 5.3.

5.2 Analysis and Optimality

Let E_i denote the ith sorted endpoint and $D_i := E_{i+1} - E_i - 1$. We have:

$$\Pr(D_i = d) = \begin{cases} \dfrac{\binom{N-d-1}{m-1}}{\binom{N}{m}} & \text{if } 0 \leq d \leq N - m, \\ 0 & \text{else.} \end{cases}$$

Indeed this corresponds, among all possible choices for m endpoints in A, to choosing the other $m - 1$ endpoints among the $N - d - 1$ values left. Since the probability does not depend on i, we simply note $D := D_i$.

Theorem 2. *The expected value of the difference (diminished by one) D between two consecutive endpoints is:*

$$\mathbb{E}[D] = \frac{N - m}{m + 1} \tag{5}$$

Proof. We have $\mathbb{E}[D] = \sum_{d=0}^{\infty} d \Pr(D = d)$. This is the expression that is addressed in pp. 175–177 of [6].

One can observe that this probability mass function has a striking similarity with a geometric distribution. Let us denote by D' a geometrically distributed random variable having the same average as D, that is:

$$\Pr(D' = d) = \left(\frac{N - m}{N + 1} \right)^d \frac{m + 1}{N + 1}.$$

Geometrically distributed data is best compressed when using schemes known as *exponential codes* such as *Rice coding* [13]. Rice coding of parameter k is a special case of Golomb coding of parameter $m = 2^k$. It works as follows (see [13] for a thorough description). Given an integer x, it outputs $\lfloor x/2^k \rfloor$ ones followed by one zero, and then the k least significant bits of x. It has been shown (see [5]) that Golomb codes are optimal to compress a geometrically distributed source. In order to select the parameter k that minimizes the rate, we can use the results of [8]. In the case of compressing endpoints, this gives:

				(bit 0)	0001	
				(bit 4)	0101	
				(bit 8)	10001	
chain 0	1		chain 0	(bit 13)	10101	
chain 1	7		chain 1	(bit 18)	0000	
chain 2	17		chain 2	(bit 22)	110011	
chain 3	31		chain 3	(bit 28)	0001	

chain 0   1   chain 0 | 1 | (bit 0) | 0001 |
chain 1   7   chain 1   5   (bit 4)   0101
chain 2   17   chain 2   9   (bit 8)   10001
chain 3   31   chain 3   13   (bit 13)   10101
chain 4   32   chain 4   0   (bit 18)   0000
chain 5   52   (1) chain 5   19 (2)   (bit 22)   110011
chain 6   54   ⇒   chain 6   1   ⇒   (bit 28)   0001
           ...   .
chain 248 4090   chain 248 14   (bit 1412) 10110
chain 249 4099   chain 249 | 3 | (bit 1417) | 0011 |
chain 250 4115   chain 250 15   (bit 1421) 10111
           ...   .

                                                    +

(bit 0)   0   0
(bit 35) 1417 249
              ...

Fig. 3. Compressed delta encoding example with parameters $N = 2^{20}$, $m = 2^{16}$, $L = \frac{m}{2^8} = 2^8$, and $k = k^{\text{opt}} = 3$. Step (1) is delta encoding (minus one) and step (2) is Rice compression and index construction.

Theorem 3. *The optimal parameter k^{opt} for the Rice coding of the differences (diminished by one) of the endpoints is:*

$$k^{\text{opt}} = 1 + \left\lfloor \log_2 \left(\frac{\log(\varphi - 1)}{\log \frac{N-m}{N+1}} \right) \right\rfloor, \tag{6}$$

with φ the golden ratio $(1 + \sqrt{5})/2$. The rate of the corresponding code is:

$$R_{k^{\text{opt}}} = k^{\text{opt}} + \frac{1}{1 - \left(\dfrac{N-m}{N+1} \right)^{2^{k^{\text{opt}}}}} \tag{7}$$

Proof. See Sect. 3.A in [8], with $\mu = \frac{N-m}{m+1}$ (from Eq. (5)). $\square$

Finally, we now address the memory usage of compressed delta encoding. Each compressed endpoint requires on average $R_{k^{\text{opt}}}$ bits as showed in Theorem 3. Additionally, each index entry comprises the position in bits of the beginning of its block, which requires $\lceil \log_2 mR_{k^{\text{opt}}} \rceil$ bits, and the chain number for possible chain reconstruction, which requires $\lceil \log_2 m \rceil$ bits. The total memory follows easily:

$$M_{\text{ep}}^{\text{cde}} = mR_{k^{\text{opt}}} + L \left(\lceil \log_2 mR_{k^{\text{opt}}} \rceil + \lceil \log_2 m \rceil \right). \tag{8}$$

5.3   Example

Figure 3 presents an example of compressed delta encoding. The parameters are $N = 2^{20}$, $m = 2^{16}$, $L = \frac{m}{2^8} = 2^8$, and $k = k^{\text{opt}} = 3$. The first step consists in computing the delta encoding of the sorted endpoints (left box) minus one. The list is divided in L blocks, with the beginning of each block marked (these are the framed numbers in Fig. 3). For instance, the second block should begin right after $\frac{N}{L} = 4096$, which corresponds in this case to chain 249. The difference is computed with respect to 4096 rather than the previous endpoint 4090, in order to make the reconstruction possible. In the second step, Rice compression is applied to these differences (top right box), and the index is built (bottom right box). In the index, we map each block with its corresponding starting bit as well as the corresponding chain number. Each entry in the index is 35 bits long, $\lceil \log_2 mR_{k^{\text{opt}}} \rceil = 19$ for the bit address of the block and $\lceil \log_2 m \rceil = 16$ for the chain number.

6   Compressing the Startpoints

In this section, we focus on the other data that must be stored: the startpoints. The main difference with the endpoints is that startpoints are not sorted. Nevertheless, there is some slack in their choice. In particular, the startpoints have been chosen in $\{0, \ldots, m_1 - 1\}$ in [1,2] (with m_1 being the total number of chains generated during the offline phase). They are, as far as we know, chosen in the same way in modern implementations, and are therefore stored on $\lceil \log_2 m_1 \rceil$ bits rather than n.

One might try to somehow compress this further, but we have found that the possible gain is very small. Indeed the startpoints and endpoints may be seen as a choice of m couples in $\{0, \ldots, m_1 - 1\} \times A$, of which there are $\binom{Nm_1}{m}$. Therefore, using the same reasoning as in Sect. 3, one finds that the size of startpoints and endpoints together is lower-bounded by:

$$M_{\text{tot}}^{\text{opt}} = \log_2 \binom{Nm_1}{m}. \tag{9}$$

If one only focuses on compressing endpoints, the total memory is lower-bounded by (and close to):

$$M_{\text{tot}} = m \lceil \log_2 m_1 \rceil + \log_2 \binom{N}{m}. \tag{10}$$

Let's take the following practical example: $N = 2^{40}$, $m = 2^{24}$, $m_1 = 25 \times m$. In this case, the theoretical lower bound for the total memory (from Eq. (9)) is a mere 0.59 % lower than the theoretical lower bound for startpoints and compressed endpoints (from Eq. (10)).

This tells us that it is not possible to do significantly better than compressing the endpoints as explained in Sect. 5, and adding the startpoints on $\lceil \log_2 m_1 \rceil$ bits. Nevertheless, recall that we have fixed the startpoints to be in $\{0, \ldots, m_1 - 1\}$. Whether other choices allowing them to be compressed more exist is an open question.

7   Experiments and Comparison

We made some theoretical and practical experiments in order to compare the two techniques (prefix-suffix decomposition and compressed delta encoding), and evaluate the gain realized with respect to the naive implementation. We also discuss on the value of L for compressed delta encoding.

7.1   Choice of the L Parameter

Recall from Sect. 5 that the compressed delta encoding technique separates the endpoints into L blocks, and requires them to be indexed. The choice of the parameter L is a trade-off between memory and online time. Indeed, if L is too big, the index part is large and the memory increases too much. If it is too small, the online time is impacted in a noticeable way.

Let us note $q = \frac{m}{L}$, that is the average number of compressed endpoints per block. As mentioned in Sect. 5.2, the average overhead to recover a point in the endpoint list is $\frac{m}{2L} = \frac{q}{2}$. This overhead should be negligible compared to the work done by computing the online chain and verifying the false alarms at each step. However, note that this additional cost is highly implementation-dependant, since the hash function can be more or less expensive to compute.

Considering that the decoding procedure relies on other computations than cryptographic hash operations, it is difficult to have a reliable point of comparison other than measured time. We implemented the decoding procedure in C, and observed in our experimental setup[7] that the decoding speed is about 18 ns/entry. What we suggest here is that recovering an endpoint should take about the time of a cryptographic hash operation. This fixes $q \approx 2^8$ in our case. For instance with $N = 2^{40}$ and $m = 2^{24}$, this results in a negligible 0.006 % increase in online time, and in a memory overhead of about 0.6 %.

7.2   Measure of the Gain

Endpoint Compression. Figure 4 shows the ratios $M_{ep}^{ps}/M_{ep}^{orig}$ and $M_{ep}^{cde}/M_{ep}^{orig}$, which are a measure of the gain realized with respectively prefix-suffix decomposition and compressed delta encoding on the memory required to store the endpoints. The two measures are contrasted with $M_{ep}^{opt}/M_{ep}^{orig}$, the optimal gain. The original method consists in storing the endpoints on $\lceil \log_2 N \rceil$ bits. In both cases, the optimal configurations are assumed, and for compressed delta encoding, a value of $L = \lfloor \frac{m}{2^8} \rfloor$ is considered. In this example, we use $N = 2^{40}$, which corresponds to a medium-sized search space for today's hardware. Using a small or bigger searching space retains the same overall picture, with similar conclusions. The horizontal axis is the number of chains m.

---

[7] This experiment has been done on a laptop with an i5 Intel Processor, with the encoded differences in RAM. We used SHA-1 as a point of comparison for a hash function.

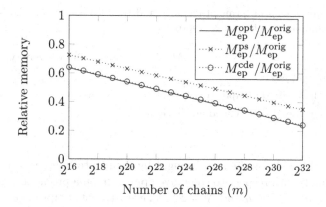

Fig. 4. Endpoints relative memory for the two techniques ($N = 2^{40}$).

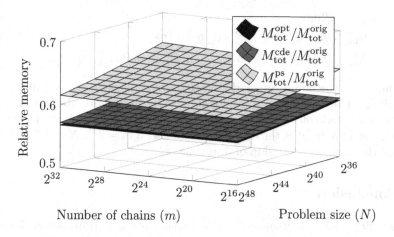

Fig. 5. Total relative memory for the two techniques.

One can observe that compressed delta encoding offers a significantly better compression than prefix-suffix decomposition, showing a 10 to 15 % improvement in terms of memory. Figure 4 also clearly indicates that compressed delta encoding is very close to the lower bound.

Total Compression. As discussed in Sect. 6, startpoints can not be compressed significantly better than when encoded on $\lceil \log_2 m_1 \rceil$ bits. When one includes the startpoints in the memory (assuming $m_1 = 25 \times m$), the relative gain appears a bit smaller, as shown in Fig. 5. It shows that compressed delta encoding is 5 to 7 % better than prefix-suffix decomposition assuming optimal configuration. However, it is hard to tell if this number is very relevant because prefix-suffix decomposition might have been used with non-optimal parameters in past implementations.

Table 1. Improvements in terms of memory and time for the two methods discussed in the paper compared to the naive approach.

	M (fixed time)	T (fixed memory)
Naive approach	–	–
Prefix-suffix decomposition	63.44 %	40.24 %
Compressed delta encoding	58.44 %	34.15 %

Finally, Table 1 shows the gain brought by the two techniques (optimal parameters assumed) with respect to the naive approach, on a problem with parameters $m = 2^{24}$, $m_1 = 25 \times m$ and $N = 2^{40}$. The startpoint compression is assumed for the two latter cases. The memory for the naive approach, the prefix-suffix decomposition, and compressed delta encoding are computed using respectively:

$$M_{\text{tot}}^{\text{orig}} = 2mn \tag{11}$$

$$M_{\text{tot}}^{\text{ps}} = m\lceil \log_2 m_1 \rceil + 2^p \lceil \log_2 m \rceil + ms \tag{12}$$

$$M_{\text{tot}}^{\text{cde}} = m\lceil \log_2 m_1 \rceil + mR_{k^{\text{opt}}} + L\left(\lceil \log_2 mR_{k^{\text{opt}}} \rceil + \lceil \log_2 m \rceil\right) \tag{13}$$

In any case, the impact of good storage optimizations on the overall memory is clearly illustrated, showing a gain of about 42 % in memory. Recall that, since time-memory trade-offs follow the rule $T \propto N^2/M^2$ as described in Sect. 2, a reduction of 42 % (as it is the case for instance with $m = 2^{24}$, $N = 2^{40}$ in Fig. 5) is about the same as a speedup of 3 in time.

8   Conclusion

In this article, we have discussed several implementation optimizations for storage in rainbow tables. In particular, we have analyzed the prefix-suffix decomposition method, and show that there is room for improvement. We have proposed the compressed delta encoding method and we show that it gets very close to the theoretical lower bound in memory usage, which contrasts with the prefix-suffix decomposition. We finally show that compressing startpoints together with endpoints can not significantly lower the memory usage further, making the compression of the startpoints (on $\lceil \log_2 m_1 \rceil$ bits) coupled with compressed delta encoding optimal for rainbow tables.

We emphasize that memory reduction is of utmost importance for time-memory trade-offs due to their nature. For instance, a reduction of 42 % in memory, which is brought by compressed delta encoding on a typical problem sizes compared to the naive approach, corresponds to a speedup of 3 in time.

References

1. Avoine, G., Junod, P., Oechslin, P.: Time-memory trade-offs: false alarm detection using checkpoints. In: Maitra, S., Veni Madhavan, C.E., Venkatesan, R. (eds.) INDOCRYPT 2005. LNCS, vol. 3797, pp. 183–196. Springer, Heidelberg (2005)
2. Avoine, G., Junod, P., Oechslin, P.: Characterization and improvement of time-memory trade-off based on perfect tables. ACM Trans. Inf. Syst. Secur. **11**(4), 1–22 (2008)
3. Biryukov, A., Shamir, A., Wagner, D.: Real time cryptanalysis of A5/1 on a PC. In: Schneier, B. (ed.) FSE 2000. LNCS, vol. 1978, pp. 1–18. Springer, Heidelberg (2001)
4. Fiat, A., Naor, M.: Rigorous time/space tradeoffs for inverting functions. In: ACM Symposium on Theory of Computing - STOC'91, pp. 534–541. ACM, ACM Press, New Orleans, Louisiana, USA, May 1991
5. Gallager, R., Van Voorhis, D.: Optimal source codes for geometrically distributed integer alphabets. IEEE Trans. Inf. Theory **21**(2), 228–230 (1975)
6. Graham, R.L., Knuth, D.E., Patashnik, O.: Concrete Mathematics: A Foundation for Computer Science. Addison-Wesley, Reading (1989)
7. Hellman, M.: A cryptanalytic time-memory trade off. IEEE Trans. Inf. Theory **IT-26**(4), 401–406 (1980)
8. Kiely, A.: Selecting the Golomb parameter in Rice coding. IPN progress report, vol. 42(159), November 2004
9. Lee, G.W., Hong, J.: A comparison of perfect table cryptanalytic tradeoff algorithms. Cryptology ePrint Archive, Report 2012/540 (2012)
10. Mentens, N., Batina, L., Preneel, B., Verbauwhede, I.: Cracking UNIX passwords using FPGA platforms. In: SHARCS - Special Purpose Hardware for Attacking Cryptographic Systems, February 2005
11. Oechslin, P.: Making a faster cryptanalytic time-memory trade-off. In: Boneh, D. (ed.) CRYPTO 2003. LNCS, vol. 2729, pp. 617–630. Springer, Heidelberg (2003)
12. Oechslin, P.: The ophcrack password cracker (2013). http://ophcrack.sourceforge.net/
13. Rice, R., Plaunt, J.: Adaptive variable-length coding for efficient compression of spacecraft television data. IEEE Trans. Commun. Technol. **19**(6), 889–897 (1971)
14. Saarinen, M.-J.O.: A time-memory tradeoff attack against LILI-128. In: Daemen, J., Rijmen, V. (eds.) FSE 2002. LNCS, vol. 2365, pp. 231–236. Springer, Heidelberg (2002)

First Multidimensional Cryptanalysis on Reduced-Round PRINCE$_{core}$

Xiaoqian Li[1,2][✉], Bao Li[1,2], Wenling Wu[3], Xiaoli Yu[3], Ronglin Hao[1,2], and Bingke Ma[1,2]

[1] State Key Laboratory of Information Security, Institute of Information Engineering, Chinese Academy of Sciences, Beijing, China
xqli@is.ac.cn
[2] University of Chinese Academy of Sciences, Beijing, China
[3] Institute of Software, Chinese Academy of Sciences, Beijing, China

Abstract. In this paper we present the first multidimensional linear attack on PRINCE$_{core}$, which uses an identical round-key for each round. Traditional one-dimensional and multidimensional linear cryptanalysis based their theoretical foundation on the independent-key assumption, so that they cannot be evaluated accurately in the case of ciphers with identical round-key. In this paper we propose a new classification technique to overcome this obstacle. In our new technique, we classify the linear trails into different subsets indexed by the XOR sum of their trail masks, deal with their correlations in each subset, and get the accurate capacity for our target linear approximation. By this technique, we build an 8-round multidimensional linear distinguisher with capacity of $2^{-57.99}$, and exhibit a key-recovery attack on 9 out of 12 round of PRINCE$_{core}$. This attack requires a data complexity of $2^{63.84}$ known plaintexts and time complexity of 2^{60} encryptions. We also present a key-recovery attack on 10-round PRINCE$_{core}$ with data complexity of $2^{63.84}$ known plaintexts and time complexity of $2^{75.68}$ encryptions.

Keywords: Linear cryptanalysis · Multidimensional cryptanalysis · Block cipher · Lightweight · PRINCE

1 Introduction

Linear cryptanalysis [2] is one of the two most prominent attacks against block ciphers, the other being differential cryptanalysis [1]. The resistance against linear cryptanalysis is usually expected in new cipher designs. Linear cryptanalysis

This work was supported by the National Basic Research Program of China (973 Project, No.2013CB338002), the National High Technology Research and Development Program of China (863 Program, No.2013AA014002), the IIE's Cryptography Research Project (No.Y3Z0027103), and the Strategic Priority Research Program of Chinese Academy of Sciences under Grant XDA06010702.

H.-S. Lee and D.-G. Han (Eds.): ICISC 2013, LNCS 8565, pp. 158–172, 2014.
DOI: 10.1007/978-3-319-12160-4_10

was introduced by Matsui in 1992 which exploits a particular linear approximation on the parity of plaintexts and ciphertexts involved by specific input masks and output masks. The idea of multidimensional linear cryptanalysis [3] is firstly suggested by Matsui in 1994. In 2010, Hermelin summarized the theory of multidimensional linear attacks on block ciphers and presented the basic attack algorithms and their complexity estimates [12].

PRINCE [14] is a lightweight block cipher proposed by Borghoff *et al.* at Asiacrypt 2012. It is designed with respect to low-latency when implemented in hardware. PRINCE is designed symmetric around the middle round, which contributes to the α-reflection property of its core function PRINCE$_{core}$: one can implement decryption by reusing the encryption implementation with a related key, so that the overhead for decryption on top of encryption is negligible. Because PRINCE$_{core}$ uses the identical round-key instead of almost independent round-keys, it is difficult to evaluate its resistance against one-dimensional and multidimensional cryptanalysis which are based on the independent round-key assumption.

The publishing of PRINCE did bring in a bunch of research from the perspective of its Even-Mansour construction and α-reflection property. At FSE 2013, Soleimany *et al.* introduced new generic distinguishers [17] on PRINCE-like ciphers due to their α-reflection property, and proposed a key-recovery attack on the full 12-round cipher for a chosen α parameter with $2^{57.95}$ known plaintexts and $2^{72.37}$ encryptions. At the same time, Jean *et al.* proposed several attacks on PRINCE and PRINCE$_{core}$ in [18], which included an integral attack on 6-round PRINCE$_{core}$ with data complexity of 2^{16} and time complexity of 2^{30}, a related-key boomerang attack on full PRINCE$_{core}$ with data complexity of 2^{39} and time complexity of 2^{39}. They also presented a single-key boomerang attack on the full cipher for a chosen α parameter with 2^{41} plaintexts and 2^{41} encryptions.

In this paper, we successfully present a multidimensional linear attack that does not suffer from the limitation of independent round-key assumption with the application of a new classification technique. In our new technique, first we set a target linear approximation, next we classify the corresponding linear trails into subsets indexed by the XOR sum of trail masks. Then, for each subset, we calculate the sum of the correlation of every trail in it, and square the sum. Finally we obtain the capacity of the target approximation by adding up all the squared values. Using this technique, we build an 8-round multidimensional linear distinguisher with capacity of $2^{-57.99}$, and recover the full key of 9-round PRINCE$_{core}$ with data complexity of $2^{63.84}$ known plaintexts and time complexity of 2^{60} encryptions. The same distinguisher is also used in a key-recovery attack on 10-round PRINCE$_{core}$ with data complexity of $2^{63.84}$ known plaintexts and time complexity of $2^{75.68}$ encryptions. To the best of our knowledge, this is the first multidimensional linear attack on PRINCE using the original α chosen by the designers.

The paper is organized as follows. In Sect. 2 the notation and the structure of PRINCE are briefly described. Section 3 presents the framework of multidimensional linear cryptanalysis, the computation of capacity, and the convolution method for marking the key candidates. Section 4 introduces the new classification technique in one-dimensional linear cryptanalysis without the independent-key assumption. In Sect. 5, our new technique is applied to construct a multidimensional linear distinguisher for 8-round PRINCE$_{core}$. Section 6 describes the attack on 9-round and 10-round PRINCE$_{core}$ using the distinguisher built in previous section. In Sect. 7, we present a multidimensional linear distinguisher for 1-step LED. Section 8 concludes this paper.

2   Preliminaries

2.1   Notations

In this paper, we use the same notations as in [5].

- x^T denotes the *transposition* of vector x.
- $x \oplus y$ denotes the *exclusive or* (XOR) of two strings x and y.
- $x \cdot y$ denotes the *inner product* of two vectors x and y.
- $x \parallel y$ denotes the *concatenation* of two strings x and y.
- $x \gg r$ denotes the bitwise *right shift* by r bits on the string x.
- $x \ggg r$ denotes the bitwise *right rotation* by r bits on the string x.
- $p * q$ denots the *convolution* of two probability distributions p and q.
- $\mathcal{E}_K(x) = \mathcal{E}(K, x)$ denotes a *block cipher* encryption of a plaintext $x \in \mathbb{Z}_2^n$ with key $K \in \mathbb{Z}_2^l$.

2.2   Brief Description of PRINCE

PRINCE [14] is a block cipher with block-length of 64-bit and key-length of 128-bit. The 128-bit key is split into two 64-bit keys, i.e., $k = k_0 \parallel k_1$. k_0 and k_0' are used as the input and output whitening keys respectively, where $k_0' = (k_0 \ggg 1) \oplus (k_0 \gg 63)$. And k_1 is used as the identical round-key of its internal function PRINCE$_{core}$ as illustrated in Fig. 1. PRINCE$_{core}$ is a 12-round SPN block cipher. Each round of PRINCE$_{core}$ consists of a round-key addition (AK), a round-constant addition (AC), an Sbox-layer (SC), and a linear layer (M). The Sbox-Layer is a 64-bit nonlinear transformation using a single 4×4 S-box 16 times in parallel. The linear

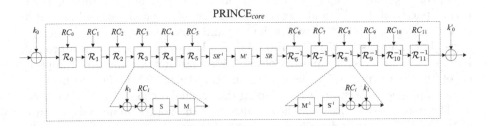

Fig. 1. The encryption scheme of PRINCE

layer M is denoted by $SR \circ MC$, where MC is a multiplication with a linear matrix M' which has a branch number of four and SR is a shifting-row permutation.

The constants of PRINCE satisfy $RC_i \oplus RC_{11-i} = \alpha$ for all $i = 0, 1, \cdots, 11$, where α is a specific constant. It allows PRINCE to decrypt a ciphertext by simply encrypting it with the key $k_0 \parallel k_1 \oplus \alpha$. This is the so-called α-reflection property.

3   Multidimensional Linear Cryptanalysis

3.1   Estimated Correlation of One-Dimensional Linear Approximation

In classic linear cryptanalysis proposed by Matsui [2], a one-dimensional linear approximation of a block cipher $\mathcal{E}_K$ with mask $(u, v, w) \in \mathbb{Z}_2^{2n+l}$ is a Boolean function defined as

$$f : \mathbb{Z}_2^n \times \mathbb{Z}_2^l \to \mathbb{Z}_2, \ f(x, K) = u \cdot x \oplus v \cdot K \oplus w \cdot \mathcal{E}_K(x).$$

The correlation of approximation f is

$$c(f) = c(u \cdot x \oplus v \cdot K \oplus w \cdot \mathcal{E}_K(x)) = 2^{-n}(\#\{x \in \mathbb{Z}_2^n : f(x) = 0\} - \#\{x \in \mathbb{Z}_2^n : f(x) \neq 0\}).$$

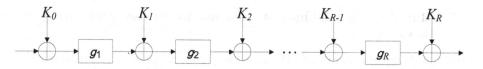

Fig. 2. Key-alternating block cipher

For a key-alternating block cipher shown in Fig. 2, the correlation can be calculated as in Theorem 1, which we call the *Correlation Theorem* [5–7].

Theorem 1 *[5–7]. Let g be the round function of an R-round key-alternating iterated block cipher $\mathcal{E}_K$ with round keys $(K_0, K_1, \cdots, K_R)$. Then for any $u \in \mathbb{Z}_2^n, v \in \mathbb{Z}_2^l$ and $w \in \mathbb{Z}_2^n$, it holds that*

$$c(u \cdot x \oplus v \cdot K \oplus w \cdot \mathcal{E}_K(x)) = \sum_{\substack{u_1, \cdots, u_{R-1} \\ u_0 = u, u_R = w}} (-1)^{u_0 \cdot K_0 \oplus \cdots \oplus u_R \cdot K_R \oplus v \cdot K} \prod_{i=1}^{R} c(u_{i-1} \cdot x \oplus u_i \cdot g_i(x)).$$

In Matsui's Algorithm 1 [2], a linear approximation with large correlation is needed. Under the assumption that the round-keys are independent, i.e., $K = K_0 \parallel K_1 \parallel \cdots \parallel K_R$, the average correlation of a target linear approximation can be calculated in Theorem 2, where only one linear trail $(u_0, u_1, \cdots, u_R) = v$ contributes to the average correlation.

Theorem 2 *[6]. Let g be the round function of an R-round key-alternating iterated block cipher $\mathcal{E}_K$ with independent round-keys $K_0, K_1, \cdots, K_R$. Then for any $u \in \mathbb{Z}_2^n, v \in \mathbb{Z}_2^l$ and $w \in \mathbb{Z}_2^n$, it holds that*

$$E_K[c(u \cdot x \oplus v \cdot K \oplus w \cdot \mathcal{E}_K(x))] = \prod_{i=1}^{R} c(u_{i-1} \cdot x \oplus u_i \cdot g_i(x)),$$

where $(u_0, u_1, \cdots, u_R) = v$.

In Matsui's Algorithm 2 [2], the strength of the linear approximation is evaluated in terms of the squared correlation. Under the key-independent assumption, the average squared correlation can be deduced in Theorem 3, which is often called as the "linear hull effect" [4–6].

Theorem 3 *[4–6]. Let g be the round function of an R-round key-alternating iterated block cipher $\mathcal{E}_K$ with independent round-keys $K_0, K_1, \cdots, K_R$. Then for any $u \in \mathbb{Z}_2^n, v \in \mathbb{Z}_2^l$ and $w \in \mathbb{Z}_2^n$, it holds that*

$$E_K[c(u \cdot x \oplus v \cdot K \oplus w \cdot \mathcal{E}_K(x))^2] = E_K[c(u \cdot x \oplus w \cdot \mathcal{E}_K(x))^2]$$

$$= \sum_{\substack{u_1, \cdots, u_R \\ u_0 = u, u_{R-1} = w}} \prod_{i=1}^{R} c(u_{i-1} \cdot x \oplus u_i \cdot g_i(x))^2.$$

3.2   Multidimensional Linear Approximation for Key-Alternating Block Cipher

Multidimensional linear cryptanalysis, which is an extension of one-dimensional linear cryptanalysis, was proposed by Matsui in 1994 [3]. Instead of one linear approximation, multiple linear approximations are exploited. An m-dimensional linear approximation can be considered as a vector boolean function

$$F : \mathbb{Z}_2^n \times \mathbb{Z}_2^l \to \mathbb{Z}_2^m, F(x, K) = U \cdot x \oplus V \cdot K \oplus W \cdot \mathcal{E}_K(x),$$

where $U = (u_0, u_1, \cdots, u_{m-1})^T, W = (w_0, w_1, \cdots, w_{m-1})^T$ are $m \times n$ matrix, $V = (v_0, v_1, \cdots, v_{m-1})^T$ are $m \times l$ matrix. In our multidimensional linear cryptanalysis, we set $V = 0$. We denote by p the probability distribution of $U \cdot x \oplus W \cdot \mathcal{E}_K(x)$, and p can be obtained by its correlations $c(a \cdot f)$, $a \in \mathbb{Z}_2^m$, which is known as the Cramér-Wold theorem [8]. The strength of multidimensional linear approximations is evaluated in terms of the *capacity* of p [5], which can be calculated in Theorem 4.

Theorem 4 *[8]. For any $F : \mathbb{Z}_2^n \times \mathbb{Z}_2^l \to \mathbb{Z}_2^m$, with probability distribution p, the capacity of p and the uniform distribution q can be calculated as*

$$C_p = \sum_{a=1}^{2^n - 1} c(a \cdot F)^2.$$

In the same setting as in [15], the space of the input mask and the space of the output mask can be split into two subspaces so that $U \in \{(u_s, u_t) \mid u_s \in \mathbb{Z}_2^s, u_t \in \mathbb{Z}_2^t\}$ and $W \in \{(w_q, w_r) \mid w_q \in \mathbb{Z}_2^q, w_r \in \mathbb{Z}_2^r\}$. Without loss of generality, we consider $(s + q)$-dimensional approximations of the form

$$(u_s, 0) \cdot x \oplus (w_q, 0) \cdot \mathcal{E}_K(x), \ u_s \in \mathbb{Z}_2^s, w_q \in \mathbb{Z}_2^q.$$

It is easy to derive the capacity as follows:

$$C_p = \sum_{(u_s, w_q)=1}^{2^{s+q}-1} c(u_s \cdot x_s \oplus (w_q, 0) \cdot \mathcal{E}_K(x_s, x_t))^2.$$

3.3 The Convolution Method

In 2009, Hermelin *et al.* described two statistical methods [10] in multidimensional linear cryptanalysis: LLR (log-likelihood) method and χ^2 method. In 2010, they presented the other convolution method [11] which has the same data complexity as the LLR-method but less time complexity. In our work, we apply the convolution method to PRINCE$_{core}$.

Given m-dimensional linear approximations, let $p = (p_0, p_1, \cdots, p_{2^m-1})$ denote the probability distribution, and the capacity C_p can be calculated using the method explained in Sect. 3.2 Suppose l is the length of the guessed key candidate, then for each $k \in \mathbb{Z}_2^l$, one can obtain the empirical distributions $q^k = (q_0^k, q_1^k, \cdots, q_{2^m-1}^k)$. Then we can sort the key candidates by the convolution $G_k = p * q^k$ which can be computed using FFT (Fast Fourier Transform) with time complexity of $m2^m$. We decide the key candidates k the right key if and only if $G_k \geq \tau$, where τ is the threshold that depends on the success probability Ps.

If the right key is ranked in the position of d from the top out of 2^l key candidates, we say that the attack has the advantage $a = l - log_2 d$ [9]. The relationship among the data complexity N, success probability Ps, capacity C, dimension of linear approximations m and the advantage a is derived in [11] as

$$N = (\sqrt{2(a+m)} + \Phi^{-1}(Ps))^2 / C,$$

where $\Phi(x) = \int_{-\infty}^{x} \frac{1}{\sqrt{2\pi}} e^{-t^2/2} dt$.

4 New Methodologies for Linear Cryptanalysis

4.1 Classification of Linear Trails

The fundamental theory of linear cryptanalysis depends on the assumption that the round-keys are independent. Clearly, PRINCE$_{core}$ does not have independent round-keys, since all the round-keys are identical to one specific key, i.e., $K = k \parallel k \parallel \cdots \parallel k$. The classic method appears to be invalid. In this section, we dig deep into the original definition of the correlation of linear approximations and gain Theorem 6, which is the key for our new technique.

Theorem 5. *Let g be the round function of an R-round key-alternating iterated block cipher $\mathcal{E}_k$ with identical round-key $k \in \mathbb{Z}_2^n$. Then for any $u, v, w \in \mathbb{Z}_2^n$, it holds that*

$$E_k[c(u \cdot x \oplus v \cdot k \oplus w \cdot \mathcal{E}_k(x))] = \sum_{\substack{u_1, \cdots, u_{R-1} \\ u_0 = u, u_R = w \\ u_0 \oplus \cdots \oplus u_R = v}} \prod_{i=1}^{R} c(u_{i-1} \cdot x \oplus u_i \cdot g_i(x)).$$

Proof. According to Theorem 1, the correlation of approximation $u \cdot x \oplus v \cdot k \oplus w \cdot \mathcal{E}_k(x)$ can be calculated as follows.

$$E_k[c(u \cdot x \oplus v \cdot k \oplus w \cdot \mathcal{E}_k(x))]$$

$$= E_k\Big[\sum_{\substack{u_1, \cdots, u_{R-1} \\ u_0 = u, u_R = w}} (-1)^{u_0 \cdot k \oplus \cdots \oplus u_R \cdot k \oplus v \cdot k} \prod_{i=1}^{R} c(u_{i-1} \cdot x \oplus u_i \cdot g_i(x))\Big]$$

$$= \sum_{\substack{u_1, \cdots, u_{R-1} \\ u_0 = u, u_R = w}} \Big(2^{-n} \sum_{k} (-1)^{(u_0 \oplus \cdots \oplus u_R \oplus v) \cdot k}\Big) \prod_{i=1}^{R} c(u_{i-1} \cdot x \oplus u_i \cdot g_i(x))$$

$$= \sum_{\substack{u_1, \cdots, u_{R-1} \\ u_0 = u, u_R = w \\ u_0 \oplus \cdots \oplus u_R = v}} \prod_{i=1}^{R} c(u_{i-1} \cdot x \oplus u_i \cdot g_i(x))$$

$\square$

As shown in Theorem 2 with independent-key assumption, only one trail $(u_0, u_1, \cdots, u_R) = v$ contributes to the average correlation for the target linear approximation. By contrast, in our new technique, linear trails whose XOR sum of trail masks is v all contribute to the average correlation. Therefore, in the case of ciphers with identical round-key, the upper bound for correlation of single trail does not imply the upper bound for correlation of any linear approximation. Furthermore, the limitation for correlation of single linear trail does not always thwart the linear attack using Matsui's Algorithm 1 [2].

Theorem 6. *Let g be the round function of an R-round key-alternating iterated block cipher $\mathcal{E}_k$ with identical round-key $k \in \mathbb{Z}_2^n$. Then for any $u \in \mathbb{Z}_2^n$ and $w \in \mathbb{Z}_2^n$, it holds that*

$$E_k[c(u \cdot x \oplus w \cdot \mathcal{E}_k(x))^2] = \sum_{\theta=0}^{2^n-1} \Big(\sum_{\substack{u_1, \cdots, u_{R-1} \\ u_0 = u, u_R = w \\ u_0 \oplus \cdots \oplus u_R = \theta}} \prod_{i=1}^{R} c(u_{i-1} \cdot x \oplus u_i \cdot g_i(x)) \Big)^2.$$

Proof. According to Theorem 1, the squared correlation of approximation $u \cdot x \oplus w \cdot \mathcal{E}_k(x)$ can be calculated as follows, where $c_{u_i, u_{i-1}}$ denotes $c(u_{i-1} \cdot x \oplus u_i \cdot g_i(x))$ for simplicity.

$$c(u \cdot x \oplus w \cdot \mathcal{E}_k(x))^2$$

$$= (\sum_{\substack{u_1,\cdots,u_{R-1} \\ u_0=u, u_R=w}} (-1)^{u_0 \cdot k \oplus \cdots \oplus u_R \cdot k} \prod_{i=1}^{R} c(u_{i-1} \cdot x \oplus u_i \cdot g_i(x)))^2$$

$$= \sum_{\substack{u_1,\cdots,u_{R-1} \\ u_0=u, u_R=w}} \sum_{\substack{u_1',\cdots,u_{R-1}' \\ u_0'=u, u_R'=w}} (-1)^{(u_0 \oplus \cdots \oplus u_R \oplus u_0' \oplus \cdots \oplus u_R') \cdot k} \prod_{i=1}^{R} c_{u_i,u_{i-1}} \prod_{j=1}^{R} c_{u_i',u_{i-1}'}.$$

Then we can compute the average squared correlation accordingly.

$$E_k[c(u \cdot x \oplus w \cdot \mathcal{E}_k(x))^2]$$

$$= 2^{-n} \sum_k \sum_{\substack{u_1,\cdots,u_{R-1} \\ u_0=u, u_R=w}} \sum_{\substack{u_1',\cdots,u_{R-1}' \\ u_0'=u, u_R'=w}} (-1)^{(u_0 \oplus \cdots \oplus u_R \oplus u_0' \oplus \cdots \oplus u_R') \cdot k} \prod_{i=1}^{R} c_{u_i,u_{i-1}} \prod_{j=1}^{R} c_{u_i',u_{i-1}'}$$

$$= \sum_{\substack{u_1,\cdots,u_{R-1} \\ u_0=u, u_R=w}} \sum_{\substack{u_1',\cdots,u_{R-1}' \\ u_0'=u, u_R'=w}} (2^{-n} \sum_k (-1)^{(u_0 \oplus \cdots \oplus u_R \oplus u_0' \oplus \cdots \oplus u_R') \cdot k}) \prod_{i=1}^{R} c_{u_i,u_{i-1}} \prod_{j=1}^{R} c_{u_i',u_{i-1}'}$$

$$= \sum_{\substack{u_1,\cdots,u_{R-1},u_1',\cdots,u_{R-1}' \\ u_0=u_0'=u, u_R=u_R'=w \\ u_0 \oplus \cdots \oplus u_R = u_0' \oplus \cdots \oplus u_R'}} \prod_{i=1}^{R} c_{u_i,u_{i-1}} \prod_{j=1}^{R} c_{u_i',u_{i-1}'}$$

$$= \sum_{\theta=0}^{2^n-1} (\sum_{\substack{u_1,\cdots,u_{R-1} \\ u_0=u, u_R=w \\ u_0 \oplus \cdots \oplus u_R = \theta}} \prod_{i=1}^{R} c_{u_i,u_{i-1}})^2.$$

□

As shown in Theorem 3, in classic linear attack with independent round-keys, squared correlation of each trails were added together as the correlation of the target one-dimensional approximation $u \cdot x \oplus w \cdot \mathcal{E}_K(x)$. On the basis of Theorem 6, in our new technique for linear attack with identical round-key, we first classify the linear trails into subsets indexed by the XOR sum of the linear masks $\theta = \sum_i u_i$. For each subset indexed by θ, we calculate the sum of the correlation of every trail in this subset and get $S_\theta = \sum_{\sum_i u_i = \theta} c(u \cdot x \oplus w \cdot \mathcal{E}_k(x))$. Then we square each sum S_θ, and add all the squared values up. Finally we obtain the average correlation as $\sum_\theta S_\theta^2$. We refer to this technique as classification technique.

4.2 Classification Technique in Calculating Capacity for Multiple Linear Approximations

Classification technique is then used to calculate the capacity of multiple approximations. For each one-dimensional approximation, we calculate its average squared correlation by Theorem 6. Then according to Theorem 4, we get the average capacity by simply summing up the average squared correlation of multiple approximations.

Furthermore, by applying this technique, we can perform a multidimensional linear attack on any key-alternating cipher with identical round-key, such as PRINCE [14] and LED [13].

5   A Multidimensional Linear Distinguisher on 8-Round PRINCE$_{core}$

In this section we apply the classification technique described in Sect. 4 to PRINCE$_{core}$.

5.1   Pattern Successions for 8-Round PRINCE$_{core}$

Set the linear mask $u \in \mathbb{Z}_2^{64}$ in terms of 16 nibbles $u = u[0]u[1] \cdots u[15]$. The *selection pattern* [16] of u is $P = P[0]P[1] \cdots P[15]$, and $u[i] \neq 0$ implies $P[i] = *$ while $u[i] = 0$ implies $P[i] = 0$. Furthermore, a linear trail $(u_0, u_1, \cdots, u_{R-1})$ corresponds to a succession of a selection pattern $P = (P_0, P_1, \cdots, P_{R-1})$.

The matrix M' used in PRINCE on the diffusion round has a branch number of four so that is not MDS (Maximum Distance Separable). In our multidimensional linear attack, we use the multiple approximations following the PRINCE Super-Box principle similar to AES [7], i.e., each of our 8-round linear trails contains 32 active S-boxes. There is another interesting property with M': if the input pattern of M' has a hamming weight of 1 (resp. 3) and the output pattern has a hamming weight of 3 (resp. 1), then each pattern maps to an unique linear trail with non-zero correlation, what's more, the trail's non-zero component mask has only one active bit. Therefore, each of our succession patterns corresponds to only one linear trail with non-zero correlation.

In our distinguisher for 8-round PRINCE$_{core}$, we find an input-output pattern and the multiple approximations satisfying this pattern have a capacity of $2^{-57.99}$. The input pattern is $P_0 = [0{*}00\ 0000\ 0000\ 0000]$ and output pattern is $P_8 = [{**}0{*}\ 0000\ 0000\ 0000]$. There are 389 pattern successions with non-zero correlation satisfying (P_0, P_8), i.e., 389 non-trivial linear trails covering 32 active S-boxes. We present one of the pattern successions in Appendix A.

For each of the pattern succession we find, there exists another inverse pattern succession starting from the output pattern and generating backwards. Due to the α-reflection property, the encryption of PRINCE is simply done just by decryption with a related key. Since the capacity is averaged over entire key space, the pattern generated backwards has the same average capacity.

5.2   Capacity Estimates of Multiple Linear Approximations for PRINCE$_{core}$

Set input-output pattern (P_0, P_R), the corresponding m-dimensional linear approximations are $U \cdot x \oplus W \cdot \mathcal{E}_k(x)$, where $U = (u_0, u_1, \cdots, u_{m-1})^T$,

$W = (w_0, w_1, \cdots, w_{m-1})^T$ satisfy $u_i \in P_0, w_i \in P_R$ for all $i = 0, 1, \cdots, m-1$. In the case of 8-round PRINCE$_{core}$ where $P_0 = [0*00\ 0000\ 0000\ 0000]$ and $P_8 = [**0*\ 0000\ 0000\ 0000]$, we have $m = 16$, since there are total of 16 active bits in (P_0, P_8). By Theorem 6 we can get average squared correlation $E_k[c(u_i \cdot x \oplus w_i \cdot \mathcal{E}_k(x))^2]$ for each one-dimensional approximation. Then according to Theorem 4, the capacity of m-dimensional approximations is

$$E_k[C] = \sum_{i=0}^{m-1} E_k[c(u_i \cdot x \oplus w_i \cdot \mathcal{E}_k(x))^2].$$

See also Algorithm 1 in Appendix B, which describes how to compute the average capacity of the multidimensional linear approximations for R-round PRINCE$_{core}$.

Algorithm 1 provides a general method for linear attacks against key-alternating ciphers with identical round-key. Compared to the classic linear attacks for calculating the capacity [5], not only do we store the correlations indexed by current linear mask, but also the XOR sum of previous linear masks, which increases the memory requirement. Both of the computation and storage complexity depend on the number of valid linear trails, i.e., the linear trails with non-zero correlation. Luckily, in PRINCE$_{core}$ there are not many of them, since each pattern succession results in only one valid linear trail. Otherwise both the computation complexity and the memory requirement will grow at an exponential rate as the number of rounds increases.

It is worth mentioning that the estimated capacity calculated by Algorithm 1 is NOT always smaller than the accurate capacity. That is determined by the accurate capacity formula in Theorem 6. When we abandon many trivial trails which have negligible correlations, the sum before squaring is biased and we cannot predict whether it is larger or smaller. Thus it leads to the estimated capacity biased in an ambiguous direction.

6   Multidimensional Linear Cryptanalysis of PRINCE$_{core}$

6.1   Break 10-Round PRINCE$_{core}$ Using Matsui's Algorithm 2

Assuming the attacked rounds are the intermediate 8 rounds from Rounds 1 to 9 of PRINCE$_{core}$, we use the 8-round distinguisher to break 8-round PRINCE$_{core}$. We denote the ith nibble of the input to round r by $x_{r-1}[i](1 \le r \le 9, 0 \le i \le 15)$, and the output of round 9 by x_9. The nibble $x_1[1]$ is affected by the 1th column of plaintext x_0, and $x_8[0], x_8[1], x_8[3]$ is affected by the $0^{th}, 1^{th}, 2^{th}$ column of ciphertext x_9 respectively. The partial encryption function of $x_1[1]$ admits the form $x_1[1] = e(x_0[4, 5, 6, 7] \oplus k[4, 5, 6, 7])$, then it suffices to compute only the 2^{16} encryptions $e(a), a \in \mathbb{Z}_2^{16}$, which can be done off-line. So in the off-line phase, for each $a \in \mathbb{Z}_2^{16}$, we computed $x_1[1] = e(a)$ and stored it in an array $T_e^{x_1[1]}(a)$. Given a key candidate $k[4, 5, 6, 7]$, the table $T^{x_1[1]}$ is permuted to obtain $T_{k[4,5,6,7]}^{x_1[1]}$ s.t. $T_{k[4,5,6,7]}^{x_1[1]}(a) = T^{x_1[1]}(a \oplus k[4, 5, 6, 7])$. For the same purpose, we constructed three other tables $T^{x_8[0]}, T^{x_8[1]}, T^{x_8[3]}$ by partial decryption.

The dimension of our multidimensional linear approximation is $m = 16$. Set $Ps = 0.95$, given the desired advantage $a = 4$, by the convolution method of Sect. 3.3, we require $N \approx 2^{63.84}$ known plaintexts to recover 64-bit identical round-key k.

1. Collect N plaintexts with corresponding ciphertexts.
2. Allocate a 8-bit counter $N_0(s_0, s_9^0, s_9^1, s_9^3)$ for each of 2^{64} possible values of $(s_0, s_9^0, s_9^1, s_9^3)$, where $s_0 = x_0[4,5,6,7]$ and $s_9^0 = x_9[0,1,2,3]$, $s_9^1 = x_9[4,5,6,7]$, $s_9^3 = x_9[12,13,14,15]$, and initialize them by zero. Calculate the numbers of pairs of plaintext-ciphertext with given value $(s_0, s_9^0, s_9^1, s_9^3)$ and save it in $N_0(s_0, s_9^0, s_9^1, s_9^3)$. In this step, N plaintext-ciphertext pairs are divided into 2^{64} different state. The number of expected pairs for each state is less than 1. So a memory space of 8-bit for each counter N_0 is sufficient.
3. Guess the 4 nibbles $k[4,5,6,7]$ of the identical round-key, obtain $T^{x_1[1]}_{k[4,5,6,7]}$, $T^{x_8[3]}_{k[4,5,6,7]}$ by permutation of table $T^{x_1[1]}$, $T^{x_8[3]}$ respectively. Allocate a counter $N_1(s_1, s_9^0, s_8^3, s_9^3)$ for each of 2^{40} possible values of $(s_1, s_9^0, s_8^3, s_9^3)$, where $s_1 = x_1[2]$ and $s_8^3 = x_8[3]$, and initialize them by zero. For all 2^{64} possible values of $(s_0, s_9^0, s_9^1, s_9^3)$, obtain $s_1 = T^{x_1[1]}_{k[4,5,6,7]}(s_0)$, $s_8^3 = T^{x_8[3]}_{k[4,5,6,7]}(s_9^1)$, and update the counter $N_1(s_1, s_9^0, s_8^3, s_9^3) = N_1(s_1, s_9^0, s_8^3, s_9^3) + N_0(s_0, s_9^0, s_9^3, s_9^3)$.
4. Guess the 4 nibbles $k[0,1,2,3]$ of the identical round-key, obtain $T^{x_8[0]}_{k[0,1,2,3]}$ by permutation of table $T^{x_8[0]}$. Allocate a counter $N_2(s_1, s_8^0, s_8^3, s_9^3)$ for each of 2^{28} possible values of $(s_1, s_8^0, s_8^3, s_9^3)$, where $s_8^0 = x_8[0]$, and initialize them by zero. For all 2^{40} possible values of $(s_0, s_9^0, s_8^3, s_9^3)$, obtain $s_8^0 = T^{x_8[0]}_{k[0,1,2,3]}(s_9^0)$ by a table access, and update the counter $N_2(s_1, s_8^0, s_8^3, s_9^3) = N_2(s_1, s_8^0, s_8^3, s_9^3) + N_1(s_0, s_9^0, s_8^3, s_9^3)$.
5. Guess the 4 nibbles $k[12,13,14,15]$ of the identical round-key, obtain $T^{x_8[1]}_{k[12,13,14,15]}$ by permutation of table $T^{x_8[1]}$. Allocate a counter $N_3(s_1, s_8^0, s_8^3, s_8^1)$ for each of 2^{12} possible values of $(s_1, s_8^0, s_8^3, s_8^1)$, where $s_8^1 = x_8[1]$, and initialize them by zero. For all 2^{28} possible values of $(s_1, s_8^0, s_8^3, s_9^3)$, obtain $s_8^1 = T^{x_8[1]}_{k[12,13,14,15]}(s_9^3)$ by a table access, and update the counter $N_3(s_1, s_8^0, s_8^3, s_8^1) = N_3(s_1, s_8^0, s_8^3, s_8^1) + N_2(s_1, s_8^0, s_8^3, s_9^3)$.
6. Allocate a counter $N(z)$ for each of 2^{16} possible values of z where z denotes the pairwise concatenating of s_1 and (s_8^0, s_8^1, s_8^3), and initialize them by zero. For all 2^{12} possible values of $(s_1, s_8^0, s_8^3, s_8^1)$, obtain z, and update the counter $N(z) = N(z) + N_3(s_8^0, s_8^3, s_8^1)$. Compute the convolution mask G_{k_g} where k_g denotes the guess key, if G_{k_g} is in the top 2^{44}, then the k_g is a possible key candidate.
7. Search the rest of 16-bit key from the top of the possible key candidates.

Attack Complexity: The memory complexity of the attack is dominated by step 2 which needs 2^{64} bytes. Step 3 requires $2^{64} \times 2^{16} \times 2 = 2^{81}$ table look-up, step 4 requires $2^{40} \times 2^{16} = 2^{56}$ table look-up, and step 5 requires $2^{28} \times 2^{16} = 2^{44}$ table look-up. Step 7 requires $2^{44} \times 2^{16} = 2^{60}$ encryptions of 10-round $PRINCE_{core}$.

If we consider one table look-up as a quarter of one round encryption, the time complexity of this attack is $(2^{81} + 2^{56} + 2^{44}) \times \frac{1}{4} \times \frac{1}{10} + 2^{60} \approx 2^{75.68}$ of 10-round PRINCE$_{core}$.

6.2 Break 9-Round PRINCE$_{core}$ Using 8-Round Distinguisher

The 8-round multidimensional linear distinguisher enables us to break 9-round PRINCE$_{core}$, and the attack is basically the version of the above 10-round attack when the last round is removed. With $Ps = 0.95, a = 4$, the attack requires $N \approx 2^{63.84}$ known plaintexts. To recover $k[4,5,6,7]$, a memory space of $2^{28} \times 8 = 2^{31}$ bytes and a time complexity of $2^{28} \times 2^{16} \times \frac{1}{4} \times \frac{1}{9} \approx 2^{38.83}$ is needed. Finally, we get the remaining 48 bits of the identical round key by exhaustive search. So the overall time complexity is $2^{38.83} + 2^{12} \times 2^{48} \approx 2^{60}$ 9-round PRINCE$_{core}$.

7 A Multidimensional Linear Distinguisher on 1-Step LED

Furthermore, this technique can be applied to all the other key-alternating ciphers with identical round-key. For example, we find several multidimensional linear approximations for 1-step LED [13], which has two identical whitening keys before the first round and after the last round. We fix the number of active S-boxes to 25 for four rounds of LED and find 16 multidimensional linear approximations with non-zero capacity. The one of maximum capacity $2^{-41.65}$ is with input pattern $P_0 = [0000\ 0*00\ 0000\ 0000]$ and output pattern $P_1 = [0000\ 0000\ 0000\ 00*0]$.

8 Conclusion

Due to its identical round-key property, block cipher PRINCE did not provide evidence on its resistance against multidimensional linear cryptanalysis which bases on round-key independent assumption. We propose a new classification technique and solve the problem. Using this new technique, we build an 8-round multidimensional linear distinguisher with capacity $2^{-57.99}$, and exhibit a key-recovery attack on 9 out of 12 round of PRINCE$_{core}$. This attack requires a data complexity of $2^{63.84}$ known plaintexts and time complexity of 2^{60} encryptions. We also present a key-recovery attack on 10-round PRINCE$_{core}$ with data complexity of $2^{63.84}$ known plaintexts and time complexity of $2^{75.68}$ encryptions.

Due to the links between multidimensional linear and multi-differential cryptanalysis [15], we hope our results will motivate the evaluation of the resistance of PRINCE and LED against multi-differential attack.

Appendix

A   An Example of a Pattern Succession over 8-Round PRINCE$_{core}$

(See Fig. 3).

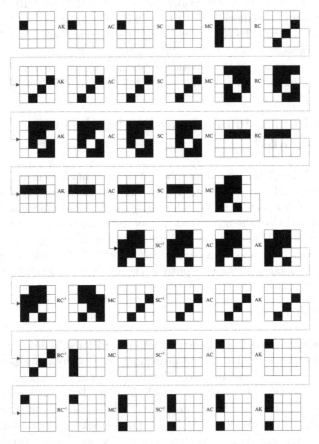

Fig. 3. A pattern succession satisfying P_0 = [0∗00 0000 0000 0000], P_8 = [∗∗0∗ 0000 0000 0000]

B   Compute the Average Capacity for R-Round Key-Alternating Cipher

---

Algorithm 1. Compute the average capacity for R-round key-alternating cipher

---

Require:

input pattern P_0 and output pattern P_R.

Ensure:

capacity of multiple linear approximations corresponding to input-output pattern.

1: search all the pattern successions $P = (P_1, \cdots, P_{R-1})$ connected to the given pattern (P_0, P_R);
2: set $sum \leftarrow 0$;
3: **for** each $u \in P_0, w \in P_R$ **do**
4:     set $sum[\theta] \leftarrow 0$ for all θ;
5:     **for** each P **do**
6:         set $\Gamma_{\text{thisRnd}}[u][\lambda] \leftarrow 1$ for $\lambda = u$;
7:         **for** $r \leftarrow 2$ to R **do**
8:             lastRnd $\leftarrow$ thisRnd;
9:             **for** each $w \in P_r$ **do**
10:                 **for** each $u \in P_{r-1}, \lambda$ **do**
11:                     $\theta \leftarrow \lambda \oplus w$;
12:                     $\Gamma_{\text{thisRnd}}[w][\theta] \leftarrow \Gamma_{\text{thisRnd}}[w][\theta] + \Gamma_{\text{lastRnd}}[u][\lambda] \cdot c_{w,u}$;
13:                 **end for**
14:             **end for**
15:         **end for**
16:         **for** each θ **do**
17:             $sum[\theta] \leftarrow sum[\theta] + \Gamma_{\text{R}}[w][\theta]$;
18:         **end for**
19:     **end for**
20:     $sum \leftarrow sum + \sum_\theta sum[\theta]^2$;
21: **end for**
22: **return** sum;

References

1. Eli, B., Shamir, A.: Differential cryptanalysis of DES-like cryptosystems. J. Cryptology 4(1), 3–72 (1991)
2. Matsui, M.: Linear cryptanalysis method for DES cipher. In: Helleseth, T. (ed.) EUROCRYPT 1993. LNCS, vol. 765, pp. 386–397. Springer, Heidelberg (1994)
3. Matsui, M.: The first experimental cryptanalysis of the data encryption standard. In: Desmedt, Y.G. (ed.) CRYPTO 1994. LNCS, vol. 839, pp. 1–11. Springer, Heidelberg (1994)
4. Nyberg, K.: Linear approximation of block ciphers. In: De Santis, A. (ed.) EUROCRYPT 1994. LNCS, vol. 950, pp. 439–444. Springer, Heidelberg (1995)

5. Hermelin, M., Nyberg, K.: Linear crypranalysis Using Multiple Linear Approximation. IACR Cryptology ePrint Archive 2011.93
6. Nyberg, K.: Correlation theorems in cryptanalysis. Discrete Appl. Math. **111**(1), 177–188 (2001)
7. Daemen, J., Rijmen, V.: The Design of Rijndael: AES - The Advanced Encryption Standard. Information Security and Cryptography. Springer, Heidelberg (2002)
8. Hermelin, M., Nyberg, K.: Multidimensional linear distinguishing attacks and Boolean functions. In: Fourth International Workshop on Boolean Functions: Cryptography and Applications (2008)
9. Selçuk, A.A.: On probability of success in linear and differential cryptanalysis. J. Cryptology **21**(1), 131–147 (2008)
10. Hermelin, M., Cho, J.Y., Nyberg, K.: Multidimensional extension of Matsui's Algorithm 2. In: Dunkelman, O. (ed.) FSE 2009. LNCS, vol. 5665, pp. 209–227. Springer, Heidelberg (2009)
11. Hermelin, M., Nyberg, K.: Dependent linear approximations: the algorithm of Biryukov and others revisited. In: Pieprzyk, J. (ed.) CT-RSA 2010. LNCS, vol. 5985, pp. 318–333. Springer, Heidelberg (2010)
12. Hermelin, M.: Multidimensional linear cryptanalysis. Ph.D. thesis, Aalto University School of Science and Technology (2010)
13. Guo, J., Peyrin, T., Poschmann, A., Robshaw, M.: The LED block cipher. In: Preneel, B., Takagi, T. (eds.) CHES 2011. LNCS, vol. 6917, pp. 326–341. Springer, Heidelberg (2011)
14. Borghoff, J., Canteaut, A., Güneysu, T., Kavun, E.B., Knezevic, M., Knudsen, L.R., Leander, G., Nikov, V., Paar, C., Rechberger, C., Rombouts, P., Thomsen, S.S., Yalçın, T.: PRINCE – a low-latency block cipher for pervasive computing applications. In: Wang, X., Sako, K. (eds.) ASIACRYPT 2012. LNCS, vol. 7658, pp. 208–225. Springer, Heidelberg (2012)
15. Blondeau, C., Nyberg, K.: New links between differential and linear cryptanalysis. In: Johansson, T., Nguyen, P.Q. (eds.) EUROCRYPT 2013. LNCS, vol. 7881, pp. 388–404. Springer, Heidelberg (2013)
16. Hakala, R.M., Kivelä, A., Nyberg, K.: Estimating resistance against multidimensional linear attacks: an application on DEAN. In: Kutyłowski, M., Yung, M. (eds.) Inscrypt 2012. LNCS, vol. 7763, pp. 246–262. Springer, Heidelberg (2013)
17. Soleimany, H., Blondeau, C., Yu, X., Wu, W., Nyberg, K., Zhang, H., Zhang, L., Wang, Y.: Reflection cryptanalysis of PRINCE-like ciphers. In: Moriai, S. (ed.) FSE 2013. LNCS, vol. 8424, pp. 71–91. Springer, Heidelberg (2013)
18. Jean, J., Nikolić, I., Peyrin, T., Wang, L., Wu, S.: Security analysis of PRINCE. In: Moriai, S. (ed.) FSE 2013. LNCS, vol. 8424, pp. 92–111. Springer, Heidelberg (2013)

Cryptanalysis 2

Rebound Attacks on Stribog

Riham AlTawy[(✉)], Aleksandar Kircanski, and Amr M. Youssef

Concordia Institute for Information Systems Engineering,
Concordia University, Montréal, QC H4B 1R6, Canada
r_altaw@encs.concordia.ca

Abstract. In August 2012, the Stribog hash function was selected as the new Russian hash standard (GOST R 34.11–2012). Stribog is an AES-based primitive and is considered as an asymmetric reply to the new SHA-3. In this paper we investigate the collision resistance of the Stribog compression function and its internal cipher. Specifically, we present a message differential path for the internal block cipher that allows us to efficiently obtain a 5-round free-start collision and a 7.75 free-start near collision for the internal cipher with complexities 2^8 and 2^{40}, respectively. Finally, the compression function is analyzed and a 7.75 round semi free-start collision, 8.75 and 9.75 round semi free-start near collisions are presented along with an example for 4.75 round 50 out of 64 bytes near colliding message pair.

Keywords: Cryptanalysis · Hash functions · Meet in the middle · Rebound attack · GOST R 34.11-2012 · Stribog

1 Introduction

Wang *et al.* attacks on MD5 [21] and SHA-1 [20] followed by the SHA-3 competition [3] have led to a flurry in the area of hash function cryptanalysis where different design concepts and various attack strategies were introduced. Many of the proposed attacks were not only targeting basic properties but they also studied any non-ideal behaviour of the hash function, compression function, internal cipher, or the used domain extender.

Stribog was proposed in 2010 [10]. It has an output length of 512/256-bit and its compression function employs a 12-round AES-like cipher with 8×8-byte internal state preceded with one round of nonlinear whitening of the chaining value. The compression function operates in Miyaguchi-Preneel mode and is plugged in Merkle-Damgård domain extender with a finalization step [6]. Stribog officially replaces the previous standard GOST R 34.11-94 which has been theoretically broken in [13,14] and recently analyzed in [11].

The rebound attack [15] is a differential attack proposed by Mendel *et al.* during the SHA-3 competition to construct differential paths for AES-based hash functions. Previous literature related to the rebound attack includes Mendel *et al.* first proposal on the ISO standard Whirlpool and the SHA-3 finalist

© Springer International Publishing Switzerland 2014
H.-S. Lee and D.-G. Han (Eds.): ICISC 2013, LNCS 8565, pp. 175–188, 2014.
DOI: 10.1007/978-3-319-12160-4_11

Grøstl [15,16]. In particular, Mendel *et al.* presented a 4.5-round collision, 5.5-round semi free-start collision and 7.5-round near collision attacks on the Whirlpool compression function. As for Grøstl-256, a 6-round semi free-start collision is given. Subsequently, rebound attacks have been applied to other AES-based hash functions such as LANE [9], JH [17], and Echo [5]. Various tweaks have been applied to the basic rebound attack in order to construct differential paths that cover more rounds such as merging multiple in-bounds [8], super Sbox cryptanalysis [4], extended 5-round inbound [8], and linearized match-in-the-middle and start-from-the-middle techniques [12]. Lastly, Sasaki *et al.* [18] presented a free-start collision and near collision attacks on Whirlpool by inserting difference in the intermediate keys to cancel the difference propagation in the message and thus creating local collisions every 4 rounds.

In this work, we investigate the security of the Stribog hash function primitives, assessing their resistance to rebound attacks. We efficiently produce free-start collision and near collision for the internal cipher (E) reduced to 5 and 7.75 rounds by employing the concept of local collisions. Specifically, we present a message differential path such that a local collision is enforced every 2 rounds. Thus we bypass the complexity of the rebound matching in the message in-bounds by using the same differentials as in the key path. Consequently, in contrast to [18], finding one key satisfying the key path is practically sufficient for finding a message pair following the message path. Finally, we present a practical 4.75 round 50 (out of 64) bytes near colliding message pair for the compression function and show that it is vulnerable to semi free-start 7.75 round collision, 8.75 and 9.75 round near collision attacks. Examples for the internal cipher attacks and the 4.75 round compression function near-collision attack are provided to validate our results.

The rest of the paper is organized as follows. In the next section, the specification of the Stribog hash function along with the notation used throughout the paper are provided. A brief overview of the rebound attack is given in Sect. 3. Afterwards, in Sects. 4 and 5, we provide detailed description of our attacks, differential patterns, and the complexities of the attacks. Finally, the paper is concluded in Sect. 6.

2   Specification of Stribog

Stribog outputs a 512 or 256-bit hash value and can process up to 2^{512}-bit message. The compression function iterates over 12 rounds of an AES-like cipher with an 8×8 byte internal state and a final round of key mixing. The compression function operates in Miyaguchi-Preneel mode and is plugged in Merkle-Damgård domain extender with a finalization step. The input message M is padded into a multiple of 512 bits by appending one followed by zeros. Given $M = m_n\|..\|m_1\|m_0$, the compression function g_N is fed with three inputs: the chaining value h_{i-1}, a message block m_{i-1}, and the number of bits hashed so far $N_{i-1} = 512 \times i$. (see Fig. 1). Let h_i be a 512-bit chaining variable. The first state is loaded with the initial value IV and assigned to h_0. The hash value of M is computed as follows:

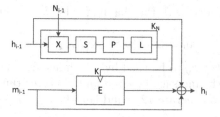

Fig. 1. Stribog's compression function g_N

$$h_i \leftarrow g_N(h_{i-1}, m_{i-1}, N_{i-1}) \text{ for } i = 1, 2, .., n+1$$
$$h_{n+2} \leftarrow g_0(h_{n+1}, |M|, 0)$$
$$h(M) \leftarrow g_0(h_{n+2}, \sum(m_0, .., m_n), 0),$$

where $h(M)$ is the hash value of M. As depicted in Fig. 1, the compression function g_N consists of:

- K_N: a nonlinear whitening round of the chaining value. It takes a 512-bit chaining variable h_{i-1} and the number of bits hashed so far N_{i-1} and outputs a 512-bit key K.
- E: an AES-based cipher that iterates over the message for 12 rounds in addition to a finalization key mixing round. The cipher E takes a 512-bit key K and a 512-bit message block m as a plaintext. As shown in Fig. 2, it consists of two similar parallel flows for the state update and the key scheduling.

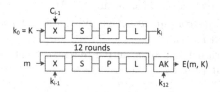

Fig. 2. The internal block cipher (E)

Both K_N and E operate on an 8×8 byte key state K. E updates an additional 8×8 byte message state M. In one round, a given state is updated by the following sequence of transformations

- AddKey(X): XOR with either a round key, a constant, or the number of bits hashed so far (N).
- SubBytes (S): A nonlinear byte bijective mapping.
- Transposition (P): Byte permutation.
- MixRows (L): Left multiplication by an MDS matrix in GF(2).

Initially, state K is loaded with the chaining value h_{i-1} and updated by K_N as follows:

$$k_0 = L \circ P \circ S \circ X[N_{i-1}](K)$$

Now K contains the key k_0 to be used by the cipher E. The message state M is initially loaded with the message block m and $E(k_0, m)$ runs the key scheduling function on state K to generate 12 round keys $k_1, k_2, .., k_{12}$ as follows:

$$k_i = L \circ P \circ S \circ X[C_{i-1}](k_{i-1}), \text{ for } i = 1, 2, .., 12,$$

where C_{i-1} is the ith round constant. The state M is updated as follows:

$$M_i = L \circ P \circ S \circ X[k_{i-1}](M_{i-1}), \text{ for } i = 1, 2, ..., 12.$$

The final round output is given by $E(k_0, m) = M_{12} \oplus k_{12}$. The output of g_N in the Miyaguchi-Preneel mode is $E(K_N(h_{i-1}, N_{i-1}), m_{i-1}) \oplus m_{i-1} \oplus h_{i-1}$ as shown in Fig. 1. For further details, the reader is referred to [1].

2.1 Notation

Let M and K be (8×8)-byte states denoting the message and key state, respectively. The following notation will be used throughout the paper:

- M_i: The message state at the beginning of round i.
- M_i^U: The message state after the U transformation at round i, where $U \in \{X, S, P, L\}$.
- $M_i[r, c]$: A byte at row r and column c of state M_i.
- $M_i[\text{row } r]$: Eight bytes located at row r of M_i state.
- $M_i[\text{col } c]$: Eight bytes located at column c of M_i state.
- $m \xrightarrow{r_i} n$: A transition from an m active bytes state at round i to an n active bytes state at round $i + 1$.
- $m \xleftarrow{r_i} n$: A transition from an n active bytes state at round $i + 1$ to an m active bytes state at round i.

Same notation applies to K.

3 The Rebound Attack

The rebound attack [15] is proposed by Mendel *et al.* for the cryptanalysis of AES-based hash functions. It is a differential attack that follows the inside-out or start from the middle approach which is used in the boomerang attack [19]. The rebound attack is composed of three phases, one inbound and two outbounds. The compression function, internal block cipher or permutation of a hash function is divided into three parts. If C is a block cipher, then C is expressed as $C = C_{fw} \circ C_{in} \circ C_{bw}$. The middle part is the inbound phase and the forward and backward parts are the two outbound phases. In the inbound phase, a low probability XOR differential path is used and all possible degrees of freedom are used to satisfy the inbound path. In the two outbound phases, high probability truncated paths [7] are used. In other words, one starts from the middle satisfying C_{in}, then hash forward and backward to satisfy C_{fw} and C_{bw} probabilistically. For an 8×8 byte state, the basic rebound attack finds two states satisfying an inbound phase over two rounds $8 \xrightarrow{r_i} 64 \xrightarrow{r_{i+1}} 8$. The main idea is to pick random differences at each of the two eight active bytes sates, then propagate both backward and forward until the output and input of the full active state Sbox, respectively. Using the Sbox differential distribution table (DDT), find values that satisfy input and output differentials. This process is further illustrated in Fig. 3. The last step of the attack is called the Sbox matching phase and its complexity depends on the Sbox DDT. If the probability of differentials that have solutions is p, then the matching probability is given by p^8. In the following, we analyze the Sbox used in Stribog and investigate how it affects the complexity of the rebound attack. The Stribog Sbox DDT has the following properties:

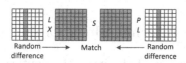

Fig. 3. The rebound attack.

- Out of the 65536 differentials, there are 27300 possible non trivial differentials, i.e., nonzero (input, output) difference pairs that have solutions. Thus the probability that a randomly chosen differential is possible $\approx 0.42 = 2^{-1.3}$.
- Each possible differential can have 2, 4, 6, or 8 solutions.
- A given input difference has a minimum of 98 and a maximum of 114 output differences.
- A given output difference has a minimum of 90 and a maximum of 128 input differences.
- For a given input (output) difference the average number of output (input) difference is 107.

From the analysis of the Sbox DDT, one can estimate the complexity of the inbound matching part of the rebound attack. Let us consider the basic inbound path $8 \xrightarrow{r_1} 64 \xrightarrow{r_2} 8$. One can find a pair of states satisfying this path as follows:

1. Compute the Sbox DDT.
2. Choose a random 8 differences for M_2^L active bytes.
3. Propagate the differences in M_2^L backwards until M_2^S (output difference).
4. For each row in M_1^P
   a. Choose a random difference for one active byte, propagate it forward to M_2^X (input difference). Propagating one active byte in M_1^P through the L transformation results in full active row in M_2^X.

    b. Using the Sbox DDT, determine if the corresponding row differences in M_2^X and M_2^S have solutions. If one byte differential pair is not possible, go to step 4.a.

One can repeat step (4.a) at most 2^8 times since we variate only one byte. However, the success probability of step 4.b. (finding solutions for the whole active row) is $2^{-1.3 \times 8} \approx 2^{-10}$ which cannot be easily satisfied by randomizing one byte difference. One would often have to restart at step 2, i.e., pick another output difference. The same situation takes place when we move to the next row and pick a new output difference. In this case we have to start from row 0. As a result, the complexity of finding solutions to the 8 rows is not purely added [15]. Based on our experimental results, the complexity of this inbound path is in the order of 2^{18}. However finding this match means finding at least 2^{64} actual state values for M_2^X, such that both M_2^X and $M_2^X \oplus$ (input difference) follow the inbound path. Each value out of the 2^{64} values is a new starting point to satisfy the two outbound paths. In the following section, we present our attack on the internal block cipher of the Stribog compression function.

4   Attacks on the Internal Block Cipher (E)

Verifying the ideal behaviour of the internal primitives of a hash function is important to evaluate its resistance to distinguishing attacks [2]. In this section we investigate the internal block cipher (E) and, by employing the idea of successive local collisions, we present a message differential path that collides every two rounds. This message differential path enables us to efficiently produce 5-round semi free-start collision and 7.75-round 40 bytes (out of 64) semi free-start near collision. The main idea of our approach is to first find a pair of keys that follows a given differential path and then use it to search for a pair of messages satisfying the message path. The approach of creating local collisions works perfectly if the key and the message flows are identical and the initial key is the input chaining value. To this end, one can keep similar differential patterns and the state message difference is cancelled after the X transformation. However, in the compression function of Stribog the key used in the internal cipher is the result of applying the K_N transformation on the input chaining value. Similar differential patterns can be obtained when considering the internal block cipher. In our attack on the Stribog internal cipher, we present a message differential path such that a local collision is enforced every two rounds. Specifically, we first search for a pair of keys that satisfies the key differential path, then we use the Sbox differentials in the key path for the message path. Consequently, we bypass the complexity caused by the Sbox DDT matching in the message differential path and only one key pair is required to search for a message pair. In [18], Sasaki et al. presented a message differential path that creates local collisions every four rounds for the Whirlpool compression function and reported that they had to try 109 key pairs to search for a message pair that collides every 4 round. Furthermore, they estimated an increase in the message search complexity by a factor of 2^7 and attributed this to the imbalance of the Sbox DDT. Given the Stribog Sbox DDT, finding one key pair that follows the 8-round differential path takes up to two hours on an 8-core Intel i7 CPU running at 2.6 GHz. Accordingly, it is important that the message differential path requires only one key pair to be satisfied. In what follows, we give the details of our approach.

4.1   5-Round Free-Start Collision

Since the Stribog's Sbox DDT is biased with possible differential probability ≈ 0.42, we bypass the Sbox matching phase by using a message differential path such that local collisions are created every two rounds. The used key and message paths are given by:

$$\text{Key: } 64 \xrightarrow{r_1} 8 \xrightarrow{r_2} 1 \xrightarrow{r_3} 8 \xrightarrow{r_4} 64$$

$$\text{Message: } 64 \xrightarrow{r_1} 0 \xrightarrow{r_2} 1 \xrightarrow{r_3} 0 \xrightarrow{r_4} 64 \xrightarrow{r_5} 0$$

This message differential path allows us to bypass the rebound matching part completely in our message search because the same input and output Sbox differences in the key path are used for the message path. Thus the matching probability is 1. Unlike the differential paths in [18], our message differential path

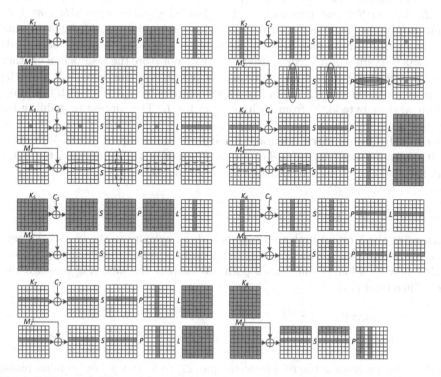

Fig. 4. 7.75 round differential path. Active bytes are coloured grey. Ellipses mark the row and column restricted by the two inbounds.

is satisfied practically using only one key pair. In this attack, we do not use the matching part of the rebound attack in either the key or the message; we only search for one byte value in the message to find a common solution between two rounds which can be considered as a meet in the middle approach. As depicted in Fig. 4, the steps for finding a key pair can be summarized as follows:

1. Choose a random difference and a random value for byte $K_2^L[3, 3]$.
2. Hash backward until K_1.
3. Hash forward until K_5.

Accordingly, we have a key pair following the given key path. Let the differences in M_2^X, M_2^S, M_4^X, and M_4^S be the same as the differences in K_2^X, K_2^S, K_4^X, and K_4^S, respectively. Having the same differences in the message states as in the key states implies that no differential matching is needed at the Sboxes of rounds 2 and 4, and guarantees that the differences in K_3 and M_3 cancel out. Similar observation applies to K_5 and M_5. To search for a conforming message pair, we need to find a common solution between the Sboxes of rounds 2 and 4 possible solutions. This can be achieved as follows. Since $M_2^X[\text{col } 3]$ and $M_2^S[\text{col } 3]$ differentials are possible, then from the Sbox DDT there are at least 2^8 values for $M_2^X[\text{col } 3]$ that satisfy the path until M_3^S. For all solution $M_2^X[\text{col } 3]$, hash forward until M_3^S. Because $M_2^X[\text{col } 3]$ is one column after the P, L, X, and S transformations, its transformed value becomes $M_3^S[\text{row } 3]$ as indicated by the ellipse in Fig. 4. We store all possible values of $M_3^S[\text{row } 3]$ in a list L. As for $M_4^X[\text{row } 3]$, and $M_4^S[\text{row } 3]$, hashing all possible solutions backwards restricts the values of $M_3^S[\text{col } 3]$. However we do not store the results in a another list. Because the two restricted results intersect in only one byte $M_3^S[3, 3]$ (the intersection of the two ellipses in Fig. 4), we compare byte $[3, 3]$ of each backward result against byte $[3, 3]$ from each entry in list L. The success probability for finding a one byte match is 2^{-8} which can be easily fulfilled by the number of entries in L. Once a match is found, we assign the matching list row to $M_3^S[\text{row } 3]$ and the backwards column to $M_3^S[\text{col } 3]$. The rest of the 49 unrestricted bytes are free and can be used to satisfy a longer outbound.

4.2   8-Round Collision and 7.75-Round Near Collision Attacks

Extending the 5 round path to 8 rounds adds complexity to the key search part because we need to use an improved version of the rebound attack to get a key pair following a longer differential path. We employ the following message and key differential paths:

$$\text{Key: } 64 \xrightarrow{r_1} 8 \xrightarrow{r_2} 1 \xrightarrow{r_3} 8 \xrightarrow{r_4} 64 \xrightarrow{r_5} 8 \xrightarrow{r_6} 8 \xrightarrow{r_7} 64$$

$$\text{Message: } 64 \xrightarrow{r_1} 0 \xrightarrow{r_2} 1 \xrightarrow{r_3} 0 \xrightarrow{r_4} 64 \xrightarrow{r_5} 0 \xrightarrow{r_6} 8 \xrightarrow{r_7} 64 \xrightarrow{r_8} 0$$

and use the start form the middle technique [12] to solve the key inbound phase between rounds 3 and 5. This approach finds states following a $1 \longrightarrow 8 \longrightarrow 64 \longrightarrow 8$ transition. Unlike the basic inbound that yields 2^{64} solutions, using this approach on Stribog results in only one solution. For AES Sboxes, a solution is expected in a time complexity of 2^8 and memory complexity of 2^8. However, for Stribog's biased Sbox DDT, one practical solution is found between 33 min to 2 h on an 8-core Intel i7 CPU running at 2.67 GHz. Accordingly, it is crucial that the key outbound phase has high probability if one is aiming for practical results and no rebound matching is used in the message search so that one key is enough to get a conforming message pair. In the following steps, we briefly describe the procedure we used for solving the $1 \longrightarrow 8 \longrightarrow 64 \longrightarrow 8$ key inbound phase. Figure 5 further illustrates the process.

1. Solve the basic inbound $8 \longrightarrow 64 \longleftarrow 8$ as explained in Sect. 3.
2. From the DDT, each byte difference in K_5^X has at least 2 and at most 8 values, such that any value satisfies the path from K_4^X to K_6.
3. To enforce the transition from 8 active bytes in K_4^X to 1 active byte in K_3^P, do the following:
   a. Create a table T_L of all possible 255 byte difference values d_3 (candidates for $K_3^P[3, 3]$) and their corresponding 8 byte difference values $L(d_3)$ (candidates for $K_4^X[\text{row } 3]$). These values are the result of applying the linear transformation L to a difference at column 3.
   b. Each candidate difference for $K_4^X[row\ 3]$ has 8 active bytes that can be manipulated independently. More precisely, to change the difference value of byte i in $K_4^X[\text{row } 3]$, one has to switch between 2^8 or more possible values of $K_5^X[\text{row } i]$. As illustrated by the ellipses in Fig. 5, a change in the values of $K_5^X[\text{row } 0]$ is reflected on the difference value of byte 0 in $K_4^X[\text{row } 3]$.
   c. Go through the entries in table T_L and change the values of K_5^X rows one by one until a match is found, if not, restart from step 1.

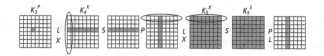

Fig. 5. Start from the middle approach.

Finally, by hashing the obtained key pair two rounds backward and two rounds forward, we get a conforming key pair that follows the key differential path. Once we have the key, we can directly get a message pair in the same way as explained in the previous section for the 5-round collision. This message pair satisfies the message differential path up until M_6^L. However, to have an 8-round collision, we need the difference in K_8 to cancel the difference in M_8 after the X transformation in round 8. Since both L and P transformations are linear, then this condition is satisfied if the 8 byte differences in K_7^S and M_7^S are equal. The difference in K_7^S is already set from the key search stage, so we randomize the 49 unrestricted bytes in M_3^S, hash forward till M_7^S and compare the resulting 8 differences with K_7^S. The probability that the 8 byte differences are equal is 2^{-64}. To verify the applicability of this attack, we have implemented a 7.75-round near collision attack where we were checking if only 5 out of 8 byte differences are equal in M_7^S and K_7^S. In Fig. 4, the implemented 7.75-round differential pattern, with 2^{40} time and 2^8 state memory complexities is given. Table 2 shows an example for a free-start 5-round collision and 7.75-round near collision for the internal cipher (E). Both the 5-round semi free-start collision and the 7.75 semi free-start near collision are demonstrated by one example because the 7.75 semi free-start near collision path collides at round 5.

5   Attacks on Stribog Compression Function

As depicted in Fig. 1, the compression function of Stribog employs a nonlinear whitening round K_N of the chaining value. This extra round randomizes the chaining value before being introduced as a key for the block cipher E. As long as there is no difference in the chaining value, most of the differential trails proposed for Whirlpool are also applicable on the Stribog compression function.

In what follows, we consider semi free-start collision attacks on the compression function. Several approaches are used to extend the inbound phase can be used to construct collision paths for the compression function. The extended 5 round inbound presented in [8] finds a pair of states satisfying the $8 \xrightarrow{r_1} 64 \xrightarrow{r_2} 8 \xrightarrow{r_3} 8 \xrightarrow{r_4} 64 \xrightarrow{r_5} 8$ transition in 2^{64} time and 2^8 memory. The main idea is to solve two independent $8 \xrightarrow{r_1} 64 \xrightarrow{r_2} 8$ and $8 \xrightarrow{r_4} 64 \xrightarrow{r_5} 8$ inbounds and use the freedom to choose key values that connect the resulting 8 differences and 64 byte values. However, unlike the basic inbound, it provides only one solution or starting point for the outbound paths. Using different outbounds with the extended inbound, a semi free-start 7.75-round collision, and 7.75-round, 8.75-round, and 9.75-round near collisions are obtained.

7.75 Round Semi Free-Start Collision. This is obtained by using two outbounds in the form of $8 \longrightarrow 1$. The probability of a transition from 8 active bytes to 1 active byte through L is $2^{-8 \times 7} = 2^{-56}$. Given the following path:

$$1 \xrightarrow{r_1} 8 \xrightarrow{r_2} 64 \xrightarrow{r_3} 8 \xrightarrow{r_4} 8 \xrightarrow{r_5} 64 \xrightarrow{r_6} 8 \xrightarrow{r_7} 1,$$

one can produce a semi free-start collision. We need two transitions from 8 to 1 in both the forward and backward directions, and the one active byte in the first and last states to be equal so that they cancel out after the feedforward. Thus, one needs to try $2^{56+56+8}$ times to satisfy the outbound phase. In other words, we need 2^{120} inbound solutions. If the complexity of one inbound solution is 2^{64}, then the time complexity of 7.75 rounds semi free-start collision is 2^{184} and the memory complexity is 2^8, as we can pass one active byte through X, S and P transformations with probability one.

7.75 Round Semi Free-Start Near Collision. While aiming for collision requires both differences in the first and last states to be exactly in the same place so that they cancel out after the feedforward, near collision requires only few differences to cancel out. A 50-byte near collision is obtained by extending the 5-round inbound with two transitions from 8 to 8 in both directions with no additional cost. Using the following path:

$$8 \xrightarrow{r_1} 8 \xrightarrow{r_2} 64 \xrightarrow{r_3} 8 \xrightarrow{r_4} 8 \xrightarrow{r_5} 64 \xrightarrow{r_6} 8 \xrightarrow{r_7} 8$$

one active byte would cancel out with probability 2^{-8} after feedforward. Consequently, The complexity of 7.75 rounds semi free-start 50-byte collision is 2^{72}. To demonstrate the correctness of the above concept, we have implemented a 4.75-round 50-byte near collision with a shorter practical inbound $8 \xrightarrow{r_2} 64 \xrightarrow{r_3} 8$ as shown in Fig. 6. A 4.75-round near colliding pair is given in Table 1 using the $IV = 0$ and $N = 0$.

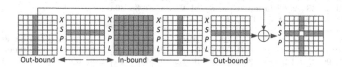

Fig. 6. 4.75 round near collision path

8.75 Round Semi Free-Start Near Collision. Using one transition from 8 to 1 in the forward outbound has a complexity of 2^{56} and results in the following path:

$$8 \xrightarrow{r_1} 8 \xrightarrow{r_2} 64 \xrightarrow{r_3} 8 \xrightarrow{r_4} 8 \xrightarrow{r_5} 64 \xrightarrow{r_6} 8 \xrightarrow{r_7} 1 \xrightarrow{r_8} 8$$

The probability that one active byte is cancelled by the feedforward is 2^{-8}. Consequently the complexity of 8.75 rounds semi free-start 50-byte collision is $2^{64+56+8} = 2^{128}$.

9.75 Round Semi Free-Start Near Collision. With a complexity of 2^{196}, a 9.75-round 50-byte near collision can be obtained with a lower complexity of 2^{184}. By adding two 8 to 1 transitions in both the forward and the backward directions for a complexity of 2^{112} and two 1 to 8 transitions in rounds one (backward) and nine (forward) for no additional cost, the following path:

$$8 \xrightarrow{r_1} 1 \xrightarrow{r_2} 8 \xrightarrow{r_3} 64 \xrightarrow{r_4} 8 \xrightarrow{r_5} 8 \xrightarrow{r_6} 64 \xrightarrow{r_7} 8 \xrightarrow{r_8} 1 \xrightarrow{r_9} 8$$

results in a 50-byte near collision. Additional complexity of 2^8 is needed for a one byte cancellation after the feedforward.

Table 1. Example of a 4.75-round near collision for the compression function.

m								m'								Difference at M_4							
cd	ed	17	46	d8	d7	f0	f3	cd	ed	17	59	d8	d7	f0	f3	00	00	00	1f	00	00	00	00
3e	d6	22	7a	99	4a	c9	ea	3e	d6	22	0c	99	4a	c9	ea	00	00	00	76	00	00	00	00
cc	5d	e2	f0	14	4f	f0	3c	cc	5d	e2	ea	14	4f	f0	3c	00	00	00	1a	00	00	00	00
4b	bc	31	41	dd	99	68	0d	4b	bc	31	4d	dd	99	68	0d	ba	38	7a	00	6f	93	95	37
b4	d1	27	0f	2d	ed	55	28	b4	d1	27	58	2d	ed	55	28	00	00	00	57	00	00	00	00
d8	ca	c8	79	22	fa	c8	14	d8	ca	c8	f6	22	fa	c8	14	00	00	00	8f	00	00	00	00
9f	06	fe	94	b3	3d	20	6a	9f	06	fe	80	b3	3d	20	6a	00	00	00	14	00	00	00	00
5a	d6	10	10	51	4c	a3	7a	5a	d6	10	2b	51	4c	a3	7a	00	00	00	3b	00	00	00	00

Table 2. Example of a 5-round collision and 7.75-round near collision for the internal block cipher (E).

m	m'	Difference at M_7^P
ba aa da d1 92 9e 95 f5	3b 16 1b b0 76 fe 1e 78	
3a 4a 35 2c 61 a8 84 f1	4c 03 4f 12 d1 a3 b4 bd	
44 38 38 e2 d2 fa 5e ec	c6 a7 81 ff 3a c7 3e 36	
27 00 09 05 4f 53 05 f2	6c 76 3e 0a d6 92 72 00	
cd 02 30 bb 3e b4 54 df	47 7e c6 e0 a4 6e 23 1a	
fc c6 de 98 54 4e 5c b6	28 a4 20 68 ee e1 01 11	d7 4d 00 c8 00 00 00 00
60 dc 52 73 dc c9 5d f1	43 20 0a 43 12 ba fe a0	ff 60 00 60 00 00 00 00
72 99 45 8d 9b c8 73 f2	8a d2 ff b3 19 f4 e4 25	15 3c 00 c9 00 00 00 00
		1b 49 00 ae 00 00 00 00
k	k'	03 81 00 42 00 00 00 00
		1a ed 00 ea 00 00 00 00
f4 d7 d6 42 05 a4 b9 7a	75 6b 17 23 e1 c4 32 f7	37 8e 00 60 00 00 00 00
2f 70 68 1a 2c 59 f4 4e	59 39 12 24 9c 52 c4 02	61 b8 00 f2 00 00 00 00
8b 7b 44 12 38 36 84 87	09 e4 fd 0f d0 0b e4 5d	
63 04 2f 7d de 3d b9 9f	28 72 18 72 47 fc ce 6d	
78 db 37 55 73 39 f7 30	f2 a7 c1 0e e9 e3 80 f5	
3f f2 8d fb 23 a9 6a 8a	eb 90 73 0b 99 06 37 2d	
20 18 3a e4 63 85 3a 81	03 e4 62 d4 ad f6 99 d0	
b5 58 8a e7 d3 34 20 4d	4d 13 30 d9 51 08 b7 9a	

6   Conclusion

In this paper, we have analyzed the Stribog compression function and its internal cipher. As for the internal cipher, we have proposed a new message differential path such that a local collision is enforced every two rounds. Accordingly, the Sbox matching complexity caused by its DDT bias is bypassed. As a result, we have efficiently produced free-start 5-round collision and 7.75-round near collision examples for the internal cipher. Moreover, the compression function is investigated and we have noted that the Stribog compression function key whitening round K_N enhances its resistance to free-start collision attacks. However, we have showed that the Stribog compression function is vulnerable to semi free-start 7.75 round collision, 8.75 and 9.75 round near collision attacks and presented an example for a 4.75 round 50-byte near colliding message pair.

Acknowledgement. The authors would like to thank the anonymous reviewers for their valuable comments and suggestions that helped improve the quality of the paper. This work is supported by the Natural Sciences and Engineering Research Council of Canada (NSERC).

References

1. The National Hash Standard of the Russian Federation GOST R 34.11-2012. Russian Federal Agency on Technical Regulation and Metrology report (2012). https://www.tc26.ru/en/GOSTR34112012/GOST_R_34_112012_eng.pdf

2. Canteaut, A., Fuhr, T., Naya-Plasencia, M., Paillier, P., Reinhard, J.-R., Videau, M.: A unified indifferentiability proof for permutation- or block cipher-based hash functions. Cryptology ePrint Archive, Report 2012/363 (2012). http://eprint.iacr.org/2012/363

3. Chang, S., Perlner, R., Burr, W.E., Turan, M., Kelsey, J., Paul, S., Bassham, L.E.: Third-round report of the SHA-3 cryptographic hash algorithm competition (2012). http://nvlpubs.nist.gov/nistpubs/ir/2012/NIST.IR.7896.pdf

4. Gilbert, H., Peyrin, T.: Super-Sbox cryptanalysis: improved attacks for AES-like permutations. In: Hong, S., Iwata, T. (eds.) FSE 2010. LNCS, vol. 6147, pp. 365–383. Springer, Heidelberg (2010)

5. Jean, J., Fouque, P.-A.: Practical near-collisions and collisions on round-reduced ECHO-256 compression function. In: Joux, A. (ed.) FSE 2011. LNCS, vol. 6733, pp. 107–127. Springer, Heidelberg (2011)

6. Kazymyrov, O., Kazymyrova, V.: Algebraic aspects of the russian hash standard GOST R 34.11-2012. Cryptology ePrint Archive, Report 2013/556 (2013). http://eprint.iacr.org/

7. Knudsen, L.R.: Truncated and higher order differentials. In: Preneel, B.I. (ed.) FSE 1995. LNCS, vol. 1008, pp. 196–211. Springer, Heidelberg (1995)

8. Lamberger, M., Mendel, F., Rechberger, C., Rijmen, V., Schläffer, M.: Rebound distinguishers: results on the full whirlpool compression function. In: Matsui, M. (ed.) ASIACRYPT 2009. LNCS, vol. 5912, pp. 126–143. Springer, Heidelberg (2009)

9. Matusiewicz, K., Naya-Plasencia, M., Nikolić, I., Sasaki, Y., Schläffer, M.: Rebound attack on the full LANE compression function. In: Matsui, M. (ed.) ASIACRYPT 2009. LNCS, vol. 5912, pp. 106–125. Springer, Heidelberg (2009)

10. Matyukhin, D., Rudskoy, V., Shishkin, V.: A perspective hashing algorithm. In: RusCrypto (2010). (In Russian)

11. Matyukhin, D.: Some methods of hash functions analysis with application to the GOST P 34.11-94 algorithm. Mat. Vopr. Kriptogr. 3(4), 71–89 (2012)

12. Mendel, F., Peyrin, T., Rechberger, C., Schläffer, M.: Improved cryptanalysis of the reduced Grøstl compression function, ECHO permutation and AES block cipher. In: Jacobson Jr, M.J., Rijmen, V., Safavi-Naini, R. (eds.) SAC 2009. LNCS, vol. 5867, pp. 16–35. Springer, Heidelberg (2009)

13. Mendel, F., Pramstaller, N., Rechberger, C.: A (second) preimage attack on the GOST hash function. In: Nyberg, K. (ed.) FSE 2008. LNCS, vol. 5086, pp. 224–234. Springer, Heidelberg (2008)

14. Mendel, F., Pramstaller, N., Rechberger, C., Kontak, M., Szmidt, J.: Cryptanalysis of the GOST hash function. In: Wagner, D. (ed.) CRYPTO 2008. LNCS, vol. 5157, pp. 162–178. Springer, Heidelberg (2008)

15. Mendel, F., Rechberger, C., Schläffer, M., Thomsen, S.S.: The rebound attack: cryptanalysis of reduced whirlpool and Grøstl. In: Dunkelman, O. (ed.) FSE 2009. LNCS, vol. 5665, pp. 260–276. Springer, Heidelberg (2009)

16. Mendel, F., Rechberger, C., Schläffer, M., Thomsen, S.S.: Rebound attacks on the reduced Grøstl hash function. In: Pieprzyk, J. (ed.) CT-RSA 2010. LNCS, vol. 5985, pp. 350–365. Springer, Heidelberg (2010)

17. Rijmen, V., Toz, D., Varıcı, K.: Rebound attack on reduced-round versions of JH. In: Hong, S., Iwata, T. (eds.) FSE 2010. LNCS, vol. 6147, pp. 286–303. Springer, Heidelberg (2010)

18. Sasaki, Y., Wang, L., Wu, S., Wu, W.: Investigating fundamental security requirements on whirlpool: improved preimage and collision attacks. In: Wang, X., Sako, K. (eds.) ASIACRYPT 2012. LNCS, vol. 7658, pp. 562–579. Springer, Heidelberg (2012)

19. Wagner, D.: The boomerang attack. In: Knudsen, L.R. (ed.) FSE 1999. LNCS, vol. 1636, pp. 156–170. Springer, Heidelberg (1999)

20. Wang, X., Yin, Y.L., Yu, H.: Finding collisions in the full SHA-1. In: Shoup, V. (ed.) CRYPTO 2005. LNCS, vol. 3621, pp. 17–36. Springer, Heidelberg (2005)

21. Wang, X., Yu, H.: How to break MD5 and other hash functions. In: Cramer, R. (ed.) EUROCRYPT 2005. LNCS, vol. 3494, pp. 19–35. Springer, Heidelberg (2005)

Bitwise Partial-Sum on HIGHT: A New Tool for Integral Analysis Against ARX Designs

Yu Sasaki[1(✉)] and Lei Wang[2]

[1] NTT Secure Platform Laboratories, Tokyo, Japan
sasaki.yu@lab.ntt.co.jp
[2] Nanyang Technological University, Singapore, Singapore
Wang.Lei@ntu.edu.sg

Abstract. In this paper, we present a new cryptanalytic tool that can reduce the complexity of integral analysis against Addition-Rotation-XOR (ARX) based designs. Our technique is based on the partial-sum technique proposed by Ferguson *et al.* at FSE 2000, which guesses sub-keys byte to byte in turn, and the data to be analyzed is compressed for each key guess. In this paper, the technique is extended to ARX based designs. Subkeys are guessed in bitwise, and the data is compressed with respect to the sum of the guessed bit position and carry values to the next bit position. We call the technique *bitwise partial-sum*. We demonstrate this technique by applying it to reduced-round HIGHT, which is one of the ISO standard ciphers. Another contribution is an independent improvement specific to HIGHT which exploits more linearity inside the round function. Together with the bitwise partial-sum, the integral analysis on HIGHT is extended from previous 22 rounds to 26 rounds.

Keywords: Integral analysis · Partial-sum · Bitwise partial-sum · HIGHT

1 Introduction

Integral analysis was firstly proposed by Daemen *et al.* for the SQUARE cipher [1], and was later unified as integral analysis by Knudsen and Wagner [2]. It consists of two phases; an *integral distinguisher* construction and a key recovery. For the first phase, an attacker prepares a set of chosen plaintexts. For these plaintexts, the corresponding states after a few encryption rounds have a certain property, *e.g.* the XOR sum of all states in the set is 0 with a probability 1 (balance). Then for the second phase, after the attacker obtains the corresponding ciphertexts of the set of chosen plaintexts, she guesses subkeys and performs the partial decryption up to the balanced state. If the guess is correct, the XOR sum of the results always becomes 0. Otherwise, the XOR sum becomes random.

Cryptanalysts are continuously developing new techniques to enhance the integral analysis. Several results improved the integral distinguisher construction, *e.g.*, multi-set analysis [3], subword multi-set [4], and bit-pattern based analysis [5]. The analysis for the ARX based structure can be seen in saturation

© Springer International Publishing Switzerland 2014
H.-S. Lee and D.-G. Han (Eds.): ICISC 2013, LNCS 8565, pp. 189–202, 2014.
DOI: 10.1007/978-3-319-12160-4_12

attack [6] and tuple analysis [7]. At the same time, techniques for the key recovery phase have been improved, which is the main motivation of this paper. We briefly illustrate two previous techniques, which are related to this paper.

Ferguson *et al.* proposed a technique called *partial-sum* [8]. It reduces the complexity of the partial decryption up to the balanced state by guessing each subkey byte one after another. We use a toy example to show its procedure and significance. Let us consider the computation, $\bigoplus S\Big(S(c_0 \oplus k_0) \oplus S(c_1 \oplus k_1) \oplus S(c_2 \oplus k_2)\Big)$, where c_0, c_1, c_2 are 8-bit variables and k_0, k_1, k_2 are 8-bit keys, and there are about 2^{24} data of (c_0, c_1, c_2). With a straightforward method, 24-bit key is exhaustively guessed and the equation is computed for all (c_0, c_1, c_2). It takes $2^{24+24} = 2^{48}$ computations. The partial-sum technique firstly guesses k_0 and k_1 and computes the sum of the first two terms c', which takes $2^{16+24} = 2^{40}$ computations. Then, 2^{24} data for 2-byte tuple (c', c_2) are generated. This causes many overlaps of the data; roughly 2^8 overlaps for each (c', c_2). The attacker only picks the values that appear odd times. This reduces the data size into 2^{16}. Finally, the entire sum is computed by guessing k_2, which takes $2^{16} \cdot 2^8 \cdot 2^{16} = 2^{40}$.

Sasaki and Wang introduced *meet-in-the-middle technique* for the key recovery phase against Feistel ciphers [9]. It exploits the property that the balanced state is represented by an XOR of two variables. Then, the XOR sum of each variable are computed independently, and the attacker checks the match of their values like a meet-in-the-middle attack. It separates the partial decryption into two independent parts, and thus the complexity can be reduced.

Our Contributions. In this paper, we extend the partial-sum technique to ARX designs, beyond the mere application to byte-oriented ciphers. We also use a toy example to illustrate our new tool. "$\oplus$" represents the bitwise XOR and "$\boxplus$" represents the modular addition. *What is the best strategy to compute* $\bigoplus[(c_0 \oplus k_0) \boxplus (c_1 \oplus k_1) \boxplus (c_2 \oplus k_2)]$? We observe that the computation can be much faster than the partial-sum technique [8] by guessing key values bit-by-bit and compressing the data for each guess. For example, let us consider the computation of the first two terms; $c' = (c_0 \oplus k_0) \boxplus (c_1 \oplus k_1)$. We guess two key bits, which are the LSB of k_0 and the LSB of k_1. Then, we can compute the LSB of c' and the carry bit to the second LSB. After this computation, 2-bit information, which are the LSB of c_0 and the LSB of c_1 are discarded. At this state, we newly obtain 2-bit information and discard 2-bit information. Hence, no advantage is generated. We then guess two key bits, which are the second LSB of k_0 and the second LSB of k_1. Then, we can compute the second LSB of c' and the carry bit to the third LSB. After this computation, 3-bit information, which are the second LSB of c_0 and c_1 and the carry value to the second LSB are discarded. In this time, we newly obtain 2-bit information, but discarded 3-bit information. Hence, the data is compressed by 1 bit. With this approach, the complexity is minimized. We call the technique *bitwise partial-sum*.

The bitwise partial-sum leads to more advantages. We focus on the computation for the MSB. As shown above, the bitwise partial-sum computes the carry

Table 1. Comparison of attack results on HIGHT

Model	Approach	#Rounds	Data	Time	Memory (bytes)	Reference
Single-key	Integral	18	2^{62}	2^{36}	2^{20}	[13]
	Integral	22	2^{62}	$2^{118.71}$	2^{64}	[14]
	Integral	22	2^{62}	$2^{102.35}$	2^{64}	[9]
	Integral	22	$2^{58.32}$	$2^{59.56}$	2^{55}	This paper
	Integral	26	2^{57}	$2^{120.55}$	$2^{99.58}$	This paper
	Imp. Diff.	18	$2^{46.8}$	$2^{109.2}$	N/A	[10]
	Imp. Diff.	25	2^{60}	$2^{126.78}$	N/A	[15]
	Imp. Diff.	26	2^{61}	$2^{119.53}$	2^{109}	[16]
	Imp. Diff.	26	$2^{61.6}$	$2^{114.35}$	$2^{87.6}$	[12]
	Imp. Diff.	27	2^{58}	$2^{126.6}$	2^{120}	[12]
Related-key	Rectangle	26	$2^{51.2}$	$2^{120.41}$	N/A	[15]
	Imp. Diff.	28	2^{60}	$2^{125.54}$	N/A	[15]
	Imp. Diff.	31	2^{64}	$2^{127.28}$	2^{117}	[16]
	Differential	32	$2^{57.84}$	$2^{125.83}$	N/A	[17]

value to the MSB when we analyze the second MSB. Therefore, the analysis on the MSB is completely linear because we do not need to compute the carry value from the MSB. Therefore, in the above equation, 3 bits for the MSBs of c_0, c_1, c_2 can be compressed into 1 bit of $c_0 \oplus c_1 \oplus c_2$ with respect to the MSB at the very beginning stage of the analysis. Moreover, for 3 bits of the MSBs of k_0, k_1, k_2, guessing only 1-bit information for their XOR relation is enough.

In this paper, we demonstrate the bitwise partial-sum technique for HIGHT [10],which was standardized by ISO as a 64-bit block-cipher [11]. As an independent improvement, we show an observation specific to HIGHT, which exploits more linearity inside the round function. By combining these two techniques, we extend the integral analysis to 26 rounds, while previous work attacked only 22 rounds. Although the best single-key attack on HIGHT breaks 27 rounds with an impossible differential attack [12], this is a significant improvement regarding the integral analysis. The attack results are summarized in Table 1.

2   Bitwise Partial-Sum

In this section, we describe our new technique called *bitwise partial-sum*, which improves the complexity of the partial-sum technique for ARX designs. Suppose that an n-bit variable Z is computed with n-bit variables X, Y and n-bit unknown keys K, K'.[1] Also suppose that 2^{2n} pairs of (X, Y) is given to the attacker and the goal of the attacker is computing Z for the exhaustive guess of

---

[1] For HIGHT, the value of n is 8. Here, we describe the analysis in a general form.

K and K'. As computations of Z, we consider the following four operations:

$$Z = (X \oplus K) \boxplus Y, \qquad\qquad Z = (X \boxplus K) \oplus Y,$$
$$Z = (X \oplus K) \boxplus (Y \oplus K'), \qquad\qquad Z = (X \boxplus K) \oplus (Y \boxplus K').$$

We describe X in bitwise with $X^{n-1}\|X^{n-2}\|\cdots\|X^1\|X^0$. The similar notations are used for Y, Z, K, and K'. We denote the carry value to bit position i by p^i.

To compute Z in each of the above operations, in the previous work, the key values K (and K') are exhaustively guessed, and for each guess, the equation is computed for all 2^{2n} pairs of (X, Y). Therefore, the complexity is $2^{2n} \cdot 2^n = 2^{3n}$ operations for the single-key cases, and $2^{2n} \cdot 2^{2n} = 2^{4n}$ operations for the two-key cases. The bitwise partial-sum can reduce the complexity to $n \cdot 2^{2n+1}$ for the single-key cases and 2^{3n+2} for the two-key cases by computing Z bit by bit.

Single-Key Cases. We start with explaining the complexity to compute $Z = (X \oplus K) \boxplus Y$ and $Z = (X \boxplus K) \oplus Y$. The procedure and the complexity for two cases are almost the same. Hence, we only explain the case for $Z = (X \oplus K) \boxplus Y$ in details. The overview is shown in Fig. 1. The analysis starts from 2^{2n} texts of (X, Y). The procedure is divided into three parts; LSB, middle bits, and MSB.

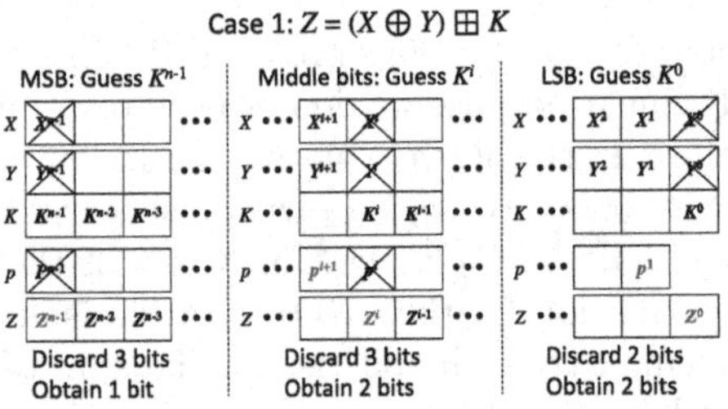

Fig. 1. Bitwise partial-sum for case 1. Each cell represents each bit. Cells with a cross are the discarded bits. Cells with red characters are the newly obtained bits.

LSB: Guess the 1-bit value K^0. For each of 2^{2n} texts, compute $(X^0 \oplus K^0) \boxplus Y^0$ to obtain 2-bit information Z^0 and p^1. After that 2-bit information X^0 and Y^0 is no longer used, and thus we can remove those 2-bit information for the further procedure. Hence, 2^{2n} texts of $(X^{n-1}\|\cdots\|X^0, Y^{n-1}\|\cdots\|Y^0)$ are updated to 2^{2n} texts of $(X^{n-1}\|\cdots\|X^1, Y^{n-1}\|\cdots\|Y^1, p^1, Z^0)$.

Middle bits (bit position i for $i = 1, 2, \ldots, n-2$): Guess the 1-bit value K^i. For each text, compute $(X^i \oplus K^i) \boxplus Y^i \boxplus p^i$ to obtain 2-bit information Z^i and p^{i+1} and then discard 3-bit information X^i, Y^i, p^i. Hence, $2^{2n-(i-1)}$ texts of $(X^{n-1}\|\cdots\|X^i, Y^{n-1}\|\cdots\|Y^i, p^i, Z^{i-1}\|\cdots\|Z^0)$ are updated to 2^{2n-i} texts of $(X^{n-1}\|\cdots\|X^{i+1}, Y^{n-1}\|\cdots\|Y^{i+1}, p^{i+1}, Z^i\|\cdots\|Z^0)$. Count how many times each tuple of $(X^{n-1}\|\cdots\|X^{i+1}, Y^{n-1}\|\cdots\|Y^{i+1}, p^{i+1}, Z^i\|\cdots\|Z^0)$ appears, and only pick the ones that appear odd times. The size of the texts will be reduced from $2^{2n-(i-1)}$ to 2^{2n-i}.

MSB: Guess the 1-bit value K^{n-1}. For each text, compute $(X^{n-1} \oplus K^{n-1} \oplus Y^{n-1} \oplus p^{n-1})$ to obtain 1-bit information Z^{n-1} and then discard 3-bit information $X^{n-1}, Y^{n-1}, p^{n-1}$. Hence, 2^{n+2} texts of $(X^{n-1}, Y^{n-1}, p^{n-1}, Z^{n-2} \| \cdots \| Z^0)$ are updated to 2^n texts of $(Z^{n-1} \| \cdots \| Z^0)$. Count how many times each tuple of $(Z^{n-1} \| \cdots \| Z^0)$ appears, and only pick the ones that appear odd times. The size of the texts will be reduced from 2^{n+2} to 2^n.

The complexity for the LSB (bit position 0) is $2 \cdot 2^{2n}$ XOR operations and $2 \cdot 2^{2n}$ addition operations, then 2^{2n} texts will remain. The complexity for bit position 1 is $2^2 \cdot 2^{2n}$ XOR operations and $2^2 \cdot 2^{2n}$ addition operations, then 2^{2n-1} texts will remain. The complexity for bit position 2 is $2^3 \cdot 2^{2n-1}$ XOR operations and $2^3 \cdot 2^{2n-1}$ addition operations, then 2^{2n-2} texts will remain. The complexity for bit position i where $i = 3, 4, \ldots, n-2$ is $2^{i+1} \cdot 2^{2n-(i-1)}$ XOR operations and $2^{i+1} \cdot 2^{2n-(i-1)}$ addition operations, then 2^{2n-i} texts will remain. The complexity for the MSB is $2^n \cdot 2^{n+2}$ XOR operations, and 2^n texts will remain. Because the complexity for each bit is about 2^{2n+2} XOR operations and addition operations, the total complexity is about $n \cdot 2^{2n+2}$ XOR operations and addition operation. This is faster than the previous analysis which requires 2^{3n} operations. For $n = 8$, the previous analysis requires 2^{24} while the bitwise partial-sum requires 2^{21}. The advantage becomes bigger for a bigger n. Three-fish block-cipher adopts a 64-bit ARX design. For $n = 64$, the previous analysis requires 2^{192} while the bitwise partial-sum only requires 2^{136}.

Optimization of the Single-Key Case. The computation of the MSB is linear, and thus the MSBs of two variables X^{n-1} and Y^{n-1} are only used in the linear computation. Hence, at the very beginning of the procedure, we can compute $X^{n-1} \oplus Y^{n-1}$, and 2^{2n} texts of (X, Y) can be compressed into 2^{2n-1} texts of $(X^{n-1} \oplus Y^{n-1}, X^{n-2} \| \cdots \| X^0, Y^{n-2} \| \cdots \| Y^0)$ This halves the complexity, and thus the total complexity is about $n \cdot 2^{2n+1}$ XOR and addition operations.

Two-Key Cases. We explain the two-key cases, *i.e.*, the complexity to compute $Z = (X \oplus K) \boxplus (Y \oplus K')$ and $Z = (X \boxplus K) \oplus (Y \boxplus K')$. The basic procedure for the two-key cases are the same as the one for the single-key case. First, we explain the case for $Z = (X \oplus K) \boxplus (Y \oplus K')$.

LSB: Guess the 2-bit values K^0 and K'^0. For each 2^{2n} texts, compute 2-bit information Z^0 and p^1 and then discard 2-bit information X^0 and Y^0. The text size after the analysis is 2^{2n}.

Middle bits (bit position i for $i = 1, 2, \ldots, n-2$): Guess the 2-bit values K^i and K'^i. For each texts, compute 2-bit information Z^i and p^{i+1} and then discard 3-bit information X^i, Y^i, p^i. Only pick the tuples of $(X^{n-1} \| \cdots \| X^{i+1}, Y^{n-1} \| \cdots \| Y^{i+1}, p^{i+1}, Z^i \| \cdots \| Z^0)$ which appears odd times, The size of the texts will be reduced from $2^{2n-(i-1)}$ to 2^{2n-i}.

MSB: Guess the 2-bit values K^{n-1} and K'^{n-1}. For each texts, compute 1-bit information Z^{n-1} and then discard 3-bit information $X^{n-1}, Y^{n-1}, p^{n-1}$. Only pick the tuples of $(Z^{n-1}\| \cdots \|Z^0)$ which appears odd times. The size of the texts will be reduced from 2^{n+2} to 2^n.

The complexity for the LSB (bit position 0) is $(2)^2 \cdot 2^{2n}$ operations, and 2^{2n} texts will remain. The complexity for bit position 1 is $(2^2)^2 \cdot 2^{2n}$ operations, and 2^{2n-1} texts will remain. The complexity for bit position 2 is $(2^3)^2 \cdot 2^{2n-1}$ operations, and 2^{2n-2} texts will remain. The complexity for bit position i where $i = 3, 4, \ldots, n-2$ is $(2^{i+1})^2 \cdot 2^{2n-(i-1)}$ operations, and 2^{2n-i} texts will remain. The complexity for the MSB is $(2^n)^2 \cdot 2^{n+2}$ operations, and 2^n texts will remain. Therefore, the total complexity is about

$$(2)^2 \cdot 2^{2n} + [(2^2)^2 \cdot 2^{2n} + (2^3)^2 \cdot 2^{2n-1} + \cdots + (2^{n-1})^2 \cdot 2^{n+3}] + (2^n)^2 \cdot 2^{n+2}.$$

The first term is smaller than 2^{2n+3}, thus the equation is smaller than

$$2^{2n+3} + 2^{2n+4} + \cdots + 2^{2n+(n+2)} = 2^{2n+3}(1 + 2^1 + 2^2 + \cdots + 2^{n-1}) < 2^{3n+3}.$$

This is faster than the previous analysis which requires 2^{4n} operations.

Optimization of the Two-Key Case. Regarding the MSBs of two variables X^{n-1} and Y^{n-1}, the same technique as the one for the single-key case can be exploited, namely, take the XOR of X^{n-1} and Y^{n-1} and compress the data by 1 bit at the very beginning of the analysis. This reduces the total complexity by 1 bit, and thus the total complexity becomes about 2^{3n+2} operations.

Moreover, the MSBs of two keys K^{n-1} and K'^{n-1} are only used in the linear operation. Therefore, instead of guessing these two key bits, guessing 1-bit relation of these bits, i.e., $K^{n-1} \oplus K'^{n-1}$, is enough. This reduces the total complexity by 1 bit, and thus the total complexity becomes about 2^{3n+1} operations.

Evaluation for $Z = (X \boxplus K) \oplus (Y \boxplus K')$. The complexity for $Z = (X \boxplus K) \oplus (Y \boxplus K')$ is a little bit worse than the complexity for $Z = (X \oplus K) \boxplus (Y \oplus K')$. This is because the equation $(X \boxplus K) \oplus (Y \boxplus K')$ contains two additions, and thus we need to store 2-bit carry values in the analysis of each bit. Compared to the case of $Z = (X \oplus K) \boxplus (Y \oplus K')$, the size of texts to be analyzed is doubled. This increases the final complexity from 2^{3n+1} to 2^{3n+2} operations.

Summary of the Bitwise Partial-Sum. The comparison of the complexities to compute each of 4 equations with the previous method (bytewise partial-sum) and ours is given in Table 2. It indicates that the advantage of the bitwise partial-sum increases as n increases. In the next section, we apply the bitwise partial-sum to HIGHT, where the size of n is 8. The impact is relatively small because the advantage is at most a factor of 2^7. Some ARX-based block-ciphers adopt a bigger n, e.g., XTEA [18] adopts $n = 32$ and Threefish [19] adopts $n = 64$. In such cases, the impact becomes much bigger.

Table 2. Summary of the complexity of the bitwise partial-sum

Target equation	Previous partial-sum	Bitwise partial-sum
$Z = (X \oplus K) \boxplus Y$	2^{3n}	$n \cdot 2^{2n+1}$
$Z = (X \boxplus K) \oplus Y$	2^{3n}	$n \cdot 2^{2n+1}$
$Z = (X \oplus K) \boxplus (Y \oplus K')$	2^{4n}	2^{3n+1}
$Z = (X \boxplus K) \oplus (Y \boxplus K')$	2^{4n}	2^{3n+2}

3 Improved Integral Analysis on HIGHT

3.1 Specification of HIGHT

HIGHT is a block-cipher proposed at CHES 2006 by Hong *et al.* [10]. The block size is 64 bits and the key size is 128 bits. It adopts the type-2 generalized Feistel structure with 8 branches and 32 rounds. The plaintext is loaded into an internal state $X_{0,7}\|X_{0,6}\| \cdots \|X_{0,0}$ where the size of each $X_{i,j}$ is 8 bits. At first, $X_{0,7}\|X_{0,6}\| \cdots \|X_{0,0}$ is updated by the pre-whitening. Then, the state $X_{i,7}\|X_{i,6}\| \cdots \|X_{i,0}$ is updated by the following operation. For $i = 0, 1, \ldots, 31$

$$X_{i+1,0} = X_{i,7} \oplus \left(F_0(X_{i,6}) \boxplus SK_{4i+3}\right), \qquad X_{i+1,1} = X_{i,0},$$
$$X_{i+1,2} = X_{i,1} \boxplus \left(F_1(X_{i,0}) \oplus SK_{4i}\right), \qquad X_{i+1,3} = X_{i,2},$$
$$X_{i+1,4} = X_{i,3} \oplus \left(F_0(X_{i,2}) \boxplus SK_{4i+1}\right), \qquad X_{i+1,5} = X_{i,4},$$
$$X_{i+1,6} = X_{i,5} \boxplus \left(F_1(X_{i,4}) \oplus SK_{4i+2}\right), \qquad X_{i+1,7} = X_{i,6},$$

where $F_0(x) = (x \lll 1) \oplus (x \lll 2) \oplus (x \lll 7)$, $F_1(x) = (x \lll 3) \oplus (x \lll 4) \oplus (x \lll 6)$, and "$\lll s$" denotes the s-bit left rotation. The swap of the byte positions is not executed in the last round. We denote the internal state between F and the key addition by $Y_{i,1}, Y_{i,3}, Y_{i,5}, Y_{i,7}$ and the internal state right after the key addition by $Z_{i,1}, Z_{i,3}, Z_{i,5}, Z_{i,7}$. Finally, the post-whitening is performed. In this paper, we denote the k-th bit of a byte $X_{i,j}$ by $X_{i,j}^k$.

Subkeys and whitening keys consist of a part of the master key K and a constant value. K is divided into each byte $K_{15}\|K_{14}\| \cdots \|K_0$ and WK_i and SK_j are derived by one of $K_{15}, \ldots, K_0$. Please refer to [10] for details. Note that [10] showed a figure with an incorrect subkey order, and the designers later fixed the problem [20]. The previous work [9,14] attacked the incorrect one though they can also be applied to the correct one. We attack the correct one, hence the subkey order is different from the previous work [9,14].

3.2 Previous Integral Analysis on 22-Round HIGHT

Zhang *et al.* presented a 17-round integral distinguisher on HIGHT [14]. For a set of 2^{56} plaintexts with the form of (A, A, A, A, A, A, A, C), the state after 17 rounds, $(X_{17,7}\|X_{17,6}\| \cdots \|X_{17,0})$, has the form of $(?,?,?,?,B^0,?,?,?)$, where B^0

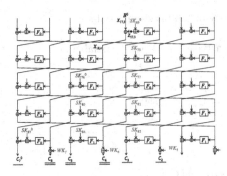 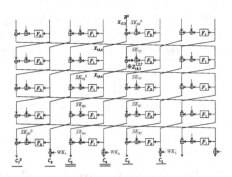

Fig. 2. Key recovery phase for 22-round HIGHT

Fig. 3. Improved key recovery phase with exploiting more linearity

stands for the balanced state with respect to the 0-th bit. By appending 5 rounds after this distinguisher, Zheng *et al.* showed a 22-round key recovery attack.

The key recovery phase was later improved by Sasaki and Wang [9]. In their attack, the condition for $\bigoplus X^0_{17,3} = 0$ is written as $\bigoplus X^0_{18,4} = \bigoplus Z^0_{17,3}$. They compute each side of the condition independently, and later check the match like the meet-in-the-middle attack. Their key recovery phase is illustrated in Fig. 2. The red color describes the computation for $Z^0_{17,3}$. The blue color describes the computation for $X^0_{18,4}$. The purple color describes the overlapped part.

3.3 Exploiting Linearly for Optimizing Matching Position

The observation of Sasaki and Wang [9] is based on the fact that the balanced bit $X^0_{17,3}$ can be written as a linear combination of two variables $X^0_{18,4}$ and $Z^0_{17,3}$. We extend this concept by exploiting more linearity inside the round function. The complexity for computing $\bigoplus Z^0_{17,3}$ is much bigger than the one for $\bigoplus X^0_{18,4}$. Therefore, we aim to reduce the number of subkeys used to compute $\bigoplus Z^0_{17,3}$.

$Z^0_{17,3}$ is computed by $SK^0_{69} \boxplus Y^0_{17,3}$. Because we only focus on the LSB, the computation is linear, *i.e.*, $Z^0_{17,3} = SK^0_{69} \oplus Y^0_{17,3}$. Therefore, SK^0_{69} can be moved to the computation of $\bigoplus X^0_{18,4}$, namely $\bigoplus (X^0_{18,4} \oplus SK^0_{69}) = \bigoplus Y^0_{17,3}$. Furthermore, by utilizing the linearity of F_0, *i.e.*, $Y^0_{17,3} = X^1_{18,3} \oplus X^2_{18,3} \oplus X^7_{18,3}$ we can move more subkey bits, and finally get the following equation.

$$\bigoplus (X^0_{18,4} \oplus SK^0_{69} \oplus X^1_{19,4} \oplus X^2_{19,4} \oplus X^7_{19,4}) = \bigoplus (Z^1_{18,3} \oplus Z^2_{18,3} \oplus Z^7_{18,3}). \quad (1)$$

The entire structure is shown in Fig. 3. This reduces the number of subkey bits in the dominant part by 17 bits and the number of ciphertexts by 8 bits, thus the complexity of the attack can be reduced roughly by a factor of 2^{25}.

3.4 Improved Integral·Analysis on 22-Round HIGHT

We explain the details of the computation of $\bigoplus(Z_{18,3}^1 \oplus Z_{18,3}^2 \oplus Z_{18,3}^7)$, which is shown in Fig. 4. With the previous method in [9], the complexity is $2^{32} \cdot 2^{56} = 2^{88}$, while our method computes it only with $2^{64.02}$.

We first compute $C_2' \leftarrow F_0(C_2)$ and $WK_5' \leftarrow F_0(WK_5)$ to exclude the F_0 function. Hence, we recover WK_5' instead of WK_5. Then, the partial decryption up to $X_{21,3}$ is written as $X_{21,3} \leftarrow C_3 \oplus (SK_{85} \boxplus (C_2' \oplus WK_5'))$. The equation is not exactly the same as 4 equations analyzed in Sect. 2, but the similar procedure can be applied. Namely, the partial-sum is updated bit by bit from the LSB to MSB. Moreover, we use the linear relations in the MSB, thus the data can be compressed with respect to the value of $C_3^7 \oplus C_2'^7$ before the analysis starts and 1-bit guess of $SK_{85}^7 \oplus WK_5'^7$ is enough for these two MSBs.

After we obtain the value of $X_{21,3}$ and the corresponding $Y_{20,3}$, another pattern of the bitwise partial-sum appears for $X_{20,3} = (C_4 \boxplus WK_6) \oplus (Y_{20,3} \boxplus SK_{81})$. However, the analysis is not simple in this time because C_4 is also used to compute $X_{21,5}$ and thus we cannot eliminate the value of C_4 after $X_{20,3}$ is computed. Such a structure makes the attack complicated. In the following, we give the detailed attack procedure to compute $\bigoplus(Z_{18,3}^1 \oplus Z_{18,3}^2 \oplus Z_{18,3}^7)$.

1. Precompute two look-up tables which return $F_0(x)$ and $F_1(x)$ for a given x.
2. Query 2^{56} plaintexts of the form (A, A, A, A, A, A, A, C). Count how many times each 4-byte tuple (C_2, C_3, C_4, C_5) appears and pick the ones that appear odd times. Hence, the number of texts to be analyzed is $2^{4*8} = 2^{32}$.
3. Convert (C_2, C_3, C_4, C_5) into (C_2', C_3, C_4, C_5) with the look-up table.
4. Compress the data with respect to $t_1 = C_2'^7 \oplus C_3^7$ and obtain 2^{31} data of $(C_2'^{0-6}, C_3^{0-6}, t_1, C_4, C_5)$.
5. For each 15-bit guess of $(SK_{85}^{0-6}, WK_5'^{0-6}, (SK_{85}^7 \oplus WK_5'^7))$, compute $X_{21,3}$ with the bitwise partial-sum. The data is compressed to 2^{24} of the form $(X_{21,3}, C_4, C_5)$. Convert them into $(Y_{20,3}, C_4, C_5)$ with the look-up table.
6. For each 8-bit guess of WK_6, update 2^{24} data $(Y_{20,3}, C_4, C_5)$ into $(Y_{20,3}, X_{21,4}, C_5)$. Then, compute $Y_{21,5}$ and add it to the data to be analyzed. Hereafter, we regard $X_{21,4}$ and $Y_{21,5}$ are independent.[2] Thus the data size increases to 2^{32}.
7. Compress the data with respect to $t_2 = C_5^7 \oplus Y_{21,5}^7$ and $t_3 = X_{21,4}^7 \oplus Y_{20,3}^7$, and obtain 2^{30} data of $(C_5^{0-6}, Y_{21,5}^{0-6}, t_2, X_{21,4}^{0-6}, Y_{20,3}^{0-6}, t_3)$.
8. For each 8-bit guess of SK_{81}, compute $X_{20,3}$ with the bitwise partial-sum technique and compress the data to 2^{23} data of the form $(C_5^{0-6}, Y_{21,5}^{0-6}, t_2, X_{20,3})$. Then, convert the set into $(C_5^{0-6}, Y_{21,5}^{0-6}, t_2, Y_{19,3})$ with the look-up table.
9. Compress the data with respect to $t_4 = t_2 \oplus Y_{19,3}^7$ and obtain 2^{22} data of the form $(C_5^{0-6}, Y_{21,5}^{0-6}, Y_{19,3}^{0-6}, t_7)$.

---

[2] By doing this, we have additional noise (wrong subkey guesses). We never miss the right key candidate and noise is later filtered out.

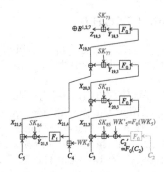

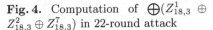

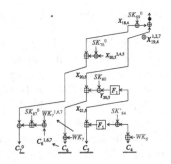

Fig. 4. Computation of $\bigoplus(Z_{18,3}^1 \oplus Z_{18,3}^2 \oplus Z_{18,3}^7)$ in 22-round attack

Fig. 5. Computation of left-hand side of Eq. (1) in 22-round attack

10. For each 15-bit guess of $(SK_{84}^{0-6}, SK_{77}^{0-6}, (SK_{84}^7 \oplus SK_{77}^7))$, compute $X_{19,3}$ with the bitwise partial-sum technique and compress the data to 2^8 data of the form $X_{19,3}$. Then, convert the set into $Y_{18,3}$ with the look-up table.

11. For 8-bit guess of SK_{73}, compute $\bigoplus(Z_{18,3}^1 \oplus Z_{18,3}^2 \oplus Z_{18,3}^7)$ with the bitwise partial-sum technique. Store the result in a table T.

We evaluate the complexity of each step. Step 1 requires 2^8 F_0 and F_1 computations. Step 2 requires 2^{56} memory access. The memory requirement is $2^{32} \cdot 4 = 2^{34}$ bytes. Step 3 requires 2^{32} table look-ups. Step 4 requires 2^{32} 1-bit XOR operations. and the data is compressed to 2^{31}. In Step 5, because 2 subkeys and 1 modular addition are involved, the complexity of the bitwise partial-sum is 2^{31+n+1}, where $n = 8$. Hence, the complexity is 2^{40} round functions. The data is compressed to 2^{24} and then 2^{24} table look-ups are performed. Step 6 requires $2^{15+8+24}$ modular additions and table look-ups, which is less than 2^{47} round functions. The data size increases to 2^{32}. Step 7 requires $2^{15+8+32}$ 2-bit XOR operation and table look-ups, which is less than $2^{15+8+32+1} = 2^{56}$ round functions. The data is compressed to 2^{30}. In Step 8, because 1 subkey is involved, the complexity of the bitwise partial-sum is $8 \cdot 2^{15+8+30+1} = 2^{57}$ round functions. The data is compressed to 2^{23}. Step 9 requires $2^{15+8+8+23}$ 1-bit XOR computations, which is less than 2^{54} round functions. The data is compressed to 2^{22}. In Step 10, because 2 subkeys and 2 modular additions are involved, the complexity of the bitwise partial-sum is $2^{15+8+8+22+(n+2)} = 2^{63}$ round functions for $n = 8$. The data is compressed to 2^8. In Step 11, because 1 subkey and 1 modular addition are involved, the complexity is $2^{8+15+8+8+15+8+1} = 2^{63}$ round functions.

The complexities for steps 1 to 5 are negligible but for 2^{56} memory access in Step 2. The complexity for the remaining part is $2^{47} + 2^{56} + 2^{57} + 2^{54} + 2^{63} + 2^{63} \approx 2^{64.02}$ round functions. After the analysis, we obtain 2^{54} values in T. Note that besides the 1-bit value of $\bigoplus(Z_{18,3}^1 \oplus Z_{18,3}^2 \oplus Z_{18,3}^7)$, we also store 15-bit values of $WK_6^{0-6}, SK_{84}^{\prime 0-6}, SK_{84}^{\prime 7} \oplus WK_6^7$, which are later used for the match. Hence, the memory requirement to construct T is $2^{54} * 16$ bits, which is 2^{55} bytes.

Left-hand-side of Eq. (1). The entire computation structure is shown in Fig. 5. Due to the limited space, we omit the detailed analysis. The left-hand-side of Eq. (1) is computed with a negligible cost compared to the other part.

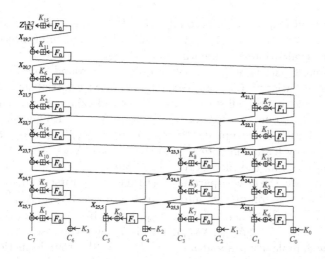

Fig. 6. Partial decryption for $\bigoplus(Z_{18,7}^1 \oplus Z_{18,7}^2 \oplus Z_{18,7}^7)$ in 26-round attack

Remaining Part. The right-hand-side of Eq. (1) involves 54 subkey bits and the left-hand-side of Eq. (1) involves 30 subkey bits. We can check the match of 1 bit of the state with Eq. (1) and 15 bits of the guessed keys (WK_6^{0-6}, $SK_{84}^{\prime 0-6}$, $SK_{84}^{\prime 7} \oplus WK_6^7$), in total 16 bits. Hence, the key space for $54 + 30 - 15 = 69$ bits are reduced by 16 bits after the analysis of 1 plaintext set. By iterating the analysis 5 times, these 69 subkey bits are recovered. The other 11 bits are exhaustively checked.

To sum up, the data complexity is $5 * 2^{56} \approx 2^{58.32}$ chosen plaintexts. The computational complexity is $5 * 2^{60.09} \approx 2^{64.02}$ round functions and $2^{58.32}$ memory access, which is equivalent to $2^{64.02}/22 \approx 2^{59.56}$ 22-round HIGHT computations and $2^{58.32}$ memory access. The memory requirement is 2^{55} bytes.

3.5 New Integral Analysis on 26-Round HIGHT

In [14], Zhang *et al.* presented another 17-round integral distinguisher. For a set of 2^{56} plaintexts with the form of (A, A, A, C, A, A, A, A), the state after 17 rounds, $(X_{17,7}\|\cdots\|X_{17,0})$, has the form of $(B^0, ?, ?, ?, ?, ?, ?, ?)$. Considering the subkey relations, we use this integral distinguisher. With the same transformation as for obtaining Eq. (1), $\bigoplus X_{17,7}^0 = 0$ can be transformed as

$$\bigoplus(X_{18,0}^0 \oplus SK_{71}^0 \oplus X_{19,0}^1 \oplus X_{19,0}^2 \oplus X_{19,0}^7) = \bigoplus(Z_{18,7}^1 \oplus Z_{18,7}^2 \oplus Z_{18,7}^7). \quad (2)$$

The computation for the right-hand side of Eq. (2) requires much more complexity than the left-hand side. Due to the limited space, we only explain how to obtain the right-hand side of Eq. (2). The partial decryption for obtaining $\bigoplus(Z_{18,7}^1 \oplus Z_{18,7}^2 \oplus Z_{18,7}^7)$ is shown in Fig. 6. We first describe a relatively simple procedure with the bytewise partial-sum. Firstly, the analysis stars from at most

2^{64} ciphertexts of $(C_0, \ldots, C_7)$. Secondly, (K_1, K_3) are guessed and the data is compressed into 2^{56} texts of $(Y_{24,7}, C_5, \ldots, C_0)$. The remaining procedure and its complexity evaluation is summarized in Table 3.

The dominant part is Step 6, which requires 2^{128} round function computations with the bytewise partial-sum. We apply the bitwise partial-sum to Step 6 to reduce the complexity. Step 6 starts from 2^{32} texts of $(Z_{20,7}, X_{24,4}, X_{24,3}, X_{23,1})$, and the goal is obtaining 2^{24} texts of $(Z_{20,7}, X_{22,2}, X_{22,1})$ with guessing two subkeys (K_8, K_{11}). At first, we update 2^{32} texts into $(Z_{20,7}, X_{24,4}, X_{24,3}, Y_{22,1})$, and we guess 1-byte key K_8 and update 2^{32} texts into $(Z_{20,7}, X_{22,2}, X_{24,3}, Y_{22,1})$. Up to here, the complexity for the guess of K_8 is less than $2^{80} \cdot 2^8 \cdot 2^{32} = 2^{120}$ round functions. We then apply the bitwise partial-sum to guess K_{11}. First of all, by exploiting the MSB, 2^{32} texts is compressed into 2^{31} texts of $(Z_{20,7}, X_{22,2}, X_{24,3}^{0-6}, Y_{22,1}^{0-6}, t^7)$, where t^7 is $X_{24,3}^7 \oplus Y_{22,1}^7$. Then, compute $X_{22,1}$ bit-by-bit from the LSB to MSB to obtain 2^{24} texts of $(Z_{20,7}, X_{22,2}, X_{22,1})$. This is a single-key case with 1 modular addition. The complexity is about $n \cdot (2^{88+31+1}) = 2^{123}$ round functions, where $n = 8$.

Finally, for a single set of chosen plaintexts, the sum of the complexity for all steps is 2^{64} memory access and $2^{80} + 2^{96} + 2^{112} + 2^{120} + (2^{120} + 2^{124}) + 2^{120} + 2^{112} + 2^{104} \approx 2^{124.25}$ round functions, which is $2^{124.25}/26 \approx 2^{119.55}$ 26-round HIGHT computations. The data complexity is 2^{56} chosen plaintexts. For each 2^{96} guess, we store guessed 12 bytes and 1-bit information for the match of the sum. Hence, the memory requirement is about $12 \cdot 2^{96} \approx 2^{99.58}$ bytes.

With one plaintext set, the left-hand side of Eq. (2) provides 2^{89} candidates and the right-hand side of Eq. (2) provides 2^{96} candidates. Hence, we check the match of 2^{185} pairs. Two computations include 72 bits in common. Therefore, together with the 1-bit of the state, we can match 73 bits. If we analyze two plaintext sets, only $2^{185-(73 \cdot 2)} = 2^{39}$ candidates will remain for the guessed key space. Because the entire guessed key space is 113 bits (all subkeys but for the 7 bits of K_9 and 8 bits of K_{13}), we need to search for the other 15 bits. This requires $2^{39+15} = 2^{54}$ 26-round HIGHT operations.

Table 3. Summary of the computation for $\bigoplus(Z_{18,7}^1 \oplus Z_{18,7}^2 \oplus Z_{18,7}^7)$. MA and RF stand for memory access and round function, respectively.

Step	Guessed keys	Data size	Texts to be analyzed	Complexity
1	-	2^{64}	$(C_0, \ldots, C_7)$	2^{64} MA
2	(K_1, K_3)	2^{56}	$(Y_{24,7}, C_5, \ldots, C_0)$	$2^{16} \cdot 2^{64} = 2^{80}$ RF
3	(K_0, K_5, K_6)	2^{48}	$(Y_{23,7}, C_5, \ldots, C_2, X_{25,1})$	$2^{16} \cdot 2^{24} \cdot 2^{56} = 2^{96}$ RF
4	(K_2, K_7, K_{10})	2^{40}	$(Y_{22,7}, C_5, X_{25,4}, X_{25,3}, X_{24,1})$	$2^{40} \cdot 2^{24} \cdot 2^{48} = 2^{112}$ RF
5	(K_{14}, K_{15})	2^{32}	$(Z_{20,7}, X_{24,4}, X_{24,3}, X_{23,1})$	$2^{64} \cdot 2^{16} \cdot 2^{40} = 2^{120}$ RF
6	(K_8, K_{11})	2^{24}	$(Z_{20,7}, X_{22,2}, X_{22,1})$	$2^{80} \cdot 2^{16} \cdot 2^{32} = 2^{128}$ RF
7	-	2^{16}	$(Y_{19,7}, X_{21,1})$	$2^{96} \cdot 2^0 \cdot 2^{24} = 2^{120}$ RF
8	-	2^8	$(Y_{18,7})$	$2^{96} \cdot 2^0 \cdot 2^{16} = 2^{112}$ RF
9	-	1	$\bigoplus(Z_{18,7}^1 \oplus Z_{18,7}^2 \oplus Z_{18,7}^7)$	$2^{96} \cdot 2^0 \cdot 2^8 = 2^{104}$ RF

In the end, two executions of the computation of the right-hand side of Eq. (2) has the overwhelming complexity, which is $2 \cdot 2^{119.55} = 2^{120.55}$ 26-round HIGHT computations. The analysis requires $2 \cdot 2^{56} = 2^{57}$ chosen plaintexts, and the memory requirement is $2^{99.58}$ bytes.

4 Concluding Remarks

In this paper, we presented the bitwise partial-sum technique that reduces the complexity of the integral analysis for ARX based designs. It computes equations bit-by-bit and compresses the data with respect to the computed value and the carry to the next bit position. We applied it to HIGHT. With an improvement specific to HIGHT, the number of attacked rounds is extended to 26.

Acknowledgment. Lei Wang is supported by the Singapore National Research Foundation Fellowship 2012 (NRF-NRFF2012-06).

References

1. Daemen, J., Knudsen, L.R., Rijmen, V.: The block cipher SQUARE. In: Biham, E. (ed.) FSE 1997. LNCS, vol. 1267, pp. 149–165. Springer, Heidelberg (1997)
2. Knudsen, L.R., Wagner, D.: Integral cryptanalysis. In: Daemen, J., Rijmen, V. (eds.) FSE 2002. LNCS, vol. 2365, pp. 112–127. Springer, Heidelberg (2002)
3. Biryukov, A., Shamir, A.: Structural cryptanalysis of SASAS. In: Pfitzmann, B. (ed.) EUROCRYPT 2001. LNCS, vol. 2045, pp. 394–405. Springer, Heidelberg (2001)
4. Nakahara Jr., J., de Freitas, D.S., Phan, R.C.-W.: New multiset attacks on Rijndael with large blocks. In: Dawson, E., Vaudenay, S. (eds.) Mycrypt 2005. LNCS, vol. 3715, pp. 277–295. Springer, Heidelberg (2005)
5. Z'aba, M.R., Raddum, H., Henricksen, M., Dawson, E.: Bit-pattern based integral attack. In: Nyberg, K. (ed.) FSE 2008. LNCS, vol. 5086, pp. 363–381. Springer, Heidelberg (2008)
6. Lucks, S.: The saturation attack - a bait for Twofish. In: Matsui, M. (ed.) FSE 2001. LNCS, vol. 2355, pp. 1–15. Springer, Heidelberg (2002)
7. Aumasson, J.P., Leurent, G., Meier, W., Mendel, F., Mouha, N., Phan, R.C.W., Sasaki, Y., Susil, P.: Tuple cryptanalysis of ARX with application to BLAKE and Skein. In: ECRYPT II Hash Workshop (2011)
8. Ferguson, N., Kelsey, J., Lucks, S., Schneier, B., Stay, M., Wagner, D., Whiting, D.L.: Improved cryptanalysis of Rijndael. In: Schneier, B. (ed.) FSE 2000. LNCS, vol. 1978, pp. 213–230. Springer, Heidelberg (2001)
9. Sasaki, Y., Wang, L.: Meet-in-the-middle technique for integral attacks against feistel ciphers. In: Knudsen, L.R., Wu, H. (eds.) SAC 2012. LNCS, vol. 7707, pp. 234–251. Springer, Heidelberg (2013)
10. Hong, D., et al.: HIGHT: a new block cipher suitable for low-resource device. In: Goubin, L., Matsui, M. (eds.) CHES 2006. LNCS, vol. 4249, pp. 46–59. Springer, Heidelberg (2006)
11. ISO/IEC 18033-3:2010: Information technology-Security techniques-Encryption Algorithms-Part 3: Block ciphers (2010)

12. Chen, J., Wang, M., Preneel, B.: Impossible differential cryptanalysis of the lightweight block ciphers TEA, XTEA and HIGHT. In: Mitrokotsa, A., Vaudenay, S. (eds.) AFRICACRYPT 2012. LNCS, vol. 7374, pp. 117–137. Springer, Heidelberg (2012)
13. Wu, W., Zhang, L.: LBlock: a lightweight block cipher. In: Lopez, J., Tsudik, G. (eds.) ACNS 2011. LNCS, vol. 6715, pp. 327–344. Springer, Heidelberg (2011)
14. Zhang, P., Sun, B., Li, C.: Saturation attack on the block cipher HIGHT. In: Garay, J.A., Miyaji, A., Otsuka, A. (eds.) CANS 2009. LNCS, vol. 5888, pp. 76–86. Springer, Heidelberg (2009)
15. Lu, J.: Cryptanalysis of block ciphers. Ph.D. thesis, Royal Holloway, University of London, England (2008)
16. Özen, O., Varici, K., Tezcan, C., Kocair, Ç.: Lightweight block ciphers revisited: cryptanalysis of reduced round PRESENT and HIGHT. In: Boyd, C., González Nieto, J. (eds.) ACISP 2009. LNCS, vol. 5594, pp. 90–107. Springer, Heidelberg (2009)
17. Koo, B., Hong, D., Kwon, D.: Related-key attack on the full HIGHT. In: Rhee, K.-H., Nyang, D.H. (eds.) ICISC 2010. LNCS, vol. 6829, pp. 49–67. Springer, Heidelberg (2011)
18. Needham, R.M., Wheeler, D.J.: TEA extensions. Technical report, Computer Laboratory, University of Cambridge (1997)
19. Ferguson, N., Lucks, S., Schneier, B., Whiting, D., Bellare, M., Kohno, T., Callas, J., Walker, J.: The Skein hash function family. Submission to NIST (Round 2) (2009)
20. Korea Internet and Security Agency: HIGHT Algorithm Specification (2009)

General Model of the Single-Key Meet-in-the-Middle Distinguisher on the Word-Oriented Block Cipher

Li Lin[1,2]($\boxtimes$), Wenling Wu[1], Yanfeng Wang[1], and Lei Zhang[1]

[1] Trusted Computing and Information Assurance Laboratory, Institute of Software, Chinese Academy of Sciences, Beijing 100190, China
{linli,wwl,wangyanfeng,zhanglei1015}@is.iscas.ac.cn
[2] Graduate University of Chinese Academy of Sciences, Beijing 100190, China

Abstract. The single-key meet-in-the-middle attack is an efficient attack against AES. The main component of this attack is a distinguisher. In this paper, we extend this kind of distinguisher to the word-oriented block cipher, such as the SPN block cipher and the Feistel-SP block cipher. We propose a general distinguisher model and find that building a better distinguisher is equivalent to a positive integer optimization problem. Then we give a proper algorithm to solve this problem. Furthermore, we analyse the limitation of the distinguisher using the efficient tabulation and give a method to search the special differential trail we need in this distinguisher. Finally, we apply the distinguisher to Crypton, mCrypton and LBlock, and give distinguishers on 4-round Crypton, 4-round mCrypton and 9-round LBlock. We also give 7-round attacks on Crypton-128 and mCrypton-96.

Keywords: Single-key MIMT · Genel distinguisher model · Word-oriented · SPN · Feistel-SPN

1 Introduction

The Rijndael block cipher was designed by Daemen and Rijmen in 1997 and accepted as the AES (Advanced Encryption Standard). Various of attacks has been proposed against AES, the single-key meet-in-the-middle attack[1] was an efficient one. The idea of this attack first came from the square attack [3], it used the δ-set to build the distinguisher. After that, Gilbert and Miner showed in [11] that this property could be used more precise to build a collisions attack on 7-round Rijndael. At FSE 2008, Demirci and Selçuk had generalized this idea using the meet-in-the-middle technique [6]. More specifically, they showed that the value of each byte of the ciphertext could be described by a function of the δ-set parameterized by 25 8-bit parameters. This function was used to build a distinguisher on 4-round AES. At ASIACRYPT 2010, Dunkelman, Keller and

---

[1] In this paper, we call this kind of attack the single-key meet-in-the-middle attack.

© Springer International Publishing Switzerland 2014
H.-S. Lee and D.-G. Han (Eds.): ICISC 2013, LNCS 8565, pp. 203–223, 2014.
DOI: 10.1007/978-3-319-12160-4_13

Shamir reduced the number of parameters from 25 to 24 [9]. Meanwhile, they developed many new ideas to solve the memory problems of the Demirci and Selçk attacks. By using the differential enumeration technique, the number of parameters was reduced largely from 24 to 16. At EUROCRYPT 2013, Derbez, Fouque and Jean developed the efficient tabulation [8] to further reduce the number of parameters from 16 to 10 which resulted in a lower memory complexity. At FSE 2013, Derbez and Fouque used the automatic search tool [1] to balance the cost of time, memory and data of the online phase and off-line phase [7].

However, the single-key meet-in-the-middle attack is rarely applied to block ciphers except AES. In this paper, we focus on the single-key meet-in-the-middle distinguisher which plays an important role in building the attack. This kind of distinguisher is extended to the word-oriented block cipher, such as the SPN block cipher and the Fetstel-SP block cipher (including the Generalized Feistel block cipher). We first define the T-δ-set which is a special set of states and the S-multiset which is a multiset of S cells, then use these definitions to get the least spread T-δ-set which has the least number of active cells and the least affected-cell-set which is affected by the least number of active cells. After that, we build a basic distinguisher model on the SPN block cipher and find that building a better distinguisher is equivalent to a positive integer optimization problem. Then a proper algorithm is given to solve this problem. Furthermore, this basic distinguisher model is applied to the Feistel-SP block cipher and the Generalized Feistel block cipher. Moreover, we analyse the limitation of the distinguisher using the efficient tabulation [8] and give a method to search the special differential trail needed in this distinguisher. We also show some viewpoints that Derbez et al don't consider in [8] about the AES distinguisher started from a 2-δ-set and the 5-round AES distinguisher. Finally we apply the distinguishers to Crypton [12,13], mCrypton [14] and LBlock [16]. We build the 4-round distinguishers on Crypton and mCrypton, then use these distinguishers to attack 7-round Crypton-128 and mCrypton-96. For Crypton, it takes a time complexity of 2^{113}, a data complexity of 2^{113} chosen plaintexts and a memory complexity of 2^{91}. For mCrypton, it takes a time complexity of 2^{77}, a data complexity of 2^{49} chosen-plaintexts and a memory complexity of $2^{52.44}$. And we give a 9-round distinguisher on LBlock with 14 guessed-nibbles.

The organization of this paper is as follows: Sect. 2 gives some definitions and a basic single-key meet-in-the-middle attack scheme. Section 3 gives the basic distinguisher model and the model using the efficient tabulation. In Sect. 4 and Sect. 5, we apply the distinguisher to Crypton, mCrypton and LBlock.

2   Definitions and Attack Scheme

In this section, we first give the definitions of the SPN block cipher, the T-δ-set and the S-multiset, then use these definitions to give a basic single-key meet-in-the-middle attack scheme. We also give the way to calculating the total number of S-multisets and the way to get the proper values of S and T. Section 2.1 gives the definition of the SPN block cipher. In Sect. 2.2, we give the definitions of the T-δ-set and S-multiset, the way to calculate the number of S-multisets and the definition of the proper parameters. In Sect. 2.3, we give the basic attack scheme.

2.1   The SPN Block Cipher

To keep our reasoning as general as possible, we give in this subsection a generic description of Substitution-Permutation Network (SPN) cipher. One round i is itself composed of three layers: a key schedule transformation layer (KS) where we can get the key used in this round, a block cipher permutation layer (BC) that updates the current state of the block cipher, a key-addition layer (AK) where a n-cell round-key rk_i is extracted from k_i and XORed to x_i.

The size of plaintext or ciphertext is n cells, and the size of key is n_K cells, each cell consist of b bits. A state means a set of n cells before or after one operation. The cipher is consist of R_{total} successive applications of a round function, and we denote x_i and k_i the successive internal states of the encryption and the key schedule, respectively. The state x_0 is initialized with the input plaintext and k_0 with the input key. We count the round-number from 0.

Definition 1 (SPN cipher [10]). *Let a block cipher $\mathscr{E}$ whose internal state is viewed as an n-cell vector, each cell representing a b-bit word, and the key schedule as an n_K-cell vector. The block cipher $\mathscr{E}$ is called an SPN cipher when its round function BC is made up of a linear function P and a non-linear permutation S, with BC=P∘S, the latter applying one or distinct b-bit Sboxes to every cell.*

The SPN cipher considered here needs to have the following properties: all operations are based on cells; if we know the input differences, we can get the output differences after the linear function, and vice versa.

2.2   Definitions

In [4], Daemen et al first proposed the definition of δ-set. After that, δ-set was used in the attacks on AES and other ciphers. In the former single-key meet-in-the-middle attacks [6–9,11], the attackers use the state structure that there is only one active byte in the first round of the distinguisher to attack AES. However, we should choose two or more all-active cells for the lightweight block cipher or other kinds of the SPN ciphers.

Definition 2 (T-δ-set). *Let a T-δ-set be a set of $2^{T\times b}$ states that are all different in T cells (the all-active cells)[2] and all equal in the other cells (the inactive cells), where b is the number of bits in a cell and $T \leq n$.*

In [9], Dunkelman, Keller and Shamir introduced the *multiset* and use the differences instead of the real values to reduce the number of guessed-cells (cells

---

[2] All-active cell: take all the values of this cell once. The active cell: the probability that the difference isn't zero is greater than 0.

need to be guessed). However, they only consider the *multiset* of one cell. We should consider the *multiset* of two or more cells for lightweight block ciphers or other kinds of the SPN ciphers.

Definition 3 (*S-Multiset*). *An S-multiset is an unordered set in which elements can occur many times, and every element of the S-multiset consists of S cells, $S \leq n$.*

Next, we will show the number of possible *S-multisets*[3]

Proposition 1 (Number of *S-Multisets*). *If one S-multiset has $2^{T \times b}$ elements, the size of each element is S cells, then the number of possible S-multisets is $\binom{2^{T \times b} + 2^{S \times b} - 1}{2^{S \times b} - 1}$.*

The chosen of S and T have a great influence on the distinguisher. We give the method to choose the proper number of S and T as follows:

Definition 4 (Proper Parameters). *The definition of the proper parameters is as follows: we choose the integer parameters S and T satisfy that $\binom{2^{T \times b} + 2^{S \times b} - 1}{2^{S \times b} - 1}$ $\gg 2^{n_K \times b}$. It means that we have a set W of size $\binom{2^{T \times b} + 2^{S \times b} - 1}{2^{S \times b} - 1}$ and its subset W' of size $2^{n_K \times b}$. If we randomly choose an element from W, the probability that it is also from W' is almost zero, we call (T,S) the proper parameters $(S \leq n, T \leq n)$.*

2.3   Attack Scheme

In this section, we present a unified view of the single-key meet-in-the-middle attack, where R rounds of the block cipher can be split into three consecutive parts of r_1, r, and r_2.

The general attack uses three successive steps as shown in Fig. 1:

Precomputation phase

1. Suppose we have built an r-round distinguisher from a T-δ-set to an S-*multiset* by guessing some internal cells, we build a lookup table $\mathcal{T}$ containing all the possible *S-multisets*;

Online phase

2. We need to identify a T-δ-set in the online phase (for the distinguisher using the efficient tabulation, the T-δ-set need to contain a pair of messages verifying the desired differential trail);
3. Finally, we partially decrypt the associated T-δ-set through the last r_2 rounds and check whether it belongs to $\mathcal{T}$.

From the statement above, if we want to make this kind of attack more efficient, a distinguisher with more rounds and less cells to be guessed need to be built. So in this paper, we focus on the distinguisher.

Since the size of $\mathcal{T}$ is less than $2^{n_K} \times b$, for the wrong key guess, the proper parameters can guarantee the *S-multiset* we get in the online phase not to be one of $\mathcal{T}$.

---

[3] We refer to [8] the number of cells n_S we need to store an *S-multiset*.

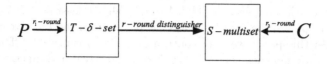

Fig. 1. The single-key meet-in-the-middle attack procedure

3   General Model of the Single-Key Meet-in-the-Middle Distinguisher

In this section, we will give a basic distinguisher model on the SPN block cipher and the Feistel-SP block cipher. In Sect. 3.1, we first define the least spread T-δ-set and the least *affected-cell-set*, then use these definitions to build a basic distinguisher model on the SPN block cipher. We find that building a distinguisher with more rounds and less cell to be guessed is equivalent to a positive integer optimization problem. Section 3.2 gives a proper algorithm to solve this problem. In Sect. 3.3, we apply the basic distinguisher model to the Feistel-SP block cipher and the Generalized Feistel block cipher. In Sect. 3.4, we analyse the limitation of the distinguisher using the efficient tabulation, then give the method to search the special differential trail we need in this distinguisher.

3.1   Distinguisher on the SPN Block Cipher

In this section, we will build a basic distinguisher model on the SPN block cipher. Firstly, we propose some definitions.

Since the propagation of T-δ-set increases the number of guessed-cells, we define the least spread T-δ-set to minimize it. Here we denote χ_i the number of active cells before the non-linear permutation of round i.

For a T-δ-set Λ, we define $\mathscr{F}_t$ as follows:

$$\mathscr{F}_t(\Lambda) = \begin{cases} (\sum_{i=1}^{\varrho-1}\chi_i, \varrho-1) & \text{if } \sum_{i=1}^{\varrho-1}\chi_i \le t \\ (\sum_{i=1}^{r}\chi_i, r) & \text{if } \sum_{i=1}^{r}\chi_i \le t, \ \sum_{i=1}^{r+1}\chi_i > t \ and \ r < \varrho-1 \end{cases}$$

where ϱ satisfies that $\chi_\varrho = n$ and $\chi_{\varrho-1} < n$. It means that before the non-linear permutation of round ϱ, all the cells just become active; but at round $\varrho-1$, there are still inactive cells.

We denote the total number of active cells before the non-linear permutation from round 1 to round r as N_r. For a given t, if $N_\varrho \le t$, then the output of $\mathscr{F}_t$ is N_ϱ and $\varrho-1$; if $N_\varrho > t$, the output is N_R and R that R satisfies $N_R \le t$ and $N_{R+1} > t$.

Definition 5 (Least Spread T-δ-set). *The least spread T-δ-set (short for the least spread T-δ-set for $\mathscr{F}_t$) is the T-δ-set that maximizes the second output of $\mathscr{F}_t$ before minimizing the first output.*

We can loop through each T-δ-set Λ to find all the least spread T-δ-sets. In the rest of this paper, the T-δ-set means the positions of the T active cells at the same time. In this paper we only concern about the truncated-difference-form (TDF) of a state, i.e. each cell only has 2 forms—active[4] and inactive.

Next, we will define the least $Affected$-$Cell$-Set. It gets rid of some guessed-cells. Oppose to the least spread T-δ-set, we start from the last round. Suppose we have an R-round encrypt procedure starting from a T-δ-set, only S cells are needed at the final round to build the S-$multiset$[4]. The definition of the $affected$-$cells$-set is as follows:

Definition 6 ($Affected$-$Cell$-Set $\mathscr{A}^{(r')}$). *Suppose we have an R-round encrypt procedure starting from a T-δ-set, for one active cell π before the non-linear permutation of round $i+1$, its value is affected by a set of active cells before the non-linear permutation of round i, i.e. the affected-cell-set $\mathscr{A}^{(1)}(\pi)$. For an S-multiset Ω, its affected-cell-set $\mathscr{A}^{(1)}(\Omega)$ is the union of the S affected-cell-sets. And*

$$\mathscr{A}^{(r')}(\Omega) = \mathscr{A}^{(r'-1)}(\mathscr{A}^{(1)}(\Omega)) = \cdots = \underbrace{\mathscr{A}^{(1)} \dots \mathscr{A}^{(1)}(\Omega)}_{r'}$$

where r' is the number of rounds. The number of the affected-cell-set is denoted by $|\mathscr{A}^{(r')}(\Omega)|$.

For an S-$multiset$ Ω, we define $\mathscr{G}_s$ as follows:

$$\mathscr{G}_s(\Omega) = \begin{cases} (\sum_{i=1}^{\varsigma-1}|\mathscr{A}^{(i)}(\Omega)|, \varsigma-1) & \text{if } \sum_{i=1}^{\varsigma-1}|\mathscr{A}^{(i)}(\Omega)| \leq s \\ (\sum_{i=1}^{r}|\mathscr{A}^{(i)}(\Omega)|, r) & \text{if } \sum_{i=1}^{r}|\mathscr{A}^{(i)}(\Omega)| \leq s, \sum_{i=1}^{r+1}|\mathscr{A}^{(i)}(\Omega)| > s \end{cases}$$

where ς satisfies that for an S-$multiset$ Ω, $|\mathscr{A}^{(\varsigma)}(\Omega)| = n$ but $|\mathscr{A}^{(\varsigma-1)}(\Omega)| < n$. It means that suppose we have an R-round encrypt procedure, Ω is affected by all the cells before the non-linear permutation of round $R - \varsigma$, but not affected by some cells of round $R - (\varsigma - 1)$.

We denote the total number of active cells that affect Ω from round $R - r$ to round $R - 1$ by N'_r. For a given s, if $N'_\varsigma \leq s$, the output of $\mathscr{G}_s$ is N'_ς and $\varsigma - 1$; if $N_\varsigma > s$, the output is N'_r and r where r satisfies $N'_r \leq s$ and $N'_{r+1} > s$.

Definition 7 (**Least** $Affected$-$Cell$-Set). *The least affected-cell-set (short for the least affected-cell-set for $\mathscr{G}_s$) is the S-multiset that maximizes the second output of $\mathscr{G}_s$ before minimizing the first output.*

We can loop through each S-$multiset$ Ω to find all the least $affected$-$cell$-sets.

Our goal is to build a distinguisher of as many rounds as possible under the condition that the time and memory complexity are both less than the exhaustive search. Distinguisher of r rounds can be split into three consecutive parts of r_1,

---

[4] S-*multiset* also means the positions of the S cells in a state.

r_2, and r_3, the number of guessed-cells of each part is n_1, n_2 and n_3. It is easy to see that $n_1 + n_2 + n_3 < n_K$.

We choose one state of the T-δ-set as the standard state, and denote it as 0. The differences mentioned below means the XORing between the states in the T-δ-set and the standard state. The main method of this distinguisher is that we can guess values of active cells in the standard state to go through the non-linear permutation. If we know the input differences of the linear function or the key-addition layer, we can get the output differences. The distinguisher can be built as follows:

1. (**The former part**) For a given n_1, get the least spread T-δ-set Λ and $\mathscr{F}_{n_1}(\Lambda) = (\chi, r_1)$. After that we can get the differences of all cells after r_1 rounds of encryption by guessing χ cells as follows:
   i. At round 0, we can get all the differences of the active cells after the non-linear permutation because we know all the values of the T active cells. Since the other cells are inactive, we can get all the differences at the beginning of round 1;
   ii. At round i $(i > 0)$, by guessing the values of the active cells in the standard state and knowing the differences before the non-linear permutation, we can get the differences after the non-linear permutation. Also by the linearity, we can get all the differences at the beginning of round $i + 1$. As a result, we can get the differences at the beginning of round $r_1 + 1$ by guessing $\chi = \sum_{i=1}^{r_1} \chi_i$ cells.
2. (**The middle part**) The middle part is the full-guessed part. Since all the n cells become active in this part, we should guess all the values of cells in the standard state before the non-linear permutation, then get all the differences at the beginning of the next round. The number of rounds and guessed-cells in this part are $r_2 = \lfloor \frac{n_2}{n} \rfloor$ and $n_2 = \lfloor \frac{n_2}{n} \rfloor \times n$, respectively.
3. (**The latter part**) For a given n_3, get the least $affected\text{-}cell\text{-}set$ Ω and $\mathscr{G}_{n_3}(\Omega) = (\omega, r_3)$. After that we can get the $S\text{-}multiset$ from the output differences of the middle part (through r_3 rounds of encryption) by guessing ω state cells as follows:
   i. If we want to get the $S\text{-}multiset$ Ω, we need to guess its $affected\text{-}cell\text{-}set$ $\mathscr{A}^{(1)}(\Omega)$ of the standard state;
   ii. If we want to get $\mathscr{A}^{(i-1)}(\Omega)$, we need to guess its $affected\text{-}cell\text{-}set$ $\mathscr{A}^{(i)}(\Omega)$ of the standard state. As a result, the total number of cells need be to guessed in the latter part is $\omega = \sum_{i=1}^{r_3} |\mathscr{A}^{(i)}(\Omega)|$.

Since our goal is to build a distinguisher with more rounds and less guessed-cells, the statement above is equivalent to a positive integer optimization problem as follows:

Problem 1.

$$\boldsymbol{Max}\ r = r_1 + r_2 + r_3\ \boldsymbol{Then}\ \boldsymbol{Min}\ M = \chi + \lfloor \frac{n_2}{n} \rfloor \times n + \omega \qquad (1)$$

$$s.t. \begin{cases} n_1 + n_2 + n_3 < n_K \\ \mathscr{F}_{n_1}(\Lambda) = (\chi, r_1), where\ \Lambda\ is\ the\ least\ spead\ T - \delta - set \\ \mathscr{G}_{n_3}(\Omega) = (\omega, r_3), where\ \Omega\ is\ the\ least\ affected - cell - set \end{cases} \qquad (2)$$

If we solve Problem 1, we can build a single-key meet-in-the-middle distinguisher of at least r rounds with a memory complexity of 2^M.[5] So we will give a proper algorithm to solve Problem 1.

3.2   Algorithm To Solve Problem 1

In this section, we will give the algorithm to solve Problem 1. Although we can loop through each possible value of n_1, n_2 and n_3, there is a better solution with the pruning method. In the algorithm below, the former part and the middle part will be combined into one part—the former part. This part will take the responsibility of propagating the T-δ-set. The latter part will take the responsibility of pruning the guessed-cells.

1. **(The former part)** Let χ_i be the number of active cells before the non-linear permutation of round i as before. We can define the function of one-round encryption — ONEROUND$(x)=(\chi, y)$, where x is a state in TDF, χ is the number of active cells of x, y is the output of x after one-round encryption.

   Next, we will define the function of r_1-round encryption—PROPAGATE(Λ, r_1), where Λ is a T-δ-set. The output of this algorithm is the number of guessed-cells and a set of r_1 internal states in TDF. This function is shown in Algorithm 1 of Appendix C.

2. **(The latter part)** The latter part is for pruning the guessed-cells. For an S-$multiset$ Ω, the meaning of $\mathscr{A}^{(j)}(\Omega)$ is the same as Definition 6. The pruning function — PRUNING$(StateSet, \chi, \Omega, FormerR)$ is given in Algorithm 2 of Appendix C, where $(\chi, StateSet)$ is the output of the former part, $FormerR$ is the number of rounds in the former part and Ω is an S-$multiset$ in TDF.

In Algorithm 3 of Appendix C, we will give a proper solution to Problem 1 combining the former part and the latter part.

Since the total number of T-δ-set is at most $\binom{n}{T}$ and the total number of S-$multiset$ is at most $\binom{n}{S}$, the maximum time complexity of Algorithm 3 is $R_{total} \times \binom{n}{T} \times \binom{n}{S}$. And we can build an r-round distinguisher on this cipher with memory complexity of $2^{\chi \times b}$ (r and χ are the output of MINROUNDGUESS() and MINNUMBER(R), respectively). We can use this distinguisher in the online phase to recover the right-key.

3.3   Applied to the Feistel Structure

The algorithm above can be also applied to the Fiestel-SP block cipher and Generalized Feistel block cipher which use the SPN structure as round functions.

The main methods and algorithms of the distinguisher are quite the same as the SPN block cipher. We give an example of the distinguisher on LBlock in Sect. 5.

---

[5] By [9], we can build a distinguisher with less guessed-cells.

3.4   The Distinguisher Using Efficient Tabulation

At [8], Derbez et al. proposed the efficient tabulation to reduce the memory complexity and made this kind of attack against 7-round AES-128 possible. The new component of the distinguisher using this technique is a special truncated differential trail. With a pair of messages satisfying this trail, we can reduce the memory complexity of the distinguisher. We call this pair the T-S **right pair**.

However, this technique doesn't work for all the SPN block ciphers because it uses **the differential-property of S**. AES has a special 4-round truncated differential trail $1 \rightarrow 4 \rightarrow 16 \leftarrow 4 \leftarrow 1$, so the two states on the both sides of the nonlinear-permutation in the third round are all active with the probability equals to 1. However, since the branch number of the mixcolumn operation [5] isn't the maximum (such as Crypton and mCrypton), there are more than 1 active cells before the mixcolumn operation (such as the 5-round AES distinguisher [8]) and so on, the states on the both sides of the non-linear permutation may have inactive cells. If it happens, the inactive cells can take all the 2^b values rather than 1. This will increase the memory complexity.

The algorithm of the distinguisher using efficient tabulation is shown in Appendix A.4. An example of distinguisher using the efficient tabulation and the computation process of memory complexity considering the limitation are shown in Sect. 4.3 and Appendix A, respectively. We also show some viewpoints on the 4-round AES distinguisher starting from a 2-δ-set and the 5-round distinguisher [8] in Appendix A.3.

4   Distinguishers and Attacks on Crypton and mCrtpton

In this section, we describe our basic distinguishers and the distinguishers using the efficient tabulation on Crypton[6] [12,13] and mCrypton [14]. In Sects. 4.1 and 4.2, we introduce the basic distinguishers on Crypton and mCrypton. Section 4.3 gives the distinguishers on Crypton and mCrypton using the efficient tabulation. Then we introduce the attacks on 7-round Crypton-128 and mCrypton-96 in Appendix B.

In this section, we use the notation as follows: $x[i]$ denote the i-th byte/nibble of an internal state, and $x[i,\ldots,j]$ for bytes/nibbles between i-th and j-th. In the i-th round, we denote the internal state after **the key-addition layer** by x_i, after **the nonlinear-permutation** by y_i, after **the bit permutation** by z_i, after **the column-to-row** by w_i.

4.1   Basic Distinguisher on Crypton

The following proposition gives a 4-round distinguisher on Crypton.

---

[6] Both V0.5 and V1.0 since we don't use the property of the key-schedule.

Proposition 2. *Consider the encryption of a $(1-)\delta$-set (of byte) $\{x_i^0, x_i^1, \ldots,$ $x_i^{255}\}$ through four full Crypton rounds. For each $(1-)$multiset*

$$\left[x_4^0[0] \oplus x_4^0[0], x_4^1[0] \oplus x_4^0[0], \ldots, x_4^0[0] \oplus x_4^{255}[0]\right]$$

is fully determined by the following 24 bytes:

$$x_{i+1}^0[0, 4, 8, 12], x_{i+2}^0[0, \ldots, 15], x_{i+3}^0[0, \ldots, 3.]$$

The proof procedure is shown in Fig. 2 and the same as the procedure of Sect. 3.1. The first and second rounds are the former part, the third round is the middle part and the last round is the latter part.

Since the *multisets* of $x_{i+4}[0]$ are totally determined by 24 bytes, it can take as many as $2^{24 \times 8} = 2^{192}$ values (out of the $2^{507.6}$ "theoretically possible" values). As a result, we treat the cipher with wrong key guess as a random function, the probability that a random value is one member of the "right set" is $2^{192-507.6} = 2^{-315.6}$. It is almost impossible.

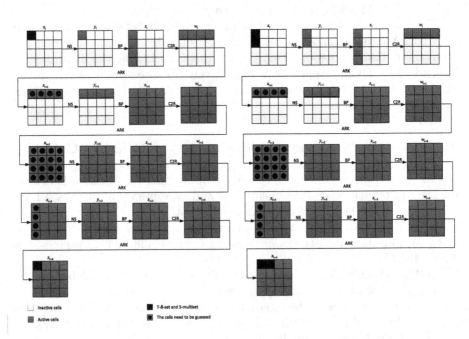

Fig. 2. The 4-rounds distinguisher of Crypton and mCrypton

4.2 Basic Distinguisher on mCrypton

Since mCrypton is a lightweight block cipher, the distinguisher on mCrypton is a little different from Crypton. mCrypton uses the $2\text{-}\delta\text{-}set$ to build the distinguisher and gets a 2-*muliset*. The following proposition gives a 4-round distinguisher on mCrypton.

Proposition 3. *Consider the encryption of a 2-δ-set $\{x_i^0[0,1], x_i^1[0,1], \ldots, x_i^{255}[0,1]\}$ through four full mCrypton rounds. For each 2-multiset*

$$[x_4^0[0,4] \oplus x_4^0[0,4], x_4^1[0,4] \oplus x_4^0[0,4], \ldots, x_4^0[0,4] \oplus x_4^{255}[0,4]]$$

is fully determined by the following 24 nibbles:

$$x_{i+1}^0[0,4,8,12], x_{i+2}^0[0,\ldots,15], x_{i+3}^0[0,\ldots,3].$$

The proof procedure is shown in Fig. 2.

4.3 Distinguishers on Crypton and mCrypton Using Efficient Tabulation

If there exists a (1-1) right pair among the δ-set of Crypton and a (2-2) right pair among the 2-δ-set of mCrypton, we can reduce the requirement for memory.

Proposition 4 ((1-1) right pair property of Crypton). *If a state x_i^0 belongs to a right pair of states conforming to the truncated differential trail, then the multisets of $\Delta x_{i+4}[0]$ obtains from the δ-set constructed from x_i^0 as the standard state can take only 2^{89} values. More precisely, the 24 bytes parameters can take only 2^{89} values and determined by 10 bytes. The 10 bytes are:*

$$\Delta y_i[0], x_{i+1}^0[0,4,8,12], \Delta z_{i+3}[0], y_{i+3}^0[0,\ldots,3].$$

The proof is shown in Fig. 3 and the same as the method in Appendix A.4.

Proposition 5 ((2-2) right pair property of mCrypton). *If a state x_i^0 belongs to a (2-2) right pair of states conforming to the truncated differential trail, then the 2-multisets of $\Delta x_{i+4}[0,1]$ obtains from the 2-δ-set constructed from x_i^0 as the standard state can take only $2^{49.44}$ values. More precisely, the 24 nibble parameters take only $2^{49.44}$ values and determined by 12 nibbles. The 12 nibbles are:*

$$\Delta y_i[0,1], x_{i+1}^0[0,4,8,12], \Delta z_{i+3}[0,1], y_{i+3}^0[0,\ldots,3].$$

The proof procedure is the same as that of Crypton and shown in Fig. 3. The number of possible *multisets* is $2^{49.44}$. The way to calculate the exact number of 2-*multisets* is shown in Appendix A.2.

4.4 Basic Attack on Crypton and mCrypton Using Efficient Tabulation

Using the distinguisher of Sect. 4.3, the attacks on 7-round Crypton-128 and mCrypton-96 can be built. For Crypton, it takes a time complexity of 2^{113}, a data complexity of 2^{113} chosen plaintexts and a memory complexity of 2^{91}. For mCrypton, it takes a time complexity of 2^{77}, a data complexity of 2^{49} chosen-plaintexts and a memory complexity of $2^{52.44}$.

The attacks are made up of 2 phase: **the precomputation phase** and **the online phase**. The online phase is also made up of three parts: **finding the right pair, creating and checking the δ-set** and **finding the secret key**. The detail of these attacks is shown in Appendix B.

5   Basic Distinguisher on LBlock

We give a 9-round distinguisher on LBlock [16] of 14 guessed-nibbles in Fig. 4. We choose the active nibbles at positions 8 and 9 of R_0 as the 2-δ-set, and the active nibbles at positions 8 and 9 of R_9 to build the 2-*multiset*. The guessed-nibbles (a, b) of round i are marked by $L_i(a, b)$.

6   Conclusion and Further Works

In this paper, we proposed the basic single-key meet-in-the-middle distinguisher model on the word-oriented block cipher and showed that building a better distinguisher is equivalent to a positive integer optimization problem. Then we gave a proper algorithm to solve this problem. Furthermore, we analyzed the limitation of the distinguisher using the efficient tabulation and the method to search the special differential trail needed in this distinguisher. What's more, we applied the distinguisher model to Crypton, mCrypton and LBlock. We gave 4-round basic distinguishers on Crypton and mCrypton. After that we gave the distinguishers with the efficient tabulation and used these distinguishers to build the attacks on 7-round Crypton-128 and mCrypton-96. For Crypton, the attack cost a time complexity of 2^{113}, a data complexity of 2^{113} chosen plaintext and a memory complexity of 2^{91}. For mCrypton, it cost a time complexity of 2^{77}, a data complexity of 2^{49} chosen-plaintexts and a memory complexity of $2^{52.44}$. For LBlock, we gave a 9-round distinguisher of 14 guessed-cells.

The research community has still a lot to learn on the way to build better distinguishers and there are many future works possible: the model to build better distinguishers of this kind with more rounds and less guessed-cells, how to apply the efficient tabulation to the Feistel-SP cipher and give a formal proof of security against this kind of distinguishers.

Acknowledgements. We would like to thank the anonymous reviewers for providing valuable comments. The research presented in this paper is supported by the National Basic Research Program of China (No. 2013CB338002) and National Natural Science Foundation of China (No. 61272476, No.61232009 and No. 61202420).

A   The Number of δ-Sets

A.1   The Number of δ-Sets for Crypton

For Crypton, since the branch number of the bit permutation is 4, in Fig. 3, the first column of z_i may not be all active. If there is one inactive byte, the result is that one column of z_{i+1} is inactive. Even if the j-th byte of the first column is active, the j-th column of z_{i+1} may have one inactive byte, and vice versa. However, the i-th byte of x_{i+2} and y_{i+2} must be both active or inactive.

If one byte at the same position of x_{i+2} and y_{i+2} is inactive, then that position can take all the 256 values out of the average $\frac{256}{255}$ values [8].

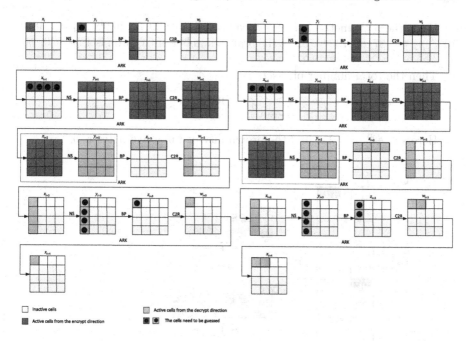

Fig. 3. The 4-rounds distinguisher of Crypton and mCrypton using efficient tabulation

We can count the exact number of *multisets* even though the maximum number of inactive bytes of x_{i+2} is 7. We find that if the input difference is {1, 2, 3, 4, 8, 12, 16, 32, 48, 64, 128, 192} then the output difference has one inactive byte.

Next we will calculate the probabilities that there are i inactive bytes in x_{i+2}, $i = 0, 1, \ldots, 7$.

0. In Fig. 3, if the active bytes of y_i, y_{i+1}, z_{i+2} and z_{i+3} don't take the 12 differences above, then the 16 bytes of x_{i+2} and y_{i+2} are all active, the probability of this happen is:
$$(\frac{255 - 12}{255})^{5 \times 2} \approx 0.6157$$

1. If the active bytes of y_i and z_{i+3} don't take the 12 differences, but one of the active bytes of y_{i+1} and z_{i+2} take the 12 differences, then 15 bytes of x_{i+2} and y_{i+2} are active(the inactive byte must be at the same position), the probability is:
$$16 \times (\frac{3}{255})^2 \times (\frac{243}{255})^8 \approx 0.0015$$

2. If the active bytes of y_i and z_{i+3} don't take the 12 differences above, but two of the active bytes of y_{i+1} and z_{i+2} take the 12 differences above, then 14 bytes of x_{i+2} and y_{i+2} are active, the probability is:
$$\binom{4}{2} \times 4 \times 3 \times (\frac{3}{255})^4 \times (\frac{243}{255})^6 \approx 1.0329 \times 10^{-6}$$

Using the same method above, we can get: $p_3 = 2.0990 \times 10^{-10}$, $p_4 = 1.4868 \times 10^{-9}$, $p_7 = 5.8718 \times 10^{-15}$. Since the branch number of Crypton is 4, $p_5 = 0$, $p_6 = 0$.

Then the total number of δ-*sets* is:

$$2^{80} \times \sum_{i=0}^{7} p_i \times s^{16-i} \times t^i \approx 2^{89}$$

Here $s = \frac{256}{255}$, $t = 256$ and the probability of i inactive bytes is p_i.

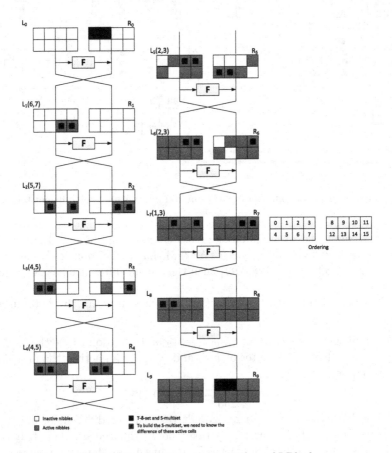

Fig. 4. The 9-rounds distinguisher of LBlock

A.2   The Number of 2-δ-*Sets* for mCryptonp

For mCrypton, since the branch number is also 4, in Fig. 3, the first column of z_i may not be all active, and the inactive nibbles can be as many as 2. As a result, there are two columns of z_{i+1} being all inactive. Even if the j-th nibble of the first column of z_i is active, the j-th column of z_{i+1} may not be all active and vice versa.

If one nibble at the same position of x_{i+2} and y_{i+2} is inactive, that position can take all the 16 values out of the average $\frac{16}{15}$ values.

We can exactly count the number of 2-*multisets* even though the maximum number of inactive nibbles of x_{i+2} is 10. If the input differences of z_i have two active nibbles, and take the values $\{(1,1), (2,2), (4,4), (8,8)\}$, then the output differences have two inactive nibbles. Else if the differences of the two active nibbles taking 52 particular values will result in 1 inactive nibble. If there is only one active nibble in a column and the difference is 1,2,4,8, after the bit permutation, the output difference of that column has 1 inactive nibble. Since the branch number of mCrypton is 4, the maximal number of inactive nibbles is 7.

The way to calculate the probability that there are i inactive nibble in x_{i+2} is the same as Crypton, we just show the probabilities of i inactive nibbles in Table 1.

Table 1. The probability of the number of inactive nibbles in x_{i+2}

i	0	1	2	3	4	7
p_i	0.0509	0.0067	2.5049×10^{-4}	2.7603×10^{-6}	2.4851×10^{-6}	3.6507×10^{-9}

Then the total number of 2-*multisets* is:

$$2^{48} \times \sum_{i=0}^{10} p_i \times s^{16-i} \times t^i \approx 2^{49.44}$$

Here $s = \frac{16}{15}$, $t = 16$ and the probability of i inactive bytes is p_i.

A.3   The Number of *Multisets* of the AES $\star$ Distinguisher and 5-Round Distinguisher in [8]

In [8], Derbez, Fouque and Jean proposed the attacks on reduced-round AES using the efficient tabulation. In Sect. 3.3 of their paper, they used a special differential trail $\star$ to reduce the time complexity of the online phase, i.e.

$$2 \xrightarrow{R_i} 4 \xrightarrow{R_{i+1}} 16 \xrightarrow{R_{i+2}} 4 \xrightarrow{R_{i+3}} 1 \qquad (\star)$$

Since $\star$ has 2 active bytes comparing to the original distinguisher, they simply calculated the memory requirement 2^8 times more than the original one.

However the branch number of AES mixcolumn operation is 5, it may have one inactive byte after the mixcolumn operation of round i, and it lead to one inactive column at x_{i+2}. From the other direction, one active byte in x_{i+4} can result in y_{i+2} being all active, this is a mismatch. The number of pairs of

$(\Delta x_i[0], \Delta x_i[2])$ which will lead to a mismatch is 1020, so we have the memory they use to store the *multisets* is:

$$2^{82} \times 2^8 \times \frac{2^{16} - 1020}{2^{16}} \approx 0.98 \times 2^{80}$$

128-bit blocks.

At Sect. 4.2 of their attack, they present an attack on 9-round AES 256, they add one round in the middle of the distinguisher, and they simply calculate the memory requirement 2^{128} times more than the original one.

They add the extra round after x_{i+2} by guessing all the values of the standard state, and use the differential property of S between x_{i+3} and y_{i+3}. Since x_{i+2} is active at all bytes, after the mixcolumn operation of round $i + 2$, it may have inactive bytes at x_{i+3}. Since one active byte at x_{i+5} will lead to all active at y_{i+3} this will lead to a mismatch. One column which includes of 4 active bytes will result in 1, 2 or 3 inactive bytes, the number of active column for each case is 6.52953×10^7, 384030, 1020. So the memory to store the *multisets* is:

$$2^{82} \times 2^{128} \times \frac{2^{32} - 6.52953 \times 10^7 - 384030 - 1020}{2^{32}} \approx 0.98 \times 2^{208}$$

128-bit blocks.

A.4   The Basic Model of Distinguisher using Efficient Tabulation

With the limitation, the search algorithm for the special truncated differential trail with the least guessed-cells is a meet-in-the-middle procedure. For the SPN cipher, we denote the pair with T active cells at the beginning of the truncated differential trail by E_T and the state with S active cells at the end by D_S. Also from the encrypt direction, the number of active cells before the non-linear permutation of round i is denoted by χ_i^E. From the decrypt direction, the number of active cells after the non-linear permutation of the i-th round from the bottom is denoted by χ_i^D. One state of the pair is dennonted by the standard state. The algorithm is as follows:

1. From the encrypt direction, starting from an E_T, we can get all the differences at the end of round 0 by guessing the differences of the active cells after the non-linear permutation. By guessing the active cells of the standard state before the non-linear permutation, we can get all the differences at the end of the i-th round. So after guessing $\sum_{i=0}^{r_E} \chi_i^E$ cells, we can get all the differences before the non-linear permutation of round $r_E + 1$;

2. From the decrypt direction, starting from a D_S, we can get all the differences at the beginning of the last round by guessing the differences of the active cells before the non-linear permutation. By guessing the active cells of the standard state after the non-linear permutation, we can get all the differences at the beginning of the i-th round from the bottom. So after guessing $\sum_{i=0}^{r_D} \chi_i^D$ cells we can get all the differences after the non-linear permutation of round $r_E + 1$;

3. The two pairs on the both sides of the non-linear permutation must be perfect match[7]. Then by the differential property of S [8], we can get one value in average for the active cells and 2^b values for the inactive cells.

4. Taken the limitation into account, we can use the guessed-cells and the retrieved values to get the *S-multisets* from the T-δ-*set* and calculate the memory complexity. If the memory complexity is greater than exhaustive search, we give up this (E_T, D_S) pair.

The goal of the algorithm is to maximize $r_E + r_D$ under the condition that the memory complexity (considering the guessed-cells and the limitation of this kind of distinguisher) is less than the exhaustive search. After that, we make the memory complexity to be the least. We can try all the possible combination of (r_E, r_D) and (E_T, D_S) to find the best distinguisher.

B   Basic Attacks on Crypton and mCrypton Using Efficient Tabulation

In this section, we will show the basic attacks on Crypton and mCrypton using the distinguishers in Sect. 4.3. The attacks are made up of 2 phases: the precomputation phase and the online phase. The online phase is also made up of three parts: finding the right pair, creating and checking δ-*set* and finding secret key.

B.1   Attacks on Crypton

1. **Precomputation phase.** In the precomputation phase of the attack, we build a lookup table containing 2^{89} *multisets* for $\Delta x_5[0]$ following the method of Sect. 4.3 and Appendix A.1.

   The lookup table of the 2^{89} possible *multisets* uses about 2^{91} 128-bit blocks to store [8]. To construct the table, we have to perform 2^{89} partial encryptions on 256 messages, which we estimate to 2^{93} encryptions.

2. **Online Phase.** The attack procedure is shown in Fig. 5. The online phase is made up of three parts: finding the right pair, creating and checking the δ-*set* and finding the secret key.

   (a) **Finding the Right Pair:**

      i. We prepare a structure of 2^{32} plaintexts where the first column takes all 2^{32} values, and the remaining 12 bytes are fixed to some constants. Hence, each of the $2^{32} \times (2^{32} - 1)/2 \approx 2^{63}$ pairs we can generate satisfies the plaintext difference. Choose 2^{81} structures and get the corresponding ciphertext. Among the $2^{63+81} = 2^{144}$ corresponding ciphertext pairs, we expect $2^{144} \times 2^{-96} = 2^{48}$ to verify the truncated-difference trail where only the third column has non-zero difference as shown in Fig. 5. Since only the third column of the ciphertext has

---

[7] The cells in the same position must be both active or inactive. If not, we give up this (E_T, D_S) pair.

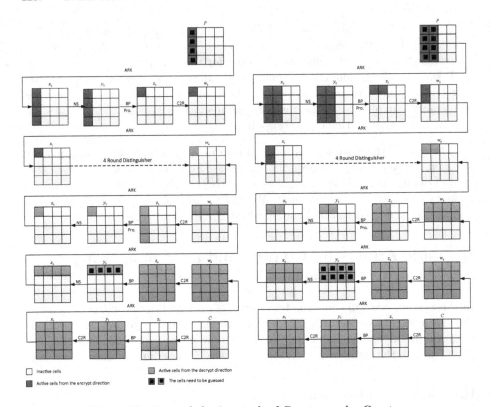

Fig. 5. The 7-rounds basic attack of Crypton and mCrypton

non-zero difference, by Observation 2 of [15], we have that only the first row of y_6 has non-zero difference. Store the leaving 2^{48} pairs in a hash table. This step requires $2^{81+32} = 2^{113}$ chosen plaintexts and their corresponding ciphertexts.

 ii. Guess the values of $k_{-1}[0, \ldots, 3]$, using the guessed values to encrypt the first column of the remaining pairs to y_0. After the bit permutation operation, we choose the pairs that have non-zero difference only in byte position 0, there are $2^{48-24} = 2^{48-24}$ pairs left.

 iii. Guess the values of $y_6[0, 4, 8, 12]$. Since we can yield the first column of Δy_6 from the third column of Δz_7, we can use the guessed values to encrypt the first row of the remaining pairs to z_5. After the bit permutation operation, we choose the pairs that have non-zero difference only in byte position 0, there are $2^{24-24} = 1$ pairs left.

(b) **Creating and Checking the *Multiset*:**

 i. For each guess of the eight bytes made in Phase (a) and for the corresponding pair, take one of the members of the pair, denote it by P^0, and find its δ-*set* using the knowledge of $k_{-1}[0, \ldots, 3]$. (This is done by using the knowledge of $k_{-1}[0, \ldots, 3]$, we can encrypt P^0 to w_0, then XOR it with the $2^8 - 1$ possible values which are different only in byte 0. Decrypt the $2^8 - 1$ obtained value through round 0 using the known subkey bytes. The resulting plaintexts are the other members of the δ-set.)

ii. Using P^0 as the standard plaintext, the other 255 plaintexts are denoted as P^1 to P^{255}, and the corresponding ciphertexts as C^0 to C^{255}. By Observation 2 of [15], knowing the knowledge of the third column in $[C^0 \oplus C^0, C^1 \oplus C^0, \ldots, C^{255} \oplus C^0]$, we can yield the knowledge of the third row of $[y_6^0 \oplus y_6^0, y_6^0 \oplus y_6^1, \ldots, y_6^{255} \oplus y_6^0]$. By the knowledge of $y_6^0[0, 4, 8, 12]$, we can yield the values of $y_6^0[0, 4, 8, 12]$ to $y_6^{255}[0, 4, 8, 12]$. By the linearity of key addition, column-to-row and bit permutation, we can yield the knowledge of byte 0 in $[y_5^0 \oplus y_5^0, y_5^1 \oplus y_5^0, \ldots, y_5^{255} \oplus y_5^0]$. Guess byte 0 of $y_5^0[0]$, we can obtain the *multiset* $[x_5^0[0] \oplus x_5^0[0], x_5^0[1] \oplus x_5^0[0], \ldots, x_5^{255}[0] \oplus x_5^0[0]]$.

iii. Checking whether the *multiset* exists in the hash table made in the Precomputation Phase. If not, discard the guessing.

(c) **Exhaustive Search the Rest of the Key:** For each remaining key guess, find the remaining key bytes by exhaustive search.

It is clear that time complexity of the online phase of the attack is dominated by encrypting 2^{113} plaintexts, and hence, the data and time complexity of this part is 2^{113}. The memory complexity is about 2^{91} 128-bit blocks, since each *multiset* contains about 512 bits. The time complexity of the preprocessing phase of the attack is approximately 2^{93} encryptions.

B.2   Attacks of mCrypton

The attack procedure of mCrypton is quite the same as Crypton and shown in Fig. 5.

The time complexity of the online phase is $2^8 \times 2^{32} \times 2^{40} = 2^{80}$ one-round mCrypton encryptions, it equals 2^{77} 7-round mCrypton encryption. The data complexity of the online phase is 2^{49}. The memory complexity of the precomputation phase is $2^{52.44}$ 64-bit blocks, since each *multiset* contains about 512 bits.

C   Algorithms

Algorithm 1. Function of r_1-Round Encryption

```
1: function PROPAGATE(Λ, r₁)
2:     StateSet of size r₁, χ ← 0
3:     (χ′, Λ) ←ONEROUND(Λ)              ▷ The first round without guessing any cells
4:     for i = 1 to r₁ − 1 do
5:         StateSet[i − 1] ← Λ            ▷ Recording the guessed-cells
6:         (χ′, Λ) ←ONEROUND(Λ)
7:         χ ← χ + χ′                     ▷ The total number of guessed-cells
8:     return (StateSet, χ)
```

Algorithm 2. Function of Pruning

1: **function** LOCALPRUNING($StateSet[i], \Omega, \chi$)   ▷ $StateSet[i]$ is one element of
    $StateSet$
2:    **for** $k = 0$ to $n - 1$ **do**
3:        **if** ($StateSet[i][k]$ is active) and ($\Omega[k]$ is inactive) **then**
4:            $\chi \leftarrow \chi - 1$ ▷ $StateSet[i][k]$ doesn't affect Ω
5:        **if** ($StateSet[i][k]$ is inactive) and $\Omega[k]$ is active **then**
6:            $\Omega[k] \leftarrow$ inactive   ▷ Local pruning for Ω
7:    **return** (Ω, χ)

1: **function** ENDINGCONDITION($StateSet[i], \Omega$)
2:    **for** $k = 0$ to $n - 1$ **do**
3:        **if** ($StateSet[i][k] \neq \Omega[k]$) **then**   ▷ One is active, the other is inactive
4:            **return** false
5:    **return** true   ▷ Return true when totally match

1: **function** PRUNING($StateSet, \Omega, \chi, r_1$) ▷ r_1 is number of round of the former part
2:    **for** $i = r_1 - 2$ to 0 **do**   ▷ Start from the last rounds of the former part
3:        $\Omega \leftarrow \mathscr{A}^{(1)}(\Omega)$ ▷ Go back one round
4:        (Ω, χ) $\leftarrow$ LOCALPRUNING($StateSet[i], \Omega, \chi$)   ▷ Local pruning
5:        **if** ENDINGCONDITION($StateSet[i], \Omega$)=true **then**
6:            **return** χ
7:    **return** χ

Algorithm 3. A Proper Solution to Problem 1

1: **function** MINROUNDNUMBER( ) ▷ The output is $Max\{r_1 + r_2 + r_3\}$ of Problem 1
2:    $RoundNum \leftarrow 0$
3:    $RoundNum \leftarrow RoundNum + 1$ ▷ Attack more round
4:    **for all** T-δ-set Λ **do**
5:        ($StateSet, \chi$) $\leftarrow$ PROPAGATE($\chi, RoundNum$)
6:        **for all** S-$Multiset$ Ω **do**
7:            $\chi \leftarrow$ PRUNING($StateSet, \Omega, \chi, RoundNum$)
8:            **if** $\chi < n_K$ **then**
9:                **return to** line 3   ▷ $\chi < n_K$ means more round is possible
10:    **return** $RoundNum - 1$ ▷ Can't build a distinguisher of $RoundNum$ rounds

1: **function** MINGUESS(R)   ▷ R is the output of MaxRoundNumber( )
2:    $MinGuess \leftarrow \infty$
3:    **for all** T-δ-set Λ **do**
4:        ($StateSet, \chi$) $\leftarrow$ PROPAGATE(χ, R)
5:        **for all** S-$Multiset$ Ω **do**
6:            $\chi \leftarrow$ PRUNING($StateSet, \Omega, \chi, R$)
7:            **if** $\chi < MinGuess$ **then**   ▷ (Λ, Ω) is a better choice
8:                $MinGuess \leftarrow \chi$
9:                $BestT$-δ-$set \leftarrow \Lambda$
10:                $BestS$-$multiset \leftarrow \Omega$
11:    **return** $MinGuess, BestT$-δ-$set, BestS$-$multiset$

References

1. Bouillaguet, C., Derbez, P., Fouque, P.-A.: Automatic search of attacks on round-reduced aes and applications. In: Rogaway, P. (ed.) CRYPTO 2011. LNCS, vol. 6841, pp. 169–187. Springer, Heidelberg (2011)
2. Cheon, J.H., Kim, M.J., Kim, K., Lee, J.-Y., Kang, S.W.: Improved impossible differential cryptanalysis of rijndael and crypton. In: Kim, K. (ed.) ICISC 2001. LNCS, vol. 2288, pp. 39–49. Springer, Heidelberg (2002)
3. Daemen, J., Knudsen, L.R., Rijmen, V.: The block cipher Square. In: Biham, E. (ed.) FSE 1997. LNCS, vol. 1267, pp. 149–165. Springer, Heidelberg (1997)
4. Daemen, J., Rijmen, V.: Aes proposal: Rijndael. In: First Advanced Encryption Standard (AES) Conference (1998)
5. Daemen, J., Rijmen, V.: The Design of Rijndael: AES-the Advanced Encryption Standard. Springer, Berlin (2002)
6. Demirci, H., Selçuk, A.A.: A meet-in-the-middle attack on 8-round AES. In: Nyberg, K. (ed.) FSE 2008. LNCS, vol. 5086, pp. 116–126. Springer, Heidelberg (2008)
7. Derbez, P., Fouque, P.-A.: Exhausting Demirci-Selçuk Meet-in-the-Middle Attacks Against Reduced-Round AES. In: Moriai, S. (ed.) FSE 2013. LNCS, vol. 2013, pp. 541–560. Springer, Heidelberg (2013)
8. Derbez, P., Fouque, P.-A., Jean, J.: Improved key recovery attacks on reduced-round AES in the single-key setting. In: Johansson, T., Nguyen, P.Q. (eds.) EURO-CRYPT 2013. LNCS, vol. 7881, pp. 371–387. Springer, Heidelberg (2013)
9. Dunkelman, O., Keller, N., Shamir, A.: Improved single-key attacks on 8-round AES-192 and AES-256. In: Abe, M. (ed.) ASIACRYPT 2010. LNCS, vol. 6477, pp. 158–176. Springer, Heidelberg (2010)
10. Fouque, P.-A., Jean, J., Peyrin, T.: Structural evaluation of AES and chosen-key distinguisher of 9-round AES-128. In: Canetti, R., Garay, J.A. (eds.) CRYPTO 2013, Part I. LNCS, vol. 8042, pp. 183–203. Springer, Heidelberg (2013)
11. Gilbert, H., Minier, M.: A Collisions Sttack on the 7-Rounds Rijndael (2000)
12. Lim, C.H.: Crypton: A New 128-bit Block Cipher. NIsT AEs Proposal (1998)
13. Lim, C.H.: A revised version of CRYPTON - CRYPTON V1.0. In: Knudsen, L.R. (ed.) FSE 1999. LNCS, vol. 1636, p. 31. Springer, Heidelberg (1999)
14. Lim, C.H., Korkishko, T.: mCrypton – a lightweight block cipher for security of low-cost RFID tags and sensors. In: Song, J.-S., Kwon, T., Yung, M. (eds.) WISA 2005. LNCS, vol. 3786, pp. 243–258. Springer, Heidelberg (2006)
15. Mala, H., Shakiba, M., Dakhilalian, M.: New impossible differential attacks on reduced-round crypton. Comput. Stand. Interface 32(4), 222–227 (2010)
16. Wu, W., Zhang, L.: LBlock: a lightweight block cipher. In: Lopez, J., Tsudik, G. (eds.) ACNS 2011. LNCS, vol. 6715, pp. 327–344. Springer, Heidelberg (2011)

Embedded System Security
and Its Implementation

Integral Based Fault Attack on LBlock

Hua Chen$^{(\boxtimes)}$ and Limin Fan

Trusted Computing and Information Assurance Laboratory,
Institute of Software, Chinese Academy of Sciences, Beijing, China
{chenhua,fanlimin}@tca.iscas.ac.cn

Abstract. LBlock is a 32-round lightweight block cipher presented at ACNS2011. In this paper, the fault attack on LBlock is explored. The first fault attack on LBlock was presented at COSADE2012, which can reveal the master key when faults are respectively induced at the end of the round from 24th to 31st round. When faults were injected at the end of the round from 25th to 31st round, the random bit fault model was adopted. While when the fault was induced into the right part of the end of 24th round encryption, the attack only worked under the semi-random model, which means the adversary must know the induce position. In this paper, we firstly applied fault attack on LBlock successfully with faults induced into the right part at the end of 24th round encryption under random nibble fault model. In our attack, eight 8-round integral distinguishers of LBlock are fully utilized to help determine the exact induce positions of faulty ciphertexts. Moreover, we also firstly apply fault attack with faults induced into the right part at the end of 23th round encryption under semi-random nibble model. Finally, the computer simulation results verify the efficiency of our attack.

Keywords: Fault attack · Integral distinguisher · Induce position

1 Introduction

In EUROCRYPT'97, the idea of fault attack was first proposed by Boneh, DeMillo and Lipton [1]. Under the idea, the attack was first successfully exploited to break an RSA CRT with both a correct and a faulty signature of the same message. Shortly after, Biham and Shamir combined the ideas of fault attack and differential attack and successfully proposed an attack on secret key cryptosystems which was called Differential Fault Analysis (DFA)[2]. Since the presentation of fault attack, a large number of fault analysis results have been published on various cryptosystems, mainly including ECC [3], 3DES [4], AES [5–9], CLEFIA [10,11], RC4 [12], Trivium [13] and so on [14–16].

LBlock is a lightweight block cipher designed by Wu et al. [17]. LBlock is a 32-round iterated block cipher with 64-bit block size and 80-bit key size. Some analysis results were originally given by the designers including differential attack, linear attack, integral attack, related-key attack and so on [17]. After

© Springer International Publishing Switzerland 2014
H.-S. Lee and D.-G. Han (Eds.): ICISC 2013, LNCS 8565, pp. 227–240, 2014.
DOI: 10.1007/978-3-319-12160-4_14

that, some other analysis work were presented, including related key impossible differential attack, biclique attack and so on [18–21].

The first fault attack on Lblock was provided at COSADE2012 [22]. By means of the differential analysis technique, fault attacks were respectively applied when faults were injected at the end of the round from 24th to 31st round. When faults were injected at the end of the round from 25th to 31st round, the random bit fault model was adopted and the last three 32-bit subkeys can be revealed. Then, through analyzing key scheduling, the master key can be recovered. However, when faults were injected at the end of the 24th round, random bit fault model failed to work. Instead, semi-random bit fault model had to be adopted, under which the attacker must know the position of the corrupted 4 bits. Whether or not random fault model can be adopted was left as an interesting open problem by the author for future work. Moreover, how to apply fault attack with faults injected at the end of the 23th round was also left as an open problem.

Our Contributions. In this paper, we successfully solve the problems left in [22], and firstly apply fault attack when faults were injected at the end of the 24th round under random fault model. In our attack, differential fault analysis is combined with integral analysis. Eight 8-round integral characteristics are fully utilized to determine the exact induce position under random fault model, based on which an effective algorithm is presented. So we call our attack "integral based fault attack". Moreover, we also firstly apply fault attack successfully when faults were injected at the end of the 23th round under semi-random fault model. Finally, the computer simulation results verify the efficiency of our attack algorithm.

The organization of this paper is as follows. In Sect. 2, some preliminary knowledge is presented. Section 3 provides the detailed FA on 24th round of LBlock and the description of algorithm **DistinFClist**. In Sect. 4, the detailed FA on 23th round of LBlock is presented. Then the data complexity analysis and the computer simulation results are provided in Sect. 5. Finally, the conclusions and future works are presented in Sect. 6.

2   Preliminaries

In this section, some notations are firstly listed, which will be used in this paper. Then a brief description of LBlock is provided. Finally, some properties of LBlock are explored, which are helpful in the following attack.

2.1   Notations

- M, C :   64-bit plaintext and ciphertext
- $C^{(\cdot)}$:   a faulty ciphertext by inducing a fault into the encryption process
- X_i :   Intermediate 32-bit output value of encryption procedure
- $X_i^{(\cdot)}$:   Intermediate 32-bit output value corresponding to $C^{(\cdot)}$:
- $X_{i,j}$:   the j-th nibble of X_i from the left, $i \in \{0, 1, ..., 33\}$, $j \in \{0, 1, ..., 7\}$, e.g. $X_{i,0}$ corresponds to 31-28 bits of X_i

- $X_{i,j}^{(\cdot)}$: the j-th nibble of $X_i^{(\cdot)}$ from the left, $i \in \{0, 1, ..., 33\}$, $j \in \{0, 1, ..., 7\}$
- $K, K_i, K_{i,j}$: 80-bit master key, 32-bit round key and the j-th nibble of round key from the left
- $F(.)$: Round function in LBlock
- $S_j(.)$: 4×4 S-box, $j \in \{0, 1, ..., 7\}$
- $\oplus, <<<$: Bitwise exclusive-OR operation and Left cyclic shift operation
- $||, [v]_2$: Concatenation operation and Binary form of an integer v
- $N_{s_j}(\Delta\alpha, \Delta\beta)$: the number of x which satisfies $S_j(x) \oplus S_j(x \oplus \Delta\alpha) = \Delta\beta$

2.2   Brief Description of LBlock

LBlock has 32-round variant Feistel structure with 64-bit block size and 80-bit key size. Denote M as a 64-bit plaintext, and the encryption procedure can be expressed as follows (Figs. 1 and 2).

Step 1. $M = X_1 || X_0$
Step 2. For $i = 2$ to 33 do
$$X_i = F(X_{i-1}, K_{i-1}) \oplus (X_{i-2} <<< 8)$$
Step 3. $C = X_{32} || X_{33}$

$F(X, K)$ can be described as follows.
$F : \{0,1\}^{32} \times \{0,1\}^{32} \rightarrow \{0,1\}^{32}$

Step 1. $Y = X \oplus K$
Step 2. Let $Y = Y_7 || Y_6 || Y_5 || Y_4 || Y_3 || Y_2 || Y_1 || Y_0$
Step 3. Let $Z = Z_7 || Z_6 || Z_5 || Z_4 || Z_3 || Z_2 || Z_1 || Z_0$
$Z_7 = S_7(Y_7), Z_6 = S_6(Y_6), Z_5 = S_5(Y_5), Z_4 = S_4(Y_4),$
$Z_3 = S_3(Y_3), Z_2 = S_2(Y_2), Z_1 = S_1(Y_1), Z_0 = S_0(Y_0),$

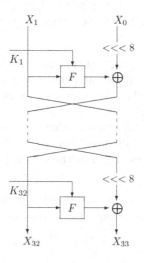

Fig. 1. Encryption process of LBlock

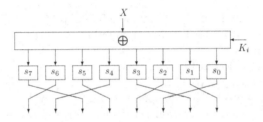

Fig. 2. Round function F

Step 4. Let $U = U_7\|U_6\|U_5\|U_4\|U_3\|U_2\|U_1\|U_0$
$\qquad U_7 = Z_6, U_6 = Z_4, U_5 = Z_7, U_4 = Z_5,$
$\qquad U_3 = Z_2, U_2 = Z_0, U_1 = Z_3, U_0 = Z_1,$

We use the same figures provided in [17] to depict the encryption procedure of LBlock and round function F. Due to the lack of space, the descriptions of decryption and key schedule of LBlock are both omitted, which does not affect the following reading.

2.3   Properties of LBlock

In [17], the designer of LBlock gives a class of 15-round integral distinguisher whose input has fifteen active nibbles. However, we only consider the inputs with one active nibble related to the fault model of our attack. Next, a class of 8-round integral characteristics is presented.

Lemma 1. *If 16 plaintexts satisfy* $(CCCC, CCCC, ACCC, CCCC)$, *the outputs of 8-round encryption must satisfy* $(B?AA, BBAA, B?B?, B?B?)$. *Denote C as a constant nibble, A as an active nibble, B as a balanced nibble, and ? as an unknown nibble respectively. For convenience, we also denote C as a ciphertext in the later section.*

Proof. When the left part of plaintexts enters into the F-function, the status of $(CCCC, CCCC)$ remains invariant, and the status of $(ACCC, CCCC)$ changes into $(CCCC, CCAC)$ after the operation $<<< 8$. So the status of one round's output is (CCCC,CCAC, CCCC,CCCC). Table 1 illustrates the detailed process of the 8-round distinguisher. Note that by changing the position of A in plaintext, we can obtain similar integral distinguishers easily. Table 2 illustrates 8 kinds of 8-round integral distinguishers, which will be used in the following attack process.

Proposition 1. *If a nibble fault is induced into the leftmost nibble position of the right part at the end of the 24th round, and $C^{(i)} = X_{32}^{(i)}\|X_{33}^{(i)}$ is the corresponding ciphertext, $N_{s_3}(\Delta\alpha, \Delta\beta) > 0$. ($\Delta\alpha = X_{32,4} \oplus X_{32,4}^{(i)}$ and $\Delta\beta = X_{33,6} \oplus X_{33,6}^{(i)}$).*

Table 1. Detailed descrption of a 8-round integral distinguisher

Rounds	Integral Distinguisher
0	$(CCCC, CCCC, ACCC, CCCC)$
1	$(CCCC, CCAC, CCCC, CCCC)$
2	$(CCCC, CCCA, CCCC, CCAC)$
3	$(CCCC, AACC, CCCC, CCCA)$
4	$(CCCC, AAAC, CCCC, AACC)$
5	$(CCAA, ACAA, CCCC, AAAC)$
6	$(CAAB, AAAA, CCAA, ACAA)$
7	$(B?AA, BBAA, CAAB, AAAA)$
8	$(?B?B, ?B?B, B?AA, BBAA)$

Table 2. Eight 8-round integral distinguishers

Ordinal	Input integral	Output integral
1	$(CCCC, CCCC, ACCC, CCCC)$	$(B?AA, BBAA, ?B?B, ?B?B)$
2	$(CCCC, CCCC, CACC, CCCC)$	$(?BAA, BBAA, ?B?B, ?B?B)$
3	$(CCCC, CCCC, CCAC, CCCC)$	$(AABB, AAB?, B?B?, B?B?)$
4	$(CCCC, CCCC, CCCA, CCCC)$	$(AABB, AA?B, B?B?, B?B?)$
5	$(CCCC, CCCC, CCCC, ACCC)$	$(BBAA, B?AA, ?B?B, ?B?B)$
6	$(CCCC, CCCC, CCCC, CACC)$	$(BBAA, ?BAA, ?B?B, ?B?B)$
7	$(CCCC, CCCC, CCAC, CCAC)$	$(AAB?, AABB, B?B?, B?B?)$
8	$(CCCC, CCCC, CCCA, CCCA)$	$(AA?B, AABB, B?B?, B?B?)$

Proof. From Table 1 we can see that, if a set of plaintexts satisfy $(CCCC, CCCC, ACCC, CCCC)$, the outputs of 7-round encryption must satisfy $(B?AA, BBAA, CAAB, AAAA)$. So if a nibble fault is induced into the leftmost nibble position (31-28 bits) of the right part at the end of the 24th round, $X_{31,0}^{(i)} = X_{31,0}$. Here, $X_{31,0}$ and $X_{31,0}^{(i)}$ are respectively denoted as the leftmost nibble of X_{31} and $X_{31}^{(i)}$, which have the inverse order compared with the denotations of S-boxes. In the 32th round encryption process, $X_{31}^{(i)}$ is rotated left 8 bit, and the invariant nibble position is changed into the 6th nibble of the 32-bit word. Since the output of 32th round's F-function equals to $X_{33} \oplus (X_{31,8} <<< 8)$, apparently, the difference of the 6th nibble of the output of F-function equals to $X_{33,6} \oplus X_{33,6}^{(i)}$. After the inverse transformation of P permutation, $X_{33,6} \oplus X_{33,6}^{(i)}$ corresponds to the output of s_3. And the corresponding input difference of s_3 is $X_{32,4} \oplus X_{32,4}^{(i)}$. So the proposition holds. Note that by changing the induce position of faults at the end of the 24th round, we can obtain similar conclusions easily.

Table 3. Corresponding position relation of $\Delta\alpha_j$, $\Delta\beta_j$

$\Delta\alpha_j$	$\Delta\beta_j$
$X_{32,0} \oplus X_{32,0}^{(i)}$	$X_{33,2} \oplus X_{33,2}^{(i)}$
$X_{32,1} \oplus X_{32,1}^{(i)}$	$X_{33,0} \oplus X_{33,0}^{(i)}$
$X_{32,2} \oplus X_{32,2}^{(i)}$	$X_{33,3} \oplus X_{33,3}^{(i)}$
$X_{32,3} \oplus X_{32,3}^{(i)}$	$X_{33,1} \oplus X_{33,1}^{(i)}$
$X_{32,4} \oplus X_{32,4}^{(i)}$	$X_{33,6} \oplus X_{33,6}^{(i)}$
$X_{32,5} \oplus X_{32,5}^{(i)}$	$X_{33,4} \oplus X_{33,4}^{(i)}$
$X_{32,6} \oplus X_{32,6}^{(i)}$	$X_{33,7} \oplus X_{33,7}^{(i)}$
$X_{32,7} \oplus X_{32,7}^{(i)}$	$X_{33,5} \oplus X_{33,5}^{(i)}$

Proposition 2. *For a faulty ciphertext $C^{(i)} = X_{32}^{(i)} \| X_{33}^{(i)}$ achieved by inducing a fault into the right part at the end of the 24th round, if $N_{s_3}(\Delta\alpha, \Delta\beta) > 0$ and for all the other $N_{s_j(0 \leq j \leq 7, j \neq 3)}$, $N_{s_j}(\Delta\alpha_j, \Delta\beta_j) = 0$, the fault must be induced into the leftmost nibble position.(The nibble position of $\Delta\beta_j$ is uniquely determined by the position of $\Delta\alpha_j$. Table 3 illustrates their relations.)*

Proof. The proposition can be deduced very easily from **Proposition 1**. Note that by changing the position of nonzero S-box in the 32th round, we can obtain similar conclusions easily.

Proposition 3. *If two different faults are induced into the leftmost nibble position of the right part at the end of the 24th round, the following expressions hold:*

$$X_{32,t}^{(i)} \neq X_{32,t}^{(j)}, X_{32,t} \notin \{X_{32,t}^{(i)}, X_{32,t}^{(j)}\}, t \in \{2, 3, 6, 7\} \tag{1}$$

where $X_{32}^{(i)}$ and $X_{32}^{(j)}$ denote the corresponding left 32-bit part of ciphertexts.

Proof. The proof can be easily achieved from Lemma 1. If plaintexts satisfy $(CCCC, CCCC, ACCC, CCCC)$, the outputs of 8-round encryption satisfy $(B?AA, BBAA, B?B?, B?B?)$. That means if two plaintexts differ from the leftmost nibble position of the right part, the 8-round outputs must differ from the 2th, 3th, 6th, and 7th nibble positions of the left 32-bit part. Note that by changing the induce position at the end of the 24th round, we can obtain similar conclusions easily.

Proposition 4. *If two different faults are induced into the leftmost nibble position of the right part at the end of the 23th round, the following expressions hold. The sets $\{X_{31}^{(i)}, X_{30}^{(i)}, X_{29}^{(i)}\}$ and $\{X_{31}^{(j)}, X_{30}^{(j)}, X_{29}^{(j)}\}$ are respectively the corresponding right parts at the end of the 31st, 30th and 29th round.*

$$\begin{cases} X_{31,t}^{(i)} \neq X_{31,t}^{(j)}, X_{31,t} \notin \{X_{31,t}^{(i)}, X_{31,t}^{(j)}\}, t \in \{2,3,6,7\} \\ X_{30,0} = X_{30,0}^{(i)} = X_{30,0}^{(j)}, X_{30,t}^{(i)} \neq X_{30,t}^{(j)}, X_{30,t} \notin \{X_{30,t}^{(i)}, X_{30,t}^{(j)}\}, t \in \{1,2,4,5,6,7\} \\ X_{29,t} = X_{29,t}^{(i)} = X_{29,t}^{(j)}, t \in \{0,1,5\} \\ X_{29,t}^{(i)} \neq X_{29,t}^{(j)}, X_{29,t} \notin \{X_{29,t}^{(i)}, X_{29,t}^{(j)}\}, t \in \{2,3,4,6,7\} \end{cases}$$

$$(2)$$

Proof. From Table 1, it is easily deduced that, when faults are induced into the leftmost nibble position of the right part at the end of the 23th round, the integral statuses of the right parts at the end of 31st round, 30th round and round are respectively $(B?AA, BBAA)$, $(CAAB, AAAA)$ and $(CCAA, ACAA)$. Apparently, the conclusion holds.

When we change the induce position into $23-20$ bit of the right part at the end of the 23th round, the following expressions also hold. The proof is similar, in which the second integral distinguisher in Table 2 is used.

$$\begin{cases} X_{31,t}^{(i)} \neq X_{31,t}^{(j)}, X_{31,t} \notin \{X_{31,t}^{(i)}, X_{31,t}^{(j)}\}, t \in \{0,1,4,5\} \\ X_{30,1} = X_{30,1}^{(i)} = X_{30,0}^{(j)}, X_{30,t}^{(i)} \neq X_{30,t}^{(j)}, X_{30,t} \notin \{X_{30,t}^{(i)}, X_{30,t}^{(j)}\}, t \in \{0,2,3,4,5,7\} \\ X_{29,t} = X_{29,t}^{(i)} = X_{29,t}^{(j)}, t \in \{0,1,2,4,5\} \\ X_{29,t}^{(i)} \neq X_{29,t}^{(j)}, X_{29,t} \notin \{X_{29,t}^{(i)}, X_{29,t}^{(j)}\}, t \in \{2,3,4,6,7\} \end{cases}$$

$$(3)$$

3   Fault Attack on 24th round of LBlock

In this section, the fault attack on 24th round of LBlock under random nibble fault model is presented. Under the fault model, only one nibble fault can be induced into the register storing the intermediate results. The adversary knows neither the location of the fault nor its concrete value. The detailed attack procedure is presented as follows.

(1) Select randomly a plaintext M, and obtain the right ciphertext C under the secret key K.

(2) Repeat inducing an unknown nibble into an unknown position of the right part at the end of the 24th round to get a set of faulty ciphertexts $TotalFCList = \{C^{(i)} | 0 \leq i \leq 119\}$.

(3) Call algorithm **DistinFClist** to divide $TotalFCList$ into $FCList7, FCList6, FCList5,...,$ and $FCList0$ through step (3.1)-(3.8), which respectively contains all 15 faulty ciphertexts achieved by inducing faults at $31-28$ bits, $27-24$ bits, $23-20$ bits,..., and $3-0$ bits of the right part at the end of the 24th round.

  (3.1) $FCList7 \leftarrow$ **DistinFClist** ($TotalFCList, 4, 6, 2, 3, 6, 7$); $TotalFCList \leftarrow TotalFCList - FCList7$

  (3.2) $FCList6 \leftarrow$ **DistinFClist** ($TotalFCList, 5, 4, 2, 3, 6, 7$); $TotalFCList \leftarrow TotalFCList - FCList6$

(3.3) $FCList5 \leftarrow$ **DistinFClist** $(TotalFCList, 6, 7, 0, 1, 4, 5); TotalFCList \leftarrow$ $TotalFCList - FCList5$

(3.4) $FCList4 \leftarrow$ **DistinFClist** $(TotalFCList, 7, 5, 0, 1, 4, 5); TotalFCList \leftarrow$ $TotalFCList - FCList4$

(3.5) $FCList3 \leftarrow$ **DistinFClist** $(TotalFCList, 0, 2, 2, 3, 6, 7); TotalFCList \leftarrow$ $TotalFCList - FCList3$

(3.6) $FCList2 \leftarrow$ **DistinFClist** $(TotalFCList, 1, 0, 2, 3, 6, 7); TotalFCList \leftarrow$ $TotalFCList - FCList2$

(3.7) $FCList1 \leftarrow$ **DistinFClist** $(TotalFCList, 2, 3, 0, 1, 4, 5); TotalFCList \leftarrow$ $TotalFCList - FCList1$

(3.8) $FCList0 \leftarrow TotalFCList$

(4) For $C^{(i)} \in FCList7$, $N_{s_3}(\Delta\alpha, \Delta\beta) > 0$. $\Delta\alpha = (X_{32,4} \oplus K_{32,4}) \oplus (X_{32,4}^{(i)} \oplus K_{32,4})$ and $\Delta\beta = X_{33,6} \oplus X_{33,6}^{(i)}$. By means of differential analysis technique, $\Delta\alpha = (X_{32,4} \oplus K_{32,4})$ can be determined. So $K_{32,4}$ can be revealed immediately. Similarly, by use of the faulty ciphertexts from $FCList6, FCList5, \ldots$, $FCList0$, the remaining bytes of K_{32} can be respectively recovered.

(5) Decrypt C and $C^{(i)}$ with K_{32}, and get the input difference and output difference of the S-boxes of 31st round. Through using the difference analysis technique, K_{31} can be recovered.

(6) With the similar procedure as (4) and (5), K_{30} can also be recovered.

(7) Since K_{32}, K_{31} and K_{30} are known, K can be recovered by analyzing the key scheduling. The detailed analysis of key scheduling is already provided in [22], which is not described here any more.

In the description of algorithm **DistinFClist**, step 2 preliminarily picks out possible faulty ciphertexts with the help of **Proposition 1** and **Proposition 3**, which respectively corresponds to the condition $2.a$ and the condition $2.b - 2.e$. In the condition $2.a$, the corresponding Sbox of N_s is actually different, but for simplicity of description, only N_s is used as an unified representation.

Step 3 firstly determines some ciphertexts which must belong to the final set of faulty ciphertexts we want to find out with the help of **Proposition 2**, which corresponds to the condition $3.a$. In the condition $3.a$, the position value j_1 has a corresponding relation with i_1, which can refer to Table 3 in Sect. 2.

The basic idea of step 4 is, if the number of candidate ciphertexts whose values of corresponding position equal to a special value is only one, the candidate ciphertext must belong to the final set of faulty ciphertexts we want to find out. For convenience of description, let $N32(i, j, L) = |\{C^{(k)} | C^{(k)} \in L, X_{32,i}^{(k)} = j, 0 \le i \le 7, 0 \le j \le 15\}|$. Step 6 further filters the wrong faulty ciphertexts with the help of **Proposition 3** which corresponds to the condition $4.a$-$4.d$.

Through repeating the steps 4–6, the 15 faulty ciphertexts achieved by inducing faults into the same nibble position can be found out one by one.

4   Fault Attack on 23th round of LBlock

In this section, the fault attack on 23th round LBlock is presented under semi-random fault model, which differs from random fault model in that the adversary

Algorithm DistinFClist

Input

TotalFCList: a set of faulty ciphertexts

Pos1,Pos2,...Pos6: the position values

Output

FCList: the special faulty ciphertexts distinguished from *TotalFCList*

Step 1. $L \leftarrow \varnothing, FCList \leftarrow \varnothing$

Step 2. For all $C^{(i)} \in TotalFCList$, if conditions (2.a)–(2.e) are all satisfied,

$$L \leftarrow L \cup \{C^{(i)}\}$$

(2.a) $N_S(X_{32,Pos1} \oplus X^{(i)}_{32,Pos1}, X_{33,Pos2} \oplus X^{(i)}_{33,Pos2}) > 0$

(2.b) $X_{32,Pos3} \neq X^{(i)}_{32,Pos3}$

(2.c) $X_{32,Pos4} \neq X^{(i)}_{32,Pos4}$

(2.d) $X_{32,Pos5} \neq X^{(i)}_{32,Pos5}$

(2.e) $X_{32,Pos6} \neq X^{(i)}_{32,Pos6}$

Step 3. For all $C^{(k)} \in L$ do

Step 3.1. if for all $i_1 \neq Pos1 (0 \leq i_1 \leq 7)$, condition (3.a) is satisfied,

$FCList \leftarrow FCList \cup \{C^{(k)}\}$ and update $L \leftarrow L - \{C^{(k)}\}$

(3.a) $N_S(X_{32,i_1} \oplus X^{(i)}_{32,i_1}, X_{33,j_1} \oplus X^{(i)}_{33,j_1}) = 0$

Step 4. For all $C^{(k)} \in L$, execute step 4.1

Step 4.1. For j=0 to 15 do

if one of conditions (4.a)-(4.d) is satisfied, $FCList \leftarrow FCList \cup \{C^{(k)}\}$

and update $L \leftarrow L - \{C^{(k)}\}$

(4.a) $N32(Pos3, j, L) = 1$

(4.b) $N32(Pos4, j, L) = 1$

(4.c) $N32(Pos5, j, L) = 1$

(4.d) $N32(Pos6, j, L) = 1$

Step 5. If $|FCList| = 15$, **return** $FCList$ and exit.

Step 6. For all $C^{(k)} \in L$ do

If there exists $C^{(t)} \in FCList$ which satisfies one of conditions (6.a)-(6.d),

update $L \leftarrow L - \{C^{(k)}\}$

(6.a) $X^{(k)}_{32,Pos3} = X^{(t)}_{32,Pos3}$

(6.b) $X^{(k)}_{32,Pos4} = X^{(t)}_{32,Pos4}$

(6.c) $X^{(k)}_{32,Pos5} = X^{(t)}_{32,Pos5}$

(6.d) $X^{(k)}_{32,Pos6} = X^{(t)}_{32,Pos6}$

Step 7. goto step 4

---

knows the location of the fault, but does not know its concrete value. The basic principle of the attack is derived from **Proposition 4** and the detailed attack procedure is as follows.

(1) Select randomly a plaintext M, and obtain the right ciphertext C under the secret key K.

(2) Respectively induce $num1$, $num2$ different nibble fault values into the $31 - 28$ and $23 - 20$ bits of the right part at the end of the 23th round, and get the corresponding faulty ciphertext sets $FCList7$, $FCList5$.

(3) Recover $K_{32,1}$, $K_{32,3}$, $K_{32,5}$ and $K_{32,7}$ with $FCList7$ through step (3.1)–(3.5).

    (3.1) Guess $K_{32,1}$, and for $GuessKey = 0$ to 15 repeat step (3.2)–(3.4)

    (3.2) $temp[0] = S(6)(X_{32,1} \oplus GuessKey) \oplus X_{33,0}$

    (3.3) For all $C^{(i)} \in FCList7$, compute $temp[i] = S(6)(X_{32,1}^{(i)} \oplus GuessKey) \oplus X_{33,0}^{(i)}$

    (3.4) If for any pair of $(temp[i], temp[j])$, $(temp[i] \neq temp[j])$ is satisfied, reserve the $GuessKey$; else discard $GuessKey$.

    (3.5) With the similar procedure as step (3.1)–(3.4), $K_{32,3}, K_{32,5}, K_{32,4}$ can be respectively recovered.

(4) With the similar procedure as step 3, $K_{32,0}$, $K_{32,2}$, $K_{32,4}$ and $K_{32,6}$ can be recovered with $FCList5$. Now the whole value of K_{32} is recovered.

(5) Decrypt C, $FCList5$ and $FCList7$ with recovered K_{32} and get the corresponding X_{31} and $X_{31}^{(i)}$.

(6) Recover $K_{31,0}$, $K_{31,1}$, $K_{31,2}$, $K_{31,4}$, $K_{31,5}$, $K_{31,6}$ and $K_{31,7}$ with $FCList7$.

    (6.1) Guess $K_{31,0}$, and for $GuessKey = 0$ to 15 repeat step (6.2)-(6.4)

    (6.2) $temp[0] = S(7)(X_{31,0} \oplus GuessKey) \oplus X_{32,2}$

    (6.3) for all $C^{(i)} \in FCList7$, compute $temp[i] = S(7)(X_{31,0}^{(i)} \oplus GuessKey) \oplus X_{32,2}^{(i)}$

    (6.4) If for any pair of $(temp[i], temp[j])$, $(temp[i] \neq temp[j])$ is satisfied, reserve the $GuessKey$; else discard $GuessKey$

    (6.5) With the similar procedure as step (6.1)-(6.4), $K_{31,1}$, $K_{31,2}$, $K_{31,5}$, $K_{31,6}$ and $K_{31,7}$ can be recovered. Specially, for $K_{31,4}$, the condition $(temp[i] \neq temp[j])$ in step (6.4) should be changed into $(temp[i] = temp[j])$

(7) With the similar procedure as step 6, $K_{31,0}$, $K_{31,1}$, $K_{31,2}$, $K_{31,3}$, $K_{31,4}$, $K_{31,6}$ and $K_{31,7}$ can be recovered with $FCList5$. Apparently, the final candidate values of $K_{31,0}$, $K_{31,1}$, $K_{31,2}$, $K_{31,4}$, $K_{31,6}$ and $K_{31,7}$ is respectively the intersection of the sets achieved from step 6 and the ones from step 7. Now the whole value of K_{31} is recovered.

(8) Decrypt C, $FCList5$ and $FCList7$ with recovered K_{32}, K_{31} and get the corresponding X_{30} and $X_{30}^{(i)}$.

(9) With the similar procedure as step 6, all the nibbles of K_{30} can be recovered with $FCList7$. Specially, for $K_{30,2}$, $K_{30,4}$ and $K_{32,6}$, the condition $(temp[i] \neq temp[j])$ should be changed into $(temp[i] = temp[j])$.

(10) With the similar procedure as step 6, all the nibbles of K_{30} also can be recovered with $FCList5$. Specially, for $K_{30,3}$, $K_{30,5}$ and $K_{32,7}$, the condition $(temp[i] \neq temp[j])$ should be changed into $(temp[i] = temp[j])$. Apparently, the final candidate values of K_{30} is the intersection of the candidate sets achieved from step 9 and the ones from step 10.

Table 4. Computer simulation with faults induced at the end of 24th round

Ordinal	actual number of distinguished faulty ciphertexts			
	15	10	6	4
1	73	90	94	96
2	83	93	96	98
3	80	84	96	97
4	77	85	94	100
5	73	84	96	95
6	78	90	96	100
7	80	88	94	99
8	79	86	93	98
9	77	86	96	94
10	74	92	97	98

Table 5. Computer simulation with faults induced at the end of 23th round

Ordinal	The value of K	induce number
1	0x47996621380c720d8729	20
2	0x435666234501421d8427	24
3	0x780906299591473d6417	22
4	0x12675421005123301110	25
5	0x13272451035222371213	24
6	0x15271457335499001614	23
7	0x34119063348044061920	23
8	0x13153376128342161221	25
9	0x00183586108592195201	21
10	0x03488922118444113309	22

(11) Since K_{32}, K_{31} and K_{30} are known, K can be recovered by analyzing the key scheduling.

5 Data Complexity and Computer Simulation

In our attack on 24th round of LBlock, eight integral distinguishers are all used, so all possible nibble values must be induced into every nibble position. The number of possible induce positions is 8, so the total induce number is $15 \times 8 = 120$. Moreover, literature [22] explored the difference distribution properties of S-boxes and got the conclusion that about three faults on average were needed to reveal the 4-bit subkey input of each S-box. Therefore, for each of the eight subsets of faulty ciphertexts, only about three faults on average are needed to reveal the 4-bit subkey input of each S-box. So the total number of faulty cipher-texts needed to reveal the master key is about $3 \times 8 = 24$. It means that, during the actual running procedure of algorithm **DistinFCList**, it is not necessary to find out all possible fifteen faulty ciphertexts, which can further increase the efficiency and success probability of the algorithm. In order to verify our attack algorithm, we conducted a number of experiments with the actual number of faulty ciphertexts found out by **DistinFCList** as a parameter. For each parameter, 10×100 fault attacks are conducted and the numbers of successful attacks are recorded, which are listed in Table 4.

In our attack on 23th round of LBlock, since only two nibble positions are induced, the maximum induce number is $Num1 + Num2 = 16 \times 2 = 32$. The experimental results listed in in Table 5 show that the actual induce number is commonly smaller than 32 to determine the unique master key.

6   Conclusion and Future Work

In this paper, an effective fault attack on LBlock is proposed. Under the attack, if faults are randomly induced into the right part at the end of 24th round encryption procedure, the master key can be recovered. Our work solves the problem left in [22], which can not recover the master key under random fault model according to the last eight rounds' encryption. In our attack, the key problem we need to solve is how to distinguish the induce position from the given faulty ciphertexts. In order to solve the problem, some integral distinguishers are explored and utilized. Based on the integral properties of LBlock, an effective algorithm is provided which can judge which position is induced from a set of faulty ciphertexts. Moveover, the same integral distinguishers also help us apply faulty attack successfully on the 23th round under semi-random fault model. The computer simulation results verify the efficiency of our attack. Our attack also provides an idea to determine the fault induce position for other similar lightweight block cipher.

In the future, there still exists some research work to be further explored. Firstly, in order to decrease the induce number of faults, it may be considered to combine the integral characteristics and key-guessing technique. Secondly, the fault attack on the 23th round under random fault model is still an interesting work in the future.

Acknowledgements. The authors would like to thank the anonymous reviewers for many helpful comments and suggestions. This work is supported by the National Basic Research Program of China (No.2013CB338002) and the National Natural Science Foundation of China (No.91118006).

References

1. Boneh, D., DeMillo, R.A., Lipton, R.J.: On the importance of checking crypto-graphic protocols for faults. In: Fumy, W. (ed.) EUROCRYPT 1997. LNCS, vol. 1233, pp. 37–51. Springer, Heidelberg (1997)

2. Biham, E., Shamir, A.: Differential fault analysis of secret key cryptosystems. In: Kaliski Jr, B.S. (ed.) CRYPTO 1997. LNCS, vol. 1294, pp. 513–525. Springer, Heidelberg (1997)

3. Biehl, I., Meyer, B., Müller, V.: Differential fault attacks on elliptic curve cryptosystems. In: Bellare, M. (ed.) CRYPTO 2000. LNCS, vol. 1880, pp. 131–146. Springer, Heidelberg (2000)

4. Hemme, L.: A differential fault attack against early rounds of (Triple-)DES. In: Joye, M., Quisquater, J.-J. (eds.) CHES 2004. LNCS, vol. 3156, pp. 254–267. Springer, Heidelberg (2004)

5. Dusart, P., Letourneux, G., Vivolo, O.: Differential fault analysis on AES. In: Zhou, J., Yung, M., Han, Y. (eds.) ACNS 2003. LNCS, vol. 2846, pp. 293–306. Springer, Heidelberg (2003)

6. Blömer, J., Seifert, J.-P.: Fault based cryptanalysis of the advanced encryption standard (AES). In: Wright, R.N. (ed.) FC 2003. LNCS, vol. 2742, pp. 162–181. Springer, Heidelberg (2003)

7. Chen, C.N., Yen, S.M.: Differential fault analysis on AES key schedule and some countermeasures. In: Safavi-Naini, R., Seberry, J. (eds.) ACISP 2003. LNCS, vol. 2727. Springer, Heidelberg (2003)

8. Giraud, C.: DFA on AES. In: Dobbertin, H., Rijmen, V., Sowa, A. (eds.) AES 2005. LNCS, vol. 3373, pp. 27–41. Springer, Heidelberg (2005)

9. Derbez, P., Fouque, P.-A., Leresteux, D.: Meet-in-the-middle and impossible differential fault analysis on AES. In: Preneel, B., Takagi, T. (eds.) CHES 2011. LNCS, vol. 6917, pp. 274–291. Springer, Heidelberg (2011)

10. Chen, H., Wu, W., Feng, D.: Differential fault analysis on CLEFIA. In: Qing, S., Imai, H., Wang, G. (eds.) ICICS 2007. LNCS, vol. 4861, pp. 284–295. Springer, Heidelberg (2007)

11. Takahashi, J., Fukunaga, T.: Improved differential fault analysis on CLEFIA. In: Fault Diagnosis and Tolerance in Cryptography-FDTC 2008, pp. 25–39. IEEE Computer Society Press, Los Alamitos (2008)

12. Biham, E., Granboulan, L., Nguyên, P.Q.: Impossible fault analysis of RC4 and differential fault analysis of RC4. In: Gilbert, H., Handschuh, H. (eds.) FSE 2005. LNCS, vol. 3557, pp. 359–367. Springer, Heidelberg (2005)

13. Hojsík, M., Rudolf, B.: Differential fault analysis of trivium. In: Nyberg, K. (ed.) FSE 2008. LNCS, vol. 5086, pp. 158–172. Springer, Heidelberg (2008)

14. Kircanski, A., Youssef, A.M.: Differential fault analysis of HC-128. In: Bernstein, D.J., Lange, T. (eds.) AFRICACRYPT 2010. LNCS, vol. 6055, pp. 261–278. Springer, Heidelberg (2010)

15. Esmaeili Salehani, Y., Kircanski, A., Youssef, A.: Differential fault analysis of SOSEMANUK. In: Nitaj, A., Pointcheval, D. (eds.) AFRICACRYPT 2011. LNCS, vol. 6737, pp. 316–331. Springer, Heidelberg (2011)

16. Gu, D.-W., Li, J.-R., Li, S., Ma, Z.-Q., Guo, Z., Liu, J. -R: Differential fault analysis on lightweight blockciphers with statistical cryptanalysis techniques. In: Bertoni, G., Gierlichs, B. (Eds.): FDTC 2012, pp. 27–33. IEEE Computer Society Press, Washington, DC (2012)

17. Wu, W., Zhang, L.: LBlock: a lightweight block cipher. In: Lopez, J., Tsudik, G. (eds.) ACNS 2011. LNCS, vol. 6715, pp. 327–344. Springer, Heidelberg (2011)

18. Minier, M., Naya-Plasencia, M.: Some Preliminary Studies on the Differential Behavior of the Lightweight Block Cipher LBlock. In: Leander, G., Standaert, F.-X. (eds.) ECRYPT Workshop on Lightweight Cryptography, pp. 35–48 (2011)

19. Minier, M., Naya-Plasencia, M.: A related key impossible differential attack against 22 rounds of the lightweight block cipher LBlock. Inf. Process. Lett. **112**(16), 624–629 (2012)

20. Wang, Y., Wu, W., Yu, X., Zhang, L.: Security on LBlock against biclique cryptanalysis. In: Lee, D.H., Yung, M. (eds.) WISA 2012. LNCS, vol. 7690, pp. 1–14. Springer, Heidelberg (2012)

21. Liu, Y., Gu, D., Liu, Z., Li, W.: Impossible differential attacks on reduced-round LBlock. In: Ryan, M.D., Smyth, B., Wang, G. (eds.) ISPEC 2012. LNCS, vol. 7232, pp. 97–108. Springer, Heidelberg (2012)

22. Zhao, L., Nishide, T., Sakurai, K.: Differential fault analysis of full LBlock. In: Schindler, W., Huss, S.A. (eds.) COSADE 2012. LNCS, vol. 7275, pp. 135–150. Springer, Heidelberg (2012)

Protecting Ring Oscillator Physical Unclonable Functions Against Modeling Attacks

Shohreh Sharif Mansouri$^{(\boxtimes)}$ and Elena Dubrova

Department of Electronic Systems, School of ICT,
KTH - Royal Institute of Technology, Stockholm, Sweden
{shsm,dubrova}@kth.se

Abstract. One of the most common types of Physical Unclonable Functions (PUFs) is the ring oscillator PUF (RO-PUF), a type of PUF in which the output bits are obtained by comparing the oscillation frequencies of different ring oscillators. One application of RO-PUFs is to be used as strong PUFs: a reader sends a challenge to the RO-PUF and the RO-PUF's response is compared with an expected response to authenticate the PUF. In this work we introduce a method to choose challenge-response pairs so that a high number of challenge-response pairs is provided but the system has a good tolerance to modeling attacks, a type of attacks in which an attacker guesses the response to a new challenge by using his knowledge about the previously-exchanged challenge-response pairs. Our method targets tag-constrained applications, i.e. applications in which there are strong limitations of cost, area and power on the system in which the PUF has to be implemented.

1 Introduction

Physical Unclonable Functions (PUFs) are a set of circuits that exploit the physical characteristics of devices to generate an instance-dependent behaviour, i.e. the behaviour of a PUF is unknown before the chip is manufactured, because it is influenced by the manufacturing tolerances of the technology [1]. Only after manufacturing, the PUF can be tested to extract its behaviour during a phase called *PUF enrollment*. It is hard (ideally impossible) to build two PUFs that behave identically. In a good PUF, once manufactured, the behavior is fixed. In practice, however, no PUF is 100 % reliable, the behaviour of all PUFs is partly influenced by environmental conditions such as temperature variations, etc., and it is possible sometimes to have slightly different outputs corresponding to the same inputs [2]. It is sometimes possible for an attacker to decapsulate a chip containing a PUF and inspect it to extract its behavior [3–5]. However, in a good PUF, any such operation inevitably and irreversibly alters the behavior of the PUF, rendering the system unusable [2].

1.1 Types of PUFs

PUF circuits can be classified in the three main groups of *strong*, *weak* and *controlled* PUFs, based on their application and security features [6].

© Springer International Publishing Switzerland 2014
H.-S. Lee and D.-G. Han (Eds.): ICISC 2013, LNCS 8565, pp. 241–255, 2014.
DOI: 10.1007/978-3-319-12160-4_15

Weak PUFs are used to derive the standard secret key for cryptographic algorithms and their outputs are never meant to be given and seen outside the chip in which the PUF is implemented. A weak PUF is a "secure storage", it has the same function as a read-only memory but is harder to attack [6–9].

Strong PUFs are used for authentication of a *tag* by a *reader* and are circuits in which the PUF, implemented on the tag, processes an input (the *challenge*) and generates an output (the *response*). To authenticate the PUF, the reader provides a challenge to the tag and compares the response with the *expected response*, obtained during PUF enrollment [6]. If an attacker manages to predict the expected response to a challenge, the system is broken because the attacker can "impersonate" the PUF. Strong PUFs are sensitive to *modeling attacks*, i.e. attacks in which an attacker listens to the challenge-response pairs (CRPs) exchanged between the reader and the PUF, records a database of previously-exchanged CRPs, uses it to build a model of the PUF and uses his model to predict the response to new challenges [6]. To avoid modeling attacks, the reader must choose carefully which CRPs he will provide: he cannot give twice the same challenge, for example, because the second time an attacker having observed the first CRP will guess the correct response. An ordered *CRP database* is determined during PUF enrollment, stored in the reader and used by the reader to take the challenge-response pairs.

Controlled PUFs work similarly to strong PUFs. However, to hinder modeling attacks, the challenge is hashed on the tag before being given as PUF input, and the PUF output is hashed before being given as response [6,10]. An attacker probing the challenge-response pairs being exchanged between tag and reader cannot directly access the inputs and outputs of the PUF and it is thus much harder, or impossible, for him to perform a modeling attack by building a model of the PUF. On the tag, the overhead of controlled PUF is higher compared to strong PUFs because the hashing algorithms, by definition, have to be implemented on the tag. Moreover, the output of a PUF, for a question of reliability, is almost never fixed to a certain value, some unreliable bits can change due to temperature variations, voltage supply variations or other environmental factors. In a strong PUF, the reader might accept as correct a response which is "almost" identical to the expected response (i.e. with only some bits difference); in a controlled PUF, if even a single bit is different in the output of the PUF, the hashing blocks can generate a completely different response that has no relation with the original response. Therefore, in a controlled PUF, an error-correction mechanism [11–13] must be inserted on the chip at the output of the PUF.

1.2 Contribution

There exists an important class of PUF systems, that we call *tag-constrained systems*, used for authentication, in which the limitations on the tag are high but the limitations on the reader are not. This class includes systems in which a portable smartcard or other passive system has to be authenticated by a fixed reader that is connected to a network and can have access to large databases and computers to execute algorithms. Guaranteeing high security in tag-constrained authentication systems is a challenge: we argue that these systems must be implemented as strong PUFs because the overhead of controlled PUFs is too high. To avoid modeling attacks, one must thus limit the number of CRPs exchanged between the reader and the tag and be careful when generating the CRP database.

RO-PUFs are a type of PUF that exploits the frequency oscillation differences between nominally-identical ring oscillators, well-suited for tag-constrained systems due to their low hardware overhead [14]. Strong RO-PUFs are also known for their vulnerability to modeling attacks [6]: to eliminate this vulnerability, one must eliminate many CRPs, remaining with a low number of them in the CRP database. As an alternative, several solutions have been proposed to obtain a high number of independent bits. Unfortunately, these methods (see Sect. 5) all require that some "complex" algorithm (such as a sort) is run in the tag, a solution that is often too expensive for tag-constrained systems. We therefore tried to determine a method to build a CRP database that contains a number of CRPs which is as high as possible, and that is as secure as possible against modeling attacks.

We recognize that the number of generated CRPs is moderate and the resistance to modeling attacks comes, at best, in the form: "the attacker can never guess the response with more than X% probability". Given the high requirements of tag-constrained systems, this is the best we could do: tag-constrained systems require strong PUFs that can never achieve the same security properties as controlled PUFs, but we still think that it is important to investigate how many single-bit challenges can be extracted from a strong RO-PUF without compromising excessively the resistance to modeling attacks. To the best of our knowledge no such study has been conducted before.

We think that our solution can at least give a satisfactory level of security to tag-constrained authentication systems against those attacks in which the attacker can probe the exchanged CRPs only for a limited period of time.

2   Ring Oscillator Strong PUFs

A RO-PUF [14] is constituted by n nominally-identical ring oscillators (chains containing an odd number of inverters in a loop) numbered RO_0 to RO_{n-1}. Its structure is shown in Fig. 1.

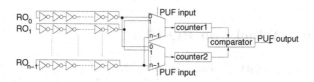

Fig. 1. RO-PUF

When manufactured, due to small manufacturing variations, each Ring Oscillator (RO) oscillates with a unique frequency, respectively f_0 to f_{n-1} (in practice, often slightly influenced by environmental variations, especially by the operating temperature).

The frequencies f_x and f_y of ring oscillators RO_x and RO_y can be compared by selecting their outputs and feeding them to the two counters: the two selected ring oscillators are left free to oscillate for a certain *comparison time* while the two counters count their oscillations; at the end of the comparison time, the comparator is used to see which of the two ROs was oscillating faster (the one with a higher value of the counter).

When RO-PUFs are used as strong PUFs, the challenges correspond to pairs of ring oscillators, i.e. a single-bit challenge takes the form:

$$\text{``}f_x > f_y?\text{''} \ with \ x > y$$

The response is *yes* if $f_x > f_y$ and *no* if $f_x < f_y$. The constraint $x > y$ is introduced to avoid meaningless challenges such as "$f_1 > f_1$?" and duplicate challenges such as "$f_2 > f_0$?" and "$f_0 > f_2$?".

We indicate challenge response pairs with the notation ("$f_x > f_y$?", *yes/no*), such as in ("$f_3 > f_2$?", *yes*).

Multi-bit challenge-response pairs are obtained by providing several single-bit challenges to the PUF and observing the responses.

Note that in Sect. 5 some alternative RO-PUF systems that use different challenges and responses are described.

3   Reliability Assumption

To keep the discussion general and be able to treat it mathematically, we do not consider the effects of reliability, i.e. we assume in this work that given a pair of ring oscillators one of the ROs is always faster than the other. With this assumption, the response to any single-bit challenge is fixed and never variates from run to run.

With this assumption all RO-PUFs are identified by a permutation of frequencies, such as $f_5 < f_0 < f_2 < f_3 < f_1 < f_4$, which is randomly determined when the chip is manufactured and then never changes.

Throughout the remainder of the paper, the reader should keep in mind this basic assumption that we made.

4   Modeling Attacks on RO-PUFs

It has been realized relatively early in the history of PUFs [6,15,16] that modeling attacks using Machine Learning (ML) techniques are a powerful tool to challenge the security of strong PUFs [16].

A modeling attack is an attack in which the attacker probes the communication channel between the reader and the tag, observes all exchanged CRPs, stores them in a database and uses the database to build a model of the PUF with the help of an ML algorithm. When a new challenge is issued, the attacker uses his model of the PUF to predict the response that the PUF would give. If the attacker is successfull in his prediction, he can impersonate the tag, fooling the reader and breaking the system.

4.1 Attacks on RO-PUFs

The number of valid single-bit challenges that can be given to a RO-PUF with n ring oscillators is equal to the total number of distinct RO pairs $\binom{n}{2} = \frac{n(n-1)}{2}$. However, if the CRP database contains all these challenges, the system can be easily broken by a modeling attack [6]. A simple proof of the fact that the bits are not independent is the fact that $\binom{n}{2}$ is way over the *entropy* of the frequency ordering, i.e. the maximal number of independent bits that can theoretically be extracted from it, which with our assumptions (see Sect. 3), is the only element that determines the responses to the challenges. Since there are only $n!$ possible frequency orderings, the entropy is $log_2 n!$.

Let us see with a simple example how modeling attacks are performed on strong RO-PUFs: we have a PUF made up by six ROs, numbered from RO_0 to RO_5 and oscillating respectively at frequencies f_0 to f_5, ordered as $f_5 < f_0 < f_2 < f_3 < f_1 < f_4$.

We distinguish three types of modeling attacks: *deterministic modeling attacks*, *indeterministic modeling attacks* and *heuristic modeling attacks*.

Deterministic Modeling Attack. If an attacker observes the challenge response pairs ("$f_3 > f_0$?", *yes*) and ("$f_5 > f_0$?", *no*), when the challenge "$f_5 > f_3$" is given the attacker can predict the correct response (*no*), because he knows that $f_5 < f_0 < f_3$.

The attack consists in determining a partial ordering of frequencies given the constraints determined by previously-exchanged CRPs, and seeing if the answer to a new challenge can be deduced from the known ordering. This type of attack is computationally feasible using a quicksort method and was first proposed in [6].

Indeterministic Modeling Attack. If the attacker observes the CRPs ("$f_5 > f_0$?", *no*), ("$f_3 > f_0$?", *yes*), ("$f_3 > f_1$?", *no*) and ("$f_4 > f_1$?", *yes*), then the attacker can determine that $f_5 < f_0 < f_3 < f_1 < f_4$. If now the new challenge "$f_4 > f_2$?" is issued, the attacker can guess the response by making a list of all the possible orderings of frequencies that satisfy the constraints given by the previously-exchanged CRPs.

$$A : f_2 < f_5 < f_0 < f_3 < f_1 < f_4 \quad ; \quad D : f_5 < f_0 < f_3 < f_2 < f_1 < f_4$$
$$B : f_5 < f_2 < f_0 < f_3 < f_1 < f_4 \quad ; \quad E : f_5 < f_0 < f_3 < f_1 < f_2 < f_4$$
$$C : f_5 < f_0 < f_2 < f_3 < f_1 < f_4 \quad ; \quad F : f_5 < f_0 < f_3 < f_1 < f_4 < f_2$$

Of the 6 possible orderings of frequencies left, only F would result in the response to the challenge being *no*. The attacker, by predicting that the response is *yes*, has a 5/6 chance of being right.

The attack consists in determining the list of all possible frequency orderings that satisfy all the constraints determined by previously-exchanged CRPs, and seeing for how many of them the response to the new challenge would be *yes* and for how many it would be *no*. It can be computationally too hard (NP-complete) to perform this attack.

Heuristic Modeling Attack. Indeterministic modeling attacks are often unfeasible due to their computational complexity. However, heuristic methods can still be used by an attacker and have success. A simple example of heuristic attack is based on this idea: if an RO RO_a has proved to be faster than other three other ROs but no RO faster than RO_a has been found yet, than it is probable that RO_a will also be faster than another random RO RO_b. However, heuristic modeling attacks can never be more accurate than indeterministic modeling attacks.

Summary. Summarizing: a *deterministic modeling attack* (computationally feasible) fails or gives to the attacker an expected response which is 100 % correct; an *indeterministic modeling attack* (often computationally unfeasible) gives to the attacker the most probable response and its exact probability; A *heuristic modeling attack* (computationally feasible) gives to the attacker a guess on the most probable response and no attached guarantee on its probability to be correct, it cannot be more accurate than an indeterministic modeling attack.

5   Related Work

Work on RO-PUFs often focuses on enhancing the reliability of RO-PUFs in presence of temperature or voltage variations, such as [11], in which the ROs are divided into groups of 8, the biggest and the smallest are determined and the pointer to the two is given as output.

Other more relevant works have been proposed to build a CRP database of independent bits for RO-PUFs. In [17], the authors proposed a non-rank-based method to extract bits, i.e. the bits are not determined only by the frequency ordering, but by a mathematical function of the distribution of the RO frequencies themselves (allowing a much higher number of bits to be extracted). The authors claim they can extract 60 K CRPs from only 16 ring oscillators. The authors statistically study their CRPs to prove that they are hard to attack, but there is no mathematical guarantee on the independence between CRPs. It remains to see if their method can be applied to other technologies.

Two rank-based methods (based only on frequency comparisons) have a more direct relevance to our approach.

The $n/2$ method [5] consists in never using any ring oscillator in more than one comparison, so that an attacker having observed the previously exchanged CRPs cannot have any clue on the response to a new challenge. In a PUF with n ROs this method generates only $n/2$ CRPs (for example, with 6 ROs, "$f_1 > f_0$?", "$f_3 > f_2$?" and "$f_5 > f_4$?").

LISA [18,19] was introduced to maximize bit extraction and is based on grouping the ROs into different groups so that the ROs belonging to the same group have all a minimal frequency difference, higher than a threshold value f_{th} to guarantee high reliability in presence of temperature variations. In each group, all ring oscillators are compared together and the frequency ordering among them is established (such as $f_5 < f_0 < f_2 < f_3 < f_1 < f_4$). With g ROs, in the group there are $g!$ possible orderings. The ordering is translated into a binary number with $log_2(g!)$ bits and given as the secret. For systems having the reliability assumption is Sect. 3, the number of CRPs is maximized by making a single group of n ROs: all n ring oscillator frequencies are extracted and sorted, obtaining a frequency ordering which is translated to a binary number $0 \le o \le n! - 1$ using a one-to-one correspondance. A single-bit challenge takes the form: "what is the value of bit X of o?". This method can give $\lfloor log_2 n! \rfloor$ independent challenge-response pairs, no other rank-based method can do better. However interesting from a theoretical point of view, this method (max-LISA) is also extremely unpractical: every time the response to a challenge must be given, the tag should test all ring oscillator frequencies, quick-sort them, determine their ordering, translate it to a number and respond with one bit.

Our approach is to introduce two possible algorithms to build the CRP database suring PUF enrollment, with a "low dependency" between CRPs. Both algorithms guarantee that all deterministic modeling attacks will fail, i.e. the attacker will never be able to obtain a 100 % certitude on the expected response. With the first algorithm, indeterministic modeling attacks are possible but require an exhaustive search among all possible orderings of CRPs, with $O(n!)$ complexity; heuristic attacks can break the system. With the second algorithm, indeterministic modeling attacks are easy to perform but are guaranteed to never find a response that has a probability higher than p_{max}, where p_{max} is chosen by the designer. Being always equal or worse in accuracy to indeterministic attacks, heuristic attacks also have the same limitation on their predicting ability. As p_{max} decreases, the number of CRPs also decreases, creating a security-to-number of CRPs tradeoff.

6   Algorithm 1

Algorithm 1 is very intuitive and works as follows:

1. The algorithm starts with the pool C of all $\binom{n}{k}$ challenges that can be given to a RO-PUF with n ROs.
2. One challenge in C is choosen randomly, eliminated from C and added at the end of the CRP database D.
3. The algorithm then ipothesizes that an attacker has observed all CRPs in D and calculates for which challenges in C he can guess the answer with 100 % probability. These challenges are eliminated from C.
4. The algorithm loops back to step 2 until C is empty.

Algorithm 1 guarantees all deterministic modeling attacks will always fail (the attacker will never be able to guess a response with 100 % probability). However, indeterministic modeling attacks can be performed with $O(n!)$ complexity and the system might be vulnerable to heuristic attacks.

A complete implementation of Algorithm 1, with $O(n^4)$ complexity, is reported in Appendix A.

7   Algorithm 2

Algorithm 2 starts with a ring oscillator pool P, initialized with all n ring oscillators. In P, one ring oscillator RO_r is picked at random. All challenges "$f_r > f_i$?" (or "$f_i > f_r$?") with $0 \leq i < n$ and $i \neq r$ are given one after the other, i.e. added to the database of the challenges that will be given to the PUF (ring oscillator RO_r is compared with all other ring oscillators).

The attacker can never guess the response to any of these challenges with 100 % certitude: f_r is always compared with a frequency f_i on which nothing is known for certain (it has not been compared with anything else before).

After having finished with all challenges, the attacker splits all ring oscillators (except RO_r) into two groups: a slow group P_s, containing all ring oscillators RO_i for which $f_i < f_r$, and a fast group P_f, containing all ring oscillators RO_j for which $f_j > f_r$.

The algorithm is recursive: on the second step, the same algorithm is applied to both P_s and to P_f. In each of the two groups, one ring oscillator is picked at random and is compared with all others, resulting in the creation of two new groups. When the algorithm moves to work on P_s and P_f, knowledge about all previously-exchanged CRPs is useless for an attacker because members of P_s and P_f have never been compared among themselves before, which guarantees that a deterministic modeling attack can never succeed.

When pools P_s and P_f have 0 or 1 members only, the algorithm stops because it is not possible to choose randomly one element and compare it with the others. The algorithm has $O(n \log n)$ complexity.

7.1   Example

As an example, let us consider a RO-PUF with $n = 6$ ring oscillators RO_0 to RO_5, with frequency ordering $f_5 < f_0 < f_2 < f_3 < f_1 < f_4$.

In the first step, $P = \{RO_0, RO_1, RO_2, RO_3, RO_4, RO_5\}$. RO_2 is selected randomly and compared with all other ring oscillators in turn, resulting in the challenges "$f_2 > f_0$?", "$f_2 > f_1$?", "$f_3 > f_2$?", "$f_4 > f_2$?" and "$f_5 > f_2$?" being added to the challenge database. Based on the challenge responses, the ring oscillators are divided into the two groups P_s and P_l, containing respectively the ROs that run slower and faster than RO_2: $P_s = \{RO_0, RO_5\}$, $P_l = \{RO_1, RO_3, RO_4\}$. The algorithm is then repeated recursively on P_s and P_l.

On P_s, RO_0 is chosen at random and compared with RO_5, resulting in the challenge "$f_5 > f_0$?" being added to the challenge database. The two groups of ring

Algorithm 2

1: P = *set of all ring oscillators*
2: generateChallenges(P)
3:
4: **function** generateChallenges(P)
5: **if** P is empty or contains only one RO **then**
6:     return;
7: **else**
8:     select one random element $RO_r \in P$
9:     remove RO_r from P
10:     $P_s = \{\}$
11:     $P_l = \{\}$
12:     **for** all elements $RO_i \in P$ **do**
13:         add the challenge "$f_i > f_r$?" or "$f_r > f_i$?" to the challenge database
14:         **if** $f_r > f_i$ **then**
15:             add RO_i to P_s
16:         **else**
17:             add RO_i to P_l
18:         **end if**
19:     **end for**
20:     generateChallenges(P_s)
21:     generateChallenges(P_l)
22:     return
23: **end if**
24: **end function**

---

oscillators in P_s faster and slower than RO_5 are respectively constituted by 0 and 1 members, so the algorithm returns. On P_l, RO_4 is chosen at random and compared with RO_3 and RO_5, resulting in the challenges "$f_4 > f_3$?" and "$f_5 > f_4$?" being added to the challenge database. The two groups of ring oscillators in P_s faster and slower than RO_4 are both constituted by 1 member only, so the algorithm returns. In total, the algorithm generates 8 CRPs.

7.2   Number of CRPs

The expected number of CRPs generated by the algorithm can be calculated mathematically.

We define as $C(n)$ the average number of challenges generated by the algorithm for a pool of n ring oscillators. By definition we have $C(0) = 0$ and $C(1) = 0$ (no pairs can be made with less than two ring oscillators).

When the algorithm is applied to a pool of $n + 1$ ring oscillators, one ring oscillator RO_r is picked at random and compared with the other n ring oscillators, resulting in n CRPs. The n remaining ring oscillators are divided into two groups P_s and P_l having sizes s and $l = n - s$. The probability distribution for the value of s is uniform between 0 and n, because nothing is known about the position of f_r in the frequency ordering among all ring oscillators: with the same probability, f_r

can be the smallest value in the pool ($s = 0$, $l = n$), or the second smallest ($s = 1$, $l = n - 1$), or ..., or the penultimate biggest ($s = n - 1$, $l = 1$), or the biggest ($s = n$, $l = 0$). The algorithm is then applied recursively on the two pools that have been generated, generating on average $C(s)$ and $C(l)$ CRPs. Therefore,

$$C(0) = C(1) = 0$$

$$C(n + 1,\ n > 0) = n + \frac{1}{n} \sum_{s=0}^{n} (C(s) + C(n - s)) = n + \frac{2}{n} \sum_{s=0}^{n} C(s)$$

The values of $C(n)$ can then be calculated recursively.

7.3   Indeterministic Modeling Attack

Indeterminstic attacks are easy to perform on a system using CRPs generated by Algorithm 2, and do not require $O(n!)$ complexity.

When the reader starts working with a new pool of ROs, an attacker does not have any information on any of the ROs in the pool because they were never compared together before, and because all of them, when compared with other ROs, always gave the same responses. The attacker has then only 50 % chance to guess the response to the challenge.

As ring oscillator r is compared with other ring oscillators in the pool, the attacker can keep track of the number s of ring oscillators for which it is known that they run at lower frequency than RO_r and the number l of ring oscillators for which it is known that they run at a higher frequency than RO_r.

It is known that in the frequency ordering among the $s + l + 1$ ring oscillators that have been compared until now (including ring oscillator r), ring oscillator r occupies the position s (it has s frequencies under it and l frequencies over it).

When comparing ring oscillator RO_i with RO_r, in the frequency ordering among all $s + l + 2$ ring oscillators that have already been compared or will now be compared, including RO_i and RO_r, f_i can randomly occupy any position with equal probability, from position 0 (it is the lowest frequency) to position $s + l + 1$ (it is the highest frequency). If it is in the first $s + 1$ positions, then $f_r > f_i$, else $f_r < f_i$.

The probability to have $f_r > f_i$ is then given by:

$$P(f_r > f_i) = \frac{s + 1}{s + l + 2}$$

For example, if in one step of the algorithm $P = \{RO_0, RO_1, RO_2, RO_3, RO_4, RO_5\}$ and $RO_r = RO_1$ has already been compared with RO_2, RO_4 and RO_5, and if it was determined that RO_2 and RO_5 are slower than RO_5 but RO_4 is faster than RO_5, then $s = 2$ and $l = 1$ and the probability to have, for example, $f_1 > f_0$ is $(s + 1)/(s + l + 2) = 3/5$.

With a simple arithmetic division, the attacker can always determine the most likely response to the challenge "$f_r > f_i$?" and its associated probability. Since indeterministic modeling attacks are so easy, it is worthless to use any heuristic attack.

We ran an indeterministic modeling attack on a RO-PUF whose challenges were determined using Algorithm 2 and calculated the average predicition probability over all the CRPs. Results were averaged over 1000 random PUFs for every value of n. based on our experiment, an attacker having observed all previously-exchanged CRPs and performing an indeterministic modeling attack has, on average, a $\sim$75 % probability to guess the response to a new challenge, instead of the 50 % probability he would have by guessing randomly. Although this number is relatively reasonable, the responses to some of the challenges are easy to guess: for $n = 100$, for example, 14 % of the CRP responses can be predicted by the attacker with a probability higher than 90 %. Note that since all challenge-response pairs used in practice are multi-bit, guessing the response to a k-bit challenge can be done on average with 0.75^k probability, which might provide a sufficient level of security for some applications.

7.4   Protecting Against Indeterministic Modeling Attacks

Since, when the CRP database is generated by Algorithm 2, it is so easy to perform an indeterminsitc modeling attack, we propose the following idea: during chip enrollment, every time a new challenge is about to be added to the CRP database D, an indeterminstic modeling attack is perfomed to determine what would be the probability for an attacker having observed all previously-exchanged CRPs to predict the answer. If this probability is above p_{max}, the challenge is "skipped" and not added to the database.

One important thing to note is that the attacker might guess wrong in an indeterminstic modeling attack. For example, his model can tell him that, with 90 % probability, $f_r > f_i$, while in reality $f_i < f_r$. The enroller (who knows the response) might be tempted to put the challenge anyhow in the CRP database, because he knows the attacker will respond wrongly. But the attacker, by seeing that the challenge has been given although he was guessing the response, will understand what the reasoning of the reader was and will respond correctly by changing its guess. Therefore, the enroller should skip all challenges for which the attacker thinks he has a high probability to guess correctly, regardless of whether he would guess correctly or not. When the enroller skips a challenge, he can freely announce what the response to that challenge was.

With $p_{max} = 1$ no challenges will be skipped (the system is only tolerant to deterministic modeling attacks). As p_{max} decreases towards 0.5, the number of skipped challenges increases and the number of given challenges decreases.

8   Number of CRPs

Table 1 reports, for different values of n: (a) the entropy; (b) the number of CRPs generated respectively by Algorithm 1 and Algorithm 2 (the values were obtained by generating 1000 random RO-PUFs, i.e. permutations of frequencies, for every value of n, applying the two algorithms, averaging the number of obtained CRPs

Table 1. Average number of CRPs generated by the two algorithms, the $n/2$ method and the max-LISA method

#ROs		$n = 10$	$n = 20$	$n = 30$	$n = 40$	$n = 50$	$n = 60$	$n = 70$	$n = 80$	$n = 90$	$n = 100$
entropy		22	61	108	159	214	272	332	395	459	525
Alg. 1		17	73	164	203	288	404	477	612	716	847
	1	21	55	108	172	250	313	359	467	512	609
	0.9	17	49	97	154	216	268	323	393	453	523
Alg. 2	0.8	17	48	86	131	166	218	266	316	376	427
$p_{max} =$	0.7	14	40	71	94	123	166	194	217	264	303
	0.6	8	26	44	59	74	97	116	148	159	167
max-LISA		22	61	108	159	214	272	332	395	459	525
$n/2$		5	10	15	20	25	30	35	40	45	50

and rounding to the nearest unit); (c) the number of CRPs generated by the "$n/2$" and the "max-LISA" methods described in Sect. 5 ($n/2$ and $\lfloor log_2 n! \rfloor$ CRPs).

The algorithms generate a number of CRPs much higher than the $n/2$ method and in the order of magnitude of those generated by max-LISA. However, the CRPs are not fully-independent as the ones generated by the other two methods. On the other hand, the max-LISA method is mostly theoretical and too complex to be applied on a tag-constrained system.

9   Conclusion

In conclusion, we have presented two algorithms to choose CRPs for strong RO-PUFs so that they are partially-protected against modeling attacks. We recognize that the level of security and number of CRPs can be unsatisfactory for some applications, but we think our method can give a satisfactory level of security to tag-constrained systems, in which the high constraints on the tag make other solutions impossible to apply.

Future work will be conducted to judge the impact of reliability issues on this solution.

Acknowledgment. This work was supported in part the research grant No 621-2010-4388 from the Swedish Research Council and in part by the research grant No SM12-0005 from the Swedish Foundation for Strategic Research.

A   Appendix

Algorithm 1 can be implemented with $O(n^4)$ complexity.

The algorithm keeps a pool C of available challenges which shrinks as challenges are selected or become unusable, and an $n \times n$ matrix O whose entry at row i and column j (entry $O(i,j)$) is 1 if it is known that $f_i > f_j$.

Algorithm 1

```
 1: for all i, j do
 2:     O(i, j) = 0
 3: end for
 4: C = set of all challenges
 5: while C ≠ {} do
 6:     select a random challenge "f_i > f_j?" ∈ C
 7:     add the challenge "f_i > f_j?" to the challenge database
 8:     remove challenge "f_i > f_j?" from C
 9:     if f_i < f_j then
10:         swap i and j
11:     end if
12:     O(i, j) = 1
13:     for k = 0; k < n; k = k + 1 do
14:         if O(k, i) = 1 then
15:             O(k, j) = 1
16:             remove challenge "f_j > f_k?" or "f_k > f_j?" from C
17:         end if
18:     end for
19:     for l = 0; l < n; l = l + 1 do
20:         if O(j, l) = 1 then
21:             O(i, l) = 1;
22:             remove challenge "f_i > f_l?" or "f_l > f_i?" from C
23:             for m = 0; m < n; m = m + 1 do
24:                 if O(m, i) = 1 then
25:                     O(m, l) = 1;
26:                     remove challenge "f_m > f_l?" or "f_l > f_m?" from C
27:                 end if
28:             end for
29:         end if
30:     end for
31: end while
```

At the beginning of the algorithm, the matrix is initialized with all zeroes and the pool of available challenges is initialized with all $\frac{n(n-1)}{2}$ possible challenges.

On the first step of the algorithm, one challenge "$f_i > f_j$?" is chosen randomly among all $\frac{n(n-1)}{2}$ possible challenges in C. The response determines the relation between f_i and f_j and a 1 is inserted in the matrix either at position $O(i, j)$ or at position $O(j, i)$.

In subsequent steps of the algorithm, when a new randomly chosen CRP determines that $f_i > f_j$, a 1 is written in the matrix at position $O(i, j)$ and also at position $O(i, k)$, with k being all the values for which matrix entry $O(j, k)$ is 1: for these entries, the attacker knows that $f_i > f_j$ and that $f_j > f_k$, and therefore can deduce that $f_i > f_k$.

Then the algorithm looks at all frequencies f_l which are known to be slower than f_j. A 1 is written in $O(i, l)$: for these entries, the attacker knows that $f_i > f_j$ and that $f_j > f_l$, and therefore can deduce that $f_i > f_l$. A 1 is also written in

$O(m, l)$, with f_m being all the frequencies that are known to be bigger than f_i (for which $O(m, i)$ is one): for these entries, the attacker knows that $f_m > f_i$, that $f_i > f_j$ and that $f_j > f_l$, and therefore can deduce that $f_m > f_l$.

Every time that a 1 is written in $O(x, y)$, the challenge "$f(x) > f(y)$?" or "$f(y) > f(x)$?" is eliminated from the pool C of available challenges because the attacker can predict the response with 100 % certitude.

References

1. Gassend, B., Clarke, D., van Dijk, M., Devadas, S.: Silicon physical random functions. In: ACM Conference on Computer and Communications Security, pp. 148–160. ACM Press (2002)
2. Sadeghi, A.-R., Naccache, D.: Towards Hardware-Intrinsic Security: Foundations and Practice, 1st edn. Springer, New York (2010)
3. Skorobogatov, S.P.: Semi-invasive attacks - a new approach to hardware security analysis. University of Cambridge, Computer Laboratory, Techical Report UCAM-CL-TR-630, April 2005
4. Mangard, S., Oswald, E., Popp, T.: Power Analysis Attacks: Revealing the Secrets of Smart Cards. Springer, New York (2007)
5. Merli, D., Schuster, D., et al.: Semi-invasive EM attack on FPGA RO pufs and countermeasures. In: Proceedings of the Workshop on Embedded Systems Security, ser. WESS '11, pp. 2:1–2:9 (2011)
6. Rührmair, U., Sehnke, F., Sölter, J., et al.: Modeling attacks on physical unclonable functions. In: Proceedings of the 17th ACM Conference on Computer and Communications Security, ser. CCS '10, pp. 237–249 (2010)
7. Kumar, S.S., Guajardo, J., Maes, R., et al.: Extended abstract: The butterfly PUF protecting IP on every FPGA. In: Proceedings of the IEEE International Workshop on Hardware-Oriented Security and Trust, pp. 67–70 (2008)
8. Selimis, G., Konijnenburg, M., Ashouei, M., et al.: Evaluation of 90nm 6T-SRAM as physical unclonable function for secure key generation in wireless sensor nodes. In: IEEE International Symposium on Circuits and Systems, pp. 567–570 (2011)
9. Guajardo, J., Kumar, S.S., Schrijen, G.-J., Tuyls, P.: FPGA intrinsic PUFs and their use for IP protection. In: Paillier, P., Verbauwhede, I. (eds.) CHES 2007. LNCS, vol. 4727, pp. 63–80. Springer, Heidelberg (2007)
10. Gassend, B., Clarke, D., et al.: Controlled physical random functions. In: Proceedings of the 18th Annual Computer Security Conference (2002)
11. Yu, M.-D.M., Devadas, S.: Secure and robust error correction for physical unclonable functions. IEEE Des. Test Comput. 27, 48–65 (2010)
12. Paral, Z., Devadas, S.: Reliable and efficient PUF-based key generation using pattern matching. In: 2011 IEEE International Symposium on Hardware-Oriented Security and Trust (HOST), pp. 128–133 (2011)
13. Suh, G.E., O'Donnell, C.W., et al.: AEGIS: A single-chip secure processor. Information Security. Techical Report, pp. 63–73 (2005)
14. Suh, G.E., Devadas, S.: Physical unclonable functions for device authentication and secret key generation. In: Proceedings of the 44th Annual Design Automation Conference, pp. 9–14 (2007)
15. Lim, D.: Extracting Secret Keys from Integrated Circuits. MIT, Cambridge (2004)
16. Sehnke, F., Osendorfer, C., Sölter, J., Schmidhuber, J., Rührmair, U.: Policy gradients for cryptanalysis. In: Diamantaras, K., Duch, W., Iliadis, L.S. (eds.) ICANN 2010, Part III. LNCS, vol. 6354, pp. 168–177. Springer, Heidelberg (2010)

17. Maiti, A., Kim, I., Schaumont, P.: A robust physical unclonable function with enhanced challenge-response set. IEEE Trans. Inf. Forensics Secur. **7**(1), 333–345 (2012)
18. Yin, C.-E., Qu, G.: Lisa: Maximizing ro puf's secret extraction. In: 2010 IEEE International Symposium on Hardware-Oriented Security and Trust (HOST), pp. 100–105 (2010)
19. Yin, C.-E., Qu, G., Zhou, Q.: Design and implementation of a group-based ro puf. In: Proceedings of the Conference on Design, Automation and Test in Europe, ser. DATE '13,pp. 416–421 (2013)

Parallel Implementations of LEA

Hwajeong Seo[1], Zhe Liu[2], Taehwan Park[1], Hyunjin Kim[1], Yeoncheol Lee[1],
Jongseok Choi[1], and Howon Kim[1]([✉])

[1] School of Computer Science and Engineering, Pusan National University, San-30,
Jangjeon-Dong, Geumjeong-Gu, Busan 609–735, Republic of Korea
{hwajeong,pth5804,moonmaker.k,lycshotgun,jschoi85,howonkim}@pusan.ac.kr
[2] Laboratory of Algorithmics, Cryptology and Security (LACS),
University of Luxembourg, 6, Rue R. Coudenhove-Kalergi,
1359 Luxembourg-Kirchberg, Luxembourg
zhe.liu@uni.lu

Abstract. LEA is a new lightweight and low-power encryption algorithm. This algorithm has a certain useful features which are especially suitable for parallel hardware and software implementations, i.e., simple ARX operations, non-S-BOX architecture, and 32-bit word size. In this paper we evaluate the performance of the LEA algorithm on ARM-NEON and GPUs by taking advantage of both the desirable features of LEA and a parallel computing platform and programming model by NEON and CUDA. Specifically, we propose novel parallel LEA implementations on representative SIMT and SIMD architectures such as CUDA and NEON. In case of CUDA, we firstly designed a thread-based computation model to fall into functional parallelism by computing several encryptions over one thread. To alleviate the memory transfer delay, we allocate memory to satisfy coalescing memory access. Secondly our method is block cipher implementation written in assembly language, which provides efficient and flexible programming environments. With these optimization techniques, we achieved 17.352 and 2.5 GBps (bytes per second) throughput without/with memory transfer. In case of NEON, we adopted pipeline instructions and SIMD-based execution models, which enhanced encryption by 49.85 % compared to previous ARM implementations.

Keywords: Low-power encryption algorithm · Single instruction multiple data · Single instruction multiple threads · NEON · GPGPU · Software implementation · Block cipher · ARM

1 Introduction

Recently, various multi-core CPU and GPU processors were introduced by Intel, AMD and NVIDIA companies, supporting parallel programming libraries

This work was supported by the Industrial Strategic Technology Development Program (No.10043907, Development of high performance IoT device and Open Platform with Intelligent Software) funded by the Ministry of Science, ICT & Future Planning (MSIF, Korea).

H.-S. Lee and D.-G. Han (Eds.): ICISC 2013, LNCS 8565, pp. 256–274, 2014.
DOI: 10.1007/978-3-319-12160-4_16

including Compute Unified Device Architecture (CUDA) and Open Computing Language (OpenCL). In [22], adopting the parallel computing power improves previous CPU based AES implementations by 5.92 times. This advanced parallel computing trend can be extended to representative embedded systems such as the ARM processors. Modern ARM processors provide a vector instruction set extensions in order to perform single instruction, multiple data (SIMD) operations. The platforms include almost all modern smart-phones and tablet PCs such as iPAD, iPhone, Galaxy Note and Galaxy S. The ARM named their SIMD model as NEON and it can compute wide word sizes of up to 64- and 128-bit in a single instruction. This new parallel computing instruction shows that traditional serialized program can be switched to parallel with high performance enhancements. In [23], ARM NEON implementation of Grøstl shows that 40 % performance enhancements than the previous fastest ARM implementation.

In this paper, we exploit parallel computing power into novel block cipher, LEA, which was released at WISA'13 [6]. The implementation of LEA is efficient in any platforms ranging from low-end embedded microprocessors to high-end personal computers. Contrary to previous implementations of LEA, mainly focused on serial computations of embedded processors and parallel computations of CPU, this paper studies the feasibility of parallel implementation of LEA on ARM-NEON and GPUs. To improve performance, we exploit SIMD and SIMT architectures and presented various novel techniques. All these methods are not limited to LEA implementation but it can be extended to other cryptography implementations without difficulties.

2 Related Works

2.1 CUDA

Traditionally, GPUs were commonly used for graphical applications by exploiting several parallel cores and graphic APIs. Before the advent of CUDA environments, these computation units were only used for limited graphical works and environments by using OPEN-GL. For this reason, crypto computations were not efficiently executable using OPEN-GL because crypto operations consist of basic integer arithmetic and logical operations while OPEN-GL does not provide these operations. Recently, NVIDIA released a programmable GPU architecture, named CUDA [4,5]. Using this parallel computing environment, a programmer can use a GPU as a parallel computing unit to execute thousands of operations in a parallel manner. This parallel computing power was straightforwardly adopted in cryptography implementations and has shown high performance enhancements. In case of block cipher, some modes of operations such as CTR and ECB do not have data dependency between each encryption session, so high parallel implementation is possible by executing several computations in a parallel way. In [10,13,15,16], many AES results have been reported. The major optimization techniques exploit multi-core computations and fast shared memory rather than global, local, or constant to preserve look-up tables. At AFRICACRYPT'13, a method for high utilization of GPU resources was reported [14]. This method manages CUDA resources such as block, thread, and register in an optimized way. Recently, assembly language programming has been made available in CUDA and feasible results have been reported in [17]. As assembly programming provides flexibility to programmer, we can write optimal and concise program and improve performance further than high-level languages.

2.2 NEON

NEON is a 128-bit SIMD architecture for the ARM Cortex-A series [1]. One of the differences between a traditional ARM processor and an ARM-NEON processor is that NEON offers registers and instructions that support a length of 64- and 128-bit. Each register is considered as a vector of elements of the same data type and this data type can be signed/unsigned 8-bit, 16-bit, 32-bit, or 64-bit. This feature provides a more precise operation and benefit to various word size computations and instructions, especially when performing the same operation in all lanes for efficiently computing multiple data. Finally, NEON technology can accelerate data processing by at least 3X that provided by ARMv5 and at least 2X that provided by ARMv6 SIMD [1]. This nice structure can boost previous implementations by converting single instruction single data model to SIMD. At CHES 2012, NEON-based cryptography implementations including Salsa20, Poly1305, Curve25519 and Ed25519 were presented in [2]. To enhance the performance, the authors provided novel bit-rotation, integration of multiplication and reduction operations exploiting NEON instructions. After then, lots of practical cryptosystem applications using NEON were presented [3,23] by using novel vector-wise instructions.

3 Parallel Implementations of LEA

In this section, we provide LEA implementation strategies over SIMT and SIMD in great detail.

3.1 Memory and Speed Trade-Off

Memory and speed have a trade-off relation. If we choose a speed-first strategy, the memory is used for saving the full round keys. This method reduces many arithmetic operations into a single memory access. On the other hand, a size-optimized strategy minimizes the code size and memory usage, taking decline of speed factor because round keys are generated during on-line. In this section, we explore two main LEA implementation algorithms over SIMT and SIMD architectures.

On-the-Fly Method. The on-the-fly method is a size-optimized method, which generates the round keys on-the-spot and uses them directly. The advantage of this method is that we do not need to pre-compute and store the round keys because the round keys in needs are directly generated during each step. We tested OFM model on both architectures. First, this method is appropriate for a CUDA machine because CUDA shows a slow performance in global memory accesses. For this reason, computing ALU operations is better than computing memory operations. In the case of NEON, OFM is favorable because an SIMD machine can compute multiple operands at once, and hence multiple round keys are computed efficiently.

Separate Encryption Method. The separate encryption method is a speed optimized model. First, we compute all round-key pairs off-line and then simply look-up the round key tables during encryption. In a CUDA machine, memory access is not recommended due to slow PCI transfer speed, but LEA encryption does not use many memory accesses so it shows better performance even with multiple memory accesses than OFM does. In the case of NEON, multiple 128-bit-wise data is accessible at once, so this method shows higher performance gain than its OFM counterpart.

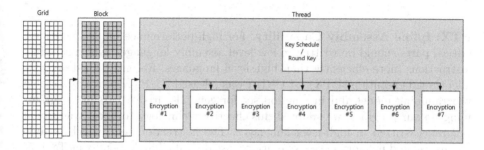

Fig. 1. Thread design in CUDA-LEA.

3.2   CUDA-LEA

In this section, we provide SIMT implementation techniques on the CUDA architecture. We tested and evaluated the performance on a computer with Window 7 operating system, GTX680 GPU, Intel i7-3770 CPU, and 8 GB RAM.

SIMT: Single Instruction Multiple Threads. CUDA consists of lots of blocks and each block is composed of thousands of threads. In previous work [13], the author claimed that one encryption per thread is optimal to utilize GPU but we imposed multiple encryptions on a single thread. To optimize each thread, we should consider limited resources such as registers that can preserve variables and provide fast access. Our target board is the Kepler architecture, which provides 65,535 registers per block. The maximum number of threads in one block is limited to 1,024. This is also a good parameter for thread scheduling because the maximum warp size is 32 and 1,024 is multiple of $32\left(\frac{1,024}{32} = 32\right)$. Finally maximum number of registers in one thread is $\frac{65,535}{1,024} = 64$(63 for general purpose and one for reserved). We designed each thread to exploit the maximum number of registers. Figure 1 shows our LEA programming architecture. We programmed seven encryption functions into one thread to provide functional parallelism. First, one round key-scheduling or look-up table access are conducted. The outputs are directed to seven encryption modules. For this reason, we could save six round key scheduling computations than separate key scheduling in each thread. The impact of the proposed method is described in Table 12. The performance is rated according to encryption per thread (E/T). The performance is significantly improved by increasing the number of factor (E/T) for both with/without memory transfer. In GPU, the performance bottleneck experienced is memory access because the PCIe bandwidth is about $100 \sim 200$ MBps. This is the main shortcoming of GPU but in near future this problem would be resolved because heterogeneous CPU and GPU architectures are being actively studied and this will combine memory architecture of CPU and GPU. For this reason, memory transfer overheads would disappear in near future.

PTX: Inline Assembly Capability. For high-performance implementations, critical parts should be written in low-level assembly languages, which schedule instructions more efficiently than high-level languages. Recently, low-level parallel thread execution (PTX) for CUDA was released [7]. PTX provides a stable programming model and instruction set for general-purpose parallel programming. In our program, we adopted this effective technology to boost traditional programs written in high-level languages. The instruction sets, which include arithmetic and memory access operations, are described in Appendix at Table 5. The main advantage of PTX is that we can use and schedule arithmetic and bit operations manually, thereby removing inefficient instructions. To demonstrate the advantages of PTX, we compared a normal CUDA-C program and an assembly program in Appendix at Table 6. These results show that assembly programming has a higher performance than CUDA-C programming. The compiler cannot follow the programmer's will, and thereby generates inefficient codes. With the aid of the Nsight tool, we can investigate disassemble codes in CUDA programming. In Appendix at Table 7, we show a comparison of some part of LEA operations. This is a simple rotation function, but in CUDA-C language, additional memory access is conducted, which is expensive in CUDA. Even though we explicitly declared the variables as register type, the compiler generated a poor source code. Unlike the CUDA-C source code in PTX, we can use registers rather than memory access to obtain high performance by avoiding expensive memory access.

Hard-Coded Delta. In round-key scheduling, delta variables are used for generating round keys. These variables are public parameters and we can pre-compute them off-line. Since the operations $(ROL_i(\delta[i \bmod 4]), ROL_{i+1}(\delta[i \bmod 4]),$

$ROL_{i+2}(\delta[i \bmod 4])$,and $ROL_{i+3}(\delta[i \bmod 4])$;) always generate constant results, we pre-computed all values listed in Appendix at Table 8 which required 1.536 KBytes of memory. For a GPU with gigabytes of memory, this memory consumption is negligible. The pre-computed delta value is not stored in memory but is explicitly hard-coded in assembly language. This means memory is not accessed but we obtained immediate variables from assembly code.

Coalescing Memory. Global memory access is much slower than kernel local registers. If variables are gathered in a group, they can be dispatched in a single access, called a coalesced memory [18]. To assign seven encryptions into one thread, we first tried to allocate seven 128-bit plaintext struct pointers for the single thread which is described in Fig. 2(a). However, this is not coalesced memory and the performance is highly degraded because the first thread TID0 accesses memory P0_0, P0_1, and P0_2. The next thread TID1 accesses memory by three offsets. This does not satisfy the coalesced memory and performance is about ten times degraded in our experiments. For better performance, the coalescing memory should be satisfied. We allocated a memory structure as shown in Fig. 2(b). In this case, thread can access to memory in grouped way such as grouping (P0_0, P0_1 and P0_2), (P1_0, P1_1 and P1_2) and (P2_0, P2_1 and P2_2) so this satisfies the coalesced memory and the performance is considerably improved than non-coalesced memory access. Our CUDA kernel is described in Table 10, and we assigned each memory pointer to each thread to align memory access properly.

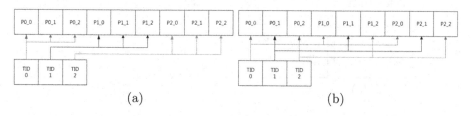

(a)   (b)

Fig. 2. Memory access models for (a) non-coalescing memory (b) coalescing memory

3.3 NEON-LEA

SIMD: Single Instruction Multiple Data. An SIMD machine computes the single operation on multiple data using instructions listed in Appendix at Table 9. In the NEON implementation, we also tested both versions, OFM and SEM. To conduct the single operation on multiple data, we grouped four 32-bit plaintext having the same index because NEON provides quad-register supporting 128-bit wise operations and four 32-bit word can fit into the quad-registers. For OFM, we assigned each 4-quad-register for delta, round key, message and temporary, respectively. In the case of SEM, we do not need to maintain delta variables so we can use the remaining registers as temporary registers or storage for preserving round keys or plaintext. In Fig. 3, we show the implementation structure. For the SIMD architecture, we assigned the same index of four secret keys into quad-registers to compute the single operation with multiple data. After key scheduling, the round keys are generated from secret keys. These values are inputted into the next encryption process. Plaintexts also have the same index and these are allocated into the quad-register to compute multiple operations. In the case of SEM, round keys are pre-computed and then stored into memory and later simply loaded from the memory rather than straight-forward computations. Furthermore, multiple data are efficiently accessed using multiple memory accesses. SEM does not need to preserve delta variables in registers so we can exploit these registers as temporal registers to load, loading more keys or plaintext variables. The impact of register usages is analyzed in the evaluation section.

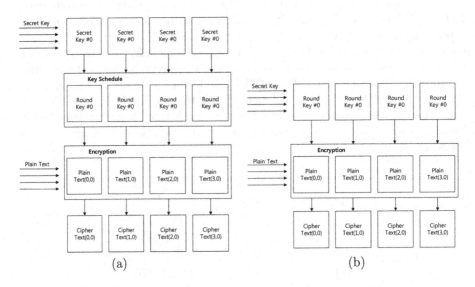

Fig. 3. Design of NEON-LEA for (a) OFM, (b) SEM.

Interleaving Delta Processing. Interleaving delta processing is derived from the characteristics of bits in constant delta variables. As we can see in Appendix at Table 11, there are four constants listed in binary representation for 128-bit encryption. In the key scheduling process, the delta variable is firstly rotated to the right or left and the results are used for round key generations. In ARM processors, the rotation instruction can be simply used to compute a single rotation instruction. Unlike the ARM processor, NEON (SIMD) does not provide rotation function so we should compute two shift instructions and one exclusive-or operation. From our observation, the delta variable has many zero bits that do not generate carry or borrow. We listed all cases that only need to compute one shift operation in Table 11, removing the instruction that does not contribute to final results. In Appendix at Table 13(a), we show one example which is the second round of key scheduling. The constant variable (0x44626b02) is left-shifted by one, two, three and four. In this case, the binary representation of variable is 0b0100, so we can remove the first, third and fourth operations which are Step 2, 12 and 17 respectively.

Elimination of Interdependency. The NEON performance is highly influenced by interdependency among instructions. If the previous instruction contributes to one register, the next instruction should avoid the register pipelining the instructions. If each instruction has interdependency, the next instruction should wait until the previous instruction is completed. In Table 13(b), we show program codes of normal and pipelined implementations. In a normal case, quad-register q8 and q1 is used in Step 1, 2 and this is also used in the subsequent Step 3, so the program is not pipelined due to interdependency of each Step. In the case of a pipelined implementation, we re-ordered all instructions, so there is no interdependency between previous and subsequent instructions. In Step 1 to 3, registers are used in this order (q8, q10, q4), (q1, q11, q5), and (q2, q13, q6). No register is used consecutively and instructions are pipelined.

4 Results

4.1 CUDA-LEA

In this section, we evaluate the performance of the CUDA implementations. The difficulty of the evaluation of GPU is that all developers' environments are different. For this reason, we should generalize our performance in an objective way. First, we compared our results with the LEA results on computers. Then we compared our results to previous GPU-based block and stream cipher implementations. Our target computer was equipped with GTX680, Intel i7-3770 CPU, and 8 GB RAM and the program was executed on Windows 7 operating system, visual studio 2012, and CUDA ver 5.5. The execution time is measured by CUDA event API in milliseconds precision, because host time-stamp function uses the explicit synchronization barrier `cudaDeviceSynchronize()` to block CPU execution and this degrades performance significantly by stalling GPU pipeline. We tested only memory transfer overheads and it was found to reach to 2.79 GBps without any other computations. This means that the GPU performance is limited to less than under 2.79 GBps. In Table 1, proposed GPU implementation results are summarized. As mentioned in [14], GPU is highly influenced by the number of block and thread. We tested various combinations and found that the largest number of blocks showed the highest performance up to 2.5, and 17.352 GBps with, without memory transfer, respectively.

Comparison with CPU Implementations. Table 2 shows the performance over CPU and its best result is 6.133 GBps when we assume that multiple cores

Table 1. CUDA-LEA results on various combinations of (block/thread).

Method	512/1024	256/1024	128/1024	64/1024
OFM				
Tp (GBps) (w/m)	2.434	2.426	2.379	2.406
Tp (GBps) (w/o m)	16.145	15.965	15.499	15.215
SEM				
Tp (GBps) (w/m)	**2.505**	2.492	2.450	2.459
Tp (GBps) (w/o m)	**17.352**	17.109	16.738	16.256

are fully used. To estimate the throughput, we first compute the throughput and the multiplied number of thread in each model. Particularly, the new Intel processor provides hyper-threading, so in this case, we multiplied the working threads by two. For example, in the case of Intel Core i7 2600K, we calculated throughput using the following equation, $6.133\,\text{GBps} = 6,133,333,333 = \frac{2,300,000,000 \times 12}{4.5}$ ($\frac{frequency \times thread}{cycles/bytes}$). Even though the GPU performance with memory transfer is lower than CPU due to slow PCI speed, GPU implementation without memory transfer shows 2.83 times faster. When we consider that the memory transfer would be removed by adopting heterogeneous computing model in near future, comparing CPU results with GPU implementations without memory transfer is meaningful.

Table 2. Previous LEA SEM implementations on CPU [6], c/b: cycle/byte, T: Throughput, '*' symbol means the Intel hyper-threading technology which delivers two processing threads per physical core. Highly threaded applications can get more work done in parallel, completing tasks sooner [9].

Platform	Speed (c/b)	T (GBps)	Mode
Intel Core 2 Quad Q6600 2.4GHz 4-core	9.29	1.033	Normal
Intel Core i5-2500 3.3GHz 4-core	9.29	1.421	Normal
AMD K10 Phenom II X4 965 3.4GHz 4-core	8.85	1.537	Normal
AMD Opteron 6176SE 2.3GHz 12-core	8.85	3.119	Normal
Intel Core 2 Quad Q6600 2.4GHz 4-core	4.51	2.129	SIMD
Intel Core i7 860 2.8GHz 4-core*	4.19	2.673	SIMD
AMD opteron 6176SE 2.3GHz 12-core	4.50	6.133	SIMD

Comparison with CUDA Implementations. We evaluated LEA implementations on GTX680 and the previous best result obtained using Salsa20/12 stream cipher on GTX590. To evaluate our performance fairly, we should scale both factors including target cipher and graphic cards. Recently, many reports argue that performance of GTX680 (Kepler) is at par with GTX580 (Fermi)

[19–21] which means the number of cores does not directly contribute to the performance. For this reason, we consider that GTX590 and GTX680 have the same performance in the CUDA computing model. In case of cipher, the previous result draws performance enhancement in stream cipher Salsa20/12 [14]. This cipher consists of 12 rounds and each round has 16 ARX (addition, rotation, and exclusive-or) operations and the output is 64-byte. In case of LEA, we should conduct the key scheduling and encryption. Each operation consists of 24 rounds and each round of key generation and encryption has four ARX operations, and the output is 16-byte. If we consider that basic instructions such as addition, rotation, and exclusive-or have same overheads, the throughput of previous work is $\frac{1}{9} = \frac{64}{12 \times 16 \times 3}$ and ours is $\frac{1}{36} = \frac{16}{24 \times 8 \times 3}$. For fair comparison, we multiplied our throughput by 4 and our works are scaled to 69.4 GBps and this is 37.4 % higher performance than previous results [14]. However, our implementation uses one trick which omits 6 key generation processes, so we scaled again by multiplying $\frac{8}{14}$ to scaled result. Finally, the result is 39.66 GBps, and this is 8.7 % lower performance than [14]. As we know, LEA and Salsa 20/12 is different algorithms so it is hard to mention which GPU implementation is faster than others so we just provided comparison results in straight-forward fashion. When it comes to other results [10–13], the scaled results are 5.7, 24, 1.64 and 9.3 GBps and these results are lagging behind our results. The second concern is slow memory transfer. When we measure our memory transfer, without any operations the performance is 2.8 GBps. This means our PCI-E memory transfer is limited and memory transfer highly depends on development environments, so we are not seriously concerned on memory transfer factor in this paper.

4.2 NEON-LEA

Comparison with ARM Implementations. For performance evaluation, we selected the target device as Cortex-A9 board operated at 1.7 GHz and programmed source code using the NDK android library. The performance is measured in system time function. We tested various NEON implementations and the results are listed in Table 4. First, OFM is implemented in normal and interleaving delta processing. The Interleaving delta processing method shows 13.4 % enhancement than the normal computation. There are no reference OFM results reported but key scheduling has a similar complexity of encryption when we assume that key scheduling has the same overheads of encryption roughly. Compared to the expected results, NEON-based OFM is improved by 25.5 %. In case of SEM, we tried to load 24- or 16-byte round keys at once because in LEA-128 three round keys are duplicated and 16-byte access is reasonable. However, to reduce interdependency we tested model to load 24-byte and removed all interdependency among round keys. Interestingly, the 24-byte pipeline method shows a slower result than the 16-byte model because memory access imposes more overheads than benefits from full pipelined code. For this reason, 16-byte round key access pipeline method shows the fastest results and performance enhancement is up-to 49.85 % than the previous result. We further implemented encryption

Table 3. Comparison of previous CUDA implementations, Tp: Throughput, S-Tp: Scaled-Tp

	D. Stefan [11]	S. Neves [12]	A. Khalid [14]	K. Iwai [13]	N. Nishikawa	This work
Algorithm	Salsa20/12	Salsa20/12	Salsa20/12	AES	AES	LEA
Block/stream	Stream	Stream	Stream	Block	Block	Block
Device	GTX 295	GTX260	GTX590	GTX285	GTX285	GTX680
Release	08/01/2009	16/06/2008	24/03/2011	15/01/2009	15/01/2009	22/3/2012
Compute capability	1.3	1.2	2.0	1.3	1.3	3.0
Cores	480	192	512	240	240	1,536
Shader freq (MHz)	1,242	1,350	1,215	1,470	1,470	1,006
Threads block	256	256	320	512	512	1,024
Program language	C	C	C	C	C	Assembly
Tp (GBps) (w/m)	-	1.3	2.8	-	2.8	2.5
Tp (GBps) (w/o m)	5.3	9	43.44	0.78	4.4	17.35
S-Tp (GBps) (w/o m)	5.7	24	43.44	1.64	9.3	69.4/39.7

Table 4. Comparison of LEA Implementations on ARM/NEON Instructions, c/b: cycle/byte, Gbps: Giga bit per second

Methods	Speed (c/b)	T (Gbps)	Instruction
OFM			
Previous works [6]	**40.12**	**0.338**	ARM
Normal	39.84	0.341	NEON
Interleaving delta processing	**34.53**	**0.394**	NEON
SEM			
Previous works [6]	**20.06**	**0.678**	ARM
Pre-compute (24-byte)	31.34	0.434	NEON
Pre-compute (24-byte)+Pipeline	11.95	1.138	NEON
Pre-compute (16-byte)	15.93	0.853	NEON
Pre-compute (16-byte)+Pipeline	**10.06**	**1.351**	NEON
Double Pre-compute (16-byte)	15.93	0.854	NEON

Table 5. The PTX instruction set used in this paper.

Operation	Syntax
add	Add two values
xor	Bitwise exclusive-OR
shl	Shift bits left, zero-fill on right
shr	Shift bits right, sign or zero fill on left
mov	Set a register variable with the value of another register register variable or an immediate value
ld	Load a register variable from an addressable state space variable
st	Store a register variable to an addressable state space variable

Table 6. Comparison of PTX and CUDA-C implementations with 65536-bit messages.

No. block	No. thread	PTX (ms)	CUDA-C (ms)	Ratio ($\frac{PTX}{CUDA-C}$)
1	512	0.064	0.29	0.22
2	256	0.063	0.27	0.23
4	128	0.064	0.24	0.27
8	64	0.066	0.23	0.29
16	32	0.063	0.23	0.28

Table 7. Comparison of program codes in CUDA-C and PTX (temp[1] = ROL(delta[0], 1)).

CUDA-C	PTX
1. ld.local.u32 %r69, [$delta\_128 + 4$];	1. shl.b32 t1, d0, 1;
2. shr.u32 %r70, %r69, 31;	2. shr.b32 t2, d0, 31;
3. ld.local.u32 %r71, [$delta\_128 + 4$];	3. xor.b32 t3, t2, t1;
4. shl.b32 %r72, %r71, 1;	
5. add.u32 %r73, %r70, %r72;	
6. st.local.u32 [$temp\_64 + 4$], %r73;	

with double plaintext size (128 × 8) and 16-byte pre-computation by exploiting remaining registers. However, this result shows similar throughput of single plaintext size (128 × 4) because performance highly depends on round key access pattern rather than other factors (Table 3).

Comparison with NEON Implementations. In NEON crypto [2], Salsa-20/12 is computed within 2.75 cycles/byte. After scaling these results to compare with LEA, the performance is 11 cycles/byte following previous assumptions in GPU evaluation. Compared to our best results 10.06 cycle/byte, our results are faster than previous Salsa20/12 NEON results by 8.54 %. As we

Table 8. Hard coded delta variables.

Hard coded delta
Oxc3efe9db, Ox87dfd3b7, OxOfbfa76f, Ox1f7f4ede, Ox88c4d604,
Ox1189ac09, Ox23135812, Ox4626b024, Oxe789f229, Oxcf13e453,
Ox9e27c8a7, Ox3c4f914f, Oxc6f98763, Ox8df30ec7, Ox1be61d8f,
Ox37cc3b1e, Ox3efe9dbc, Ox7dfd3b78, Oxfbfa76f0, Oxf7f4ede1,
Ox8c4d6048, Ox189ac091, Ox31358122, Ox626b0244, Ox789f229e,
Oxf13e453c, Oxe27c8a79, Oxc4f914f3, Ox6f98763c, Oxdf30ec78,
Oxbe61d8f1, Ox7cc3b1e3, Oxefe9dbc3, Oxdfd3b787, Oxbfa76f0f,
Ox7f4ede1f, Oxc4d60488, Ox89ac0911, Ox13581223, Ox26b02446,
Ox89f229e7, Ox13e453cf, Ox27c8a79e, Ox4f914f3c, Oxf98763c6,
Oxf30ec78d, Oxe61d8f1b, Oxcc3b1e37, Oxfe9dbc3e, Oxfd3b787d,
Oxfa76f0fb, Oxf4ede1f7, Ox4d60488c, Ox9ac09118, Ox35812231,
Ox6b024462, Ox9f229e78, Ox3e453cf1, Ox7c8a79e2, Oxf914f3c4,
Ox98763c6f, Ox30ec78df, Ox61d8f1be, Oxc3b1e37c, Oxe9dbc3ef,
Oxd3b787df, Oxa76f0fbf, Ox4ede1f7f, Oxd60488c4, Oxac091189,
Ox58122313, Oxb0244626, Oxf229e789, Oxe453cf13, Oxc8a79e27,
Ox914f3c4f, Ox8763c6f9, Ox0ec78df3, Ox1d8f1be6, Ox3b1e37cc,
Ox9dbc3efe, Ox3b787dfd, Ox76f0fbfa, Oxede1f7f4, Ox60488c4d,
Oxc091189a, Ox81223135, Ox0244626b, Ox229e789f, Ox453cf13e,
Ox8a79e27c, Ox14f3c4f9, Ox763c6f98, Oxec78df30, Oxd8f1be61,
Oxb1e37cc3

Table 9. The NEON instruction set used in this paper.

Operation	Syntax
vadd	Adds the vector-wise values in the operand registers
veor	Performs bitwise logical operations between two registers
vshl	Left shift them by an immediate value
vsri	Right shifts them by an immediate value, and inserts the results in the destination vector
vldmia	Load multiple register variables from an addressable state space variables
vstmia	Store multiple register variables to an addressable state space variables

mentioned before, we only provide comparison results which does not mean that our implementation is faster than previous results [2] due to different architectures in each algorithm.

Table 10. Coalescing memory call in CUDA kernel, mi_j means 32-bit plain text where 'i' is message number and 'j' is index in a message.

```
const int idx = (blockIdx.x * blockDim.x) + threadIdx.x;
LEA_encrypt( &(m0_0[idx]), &(m0_1[idx]), &(m0_2[idx]), &(m0_3[idx]),
    &(m1_0[idx]), &(m1_1[idx]), &(m1_2[idx]), &(m1_3[idx]),
    &(m2_0[idx]), &(m2_1[idx]), &(m2_2[idx]), &(m2_3[idx]),
    &(m3_0[idx]), &(m3_1[idx]), &(m3_2[idx]), &(m3_3[idx]),
    &(m4_0[idx]), &(m4_1[idx]), &(m4_2[idx]), &(m4_3[idx]),
    &(m5_0[idx]), &(m5_1[idx]), &(m5_2[idx]), &(m5_3[idx]),
    &(m6_0[idx]), &(m6_1[idx]), &(m6_2[idx]), &(m6_3[idx]), &(key[0]));
```

Table 11. Interleaving delta processing method

Hexadecimal	Interleaving index
0xc3efe9db	$29, 28, 27, 26, 20, 12, 10, 9, 5, 3$
0x44626b02	$31, 29, 28, 27, 25, 24, 23, 20, 19, 18, 16, 15, 12, 10, 7, 6, 5, 4, 3, 2, 0$
0x79e27c8a	$31, 26, 25, 20, 19, 18, 16, 15, 9, 8, 6, 5, 4, 2, 0$
0x78df30ec	$31, 26, 25, 24, 21, 15, 14, 11, 10, 9, 8, 4, 1, 0$

Table 12. Performance comparison of encryption per thread, GBps: Giga byte per second, w/m: with memory transfer, w/o m: without memory transfer.

Encryption/thread	1	2	3	4	5	6	7
Throughput (GBps) (w/m)	2.16	2.29	2.34	2.37	2.39	2.42	2.43
Throughput (GBps) (w/o m)	9.36	12.94	14.52	15.16	15.03	15.82	16.14

Table 13. First and second tables denote (a) and (b), respectively, (a) Interleaving delta processing, in case of computing the second round of constant(0x44626b02), (b) Normal and pipelined program codes for one round of encryption in NEON instructions.

Normal	Interleaving delta
1. vshl.i32 q4, q1, #1	1. vshl.i32 q4, q1, #1
2. vsri.32 q4, q1, #31	2. pass
3. vadd.i32 q12,q4, q12	3. vadd.i32 q12,q4, q12
4. vshl.i32 q4, q12, #1	4. vshl.i32 q4, q12, #1
5. vsri.32 q4, q12, #31	5. vsri.32 q4, q12, #31
6. vshl.i32 q5, q1, #2	6. vshl.i32 q7, q1, #2
7. vsri.32 q5, q1, #30	7. vsri.32 q7, q1, #30
8. vadd.i32 q13,q5, q13	8. vadd.i32 q13,q7, q13
9. vshl.i32 q5, q13, #3	9. vshl.i32 q5, q13, #3
10. vsri.32 q5, q13, #29	10. vsri.32 q5, q13, #29
11. vshl.i32 q6, q1, #3	11. vshl.i32 q6, q7, #1
12. vsri.32 q6, q1, #29	12. pass
13. vadd.i32 q14,q6,q14	13. vadd.i32 q14,q6,q14
14. vshl.i32 q6, q14, #6	14. vshl.i32 q6, q14, #6
15. vsri.32 q6, q14, #26	15. vsri.32 q6, q14, #26
16. vshl.i32 q7, q1, #4	16. vshl.i32 q7, q7, #2
17. vsri.32 q7, q1, #28	17. pass
18. vadd.i32 q15,q7,q15	18. vadd.i32 q15,q7,q15
19. vshl.i32 q7, q15, #11	19. vshl.i32 q7, q15, #11
20. vsri.32 q7, q15, #21	20. vsri.32 q7, q15, #21
Normal	Pipeline
1. veor q8, q10, q4	1. veor q8, q10, q4
2. veor q1, q11, q5	2. veor q1, q11, q5
3. vadd.i32 q8,q8,q1	3. veor q2, q13, q6
4. vshl.i32 q1, q8, #9	4. veor q9, q12, q5
5. vsri.32 q1, q8, #23	5. veor q3, q15, q7
6. veor q9, q12, q5	6. veor q0, q14, q6
7. veor q2, q13, q6	7. vadd.i32 q8,q8,q1
8. vadd.i32 q9,q9,q2	8. vadd.i32 q9,q9,q2
9. vshl.i32 q2, q9, #27	9. vadd.i32 q0,q0,q3
10. vsri.32 q2, q9, #5	10. vshl.i32 q1, q8, #9
11. veor q0, q14, q6	11. vshl.i32 q2, q9, #27
12. veor q3, q15, q7	12. vshl.i32 q3, q0, #29
13. vadd.i32 q0,q0,q3	13. vsri.32 q1, q8, #23
14. vshl.i32 q3, q0, #29	14. vsri.32 q2, q9, #5
15. vsri.32 q3, q0, #3	15. vsri.32 q3, q0, #3

5   Conclusion

In this paper, we presented parallel implementation methods of LEA on representative SIMT and SIMD architectures such as CUDA and NEON. We achieved performance enhancement to 17.352 GBps (bytes per second) without memory transfer, which is 2.83 times faster than the CPU counterparts. In case of NEON, we achieved 10.06 cycle/byte and 0.84 Gbps (bits per second) which improved the traditional ARM results by 49.85 %.

Appendix

Algorithm 1. Key Schedule with a 128-bit Key.

Input: master key K, constants δ.
Output: round key RK.
1. $T[0] = K[0]$, $T[1] = K[1]$, $T[2] = K[2]$, $T[3] = K[3]$.
2. for $i \leftarrow 0$ to 23
3. $T[0] \leftarrow ROL_1(T[0] \boxplus ROL_i(\delta[i \bmod 4]))$
4. $T[1] \leftarrow ROL_3(T[1] \boxplus ROL_{i+1}(\delta[i \bmod 4]))$
5. $T[2] \leftarrow ROL_6(T[2] \boxplus ROL_{i+2}(\delta[i \bmod 4]))$
6. $T[3] \leftarrow ROL_{11}(T[3] \boxplus ROL_{i+3}(\delta[i \bmod 4]))$
7. $RK_i \leftarrow (T[0], T[1], T[2], T[1], T[3], T[1])$
8. end for
9. return RK

Algorithm 2. Encryption with a 128-bit Key.

Input: plaintext P, round key RK.
Output: ciphertext C
1. $X_0[0] = P[0]$, $X_0[1] = P[1]$, $X_0[2] = P[2]$, $X_0[3] = P[3]$.
2. for $i \leftarrow 0$ to 23
3. $X_{i+1}[0] \leftarrow ROL_9(X_i[0] \oplus RK_i[0]) \boxplus (X_i[1] \oplus RK_i[1])$
4. $X_{i+1}[1] \leftarrow ROR_5(X_i[1] \oplus RK_i[2]) \boxplus (X_i[2] \oplus RK_i[3])$
5. $X_{i+1}[2] \leftarrow ROR_3(X_i[2] \oplus RK_i[4]) \boxplus (X_i[3] \oplus RK_i[5])$
6. $X_{i+1}[3] \leftarrow X_i[0]$
7. end for
8. $C[0] = X_{24}[0]$, $C[1] = X_{24}[1]$, $C[2] = X_{24}[2]$, $C[3] = X_{24}[3]$.
9. return C

Algorithm 3. On the Fly Mode, 128-bit Key

Input: master key K, constants δ, plaintext P.
Output: ciphertext C.

1. $T[0] = K[0]$, $T[1] = K[1]$, $T[2] = K[2]$, $T[3] = K[3]$.
2. $X_0[0] = P[0]$, $X_0[1] = P[1]$, $X_0[2] = P[2]$, $X_0[3] = P[3]$.
2.   for $i \leftarrow 0$ to 23
4. $T[0] \leftarrow ROL_1(T[0] \boxplus ROL_i(\delta[i \bmod 4))$
5. $T[1] \leftarrow ROL_3(T[1] \boxplus ROL_{i+1}(\delta[i \bmod 4))$
6. $T[2] \leftarrow ROL_6(T[2] \boxplus ROL_{i+2}(\delta[i \bmod 4))$
7. $T[3] \leftarrow ROL_{11}(T[3] \boxplus ROL_{i+3}(\delta[i \bmod 4))$
8. $X_{i+1}[0] \leftarrow ROL_9(X_i[0] \oplus T[0]) \boxplus (X_i[1] \oplus T[1])$
9. $X_{i+1}[1] \leftarrow ROR_5(X_i[1] \oplus T[2]) \boxplus (X_i[2] \oplus T[1])$
10. $X_{i+1}[2] \leftarrow ROR_3(X_i[2] \oplus T[3]) \boxplus (X_i[3] \oplus T[1])$
11. $X_{i+1}[3] \leftarrow X_i[0]$
12.   end for
13. $C[0] = X_{24}[0]$, $C[1] = X_{24}[1]$, $C[2] = X_{24}[2]$, $C[3] = X_{24}[3]$.
14.   return C

Algorithm 4. Separate Encryption Mode, 128-bit Key

Input: master key K, constants δ, plaintext P.
Intermediate: round key RK.
Output: ciphertext C.

1. $T[0] = K[0]$, $T[1] = K[1]$, $T[2] = K[2]$, $T[3] = K[3]$.
2.   for $i \leftarrow 0$ to 23
3. $T[0] \leftarrow ROL_1(T[0] \boxplus ROL_i(\delta[i \bmod 4))$
4. $T[1] \leftarrow ROL_3(T[1] \boxplus ROL_{i+1}(\delta[i \bmod 4))$
5. $T[2] \leftarrow ROL_6(T[2] \boxplus ROL_{i+2}(\delta[i \bmod 4))$
6. $T[3] \leftarrow ROL_{11}(T[3] \boxplus ROL_{i+3}(\delta[i \bmod 4))$
7. $RK_i \leftarrow (T[0], T[1], T[2], T[1], T[3], T[1])$
8.   end for
9. $X_0[0] = P[0]$, $X_0[1] = P[1]$, $X_0[2] = P[2]$, $X_0[3] = P[3]$.
10.   for $i \leftarrow 0$ to 23
11. $X_{i+1}[0] \leftarrow ROL_9(X_i[0] \oplus RK_i[0]) \boxplus (X_i[1] \oplus RK_i[1])$
12. $X_{i+1}[1] \leftarrow ROR_5(X_i[1] \oplus RK_i[2]) \boxplus (X_i[2] \oplus RK_i[3])$
13. $X_{i+1}[2] \leftarrow ROR_3(X_i[2] \oplus RK_i[4]) \boxplus (X_i[3] \oplus RK_i[5])$
14. $X_{i+1}[3] \leftarrow X_i[0]$
15.   end for
16. $C[0] = X_{24}[0]$, $C[1] = X_{24}[1]$, $C[2] = X_{24}[2]$, $C[3] = X_{24}[3]$.
17.   return C

References

1. NEON. http://www.arm.com/products/processors/technologies/neon.php. Accessed 2013
2. Bernstein, D.J., Schwabe, P.: NEON crypto. In: Prouff, E., Schaumont, P. (eds.) CHES 2012. LNCS, vol. 7428, pp. 320–339. Springer, Heidelberg (2012)
3. Sánchez, A.H., Rodríguez-Henríquez, F.: NEON implementation of an attribute-based encryption scheme. In: Jacobson, M., Locasto, M., Mohassel, P., Safavi-Naini, R. (eds.) ACNS 2013. LNCS, vol. 7954, pp. 322–338. Springer, Heidelberg (2013)
4. Nvidia: CUDA C programming guide (2012)
5. Nvidia: CUDA best practices guide (2012)
6. Hong, D., Lee, J.-K., Kim, D.-C., Kwon, D., Ryu, K.H., Lee, D.-G.: LEA: a 128-bit block cipher for fast encryption on common processors. In: Kim, Y., Lee, H., Perrig, A. (eds.) WISA 2013. LNCS, vol. 8267, pp. 1–24. Springer, Heidelberg (2014)
7. Nvidia: Parallel thread execution ISA version 3.1. http://docs.nvidia.com/cuda/pdf/ptx_isa_3.1.pdf. Accessed 2013
8. Scott, M., Szczechowiak, P.: Optimizing multiprecision multiplication for public key cryptography. IACR Cryptology ePrint Archive 2007:299 (2007)
9. Intel Corporation. http://ark.intel.com/. Accessed 2013
10. Iwai, K., Kurokawa, T., Nisikawa, N.: AES encryption implementation on CUDA GPU and its analysis. In: 2010 First International Conference on Networking and Computing (ICNC), pp. 209–214. IEEE (2010)
11. Stefan, D.: Analysis and Implementation of eSTREAM and SHA-3 Cryptographic Algorithms. Ph.D. dissertation, COOPER UNION (2011)
12. Neves, S., Arajo, F.: Cryptography in GPUs. Ph.D. dissertation, Masters thesis, Universidade de Coimbra, Coimbra (2009)
13. Iwai, K., Nishikawa, N., Kurokawa, T.: Acceleration of AES encryption on CUDA GPU. Int. J. Netw. Comput. 2(1), 131 (2012)
14. Khalid, A., Paul, G., Chattopadhyay, A.: New speed records for Salsa20 stream cipher using an autotuning framework on GPUs. In: Youssef, A., Nitaj, A., Hassanien, A.E. (eds.) AFRICACRYPT 2013. LNCS, vol. 7918, pp. 189–207. Springer, Heidelberg (2013)
15. Liu, G., An, H., Han, W., Xu, G., Yao, P., Xu, M., Hao, X., Wang, Y.: A program behavior study of block cryptography algorithms on GPGPU. In: Fourth International Conference on Frontier of Computer Science and Technology, 2009 FCST'09, pp. 33–39. IEEE (2009)
16. Di Biagio, A., Barenghi, A., Agosta, G., Pelosi, G.: Design of a parallel AES for graphics hardware using the CUDA framework. In: IEEE International Symposium on Parallel & Distributed Processing, 2009. IPDPS 2009, pp. 1–8. IEEE (2009)
17. Bernstein, D.J., Chen, H.-C., Cheng, C.-M., Lange, T., Niederhagen, R., Schwabe, P., Yang, B.-Y.: Usable assembly language for GPUs: a success story. IACR Cryptology ePrint Archive 2012:137 (2012)
18. Cook, S.: CUDA Programming: A Developer's Guide to Parallel Computing with GPUs. Newnes, Boston (2012)
19. Benchmarking the new Kepler (GTX 680). http://blog.accelereyes.com/blog/2012/04/26/benchmarking-kepler-gtx-680/. Accessed 2013
20. GeForce GTX 680 2 GB review: Kepler sends Tahiti on vacation. http://www.tomshardware.com/reviews/geforce-gtx-680-review-benchmark,3161-15.html. Accessed 2013

21. GPGPU face-off: K20 vs 7970 vs GTX680 vs M2050 vs GTX580. http://wili.cc/blog/gpgpu-faceoff.html. Accessed 2013
22. Manavski, S.A.: CUDA compatible GPU as an efficient hardware accelerator for AES cryptography. In: IEEE International Conference on Signal Processing and Communications, 2007, ICSPC 2007, pp. 65–68. IEEE (2007)
23. Holzer-Graf, S., Krinninger, T., Pernull, M., Schläffer, M., Schwabe, P., Seywald, D., Wieser, W.: Efficient vector implementations of AES-based designs: a case study and new implemenations for Grøstl. In: Dawson, E. (ed.) CT-RSA 2013. LNCS, vol. 7779, pp. 145–161. Springer, Heidelberg (2013)

Primitives for Cryptography

Invertible Polynomial Representation
for Private Set Operations

Jung Hee Cheon$^{(\boxtimes)}$, Hyunsook Hong, and Hyung Tae Lee

CHRI and Department of Mathematical Sciences, Seoul National University,
1 Gwanak-ro, Gwanak-gu, Seoul 151-747, Korea
{jhcheon,hongsuk07,htsm1138}@snu.ac.kr

Abstract. In many private set operations, a set is represented by a polynomial over a ring $\mathbb{Z}_\sigma$ for a composite integer σ, where $\mathbb{Z}_\sigma$ is the message space of some additive homomorphic encryption. While it is useful for implementing set operations with polynomial additions and multiplications, it has a limitation that it is hard to recover a set from a polynomial due to the hardness of polynomial factorization over $\mathbb{Z}_\sigma$.

We propose a new representation of a set by a polynomial over $\mathbb{Z}_\sigma$, in which σ is a composite integer with known factorization but a corresponding set can be efficiently recovered from a polynomial except negligible probability. Since $\mathbb{Z}_\sigma[x]$ is not a unique factorization domain, a polynomial may be written as a product of linear factors in several ways. To exclude irrelevant linear factors, we introduce a special encoding function which supports early abort strategy. Our representation can be efficiently inverted by computing all the linear factors of a polynomial in $\mathbb{Z}_\sigma[x]$ whose roots locate in the image of the encoding function.

As an application of our representation, we obtain a constant-round private set union protocol. Our construction improves the complexity than the previous without honest majority.

Keywords: Polynomial representation · Polynomial factorization · Root finding · Privacy-preserving set union

1 Introduction

Privacy-preserving set operations (PPSO) are to compute set operations of participants' dataset without revealing any information other than the result. There have been many proposals to construct PPSO protocols with various techniques such as general MPC [1,9], polynomial representations [7,8,10,12,18], pseudorandom functions [11], and blind RSA signatures [4,5]. While the last two techniques are hard to be generalized into multi-party protocols, polynomial representations combining with additive homomorphic encryption (AHE) schemes enable us to have multi-party PPSO protocols for various operations including set intersection [8,12,18], (over-)threshold set union [12], element reduction [12]

This work includes some part of the third author's PhD thesis [14].

© Springer International Publishing Switzerland 2014
H.-S. Lee and D.-G. Han (Eds.): ICISC 2013, LNCS 8565, pp. 277–292, 2014.
DOI: 10.1007/978-3-319-12160-4_17

and so on. Among these constructions, set intersection protocols run in constant rounds, but others run in linear of the number of participants.

Let us focus on privacy-preserving set union protocols. There are two obstacles to construct constant round privacy-preserving multi-party set union protocols based on the polynomial representation with AHE schemes. First, in the polynomial representation set union corresponds to polynomial multiplication, which is not supported by an AHE scheme in constant rounds. Second, to recover the union set from the resulting polynomial, we need a root finding algorithm of a polynomial over $\mathbb{Z}_\sigma$, where $\mathbb{Z}_\sigma$ is the message space of the AHE scheme.

Recently, Seo et al. [19] proposed a constant round set union protocol based on a novel approach in which a set is represented as a rational function using the reversed Laurent series. In their protocol, each participant takes part in the protocol with a rational function whose poles consist of the elements of his set and at the end of the protocol he obtains a rational function whose poles correspond to the set union. Then each participant recovers the denominator of the rational function using the extended Euclidean algorithm and finds the roots of the denominator. Since each rational function is summed up to the resulting function after encrypted under an AHE scheme, the first obstacle is easily overcome.

However, a root finding is still problematic on the message space $\mathbb{Z}_\sigma$ of the AHE schemes. Since the message space has unknown order [16] or is not a unique factorization domain (UFD) [2,15,17] in the current *efficient* AHE schemes, there is no proper polynomial factorization or root finding algorithm working on the message space. To avoid this obstacle, the authors in [19] utilized a secret sharing scheme. However, it requires computational and communicational costs heavier than the previous and requires an honest majority for security since their protocol exploits a secret sharing scheme to support privacy-preserving multiplications in constant rounds.

Our Contribution. Let $\sigma = \prod_{j=1}^{\bar{\ell}} q_j$ for distinct primes q_j, which is larger than the size of the universe of set elements. We propose a new representation of a set by a polynomial over $\mathbb{Z}_\sigma$ in which a corresponding set can be efficiently recovered from a polynomial except negligible probability when the factorization of σ is given.

For a given polynomial $f(x) = \prod_{i=1}^{d}(x - s_i) \in \mathbb{Z}_\sigma[x]$, if the factorization of σ is given, one can obtain all roots of f in $\mathbb{Z}_{q_j}$ for each j by exploiting a polynomial factorization algorithm over a finite field $\mathbb{Z}_{q_j}$ [22]. By reassembling the roots of f in $\mathbb{Z}_\sigma$ using the Chinese Remainder Theorem (CRT), we can obtain all the candidates. However, the number of candidates amounts to d^ℓ, which is exponential in the size of the universe.

We introduce a special encoding function ι to exclude irrelevant candidates efficiently. For a polynomial $f = \prod_{i=1}^{d}(x - \iota(s_i)) \in \mathbb{Z}_\sigma[x]$, our encoding function aborts most irrelevant candidates without d^ℓ CRT computations, by giving a certain relation among roots of f in $\mathbb{Z}_{q_j}[x]$ and roots of f in $\mathbb{Z}_{q_{j+1}}[x]$. As a

Table 1. Comparison with previous set-union protocols

HBC	Rounds	Communication cost	Computational cost	# of honest party
[12]	$O(n)$	$O(n^3 k \tau_N)$	$O(n^4 k^2 \tau_N \rho_N)$	≥ 1
[8]	$O(n)$	$O(n^2 k \tau_N)$	$O(n^2 k^2 \tau_N \rho_N)$	≥ 1
[19]	$O(1)$	$O(n^4 k^2 \tau_{p'})$	$O(n^5 k^2 \rho_{p'})$	$\geq n/2$
Ours	$O(1)$	$O(n^3 k \tau_N)$	$O(n^3 k^2 \tau_N \rho_N)$	≥ 1
Malicious	Rounds	Communication cost	Computational cost	# of honest party
[8]	$O(n)$	$O((n^2 k^2 + n^3 k)\tau_N)$	$O(n^2 k^2 \tau_N \rho_N)$	≥ 1
[19]	$O(1)$	$O(n^4 k^2 \tau_p)$	$O(n^5 k^2 \tau_p \rho_p)$	$\geq n/2$
Ours	$O(1)$	$O(n^3 k^2 \tau_N)$	$O(n^3 k^2 \tau_N \rho_N)$	≥ 1

n: the number of participants, k: the maximum size of sets

$\tau_N, \tau_{p'}, \tau_p$: the size of modulus N for Paillier encryption scheme or NS encryption scheme, the size p' of representing domain, the order p of a cyclic group for Pedersen commitment scheme, respectively

$\rho_N, \rho_{p'}, \rho_p$: modular multiplication cost of modulus N for Paillier encryption scheme or NS encryption scheme, p' for the size of representing domain, p for the order of a cyclic group for Pedersen commitment scheme, respectively

result, our encoding function enables us to efficiently recover all the roots of f with negligible failure probability if they are in the image of ι.

As an application of our representation, combining with Naccache-Stern (NS) AHE scheme which is the factorization of σ is public, we obtain an efficient constant round privacy-preserving set union protocol without an honest majority. In Table 1, we compare our set union protocols with the previous main results [8, 12, 19].

Organization. In Sect. 2 we look into some components of our privacy-preserving set union protocol, including polynomial representation and AHE schemes. We provide our new polynomial representation that enables us to uniquely factorize a polynomial satisfying some criteria in Sect. 3. Our constant round privacy-preserving set union protocols are presented in Sect. 4. Some supplying materials including analysis of our representation are given in Appendix.

2 Preliminaries

In this section, we look into the polynomial representation of a set for PPSO protocols and introduce efficient AHE schemes utilized in PPSO protocols to support polynomial operations between encrypted polynomials.

2.1 Basic Definitions and Notations

Throughout the paper, let $\mathcal{U}$ be the universe, n the number of participants in the protocol, and k the maximum size of participants' datasets S_i's. Also, d denotes the size of (multi-)set union among participants' datasets in the protocol.

Let $R[x]$ be a set of polynomials defined over a ring R and $R(x)$ be a set of rational functions defined over R, i.e., $R[x] = \{f(x)|f(x) = \sum_{i=0}^{\deg f} f[i]x^i$ and $f[i] \in R$ for all $i\}$ and $R(x) = \{\frac{f(x)}{g(x)}|f(x), g(x) \in R[x], g(x) \neq 0\}$. For a polynomial $f \in R[x]$, we denote the coefficient of x^i in a polynomial f by $f[i]$, i.e., $f(x) = \sum_{i=0}^{\deg f} f[i]x^i \in R[x]$. For a polynomial $f(x) = \sum_{i=0}^{\deg f} f[i]x^i \in \mathbb{Z}_\sigma[x]$ and a factor q of σ, $f \bmod q$ denotes a polynomial $\sum_{i=0}^{\deg f}(f[i] \bmod q)x^i \in \mathbb{Z}_q[x]$.

We also define a negligible function as follows: a function $g : \mathbb{N} \to \mathbb{R}$ is *negligible* if for every positive polynomial $\mu(\lambda)$, there exists an integer N such that $g(\lambda) < 1/\mu(\lambda)$ for all $\lambda > N$.

2.2   Polynomial Representation of a Set

Let R be a commutative ring with unity and S be a subset of R. We may represent a set S by a polynomial or a rational function over R.

Polynomial Representation. In some previous works [7,8,10,12,19], a set S can be represented by a polynomial $f_S(x) \in R[x]$ whose roots are the elements of S. That is, $f_S(x) := \prod_{s_i \in S}(x - s_i)$. This representation gives the following relation: $f_S(x) + f_{S'}(x) = \gcd(f_S(x), f_{S'}(x)) \cdot u(x)$ for some polynomial $u(x) \in R[x]$ and hence the roots of a polynomial $f_S(x) + f_{S'}(x)$ are the elements of $S \cap S'$ with overwhelming probability. Also, the roots of $f_S(x) \cdot f_{S'}(x)$ are the elements of $S \cup S'$ as multi-sets.

Rational function Representation. Recently, Seo et al. [19] introduced a novel representation of a set $S \subset R$ by a rational function F_S over R whose poles consist of the elements of S. That is, $F_S(x) := \dfrac{1}{\prod_{s_i \in S}(x - s_i)} = \dfrac{1}{f_S(x)}$. This representation provides the following relation:

$$F_S(x) + F_{S'}(x) = \frac{f_S(x) + f_{S'}(x)}{f_S(x) \cdot f_{S'}(x)} = \frac{\gcd(f_S(x), f_{S'}(x)) \cdot u(x)}{f_S(x) \cdot f_{S'}(x)}$$
$$= \frac{u(x)}{\operatorname{lcm}(f_S(x), f_{S'}(x))}$$

for some polynomial $u(x) \in R[x]$ which is relatively prime to $\operatorname{lcm}(f_S(x), f_{S'}(x))$ with overwhelming probability. Hence the poles of $F_S(x) + F_{S'}(x)$ are exactly the roots of $\operatorname{lcm}(f_S(x), f_{S'}(x))$, which are the elements of $S \cup S'$ as sets, not multi-sets, if $u(x)$ and $\operatorname{lcm}(f_S(x), f_{S'}(x))$ have no common roots. This rational function is represented again by an infinite formal power series, so called a *Reversed Laurent Series* (RLS), in [19].

2.3   Additive Homomorphic Encryption

Let us consider a commutative ring R with unity and a R-module G where $r \cdot g := g^r$ for $r \in R$ and $g \in G$. Let $\mathsf{Enc}_{\mathsf{pk}} : R \to G$ be a public key encryption under the public key pk. We can define a public key encryption for a polynomial $f = \sum_{i=0}^{\deg f} f[i]x^i \in R[x]$ as follows: $\mathcal{E}_{\mathsf{pk}}(f) := \sum_{i=0}^{\deg f} \mathsf{Enc}_{\mathsf{pk}}(f[i])x^i$.

Assume $\mathsf{Enc}_{\mathsf{pk}}$ has an additive homomorphic property. Then one can easily induce polynomial addition between encrypted polynomials and polynomial multiplication between an unencrypted polynomial and an encrypted polynomial.

There have been several efficient AHE schemes [15–17]: Under the assumption that factoring $N = p^2 q$ is hard, Okamoto and Uchiyama [16] proposed a scheme with $R = \mathbb{Z}_p$ and $G = \mathbb{Z}_N$, in which the order p of the message space R is hidden. With the decisional composite residuosity assumption, Paillier scheme [17] has $R = \mathbb{Z}_N$ and $G = \mathbb{Z}_{N^2}$ for $N = pq$, in which the size of message spaces is a hard-to-factor composite integer N. Naccache and Stern [15] proposed a scheme with $R = \mathbb{Z}_\sigma$ and $G = \mathbb{Z}_N$ under the higher residuosity assumption, where $N = pq$ is a hard-to-factor integer and σ is a product of small primes dividing $\phi(N)$ for Euler's totient function ϕ.

In the above schemes, it is hard to find the roots of a polynomial in $R[x]$ without knowing a secret key. For the second case, in fact, Shamir [20] showed that to find a root of a polynomial $f(x) = \prod_{i=1}^{d}(x - s_i) \in \mathbb{Z}_N[x]$ is equivalent to factor N. While, in the NS scheme, it may be possible to compute some roots of a polynomial in $\mathbb{Z}_\sigma[x]$ since the factorization of σ is public. But $\mathbb{Z}_\sigma[x]$ is not a UFD and hence the number of roots of a polynomial $f \in \mathbb{Z}_\sigma[x]$ can be larger than $\deg f$. In fact, if $f(x) = \prod_{i=1}^{d}(x - s_i) \in R[x]$, then the number of candidates of roots of the polynomial f is $d^{\bar{\ell}}$ where $\bar{\ell}$ is the number of prime factors of σ. We will use the NS scheme by presenting a method to efficiently recover all the roots of a polynomial $f \in \mathbb{Z}_\sigma[x]$ satisfying some criteria.

3   Invertible Polynomial Representation

In this section, we provide our new polynomial representation that enables us to efficiently recover the exact corresponding set from the polynomial represented by our suggestion.

Focus on the fact that the factorization of σ is public in the NS encryption scheme. Using this fact, given a polynomial $f = \prod_{i=1}^{d}(x - s_i) \in \mathbb{Z}_\sigma[x]$ for a set $S = \{s_1, \ldots, s_d\}$, one can obtain all roots of $f \mod q_j$ for each j by applying a polynomial factorization algorithm over a finite field $\mathbb{Z}_{q_j}$ such as Umans' [22]. To recover S, one can perform CRT computation for obtaining less than $d^{\bar{\ell}}$ candidates of roots of f over $\mathbb{Z}_\sigma$. In general, however, the number of roots of f over $\mathbb{Z}_\sigma$ is larger than $\deg f$ and there is no criteria to determine the exact set S. To remove irrelevant roots which are not in S, we give some relations among all roots of polynomials $f \mod q_j$'s by providing an encoding function.

3.1   Our Polynomial Representation

We present our polynomial representation for supporting to recover a set from a polynomial over $\mathbb{Z}_\sigma$ represented by our suggestion.

Parameter Setting. Let us explain parameters for our polynomial representation and PPSO protocols. First, set the bit size of the modulus N of the NS encryption scheme by considering a security parameter λ. For the given universe $\mathcal{U}$ and the maximum size d of the resulting set union (here, $d = nk$ for the number n of participants and the maximum size k of participants' datasets), let $d_0 = \max\{d, \lceil \log N \rceil\}$ and set $\tau = \frac{1}{3}(\log d + 2\log d_0)$. This setting comes from the computational complexity analysis of our set union protocol and the value τ will influence the bit size of prime factors of σ and the size of the message space of the NS encryption scheme. See Sect. 4 for details.

Set the parameter ℓ and α so that ℓ is the smallest positive integer such that $\mathcal{U} \subseteq \{0,1\}^{3\tau\alpha\ell}$ for some rational number $0 < \alpha < 1$ satisfying $3\alpha\tau$ and $3(1 - \alpha)\tau$ are integers. Note that the proper size of α is $\frac{1}{3}$, i.e., $\mathcal{U} \subseteq \{0,1\}^{\tau\ell}$ for optimization. If $\alpha \neq \frac{1}{3}$, the expected computation is in polynomial time only when the size of the universe is restricted. Details about the proper size of α is given in the full version of this paper [3].

Then, set the proper size $\bar{\ell}$ larger than ℓ and let $\ell' = \bar{\ell} - \ell$. The analysis of the proper size of $\bar{\ell}$ will be discussed at the end of Sect. 3.1. Choose $\bar{\ell}$ $(3\tau + 1)$-bit distinct primes q_j's and set $\sigma = \prod_{j=1}^{\bar{\ell}} q_j$. Note that the size of the message space of the NS encryption scheme is less than $\frac{N}{4}$ for its security [15]. Hence, the parameters have to be satisfied the condition $\sigma < \frac{N}{4}$ and so $\bar{\ell} < \frac{\lfloor \log N \rfloor - 2}{3\tau}$. Also, we assume that $\bar{\ell}$ is smaller than d for optimal complexity of our proposed protocol. In summary, the parameter $\bar{\ell}$ is smaller than $\min\{d, \frac{\lfloor \log N \rfloor - 2}{3\tau}\}$ (Fig. 1).

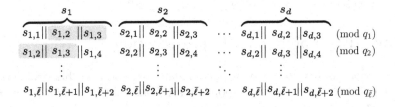

Fig. 1. Our encoding function ι

Encoding by Repetition. Let $h : \{0,1\}^* \to \{0,1\}^{2\tau}$ and $h_j : \{0,1\}^* \to \{0,1\}^\tau$ be uniform hash functions for $1 \leq j \leq \ell'$. Parse a message $s_i \in \mathcal{U} \subseteq \{0,1\}^{\tau\ell}$ into ℓ blocks $s_{i,1}, \ldots, s_{i,\ell}$ of τ-bit so that $s_i = s_{i,1} \| \cdots \| s_{i,\ell}$. Let $s_{i,\ell+j} = h_j(s_i)$ for $1 \leq j \leq \ell'$ and parse $h(s_i)$ into two blocks $s_{i,\bar{\ell}+1}$ and $s_{i,\bar{\ell}+2}$ of τ-bit. We define our encoding function $\iota : \mathcal{U} \subseteq \{0,1\}^{\tau\ell} \to \mathbb{Z}_\sigma$, in which $\iota(s_i)$ is the unique element in $\mathbb{Z}_\sigma$ satisfying $\iota(s_i) \equiv s_{i,j} \| s_{i,j+1} \| s_{i,j+2} \mod q_j$ for $1 \leq j \leq \bar{\ell}$. Then a set S is represented as a polynomial $f_S(x) = \prod_{s_i \in S} (x - \iota(s_i)) \in \mathbb{Z}_\sigma[x]$.

Decoding Phase. Denote by $s_j^{(i)} := \iota(s_i) \mod q_j$ for each message $s_i = s_{i,1} \| \cdots \| s_{i,\ell}$. For $1 \leq j \leq \bar{\ell} - 1$, we define $(s_j^{(i)}, s_{j+1}^{(i')}) \in \mathbb{Z}_{q_j} \times \mathbb{Z}_{q_{j+1}}$ to be a *linkable pair* if the last (2τ)-bit of $s_j^{(i)}$ is equal to the first (2τ)-bit of $s_{j+1}^{(i')}$, i.e., $s_{i,j+1} \| s_{i,j+2} = s_{i',j+1} \| s_{i',j+2}$. Inductively, we also define $(s_1^{(i_1)}, \cdots, s_{j+1}^{(i_{j+1})}) \in \mathbb{Z}_{q_1} \times \cdots \times \mathbb{Z}_{q_{j+1}}$ to be a *linkable pair* if $(s_1^{(i_1)}, \cdots, s_j^{(i_j)})$ and $(s_j^{(i_j)}, s_{j+1}^{(i_{j+1})})$ are linkable pairs (Fig. 2).

$$s_1^{(i_1)} = s_{i_1,1}||s_{i_1,2}||s_{i_1,3}$$
$$s_2^{(i_2)} = \phantom{s_{i_1,1}||}s_{i_2,2}||s_{i_2,3}||s_{i_2,4}$$
$$s_3^{(i_3)} = \phantom{s_{i_1,1}||s_{i_1,2}||}s_{i_3,3}||s_{i_3,4}||s_{i_3,5}$$
$$\Rightarrow \left(s_1^{(i_1)}, s_2^{(i_2)}, s_3^{(i_3)}\right) \text{ is a linkable pair.}$$

Fig. 2. Linkable pair

Let $\iota(s_i)$ and $\iota(s_{i'})$ be images of elements s_i and $s_{i'}$ of the function ι with $s_i \neq s_{i'}$. We can easily check the following properties:

- $\left(s_1^{(i)}, \cdots, s_{j+1}^{(i)}\right)$ is always a linkable pair.
- When s_i and $s_{i'}$ are uniformly chosen strings from $\{0,1\}^{\tau\ell}$,

$$\Pr[(s_j^{(i)}, s_j^{(i')}) \text{ is a linkable pair}] = \Pr\left[s_{i,j+1}||s_{i,j+2} = s_{i',j+1}||s_{i',j+2}\right]$$
$$= \frac{1}{2^{2\tau}} \tag{1}$$

for a fixed $1 \leq j \leq \bar{\ell}$.

At decoding phase, when a polynomial $f(x) = \prod_{i=1}^{d}(x - \iota(s_i)) \in \mathbb{Z}_\sigma[x]$ is given, we perform two phases to find the correct d roots of the polynomial $f(x)$. In the first stage, one computes all the roots $\{s_j^{(1)}, \cdots, s_j^{(d)}\}$ over $\mathbb{Z}_{q_j}[x]$ for each j. For each j sequentially from 1 to $\bar{\ell} - 1$, we find all the linkable pairs among $\{s_j^{(1)}, \cdots, s_j^{(d)}\}$ and $\{s_{j+1}^{(1)}, \cdots, s_{j+1}^{(d)}\}$ by checking whether the last (2τ)-bit of $s_j^{(i)}$ and the first (2τ)-bit of $s_{j+1}^{(i')}$ are the same. It can be done by d^2 comparisons or $O(d \log d)$ computations using sorting and determining algorithms.

After $\bar{\ell} - 1$ steps, we obtain d' linkable pairs of $\bar{\ell}$-tuple, which are candidates of roots of the polynomial f and elements of the set. It includes the d elements corresponding to $\iota(s_1), \ldots, \iota(s_d)$. If d' is much larger than d, it can be a burden. However, we can show that the expected value of d' is at most $3d$ in Theorem 1. See the end of this section.

After obtaining d' linkable pairs of $\bar{\ell}$-tuple, in the second phase, we check whether each pair belongs to the image of ι with the following equalities:

$$s_{i,\ell+j} = h_j(s_i) \quad \text{for all } 1 \leq j \leq \ell', \tag{2}$$
$$s_{i,\bar{\ell}+1}|| s_{i,\bar{\ell}+2} = h(s_i). \tag{3}$$

The linkable pairs of $\bar{\ell}$-tuple, corresponding to $\iota(s_i)$ for some i clearly satisfies the above equations. However, for a random $\bar{\ell}$-tuple in $\mathbb{Z}_{q_1} \times \cdots \times \mathbb{Z}_{q_{\bar{\ell}}}$, the probability that it satisfies the relation (2) is about $\frac{1}{2^{\tau\ell'}}$ and the probability that it satisfies the relation (3) is about $\frac{1}{2^{2\tau}}$ under the assumption that h and h_j's are uniform hash functions. Hence, the expected number of wrong $\bar{\ell}$-tuples passing both phases is less than $d \times \frac{1}{2^{\tau(2+\ell')}}$. It is less than $2^{-\lambda}$ for a security parameter λ if we take the parameter ℓ' to satisfy

$$\ell' > \frac{3(\lambda + \log d)}{\log d + 2 \log d_0} - 2. \tag{4}$$

For example, when $\lambda = 80$ and $d \approx d_0 \approx 2^{10}$, then ℓ' is about 8. Therefore, one can recover a set from the given polynomial represented by our suggestion without negligible failure probability in the security parameter.

3.2 Analysis of Our Polynomial Representation

Computational Complexity. Let us count the computational cost of our representation. The encoding phase consists of two steps: (1) the CRT computation per each element to obtain a value of the encoding function ι and (2) the polynomial expansion. The first step requires $O(d \log^2 \sigma)$ bit operations for d elements and the second step requires $O(d^2)$ multiplications. Hence, the complexity for the encoding phase is $O(d^2)$ multiplications.

The decoding phase may be divided into three steps: (1) finding roots of a polynomial f in $\mathbb{Z}_{q_j}$ for each j, (2) finding all linkable pairs of length $\bar{\ell}$, and (3) checking the Eqs. (2) and (3). These steps require $O(\bar{\ell} d^{1.5})$ multiplications, $O(\bar{\ell} d \log d)$ bit operations, and $O(\ell' d)$ hash computations, respectively. Hence, the complexity for the decoding phase is dominated by $O(\bar{\ell} d^{1.5})$ multiplications.

The Expected Number of Linkable Pairs. We analyze the expected number of linkable pairs of $\bar{\ell}$-tuple when we recover a set from a polynomial of degree d, represented by our suggestion. Theorem 1 gives a rigorous analysis of the upper bound of the expected number of linkable pairs of $\bar{\ell}$-tuple. The proof is given in Appendix A.

Theorem 1. *Assume that $S = \{s_1, \ldots, s_d\}$ is a uniformly and randomly chosen set in the set of subsets of cardinality d of the set $\{0,1\}^{\tau\ell}$. Define an encoding function $\iota : \{0,1\}^{\tau\ell} \to \mathbb{Z}_\sigma$ so that $\iota(s_i)$ is the unique element in $\mathbb{Z}_\sigma$ satisfying $\iota(s_i) \equiv s_{i,j}||s_{i,j+1}||s_{i,j+2} \mod q_j$ for all $1 \le j \le \bar{\ell}$ when $s_i = s_{i,1}||\ldots||s_{i,\ell}$ and $s_{i,j}$'s are τ-bit. Assume h and h_j's utilized in the encoding function ι are uniform hash functions. Then the expected number of linkable pairs of $\bar{\ell}$-tuple is at most $3d$ for all polynomials $f_S = \prod_{s_i \in S}(x - \iota(s_i))$.*

4   Applications: Set Union for Honest-but-Curious Case

In this section, we present our set union protocol based on our polynomial representation described in Sect. 3. Our construction exploits the NS AHE scheme to encrypt a rational function whose denominator corresponds to a participant's set. For this we generalize a reversed Laurent series presented in [19] to work on $\mathbb{Z}_\sigma$ with a composite σ, which the domain of the NS scheme. As a result, we obtain set union protocols which improve the complexity than the previous.

4.1 Set Union for Honest-but-Curious Case

Rational Function Representation. We adopt the rational function representation presented in [19]. To represent a set as a rational function, the authors in [19] exploited a reversed Laurent series (RLS): For a positive integer q, a RLS over $\mathbb{Z}_q$ is a singly infinite, formal sum of the form $f(x) = \sum_{i=-\infty}^{m} f[i]x^i$ ($f[m] \neq 0$) with an integer m and $f[i] \in \mathbb{Z}_q$ for all i. For a RLS $f(x)$, we denote $f(x)_{[d_1,d_2]} = \sum_{i=d_1}^{d_2} f[i]x^i$. For polynomials $f, g \in \mathbb{Z}_q[x]$ with $g \neq 0$, we define *the RLS representation of a rational function* f/g by a RLS of f/g. In Fig. 3, we provide an algorithm which takes polynomials $f, g \in \mathbb{Z}_q[x]$ with $\deg f < \deg g$ and an integer k larger than $\deg g$ as inputs and outputs k higher-order terms of the RLS representation of f/g. We also note that if one knows $2 \deg g$ higher-order terms of the RLS representation of a rational function f/g, one can recover f' and g' such that $\frac{f'}{g'} = \frac{f}{g}$ [19].

Input $f(x), g(x) \in \mathbb{Z}_q[x]$ with $\deg f < \deg g$ and an integer $k > \deg g$
Output k higher-order terms of the RLS representation of a rational function f/g

1. $F(x) \leftarrow f(x) \cdot x^k$
2. Compute $Q(x), R(x)$ such that $F(x) = g(x)Q(x) + R(x)$ and $\deg R < \deg g$ using a polynomial division algorithm
3. **Return** $Q(x) \cdot x^{-k}$

Fig. 3. RationalToRLS(f, g, k)

While Seo et al.'s constructions work on $\mathbb{Z}_q[x]$ for a prime q, our constructions are based on $\mathbb{Z}_\sigma[x]$ for a composite σ. Hence, one may doubt a RLS representation works well on $\mathbb{Z}_\sigma[x]$. In our protocol, we will represent each participant's set S_i as our polynomial representation $f_{S_i} := \prod_{s_{i,j} \in S_i} (x - \iota(s_{i,j})) \in \mathbb{Z}_\sigma[x]$ with our encoding function ι. Then we convert a rational function of $1/f_{S_i}$ to its RLS over $\mathbb{Z}_\sigma$. Since $\mathbb{Z}_\sigma$ is not a Euclidean domain, one may doubt whether the RationalToRLS algorithm works on $\mathbb{Z}_\sigma[x]$. However, in our protocol, since the conversion requires polynomial divisions only by monic polynomials, it works well on $\mathbb{Z}_\sigma[x]$.

After the end of interactions among participants in our protocol, each participant obtains the $2nk$ higher-order terms of the RLS representation of a rational function $\frac{u(x)}{U(x)} = \frac{r_1}{f_{S_1}} + \frac{r_2}{f_{S_2}} + \cdots + \frac{r_n}{f_{S_n}}$ where $U(x) = \operatorname{lcm}(f_{S_1}(x), \ldots, f_{S_n}(x))$ and r_i's are hidden polynomials. There is no algorithm to recover $u'(x)$ and $U'(x)$ in $\mathbb{Z}_\sigma[x]$ such that $\frac{u(x)}{U(x)} = \frac{u'(x)}{U'(x)}$. However, from our polynomial representation, it only requires $U'(x) \mod q_j$ for each j and we can obtain $U'(x) \mod q_j$ from the RLS representation modulo q_j by running polynomial recovering algorithm on $\mathbb{Z}_{q_j}[x]$'s.

The correctness and the security of our set union protocol are induced from properties of a RLS representation. We omit the details due to the space limitation. See the full version [3] of this paper for these.

Threshold Naccache-Stern Encryption. For a group decryption, it requires a semantically secure, threshold NS AHE scheme in our protocol. One can easily construct a threshold version of the NS encryption scheme using the technique of Fouque et al. [6], which transforms the original Paillier homomorphic encryption scheme into a threshold version working from Shoup's technique [21].

Parameter Setting. Let $\mathcal{U}$ be the universe, n be the number of participants, and k be the maximum size of participants' datasets. Let d be the possible maximum size of the set union, i.e., $d = nk$. Take the bit size of N by considering the security of the threshold NS AHE scheme, which is the modulus of the threshold NS AHE scheme. Put $d_0 = \max\{d, \lceil \log N \rceil\}$ and $\tau = \frac{1}{3}(\log d + 2 \log d_0)$. Set ℓ so that $\mathcal{U} \subseteq \{0,1\}^{\tau\ell}$, a proper size of ℓ' so that ℓ' satisfies the relation (4) and let $\bar{\ell} = \ell + \ell'$. Note that $\bar{\ell}$ is to be smaller than $\min\left\{d, \frac{\lfloor \log N \rfloor - 2}{3 \log \log N}\right\}$ since $\tau \geq \log \log N$. Generate the parameters of the threshold NS encryption scheme, including the size of message space σ, which is a product of $\bar{\ell}\,(3\tau+1)$-bit distinct primes q_j's.

Our Set Union Protocol for Honest-but-Curious Case. Our set union protocol against honest-but-curious (HBC) adversaries is described in Fig. 4. In our set union protocol, each participant computes the $2nk$ higher-order terms of the RLS representation of $F_{S_i} = \frac{1}{f_{S_i}} \in \mathbb{Z}_\sigma[x]$ where $f_{S_i} = \prod_{s_{i,j} \in S_i}(x - \iota(s_{i,j}))$ for our encoding function ι and sends its encryption to all others. With the received encryptions of F_{S_j} for $1 \leq j \leq n$, each participant $\mathcal{P}_i$ multiplies a polynomial $r_{i,j}$ using additive homomorphic property, which is a randomly chosen polynomial by the participant $\mathcal{P}_i$ and adds all the resulting polynomials to obtain the encryption of $\phi_i(x) = \sum_{j=1}^n F_{S_j} \cdot r_{i,j}$. Then, he sends the encryption of $\phi_i(x)$ to all others. After interactions among participants, each participant can obtain the $2nk$ high-order term of the RLS representation of $F(x) = \sum_{i=1}^n \left(\sum_{j=1}^n \frac{1}{f_{S_j}} \cdot r_{i,j}\right) \in \mathbb{Z}_\sigma[x]$. Then each participant obtains the $2nk$ high-order terms of the RLS representation of F in $\mathbb{Z}_\sigma[x]$ with group decryption and recovers polynomials $u_j(x)$ and $U_j(x)$ such that $\left(\frac{u_j(x)}{U_j(x)}\right)_{[-2nk,-1]} = (F(x) \bmod q_j)_{[k-1,(2n+1)k-2]} \cdot x^{-(2n+1)k+1}$ and $\gcd(u_j(x), U_j(x)) = 1$ in $\mathbb{Z}_{q_j}[x]$ from these values. Thereafter, each participant extracts all roots of $U_j(x)$ over $\mathbb{Z}_{q_j}$ for each j and recovers all elements based on the criteria of our representation.

4.2   Analysis

Security Analysis. Now, we consider the correctness and privacy of our proposed protocol described in Fig. 4. The following theorems guarantee the correctness

Input: There are $n \geq 2$ HBC participants $\mathcal{P}_i$ with a private input set $S_i \subseteq \mathcal{U}$ of cardinality k. Set $d = nk$. The participants share the secret key sk, to which pk is the corresponding public key to the threshold NS AHE scheme. Let $\iota : \{0,1\}^* \to \mathbb{Z}_\sigma$ be the encoding function provided in Section 3.

Each participant $\mathcal{P}_i$, $i = 1, \ldots, n$:

1. (a) constructs the polynomial $f_{S_i}(x) = \prod_{s_{i,j} \in S_i} (x - \iota(s_{i,j})) \in \mathbb{Z}_\sigma[x]$, runs

   RationalToRLS$(1, f_{S_i}, (2n+1)k - 1)$ to obtain $\left(\frac{1}{f_{S_i}(x)} \right)_{[-(2n+1)k+1, -k]}$, and

   computes $F_{S_i}(x) = \left(\frac{1}{f_{S_i}(x)} \right)_{[-(2n+1)k+1, -k]} \cdot x^{(2n+1)k-1}$.

   (b) computes $\tilde{F}_{S_i}$, the encrypted polynomial of F_{S_i}, and sends $\tilde{F}_{S_i}$ to all other participants.

2. (a) chooses random polynomials $r_{i,j}(x) \in \mathbb{Z}_\sigma[x]$ of degree at most k for all $1 \leq j \leq n$.

   (b) computes the encryption, $\tilde{\phi}_i$, of the polynomial $\phi_i(x) = \sum_{j=1}^n F_{S_j} \cdot r_{i,j}$ and sends it to all participants.

3. (a) calculates the encryption of the polynomial $F(x) = \sum_{i=1}^n \phi_i(x)$.

   (b) performs a group decryption with all other players to obtain the $2nk$ higher-order terms of $F(x)$.

4. (a) recovers a polynomial pair of $u_j(x)$ and $U_j(x)$ in $\mathbb{Z}_{q_j}[x]$ for all $1 \leq j \leq \bar{\ell}$

   such that $\left(\frac{u_j(x)}{U_j(x)} \right)_{[-2nk, -1]} = (F(x) \bmod q_j)_{[k-1, (2n+1)k-2]} \cdot x^{-(2n+1)k+1}$

   and $\gcd(u_j(x), U_j(x)) = 1$ in $\mathbb{Z}_{q_j}[x]$, using the $2nk$ higher-order terms of $F(x)$ obtained in Step 3 (b).

   (b) extracts all roots of $U_j(x)$ in $\mathbb{Z}_{q_j}[x]$ for all j using a factorization algorithm.

   (c) determines the set union using the encoding rule of ι.

Fig. 4. PPSU-HBC protocol in the HBC case

and privacy of our construction in Fig. 4. We provide proofs of the following theorems in the full version of this paper [3].

Theorem 2. *In the protocol described in Fig. 4, every participant learns the set union of private inputs participating players, with high probability.*

Theorem 3. *Assume that the utilized additive homomorphic encryption scheme is semantically secure. Then, in our set union protocol for the HBC case described in Fig. 4, any adversary $\mathcal{A}$ of colluding fewer than n HBC participants learns no more information than would be gained by using the same private inputs in the ideal model with a trusted third party.*

Performance Analysis. It is clear that our protocol runs in $O(1)$ rounds. Let us count the computational and communicational costs for each participant.

Step 1 (a) requires $\tilde{O}(k)$ multiplications in $\mathbb{Z}_\sigma$ for a polynomial expansion of degree k and $O(kd)$ multiplications to run the RationalToRLS algorithm and compute F_{S_i}.

Step 1 (b) requires $O(d)$ exponentiations for $2d$ encryptions and $O(nd)$ communication costs.

Step 2 (b) requires $O(d^2)$ exponentiations for computing the encryption $\tilde{\phi}_i := \sum_{j=1}^n \bar{F}_{S_j} \cdot r_{i,j}$ using additive homomorphic property and $O(nd)$ communication costs.

Step 3 (a) requires $O(nd)$ multiplications for computing $\sum_{i=1}^n \tilde{\phi}_i$.

Step 3 (b) requires $O(d)$ exponentiations for decryption share computation for $2d$ ciphertexts and $O(\bar{\ell}\sqrt{dq_j})$ multiplications for solving d DLPs for $\bar{\ell}$ groups of order q_j's.[1] The communication cost is $O(nd)$.

Step 4 (a) requires $O(d^2)$ multiplications in $\mathbb{Z}_{q_j}$ to recover $U_j(x)$ using extended Euclidean algorithm for each j.

Step 4 (b) requires $O(d^{1.5+o(1)})$ multiplications in $\mathbb{Z}_{q_j}$ for each j to factor a polynomial of degree d.

Step 4 (c) requires $O(\bar{\ell}d\log d\log q_j)$ bit operations for sorting and $O(d)$ hash computations.

Then the computational complexity is dominated by one of terms $O(d^2)$ exponentiations in Step 2 (b) and $O(\bar{\ell}\sqrt{dq_j})$ multiplications in Step 3 (b). Since one modular exponentiation for a modulus N requires $O(\log N)$ multiplications and $\bar{\ell} < \min\left\{d, \frac{\lfloor \log N \rfloor - 2}{3\log\log N}\right\}$, the computational complexity for each participant is dominated by $O(d^2) = O(n^2k^2)$ exponentiations in $\mathbb{Z}_N$ and the total complexity is $O(n^3k^2)$ exponentiations in $\mathbb{Z}_N$. The total communication cost for our protocol is $O(n^2d) = O(n^3k)$ $(\log N)$-bit elements.

For the malicious case, we can also obtain the set union protocol using the techniques in [12,19]. We omit the details about our set union protocol for malicious case due to the space limitation. See the full version [3] of this paper.

5   Conclusion

In this paper, we provided a new representation of a set by a polynomial over $\mathbb{Z}_\sigma$, which can be efficiently inverted by finding all the linear factors of a polynomial whose root locates in the image of our encoding function, when the factorization of σ is public. Then we presented an efficient constant-round set union protocols, transforming our representation into a rational function and then combining it with threshold NS AHE scheme.

We showed that our encoding function is quite efficient on average-case, but it still requires exponential time in the degree of a polynomial to recover a set from the polynomial represented by our encoding function at worst-case although the probability of the worst-case is sufficiently small. Hence it would be interesting to construct an encoding function that enables us to recover a set in polynomial time even at worst-case.

---

[1] Note that one has to solve $\bar{\ell}$ DLPs over a group of order q_j for one decryption in the NS encryption scheme. In Step 3 (b), one has to solve $2d = 2nk$ DLPs over a group of order q_j for each q_j. It requires $O(\sqrt{dq_j})$ multiplications to solve d DLPs over a group of order q_j [13] and hence total complexity of this step is $O(\bar{\ell}\sqrt{dq_j})$ multiplications.

Acknowledgements. We thank Jae Hong Seo for helpful comments on our preliminary works and anonymous reviewers for their valuable comments. This work was supported by the IT R&D program of MSIP/KEIT. [No. 10047212, Development of homomorphic encryption supporting arithmetics on ciphertexts of size less than 1kB and its applications].

A Proof of Theorem 1

Let E_j be the expected number of linkable pairs of j-tuple in $\mathbb{Z}_{q_1} \times \cdots \times \mathbb{Z}_{q_j}$ for $j \geq 2$. For $1 \leq j \leq j' \leq \bar{\ell}$, let $S_{j'-j+1}(i_j, \ldots, i_{j'})$ be the event that $(s_j^{(i_j)}, \ldots, s_{j'}^{(i_{j'})})$ is a linkable pair. Then,

$$
\begin{aligned}
E_2 &= \sum_{i_1, i_2 \in \{1, \ldots, d\}} 1 \cdot \Pr[S_2(i_1, i_2)] \\
&= \sum_{i_1, i_2 \in \{1, \ldots, d\}} \Pr[S_2(i_1, i_2) \wedge (i_1 = i_2)] + \sum_{i_1, i_2 \in \{1, \ldots, d\}} \Pr[S_2(i_1, i_2) \wedge (i_1 \neq i_2)] \\
&= d + d(d-1)\frac{1}{2^{2\tau}} = d\left(1 + \frac{d-1}{2^{2\tau}}\right)
\end{aligned}
$$

since $\Pr[S_2(i_1, i_1)] = 1$ for $i_1 \in \{1, \ldots, d\}$ and $\Pr[S_2(i_1, i_2)] = \frac{1}{2^{2\tau}}$ for distinct $i_1, i_2 \in \{1, \ldots, d\}$ from the Eq. (1).

Now, we consider the relation between E_j and E_{j+1}. When $(s_1^{(i_1)}, \ldots, s_j^{(i_j)})$ is a linkable pair, consider the case that $(s_1^{(i_1)}, \ldots, s_j^{(i_j)}, s_{j+1}^{(i_{j+1})})$ is a linkable pair. One can classify this case into the following three cases:

1. $i_{j+1} = i_j$,
2. $(i_{j+1} \neq i_j) \wedge (i_{j+1} = i_{j-1})$,
3. $(i_{j+1} \neq i_j) \wedge (i_{j+1} \neq i_{j-1})$.

At the first case, if $i_{j+1} = i_j$ and $(s_1^{(i_1)}, \ldots, s_j^{(i_j)})$ is a linkable pair, then $(s_1^{(i_1)}, \ldots, s_j^{(i_j)}, s_{j+1}^{(i_{j+1})})$ is always a linkable pair. Hence,

$$
\begin{aligned}
E_{j+1}^{(1)} &:= \sum_{i_1, \ldots, i_{j+1}} \Pr\left[S_{j+1}(i_1, \ldots, i_j, i_{j+1}) \wedge (i_{j+1} = i_j)\right] \\
&= \sum_{i_1, \ldots, i_j} \Pr\left[S_j(i_1, \ldots, i_j)\right] = E_j.
\end{aligned}
$$

At the second case, if $i_{j+1} = i_{j-1} \neq i_j$ and $(s_1^{(i_1)}, \ldots, s_j^{(i_j)})$ is a linkable pair, then the relation $s_{i_{j-1}, j+1} = s_{i_j, j+1} = s_{i_{j+1}, j+1}$ is satisfied from the encoding rule of ι. Hence,[2]

---

[2] Due to the space limitation, the detailed computation of Eqs. (5) and (6) are given in the full version of this paper [3].

$$E_{j+1}^{(2)} := \sum_{i_1,\ldots,i_{j+1}\in\{1,\ldots,d\}} \Pr[S_{j+1}(i_1,\ldots,i_j,i_{j+1}) \wedge (i_{j+1} = i_{j-1} \neq i_j)]$$

$$\leq \frac{1}{2^\tau} \sum_{i_1,\ldots,i_j\in\{1,\ldots,d\}} \Pr[S_j(i_1,\ldots,i_j)] = \frac{1}{2^\tau}E_j. \tag{5}$$

At the last case, we can obtain the following result:

$$E_{j+1}^{(3)} := \sum_{i_1,\ldots,i_{j+1}\in\{1,\ldots,d\}} \Pr[S_{j+1}(i_1,\ldots,i_j,i_{j+1}) \wedge ((i_{j+1} \neq i_j) \wedge (i_{j+1} \neq i_{j-1}))]$$

$$\leq \frac{d-1}{2^{2\tau}} \sum_{i_1,\ldots,i_j\in\{1,\ldots,d\}} \Pr[S_j(i_1,\ldots,i_j)] = \frac{d-1}{2^{2\tau}}E_j. \tag{6}$$

From the above results, we obtain the recurrence formula of E_j as follows:

$$E_{j+1} = E_{j+1}^{(1)} + E_{j+1}^{(2)} + E_{j+1}^{(3)} \leq \left(1 + \frac{1}{2^\tau} + \frac{d-1}{2^{2\tau}}\right)E_j$$

for $j \geq 2$ and hence $E_{\bar{\ell}} \leq d\left(1 + \frac{1}{2^\tau} + \frac{d-1}{2^{2\tau}}\right)^{\bar{\ell}-1}$ since $E_2 = d\left(1 + \frac{d-1}{2^{2\tau}}\right) \leq d\left(1 + \frac{1}{2^\tau} + \frac{d-1}{2^{2\tau}}\right)$.

Now, we show that $\bar{\ell} \leq \frac{2^{2\tau}}{2^\tau+d}$. From the parameter setting, it is satisfied that $\bar{\ell} \leq \min\{d, \frac{\lfloor\log N\rfloor-2}{3\tau}\}$. When $d_0 \geq 8d$, it holds

$$\min\left\{d, \frac{\lfloor\log N\rfloor-2}{3\tau}\right\} \leq d \leq \frac{d_0^{1/3}d^{2/3}}{2}.$$

Consider the case that $d_0 < 8d$. Then, it also holds

$$\min\left\{d, \frac{\lfloor\log N\rfloor-2}{3\tau}\right\} \leq \frac{\lfloor\log N\rfloor-2}{3\tau} \leq \frac{d_0}{3\tau} \leq \frac{d_0^{1/3}d^{2/3}}{2}$$

since $\tau \geq 3$. Hence

$$\bar{\ell} \leq \min\left\{d, \frac{\lfloor\log N\rfloor-2}{3\tau}\right\} \leq \frac{d_0^{1/3}d^{2/3}}{2} \leq \frac{(d_0^2 d)^{2/3}}{2d_0} \leq \frac{2^{2\tau}}{2^\tau+d}$$

since $2d_0 > 2^\tau + d$. Therefore we obtain the following result:

$$E_{\bar{\ell}} \leq d\left(1 + \frac{1}{2^\tau} + \frac{d-1}{2^{2\tau}}\right)^{\bar{\ell}-1} < ed < 3d,$$

where $e \approx 2.718$ is the base of the natural logarithm. In other words, the upper bound of the expected number of linkable pairs of $\bar{\ell}$-tuple is $3d$. $\square$

References

1. Ben-Or, M., Goldwasser, S., Wigderson, A.: Completeness theorems for non-cryptographic fault-tolerant distributed computation (extended abstract). In: Simon, J. (ed.) ACM Symposium on Theory of Computing (STOC), pp. 1–10. ACM (1988)
2. Camenisch, J., Shoup, V.: Practical verifiable encryption and decryption of discrete logarithms. In: Boneh, D. (ed.) CRYPTO 2003. LNCS, vol. 2729, pp. 126–144. Springer, Heidelberg (2003)
3. Cheon, J.H., Hong, H., Lee, H.T.: Invertible polynomial representation for set operations. Cryptology ePrint Archive, Report 2012/526 (2012). http://eprint.iacr.org/2012/526
4. De Cristofaro, E., Kim, J., Tsudik, G.: Linear-complexity private set intersection protocols secure in malicious model. In: Abe, M. (ed.) ASIACRYPT 2010. LNCS, vol. 6477, pp. 213–231. Springer, Heidelberg (2010)
5. De Cristofaro, E., Tsudik, G.: Practical private set intersection protocols with linear complexity. In: Sion, R. (ed.) FC 2010. LNCS, vol. 6052, pp. 143–159. Springer, Heidelberg (2010)
6. Fouque, P.-A., Poupard, G., Stern, J.: Sharing decryption in the context of voting or lotteries. In: Frankel, Y. (ed.) FC 2000. LNCS, vol. 1962, pp. 90–104. Springer, Heidelberg (2001)
7. Freedman, M.J., Nissim, K., Pinkas, B.: Efficient private matching and set intersection. In: Cachin, C., Camenisch, J.L. (eds.) EUROCRYPT 2004. LNCS, vol. 3027, pp. 1–19. Springer, Heidelberg (2004)
8. Frikken, K.B.: Privacy-preserving set union. In: Katz, J., Yung, M. (eds.) ACNS 2007. LNCS, vol. 4521, pp. 237–252. Springer, Heidelberg (2007)
9. Goldreich, O., Micali, S., Wigderson, A.: How to play any mental game or a completeness theorem for protocols with honest majority. In: Aho, A.V. (ed.) ACM Symposium on Theory of Computing (STOC), pp. 218–229. ACM (1987)
10. Hong, J., Kim, J.W., Kim, J., Park, K., Cheon, J.H.: Constant-round privacy preserving multiset union. Bull. Korean Math. Soc. **50**(6), 1799–1816 (2013)
11. Jarecki, S., Liu, X.: Efficient oblivious pseudorandom function with applications to adaptive OT and secure computation of set intersection. In: Reingold, O. (ed.) TCC 2009. LNCS, vol. 5444, pp. 577–594. Springer, Heidelberg (2009)
12. Kissner, L., Song, D.: Privacy-preserving set operations. In: Shoup, V. (ed.) CRYPTO 2005. LNCS, vol. 3621, pp. 241–257. Springer, Heidelberg (2005)
13. Kuhn, F., Struik, R.: Random walks revisited: extensions of pollard's rho algorithm for computing multiple discrete logarithms. In: Vaudenay, S., Youssef, A.M. (eds.) SAC 2001. LNCS, vol. 2259, pp. 212–229. Springer, Heidelberg (2001)
14. Lee, H.T.: Polynomial Factorization and Its Applications. Ph.D. thesis, Seoul National University, February 2013
15. Naccache, D., Stern, J.: A new public key cryptosystem based on higher residues. In: Gong, L., Reiter, M.K. (eds.) ACM Conference on Computer and Communications Security (ACM CCS), pp. 59–66. ACM (1998)
16. Okamoto, T., Uchiyama, S.: A new public-key cryptosystem as secure as factoring. In: Nyberg, K. (ed.) EUROCRYPT 1998. LNCS, vol. 1403, pp. 308–318. Springer, Heidelberg (1998)
17. Paillier, P.: Public-key cryptosystems based on composite degree residuosity classes. In: Stern, J. (ed.) EUROCRYPT 1999. LNCS, vol. 1592, pp. 223–238. Springer, Heidelberg (1999)

18. Sang, Y., Shen, H.: Efficient and secure protocols for privacy-preserving set operations. ACM Trans. Inf. Syst. Secur. **13**(1), 9:1–9:35 (2009)
19. Seo, J.H., Cheon, J.H., Katz, J.: Constant-round multi-party private set union using reversed Laurent series. In: Fischlin, M., Buchmann, J., Manulis, M. (eds.) PKC 2012. LNCS, vol. 7293, pp. 398–412. Springer, Heidelberg (2012)
20. Shamir, A.: On the generation of multivariate polynomials which are hard to factor. In: Kosaraju, S.R., Johnson, D.S., Aggarwal, A. (eds.) ACM Symposium on Theory of Computing (STOC), pp. 796–804. ACM (1993)
21. Shoup, V.: Practical threshold signatures. In: Preneel, B. (ed.) EUROCRYPT 2000. LNCS, vol. 1807, pp. 207–220. Springer, Heidelberg (2000)
22. Umans, C.: Fast polynomial factorization and modular composition in small characteristic. In: Dwork, C. (ed.) ACM Symposium on Theory of Computing (STOC), pp. 481–490. ACM (2008)

On the Efficacy of Solving LWE by Reduction to Unique-SVP

Martin R. Albrecht[1], Robert Fitzpatrick[2(✉)], and Florian Göpfert[3]

[1] Technical University of Denmark, Kongens Lyngby, Denmark
maroa@dtu.dk
[2] ISG, Royal Holloway, University of London, Egham, UK
robert.fitzpatrick.2010@live.rhul.ac.uk
[3] CASED, TU Darmstadt, Darmstadt, Germany
fgoepfert@cdc.informatik.tu-darmstadt.de

Abstract. We present a study of the concrete complexity of solving instances of the unique shortest vector problem (uSVP). In particular, we study the complexity of solving the Learning with Errors (LWE) problem by reducing the Bounded-Distance Decoding (BDD) problem to uSVP and attempting to solve such instances using the 'embedding' approach. We experimentally derive a model for the success of the approach, compare to alternative methods and demonstrate that for the LWE instances considered in this work, reducing to uSVP and solving via embedding compares favorably to other approaches.

1 Introduction

The Learning with Errors (LWE) problem is a generalisation to large moduli of the Learning Parity with Noise (LPN) problem. Since its introduction by Regev [20], it has proved a remarkably flexible base for building cryptosystems. For example, Gentry, Peikert and Vaikuntanathan presented in [11] LWE-based constructions of identity-based encryption and many recent (fully) homomorphic encryption constructions are related to LWE [2,7,10]. Besides the flexibility of LWE, the main reason for the popularity of this problem is the convincing theoretical arguments underlying its hardness, namely a reduction from worst-case lattice problems such as GapSVP and SIVP to average-case LWE.

Definition 1 (LWE [20]). *Let n, q be positive integers, χ be a probability distribution on $\mathbb{Z}$ and s be a secret vector following the uniform distribution on $\mathbb{Z}_q^n$. We denote by $L_{s,\chi}$ the probability distribution on $\mathbb{Z}_q^n \times \mathbb{Z}_q$ obtained by choosing a from the uniform distribution on $\mathbb{Z}_q^n$, choosing $e \in \mathbb{Z}$ according to χ and returning $(a, c) = (a, \langle a, s \rangle + e) \in \mathbb{Z}_q^n \times \mathbb{Z}_q$. The LWE problem is then, given a set of samples, to determine whether they originated from $L_{s,\chi}$ for some s or whether they follow the uniform distribution on $\mathbb{Z}_q^n \times \mathbb{Z}_q$.*

The modulus is typically taken to be polynomial in n and χ is the discrete Gaussian $D_{\mathbb{Z}, \alpha \cdot q}$ with mean 0 and standard deviation $\sigma = \alpha \cdot q / \sqrt{2\pi}$ for some

© Springer International Publishing Switzerland 2014
H.-S. Lee and D.-G. Han (Eds.): ICISC 2013, LNCS 8565, pp. 293–310, 2014.
DOI: 10.1007/978-3-319-12160-4_18

α. For these choices it was shown in [6,21] that if $\alpha q > 2\sqrt{n}$ then (worst-case) GapSVP-$\tilde{\mathcal{O}}(n/\alpha)$ reduces to (average-case) LWE.

However, while the asymptotic hardness of LWE is well-understood, current understanding of the concrete hardness of solving particular instances of LWE leaves much to be desired. In this work, we examine the applicability of Kannan's embedding technique [13] to LWE and present the results of experiments using the Lenstra-Lenstra-Lovasz (LLL) and block Korkine-Zolotarev (BKZ) algorithms. While the embedding approach has been successfully employed in several past works, the approach remains somewhat mysterious with our current understanding of the efficacy of the approach being comparatively poor.

1.1   Related Work

In [16] Liu et. al. investigate similar questions, though their work lacks an experimental component which, in our opinion, form an indispensable part of any such work, given the current state of knowledge regarding the concrete complexity of unique-SVP. The current understanding of how a particular gap is related to the success of a particular reduction algorithm in disclosing a shortest vector, is poor. In [9] the results of a number of experiments were reported in which the authors examined the success of a number of algorithms in disclosing a shortest vector when (at least) a good approximation to the gap was known (though not in bounded-distance decoding/LWE cases). A simple model was proposed as a criterion for the success of a particular algorithm and particular class of lattices, with 'explaining the uSVP phenomenon' being posed as an open question.

1.2   Contribution and Organisation

We provide some background in Sect. 2 and discuss the embedding gap in Sect. 3.1. In Sect. 4 we apply the embedding approach to lattices derived from LWE instances. Finally, in Sect. 5 we discuss the limits of the embedding approach and compare our results with results from the literature.

2   Background and Notation

2.1   Lattices and Discrete Gaussians

A *lattice* Λ in $\mathbb{R}^m$ is a discrete additive subgroup. We view a lattice as being generated by a (non-unique) basis $\mathbb{B} = \{b_0, \ldots, b_{n-1}\} \subset \mathbb{Z}^m$ of linearly-independent integer vectors:

$$\Lambda = \mathcal{L}(\mathbf{B}) = \mathbb{Z}^m \cdot \mathbf{B} = \left\{ \sum_{i=0}^{m-1} x_i \cdot b_i : x_i \in \mathbb{Z} \right\}$$

The *rank* of the lattice $\mathcal{L}(\mathbf{B})$ is defined to be the rank of the matrix $\mathbf{B}$ with rows consisting of the basis vectors. If $m = n$ we say that $\mathcal{L}(\mathbf{B})$ is *full-rank*.

We are only concerned with such lattices in this work and henceforth assume that the lattices we deal with are full-rank. In addition, in this work we are only concerned with q-ary lattices which are those such that $q\mathbb{Z}^m \subseteq \Lambda \subseteq \mathbb{Z}^m$. Note that every q-ary lattice is full-rank. Throughout, we adopt the convention that a lattice is generated by integer combinations of row vectors, to match software conventions.

Given a lattice Λ we denote by $\lambda_i(\Lambda)$ the i-th minimum of Λ:

$$\lambda_i(\Lambda) := \inf \left\{ r \mid \dim(\mathrm{span}(\Lambda \cap \bar{\mathcal{B}}_m(\mathbf{0}, r))) \geq i \right\}$$

where $\bar{\mathcal{B}}_m(\mathbf{0}, r)$ denotes the closed, zero-centered m-dimensional (Euclidean) ball of radius r.

The determinant $\det(\mathcal{L})$ of a full-rank lattice is the absolute value of the determinant of any basis of the lattice.

Throughout, we work exclusively in the Euclidean norm unless otherwise stated and omit norm subscripts i.e. $\|x\| = \|x\|_2$. Given a point $t \in \mathbb{R}^m$ and a lattice Λ, we define the minimum distance from t to the lattice by $\mathrm{dist}(t, \Lambda) = \min \{\|t - x\| \mid x \in \Lambda\}$.

The following are some computational problems on lattices which will be of relevance to our discussion

- ζ-Approx SVP (ζ-Approx-SVP), $\zeta \geq 1$: Given a lattice $\mathcal{L}$, find a vector $v \in \mathcal{L}$ such that $0 < \|v\| \leq \zeta \cdot \lambda_1(\mathcal{L})$
- κ-Hermite SVP (κ-HSVP), $\kappa \geq 1$: Given a lattice $\mathcal{L}$, find a vector $v \in \mathcal{L}$ such that $0 < \|v\| \leq \kappa \cdot \det(\mathcal{L})^{1/n}$
- η-Bounded Distance Decoding (BDD$_\eta$) ($\eta \leq 1/2$): Given a lattice $\mathcal{L}$ and a vector t such that $dist(t, \mathcal{L}) < \eta\lambda_1(\mathcal{L})$, output the lattice vector y closest to t
- ϱ-Unique Shortest Vector Problem (ϱ-uSVP): Given a lattice $\mathcal{L}$ such that $\lambda_2(\mathcal{L}) > \varrho \cdot \lambda_1(\mathcal{L})$, find the shortest non-zero lattice vector in $\mathcal{L}$

If we have an algorithm which solves κ-Hermite SVP for lattices of dimension n, we say that the algorithm attains a *root Hermite factor* of $\delta_0 := \kappa^{1/n}$. It is an experimentally-verified heuristic [9] that the root Hermite factor a given algorithm attains converges swiftly with increasing dimension. Now, if we have an algorithm which can solve Hermite-SVP with approximation factor κ, we can use this algorithm linearly many times [17] to solve Approx-SVP with approximation factor κ^2. Hence, we can use our κ-HSVP algorithm to solve uSVP instances in which the gap is at least κ^2. Similarly, if we have a root Hermite factor δ_0 characterising our Hermite-SVP algorithm, we can solve uSVP instances of gap δ_0^{2m}. However, one of the conclusions from [9], as we discuss later, is that, as with the gulf between the theoretical and practical performance of lattice reduction algorithms, we can generally solve uSVP instances with much smaller gap. More specifically, the results of [9] indicate that, while an exponential gap is still required to solve uSVP, the size of the gap only needs to grow on the order of the Hermite factor rather than its square, as indicated by the theoretical (worst-case) results. To the best of our knowledge, this behaviour remains unexplained and the practical performance of lattice reduction algorithms on lattices possessing a λ_2/λ_1 gap remains somewhat mysterious.

We always start counting from zero and denote vectors and matrices in lower-case and upper-case bold, respectively. We always assume that a lattice is generated by row combinations and that, when treating a collection of LWE samples as a 'matrix-LWE' sample, we assume this takes the form $b = A^T s + e$. Given a random variable X, E[X] denotes the expected value of X.

All experiments were carried out using the NTL implementation of BKZ and all LWE instances were generated using the LWE instance generator [3]. BKZ is parameterised (in part) by the choice of a block-size with higher block-sizes leading to 'stronger' basis reduction. In this work, due to the probabilistic nature of our experiments (as opposed to one-off reductions), we are constrained to experiments in relatively low block-size. Here, we report the results of experiments using block-sizes of 5 and 10 (with no pruning) which collectively took around 2 months on two servers. Partial results for BKZ with a block-size of 20 indicate no discrepancy with our conclusions. While much larger block-sizes, in particular with pruning, have been achieved, our experiments required the execution of a large number (100) of reductions for each attempt at a solution. For simplicity, we assume throughout that enough LWE samples are exposed by a cryptosystem to allow the employment of the embedding technique in the optimal lattice dimension. While this may not always be the case in reality, in this work we are concerned primarily with the LWE problem "in theory" and note that, as observed in [22], given a fixed polynomial number of LWE samples, one can generate arbitrarily many additional equations which are (essentially) as good as the original samples, suffering only a slight increase in the deviation of the noise distribution.

The discrete Gaussian distribution with parameter s, denoted $D_{\Lambda,s}$, over a lattice Λ is defined to be the probability distribution with support Λ which, for each $x \in \Lambda$, assigns probability proportional to $\exp(-\pi\|x\|^2/s^2)$. When we refer to the value s in this work with regard to LWE instantiations, we mean a discrete Gaussian with parameter s over the integer lattice. In an abuse of notation, we also use $D_{\Lambda,s}$ to denote a random variable following this distribution.

The following tail bound on discrete Gaussians is needed. This tail bound is obtained by employing the tail-bound on $D_{\mathbb{Z},s}$ from [5] and then observing that the product distribution of n copies of this distribution gives $D_{\mathbb{Z}^n,s}$.

Lemma 1. *Let $c \geq 1$ and $C = c \cdot \exp((1 - c^2)/2) < 1$. Then for any real $s > 0$ and any integer $n \geq 1$ we have*

$$\Pr[\|D_{\mathbb{Z}^n,s}\| \geq c \cdot \frac{s\sqrt{n}}{\sqrt{2\pi}}] \leq C^n.$$

2.2   The Concrete Complexity of BKZ and BKZ 2.0

A central difficulty which arises in all works which require the use of 'strong' lattice reduction (by which we mean BKZ and improved variants) is the prediction of the concrete complexity of such algorithms. In [8] the authors present a study of 'BKZ 2.0', the amalgamation of three folklore techniques to improve the performance of BKZ: pruned enumeration; pre-processing of local blocks and early termination. While no implementations of such algorithms are publicly available, the authors of [8] present a simulator to predict the behaviour of out-of-reach BKZ computations. In [14] a model for the running time of BKZ 2.0 is proposed by running a limited set of experiments using the standard NTL implementation of BKZ and then adjusting the extrapolated running times by a certain factor to try and account for the improved running times promised by BKZ 2.0. The model arrived at is

$$\log_2 T_{sec} = 1.8/\log_2 \delta_0 - 110$$

We note that, while [14] pre-dates [8], the model in [14] aimed to account for the improvements in running time allowed for by the then-folklore techniques, later formalised by [8]. In a recent work [15], the authors re-visit this model and compare the predictions to the BKZ 2.0 simulator of [8] in a few cases. In the cases examined in [15], the running-time predictions obtained by the use of the BKZ 2.0 simulator are quite close to those obtained by the model of Lindner and Peikert.

However, based on the data-points provided in [15] and converting these to the same metric as in the Lindner-Peikert model, the function

$$\log_2 T_{sec}^{\text{BKZ2.0}} = 0.009/\log_2^2 \delta_0 - 27$$

provides a close approximation to the running-time output of the simulator for these particular cases.

This is a non-linear approximation and hence naturally grows faster than the approximation in [14]. However, given the greater sophistication of the latter 'BKZ 2.0' extrapolations derived from the simulator of [8], we expect this model to provide more accurate approximations of running times than the model of [14].

We note that a BKZ logarithmic running-time model which is non-linear in $\log_2 \delta_0$ appears more intuitive than a linear model. While, in practice, the root Hermite factors achievable through the use of BKZ with a particular blocksize β are much better than their best provable upper bounds, the root Hermite factor achievable appears to behave similarly to the upper bounds as a function of β. Namely, the best proven upper bounds on the root Hermite factor are of the form $\sqrt{\gamma_\beta}^{1/(\beta-1)}$, where γ_β denotes the best known upper bound on the Hermite constant for lattices of dimension β. Now since, asymptotically, γ_β grows linearly in β, if we assume that the root Hermite factor achievable in practice displays asymptotic behaviour similar to that of the best-known upper bound, then the root Hermite factor achievable as a function of β, denoted $\delta_0(\beta)$, is such that $\delta_0(\beta) \in \Omega(1/\beta)$. Since the running time of BKZ appears to be doubly-exponential in β, we can derive that $\log T_{sec}$ is non-linear in $1/\log \delta_0$, as is borne out by the results in [15]. In Sect. 4, we employ both models for completeness and comparison.

2.3   Alternative Algorithms for Solving LWE

Several previous works examine algorithms for solving LWE instances. The main methods for solving LWE consist of

1. Using combinatorial methods or lattice reduction to find a short (scaled) dual-lattice vector, permitting to distinguish LWE samples from uniform [1,19]
2. Employing lattice reduction on the primal lattice then employing Babai's nearest-plane algorithm or a decoding variant thereof [14,15]
3. Reduce the problem to noise-free non-linear polynomial system solving as proposed by Arora and Ge [4].

While, asymptotically, combinatorial methods for finding short (scaled) dual-lattice vectors are most efficient even for moderate parameter sizes [1], the exponential space requirements of these algorithms imply that lattice-based methods are more suitable for attacking practical instantiations of LWE. The algorithm due to Arora and Ge, at present, is largely of theoretical interest and impractical in its current form.

2.4   Concrete Hardness of uSVP

It is folklore that the presence of a significant gap between the first and second minima of a lattice makes finding a shortest non-zero vector somewhat easier than would otherwise be the case, with an exponential gap allowing a shortest non-zero vector to be disclosed by application of LLL. However, in cases with sub-exponential gap, the success of lattice reduction algorithms in disclosing shortest non-zero vectors is poorly understood with a brief investigation in [9] being (to the best of our knowledge) the only practical investigation of such effects.

In [9] it was posited that given a lattice-reduction algorithm which we assume to be characterised by a root Hermite factor δ_0 and a (full-rank) m-dimensional lattice Λ, the algorithm will be successful in disclosing a shortest non-zero vector with high probability when $\lambda_2(\Lambda)/\lambda_1(\Lambda) \geq \tau \cdot \delta_0^m$, where τ was taken to be a constant depending both on the nature of the lattices examined and also on the lattice reduction algorithm applied. In [9] values of τ ranging between 0.18 and 0.48 were experimentally-derived for various classes of lattices (though not LWE-derived lattices) and algorithms. However, the phrase 'with high probability' was not elaborated on in [9] and thus it is unclear as to whether a fixed threshold was used throughout the experiments in [9] or a variable threshold.

3   The Embedding Approach

In this section we outline and examine our application of Kannan's embedding technique, the resulting λ_2/λ_1-gap distributions and the resulting implications for the success of the approach.

3.1   Construction of Embedding Lattices

Given a set of m LWE samples $(\boldsymbol{a}_i, c_i)$, we construct a Matrix-LWE instance of dimension m by constructing a matrix $\mathbf{A}'$ by taking the $\boldsymbol{a}_i$ vectors to be the columns of $\mathbf{A}'$ and form the vector $\mathbf{c}$ from the c_i's to obtain $\mathbf{c} = \mathbf{A}'^T \mathbf{s} + \mathbf{e}$. We consider the problem of being given a matrix-LWE instance $(\mathbf{A}', \mathbf{c})$ of dimension m and forming a lattice basis as follows. We take the matrix $\mathbf{A}' \in \mathbb{Z}_q^{n \times m}$ and calculate the reduced echelon form $\mathbf{A}'' \in \mathbb{Z}_q^{n \times m}$. For the right permutation matrix $\mathbf{P} \in \mathbb{Z}^{m \times m}$, we obtain the form $\mathbf{A}'' \cdot \mathbf{P} = (\mathbf{I}\,\overline{\mathbf{A}})$ with $\mathbf{I} \in \mathbb{Z}_q^{n \times n}$ and $\overline{\mathbf{A}} \in \mathbb{Z}_q^{n \times (m-n)}$. If we interpret this matrix as a matrix over $\mathbb{Z}$, extend it with $(\mathbf{0}\ q\mathbf{I}) \in \mathbb{Z}^{(m-n) \times m}$ and define

$$\mathbf{A} = \begin{pmatrix} \mathbf{I}\ \overline{\mathbf{A}} \\ \mathbf{0}\ q\mathbf{I} \end{pmatrix} \mathbf{P}^{-1},$$

$\mathbf{A}$ is a basis of the lattice $\{\mathbf{v} \in \mathbb{Z}^m \mid \exists \mathbf{x} \in \mathbb{Z}_q^n : \mathbf{x}\mathbf{A} = \mathbf{v} \mod q\}$. Now, given this $\mathbf{A}$ and a target vector $\mathbf{t} \in \mathbb{Z}_q^m$ and attempting to solve the LWE instance by reducing the embedding lattice basis

$$\mathbf{B}_{(\mathbf{A}, \mathbf{t}, t)} := \begin{pmatrix} \mathbf{A}\ \mathbf{0} \\ \mathbf{t}\ t \end{pmatrix}$$

where $t > 0$ is an embedding factor to be determined. We then define $\Lambda_e := \mathcal{L}(\mathbf{B})$. Note that, with overwhelming probability, $\det(\Lambda_e) = t \cdot q^{m-n}$, i.e. $\mathbf{A}'$ has full rank over $\mathbb{Z}_q$.

It is well-known [18] that $1/(2\gamma)$-BDD can be reduced to solving γ-USVP by setting the embedding factor $t \geq \text{dist}(\mathbf{t}, \mathcal{L}(\mathbf{A}))$. In practice, however, employing a smaller embedding factor generally allows us to create a unique-SVP instance with larger λ_2/λ_1 gap than by setting $t = \text{dist}(\mathbf{t}, \mathcal{L}(\mathbf{A}))$. However, by setting $t < \text{dist}(\mathbf{t}, \mathcal{L}(\mathbf{A}))$, with non-zero probability there exists a vector $\mathbf{v} \in \Lambda$ such that $\|\mathbf{v} + c \cdot [\mathbf{t}\ \ t]\| < \|[\mathbf{e}\ \ t]\|$ where $c \in \mathbb{Z}$ and, in general, if $t < \text{dist}(\mathbf{t}, \mathcal{L}(\mathbf{A}))$, we will have $\lambda_2(\Lambda_e) < \lambda_1(\mathcal{L}(\mathbf{A}))$. Thus when we reduce t, quantification of the resulting λ_2/λ_1 gap becomes difficult.

To the best of our knowledge, no good model exists to determine the distribution of the lattice gap when taking an embedding factor smaller than $\|\mathbf{e}\|$. To attempt circumvention of such difficulties, we conduct experiments on LWE-derived uSVP lattices, examining firstly the λ_2/λ_1 gap required for success when we set $t = \lceil \text{dist}(\mathbf{t}, \mathcal{L}(\mathbf{A})) \rceil$ (where we know λ_2/λ_1) and then for the case $t = 1$, under the assumption that the 'necessary gap' is unlikely to change, allowing us to derive analogous models.

3.2   On the Determination of τ When $t = \lceil \|\mathbf{e}\| \rceil$

As mentioned in 2.4, we employ the simple model of Gama and Nguyen for predicting the success of a particular basis-reduction algorithm in recovering a shortest non-zero vector, namely that there exist values of τ such that, for a given probability, basis-reduction algorithm and lattice class, the basis-reduction algorithm finds a shortest non-zero vector with probability greater or equal than the given probability over the random choice of lattices in the class whenever $\lambda_2(\Lambda)/\lambda_1(\Lambda) \geq \tau \cdot \delta_0^m$ where Λ represents a random choice of lattice in the class with dimension m. Thus, if we are able to sample such lattices randomly, determining a particular value of τ requires us to know (at least approximately) the λ_2/λ_1 gap of the lattices we are dealing with.

In the q-ary lattices we consider (i.e. lattices of the form $\mathcal{L}(\mathbf{A})$), unfortunately, there is no known good bound (in the Euclidean norm) on the first minimum when $m < 5n\log_2 q$. The case of $m \geq 5n\log_2 q$ is dealt with in [23]. For the case of random lattices (in the sense of [12]), it is known that with overwhelming probability the minima of such an n-dimensional lattice are all asymptotically close to the Gaussian heuristic i.e.

$$\frac{\lambda_i(\Lambda)}{\mathrm{vol}(\Lambda)^{1/n}} \approx \frac{\Gamma(1+n/2)^{1/n}}{\sqrt{\pi}}.$$

Now the q-ary lattices (e.g. $\mathcal{L}(\mathbf{A})$) widely employed in lattice-based cryptography are not random in this sense, being instead 'Ajtai' or LWE lattices, endowed with the worst-to-average-case properties. However, in all cases, it appears that the Gaussian heuristic appears to hold exceedingly well for such lattices (at least for the first minimum and with the added property that we always have vectors of norm q within the lattice), thus we assume throughout that the first minimum of such lattices is lower-bounded by the Gaussian heuristic with overwhelming probability.

For the first minimum of the embedding lattices, we only deal with this explicitly in the 'known-λ_1' case where we take this to be $\lambda_1(\Lambda_e) = \sqrt{2} \cdot \|\mathbf{e}\|$.

Then we can state the following lemma.

Lemma 2. *Let $\mathbf{A} \in \mathbb{Z}_q^{n \times m}$, let $s > 0$ and let $c > 1$. Let $\mathbf{e}$ be drawn from $D_{\mathbb{Z}^m,s}$. Under the assumption that $\lambda_1(\Lambda(\mathbf{A})) \geq \mathrm{GH}_{q,n,m}$[1] and that the rows of $\mathbf{A}$ are linearly-independent over $\mathbb{Z}_q$, we can create an embedding lattice Λ_e with λ_2/λ_1-gap greater than*

$$\frac{\min\left\{q, \dfrac{q^{1-\frac{n}{m}}\Gamma(1+\frac{m}{2})^{\frac{1}{m}}}{\sqrt{\pi}}\right\}}{\frac{cs\sqrt{m}}{\sqrt{\pi}}} \approx \frac{\min\left\{q, q^{1-\frac{n}{m}}\sqrt{\frac{m}{2\pi e}}\right\}}{\frac{cs\sqrt{m}}{\sqrt{\pi}}}$$

with probabillity greater than $1 - (c \cdot \exp((1-c^2)/2))^m$.

Proof. Omitted

We wish to obtain the value of m for which we can expect to gain the largest gaps (again, probabilistically).

Corollary 1. *Under the assumptions stated in Lemma 2 and for a fixed value of c $(c > 1)$, we can construct embedding lattices with the largest possible gap when*

$$q = \frac{q^{1-\frac{n}{m}}\Gamma(1+\frac{m}{2})^{\frac{1}{m}}}{\sqrt{\pi}}.$$

---

[1] We employ the notation $\mathrm{GH}_{q,n,m}$ to denote the application of the Gaussian heuristic to an LWE lattice formed from m LWE samples of dimension n, with modulus q.

Proof. We assume that the approximation is close enough such that the maximum occurs for the same value of m. Consider the functions:

- $f_0(m) = \frac{\sqrt{\pi}q^{1-\frac{n}{m}}\sqrt{\frac{m}{2\pi e}}}{cs\sqrt{m}}$ where $c > 1$, $s > 0$.
- $f_1(m) = \frac{q\sqrt{\pi}}{cs\sqrt{m}}$ where $c, m > 1$ and $s > 0$.

Then $f_1(m)$ is clearly monotonically-decreasing and $f_0(m)$ has the form $f_0(m) = d \cdot q^{1-\frac{n}{m}}$, where d is a positive constant, hence is clearly monotonically-increasing under the conditions given. $\square$

Thus, in our experiments, it appears valid to derive values of τ by assuming the Gaussian heuristic holds and that the (Euclidean) norm of the noise vector is equal to the expected value.

3.3   On the Determination of τ When $t < \lceil \|e\| \rceil$

However, as mentioned, the employment of an embedding factor smaller than the norm of the noise vector e generally leads to a modest decrease in the size of the second minimum of the resulting lattice. In all cases observed, however, this decrease in the second minimum is less than the corresponding decrease in the first minimum (as a result of making the target vector shorter), leading to a more effective attack. However, quantification of the resulting gap is not simple – we know of no efficient method for determining the distribution of the λ_2/λ_1 gap under such conditions.

In an attempt to circumvent the lack of knowledge of the distribution of the λ_2/λ_1 gap when we take an embedding factor t such that $t < \|e\|$, we assume that (for the same probabilistic success of a given basis-reduction algorithm) the same size of gap is required as in the case where we take $t = \lceil \|e\| \rceil$ and then derive a modified value for τ. That is, we assume that the basis-reduction algorithm is in some sense oblivious to the embedding factor, with the size of the gap being the 'deciding factor'. While this is a somewhat arbitrary assumption, we believe it to be reasonable and intuitive. We denote the value of τ when $t = \lceil \|e\| \rceil$ by $\tau_{\|e\|}$ and the analogous value of τ when $t = 1$ by τ_1. Given a particular value of n and knowing $\tau_{\|e\|}$, we hence know (approximately) the gap required, denoted by $g_{\|e\|}$ and hence a corresponding minimum lattice dimension which we denote by $m_{\|e\|}$. Then, denoting by m_1 the minimum lattice dimension in the case $t = 1$ and assuming that the minimum required gap in the second case, denoted by g_1, is the same, we can write

$$\tau_1 = \min\left\{\tau_{\|e\|} \cdot \delta_0^{(m_{\|e\|}-m_1)}, 1\right\}.$$

However, for easier and more intuitive comparison, we wish to express τ values for the case $t = 1$ when using the gaps from the $t = \lceil \|e\| \rceil$ cases. For this comparison, we simply use the λ_2/λ_1 gaps from the case $t = \lceil \|e\| \rceil$ and plug in the minimum dimension values from the case $t = 1$. We denote these 'illustrative' values of τ by τ'.

4   Application to LWE and Comparisons

We now examine in more detail the model of [9] when applied to such unique-SVP instances. One difficulty with this model is that, while Gama and Nguyen state that success will occur with 'high probability', this probability is not explained. In the cases examined in this work, it appears to be often impossible to exceed a certain success probability regardless of the lattice λ_2/λ_1 gap (when fixing a particular algorithm and parameterisation) and forms, in our opinion, an interesting subject for future work. For instance, Fig. 1 demonstrates success probabilities for LLL for the case of Regev's parameterisation with $n \in \{35, 40, 45\}$ ($t = \|e\|$) and increasing values of m, with between 50 and 100 cases being run for each value of m.

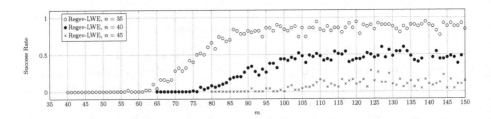

Fig. 1. Experimental success rates, Regev-LWE, LLL, $n \in \{35, 40, 45\}$, $t = \|e\|$

We treat only the LWE parameterisations proposed by Regev [21] and Lindner/Peikert [14] and view each family of LWE instances as being parameterised by a value of n, from which values of s and q are derived. We then wish to examine the conditions under which applying the embedding approach yields a basis in which the target vector is present (though not necessarily the shortest vector in this reduced basis).

As in [9], our experiments indicate that the target vector lies in the reduced basis with some (fixed) probability whenever the gap is large enough such that

$$\frac{\lambda_2(\Lambda_m)}{\lambda_1(\Lambda_m)} \geq \tau \cdot \delta_0^m$$

where τ is some real constant such that $0 < \tau \leq 1$ depending on the desired probability level, the 'nature' of the lattices considered and the basis-reduction algorithm used. Our experiments proceed by fixing values of n to obtain corresponding LWE parameterisations then generating instances with increasing values of m – using [3] – until finding the minimum such value that recovery of the target vector is possible with the desired probability. We denote such values of m by $m_{\min}(n)$. In the $t = \lceil \|e\| \rceil$ case, plugging this value $m_{\min}(n)$ in $\frac{\lambda_2(\Lambda_m)}{\lambda_1(\Lambda_m)} = \tau \cdot \delta_0^m$ for m where we use Lemma 2 then recovers $\tau_{\|e\|}$. From this value and experimental data for $t = 1$ we can then derive $\tau_1 = \min \left\{ \tau_{\|e\|} \cdot \delta_0^{(m_{\|e\|} - m_1)}, 1 \right\}$ and τ'

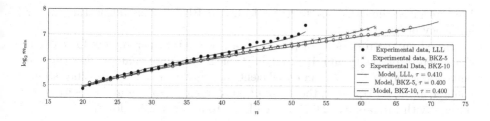

Fig. 2. Minimum lattice dimension, Regev-LWE, success rate 10 %, $t = \|e\|$.

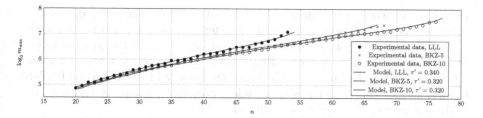

Fig. 3. Minimum lattice dimension, Regev-LWE, success rate 10 %, $t = 1$.

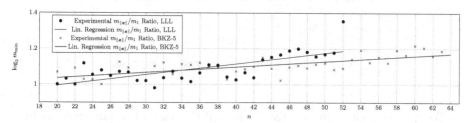

Fig. 4. $m_{\|e\|}/m_1$ Ratios, Regev-LWE, LLL and BKZ-5

by solving $\frac{\lambda_2(\Lambda_m)}{\lambda_1(\Lambda_m)} = \tau' \cdot \delta_0^{m_1}$. Throughout, the experimental data points indicate the minimum lattice dimension for which the lattice basis reduction algorithm succeeds in recovering the target vector with success rate 10 %.

In all experiments carried out, we artificially force that every $\|e\|$ takes value $\approx \mathrm{E}[\|e\|]$. This allows us to gain a good estimate of the λ_2/λ_1 gap in the $t = \|e\|$ case. In addition, for the $m_{\min}$ calculations, we used the experimentally-derived root Hermite factors (see Appendix A) with linear interpolation.

4.1   Regev's Parameters

We firstly examine the case of Regev's original parameters as proposed in [20]. We take $q \approx n^2$ and set $\alpha = 1/(\sqrt{n} \cdot \log_2^2 n)$, $s = \alpha q$. Figure 2 illustrates the predicted feasible regions when $t = \lceil \|e\| \rceil$. Similarly, Fig. 3 gives analogous plots in the case $t = 1$, using the 'illustrative' values of τ' mentioned in Sect. 3.3.

Figure 4 gives the $m_{\|e\|}/m_1$ ratio for LLL and BKZ-5, illustrating the greater efficiency of using $t = 1$.

Based on the results as displayed above, we obtain parameters for embedding factors of $\lceil\|e\|\rceil$ and 1, given in Table 2. We note that, while using an embedding factor $t = 1$ is most efficient, obtaining $\tau_1 > \tau_{\|e\|}$ possibly seems counter-intuitive. However, the assumption of a fixed gap required for success to occurs (with probability ≈ 0.1) indeed leads to a larger value for τ_1.

4.2 Lindner and Peikert's Parameters

In [14], parameters for an improved LWE-based cryptosystem were proposed. For more details on this variant, the reader is refered to [14]. For our purposes, the principal difference from the Regev-LWE case is the smaller moduli employed by Lindner and Peikert. As in the Regev-LWE case, we choose a series of values for n and generate parameters accordingly, then apply LLL, BKZ-5 and BKZ-10 to solve such instances as far as is possible. Specifically, Table 1 gives a selection of the parameters considered as produced by [3].

Table 1. Selected Lindner/Peikert LWE parameters

n	20	30	40	50	60	70	80
q	2053	2053	2053	2053	2053	2053	2053
s	9.026	8.566	8.225	7.953	7.728	7.536	7.369

We proceed similarly to the Regev-LWE case, with minimum lattice dimensions being given in Fig. 5 for the $t = \|e\|$ case and in Fig. 6 for the $t = 1$ case. Table 2 also gives the derived values of τ for Lindner and Peikert's parameterisation.

We note that the values of τ derived seem consistent and do not vary widely between parameterisations. Of course, the value of τ may be expected to change when using 'stronger' algorithms than BKZ-10 or BKZ-20, however our limited experiments, and the results reported in [9] appear to indicate that the use of

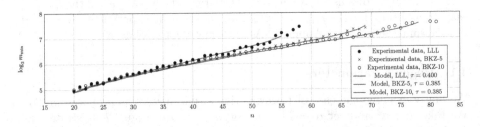

Fig. 5. Minimum lattice dimension, Lindner/Peikert Parameterisation, success rate 10%, $t = \|e\|$

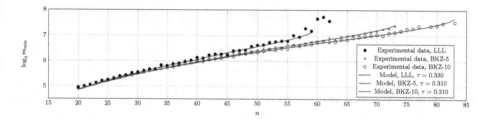

Fig. 6. Minimum lattice dimension, Lindner/Peikert Parameterisation, success rate 10%, $t = 1$

Table 2. Parameters for finding e with success rate 10%, Regev's and Lindner & Peikert's parameters.

Regev	LLL	BKZ-5	BKZ-10	Lindner and Peikert	LLL	BKZ-5	BKZ-10
τ $(t = \|e\|)$	0.410	0.400	0.400	τ $(t = \|e\|)$	0.400	0.385	0.385
τ $(t = 1)$	0.467	0.464	0.444	τ $(t = 1)$	0.435	0.431	0.439
τ' $(t = 1)$	0.340	0.320	0.320	τ' $(t = 1)$	0.330	0.310	0.310

'stronger' basis reduction algorithms leads to modest decreases in the values of τ. Thus, when we project these results in Sect. 5.1, we use the experimentally-derived τ values and thus expect the resulting complexity predictions to be somewhat conservative.

5   Limits of the Embedding Approach

Using the above model, we can derive an estimation of the limits of applicability of the embedding approach. Given a values (δ_0, τ), we can define the maximum value of n for which we can recover the target vector using the embedding approach to be

$$n_{\max} := \max\left\{ n : \exists m \quad \text{s.t.} \frac{\lambda_2(\Lambda_e(n, m))}{\lambda_1(\Lambda_e(n, m))} = \tau \cdot \delta_0^m \right\}$$

The goal is to determine the values of $n_{\max}$. Lemma 2 shows that we can construct a gap of size (under the assumption that we use basis-reduction algorithms with δ_0 small enough that $q^{1-(n/m)}\sqrt{m/(2\pi e)} < q$)

$$\frac{\lambda_2}{\lambda_1} \approx \frac{q^{1-\frac{n}{m}}\sqrt{\frac{1}{2e}}}{cs}.$$

If we want to solve an LWE instance with secret-dimension n, we have to find m such that

$$\frac{q^{1-\frac{n}{m}}\sqrt{\frac{1}{2e}}}{cs \cdot \tau \cdot \delta_0^m} \geq 1.$$

In order to determine the optimal m, we want to maximize the function

$$f_n(m) = \frac{q^{1-\frac{n}{m}} \sqrt{\frac{1}{2e}}}{c \cdot s \cdot \tau \cdot \delta_0^m}.$$

the first derivative of which is zero only when

$$\frac{n \log q}{m^2} = \log \delta_0,$$

and therefore $m = \sqrt{\frac{n \log q}{\log \delta_0}}$ is the optimal sub-dimension. In other words, we expect the attack to succeed if

$$\frac{q^{\left(1 - \frac{n}{\sqrt{\frac{n \log q}{\log \delta_0}}}\right)} \sqrt{\frac{1}{2e}}}{c \cdot s \cdot \tau \cdot \delta_0^{\sqrt{\frac{n \log q}{\log \delta_0}}}} \geq 1$$

Thus, we only need to consider the optimal sub-dimension to ascertain whether we can expect the attack to succeed (with the given probability). Since, in our experiments we force $\|e\| \approx \mathrm{E}[\|e\|]$, we increase the value of c to cover all but the upper-tail of the distribution of $\|e\|$. We can then state the following:

Assumption 1. *Given a fixed LWE parameterisation and a given value of τ (derived as above using $\|e\| \approx \mathrm{E}[\|e\|]$ instances and also corresponding to a fixed δ_0) corresponding to a fixed success rate p_s, we can solve general instances from the parameterisation with secret-dimension n with a particular value of m with probability*

$$p_c \geq p_s \cdot \left(1 - (c \cdot \exp((1 - c^2)/2))^m\right) \tag{1}$$

if

$$\frac{q^{\left(1 - \frac{n}{\sqrt{\frac{n \log q}{\log \delta_0}}}\right)} \sqrt{\frac{1}{2e}}}{c \cdot s \cdot \tau \cdot \delta_0^{\sqrt{\frac{n \log q}{\log \delta_0}}}} \geq 1 \tag{2}$$

We note that this assumption follows immediately from the above discussion and Lemma 1. Thus, given a target success probability, we attempt to satisfy conditions (1) and (2) (Table 3).

5.1   Comparisons

We briefly compare the application of BKZ in both the embedding approach and the short dual-lattice vector distinguishing approach. For all embedding approach predictions, we take success probability slightly lower than 0.1, employing Assumption 1 - we choose c such that condition 1 holds for $p_c \geq 0.099$. While the

Table 3. Estimated cost of finding e with success rate 0.099, Regev's parameters.

n	64	96	128	160	192	224	256	288	320
δ_0	1.0159	1.0111	1.0085	1.0069	1.0058	1.0050	1.0045	1.0040	1.0036
$\log_2(\sec) = 1.8/\log_2 \delta_0 - 110$	negl.	negl.	37.41	71.44	105.74	140.16	167.88	202.54	237.20
$\log_2(\sec) = 0.009/\log_2^2 \delta_0 - 27$	negl.	negl.	33.36	64.45	102.29	146.83	187.50	244.37	307.85

dual-lattice distinguishing approach is not the best-known attack (the best practical attacks being that in [14] or modified versions [15]), it is easy to analyse in comparison to reduction-then-decode algorithms. We consider the application of BKZ in both situations. In the distinguishing approach, we can choose a desired distinguishing advantage ϵ and set $\gamma = q/s \cdot \sqrt{\ln(1/\epsilon)/\pi}$, from which we can compute a required root Hermite factor of $\delta_0 = 2^{\log_2^2(\gamma)/(4n \log_2 q)}$. So, for instance, with $n = 128$, we require $\delta_0 \approx 1.0077$ to gain a distinguishing advantage of ≈ 0.099, i.e. significantly worse than the 1.0085 required for the embedding attack. In Table 4 we give comparable estimated costs for distinguishing between LWE samples and uniformly random samples using the approach of Micciancio and Regev.

Table 4. Estimated cost of solving decision-LWE, advantage ~ 0.099, Regev's parameters, dual-lattice distinguisher

n	64	96	128	160	192	224	256	288	320
δ_0	1.0144	1.0099	1.0077	1.0063	1.0053	1.0046	1.0040	1.0036	1.0033
$\log_2(\sec) = 1.8/\log_2 \delta_0 - 110$	negl.	negl.	53.15	89.99	126.44	162.56	198.39	234.00	269.38
$\log_2(\sec) = 0.009/\log_2^2 \delta_0 - 27$	negl	negl	46.93	84.10	128.29	179.35	237.18	301.70	372.81

However, we note that the expression of Lindner and Peikert for the advantage of the dual-lattice distinguishing approach gives an upper-bound on the advantage obtained through the use of a specific algorithm. While the approximation is close overall, in the high-advantage regime the model is somewhat optimistic in estimating the advantage obtainable.

More rigorous comparison to the dual-lattice distinguishing attack is difficult, however, since the optimal strategy for said attack is to run a large number of low-advantage attacks and we can only analyse the embedding approach for high-advantages due to the (current) practical component of the analysis. We also note that if the embedding approach is used with $t = \|e\|$ and fails, we can extract the resulting reduced basis of the lattice Λ and can then we proceed to run enumeration/decoding procedures, a strategy worthy of further investigation.

In conclusion, we provide evidence that the model of Gama and Nguyen is applicable to the solution of unique-SVP instances constructed from LWE instances and experimentally derive the constants which embody the performance of the approach. Based on the models used and assumptions made, we show that the embedding approach outperforms the dual-lattice distinguishing approach of Micciancio and Regev (in the high-advantage regime).

Open Questions. We view a more in-depth comparison of the efficiency of the embedding technique and enumeration techniques as a pressing research question. The practical behaviour of lattice-reduction algorithms on unique-SVP instances remains mysterious, with (to the best of our knowledge) no recent progress in explaining the phenomena observed.

A Root Hermite Factors for LWE-Derived Lattices

It is a generally-accepted heuristic that the norms of shortest lattice vectors found by lattice basis reduction algorithms can be approximated by (Table 5)

$$\|\boldsymbol{b}_1\| \approx \det(\mathcal{L})^{1/m} \cdot \delta_0(m)^m$$

where $\delta_0(m)$ rapidly converges to a constant, denoted δ_0, as m grows. The following tables give experimentally-derived root Hermite factors for LLL and some BKZ algorithms as applied to the LWE-derived lattices studied in this work – all root Hermite factors being obtained for the minimum dimension in which the given algorithm solves the LWE-n instance with probability 0.1 (Tables 6 and 7).

Table 5. Root Hermite factors, LLL, Regev's parameters

n	20	25	30	35	40	45	50
δ_0	1.0151	1.0169	1.0178	1.0182	1.0192	1.0204	1.0204

Table 6. Root Hermite factors, BKZ-5, Regev's parameters

n	20	25	30	35	40	45	50	55	60
δ_0	1.0138	1.0146	1.0147	1.0147	1.0148	1.0157	1.0161	1.0159	1.0160

Table 7. Root Hermite factors, BKZ-10, Regev's parameters

n	20	25	30	35	40	45	50	55	60	65
δ_0	1.0121	1.0129	1.0136	1.0139	1.0138	1.0141	1.0145	1.0145	1.0146	1.0143

References

1. Albrecht, M.R., Cid, C., Faugère, J.-C., Fitzpatrick, R., Perret, L.: On the complexity of the BKW algorithm on LWE. Des. Codes and Cryptogr. 1–30 (2013)
2. Albrecht, M.R., Farshim, P., Faugère, J.-C., Perret, L.: Polly cracker, revisited. In: Lee, D.H., Wang, X. (eds.) ASIACRYPT 2011. LNCS, vol. 7073, pp. 179–196. Springer, Heidelberg (2011)
3. Albrecht, M.R., Fitzpatrick, R., Cabracas, D., Göpfert, F., Schneider, M.: A generator for LWE and Ring-LWE instances (2013). http://www.iacr.org/news/files/2013-04-29lwe-generator.pdf
4. Arora, S., Ge, R.: New algorithms for learning in presence of errors. In: Aceto, L., Henzinger, M., Sgall, J. (eds.) ICALP 2011, Part I. LNCS, vol. 6755, pp. 403–415. Springer, Heidelberg (2011)
5. Banaszczyk, W.: New bounds in some transference theorems in the geometry of numbers. Math. Ann. **296**(1), 625–635 (1993)
6. Brakerski, Z., Langlois, A., Peikert, C., Regev, O., Stehlé, D.: Classical hardness of Learning with Errors. To appear STOC 2013 (2013)
7. Brakerski, Z., Vaikuntanathan, V.: Efficient fully homomorphic encryption from (standard) LWE. In: Ostrovsky, R. (ed.) IEEE 52nd Annual Symposium on Foundations of Computer Science, FOCS 2011, pp. 97–106. IEEE (2011)
8. Chen, Y., Nguyen, P.Q.: BKZ 2.0: better lattice security estimates. In: Lee, D.H., Wang, X. (eds.) ASIACRYPT 2011. LNCS, vol. 7073, pp. 1–20. Springer, Heidelberg (2011)
9. Gama, N., Nguyen, P.Q.: Predicting lattice reduction. In: Smart, N.P. (ed.) EUROCRYPT 2008. LNCS, vol. 4965, pp. 31–51. Springer, Heidelberg (2008)
10. Gentry, C.: A fully homomorphic encryption scheme. Ph.D. thesis, Stanford University (2009). http://crypto.stanford.edu/craig
11. Gentry, C., Peikert, C., Vaikuntanathan, V.: Trapdoors for hard lattices and new cryptographic constructions. In: STOC 08: Proceedings of the 40th Annual ACM Symposium on Theory of Computing, pp. 197–206. ACM (2008)
12. Goldstein, D., Mayer, A.: On the equidistribution of Hecke points. Forum Mathematicum **15**, 165–189 (2003)
13. Kannan, R.: Minkowski's convex body theorem and integer programming. Math. Oper. Res. **12**(3), 415–440 (1987)
14. Lindner, R., Peikert, C.: Better key sizes (and attacks) for LWE-based encryption. In: Kiayias, A. (ed.) CT-RSA 2011. LNCS, vol. 6558, pp. 319–339. Springer, Heidelberg (2011)
15. Liu, M., Nguyen, P.Q.: Solving BDD by enumeration: an update. In: Dawson, E. (ed.) CT-RSA 2013. LNCS, vol. 7779, pp. 293–309. Springer, Heidelberg (2013)
16. Liu, M., Wang, X., Xu, G., Zheng, X.: Shortest lattice vectors in the presence of gaps. Cryptology ePrint Archive, Report 2011/139 (2011). http://eprint.iacr.org/. Accessed 4 March 2012
17. Lovász, L.: An algorithmic theory of numbers, graphs, and convexity. In: CBMS-NSF Regional Conference Series in Applied Mathematics. Society for Industrial and Applied Mathematics, Philadelphia (1986)
18. Lyubashevsky, V., Micciancio, D.: On bounded distance decoding, unique shortest vectors, and the minimum distance problem. In: Halevi, S. (ed.) CRYPTO 2009. LNCS, vol. 5677, pp. 577–594. Springer, Heidelberg (2009)
19. Micciancio, D., Regev, O.: Lattice-based cryptography. In: Bernstein, D.J., Buchmann, J., Dahmen, E. (eds.) Post-Quantum Cryptography, pp. 147–191. Springer, Heidelberg (2009)

20. Regev, O.: On lattices, learning with errors, random linear codes, and cryptography. In: Gabow, H.N., Fagin, R. (eds.) STOC, pp. 84–93. ACM (2005)
21. Regev, O.: On lattices, learning with errors, random linear codes, and cryptography. J. ACM **56**(6), 1–40 (2009)
22. Regev, O.: The learning with errors problem (invited survey). In: IEEE Conference on Computational Complexity, pp. 191–204. IEEE Computer Society (2010)
23. Stehlé, D., Steinfeld, R., Tanaka, K., Xagawa, K.: Efficient public key encryption based on ideal lattices. In: Matsui, M. (ed.) ASIACRYPT 2009. LNCS, vol. 5912, pp. 617–635. Springer, Heidelberg (2009)

A Family of Cryptographically Significant Boolean Functions Based on the Hidden Weighted Bit Function

Qichun Wang[✉], Chik How Tan, and Timothy Foo

Temasek Laboratories, National University of Singapore, Singapore 117411, Singapore
{tslwq,tsltch,tslfcht}@nus.edu.sg

Abstract. Based on the hidden weighted bit function, we propose a family of cryptographically significant Boolean functions. We investigate its algebraic degree and use Schur polynomials to study its algebraic immunity. For a subclass of this family, we deduce a lower bound on its nonlinearity. Moreover, we give an infinite class of balanced functions with very good cryptographic properties: optimum algebraic degree, optimum algebraic immunity, high nonlinearity (higher than the Carlet-Feng function and the function proposed by [25]) and a good behavior against fast algebraic attacks. These functions seem to have the best cryptographic properties among all currently known functions.

Keywords: Boolean function · Hidden weighted bit function · Algebraic immunity · Nonlinearity

1 Introduction

To resist the main known attacks, Boolean functions used in stream ciphers should be balanced, with high algebraic degree, with high algebraic immunity, with high nonlinearity and with good immunity to fast algebraic attacks. It is hard to construct Boolean functions satisfying all these criteria. Many classes of Boolean functions with optimum algebraic immunity have been introduced [3,5,9,10,15,16,20]. However, the nonlinearity of these functions is not good. In 2008, Carlet and Feng studied a class of functions which had been introduced by [11], and they found that these functions seem to satisfy all the cryptographic criteria [4]. Based on the Carlet-Feng function, some researchers proposed several classes of cryptographically significant Boolean functions [12,22,24–26,29–31,33]. In [21], the authors construct another class of almost fully optimized functions with very high nonlinearity and a little worse behavior against fast algebraic attacks, compared to the Carlet-Feng function.

The hidden weighted bit function which was proposed by Bryant [1], seems to be the simplest one with exponential BDD size [14]. In [27,32], the authors investigated the cryptographic properties of the HWBF and found that it could be a very good candidate for being used in real ciphers. Based on the hidden

© Springer International Publishing Switzerland 2014
H.-S. Lee and D.-G. Han (Eds.): ICISC 2013, LNCS 8565, pp. 311–322, 2014.
DOI: 10.1007/978-3-319-12160-4_19

weighted bit function, we propose a family of Boolean functions. We investigate the cryptographic properties of these functions and give an infinite class of balanced functions with very good cryptographic properties: optimum algebraic degree, optimum algebraic immunity, high nonlinearity (higher than the Carlet-Feng function and the functions proposed by [25]) and a good behavior against fast algebraic attacks.

The paper is organized as follows. In Sect. 2, the necessary background is established. We investigate the properties of a family of Boolean functions in Sect. 3. In Sect. 4, we give an infinite class of balanced functions with very good cryptographic properties. We end in Sect. 5 with conclusions.

2   Preliminaries

Let $\mathbb{F}_2^n$ be the n-dimensional vector space over the finite field $\mathbb{F}_2$. We denote by B_n the set of all n-variable Boolean functions, from $\mathbb{F}_2^n$ into $\mathbb{F}_2$.

Any Boolean function $f \in B_n$ can be uniquely represented as a multivariate polynomial in $\mathbb{F}_2[x_1, \cdots, x_n]$,

$$f(x_1, \ldots, x_n) = \sum_{K \subseteq \{1,2,\ldots,n\}} a_K \prod_{k \in K} x_k,$$

which is called its algebraic normal form (ANF). The algebraic degree of f, denoted by $\deg(f)$, is the number of variables in the highest order term with nonzero coefficient.

A Boolean function f is affine if $\deg(f) \leq 1$ and the set of all affine functions is denoted by A_n.

Let

$$1_f = \{x \in \mathbb{F}_2^n | f(x) = 1\}, \ 0_f = \{x \in \mathbb{F}_2^n | f(x) = 0\},$$

be the support of a Boolean function f, respectively, its complement. The cardinality of 1_f is called the Hamming weight of f, and will be denoted by $wt(f)$. The Hamming distance between two functions f and g is the Hamming weight of $f + g$, and will be denoted by $d(f, g)$. We say that an n-variable Boolean function f is *balanced* if $wt(f) = 2^{n-1}$.

Let $f \in B_n$. The nonlinearity of f is its distance from the set of all n-variable affine functions, i.e.,

$$nl(f) = \min_{g \in A_n} d(f, g).$$

The nonlinearity of an n-variable Boolean function is bounded above by $2^{n-1} - 2^{n/2-1}$, and a function is said to be bent if it achieves this bound. Clearly, bent functions exist only for even n and it is known that the algebraic degree of a bent function is bounded above by $\frac{n}{2}$ [2,8,23].

For any $f \in B_n$, a nonzero function $g \in B_n$ is called an annihilator of f if $fg = 0$, and the algebraic immunity of f, denoted by $\mathcal{AI}(f)$, is the minimum value of d such that f or $f + 1$ admits an annihilator of degree d [19]. It is known that the algebraic immunity of an n-variable Boolean function is bounded above by $\lceil \frac{n}{2} \rceil$ [7].

To resist fast algebraic attacks, a high algebraic immunity is not sufficient. If we can find g of low degree and h of algebraic degree not much larger than $n/2$ such that $fg = h$, then f is considered to be weak against fast algebraic attacks [6,13]. To resist fast algebraic attacks, a Boolean function should have a large distance to bent functions [28].

The Walsh transform of a given function $f \in B_n$ is the function over $\mathbb{F}_{2^n}$ defined by

$$W_f(\omega) = \sum_{x \in \mathbb{F}_{2^n}} (-1)^{f(x)+tr(\omega x)},$$

where $tr(x) = \sum_{i=0}^{n-1} x^{2^i}$ is the trace function from $\mathbb{F}_{2^n}$ to $\mathbb{F}_2$. It is easy to see that a Boolean function f is balanced if and only if $W_f(0) = 0$. Moreover, the nonlinearity of f can be determined by

$$nl(f) = 2^{n-1} - \frac{1}{2} \max_{\omega \in \mathbb{F}_{2^n}} |W_f(\omega)|.$$

3   A Family of Boolean Functions

Let $0 \leq l \leq 2^m - 1$. Then l can be uniquely represented as $l_0 + l_1 * 2 + ... + l_{m-1} * 2^{m-1}$, where $l_i \in \mathbb{F}_2$, $0 \leq i \leq m - 1$. Hence, we can identify l with a vector $(l_0, l_1, ..., l_{m-1}) \in \mathbb{F}_2^m$. Let $g \in B_m$. In the following, we use $g(l)$ to denote $g(l_0, l_1, ..., l_{m-1})$ and $wt(l) = l_0 + l_1 + ... + l_{m-1}$.

Let $h \in B_m$ be the hidden weighted bit function. That is,

$$h(x) = \begin{cases} 0 & \text{if } x = 0, \\ x_{wt(x)} & \text{otherwise,} \end{cases}$$

where $x = (x_1, x_2, ..., x_m)$ and $wt(x) = x_1 + x_2 + ... + x_m$.

Construction 1. *Let α be a primitive element of $\mathbb{F}_{2^n}$. We define f, a Boolean function from $\mathbb{F}_{2^n}$ into $\mathbb{F}_2$ which is defined by*

$$\begin{cases} f(0) = 0, \\ f(\alpha^i) = h(i \mod 2^m), \ 1 \leq i \leq 2^n - 1, \end{cases}$$

where $1 \leq m \leq n$ and $h \in B_m$ is the hidden weighted bit function.

Clearly, the Carlet-Feng function can be viewed as a special case of the construction for $m = 1$.

3.1   Algebraic Degree

Theorem 1. *The function f is balanced.* $\deg(f) = n - 1$ *if and only if*

$$\sum_{\substack{j=1 \\ j \in 1_h}}^{2^m - 1} \alpha^j \neq 0.$$

Proof. We have $|1_h| = 2^{m-1}$, since $h \in B_m$ is balanced. Therefore,

$$|1_f| = 2^{n-m} * 2^{m-1} = 2^{n-1}$$

and f is a balanced function. Let the univariate representation of f be

$$f(x) = \sum_{i=0}^{2^n - 1} a_i x^i.$$

Then $a_0 = a_{2^n - 1} = 0$, since f is balanced and $f(0) = 0$. For $1 \leq i \leq 2^n - 2$, we have

$$
\begin{aligned}
a_i &= \sum_{j=0}^{2^n - 2} f(\alpha^j) \alpha^{-ij} \\
&= \sum_{\substack{j=1 \\ j \mod 2^m \in 1_h}}^{2^n - 1} \alpha^{-ij} \\
&= \sum_{\substack{j=1 \\ j \in 1_h}}^{2^m - 1} \alpha^{-ij} \sum_{k=0}^{2^{n-m} - 1} \alpha^{-ik2^m} \\
&= \frac{1 - \alpha^{-i}}{1 - \alpha^{-i2^m}} \sum_{\substack{j=1 \\ j \in 1_h}}^{2^m - 1} \alpha^{-ij}.
\end{aligned}
$$

Clearly, $\deg(f) = n - 1$ if and only if there exists an i such that $wt(i) = n - 1$ and $a_i \neq 0$. That is, there exists an i satisfying $wt(i) = 1$ and $a_{2^n - 1 - i} \neq 0$. For $0 \leq t \leq n - 1$, we have

$$a_{2^n - 1 - 2^t} = \left(\frac{1 - \alpha}{1 - \alpha^{2^m}} \sum_{\substack{j=1 \\ j \in 1_h}}^{2^m - 1} \alpha^j \right)^{2^t}.$$

Clearly, $\frac{1-\alpha}{1-\alpha^{2^m}} \neq 0$. Therefore, $\deg(f) = n - 1$ if and only if

$$\sum_{\substack{j=1 \\ j \in 1_h}}^{2^m - 1} \alpha^j \neq 0.$$

Remark 1. Let $p(x) \in \mathbb{F}_2[x]$ be of degree n and primitive. If $p(\alpha) = 0$, then f has the optimum algebraic degree $n - 1$ if and only if

$$p(x) \nmid \sum_{\substack{j=1 \\ j \in 1_h}}^{2^m - 1} x^j.$$

That is,

$$p(x) \nmid \sum_{\substack{j=1 \\ j \in 1_h}}^{2^m - 1} x^{j-1}.$$

Remark 2. If $m < \log_2(n+2)$, then $\deg(f) = n-1$. Moreover, if $m < \log_2(\varphi(2^n - 1)+2)$, then there is a primitive element α such that f has the optimum algebraic degree, where φ is the Euler's totient function. Particularly, if $2^n - 1$ is a prime, then there always exists a primitive element α such that $\deg(f) = n - 1$, for any $1 \leq m \leq n$.

3.2   Algebraic Immunity

Given a partition

$$d = d_1 + d_2 + ... + d_t, \ d_1 \geq d_2 \geq ... \geq d_t,$$

where each d_i is a non-negative integer. Let

$$a_{(d_1+t-1, d_2+t-2, ..., d_t)}(x_1, ..., x_t) = \det \begin{pmatrix} x_1^{d_1+t-1} & x_2^{d_1+t-1} & ... & x_t^{d_1+t-1} \\ x_1^{d_2+t-2} & x_2^{d_2+t-2} & ... & x_t^{d_2+t-2} \\ ... & ... & ... & ... \\ x_1^{d_t} & x_2^{d_t} & ... & x_t^{d_t} \end{pmatrix}.$$

The Schur polynomial is defined as follows

$$s_{(d_1, d_2, ..., d_t)}(x_1, x_2, ..., x_t) = \frac{a_{(d_1+t-1, d_2+t-2, ..., d_t)}(x_1, ..., x_t)}{a_{(t-1, t-2, ..., 0)}(x_1, ..., x_t)}.$$

Let $J = \{j | wt(j) < \lceil \frac{n}{2} \rceil\} = \{j_1, ..., j_r\}$, where $r = \sum_{i=0}^{\lceil \frac{n}{2} \rceil - 1} \binom{n}{i}$. Let $I_1 = \{1 \leq i \leq 2^n - 1 | \alpha^i \in 1_f\} = \{i_1, ..., i_{2^{n-1}}\}$ and $I_2 = \{1, 2, ..., 2^n - 1\} - I_1$.

Proposition 1. *Let n be odd. Then $f \in B_n$ has optimum algebraic immunity if and only if*

$$s_{(d_1, d_2, ..., d_{2^{n-1}})}(\alpha^{j_1}, \alpha^{j_2}, ..., \alpha^{j_{2^{n-1}}}) \neq 0,$$

where $s_{(d_1, d_2, ..., d_{2^{n-1}})}$ is the Schur polynomial and $d_k = i_{2^{n-1}+1-k} - 2^{n-1} + k$, for $1 \leq k \leq 2^{n-1}$.

Proof. Let $g \in B_n$ be of degree $< \lceil \frac{n}{2} \rceil$ and $g(\alpha^i) = 0$, for $i \in I_1$. Denote $g(x)$ as $\sum_{j \in J} c_j x^j$, where $c_j \in \mathbb{F}_{2^n}$. Then we have

$$
\begin{pmatrix}
\alpha^{i_1 j_1} & \alpha^{i_1 j_2} & \cdots & \alpha^{i_1 j_{2^{n-1}}} \\
\alpha^{i_2 j_1} & \alpha^{i_2 j_2} & \cdots & \alpha^{i_2 j_{2^{n-1}}} \\
\cdots & \cdots & \cdots & \cdots \\
\alpha^{i_{2^{n-1}} j_1} & \alpha^{i_{2^{n-1}} j_2} & \cdots & \alpha^{i_{2^{n-1}} j_{2^{n-1}}}
\end{pmatrix}
\begin{pmatrix}
c_{j_1} \\
c_{j_2} \\
\cdots \\
c_{j_{2^{n-1}}}
\end{pmatrix}
= 0.
$$

Clearly, $\mathcal{AI}(f) = \lceil \frac{n}{2} \rceil$ if and only if the above coefficient matrix is nonsingular. That is, for $1 \le k \le 2^{n-1}$ and $d_k = i_{2^{n-1}+1-k} - 2^{n-1} + k$, we have

$$
s_{(d_1, d_2, \ldots, d_{2^{n-1}})}(\alpha^{j_1}, \alpha^{j_2}, \ldots, \alpha^{j_{2^{n-1}}}) \ne 0.
$$

Similarly, we have the following proposition.

Proposition 2. *Let n be even. Then $f \in B_n$ has optimum algebraic immunity if and only if the following two conditions hold*
   1) For $1 \le k \le r$, there exist $i'_1 < i'_2 < \ldots < i'_r \in I_1$ such that $d'_k = i'_{r+1-k} - r + k$ and

$$
s_{(d'_1, d'_2, \ldots, d'_r)}(\alpha^{j_1}, \alpha^{j_2}, \ldots, \alpha^{j_r}) \ne 0.
$$

   2) For $1 \le k \le r$, there exist $i''_1 < i''_2 < \ldots < i''_r \in I_2$ such that $d''_k = i''_{r+1-k} - r + k$ and

$$
s_{(d''_1, d''_2, \ldots, d''_r)}(\alpha^{j_1}, \alpha^{j_2}, \ldots, \alpha^{j_r}) \ne 0.
$$

3.3   Nonlinearity

Let χ be the primitive character of $\mathbb{F}_{2^n}^*$ defined by $\chi(\alpha^j) = \zeta^j$ $(0 \le j \le 2^n - 2)$, where $\zeta = e^{\frac{2\pi\sqrt{-1}}{2^n-1}}$. Let $\chi(0) = 0$. Then

$$
G(\chi^\mu) = \sum_{x \in \mathbb{F}_{2^n}} \chi^\mu(x)(-1)^{tr(x)}
$$

is a Gauss sum, where $0 \le \mu \le 2^n - 2$. We have $G(\chi^0) = -1$ and $\mid G(\chi^\mu) \mid = 2^{\frac{n}{2}}$ for $1 \le \mu \le 2^n - 2$ [17].
   From calculus, we have the following lemma.

Lemma 1. *For $0 < x < \frac{\pi}{4}$, we have $y = x^2 \sin x + 5 \sin x - 5x > 0$. That is, $\frac{1}{\sin x} < \frac{1}{x} + \frac{x}{5}$.*

Theorem 2. *Let $m = 3$, $n \ge 5$ and $f \in B_n$ be the function defined in Construction 1. Then*

$$
nl(f) \ge 2^{n-1} - (\frac{10n \ln 2}{3\pi} - 0.8)2^{n/2}
$$

Proof. Let $q = 2^n$ and $\omega = \alpha^l$. Since

$$(-1)^{tr(\alpha^j)} = \frac{1}{q-1} \sum_{\mu=0}^{q-2} G(\chi^\mu)\overline{\chi}^\mu(\alpha^j),$$

where $0 \leq j \leq q-2$, We have

$$\sum_{x \in 1_f} (-1)^{tr(\omega x)} = \frac{1}{q-1} \sum_{\mu=0}^{q-2} G(\chi^\mu) \sum_{\substack{i \bmod 2^m \in 1_h \\ 1 \leq i \leq q-1}} \overline{\chi}^\mu(\alpha^{l+i})$$

$$= \frac{1}{q-1}\left(\sum_{\mu=1}^{q-2} G(\chi^\mu) \sum_{\substack{i \bmod 2^m \in 1_h \\ 1 \leq i \leq q-1}} \zeta^{-\mu(l+i)} - \frac{q}{2}\right).$$

Then,

$$\left|\sum_{x \in 1_f} (-1)^{tr(\omega x)}\right| \leq \frac{1}{q-1}\left(\sqrt{q} \sum_{\mu=1}^{q-2} |\zeta^{-\mu} + \zeta^{-3\mu} + \zeta^{-6\mu} + \zeta^{-7\mu}|\left|\frac{1-\zeta^{-\mu q}}{1-\zeta^{-8\mu}}\right| + \frac{q}{2}\right)$$

$$\leq \frac{2\sqrt{q}}{q-1} \sum_{\mu=1}^{q-2} \left|\frac{1-\zeta^{-\mu}}{1-\zeta^{-8\mu}}\right| + \frac{q}{2(q-1)}$$

$$= \frac{\sqrt{q}}{4(q-1)} \sum_{\mu=1}^{q-2} \left|\frac{1}{\cos\theta\cos 2\theta\cos 4\theta}\right| + \frac{q}{2(q-1)}$$

$$\leq \frac{2\sqrt{q}}{q-1} \sum_{\mu=7q/16}^{q/2-1} \left|\frac{1}{\cos\theta\cos 2\theta\cos 4\theta}\right| + \frac{16}{31},$$

where $\theta = \frac{\pi\mu}{q-1}$. Since $|\cos 2\theta\cos 4\theta| > 0.6$, for $\frac{7q\pi}{16(q-1)} < \theta < \frac{\pi}{2}$, we have

$$\left|\sum_{x \in 1_f} (-1)^{tr(\omega x)}\right| \leq \frac{10\sqrt{q}}{3(q-1)} \sum_{\mu=7q/16}^{q/2-1} \frac{1}{\cos\theta} + \frac{16}{31},$$

Then by Lemma 1 and $1 + \frac{1}{3} + \cdots + \frac{1}{2^{n-3}-1} < \frac{n-3}{2}\ln 2 + 0.64$, we have

$$\left|\sum_{x \in 1_f} (-1)^{tr(\omega x)}\right| \leq \frac{10\sqrt{q}}{3(q-1)} \sum_{\mu=7q/16}^{q/2-1} \left(\frac{2}{\pi-2\theta} + \frac{\pi-2\theta}{10}\right) + \frac{16}{31}$$

$$\leq \frac{10\sqrt{q}}{3(q-1)}\left(\frac{2(q-1)}{\pi}\left(\frac{n-3}{2}\ln 2 + 0.64\right) + \frac{q\pi}{2560}\right) + \frac{16}{31}$$

$$< \left(\frac{10n\ln 2}{3\pi} - 0.8\right)\sqrt{q}.$$

Table 1. Cryptographic properties of f and nonlinearities of functions in [4, 25]

n	$\deg(f)$	$\mathcal{AI}(f)$	$nl(f)$	$nl(CF)$	$nl(MCF)$
8	7	4	112	112	108
9	8	5	232	232	
10	9	5	484	484	476
11	10	6	984	980	
12	11	6	1990	1970	1982
13	12	7	4004	3988	
14	13	7	8074	8036	8028
15	14	8	16216	16212	

Therefore,

$$|W_f(\omega)| = 2\left| \sum_{x \in 1_f} (-1)^{tr(\omega x)} \right| < \left(\frac{20n \ln 2}{3\pi} - 1.6 \right) 2^{n/2},$$

and the result follows.   □

4   An Infinite Class of Balanced Functions with Very Good Cryptographic Properties

Construction 1 provides many functions with good cryptographic properties. Taking $m = 1$, we get the Carlet-Feng function. Taking $m = n$, we can get the following function $f \in B_n$

$$\begin{cases} f(0) = 0, \\ f(\alpha^i) = h(i), \ 1 \le i \le 2^n - 1, \end{cases}$$

where $h \in B_n$ is the hidden weighted bit function.

In Table 1, we give some cryptographic properties of the function $f \in B_n$. We also give the nonlinearity of the Carlet-Feng function which is denoted by $nl(CF)$, and the nonlinearity of the even-variable balanced function proposed by [25] which is denoted by $nl(MCF)$. Clearly, f has quite good cryptographic properties: balancedness, optimum algebraic degree, optimum algebraic immunity and high nonlinearity (higher than $nl(CF)$ and $nl(MCF)$).

We then observe its behavior against fast algebraic attacks.

Let $\deg(g_1) = d < \mathcal{AI}(f)$ and $f \cdot g_1 = g_2$. Let $\deg(g_2) = e$. To behave well against fast algebraic attacks, for any g_1 of low degree, we expect that e is as high as possible. For $8 \le n \le 13$, in Table 2, we give the lowest possible values of (d, e). Clearly, $d + e \ge n - 1$ for $n = 8, 10, 11, 12, 13$, and $d + e = n$ for $n = 9$. This is the optimum case for a balanced function to resist the fast algebraic attacks [18]. It seems that $f \in B_n$ has optimal resistance to fast algebraic attacks for any n.

Table 2. Behavior of the function f against Fast Algebraic Attacks

n	8	9	10	11	12	13
(d, e)	(1,6)	(1,8)	(1,8)	(1,10)	(1,10)	(1,12)
	(2,5)	(2,7)	(2,8)	(2,8)	(2,9)	(2,11)
	(3,4)	(3,6)	(3,7)	(3,8)	(3,8)	(3,10)
		(4,5)	(4,6)	(4,7)	(4,8)	(4,8)
				(5,6)	(5,7)	(5,8)
						(6,7)
$\min\{d + e\}$	7	9	9	10	11	12

Example 1. Take $n = m = 12$. We observe the cryptographic properties of $f \in B_{12}$. From Tables 1 and 2, we have $\deg(f) = 11$, $\mathcal{AI}(f) = 6$, $nl(f) = 1990$ and f has optimal resistance to fast algebraic attacks. As a comparison, $nl(CF)$ is only 1970, and $nl(MCF)$ equals 1982. The function f is balanced and has optimal algebraic degree, optimal algebraic immunity and optimal resistance to fast algebraic attacks. It has the highest nonlinearity among all these functions. The truth table of f can be found in Appendix, where it is represented in hexadecimal.

5   Conclusion

This paper proposes a family of cryptographically significant Boolean functions. We investigate the cryptographic properties of these functions and give an infinite class of balanced functions with optimum algebraic degree, optimum algebraic immunity, high nonlinearity (higher than the Carlet-Feng function and the functions proposed by [25]) and a good behavior against fast algebraic attacks. These functions seem to have the best cryptographic properties among all currently known functions.

Construction 1 contains many Boolean functions with very good cryptographic properties. This work is just a start-up, and we will investigate that family further in the future work.

Acknowledgment. The first author would like to thank the financial support from the National Natural Science Foundation of China (Grant No. 61202463) and Shanghai Key Laboratory of Intelligent Information Processing, China (Grant No. IIPL-2011-005).

Appendix

The truth table of f in Example 1:

7076	$C0E7$	$6DE7$	$1AE6$	$C208$	2149	$EC73$	$03D3$
$2F63$	$777B$	$91F4$	$471C$	0309	$A268$	$76F6$	$2A79$
7204	$E561$	$C9E6$	$C229$	$18ED$	$19E9$	$CB48$	$7D2B$
$F6B0$	$BBA4$	$AAB5$	$E13E$	$845A$	$88C7$	$D7BB$	$C93A$
$A0EA$	$6FC9$	$03C5$	$53D8$	$9F7C$	$45D2$	$87D5$	$B3B5$
$BEAE$	9348	$DEAC$	$1B5A$	8672	$CD36$	$516E$	$F3B0$
$01C7$	$707F$	$A956$	$315E$	3533	$398E$	6575	$E901$
$A78D$	$8E22$	$A75B$	$6BC9$	6851	$B036$	$6D34$	$F033$
$ABBF$	$01B2$	$5A24$	$49B5$	$99F1$	$16CE$	8878	$057D$
2406	$E617$	$DEEC$	$287A$	$7B50$	$1DEC$	$14F9$	$A98A$
7202	2303	$1EF0$	$CF7D$	8567	3107	$6C10$	$CCBB$
$3BD2$	5891	$090D$	7881	$D5B8$	$A782$	$10B6$	$50E7$
$66FE$	$6BD8$	$D89D$	8480	3325	$D481$	$F06D$	$5C03$
6088	$D479$	$703C$	$7D8B$	$875D$	$C0AC$	6124	$67DC$
7741	$2E0E$	$7B9B$	$EA91$	$BAE4$	$8CB8$	$D250$	$29BC$
$C3AE$	$449C$	$74EF$	$E8A3$	$4A0E$	$B446$	$81D9$	$D479$
$3B70$	1690	$7FBC$	$52E2$	$8EA2$	$F3ED$	$EFAD$	$B0A8$
$BD1E$	$406C$	$F483$	$6D8A$	$3BA7$	5939	$D954$	$404A$
$B5C7$	$E6A7$	0153	$65A2$	8527	4586	$725B$	$A023$
$E438$	$44B9$	$9A8C$	$1A4F$	$6DCF$	6624	$3A38$	$1B3A$
$48F3$	9972	$F2B4$	$F9E1$	$FC0A$	$11B9$	$2B81$	$D04E$
$2FEE$	$C341$	$60BE$	$DF50$	$A39F$	$FC9F$	$2B87$	$B876$
$F021$	$1DD7$	$AE3F$	$3C9E$	$FF58$	$B914$	$C879$	$3FE5$
$0EDC$	$205F$	$11D1$	$37B1$	$65FD$	$145A$	$DC9F$	6758
$83C3$	8967	$C721$	$043B$	$0C7D$	$3E15$	$A68B$	$7BF6$
9678	$FAEA$	6857	$B6BE$	$19FB$	$E594$	$C40F$	$9BE9$
$D2FB$	3936	$1DAB$	$A634$	$C06E$	$F84B$	$A01C$	$A610$
$3E84$	$889C$	$07BB$	5386	$C1F4$	$F2AB$	$E1D9$	$1C09$
$E640$	$4EFA$	$D18A$	$7E23$	$C912$	$3A38$	8213	$7CE4$
$32BB$	$8A8B$	$7D16$	$B97F$	$9DF1$	$EA67$	$733A$	$309F$
$0FD2$	$759A$	$4EA9$	$7E17$	$A05E$	$1B00$	$032E$	$AAB0$
$C611$	$DB0A$	$B98F$	$ED5B$	$7F6D$	$0C18$	$0CDF$	$D03A$

References

1. Bryant, R.E.: On the complexity of VLSI implementations and graph representations of boolean functions with application to integer multiplication. IEEE Trans. Comput. **40**(2), 205–213 (1991)
2. Carlet, C.: Boolean Models and Methods in Mathematics, Computer Science, and Engineering. In: Boolean Functions for Cryptography and Error Correcting Codes. Cambridge University Press, pp. 257–397 (2010). http://www-roc.inria.fr/secret/Claude.Carlet/pubs.html

3. Carlet, C., Dalai, D.K., Gupta, K.C., Maitra, S.: Algebraic immunity for cryptographically significant Boolean functions: analysis and construction. IEEE Trans. Inf. Theory **52**(7), 3105–3121 (2006)

4. Carlet, C., Feng, K.: An infinite class of balanced functions with optimal algebraic immunity, good immunity to fast algebraic attacks and good nonlinearity. In: Pieprzyk, J. (ed.) ASIACRYPT 2008. LNCS, vol. 5350, pp. 425–440. Springer, Heidelberg (2008)

5. Carlet, C., Zeng, X., Li, C., Hu, L.: Further properties of several classes of Boolean functions with optimum algebraic immunity. Des. Codes Cryptogr. **52**, 303–338 (2009)

6. Courtois, N.T.: Fast algebraic attacks on stream ciphers with linear feedback. In: Boneh, D. (ed.) CRYPTO 2003. LNCS, vol. 2729, pp. 176–194. Springer, Heidelberg (2003)

7. Courtois, N., Meier, W.: Algebraic attacks on stream ciphers with linear feedback. In: Biham, E. (ed.) EUROCRYPT 2003. LNCS, vol. 2656, pp. 345–359. Springer, Heidelberg (2003)

8. Cusick, T.W., Stănică, P.: Cryptographic Boolean Functions and Applications. Elsevier-Academic Press, Stuanicua (2009)

9. Dalai, D.K., Gupta, K.C., Maitra, S.: Cryptographically significant Boolean functions: construction and analysis in terms of algebraic immunity. In: Gilbert, H., Handschuh, H. (eds.) FSE 2005. LNCS, vol. 3557, pp. 98–111. Springer, Heidelberg (2005)

10. Dalai, D.K., Maitra, S., Sarkar, S.: Baisc theory in construction of Boolean functions with maximum possible annihilator immunity. Des. Codes Crypt. **40**(1), 41–58 (2006)

11. Feng, K., Liao, Q., Yang, J.: Maximum values of generalized algebraic immunity. Des. Codes Crypt. **50**(2), 243–252 (2009)

12. Fu, S., Li, C., Qu, L.: Generalized construction of Boolean function with maximum algebraic immunity using univariate polynomial representation. IEICE Trans. **E96.A**(1), 360–362 (2013)

13. Hawkes, P., Rose, G.G.: Rewriting variables: the complexity of fast algebraic attacks on stream ciphers. In: Franklin, M. (ed.) CRYPTO 2004. LNCS, vol. 3152, pp. 390–406. Springer, Heidelberg (2004)

14. Knuth, D.E.: The Art of Computer Programming. Fascicle 1: Bitwise tricks & techniques; Binary Decision Diagrams, vol. 4. Addison-Wesley Professional, Massachusetts (2009)

15. Li, N., Qi, W.-F.: Construction and analysis of boolean functions of $2t+1$ variables with maximum algebraic immunity. In: Lai, X., Chen, K. (eds.) ASIACRYPT 2006. LNCS, vol. 4284, pp. 84–98. Springer, Heidelberg (2006)

16. Li, N., Qu, L., Qi, W., Feng, G., Li, C., Xie, D.: On the construction of boolean functions with optimal algebraic immunity. IEEE Trans. Inf. Theory **54**(3), 1330–1334 (2008)

17. Lidl, R., Niederreiter, H.: Introduction to Finite Fields and Their Applications. Cambridge University Press, Cambridge (1986)

18. Liu, M., Zhang, Y., Lin, D.: Perfect algebraic immune functions. In: Wang, X., Sako, K. (eds.) ASIACRYPT 2012. LNCS, vol. 7658, pp. 172–189. Springer, Heidelberg (2012)

19. Meier, W., Pasalic, E., Carlet, C.: Algebraic attacks and decomposition of boolean functions. In: Cachin, C., Camenisch, J.L. (eds.) EUROCRYPT 2004. LNCS, vol. 3027, pp. 474–491. Springer, Heidelberg (2004)

20. Pasalic, E.: Almost fully optimized infinite classes of boolean functions resistant to (fast) algebraic cryptanalysis. In: Lee, P.J., Cheon, J.H. (eds.) ICISC 2008. LNCS, vol. 5461, pp. 399–414. Springer, Heidelberg (2009)

21. Pasalic, E., Wei, Y.: On the construction of cryptographically significant boolean functions using objects in projective geometry spaces. IEEE Trans. Inf. Theory 58(10), 6681–6693 (2012)

22. Rizomiliotis, P.: On the resistance of boolean functions against algebraic attacks using univariate polynomial representation. IEEE Trans. Inf. Theory 56(8), 4014–4024 (2010)

23. Rothaus, O.S.: On bent functions. J. Comb. Theory - Ser. A 20(3), 300–305 (1976)

24. Tan, C., Goh, S.: Several classes of even-variable balanced boolean functions with optimal algebraic immunity. IEICE Trans. E94.A(1), 165–171 (2011)

25. Tang, D., Carlet, C., Tang, X.: Highly nonlinear boolean functions with optimal algebraic immunity and good behavior against fast algebraic attacks. IEEE Trans. Inf. Theory 59(1), 653–664 (2013)

26. Tu, Z., Deng, Y.: A conjecture about binary strings and its applications on constructing Boolean functions with optimal algebraic immunity. Des. Codes Crypt. 60(1), 1–14 (2011)

27. Wang, Q., Carlet, C., Stuanicua, P., Tan, C.H.: Cryptographic properties of the hidden weighted bit function. Discrete Appl. Math. 174, 1–10 (2014)

28. Wang, Q., Johansson, T.: A note on fast algebraic attacks and higher order nonlinearities. In: Lai, X., Yung, M., Lin, D. (eds.) Inscrypt 2010. LNCS, vol. 6584, pp. 404–414. Springer, Heidelberg (2011)

29. Wang, Q., Peng, J., Kan, H., Xue, X.: Constructions of cryptographically significant boolean functions using primitive polynomials. IEEE Trans. Inf. Theory 56(6), 3048–3053 (2010)

30. Wang, Q., Tan, C.H.: Balanced Boolean functions with optimum algebraic degree, optimum algebraic immunity and very high nonlinearity. Discrete Appl. Math. 1673, 25–32 (2014)

31. Wang, Q., Tan, C.H.: A new method to construct boolean functions with good cryptographic properties. Inform. Process. Lett. 113(14), 567–571 (2013)

32. Wang, Q., Tan, C.H., Stuanicua, P.: Concatenations of the hidden weighted bit function and their cryptographic properties. Adv. Math. Commun. 8(2), 153–165 (2014)

33. Zeng, X., Carlet, C., Shan, J., Hu, L.: More balanced boolean functions with optimal algebraic immunity, and good nonlinearity and resistance to fast algebraic attacks. IEEE Trans. Inf. Theory 57(9), 6310–6320 (2011)

Digital Signature

Ambiguous One-Move Nominative Signature Without Random Oracles

Dennis Y.W. Liu[1,2(✉)], Duncan S. Wong[2], and Qiong Huang[3]

[1] School of Professional and Continuing Education,
University of Hong Kong, Pok Fu Lam, Hong Kong
[2] Department of Computer Science, City University of Hong Kong,
Kowloon Tong, Hong Kong
dennis.liu@hkuspace.hku.hk, duncan@cityu.edu.hk
[3] College of Informatics, South China Agricultural University, Guangzhou, China
csqhuang@gmail.com

Abstract. Nominative Signature is a useful tool in situations where a signature has to be created jointly by two parties, a nominator (signer) and a nominee (user), while only the user can verify and prove to a third party about the validity of the signature. In this paper, we study the existing security models of nominative signature and show that though the existing models have captured the essential security requirements of nominative signature in a strong sense, especially on the unforgeability against malicious signers/users and invisibility, they are yet to capture a requirement regarding the privacy of the signer and the user, and this requirement has been one of the original ones since the notion of nominative signature was first introduced. In particular, we show that it is possible to build a highly efficient nominative signature scheme which can be proven secure in the existing security models, while in practice it is obvious to find out from the component(s) of a nominative signature on whether a particular signer or user has involved in the signature generation, which may not be desirable in some actual applications. We therefore propose an enhanced security property, named "Ambiguity", and also propose a new *one-move* nominative scheme for fulfilling this new security requirement without random oracles, and among the various types of nominative signature, one-move is the most efficient type. Furthermore, this new scheme is at least 33 % more efficient during signature generation and 17 % shorter in signature size when compared with the existing one-move signature schemes without random oracles even that the existing ones in the literature may not satisfy this new Ambiguity requirement.

Keywords: Nominative signature · Undeniable signature · Non-self-authenticating signature · Security model

1 Introduction

In nominative signature (NS) [13,19], there are two parties: a signer (or *nominator*) A and a user (or *nominee*) B. To generate a nominative signature σ,

© Springer International Publishing Switzerland 2014
H.-S. Lee and D.-G. Han (Eds.): ICISC 2013, LNCS 8565, pp. 325–341, 2014.
DOI: 10.1007/978-3-319-12160-4_20

A and B have to work together. However, once σ is generated, no one can verify its validity unless B and B is the only one who can show the validity or invalidity of an alleged nominative signature to a third party via running a confirmation/disavowal protocol. NS is useful in applications that there is a need in the division of signing and verifying abilities that two parties have to jointly create a non-self-authenticating signature, and only one of them is able to perform the verification of the signature, both to himself and to any third-parties. In [9], Huang et al. exemplified a practical application of NS in a healthcare system. In the system, a hospital may certify some personal medical records for a patient, for example, after a body checkup. For privacy, the patient would like to control on who can verify these personal medical records and how many of these records that a third party, for example, an insurance company, can verify. By using NS, the hospital and the patient will serve as the signer (or the nominator) and the user (or the nominee), respectively. Some may note that the hospital may simply release a medical document without participating in the nominative signature generation, but the patient can accuse the hospital of making false claims on the patient's medical records. The role of NS in this scenario is to produce a mutual agreement on the validity of the patient's personal medical records.

Since its introduction in 1996 [13], NS has been refined on its definitions and security models, and most of the security requirements of NS have been properly modeled to date [9,16,17,19,20] that include (1 and 2): unforgeability against malicious signers and users, (3) non-transferrability, (4) invisibility and (5) user-only conversion. Unforgeability against malicious signers (*resp.* users) prevents a signer (*resp.* user) from generating a nominative signature alone. A signer and a user have to work together in order to generate a valid one. Non-transferrability requires that a third party is not able to transfer the proof transcript of a confirmation/disavowal protocol to further convince other verifiers on the validity/invalidity of an alleged nominative signature. Invisibility is another main requirement of NS and restricts any party but the user to tell the validity of an alleged nominative signature, and user-only conversion is an optional property of NS that allows only the user to transform a valid nominative signature to a publicly verifiable one.

Despite the well modeling [9,16,17,19,20] of the five security requirements above, we have an ingrained view that a nominative signature σ is valid only if all the components of σ are verified positively. Suppose a nominative signature σ consists of 5 tuples $\sigma = (\alpha, \beta, \Delta, \Lambda, \theta)$, the nominative signature verification carried out by a user always checks the well-formedness and the validity of all these 5 tuples, and if any of the tuples is found to be invalid, σ is considered invalid. However, an invalid σ may contain some valid and **self-authenticating** components and these components might have already leaked the involvement of the signer A or the user B in the nominative signature generation. For example, suppose (α, β) in σ represents a digital signature generated by a signer A. If the other components $(\Delta, \Lambda, \theta)$ in σ are invalid, σ is deemed invalid. However, from (α, β), one can already tell that A has indeed involved in the generation of σ regardless whether σ is valid or not, as only the user B can determine its validity (note that σ can still be invalid even if (α, β) is a valid digital signature generated by A as the other components $(\Delta, \Lambda, \theta)$ can be invalid while only B can determine their validity and which makes such a scheme satisfy the invisibility requirement). More details are given in Sect. 3.2.

Let us use the aforementioned hospital-and-patient scenario as an illustration. Suppose the above NS is used and there is an alleged nominative signature $\sigma = (\alpha, \beta, \Delta, \Lambda, \theta)$ for certifying a patient's personal medical records. The hospital is the signer A and the patient is the user B in the NS. When issuing a certificate for B's personal medical records, the hospital A works jointly with B and generates a nominative signature σ. Although the validity of σ is unknown to the public due to non-transferrability and invisibility of the NS, everyone can check the validity of the digital signature components (α, β) of the hospital in σ. This may leak the fact that the hospital A has indeed got involved on issuing a certificate regarding B's personal medical records though σ as a whole is not able to be verified by the public.

Our Results. In this paper, we describe an NS scheme and proves that it is secure in the existing security models which capture the five conventional security requirements, namely unforgeability against malicious signers or users, non-transferrability, invisibility, and user-only conversion. Then we show that this nominative signature leaks the information on the involvement of a particular signer A. For capturing that no one, except the user B, is able to tell whether a particular signer or a user has participated in the generation of a nominative signature, we formalize a new security model, called "Ambiguity" and show that any NS scheme which can be proven secure under this new security model would not contain any sensible components which may leak the involvement of any particular party.

Besides the new Ambiguity model, we propose a new and highly efficient NS scheme which is proven secure under the existing models with respect to the five conventional security requirements. The new scheme is at least 33 % more efficient, in terms of modular exponentiations during signature generation, and 17 % shorter in signature size when compared with the most efficient NS schemes in the literature that has been proven secure without the random oracles. Also, we propose an improved NS scheme which satisfies not only the existing models, but also the new Ambiguity security requirement.

2   Nominative Signature: Definitions

A *One-Move* Nominative Signature (NS) consists of six probabilistic polynomial-time (PPT) algorithms (SystemSetup, SKeyGen, UKeyGen, NSVer, Conv, Ver) and three protocols (SigGen, Confirmation and Disavowal).

1. SystemSetup: On input a security parameter 1^k, where $k \in \mathbb{N}$, it outputs a list of system parameters denoted by param.
2. SKeyGen: On input param, it generates a public/private key pair (pk_A, sk_A) for the signer (i.e. nominator).

3. UKeyGen: On input param, it generates a public/private key pair (pk_B, sk_B) for the user (i.e. nominee).
4. NSVer: On input a message $m \in \{0,1\}^*$, a nominative signature σ, a signer public key pk_A and a user private key sk_B, it outputs valid or invalid.
5. Conv: On input a message-signature pair (m, σ), pk_A and sk_B, it outputs a standard (publicly verifiable) signature σ^{std} if valid $\leftarrow$ NSVer(m, σ, pk_A, sk_B); otherwise, it outputs $\perp$ symbolizing the failure of conversion.
6. Ver: On input $(m, \sigma^{std}, pk_A, pk_B)$, it outputs valid or invalid.
7. SigGen Protocol: A one-move protocol in which A makes one-move message transfer to B only. The common input of A and B is (param, m, pk_A, pk_B). A and B take sk_A, sk_B as their secret inputs, respectively. At the end of the protocol, A outputs nothing and B outputs a nominative signature σ. Let $\mathcal{S}(pk_A, pk_B)$ be the signature space.
8. Confirmation/Disavowal Protocol: On input (m, σ, pk_A, pk_B), B sets a bit μ to 1 if valid $\leftarrow$ NSVer(m, σ, pk_A, sk_B); otherwise, μ is set to 0. B then sends μ to C. If $\mu = 1$, Confirmation protocol is carried out; otherwise, Disavowal protocol is carried out. At the end of the protocol, C outputs either accept or reject while B has no output.

An NS scheme proceeds as follows. SystemSetup is first invoked. SKeyGen and UKeyGen are then executed to initialize a signer A and a user B. On a message m, A and B carries out SigGen protocol. As SigGen is one-move, A generates a *partial* nominative signature denoted by σ' and sends it to B. B then generates and outputs a nominative signature denoted by σ. Formally, SigGen consists of two algorithms, (Sign, Receive), which are carried out by signer A (who is holding (pk_A, sk_A)) and user B (who is holding (pk_B, sk_B)), respectively. SigGen protocol proceeds as follows:

1. A generates $\sigma' \leftarrow$ Sign(param, pk_B, m, sk_A) and sends σ' to B;
2. B generates $\sigma \leftarrow$ Receive(param, pk_A, m, σ', sk_B).

At the end of the protocol, B either outputs a nominative signature σ or $\perp$ indicating the failure of the protocol run.

Unlike the original definition in [19], the SigGen protocol defined above is specific to the one-move setting, that is, signer A initiates and generates a *partial* nominative signature σ', then B generates the final nominative signature σ upon receiving σ'. Note that the signature space should be specified explicitly in each NS construction.

For a nominative signature σ in the signature space $\mathcal{S}(pk_A, pk_B)$ (defined above in SigGen), the validity of σ can be determined by B using NSVer. If σ is valid, B can prove its validity to a third party C using the Confirmation protocol, otherwise, B can prove its invalidity to C using the Disavowal protocol.

Correctness can be defined naturally. Soundness requires that no PPT user can convince a third party that an invalid (resp. invalid) nominative signature is valid (resp. invalid). We defer their formal definitions to the full version of this paper [18].

Before describing the security games for NS, we begin with the description of oracles.

- OCreateSigner: This oracle generates a key pair (pk_A, sk_A) using SKeyGen, and returns pk_A.
- OCreateUser: This oracle generates a key pair (pk_B, sk_B) using UKeyGen, and returns pk_B.
- OCorrupt: On input a public key pk, if pk is generated by OCreateSigner or OCreateUser, the corresponding private key is returned; otherwise, $\perp$ is returned. pk is said to be *corrupted*.
- OSign: On input a message m, two distinct public keys, pk_1 (signer) and pk_2 (user), it returns σ' where σ' is a partial nominative signature generated using Sign.
- OReceive: On input a message m, a partial nominative signature σ', two distinct public keys, pk_1 (signer) and pk_2 (user), it returns a nominative signature σ.
- OProof: On input a message m, a nominative signature σ and two public keys pk_1 (signer) and pk_2 (user), the oracle, acting as the user (prover) and runs $\mathsf{NSVer}(m, \sigma, pk_1, sk_2)$ where sk_2 is the corresponding private key of pk_2. If the output of NSVer is valid, the oracle returns 1 and carries out the Confirmation protocol. Otherwise, it returns 0 and runs the Disavowal protocol.
- OConvert: On input (m, σ, pk_1, pk_2) such that valid $\leftarrow \mathsf{NSVer}(m, \sigma, pk_1, sk_2)$, it runs Convert and returns σ^{std}.

In all the oracles described above, the public keys in the queries of the oracles are assumed to be generated by the corresponding OCreateSigner or OCreateUser. This approach aligns with the multi-user setting and also the usual formalization under the registered-key model [1] and is based on that of [20].

A secure nominative signature should satisfy the following requirements [9, 16, 17, 19, 20]: (1) **Unforgeability Against Malicious Users**, (2) **Unforgeability Against Malicious Signers**, (3) **Invisibility**, (4) **Non-transferability**, and (5) **User-only Conversion**. Please refer to Appendix B for details.

3 Nominative Signature Supporting Ambiguity

In this section, we motivate the formalization of a new security requirement, "Ambiguity". It helps prevent an adversary from determining whether a signer A or a user B has involved in the generation of an alleged nominative signature σ. To the best of our knowledge, although Ambiguity has been considered as a folklore in the research of nominative signature for all these years since its first introduction in 1996 [13] and has also been studied in many other related cryptographic primitives, for example, the Ambiguous Optimistic Fair Exchange (AOFE) [11], it has never been formalized in the context of nominative signature, while it is an important and practical requirement. In the following, we first give a new NS construction that satisfies the existing security models (as defined in Sect. 2 above). The new construction is also more efficient, in terms computational complexity and signature size, than existing NS schemes. We, however, show that a nominative signature generated using this NS already leaks the involvement of a particular signer regardless the validity of the nominative signature. We make use of this NS scheme to illustrate the importance and practicality of this new "Ambiguity" security requirement.

3.1 An Efficient NS Construction (Our Scheme I)

This scheme employs the Boneh-Boyen short signature (BB) [2] and the Huang-Wong short convertible undeniable signature (HW) [10]. Particularly in SigGen, a signer A generates a BB signature $\sigma' = (\sigma^{BB}, r_A)$ and sends it to a user B, which signs on σ' using HW convertible undeniable signature.

> SystemSetup: Given a security parameter $k \in \mathbb{N}$, the algorithm selects a bilinear group G with generator g of prime order p, and a collision resistant hash function $H : \{0,1\}^* \to \mathbb{Z}_p$. It also selects a keyed group hash function [8] $\mathcal{H} = (\mathsf{PHF.Gen}, \mathsf{PHF.Eval})$, such that $\kappa \leftarrow \mathsf{PHF.Gen}(1^k)$ is the key, and we denote $\mathcal{H}_\kappa(m) = \mathsf{PHF.Eval}(\kappa, m)$, where $m \in \{0,1\}^*$. Let $\mathsf{param} = (k, H, \mathcal{H}, G, g, p)$.
>
> SKeyGen: On input param, it randomly generates $x_{A_1}, x_{A_2} \in_R \mathbb{Z}_p^*$ and calculates $y_{A_1} = g^{x_{A_1}}$ and $y_{A_2} = g^{x_{A_2}}$. Set the public key $pk_A = (y_{A_1}, y_{A_2})$ and private key $sk_A = (x_{A_1}, x_{A_2})$ for signer A.
>
> UKeyGen: On input param, it randomly picks $x_{B_1}, x_{B_2} \in_R \mathbb{Z}_p, \eta \in_R G$ and gets $\kappa \leftarrow \mathsf{PHF.Gen}(1^k)$. Calculate $y_{B_1} = g^{x_{B_1}}, y_{B_2} = g^{1/x_{B_2}}$, and set the public key $pk_B = (y_{B_1}, y_{B_2}, \eta, \kappa)$ and private key $sk_B = (x_{B_1}, x_{B_2})$ for user B.
>
> SigGen Protocol: On input a message $m \in \{0,1\}^*$, A and B carry out the following:
> 1. A randomly picks $r_A \in \mathbb{Z}_p \setminus \{\frac{x_{A_1} + H(m\|y_B)}{x_{A_2}}\}$ where $y_B = y_{B_1}\|y_{B_2}\|\eta\|\kappa$, computes $\sigma^{BB} = g^{1/(x_{A_1} + H(m\|y_B) + x_{A_2} r_A)}$, and sends $\sigma' \leftarrow (\sigma^{BB}, r_A)$ to B. Here, the inverse $1/(x_{A_1} + H(m\|y_B) + x_{A_2} r_A)$ is computed modulo p.
> 2. B verifies if $e(g, g) \stackrel{?}{=} e(\sigma^{BB}, y_{A_1} g^{H(m\|y_B)} y_{A_2}^{r_A})$. B then randomly picks $\tau \in_R \mathbb{Z}_p$, computes $\Delta \leftarrow \mathcal{H}_\kappa(\sigma')^{1/(x_{B_1} + \tau)}$, $\Lambda \leftarrow y_{B_2}^\tau$, $\theta \leftarrow \eta^\tau$, and sets $\sigma_U = (\Delta, \Lambda, \theta)$. The nominative signature is set to $\sigma = (\sigma', \sigma_U)$.

Signature Space: $\sigma = (\sigma', \sigma_U)$ is said to be in the signature space $\mathcal{S}(pk_A, pk_B)$ if σ' is a valid BB signature under pk_A on $m\|y_B$ and $\Delta, \Lambda, \theta \in G$.

> NSVer: On input (m, σ, pk_A, sk_B), if $e(\Delta, y_{B_1}\Lambda^{x_{B_2}}) = e(\mathcal{H}_\kappa(\sigma'), g)$ and $e(\Lambda^{x_{B_2}}, \eta) = e(g, \theta)$, it outputs valid; otherwise, it outputs invalid.
>
> Confirmation/Disavowal Protocol: If valid $\leftarrow$ NSVer(m, σ, pk_A, sk_B), B sends $\mu = 1$ and carries out the following proof system for showing the validity of σ_U to a verifier:
>
> $$PoK\{x_{B_2} : e(\Delta, \Lambda)^{x_{B_2}} = e(\mathcal{H}_\kappa(\sigma'), g) \cdot e(\Delta, y_{B_1})^{-1}\};$$

otherwise, B sends $\mu = 0$ and carries out the following proof system with the verifier:

$$PoK\{x_{B_2} : \ e(\Delta, \Lambda)^{x_{B_2}} \neq e(\mathcal{H}_\kappa(\sigma'), g) \cdot e(\Delta, y_{B_1})^{-1}\}.$$

There exist efficient (3-move) *special honest-verifier zero-knowledge* protocols [4,5] for the instantiation of above proof systems. They can also be transformed into 4-move perfect zero-knowledge proofs of knowledge [6] so that there exists a PPT simulator that produces indistinguishable views for any verifier.

Conv: On input (m, σ, pk_A, sk_B) where σ is a valid nominative signature on m respect to pk_A and pk_B, the algorithm computes $cvt = \Lambda^{x_{B_2}}$ and sets $\sigma_U^{std} = (\sigma_U, cvt)$. It outputs a digital signature as $\sigma^{std} = (\sigma', \sigma_U^{std})$.
Ver: On input $(m, \sigma^{std}, pk_A, pk_B)$, it outputs valid if (1) $e(\Delta, y_{B_1} cvt) = e(\mathcal{H}_\kappa(\sigma'), g)$, and (2) $e(cvt, \eta) = e(g, \theta)$; otherwise, it outputs invalid.

For Invisibility, we define $\sigma^{invalid} \leftarrow \mathsf{NSSim}(param, pk_A, pk_B, m, \sigma^{valid})$ as follows. Given $\sigma^{valid} := (\sigma', \sigma_U)$, NSSim outputs $\sigma^{invalid}$ as (σ', σ_U^*) for randomly chosen $\Delta^*, \Lambda^*, \theta^* \in_R G$.

The security analysis for the scheme above will be given in the full version of this paper [18].

3.2 Security Model: Ambiguity

The existing security model treats a nominative signature σ *as a whole* when determining its validity, that is, σ is considered valid if all individual components of σ are considered valid. However, this security model does not consider the **self-authenticating** individual components in σ. Those components may leak certain important information, for example, a particular signer/user's involvement in the signature generation. In our construction given in Sect. 3.1, the signer A creates a partial NS signature σ' which is a standard signature on $(m\|pk_B)$. The user B then creates an undeniable signature σ_U on σ' to form the final NS signature $\sigma = (\sigma', \sigma_U)$. Note that σ' can only be generated by A while the unforgeability property of the NS scheme still holds as neither A nor B is able to forge the entire signature σ alone. On invisibility, as the second part of σ, that is, σ_U, can only be verified by B while the public (including A) cannot tell whether σ_U is valid or not, even σ' is publicly verifiable, no one (including A) can conclude on whether the nominative signature σ *as a whole* is valid or not. However, the partial NS signature σ' is self-authenticated and already reveals A's participation in the signature generation regardless the validity or invalidity of the second part σ_U. We believe that this may act against the interest of the signer/user in real life situations. The hospital-and-patient scenario mentioned previously provides a good example. Though the certificate (i.e. σ) of a patient's personal medical records may not be self-authenticated that public verifiers are not able to check whether the certificate (*as a whole*) is valid or invalid, the first part of the certificate, i.e. σ', has already leaked the fact that the patient's personal medical records had been signed by a specific hospital. The patient, however, may not be happy to disclose this fact to the public. In real life situations, we believe that it is crucial to hide completely the information about whether a particular signer A or user B has got involved in the generation of an alleged nominative signature σ.

Informally speaking, given an alleged NS signature, we require that other than user B, no one (including signer A) can tell whether A or B has been involved in the signature generation protocol SigGen. Here, we propose two games for formalizing Signer Ambiguity and User Ambiguity.

Game Signer Ambiguity: The initialization and attacking phases are the same as that of Game Unforgeability Against Malicious Signers. In particular, the challenger S runs $(pk_B, sk_B) \leftarrow$ UKeyGen(param) and sends pk_B to the adversary/distinguisher D_A while keeping sk_B secret. Below are the subsequent phases.

1. (*Challenge Selection Phase*) D_A arbitrarily chooses and sends two distinct challenge messages m_0^*, m_1^* and key pairs (pk_{A_0}, sk_{A_0}) and (pk_{A_1}, sk_{A_1}) of two signers to S. D_A then further runs $\sigma_i' \leftarrow$ Sign(param, pk_B, m_i^*, sk_{A_i}) and sends σ_i' to S, for $i = 0, 1$.
2. (*Challenge Signature Generation Phase*) Upon receiving $\langle m_0^*, m_1^*, (pk_{A_0}, sk_{A_0}), (pk_{A_1}, sk_{A_1}), \sigma_0', \sigma_1' \rangle$, S tosses a coin $b \in_R \{0, 1\}$ and sends $\sigma^* \leftarrow$ Receive(param, $pk_{A_b}, m_b^*, \sigma_b', sk_B$) to D_A.
3. (*Guess Phase*) D_A outputs a guess bit b' for b.

D_A *wins* the game if $b' = b$ provided that

1. D_A has never queried OCorrupt(pk_B) for getting sk_B;
2. (pk_{A_0}, sk_{A_0}) and (pk_{A_1}, sk_{A_1}) are created by querying OCreateSigner;
3. $(m^*, \sigma^*, pk_{A_i}, pk_B)$ has never been queried to OProof or OConvert, for $i = 0, 1$.

D_A's advantage in this game is defined as $P[b' = b] - \frac{1}{2}$.

Definition 1. An NS has the property of Signer Ambiguity if no PPT distinguisher D_A has a non-negligible advantage in Game Signer Ambiguity.

Game User Ambiguity: The initialization and attacking phases are the same as that of Game Unforgeability Against Malicious Signers. In particular, the challenger S generates $(pk_{B_0}, sk_{B_0}) \leftarrow$ UKeyGen(param) and $(pk_{B_1}, sk_{B_1}) \leftarrow$ UKeyGen (param) and sends pk_{B_0} and pk_{B_1} to the adversary/distinguisher D_A while keeping sk_{B_0} and sk_{B_1} secret. Below are the subsequent phases.

1. (*Challenge Selection Phase*) D_A arbitrarily chooses and sends two distinct challenge messages m_0^*, m_1^* and a pair (pk_A, sk_A) to S. D_A further runs $\sigma_i' \leftarrow$ Sign(param, pk_{B_i}, m_i^*, sk_A) and sends σ_i' to S, for $i = 0, 1$.
2. (*Challenge Signature Generation Phase*) Upon receiving $\langle m_0^*, m_1^*, pk_A, sk_A, \sigma_0', \sigma_1' \rangle$, S tosses a coin $b \in_R \{0, 1\}$, computes $\sigma_b^* \leftarrow$ Receive(param, $pk_A, m_b^*, \sigma_b', sk_{B_b}$), and sends σ_b^* to D_A.
3, (*Guess Phase*) D_A outputs a guess bit b' for b.

D_A *wins* the game if $b' = b$ provided that

1. D_A has never queried $\mathsf{OCorrupt}(pk_{B_i})$ for getting sk_{B_i} for $i = 0, 1$;
2. (pk_A, sk_A) is created by querying $\mathsf{OCreateSigner}$;
3. $(m^*, \sigma^*, pk_A, pk_{B_i})$ has never been queried to OProof or $\mathsf{OConvert}$, for $i = 0, 1$.

D_A's advantage in this game is defined as $\mathsf{P}[b' = b] - \frac{1}{2}$.

Definition 2. An NS has the property of User Ambiguity if no PPT distinguisher D_A has a non-negligible advantage in Game User Ambiguity.

[16,17] does not satisfy User Ambiguity as the adversary can make use of r_A, which is generated by the adversary as signer A but is not masked in σ_b^*, to tell whether σ_0' or σ_1' is used in the generation of σ_b^* in the Game User Ambiguity above.

Definition 3. An NS has the property of ambiguity if it satisfies both Signer Ambiguity and User Ambiguity.

We say that a secure nominative signature (NS) scheme satisfies: (1) **Unforgeability Against Malicious Users**, (2) **Unforgeability Against Malicious Signers**, (3) **Invisibility**, (4) **Non-transferability**, (5) **User-only Conversion** and (6) **Ambiguity**.

4 A New NS Construction Supporting Ambiguity (Our Scheme II)

We propose a new NS scheme for achieving "Ambiguity". The scheme is based on the one in [16,17], and major modifications include the encryption of the randomness, r_A, using ElGamal encryption (EGE), and the inclusion of the ciphertext in the signature. We will also describe an alternative approach using Linear Encryption (LE) later in the same section.

SystemSetup: On input a security parameter $k \in \mathbb{N}$, the algorithm sets three cyclic groups G_1, G_2, and G_T of prime order $p \geq 2^k$ and a bilinear map $e : G_1 \times G_2 \to G_T$. It also picks a collision resistant hash function $H : \{0,1\}^* \to \mathbb{Z}_p$, and randomly selects generators $g_1 \in G_1$, $g_2 \in G_2$, and $g_3 \in \mathbb{Z}_p^*$. Set param $= (p, G_1, G_2, G_T, g_1, g_2, g_3, H)$.

SKeyGen: On input param, it randomly picks $x_{A_1}, x_{A_2} \in_R \mathbb{Z}_p^*$, and computes $y_{A_1} = g_2^{x_{A_1}}$ and $y_{A_2} = g_2^{x_{A_2}}$. Set public key $pk_A = (y_{A_1}, y_{A_2})$, and private key $sk_A = (x_{A_1}, x_{A_2})$ for signer A.

UKeyGen: On input param, it randomly generates $x_{B_1}, x_{B_2}, x_{B_3}, x_{B_4} \in_R \mathbb{Z}_p^*$, and computes $y_{B_1} = g_2^{x_{B_1}}$, $y_{B_2} = g_2^{x_{B_2}}$, $y_{B_3} = g_1^{x_{B_3}}$ and $y_{B_4} = g_3^{x_{B_4}}$. Set public key $pk_B = (y_{B_1}, y_{B_2}, y_{B_3}, y_{B_4})$ and private key $sk_B = (x_{B_1}, x_{B_2}, x_{B_3}, x_{B_4})$ for user B.

SigGen Protocol: On input a message $m \in \{0,1\}^*$, A and B carry out the following.

1. A randomly picks $r_A \in_R \mathbb{Z}_p \setminus \{\frac{x_{A_1} + H(m\|y_B)}{x_{A_2}}\}$ where $y_B = y_{B_1}\|y_{B_2}\|y_{B_3}\|y_{B_4}$, computes $\sigma^{BB} = g_1^{1/(x_{A_1} + H(m\|y_B) + x_{A_2}r_A)}$, and sends $\sigma' \leftarrow (\sigma^{BB}, r_A)$ to B.

2. B checks if $e(g_1, g_2) \stackrel{?}{=} e(\sigma^{BB}, y_{A_1} g_2^{H(m\|y_B)} y_{A_2}^{r_A})$. If so, B computes $\sigma_1 = \sigma^{BB} y_{B_3}^{r_1}$ and $\alpha_1 = g_1^{r_1}$ where $r_1 \in_R \mathbb{Z}_p$, then randomly picks $r_B \in_R \mathbb{Z}_p \setminus \{\frac{x_{B_1} + H(\sigma_1)}{x_{B_2}}\}$, and computes $\sigma_2 = g_1^{1/(x_{B_1} + H(\sigma_1) + x_{B_2}r_B)} y_{B_3}^{r_2}$ and $\alpha_2 = g_1^{r_2}$ where $r_2 \in_R \mathbb{Z}_p$. B also computes $c_A = r_A y_{B_4}^{r_3}$, $\alpha_3 = g_3^{r_3}$ where $r_3 \in_R \mathbb{Z}_p$. The signature is $\sigma = (\sigma_1, \sigma_2, c_A, r_B, \alpha_1, \alpha_2, \alpha_3)$.

Signature Space: σ is said to be in the signature space $\mathcal{S}(pk_A, pk_B)$ if $\sigma_1, \sigma_2, \alpha_1, \alpha_2 \in G_1$, $c_A, \alpha_3 \in \mathbb{Z}_p^*$, $r_B \in \mathbb{Z}_p$.

NSVer: On input (m, σ, pk_A, sk_B) where σ is in $\mathcal{S}(pk_A, pk_B)$, set $r_A' = c_A/\alpha_3^{x_{B_4}}$ and check if

$$e(\alpha_1, y_{A_1} g_2^{H(m\|y_B)} y_{A_2}^{r_A})^{x_{B_3}} \stackrel{?}{=} e(\sigma_1, y_{A_1} g_2^{H(m\|y_B)} y_{A_2}^{r_A})/e(g_1, g_2)$$
$$\wedge \ e(\alpha_2, y_{B_1} g_2^{H(\sigma_1)} y_{B_2}^{r_B})^{x_{B_3}} \stackrel{?}{=} e(\sigma_2, y_{B_1} g_2^{H(\sigma_1)} y_{B_2}^{r_B})/e(g_1, g_2)$$

If so, output valid; otherwise, output invalid.

Confirmation/Disavowal Protocol: If valid $\leftarrow$ NSVer(m, σ, pk_A, sk_B), B sends $\mu = 1$ and carries out the following zero-knowledge proof of knowledge with a verifier:

$$PoK\{(x_{B_3}, x_{B_4}, r_A) : g_1^{x_{B_3}} = y_{B_3} \wedge g_3^{x_{B_4}} = y_{B_4}$$
$$\wedge \ e(\alpha_1, y_{A_1} g_2^{H(m\|y_B)} y_{A_2}^{r_A})^{x_{B_3}} = e(\sigma_1, y_{A_1} g_2^{H(m\|y_B)} y_{A_2}^{r_A})/e(g_1, g_2)$$
$$\wedge \ e(\alpha_2, y_{B_1} g_2^{H(\sigma_1)} y_{B_2}^{r_B})^{x_{B_3}} = e(\sigma_2, y_{B_1} g_2^{H(\sigma_1)} y_{B_2}^{r_B})/e(g_1, g_2)\};$$

otherwise, B sends $\mu = 0$ and carries out the following zero-knowledge proof of knowledge with the verifier:

$$PoK\{(x_{B_3}, x_{B_4}, r_A) : g_1^{x_{B_3}} = y_{B_3} \wedge g_3^{x_{B_4}} = y_{B_4}$$
$$\wedge \ (e(\alpha_1, y_{A_1} g_2^{H(m\|y_B)} y_{A_2}^{r_A})^{x_{B_3}} \neq e(\sigma_1, y_{A_1} g_2^{H(m\|y_B)} y_{A_2}^{r_A})/e(g_1, g_2)$$
$$\vee \ e(\alpha_2, y_{B_1} g_2^{H(\sigma_1)} y_{B_2}^{r_B})^{x_{B_3}} \neq e(\sigma_2, y_{B_1} g_2^{H(\sigma_1)} y_{B_2}^{r_B})/e(g_1, g_2))\}.$$

Conv: On input (m, σ, pk_A, sk_B) where σ is a valid nominative signature on m respect to pk_A and pk_B, the algorithm computes $r_A = c_A/\alpha_3^{x_{B_4}}$, then randomly picks $r_4 \in_R \mathbb{Z}_p$, and sets $\delta = (\delta_1, \delta_2, r_A, r_4)$ where $\delta_1 = \sigma_1/\alpha_1^{x_{B_3}}$ and $\delta_2 = g_1^{1/(x_{B_1} + H(\delta_1) + x_{B_2}r_4)}$.

Ver: On input (m, δ, pk_A, pk_B), it outputs valid if $e(g_1, g_2) = e(\delta_1, y_{A_1} g_2^{H(m\|y_B)} y_{A_2}^{r_A})$ and $e(g_1, g_2) = e(\delta_2, y_{B_1} g_2^{H(\delta_1)} y_{B_2}^{r_4})$; otherwise, it outputs invalid.

For Invisibility, we define $\sigma^{invalid} \leftarrow$ NSSim(param, $pk_A, pk_B, m, \sigma^{valid}$) as follows. Given $\sigma^{valid} := (\sigma_1, \sigma_2, c_A, r_B, \alpha_1, \alpha_2, \alpha_3)$, NSSim outputs $\sigma^{invalid}$ as $(\sigma_1^*, \sigma_2^*, c_A, r_B, \alpha_1, \alpha_2, \alpha_3)$ where $\sigma_1^* = \sigma_1 R_1$, $\sigma_2^* = \sigma_2 R_2$ where R_1 and R_2 are randomly chosen from G_1. An alternative approach is to use Linear Encryption [3], a natural extension of ElGamal encryption, to encrypt σ^{BB}. Linear encryption (LE) can be secure even in groups where a DDH-deciding algorithm exists. By using LE, we need to change pk_B to a triple of generators $g_i, g_{ii}, g_{iii} \in G_1$, and sk_B to exponents $x_i, x_{ii} \in \mathbb{Z}_p$ such that $g_i^{x_i} = g_{ii}^{x_{ii}} = g_{iii}$. To encrypt σ^{BB}, we randomly choose $a, b \in_R \mathbb{Z}_p$ and compute $(T_1, T_2, T_3) = (g_i^a, g_{ii}^b, \sigma^{BB} g_{iii}^{a+b})$. To recover σ^{BB}, we compute $T_3/(T_1^{x_i} T_2^{x_{ii}})$. LE is semantically secure against chosen-plaintext attacks, assuming the Decision Linear Problem (DLIN) assumption holds, which is a weaker assumption and the scheme can remain secure even in groups where a DDH-deciding algorithm exists. This LE-based variant can therefore provide a potentially larger class of groups to choose from during implementation, while it is less efficient than the original EGE-based scheme. A detailed comparison will be given in Sect. 5.

Theorem 1 (Ambiguity). *The NS scheme proposed above satifies Ambiguity (Definition 3) if the scheme is unforgeable and ElGamal encryption satisfies ANO-CPA and IND-CPA.*

The completed proof will be given in the full version of this paper [18]. The improved NS scheme also satisfies (1) **Unforgeability Against Malicious Users**, (2) **Unforgeability Against Malicious Signers**, (3) **Invisibility**, (4) **Non-transferability**, (5) **User-only Conversion**. The proof is similar to that for the scheme in [16,17] and is omitted here.

5   Efficiency Analysis and Comparison

In Table 1, we compare our Scheme I (the one does not satisfy Ambiguity) and Scheme II (the one supports Ambiguity) with the most efficient NS schemes in the literature. The comparison includes signature size, signer A and user B key sizes (termed as A_{Key} and B_{Key}), signature generation efficiency in terms of modular exponentiation calculation by A (Sign) and B (Receive) individually, and the security assumptions for unforgeability and invisibility. The table also shows whether the schemes satisfy Ambiguity, and whether the schemes can be proven secure without the assumption of random oracles. Our first efficient scheme is 33 % more efficient, in terms of the number of modular exponentiation operations during signature generation, and 17 % shorter in signature size than those in Liu et al's scheme [16,17], which is known to be the most efficient NS scheme proven secure without random oracles to date. The schemes [24] and [20] also satisfy the Ambiguity property, while the scheme in [24] relies on the random oracle assumption and in [20], the number of components in signer A's key is linear to the security parameter. Our Scheme II (EGE), the ElGamal encryption based variant of Scheme II, has constant size key and is proven without random oracles. In Scheme II (LE), the linear encryption based variant, though

Table 1. Comparison with Existing One-Move NS Schemes

Scheme	σ	A_{Key}	B_{Key}	$SigGen^a$
ZY09 [24]	1G	$2G+2\mathbb{Z}_p^*$	$2G+2\mathbb{Z}_p^*$	$1+2$
SH11 [20]	$3G+\mathbb{Z}_p$	$2G+(n+2)\mathbb{Z}_p^{\,b}$	$5G+[2(n+1)+3]\mathbb{Z}_p$	$3+8$
LW12 [16,17]	$4G+2\mathbb{Z}_p$	$2G+2\mathbb{Z}_p$	$3G+3\mathbb{Z}_p$	$1+5$
Our Scheme I	$4G+1\mathbb{Z}_p$	$2G+2\mathbb{Z}_p$	$[3+(m+1)]G+2\mathbb{Z}_p^{\,c}$	$1+3$
Our Scheme II (EGE)	$4G+3\mathbb{Z}_p$	$2G+2\mathbb{Z}_p$	$3G+5\mathbb{Z}_p$	$1+7$
Our Scheme II (LE)	$6G+3\mathbb{Z}_p$	$2G+2\mathbb{Z}_p$	$6G+5\mathbb{Z}_p$	$1+9$
	Unforgeability	Invisibility	Ambiguity	No ROM
ZY09 [24]	√	√	√	×
SH11 [20]	√	√	√	√
LW12 [16,17]	√	√	×	√
Our Scheme I	√	√	×	√
Our Scheme II (EGE)	√	√	√	√
Our Scheme II (LE)	√	√	√	√

[a] No. of modular exponentiation operations in signature generation (Sign + Receive)
[b] n: No. of bits of each message to be signed
[c] m: The public generators of group G included in the key of the programmable hash function (PHF)

the performance is slightly lower than Scheme II (EGE), it relies on a weaker assumption (DLIN) and the scheme will remain secure even in groups where a DDH-deciding algorithm exists.

6   Conclusion

We proposed a new security notion called Ambiguity to Nominative Signature. This new notion ensures that a nominative signature will remain anonymous in the sense that no one (including the signer) but the user can tell whether a particular signer or user has involved in the generation of an alleged nominative signature. We no longer restrict ourselves to look into a nominative signature *as a whole*, but also require that any individual components of a nominative signature should not leak any information regarding the involvement of any particular party with respect to the generation of an alleged nominative signature. We formalized the Ambiguity notion, showed that it is possible to build a highly efficient nominative signature secure in the existing model but not satisfying the ambiguity requirement. We also proposed a new and secure nominative signature scheme which also satisfies the ambiguity requirement. The new scheme is proven secure without the random oracle assumption.

Acknowledgements. Q. Huang is supported by National Natural Science Foundation of China (No. 61103232), the Research Fund for the Doctoral Program of Higher Education of China (No. 20114404120027), Guangdong Natural Science Foundation (No. S2013010011859), and the Foundation for Distinguished Young Talents in Higher Education of Guangdong, China (No. LYM11033).

A   Related Work

Nominative Signature (NS) was introduced by Kim et al. [13]. In their seminal paper, they also proposed the first NS, which was later found insecure [12]. The notion convertible nominative signature was also introduced in [12] and the first construction of a convertible nominative signature was proposed. In [21], an attack against the scheme in [12] was described. Though the attack was later found invalid [7], new attacks against the scheme in [12] was found in [7,22].

In [19], Liu et al. proposed the first set of formal definitions and security models for Convertible NS (for simplicity, we use NS to represent convertible NS as well). They also proposed the first provably secure NS scheme under the models they defined. Their scheme requires at least four rounds of communication between the signer and the user during signature generation. More efficient nominative signature schemes were later proposed [14,15]. The scheme in [14] requires two rounds during nominative signature generation and the scheme in [15] is the first *one-move* (non-interactive) NS in the literature. Later, more one-move NS schemes [9,23,24] were proposed and proven secure in random oracle model. In [20], Schuldt et al. proposed a new NS scheme without random oracles, and recently in [16,17], a more efficient NS scheme than that in [20] was proposed. The new scheme achieved constant-size keys.

B   Security Model

B.1   Unforgeability Against Malicious Users

We require that a user cannot forge a nominative signature without the involvement of a signer.

Game Unforgeability Against Malicious Users: Let S be a challenger and F a forger.

1. (*Initialization*) Let $k \in \mathbb{N}$ be a security parameter. S runs param $\leftarrow$ System Setup(1^k) and $(pk_A, sk_A) \leftarrow$ SKeyGen(param), then invokes F with (param, pk_A).
2. (*Attacking Phase*) F adaptively queries OCreateSigner, OCreateUser, OCorrupt, and OSign.
3. (*Output Phase*) F outputs $(m^*, \sigma^*, pk_B, sk_B)$.

F *wins* the game if valid $\leftarrow$ NSVer($m^*, \sigma^*, pk_A, sk_B$) provided that

1. F has never queried OCorrupt(pk_A) for getting sk_A;
2. (pk_B, sk_B) is created through querying OCreateUser;
3. (m^*, pk_A, pk_B) has never been queried to OSign.

F's advantage in this game is defined as the probability that F wins.

Definition 4. An NS is unforgeable against malicious users if no PPT forger F has a non-negligible advantage in Game Unforgeability Against Malicious Users.

Oracles OProof and OConvert are not provided in the game as F can readily carry out these protocol/algorithm as a (malicious) user by making use of OCreateUser and OCorrupt oracles.

B.2   Unforgeability Against Malicious Signers

A malicious signer should not be able to forge a nominative signature without the help of a user.

Game Unforgeability Against Malicious Signers: Let S be a challenger and F a forger.

1. (*Initialization*) On input a security parameter $k \in \mathbb{N}$, S runs param $\leftarrow$ SystemSetup(1^k) and (pk_B, sk_B) $\leftarrow$ UKeyGen(param) and invokes F with (param, pk_B).
2. (*Attacking Phase*) F adaptively queries OCreateSigner, OCreateUser, OCorrupt, OReceive, OProof and OConvert.
3. (*Output Phase*) F outputs $(m^*, \sigma^*, pk_A, sk_A)$.

F *wins* the game if valid $\leftarrow$ NSVer($m^*, \sigma^*, pk_A, sk_B$) provided that

1. F has never queried OCorrupt(pk_B) for getting sk_B;
2. (pk_A, sk_A) is created through OCreateSigner;
3. $(m^*, \sigma'^*, pk_A, pk_B)$ has never been queried to OReceive such that σ^* is the return.

F's advantage in this game is defined as the probability that F wins.

Definition 5. An NS is unforgeable against malicious signers if no PPT forger F has a non-negligible advantage in Game Unforgeability Against Malicious Signers.

OSign is not provided in the game above as F can readily carry out Sign as (malicious) signers by making use of OCreateSigner and OCorrupt.

B.3   Invisibility

We require that no verifier C (including signer A) but user B can tell the validity of a nominative signature. In the formalization, we define an auxiliary algorithm called NSSim (Nominative Signature Simulator). The algorithm takes (param, $pk_A, pk_B, m, \sigma^{valid}$) as input, where σ^{valid} is a valid nominative signature for message m under pk_A and pk_B, outputs $\sigma^{invalid}$ so that $\sigma^{invalid} \in \mathcal{S}(pk_A, pk_B)$ but $\sigma^{invalid}$ is no longer a valid nominative signature for m under (pk_A, pk_B). The purpose of introducing NSSim is to explicitly define the capability of the public to convert a valid nominative signature to an invalid one while both σ^{valid} and $\sigma^{invalid}$ should look indistinguishable to C, and only B can tell which signature is valid and which one is not. Also note that NSSim has to be explicitly described in the construction of an NS scheme in order to have the new scheme be proven satisfying the Invisibility requirement.

Game Invisibility: The adversary in the game is a distinguisher D.

1. (*Initialization*) Same as that of Game Unforgeability Against Malicious Signers.
2. (*Attacking Phase*) Same as that of Game Unforgeability Against Malicious Signers.

3. (*Challenge Signature Generation Phase*) D chooses and sends a message m^* and (pk_A, pk_B) to the challenger while acting as a signer (indexed by pk_A) to carry out a run of SigGen with the challenger which acts as a user (indexed by pk_B). Let σ^{valid} be the nominative signature generated by the challenger in a SigGen protocol run, that is, valid $\leftarrow$ NSVer($m^*, \sigma^{valid}, pk_A, sk_B$). The challenger then tosses a random coin $b \in_R \{0, 1\}$. If $b = 1$, the challenges sends σ^{valid} to D; otherwise, the challenge sends $\sigma^* \leftarrow$ NSSim(param, $pk_A, pk_B, m, \sigma^{valid}$) to D.

4. (*Guess Phase*) D continues querying the oracles until it outputs a guess b'.

D *wins* the game if $b' = b$ provided that

1. D has never queried OCorrupt(pk_B) for getting sk_B;
2. (pk_A, sk_A) is created by querying OCreateSigner;
3. $(m^*, \sigma'^*, pk_A, pk_B)$ has never been queried to OReceive such that it returns σ^*;
4. $(m^*, \sigma^*, pk_A, pk_B)$ has never been queried to OProof or OConvert.

D's advantage in this game is defined as $P[b' = b] - \frac{1}{2}$.

Definition 6. An NS satisfies invisibility if no PPT distinguisher D has a non-negligible advantage in Game Invisibility.

B.4   Non-transferability

This security property requires that a verifier C cannot convince other verifiers using a previous confirmation/disavowal proof transcript about the validity/invalidity of a given nominative signature. For a secure NS scheme, the Confirmation and Disavowal protocols should be perfect zero-knowledge so that no PPT verifier (including the signer) can transfer the proof transcript. The perfect zero-knowledge property implies non-transferability of proof transcripts as a verifier C can simulate the proof transcripts that look indistinguishable from the actual proof transcripts. A third party C can sample a signature from the signature space and create a proof transcript which looks indistinguishable from those generated from the Confirmation/Disavowal protocols running between the corresponding user B and the third party C.

B.5   User-Only Conversion

The following game captures the requirement that no one but the user can convert a valid nominative signature to a publicly-verifiable one.
Game User-only Conversion: Let C be an adversary.

- (*Initialization*) Same as that of Game Unforgeability Against Malicious Signers.
- (*Attacking Phase*) Same as that of Game Unforgeability Against Malicious Signers.

- (*Challenge Signature Generation Phase*) C is given a challenge message-nominative-signature pair (m^*, σ^*) and the public keys of signer and user, respectively, (pk_A, pk_B) such that σ^* is valid on m^* under (pk_A, pk_B).
- (*Conversion Phase*) C outputs (m^*, σ^{std}).

C *wins* if valid $\leftarrow$ Ver$(m, \sigma^{std}, pk_A, pk_B)$ provided that

1. C has never queried OCorrupt(pk_B) for getting sk_B;
2. (pk_A, sk_A) is created by querying OCreateSigner;
3. $(m^*, \sigma^*, pk_A, pk_B)$ has never been queried to OProof or OConvert.

C's advantage is defined as the probability that C wins.

Definition 7. An NS satisfies user-only conversion if no PPT adversary C has a non-negligible advantage in Game User-only Conversion.

Theorem 2 ([16, 17]). *If an NS satisfies invisibility with respect to Definition 6, the scheme satisfies user-only conversion.*

References

1. Barak, B., Canetti, R., Nielsen, J.B., Pass, R.: Universally composable protocols with relaxed set-up assumptions. In: FOCS 2004, pp. 186–195. IEEE Computer Society, (2004)
2. Boneh, D., Boyen, X.: Short signatures without random oracles and the SDH assumption in bilinear groups. J. Cryptol. **21**(2), 149–177 (2008)
3. Boneh, D., Boyen, X., Shacham, H.: Short group signatures. In: Franklin, M. (ed.) CRYPTO 2004. LNCS, vol. 3152, pp. 41–55. Springer, Heidelberg (2004)
4. Bresson, E., Stern, J.: Proofs of knowledge for non-monotone discrete-log formulae and applications. In: Chan, A.H., Gligor, V.D. (eds.) ISC 2002. LNCS, vol. 2433, pp. 272–288. Springer, Heidelberg (2002)
5. Camenisch, J.L., Shoup, V.: Practical verifiable encryption and decryption of discrete logarithms. In: Boneh, D. (ed.) CRYPTO 2003. LNCS, vol. 2729, pp. 126–144. Springer, Heidelberg (2003)
6. Cramer, R., Damgård, I.B., MacKenzie, P.D.: Efficient zero-knowledge proofs of knowledge without intractability assumptions. In: Imai, H., Zheng, Y. (eds.) PKC 2000. LNCS, vol. 1751, pp. 354–373. Springer, Heidelberg (2000)
7. Guo, L., Wang, G., Wong, D.S., Hu, L.: Further discussions on the security of a nominative signature scheme. In: SAM 2007, pp. 566–572. CSREA Press, June 2007
8. Hofheinz, D., Kiltz, E.: Programmable hash functions and their applications. In: Wagner, D. (ed.) CRYPTO 2008. LNCS, vol. 5157, pp. 21–38. Springer, Heidelberg (2008)
9. Huang, Q., Liu, D.Y.W., Wong, D.S.: An efficient one-move nominative signature scheme. IJACT **1**(2), 133–143 (2008)
10. Huang, Q., Wong, D.S.: Short and efficient convertible undeniable signature schemes without random oracles. Theor. Comput. Sci. **476**, 67–83 (2013)
11. Huang, Q., Yang, G., Wong, D.S., Susilo, W.: Ambiguous optimistic fair exchange. In: Pieprzyk, J. (ed.) ASIACRYPT 2008. LNCS, vol. 5350, pp. 74–89. Springer, Heidelberg (2008)

12. Huang, Z., Wang, Y.-M.: Convertible nominative signatures. In: Wang, H., Pieprzyk, J., Varadharajan, V. (eds.) ACISP 2004. LNCS, vol. 3108, pp. 348–357. Springer, Heidelberg (2004)
13. Kim, S.J., Park, S.J., Won, D.H.: Zero-knowledge nominative signatures. In: PragoCrypt'96, pp. 380–392 (1996)
14. Liu, D.Y.W., Chang, S., Wong, D.S.: A more efficient convertible nominative signature. In: SECRYPT 2007, pp. 214–221. INSTICC Press (2007)
15. Liu, D.Y.W., Chang, S., Wong, D.S., Mu, Y.: Nominative signature from ring signature. In: Miyaji, A., Kikuchi, H., Rannenberg, K. (eds.) IWSEC 2007. LNCS, vol. 4752, pp. 396–411. Springer, Heidelberg (2007)
16. Liu, D.Y.W., Wong, D.S.: One-move convertible nominative signature in the standard model. In: Takagi, T., Wang, G., Qin, Z., Jiang, S., Yu, Y. (eds.) ProvSec 2012. LNCS, vol. 7496, pp. 2–20. Springer, Heidelberg (2012)
17. Liu, D.Y.W., Wong, D.S.: One-move convertible nominative signature in the standard model. Security and Communication Networks, July 2013. http://dx.doi.org/10.1002/sec.812
18. Liu, D.Y.W., Wong, D.S., Huang, Q.: Ambiguous one-move nominative signature without random oracles. Cryptology ePrint Archive, Report 2013/711, 2013. http://eprint.iacr.org/
19. Liu, D.Y.W., Wong, D.S., Huang, X., Wang, G., Huang, Q., Mu, Y., Susilo, W.: Formal definition and construction of nominative signature. In: Qing, S., Imai, H., Wang, G. (eds.) ICICS 2007. LNCS, vol. 4861, pp. 57–68. Springer, Heidelberg (2007)
20. Schuldt, J.C.N., Hanaoka, G.: Non-transferable user certification secure against authority information leaks and impersonation attacks. In: Lopez, J., Tsudik, G. (eds.) ACNS 2011. LNCS, vol. 6715, pp. 413–430. Springer, Heidelberg (2011)
21. Susilo, W., Mu, Y.: On the security of nominative signatures. In: Boyd, C., González Nieto, J.M. (eds.) ACISP 2005. LNCS, vol. 3574, pp. 329–335. Springer, Heidelberg (2005)
22. Wang, G., Bao, F.: Security remarks on a convertible nominative signature scheme. In: Venter, H., Eloff, M., Labuschagne, L., Eloff, J., von Solms, R. (eds.) SEC 2007. IFIP, vol. 232, pp. 265–275. Springer, US (2007)
23. Zhao, W., Lin, C., Ye, D.: Provably secure convertible nominative signature scheme. In: Yung, M., Liu, P., Lin, D. (eds.) Inscrypt 2008. LNCS, vol. 5487, pp. 23–40. Springer, Heidelberg (2009)
24. Zhao, W., Ye, D.: Pairing-based nominative signatures with selective and universal convertibility. In: Bao, F., Yung, M., Lin, D., Jing, J. (eds.) Inscrypt 2009. LNCS, vol. 6151, pp. 60–74. Springer, Heidelberg (2010)

A Provably Secure Signature and Signcryption Scheme Using the Hardness Assumptions in Coding Theory

K. Preetha Mathew[1]([✉]), Sachin Vasant[2], and C. Pandu Rangan[1]

[1] Theoretical Computer Science Lab, Department of Computer Science and Engineering, Indian Institute of Technology Madras, Chennai, India
{kpreetha,prangan}@cse.iitm.ac.in
[2] Department of Computer Science, Boston University, Boston, USA
sachinv@cs.bu.edu

Abstract. Signcryption is a cryptographic protocol that provides authentication and confidentiality as a single primitive at a cost lower than the combined cost of sign and encryption. Code-based cryptography, a likely candidate for post-quantum cryptography, provides an exciting alternative to number-theoretic cryptography. Courtois, Finiasz and Sendrier proposed the only practical code-based signature(CFS signature) at Asiacrypt 2001. But that signature scheme currently lacks a formal proof of security due to the existence of the high rate distinguisher proposed by Faugère et al. In this paper, we make use of an alternate key-construct for the CFS signature, and thus prove its existential unforgeability under chosen message attacks (EUF-CMA). Also, we propose a code-based signcryption scheme and prove its security. To the best of our knowledge, this is the first code-based, provably secure signature and signcryption scheme in literature.

Keywords: Signature · Signcryption · Code-based cryptography · CFS signature · Syndrome decoding

1 Introduction

Authentication and confidentiality of a message are among important security goals achieved using cryptography. Confidentiality is achieved by encryption and signature achieves authentication. Signcryption as a primitive, aims at attaining the above goals at a lower cost than individually signing and encrypting or vice-versa. Zheng [32], in 1997 proposed the first digital signcryption scheme. Later, a formal model of security for signcryption schemes was provided by Baek et al. in [2], which includes signcrypted text indistinguishable under chosen ciphertext attack (SC-IND-CCA2) for confidentiality and signature on the signcrypted text is existential unforgeable under chosen message attack (SC-EUF-CMA) for unforgeability. Also, a stronger notion of security called *insider*

© Springer International Publishing Switzerland 2014
H.-S. Lee and D.-G. Han (Eds.): ICISC 2013, LNCS 8565, pp. 342–362, 2014.
DOI: 10.1007/978-3-319-12160-4_21

security was introduced by An et al. in [1], which proposed that a signcryption scheme needs to offer confidentiality even if all the private-keys except the receiver's private key are known (the private key of the sender in particular, is known to the adversary), and it must be unforgeable even if all the private keys except the private-key of the sender are known (in particular, the private key of the receiver is known to the adversary).

The notion of code-based cryptography was initiated by the encryption scheme proposed by McEliece [28] in 1978, which was based on the Bounded Decoding Problem. The aforementioned problem is NP-complete [5]. Niederreiter [18] proposed an encryption scheme which was effectively on the dual of the code used in the McEliece encryption scheme. In the Niederreiter system, the security was based on the hardness of the Syndrome Decoding Problem. The security of the schemes by McEliece [28] and Niederreiter [18] are shown to be equivalent in [22]. Stern [30] proposed an efficient code-based identification scheme, which does not require a trapdoor like Goppa codes and its corresponding decoding mechanism, unlike the above cryptosystems. But, to obtain a signature scheme based on [30] is practically infeasible as the signature size is very large. Courtois et al.[9] in 2001 proposed a signature scheme (CFS signature scheme) based on the hardness of Syndrome Decoding Problem. These signatures are practical only for high-rate linear codes (as the density of non-decodable syndromes is sparse). Although it has a relatively large signing time, the signature scheme was an exciting breakthrough, as it laid a foundation-stone for development of many code-based schemes in various cryptographic primitives. Barreto et al. [4] proposed one-time signature and Kabatianskii et al. [19] also proposed a signature which is secure only for few signatures. Otmani et al. [25] proved an attack on the above two schemes.

Motivation. The first practical code based signature scheme was reported in 2001 by Courtois et al. [10]. Later the authors added few more details in the scheme presented in [9]. The running time of the signing algorithm, is estimated to be $O(t^2 t! \log(n)^3)$, where t is the number of errors that can be corrected and n is the length of the code word. The formal proof for the signature was not presented in the paper, but to arrive at safe parameter values, the authors considered the attacks like Canteaut Chabaud (CC) attack [7] and Lee Brickell (LB) attack [20]. Assuming a threshold of 2^{80} binary work factor for security against specific attack, $(\log(n), t)$ values that would withstand the attacks and the corresponding signing times were estimated. Specifically in order to resist the attacks like the CC attack and LB attack, [9] suggests that the values such as (15,10), (16,9) are appropriate for $(\log(n), t)$. They have also shown that the running time of the signature algorithm is reasonable for these choice of parameters. In 2009, Finiasz et al. [16] considered an attack due to Daniel Bleichenbacher (communicated through the private communication to the authors of [16], but never published). The authors of [16] suggested the parameters must be set to (15,12) or (16,12) etc. for $(\log(n), t)$ values in view of this new attack. Subsequently, in 2011, Sendrier [29] studied another attack, namely decoding one out of many. The revised parameters that can be chosen according to [29] are (18,13), (19,12), (20,11) for $(\log(n), t)$. In 2007, a formal proof was given by Dallot [11] assuming the hardness of syndrome decoding and code indistinguishability. In 2010, Faugere et al. [14] cryptanalysed the McEliece variants with compact keys algebraically, which was subsequently extended in [12]. The analysis of [12] is an extended analysis of a high rate distinguisher for McEliece encryption in [13]. This result gives that the t values (the error-correcting capacities) must be set higher than previous estimates to achieve a provably secure system. In particular if $\log(n)$ (n is the length of the code) is chosen as 18, 19 or 20 then t values must be set to 85, 114, 157 respectively. But, these parameters lead to impractical signing times ($>2^{220}$ operations).

Still the distinguisher does not imply a concrete attack on the scheme in [11] or in [9]. In fact, the randomised CFS signature has widely been conjectured to be unforgeable, even though a formal security argument does not exist currently. Hence, we need to explore alternatives to overcome the distinguisher to arrive at a proof of security.

Signcryption is an important primitive in applications such as e-commerce, secure and authentic e-mails, etc., because it offers both confidentiality and authentication simultaneously. However, designing a signcryption scheme using the paradigm 'sign-then-encrypt' will lead to an inefficient scheme in code based scenario.

Our Contribution. In this paper, we alter the key-construct of the CFS signature [9] (based on the key construct in [17]) and formally argue the security of the proposed signature in the EUF-CMA model. To do so, we introduce a new distinguishability assumption, which is weaker than the current Goppa-code distinguishability assumption. We also propose the first code-based signcryption scheme (also, the first signcryption not using the classical number-theoretic assumptions, to the best of our knowledge) using the Niederreiter's system [18] and the CFS signature, both using the modified key-construct. The signcryption scheme is loosely based on the construction in [21]. We formally prove the confidentiality (in the SC-IND-CCA2) and unforgeability (in the SC-EUF-CMA).

Organisation of paper. In the next section we provide some preliminaries. In Sect. 3, we briefly introduce our weaker distinguishability assumptions. We also argue (informally) as to why it is weaker than the conventional distinguishability assumptions. In Sect. 4, we give the proposed signature scheme along with the security proof. In Sect. 5, we give the proposal for signcryption and provide a sketch of its security and identify a few secure parameters for the scheme. We conclude in Sect. 6. The formal proof of security of the signcryption scheme is given in Appendix A.

2   Preliminaries

Before proceeding to the preliminaries, one should note that $\mathsf{negl}(n)$ is a negligible value with respect to the parameter n. We now enlist some basics of coding theory and the definitions of the primitives involved.

2.1   Coding Theory

A binary linear-error correcting code of length n and dimension k or a $[n, k]$- code is a k-dimensional subspace of $\mathbb{F}_2^n$. If the minimum distance between code-words is d, then we denote the code as an $[n, k, d]$ code, where d is called the Hamming distance. The error correcting capability of the code is $t = \lfloor \frac{d-1}{2} \rfloor$. The generator matrix $G \in \mathbb{F}_2^{k \times n}$ of a $[n, k]$ linear code $\mathcal{C}$ is a matrix of rank k whose rows span the code $\mathcal{C}$. The parity-check matrix $H \in \mathbb{F}_2^{n-k \times n}$ of a $[n, k]$ code $\mathcal{C}$ is defined as a matrix satisfying $HG^T = 0$. Hence, we can define the code $\mathcal{C}$ as $\{mG : \forall m \in \mathbb{F}_2^k\}$ or $\{c : Hc^T = 0\}$. We now proceed to list the hard problems.

Definition 1 Syndrome Decoding Problem. *For some parameters $[n, k, 2t+1]$ given an* $\mathbf{a} \in \mathbb{F}_2^{n-k}$ *and a random matrix $H \in \mathbb{F}_2^{n-k \times n}$, find a vector* $\mathbf{e} \in \mathbb{F}_2^n$ *with weight* $\mathsf{wt}(\mathbf{e}) \leq t$ *such that $H\mathbf{e}^T = \mathbf{a}$.*

The advantage of a probabilistic polynomial time (PPT) algorithm $\mathcal{D}$ of solving the syndrome decoding problem for $[n, k, 2t+1]$ code is denoted by $\mathsf{Adv}_{\mathcal{D}}^{\mathsf{SD}}(n, k, t)$. Syndrome Decoding Problem is hard (worst-case) for any random code [5]. Hence, $\mathsf{Adv}_{\mathcal{D}}^{\mathsf{SD}}(n, k, t) = \mathsf{negl}(n)$. But, for Goppa codes, there is a polynomial time algorithm for syndrome decoding.

Definition 2 Punctured Codes [31]. *Let C be a code of length n and $S \subset N$ where N denotes the set $\{1, ..., n\}$. Let C_S denote the code which is obtained by deleting all coordinates of C in N/S. C_S is called punctured code of C in N/S.*

Definition 3 Equivalent Codes [26,31]. *Let C and D be two codes over the same field and of same length n. C and D are called equivalent, if there is a permutation $\pi : \{1, ..., n\} \rightarrow \{1, ..., n\}$ such that $(c_1, ..., c_n) \in C \Leftrightarrow (c_{\pi(1)}, ..., c_{\pi(n)}) \in D$.*

The problem of finding code equivalence is proven to be harder than graph isomorphism problem [27].

Consider the problem with C be a code of length n and D a code of length m, such that $m \leq n$, Does there exist a subset $S \subset \{1, ..., n\}$, such that C_S and D are equivalent? can be viewed as a punctured code equivalence problem.

Definition 4. *Let M be a $k \times n$ matrix over a field F with columns $m_1, ..., m_n$ and $\tau : \{1, ..., q\} \rightarrow \{1, .., n\}$ an injection, such that $(q \leq n)$. The $k \times q$ matrix consists of the columns $m_{\tau(1)}, ..., m_{\tau(q)}$ (in this order) is denoted by M_τ.*

Definition 5 Equivalent Punctured Codes (EPC) [31]. *Let M be a $k \times n$ matrix and H be a $k \times m$ matrix where $m \leq n$ over a field F, Does there exist a non-singular matrix $k \times k$ matrix T and an injective map τ such that $(TM)_\tau = TM_\tau = H$.*

The EPC problem was shown to be NP-complete by reducing three dimensional matching (3DM) problem to Equivalent Punctured code problem [24,31]. In fact, the hardness of EPC problem is the basis of the encryption scheme given in [31]. Thus we are justified in the following assumption.

Assumption 1. *There is no PPT algorithm $\mathcal{D}$ that can find a non-singular matrix $k \times k$ matrix T and an injective map τ such that $(TM)_\tau = TM_\tau = H$, given M and H.*

In the construction of the signature presented in this paper, the security of private key is based on Equivalent Punctured Code problem.

2.2   Signature

Definition 6. *A signature scheme consists of a triple of algorithms (KeyGen, Sign, Verify) where,*

KeyGen *is a PPT algorithm that takes as input the security parameter κ (or 1^κ) to return the key-pair (sk, pk), where sk is the signing-key which is kept as secret with the signer, and pk is the verification-key which is made public.*

Sign *is a PPT algorithm that takes as input the secret signing key sk and the document/message m from the message space and outputs a signature σ.*

Verify *is a polynomial time algorithm that takes as input the public verification key pk, the document/message m and the signature σ on the message and outputs ACCEPT if σ is valid and REJECT otherwise.*

Definition 7 (Existential Unforgeability under Chosen Message Attack). *A signature scheme is said to be existentially unforgeable against chosen-message insider attack (EUF-CMA) if no PPT forger $\mathcal{F}$ has a non-negligible advantage in the following game:*

1. *The challenger runs KeyGen to generate a key pair (sk, pk). sk is kept secret while pk is given to the adversary $\mathcal{F}$.*
2. *The forger $\mathcal{F}$ adaptively makes a polynomial number of queries to the signature oracle and the hash oracles (if any).*
3. *The forger $\mathcal{F}$ produces a signature σ and wins the game if :*
   - *Verify(pk,m,σ) outputs ACCEPT and*
   - *(m, σ) is not the output of any signature oracle, described in step 2.*

The probability that, for a parameter n a forger is able to forge a signature is denoted by $\mathsf{Succ}_{\mathcal{F}}^{euf-cma}(n)$.

2.3   Signcryption

We first begin by formally defining a signcryption scheme. This formal definition is based on the definition given in [21].

Definition 8. *A signcryption scheme is a triple of algorithms (UK$_g$, $\overline{S}$, $\overline{U}$) for a security parameter 1^k.*

$(sk, pk) \leftarrow UK_g(1^k)$ *is the **Key-generation** algorithm which takes a security parameter k to generate the private/public key pair (sk,pk).*

$\sigma \leftarrow \overline{S}(1^k, m, sk_S, pk_R)$ is the **Signcryption** is a PPT algorithm which takes a security parameter k, the message m from a message space M, the sender's private key sk_S and receiver's public key pk_R, to output the signcrypted text σ.

$((m, s), \mathsf{Accept})/\mathsf{Reject} \leftarrow \overline{U}(1^k, \sigma, sk_R, pk_S)$ is the **De-signcrypt** algorithm. The **De-Signcrypt** algorithm is as follows. It takes security parameter k, the signcrypted text σ and the receiver's private key sk_R and sender's public key pk_S as input to decrypt and get the signed message m, or Reject which indicates failure of De-signcrypt when message was not encrypted or signed correctly.

The security notions of confidentiality and unforgeability (that also model the insider security notion) are described here. The notion is based on the notion mentioned in [21].

Definition 9 (Confidentiality). *A signcryption scheme is semantically secure against chosen ciphertext attack (SC-IND-CCA2) if no PPT adversary $\mathcal{A}$ has a non-negligible advantage in the following game:*

1. *The challenger runs UK_g to generate a key pair (sk_U, pk_U). sk_U is kept secret while pk_U is given to the adversary $\mathcal{A}$. For the others users U' (say), the challenger runs UK_g to generate $(sk_{U'}, pk_{U'})$, and sends the tuple to the adversary. (Insider security).*
2. *In the first stage, $\mathcal{A}$ makes a polynomial number of queries to the following oracles:*
   Signcryption Oracle: *$\mathcal{A}$ prepares a message $m \in M$ and a public key pk_R, and queries the Signcryption Oracle (simulated by the challenger) for the result of $\overline{S}(m, sk_U, pk_R)$. The result is returned if $pk_R \neq pk_U$ and pk_R is valid in the sense that pk_R is in the range of UK_g with respect to the security parameter. Otherwise, a symbol '$\perp$' is returned for rejection.*
   De-signcryption Oracle: *$\mathcal{A}$ produces a signcrypted text σ and queries for the result of $\overline{U}(\sigma, sk_U, pk_S)$. The message is returned if the de-signcryption is successful and the signature is valid under the sender's public key. Otherwise, a symbol '$\perp$' is returned for rejection.*
   The queries may be asked adaptively, i.e., each query may depend on the answers to the previous queries.
3. *$\mathcal{A}$ produces two messages $m_0, m_1 \in M$ of equal length and a valid private key sk_S. The challenger takes a random $b \xleftarrow{R} \{0,1\}$ and computes a signcryption $\sigma^* = \overline{S}(m_b, sk_S, pk_U)$ of m_b with the sender's private key sk_S under the receiver's public pk_U. σ^* is sent to $\mathcal{A}$ as a challenge.*
4. *$\mathcal{A}$ makes a number of queries as in the first stage with the restriction that it cannot query the de-signcryption oracle with σ^*.*
5. *At the end of the game, $\mathcal{A}$ outputs a bit b' and wins if $b' = b$.*

$\mathcal{A}$'s advantage is defined as $Adv^{ind-cca}(\mathcal{A}) = Pr[b = b'] - \frac{1}{2}$ and the probability that $b = b'$ is the probability that $\mathcal{A}$ wins the game.

Definition 10 (Unforgeability). *A signcryption scheme is said to be existentially unforgeable against chosen-message insider attack (SC-EUF-CMA) if no PPT forger $\mathcal{F}$ has a non-negligible advantage in the following game:*

1. *Follow the first two steps as that of confidentiality game.*
2. *The forger $\mathcal{F}$ produces a signcrypted text σ and a valid key pair (sk_R, pk_R) and wins the game if :*
   - $\overline{U}(\sigma, sk_R, pk_U)$ *returns a tuple (m, s) such that the output of verification on (m, s) for the verification key pk_U is Accept.*
   - σ *is not the output of the signcryption oracle.*

3 Weak Distinguishability Assumptions

In this section, we introduce a weak Goppa distinguishability assumption. We assume that the public key construct using Goppa code is computationally indistinguishable from a random matrix. The public key and private key pair must be constructed in such a way that given public key, it should not be possible to reconstruct the private key [8]. Therefore signature scheme is a variant of the CFS, but uses an alternate public key construction such that the public key is no longer the permutation equivalent of the private code. The key construct is some what similar to the one used in [17], but there are subtle differences. The private keys used for signing are Q, H, P, where Q is an $(n-k) \times (n-k)$ invertible matrix, H a Parity Check Matrix of a binary code $\mathcal{C}$ of type $Goppa(n, k, t)$, which is always a nonzero matrix, and a random $n \times n$ permutation matrix P as per the CFS signature. But the public key $\widetilde{H}$ used in our scheme is $(n-k+1) \times n$ matrix, unlike $(n-k) \times n$ parity check matrix used as the public key in the CFS signature. Therefore the public key is no longer a permuted randomised parity check matrix of a Goppa code. Also the matrix Q is computed as a product of two randomly generated matrices H' of size $(n-k) \times n'$, where $n' = n-k+1$ and Q' of size $n' \times (n-k)$. The process is repeated until Q is invertible. We see that Q is invertible with probability at least 0.288 [6]. Hence, in roughly 4 trials we can expect to obtain an invertible Q. Also, $\mathbf{a}$ is selected such that $H'\mathbf{a}^T = 0$. Due to all these differences, we obtain a novel and provably secure signature scheme.

3.1 Key-Construct

The key generation involves the following steps

- Select H, a Parity Check Matrix of a binary code $\mathcal{C}$ of type $Goppa(n, k, t)$. and a random $n \times n$ permutation matrix P .
- Select randomly a $H' \in_R \mathbb{F}_2^{(n-k) \times n'}$ and a $Q' \in_R \mathbb{F}_2^{n' \times (n-k)}$, such that Q' is full-rank and compute matrix $Q = H'Q'$. Repeat the step until Q is invertible.
- Select an $\mathbf{a} \in \mathbb{F}_2^{n'}$, such that $H'\mathbf{a}^T = 0$ and Select $\mathbf{b} \in_R \mathbb{F}_2^n$..
- Compute a parity check matrix $\widetilde{H}$ as $\widetilde{H} = Q'HP \oplus \mathbf{a}^T\mathbf{b}$. $\widetilde{H}$ is a $n' \times n$ matrix. If $\widetilde{H}$ is not full-rank, repeat the process with a different random $\mathbf{b}$, until we obtain a full-rank $\widetilde{H}$.

3.2 Assumption

For the aforementioned key construct we make the following hardness assumptions which is weaker than Goppa code Distinguishability assumption. The symbols in this section are as defined in the key construct (unless specified otherwise).

Assumption 2. *There is no PPT distinguisher $\mathcal{D}$ that can distinguish $\widetilde{H}$ from a parity check matrix R of a random $(n, k-1, 2t+1)$ linear code.*

Let the advantage of such a distinguisher be $\mathsf{Adv}_{\mathcal{D}}^{\mathsf{Dist}}(n, k) = |Pr[\mathcal{D}(\widetilde{H}) \to 1] - Pr[\mathcal{D}(R) \to 1]|$. We consider Assumption 2 to be weaker than the Goppa-code distinguishability assumption. The reason for this can be explained based on another assumption based on Equivalent Punctured code Problem and the high rate code distinguisher.

Assumption 3. *Given $\widetilde{H}$, it is infeasible to retrieve H, a and b.*

Given $\widetilde{H}$ it is infeasible to find H'. The corresponding decisional version of Assumption 3 is "*Given $\widetilde{H}$, does there exist a H' such that $H'\widetilde{H} = QHP$ for some Goppa code with parity matrix H, some $(n-k) \times (n-k)$ invertible matrix Q and $n \times n$ permutation matrix P*". This is clearly Assumption 2 (if there doesn't exists such a H' then the input matrix is random). This is a generalisation of the Equivalent Punctured Code problem. To elaborate, suppose this decision problem is solved, then we can solve the following problem, *For two matrices M and H does there exist a T and selections S_1, $S_2 \subseteq \{1, 2, \ldots n\}$ such that* $(TM)_{S_1} = H_{S_2}$.

Another reason, why we consider this problem to be weaker than the Goppa distinguishability is based on the equations for the distinguisher. It is seen that the public key is not a parity check matrix of a permutation equivalent code of the secret code. We take the generator matrix corresponding to the public matrix. Hence, to solve the system to obtain the private keys, the following system of equations have to be solved.

$$\{g_{i1}(X_1^j Y_1 + a_j b_1) + \ldots + g_{in}(X_n^j Y_n + a_j b_n) = 0 \mid i \in \{1, \ldots, k\} \ \& \ j \in \{0, \ldots, (n-k)\}\}\}$$

where g_{ij} is the element of the generator matrix at the ith row and j^{th} column. Unlike the system in [13], the system here is not trivially linearisable. Hence, the distinguishing based on the dimension may not hold good.

4 Proposed Signature Scheme

4.1 Scheme

System Parameters(κ). The following system parameters are used:

– Parameters of the code n, k, t for any $[n, k, 2t+1]$ linear code, with n, k determined by the security parameter κ, and $t = \frac{(n-k)}{\log_2 n}$.

- We define $n' = n - k + 1$.
- Hash function $\mathcal{G} : \mathbb{F}_2^n \times \{0,1\}^n \to \mathbb{F}_2^{n'}$.

Key Generation$(\kappa, parameters)$. The key generation is as mentioned in Sect. 3 and we have

private key: H, P, Q, H'; **public key:** $\widetilde{H}$; **parameters:** $[n, k, t], n', \mathcal{G}$

Sign(m, H, P, Q, H'). To sign a message $m \in \{0,1\}^l$

- **repeat**

  $r \xleftarrow{R} \mathbb{F}_2^n$

  $m_1' \leftarrow \mathcal{G}(r, m)$

  $m_1 = H'm_1'^T$

  $s_1 = P^T Decode_H(Q^{-1}m_1)$ //If m_1 is not decodable for H, the decoding algorithm sets $s_1 = \perp$.

  until$(s_1 \neq \perp \;\&\&\; m_1' = \widetilde{H}s_1^T)$
- The signature is $\sigma = (s_1, r)$

Verify$(m, \sigma, \widetilde{H})$. Verification of the signature $\sigma = (s_1, r)$ on m is done by checking $\widetilde{H}s_1^T \overset{?}{=} \mathcal{G}(r, m)$ and $wt(s_1) \leq t$. If TRUE then return ACCEPT, else return REJECT.

Note that m_1 is made a syndrome for H' for the word m_1', and m_1 also made a syndrome for code word s_1 for QHP. When m_1' is replaced with $\widetilde{H}s_1^T$ according to the signing procedure in $m_1 = H'm_1'^T$, observe that it becomes a syndrome for code word s_1 for QHP.

Note 1. To elaborate on the scheme, we take two cases.

- In the first case, assume m_1' is a decodable syndrome for $\widetilde{H}$, i.e., there exists an s_1 such that $m_1' = \widetilde{H}s_1^T$ and $wt(s_1) \leq t$. Then it is seen that $m_1 = H'm_1'^T = H'(Q'HP \oplus \mathbf{a}^T\mathbf{b})s_1^T = QHPs_1^T$ (since $Q = H'Q'$ and $H'\mathbf{a}^T = 0$). Hence, it is possible to decode m_1 using the decoding algorithm on H to obtain s_1 which is the solution of syndrome decoding of m_1' for $\widetilde{H}$.
- In the second case, assume m_1' is not decodable for $\widetilde{H}$. Hence, there does not exist any s_1 unlike the first case. But m_1 can either be decodable or not decodable for H. It is the property of any binary linear code of length n' and dimension k', to partition the space $\mathbb{F}_2^{n'}$ into $2^{n'-k'}$ partitions of size $2^{k'}$, using the syndromes. Hence, for H' (which has dimension 1), exactly two values m_1' and m_2'(say) map to the same syndrome m_1. If m_1 is not decodable for H then both m_1' and m_2' are not decodable for $\widetilde{H}$. But, if m_1 is decodable (and can be decoded to s (say)) , then one of the two the values m_1' and m_2' is of the form $\widetilde{H}s^T$, whereas the other is not decodable. This can be proved by contradiction. Assuming both m_1' and m_2' are decodable for $\widetilde{H}$, into s_1 and s_2 repsepctively. Then, $H'm_1'$ and $H'm_2'$ are also correspondingly decodable into s_1 and s_2 for H. But, we know that $H'm_1' = H'm_2' = m_1$. Hence, it is a contradiction that m_1 decodes into two vectors (both of weight $\leq t$). Therefore, only one vector is decodable, while the other is not decodable.

Hence, the expected time taken [9] for the above signature is $O(t!t^2m^3)$.

4.2   Security of the Scheme

We now proceed to prove the unforgeability of the scheme under the EUF-CMA security notion in random oracle model. The proof follows the same line as that of [11].

Theorem 1. *The given scheme is EUF-CMA (under the random oracle model) if the syndrome decoding (SD) is hard to solve and the public key is computationally indistinguishable from the parity matrix of a random $(n, k-1, t)$ code R.*

Proof: We build the proof, by constructing a challenger C through a sequence of games **Game0, Game1,$\cdots$**. **Game0** is played by using the protocol as mentioned in EUF-CMA game. Successive games are obtained by small modifications of the preceding games, in such a way that the difference of the view in consecutive games is easily quantifiable. Let $q_{\mathcal{G}}, q_s$ be the maximum number of queries made by the forger $\mathcal{F}$ to the hash oracle of $\mathcal{G}$ and the signature oracle. We want to show that the advantage for the adversary $\mathcal{F}$ is equivalent to the advantage of solving the hard problem SD for a random code with parity check matrix R and some syndrome s.

To answer the hash queries and the signature queries, we maintain the lists, $\mathcal{G}^{list}, \sigma^{list}$ and Λ. If there is no value in a list we denote its output by $\perp$.

- The list $\mathcal{G}^{list}$ contains a tuple $((x, s), a)$ indexed by (r, m).
- The σ^{list} (the signature list) consists of entries of the form $(m, \sigma = (s, r))$.
- The list Λ consists of indices r of $\Lambda(m)$ for which the simulator is able to produce a signature on $\mathcal{G}(m, \Lambda(m))$,i.e., the list of r for which $\mathcal{G}(m, \Lambda(m))$ is a decodable syndrome.

Game 0. Here the challenger employs the actual scheme according to the EUF-CMA game. The private and public key pair are obtained by running the key generation algorithm given the scheme, to obtain secret key (Q, H, P, H'), where $H \leftarrow$ Goppa(n, k) (a binary Goppa code), and the public key $\tilde{H} = Q'HP \oplus a^T b$. $\tilde{H}$ is given to $\mathcal{F}$. Also, $\mathcal{F}$ is given access to the hash oracle $\mathcal{G}$. The signature oracle functions as mentioned in the scheme. Let X_0 be the event that $\mathcal{F}$ wins Game 0. It is seen that Game 0 runs the EUF-CMA game on the proposed scheme perfectly. Hence,

$$Pr[X_0] = \mathsf{Succ}^{euf-cma}(\mathcal{F})$$

Game 1. (Simulation of hash oracle) In this game, the hash oracle for $\mathcal{G}$ is simulated, while the rest of the protocol is executed as in the previous game. The oracle is simulated as follows:
For the query on $\mathcal{G}$ of the form (m, r), we have two situations, depending on whether $r \in \Lambda(m)$. The simulation of the oracle is given below:
Input: A tuple (m, r)
Output: A syndrome x
if $r \neq \Lambda(m)$ **then**
    if $s =\perp$ **then**

$s_1 \xleftarrow{R} \mathbb{F}_2^n$ // Since, the challenger may not be able to decode $\mathcal{G}(m,r)$,
$x \leftarrow \widetilde{H} s_1{}^T$ // we take a s randomly, and may not have weight $< t$
$s \leftarrow \perp$ $\mathcal{G}^{list}(m,r) \leftarrow ((x,s), s_1)$
end
return $\mathcal{G}(m,r) = x$
else
  if $x = \perp$ **then**
    $s_1 \xleftarrow{R} \mathbb{F}_2^n$ such that $wt(s_1) = t$
    $x \leftarrow \widetilde{H} s_1^T$ // x is decodable, since $wt(s_1) \leq t$
    $s \leftarrow s_1$ $\mathcal{G}^{list}(m,r) \leftarrow ((x,s), s_1)$
  end
  return $\mathcal{G}(m,r) = x$
end

It is seen that, while the oracles are simulated in the Game 1, the distribution of these oracles remain unchanged from Game 0 (i.e., the randomness is maintained). Let the event that $\mathcal{F}$ wins Game 1 be denoted by X_1. Hence

$$Pr[X_1] = Pr[X_0]$$

Game 2. (Simulation of the signing oracle.) The signing oracle is simulated as follows:

Input: the message m of length l **Output:** A signature $\sigma = (s_1, r)$
if $\Lambda(m) = \perp$ **then**
  $r \xleftarrow{R} \mathbb{F}_2^n$ //Fix a r such that $\mathcal{G}(m,r)$ is decodable, and
  $\Lambda(m) \leftarrow r$ // s such that $\widetilde{H} s_1^T = \mathcal{G}(m,r)$ and $wt(s) \leq t$
end
$((x, s_1), s_1) \leftarrow \mathcal{G}(m, \Lambda(m))$
if $(s_1 = \perp)$ **then**   //Incoherence, as $\mathcal{G}(m,r)$ was set earlier, when $r \neq \Lambda(m)$
  ABORT
else
  $r \leftarrow \Lambda(m)$
  $\Lambda(m) \leftarrow \perp$
Return $\sigma = (s_1, r)$.

The signature produced by the signing oracle, is valid according to the verification algorithm, since, $\widetilde{H} s_1^T = \mathcal{G}(m,r)$ and $wt(s_1) \leq t$.

In Game 2, incoherence occurs if the oracle to $\mathcal{G}$ is queried initially for some (m,r) such that later r is set to $\Lambda(m)$. This happens with the probability $\frac{q_s}{2^n}$ (since the indices Λ are defined only when the signature oracle is queried). It can be noted that this incoherence is the only scenario in which $\mathcal{F}$ can distinguish Game 2 from Game 1. Therefore, for the event X_2 that $\mathcal{F}$ wins Game 2,

$$|Pr[X_1] - Pr[X_2]| \leq \frac{q_s}{2^n}$$

Game 3. (Changing the key generation algorithm) The parity check matrix R, for which the syndrome decoding problem needs to be solved, is taken as the private key, i.e., $H = R$. The public key is $\widetilde{H} = R'$, where $R'^T = [R^T | z^T]$

where $z \in_R \mathbb{F}_2^n$. The verification key $\widetilde{H}$ is given to the forger $\mathcal{F}$, while $\mathcal{C}$ keeps the remaining secret keys. By Assumption 2

$$|Pr[X_2] - Pr[X_3]| \leq \mathsf{Adv}_{\mathcal{C}}^{\mathsf{Dist}}(n, k)$$

Game 4. In this game, the challenger modifies the winning condition. The challenger first gets a random $c \xleftarrow{R} \{1, \ldots, q_s + q_{\mathcal{G}} + 1\}$. $\mathcal{F}$ wins the Game if, in addition to the above conditions (as given in the previous game), the forgery was made on the c-th query to the hash oracle $\mathcal{G}$. This occurs with the probability $\frac{1}{q_s + q_{\mathcal{G}} + 1}$. For the event that $\mathcal{F}$ wins Game 4, X_4, we obtain

$$Pr[X_4] = \frac{Pr[X_3]}{q_s + q_{\mathcal{G}} + 1}$$

Game 5. In this game the challenger modifies the hash oracle, incorporating the problem instance (syndrome s) in the $c - th$ query. Since, the key used is R' and not R, we require a syndrome of length n'. Hence, a bit generated uniformly at random, s_c, is appended to the end of s. Therefore, the output of the hash oracle for the $c - th$ query is s' such that $s'^T = [s^T | s_c]$. Since, in game 5, the forger can output a forgery only if the final bit s_c has been guessed correctly (then s' is consistent with s),

$$Pr[X_5] = Pr[X_4]/2$$

Let s^* be the signature output by the forger. It is seen that s^* is the solution to the bounded decoding problem on the syndrome s' for $\widetilde{H}$. Also, s^* is guaranteed to be the solution for the syndrome Rs^T on R. Hence, we have

$$Pr[X_5] \leq \mathsf{Adv}_{\mathcal{C}}^{SD}(n, k)$$

Now, combining all results and use of triangular inequality, we have:
$Succ^{euf-cma}(\mathcal{F}) \leq \frac{q_s}{2^n} + \mathsf{Adv}_{\mathcal{C}}^{\mathsf{Dist}}(n, k) + 2(q_s + q_{\mathcal{G}} + 1)\mathsf{Adv}_{\mathcal{C}}^{SD}(n, k)$.
The detailed reduction of the equations to arrive at the final bound is available in the full version of the paper.

Hence, the success of probability of the forger is bound by the advantage the challenger has in solving the syndrome decoding problem. This implies the signature is unforgeable as long as the corresponding syndrome decoding instance is hard to solve. $\qquad \square$

Since the scheme avoids the distinguisher attack, the parameters that can be used in this scheme can be as that of the parameters suggested by [29] and the signing time will be slightly greater than the signing time of the [9].

5   Proposed Signcryption Scheme

The proposed scheme is the first code-based signcryption scheme (to the best of our knowledge). This scheme, takes into consideration the idea of construction used in [21,23].

5.1   Scheme

System Parameters(κ). The following system parameters are used:

- Parameters of the code n, k, t for any $[n, k, 2t + 1]$ linear code, with n, k determined by the security parameter κ, and $t = \frac{(n-k)}{\log_2 n}$.
- We define $n' = n - k + 1$.
- Cryptographic Hash functions $\mathcal{H} : \mathbb{F}_2^{n' \times n} \times \mathbb{F}_2^{n'} \times \mathbb{F}_2^{n} \rightarrow \{0, 1\}^l$ (assuming messages of length l) and $\mathcal{G} : \mathbb{F}_2^{n} \times \{0, 1\}^n \times \mathbb{F}_2^{n' \times n} \times \mathbb{F}_2^{n' \times n} \rightarrow \mathbb{F}_2^{n'}$.

Key Generation$(\kappa, parameters)$. For a user U the key generation involves the following steps

- Select H_U, a Parity Check Matrix of a binary code $\mathcal{C}$ of type $Goppa(n, k, t)$.
- Select randomly a $n \times n$ permutation matrix P_U.
- Select $\mathbf{b}_U \in_R \mathbb{F}_2^n$.
- Select randomly H'_U of size $(n - k) \times n'$ and $Q'_U \in_R \mathbb{F}_2^{n' \times (n-k)}$, such that Q'_U is full-rank and compute the matrix $Q_U = H'_U Q'_U$. Repeat until Q_U is invertible.
- Select $\mathbf{a}_U$, such that, $H'_U \mathbf{a}_U^T = 0$.
- Compute a parity check matrix $\tilde{H}_U$ as $\tilde{H}_U = Q'_U H_U P_U \oplus \mathbf{a}_U^T \mathbf{b}_U$. $\tilde{H}_U$ is a $n' \times n$ matrix. If $\tilde{H}_U$ is not a full-rank matrix, we repeat the process with different random $\mathbf{b}_U$ until we obtain a full-rank $\tilde{H}_U$.

Thus we have

private key: H_U, P_U, Q_U, H'_U; **public key:** $\tilde{H}_U$; **parameters:** $\mathcal{H}, \mathcal{G}, n, k, t, n'$

Signcrypt$(m, H_S, P_S, Q_S, H'_S, \tilde{H}_R)$. To signcrypt a message $m \in \{0, 1\}^n$ from a sender S and a receiver R

- **repeat**
   $r \xleftarrow{R} \mathbb{F}_2^n$, such that $wt(r) \leq t$;
   $m'_1 \leftarrow \mathcal{G}(r, m, \tilde{H}_R, \tilde{H}_S)$
   $m_1 = H'_S {m'_1}^T$
   $s_1 = P_S^T Decode_{H_S}(Q_S^{-1} m_1)$
  until$(s_1 \neq \perp \ \&\& \ m'_1 = \tilde{H}_S s_1^T)$
- Compute $U = \tilde{H}_R r^T$
- Compute $V = m \oplus \mathcal{H}(\tilde{H}_R, U, r)$
- The signcrypted text is $\sigma = (U, V, s_1)$

De-signcrypt$(\sigma, H_R, P_R, Q_R, H'_R, \tilde{H}_S)$. When the signcrypted text $\sigma = (U, V, s_1)$ is received R does the following:
   $Compute \ U' = H'_R U^T$
   $r' = P_R^T Decode_{H_R}(Q_R^{-1} U')$.
   $if(r' = \perp \ || U \neq \tilde{H}_R {r'}^T || wt(s_1) > t)$
      $Return \ \textsf{Reject}$

 else
  Compute $m' = V \oplus \mathcal{H}(\widetilde{H}_R, U, r')$
  if $(\widetilde{H}_S s_1{}^T \neq \mathcal{G}(r', m', \widetilde{H}_R, \widetilde{H}_S))$
   Return Reject
  else
   Return $((m', s_1),$Accept$)$
 end

Note 1: The signcryption scheme is more efficient than individually signing and encrypting, for the following reasons:

1. The scheme uses the same key-pair for both confidentiality and authentication.
2. Avoids the use of independently generated randomness and ephemeral keys while individually signing and authenticating.
3. The scheme avoids the use of additional authenticating mechanism which is required for non-malleability of the ciphertext.

5.2   Security of the Scheme

The security of the scheme is argued based on the security models given in Definitions 9 and 10 in random oracle model.

Theorem 2 (Confidentiality). *The given scheme is secure in the sense of SC-IND-CCA2 (under the random oracle model) if the syndrome decoding (SD) is hard to solve and the public key is computationally indistinguishable from the parity matrix of a random $(n, k - 1, t)$ code R.*

We build the proof, by constructing a challenger $\mathcal{C}$ through a sequence of games **Game0, Game1,** $\cdots$. The complete proof is in Appendix A.

Theorem 3 (Unforgeability). *The given scheme is unforgeable in the sense of SC-EUF-CMA (under the random oracle model) if the syndrome decoding (SD) is hard to solve and the public key is computationally indistinguishable from the parity matrix of a random $(n, k - 1, t)$ code R.*

The proof of this theorem, follows the line of proof in theorem 1 and theorem 2. Hence, we do not elaborate on the same.

5.3   Parameters Selection

We give some of the parameters for which our scheme will be practical and remain secure. The security proof explains the dependence of the scheme on the SD problem for security. The best-known attack for the signature is that by Bleichenbacher which is given in [16]. Also, the best known attack for syndrome decoding is Information-set decoding. A lower bound of the work factor for the attack is given in [16]. The parameters are selected according to [29]. In Table 1 we present a few secure parameters and the signing times of our signature scheme.

Table 1. Secure parameters for the scheme based on the bounds in [16]

$(\log_2(n), t)$	Key (Matrix of size $(n-k) \times n$)	Security factor for Confidentiality in $\log_2$	Security factor for Authentication in $(\log_2$	Time complexity of signing in the proposed scheme(in $\log_2$)
(18,13)	234×2^{18}	102.05	93.7	53.44
(19,12)	228×2^{19}	100.34	83.6	49.74
(20,11)	220×2^{20}	105.91	87.6	46.2

6   Conclusion

In the paper, we introduced a weaker distinguishability assumption. This results in a modification of CFS signature, which allows a formal proof of security, reducing the unforgeability problem to syndrome decoding problem and the introduced assumption. Hence it overcomes the problems associated with the high rate distinguisher in [13]. This lays the foundation stone for the use of CFS schemes in various primitives. Also, existing primitives which have made use of the CFS signature can now be altered appropriately to achieve provable security. Also, in this paper we present a signcryption scheme. The scheme can be used in applications which require both confidentiality and authentication, instead of individually signing and encrypting, as the efficiency is improved. It can be noted that the key-construct in [3] can also be used for constructing the signature and the signcryption scheme. The parameters of the proposed signcryption could be improved by using the Parallel-CFS [15].

Also, it is interesting to investigate the possibility of using LDPC codes, and other codes with better decoding properties. The key construct may be sufficiently altered to enable the secure use of such codes. The subsequent improvement in efficiency has to be investigated further.

A   Proof of Confidentiality for the Signcryption Scheme

Theorem 4 (Confidentiality). *The given scheme is secure in the sense of SC-IND-CCA2 (under the random oracle model) if the syndrome decoding (SD) is hard to solve and the public key is computationally indistinguishable from the parity matrix of a random $(n, k-1, t)$ code R.*

Proof: We build the proof, by constructing a challenger C through a sequence of games **Game0, Game1,** $\cdots$. **Game0** is the adaptation of the protocol to the SC-IND-CCA2 game. Successive games are obtained by small modifications of the preceding games, in such a way that the difference of the adversarial advantage in consecutive games is easily quantifiable.

Let $q_{\mathcal{H}}, q_{\mathcal{G}}, q_s, q_u$ be the maximum number of queries made by the adversary $\mathcal{A}$ to the oracles for the hash queries $\mathcal{H}, \mathcal{G}$, the signcryption oracle and the designcryption oracle. We want to show that the advantage for the adversary $\mathcal{A}$ is bounded by the advantage of solving the hard problem SD for a random code with parity check matrix R.

To answer the hash queries and the signcryption and the de-signcryption queries, we maintain the lists, $\mathcal{G}^{list}, \mathcal{H}^{list}, \sigma^{list}$ and Λ. If there is no value in a list we denote its output by $\perp$.

- The list $\mathcal{G}^{list}$ contains a tuple $((x,s),a)$ indexed by $(r,m,\widetilde{H}_R,\widetilde{H}_S)$.
- The list $\mathcal{H}^{list}$ consists of strings $\rho \in \{0,1\}^l$ indexed by $(\widetilde{H}_R,U,r)$ where $\widetilde{H}_R$ and $\widetilde{H}_S$ are $(n-k) \times n$ sized parity check matrices, and $U \in \mathbb{F}_2^{n-k}$ and $r \in \mathbb{F}_2^n$ such that $wt(r) \leq t$.
- The σ^{list} (the signature list) consists of entries of the form $(m, \sigma = (U,V,s))$.
- The list Λ consists of indices r of $\Lambda(m)$ for which the simulator is able to produce a signature on $\mathcal{G}(m, \Lambda(m, \widetilde{H}_R, \widetilde{H}_S)), \widetilde{H}_R, \widetilde{H}_S)$, i.e., the list of r for which $\mathcal{G}(m, \Lambda(m, \widetilde{H}_R, \widetilde{H}_S)), \widetilde{H}_R, \widetilde{H}_S)$ is a decodable syndrome.

Game 0. This is the standard SC-IND-CCA2 game. The private and public key pair are obtained by running the key generation algorithm given the scheme, to obtain secret key (Q_U, H_U, P_U, H'_U), where $H_U \leftarrow \mathsf{Goppa}(n,k)$ (a binary Goppa code), and the public key $\widetilde{H}_U = Q'_U H_U P_U \oplus a_U b_U^T$. $\widetilde{H}_U$ is given to $\mathcal{A}$. Also, $\mathcal{A}$ is given access to the hash oracles $\mathcal{H}$ and $\mathcal{G}$. The signcryption oracle and designcryption oracle function as mentioned in the scheme. Let X_0 be the event that $\mathcal{A}$ wins Game 0. It is seen that Game 0 runs the SC-IND-CCA2 game on the proposed scheme perfectly.
Therefore $Pr[X_0] - \frac{1}{2} = Adv_{\mathcal{A}}^{ind-cca}(n,k)$.

Game 1. (Simulation of hash oracles) In this game, the hash oracles for $\mathcal{G}$ and $\mathcal{H}$ are simulated, while the rest of the protocol is executed as in the previous game. The two oracles are simulated as follows:
For the query on $\mathcal{G}$ of the form $(r,m,\widetilde{H}_R,\widetilde{H}_S)$, we have two situations, depending on whether $r = \Lambda(m,\widetilde{H}_R,\widetilde{H}_S)$. The simulation of the oracle is given below:

Input: A tuple $(m,r,\widetilde{H}_R,\widetilde{H}_S)$
Output: A syndrome x
if $r \neq \Lambda(m,\widetilde{H}_R,\widetilde{H}_S)$ **then**
    if $s_1 = \perp$ **then**
        $s_1 \xleftarrow{R} \mathbb{F}_2^n$
        $x \leftarrow \widetilde{H}_S s_1^T$
        $\mathcal{G}^{list}(r,m,\widetilde{H}_R,\widetilde{H}_S) \leftarrow ((x,\perp),s_1)$
    end
    return $\mathcal{G}(r,m,\widetilde{H}_R,\widetilde{H}_S) = x$
else
    if $x = \perp$ **then**
        $s_1 \xleftarrow{R} \mathbb{F}_2^n$ such that $wt(s_1) = t$
        $x \leftarrow \widetilde{H}_S s_1^T$
        $\mathcal{G}^{list}(r,m,\widetilde{H}_R,\widetilde{H}_S) \leftarrow ((x,s_1),s_1)$
    end

return $\mathcal{G}(r, m, \widetilde{H}_R, \widetilde{H}_S) = x$
end

For the query to $\mathcal{H}$ of the form $(\widetilde{H}_R, U, r)$, the challenger searches $\mathcal{H}^{list}$ for the tuple $(\widetilde{H}_R, U, r)$. If found, the corresponding value from the list is returned, else return a random string $\rho \xleftarrow{R} \{0,1\}^l$ and store the tuple $((\widetilde{H}_R, U, r), \rho)$ in $\mathcal{H}^{list}$. Let X_1 be the event that $\mathcal{A}$ wins Game 1. It is seen that, while the oracles are simulated in Game 1, the distribution of the output of these oracles remain unchanged (i.e., the randomness is maintained) from Game 0.

Hence $Pr[X_1] = Pr[X_0]$

Game 2. (Simulation of the signcryption oracle.) The signcryption oracle is simulated as follows:

Input: the tuple $(m, \widetilde{H}_R, \widetilde{H}_U)$ **Output:** A signcrypted text $\sigma = (U, V, s_1)$
if $\Lambda(m, \widetilde{H}_R, \widetilde{H}_U) = \bot$ then
$\quad r \xleftarrow{R} \mathbb{F}_2^n$, such that $wt(r) \leq t \quad \Lambda(m, \widetilde{H}_R, \widetilde{H}_U) \leftarrow r$
end
$((x, s_1), s_1) \leftarrow \mathcal{G}(\Lambda(m, \widetilde{H}_R, \widetilde{H}_U), m, \widetilde{H}_R, \widetilde{H}_U)$
if$(s_1 = \bot)$ then $\quad$ ABORT
else
$\quad r \leftarrow \Lambda(m, \widetilde{H}_R, \widetilde{H}_U) \quad \Lambda(m, \widetilde{H}_R, \widetilde{H}_U) \leftarrow \bot \quad U = \widetilde{H}_R r^T$
$\quad V = m \oplus \mathcal{H}(\widetilde{H}_R, U, r)$
end
Return $\sigma = (U, V, s_1)$.

The simulation of the signcryption is an extension of the signing oracle simulation presented in the previous proof. It is thus, seen that the s_1 is a valid signature on m for verification key $\widetilde{H}_U$. Also, the remaining signcrypted text is also valid, and follows from the signcrypt algorithm given in the scheme. In Game 2, incoherence occurs if the oracle to $\mathcal{G}$ is queried initially for some $(r, m, \widetilde{H}_R, \widetilde{H}_S)$ such that later r is set to $\Lambda(m, \widetilde{H}_R, \widetilde{H}_S)$. This happens with the probability $\dfrac{q_s}{\binom{n}{t}}$ (since the indices Λ are defined only when the signcryption oracle is queried). It can be noted that this incoherence is the only scenario in which $\mathcal{F}$ can distinguish Game 2 from Game 1. Therefore, for the event X_2, that $\mathcal{A}$ wins the Game 2, we obtain, $|Pr[X_1] - Pr[X_2]| \leq \dfrac{q_s}{\binom{n}{t}}$.

Game 3. (Simulation of the designcryption oracle.) For the designcryption oracle queried on $(s_1, U, V, \widetilde{H}_U, \widetilde{H}_S)$ the following is done:

- The challenger searches the $\mathcal{H}^{list}$ for the tuple $(\widetilde{H}_U, U, \lambda)$ such that $\widetilde{H}_U \lambda^T = U$. If it exists in the list, then the corresponding vector X is given as output. If no such tuple is found (i.e., the hash for such a tuple has not been queried) then it fixes $\lambda = \bot$ and gives the corresponding output from the hash oracle as X.
- It obtains $m' = V \oplus X$.

- The challenger then searches $\mathcal{G}^{list}$ for the tuple of the form $(\lambda, m', \widetilde{H}_U, \widetilde{H}_S)$ where $\widetilde{H}_U \lambda^T = U$ or $\lambda = \perp$. If the tuple is not in $\mathcal{G}^{list}$, the challenger adds it to the list.
- Now the challenger verifies if $\widetilde{H}_U s_1{}^T \stackrel{?}{=} \mathcal{G}(\lambda, m', \widetilde{H}_U, \widetilde{H}_S)$. If the condition holds and $\widetilde{H}_U \lambda^T = U$, then the challenger returns m' as the message. If condition holds but $\lambda = \perp$ then challenger ABORTS citing failure. If the condition does not hold at all, then the challenger returns $\perp$, as symbol of rejection of invalid signcrypted text.

In the above game, if the challenger aborts, it implies that the adversary created the signcrypted text without querying the hash oracles. Hence, the probability of aborting is $\frac{q_d}{2^t}$. This scenario (of ABORT) would not occur in Game 2. Hence, for the event X_3 that $\mathcal{A}$ wins Game 3, we have $|Pr[X_3] - Pr[X_2]| \leq \frac{q_d}{2^t}$.

Game 4. (Changing the key generation algorithm) The adversary has access to the private keys of all users except the user U. Hence, for the other users, the keys are generated as in the scheme, and given to the adversary. For the user U, $\mathcal{C}$ selects the private key $H_U = R$. The public key is $\widetilde{H}_U = R'$, where $R'^T = [R^T | z^T]$ where $z \in_R \mathbb{F}_2^n$. The verification key $\widetilde{H}_U$ is given to the adversary $\mathcal{A}$. It follows from Assumption 2 that $|Pr[X_3] - Pr[X_4]| \leq \mathsf{Adv}_\mathcal{C}^{\mathsf{Dist}}(n, k)$ where X_4 is the event that $\mathcal{A}$ wins Game 4.

Game 5. (Challenge ciphertext) The challenger takes the message m_b, and does the following to create the challenge, which would aid the challenger in solving the problem instance, syndrome s (where $wt(s) > 2t + 1$). The challenger wants to find $r \in \mathbb{F}_2^n$ with $wt(r) \leq t$ such that $s = Rr^T$. The challenger generates the challenge cipher-text as follows:

- $\mathcal{C}$ sets $U^* = s'$, where $s'^T = [s^T | s_c]$ where s_c is a randomly generated bit.
- For the query on $\mathcal{H}$, $\mathcal{C}$ sets a special symbol $\top$, randomly generates a vector y and stores it in $\mathcal{H}^{list}$ as $(\widetilde{H}_U, U^*, \top, y)$. And for the query on $\mathcal{G}$, again uses the special symbol $\top$, also a random decodable syndrome (say x, with the decoded vector s_1) is given (just as in the simulation in $\mathcal{G}$ oracle and the Signcrypt oracle), and stores in $\mathcal{G}^{list}$ the tuple $(m_b, \top, \widetilde{H}_U, \widetilde{H}_S, (x, s_1), s_1)$. The signing is simulated just as in signcryption oracle.
- The challenger set $V = m_b \oplus y$.

Also, the challenger has to now alter the answer to the hash queries in the following way:

- For the $\mathcal{H}$ oracle, for any query $(\widetilde{H}_U, \widetilde{H}_U s^T, r)$ where $\widetilde{H}_U r^T \neq \widetilde{H}_U s^T$, some random value is returned. If $\widetilde{H}_U r^T = U^*$ and $weight(r) \leq t$, then the value y is returned, and $\top$ is replaced by r in the tuple. The valid r thus obtained is the solution to the problem instance.
- For the $\mathcal{G}$ oracle, for any query $(m, r, \widetilde{H}_U, \widetilde{H}_S)$ if $\widetilde{H}_U r^T = U^*$ and $m = m_b$ output x, else output any random syndrome. The valid r thus obtained is the solution to the problem instance.

Just as in the proof of unforgeability, the decodability of U^* depends on correctly predicting s_c, which occurs with probability $\frac{1}{2}$. If X_5 be the event that $\mathcal{A}$

wins Game 5, we can clearly claim that, $|Pr[X_4] - Pr[X_5]| \leq \mathsf{Adv}_{\mathcal{C}}^{SD}(n,k)/2$ where $\mathsf{Adv}_{\mathcal{C}}^{SD}(n,k)$ is the advantage that some PPT algorithm $\mathcal{C}$ has at solving the syndrome decoding problem (SD) on R.

Game 6. (Challenge ciphertext) In this game, the challenger C again alters the procedure of producing the challenge ciphertext. For the ciphertext, the process of creating U and s is the same, but changes for V. The challenger C sets $V = z$, where $z \xleftarrow{R} \{0,1\}^l$. Clearly, now the challenge ciphertext generated is completely random. But, even in game 5, the ciphertext generated was random as we blinded the message with a completely random component. Hence, there is no change in the distribution of the ciphertext space, i.e., $Pr[X_5] = Pr[X_6]$, where X_6 is the event that $\mathcal{A}$ wins Game 6. Also, it can noted that the probability of correctly guessing the choice b by the adversary $\mathcal{A}$ is exactly half, i.e., $Pr[X_6] = \frac{1}{2}$.

Accumulating all the above results and using triangular inequality we have the following result: $Adv^{ind-cca2}(\mathcal{A}) \leq \dfrac{q_s}{\dbinom{n}{t}} + \dfrac{q_d}{2^l} + \mathsf{Adv}_{\mathcal{C}}^{\mathsf{Dist}}(n,k) + \mathsf{Adv}_{\mathcal{C}}^{SD}(n,k)/2.$

Hence, the advantage of the adversary is bound by the advantage of the challenger in solving the syndrome decoding problem and the weak distinguishability.   □

References

1. An, J.H., Dodis, Y., Rabin, T.: On the security of joint signature and encryption. In: Knudsen, L.R. (ed.) EUROCRYPT 2002. LNCS, vol. 2332, pp. 83–107. Springer, Heidelberg (2002)
2. Baek, J., Steinfeld, R., Zheng, Y.: Formal proofs for the security of signcryption. In: Naccache, D., Paillier, P. (eds.) PKC 2002. LNCS, vol. 2274, p. 80. Springer, Heidelberg (2002)
3. Baldi, M., Bianchi, M., Chiaraluce, F., Rosenthal, J., Schipani, D.: Enhanced public key security for the McEliece cryptosystem. CoRR, abs/1108.2462 (2011)
4. Barreto, P.S.L.M., Misoczki, R.: One-time signature scheme from syndrome decoding over generic error-correcting codes. J. Syst. Softw. **84**(2), 198–204 (2011). http://dx.doi.org/10.1016/j.jss.2010.09.016
5. Berlekamp, E.R., McEliece, R.J., Vantilborg, H.C.: On the inherent intractability of certain coding problems. IEEE Trans. Inf. Theory **24**, 384–386 (1978)
6. Blake, I.F., Studholme, C.: Properties of random matrices and applications (2006). http://www.cs.utoronto.ca/~cvs/coding/random_report.pdf. Accessed 15 Dec 2006
7. Canteaut, A., Chabaud, F.: A new algorithm for finding minimum-weight words in a linear code: application to McEliece's cryptosystem and to narrow-sense BCH codes of length 511. IEEE Trans. Inf. Theory **44**(1), 367–378 (1998)
8. Corbella, I.M., Pellikaan, R.: Error-correcting pairs for a public-key cryptosystem. CoRR, abs/1205.3647 (2012)
9. Courtois, N.T., Finiasz, M., Sendrier, N.: How to achieve a McEliece-based digital signature scheme. In: Boyd, C. (ed.) ASIACRYPT 2001. LNCS, vol. 2248, pp. 157–174. Springer, Heidelberg (2001)

10. Courtois, N., Finiasz, M., Sendrier, N.: How to achieve a McEliece-based digital signature scheme. INRIA Report (2001)
11. Dallot, L.: Towards a concrete security proof of courtois, finiasz and sendrier signature scheme. In: Lucks, S., Sadeghi, A.-R., Wolf, C. (eds.) WEWoRC 2007. LNCS, vol. 4945, pp. 65–77. Springer, Heidelberg (2008)
12. Faugére, J.-C., Otmani, A., Perret, L., Tillich, J.-P.: Algebraic cryptanalysis of McEliece variants with compact keys - toward a complexity analysis. In: SCC '10: Proceedings of the 2nd International Conference on Symbolic Computation and Cryptography, pp. 45–55. RHUL, June 2010
13. Faugère, J-C., Gauthier, V., Otmani, A., Perret, L., Tillich, J.-P.: A distinguisher for high rate McEliece cryptosystems. In: IEEE Information Theory Workshop (ITW) (2011)
14. Faugère, J.-C., Otmani, A., Perret, L., Tillich, J.-P.: Algebraic cryptanalysis of mceliece variants with compact keys. In: Gilbert, H. (ed.) EUROCRYPT 2010. LNCS, vol. 6110, pp. 279–298. Springer, Heidelberg (2010)
15. Finiasz, M.: Parallel-CFS: strengthening the CFS McEliece-based signature scheme. In: Biryukov, A., Gong, G., Stinson, D.R. (eds.) SAC 2010. LNCS, vol. 6544, pp. 159–170. Springer, Heidelberg (2011)
16. Finiasz, M., Sendrier, N.: Security bounds for the design of code-based cryptosystems. In: Matsui, M. (ed.) ASIACRYPT 2009. LNCS, vol. 5912, pp. 88–105. Springer, Heidelberg (2009)
17. Gabidulin, E.M., Kjelsen, O.: How to avoid the Sidel'nikov-Shestakov attack. In: Chmora, A., Wicker, S.B. (eds.) Information Protection 1993. LNCS, vol. 829, pp. 25–32. Springer, Heidelberg (1994)
18. Niederreiter, H.: Knapsack-type cryptosystems and algebraic coding theory. Prob. Contr. Inform. Theor. **15**, 159–166 (1986)
19. Kabatianskii, G., Krouk, E., Smeets, B.J.M.: A digital signature scheme based on random error-correcting codes. In: Darnell, M.J. (ed.) Cryptography and Coding 1997. LNCS, vol. 1355, pp. 161–167. Springer, Heidelberg (1997)
20. Lee, P.J., Brickell, E.F.: An observation on the security of McEliece's public-key cryptosystem. In: Günther, C.G. (ed.) EUROCRYPT 1988. LNCS, vol. 330, pp. 275–280. Springer, Heidelberg (1988)
21. Li, C.K., Yang, G., Wong, D.S., Deng, X., Chow, S.S.M.: An efficient signcryption scheme with key privacy. In: López, J., Samarati, P., Ferrer, J.L. (eds.) EuroPKI 2007. LNCS, vol. 4582, pp. 78–93. Springer, Heidelberg (2007)
22. Li, Y.X., Deng, R.H., Wang, X.M.: On the equivalence of McEliece's and Niederreiter's public-key cryptosystems. IEEE Trans. Inf. Theory **40**(1), 271–274 (1994)
23. Malone-Lee, J., Mao, W.: Two birds one stone: signcryption using RSA. In: Joye, M. (ed.) CT-RSA 2003. LNCS, vol. 2612, pp. 211–225. Springer, Heidelberg (2003)
24. Garey, M., Johnson, D.: Computers and intractability. A guide to the theory of incompleteness (1979)
25. Otmani, A., Tillich, J.-P.: An efficient attack on all concrete KKS proposals. In: Yang, B.-Y. (ed.) PQCrypto 2011. LNCS, vol. 7071, pp. 98–116. Springer, Heidelberg (2011)
26. Overbeck, R., Sendrier, N.: Code-based cryptography. pp. 95–137 (2008)
27. Petrank, E., Roth, R.M.: Is code equivalence easy to decide? IEEE Trans. Inf. Theory **43**, 1602–1604 (1997)
28. McEliece, R.J.: A public-key cryptosystem based on algebraic coding theory. JPL DSN Progress Report, pp. 114–116 (1978)
29. Sendrier, N.: Decoding one out of many. In: Yang, B.-Y. (ed.) PQCrypto 2011. LNCS, vol. 7071, pp. 51–67. Springer, Heidelberg (2011)

30. Stern, J.: A new identification scheme based on syndrome decoding. In: Stinson, D.R. (ed.) CRYPTO 1993. LNCS, vol. 773, pp. 13–21. Springer, Heidelberg (1994)
31. Wieschebrink, C.: Two NP-complete problems in coding theory with an application in code based cryptography. In: IEEE International Symposium on Information Theory, pp. 1733–1737 (2006)
32. Zheng, Y.: Digital signcryption or how to achieve cost(signature & encryption) ≪ cost(signature) + cost(encryption). In: Kaliski Jr., B.S. (ed.) CRYPTO 1997. LNCS, vol. 1294, pp. 165–179. Springer, Heidelberg (1997)

An Anonymous Reputation System
with Reputation Secrecy for Manager

Toru Nakanishi$^{(\boxtimes)}$, Tomoya Nomura, and Nobuo Funabiki

Department of Communication Network Engineering,
Okayama University, 3-1-1 Tsushima-Naka, Okayama 700-8530, Japan
nakanisi@cne.okayama-u.ac.jp

Abstract. In anonymous reputation systems, where after an interaction between anonymous users, one of the user evaluates the peer by giving a rating. Ratings for a user are accumulated, which becomes the reputation of the user. By using the reputation, we can know the reliability of an anonymous user. Previously, anonymous reputation systems have been proposed, using an anonymous e-cash scheme. However, in the e-cash-based systems, the bank grasps the accumulated reputations for all users, and the fluctuation of reputations. These are private information for users. Furthermore, the timing attack using the deposit times is possible, which makes the anonymity weak. In this paper, we propose an anonymous reputation system, where the reputations of users are secret for even the reputation manager such as the bank. Our approach is to adopt an anonymous credential certifying the accumulated reputation of a user. Initially a user registers with the reputation manager, and is issued an initial certificate. After each interaction with a rater, the user as the ratee obtains an updated certificate certifying the previous reputation summed up by the current rating. The update protocol is based on the zero-knowledge proofs, and thus the reputations are secret for the reputation manager. On the other hand, due to the certificate, the user cannot maliciously alter his reputation.

Keywords: Reputation system · Anonymity · Anonymous credentials · Pairings

1 Introduction

Users interact with each other in various services, over the Internet. The popular example is marketplaces such as eBay. In such P2P services, the anonymity of users is desirable to protect their privacy for even service providers. However, in the anonymous situation, it has a problem that a user cannot guess the reliability of the peer. Some anonymous seller may repeat misbehaviours such as sending faked items.

One of the solutions is an *anonymous reputation system* [3,5,11,12]. In the reputation system, after an interaction between users, an anonymous user evaluates the anonymous peer by giving a rating. Ratings for a user are accumulated,

© Springer International Publishing Switzerland 2014
H.-S. Lee and D.-G. Han (Eds.): ICISC 2013, LNCS 8565, pp. 363–378, 2014.
DOI: 10.1007/978-3-319-12160-4_22

which becomes the reputation of the user. A user can check the reputations of anonymous peer candidates to know how much evaluations the candidates have obtained in the history of interactions.

In [3], an anonymous reputation system was proposed. In this system, using an anonymous e-cash scheme, the strong anonymity with unlinkability is satisfied: It is infeasible to decide a ratee in a rating protocol to send the rating is the same as one in another rating protocol. In this scheme, a rater withdraws an e-coin from the bank in advance. After an interaction, the rater anonymously pays the e-coin to the ratee. Then, the ratee anonymously deposits the e-coin to the bank, and instead obtains a blind signature to ensure the anonymous deposit. Finally, the ratee returns the blind signature to the bank, which updates the database where the ratee's reputation is increased by the rating. Due to the blind signature, the unlinkability is satisfied. However, this system has a problem: the ratee can discard a negative rating to prevent the rating from be accumulated.

In [11], the extended version of the anonymous reputation system [3] based on the e-cash scheme was proposed. This system uses three types of e-coins: an interaction coin, a positive rating coin, and a negative rating coin with the same serial number. Before the interaction between the rater and the ratee, the rater spends the interaction coin to the ratee, who deposits the coin in the bank. After the interaction, the rater spends the positive or negative rating coin to the ratee, and the ratee deposits the coin. The bank can check the consistency, and if it is inconsistent, the following deposit will be rejected. Thus, the ratee cannot discard the negative coin.

However, in both the e-cash-based systems, the bank grasps the accumulated reputations for all users, and the fluctuation of reputations. These are private information for users. Furthermore, as pointed in [11], the time of deposit may make the anonymity weak: After the ratee obtains e-coins, he usually deposits them to the bank without a significant delay. Thus, the bank can decrease the candidates of users obtaining the e-coins. The countermeasure proposed in [11] is the batching: e-coin transfers during a fixed time are batched, and the batched e-coins are deposited to the bank all at once. However, to obtain the strong anonymity, we need to batch the e-coin transfers in relatively long time. On the other hand, before the deposit is finished, malicious users can show incorrect reputations which do not reflect negative ratings.

In this paper, we propose an anonymous reputation system, where the reputations of users are secret for even the reputation manager such as the bank in the e-cash-based systems. Our approach is to adopt an anonymous credential certifying the accumulated reputation of a user. Initially a user registers with the reputation manager (RM), and is issued an initial certificate. After each interaction with a rater, the user as the ratee obtains an updated certificate certifying the previous reputation summed up by the current rating. The update protocol is based on the zero-knowledge proofs, and thus the reputations are secret for RM. On the other hand, due to the certificate, the user cannot maliciously alter his reputation. Using the show protocol, the user can reveal an integer range which his reputation rep lies in such as $2^{\ell-1} \leq rep \leq 2^\ell - 1$ for an integer ℓ in the zero-knowledge fashion. This is why the user's concrete reputation is kept secret and the anonymity is preserved.

Our system counters the issue of negative ratings: The show protocol corresponding to a P2P interaction is numbered by i, which is maintained in a list. Also, i is embedded into the certificate. In the show protocol, the verifier can check whether the interactions for all i in the certificate are not rated. This is why, if the user with a negative rating has not updated the certificate, the user cannot execute the show protocol.

In our system, the accumulated reputation of the user is revealed via the range proof. Thus, the verifier cannot grasp the average of ratings. In our system, the number of ratings is also embedded into the certificate, and the user proves the range which the number of ratings lies in.

2 Preliminaries

2.1 Bilinear Groups

Our scheme utilizes the following bilinear groups:

1. $\mathcal{G}$ and $\mathcal{T}$ are multiplicative cyclic groups of prime order p,
2. g is a randomly chosen generator of $\mathcal{G}$,
3. e is an efficiently computable bilinear map: $\mathcal{G} \times \mathcal{G} \to \mathcal{T}$, i.e., (1) for all $u, v \in \mathcal{G}$ and $a, b \in Z$, $e(u^a, v^b) = e(u, v)^{ab}$, and (2) $e(g, g) \neq 1_{\mathcal{T}}$.

2.2 Assumptions

The security of our system is based on the SDH (Strong DH) assumption [6], the q-SFP (Simultaneous Flexible Pairing) assumption [2], and n-DHE (DH Exponent) assumption [9].

Definition 1 (q-SDH assumption). *For all PPT algorithm $\mathcal{A}$, the probability*

$$\Pr[\mathcal{A}(g, g^a, \ldots, g^{a^q}) = (b, g^{1/(a+b)}) \wedge b \in Z_p]$$

is negligible, where $g \in_R \mathcal{G}$ and $a \in_R Z_p$.

Definition 2 (q-SFP assumption). *For all PPT algorithm $\mathcal{A}$, the probability*

$$\Pr[\mathcal{A}(g_z, h_z, g_r, h_r, a, \tilde{a}, b, \tilde{b}, \{(z_j, r_j, s_j, t_j, u_j, v_j, w_j)\}_{j=1}^q)$$
$$= (z^*, r^*, s^*, t^*, u^*, v^*, w^*) \in \mathcal{G}^7$$
$$\wedge e(a, \tilde{a}) = e(g_z, z^*)e(g_r, r^*)e(s^*, t^*) \wedge e(b, \tilde{b}) = e(h_z, z^*)e(h_r, u^*)e(v^*, w^*)$$
$$\wedge z^* \neq 1_{\mathcal{G}} \wedge z^* \neq z_j \text{ for all } 1 \leq j \leq q]$$

is negligible, where $(g_z, h_z, g_r, h_r, a, \tilde{a}, b, \tilde{b}) \in \mathcal{G}^8$ and all tuples $\{(z_j, r_j, s_j, t_j, u_j, v_j, w_j)\}_{j=1}^q$ satisfy the above relations.

Definition 3 (n-DHE assumption). *For all PPT algorithm $\mathcal{A}$, the probability*

$$\Pr[\mathcal{A}(g, g^a, \ldots, g^{a^n}, g^{a^{n+2}}, \ldots, g^{a^{2n}}) = g^{a^{n+1}}]$$

is negligible, where $g \in_R \mathcal{G}$ and $a \in_R Z_p$.

2.3 Structure-Preserving Signatures (AHO Signatures)

We need the structure-preserving signatures for signing L $\mathcal{G}$-elements, and we adopt the AHO signature scheme in [1,2].

AHOKeyGen: Select bilinear groups $\mathcal{G}, \mathcal{T}$ with a prime order p and a bilinear map e. Select $g, G_r, H_r \in_R \mathcal{G}$, and $\mu_z, \nu_z, \mu_1 \ldots, \mu_L, \nu_1, \ldots, \nu_L, \alpha_a, \alpha_b \in_R Z_p$. Compute $G_z = G_r^{\mu_z}, H_z = H_r^{\nu_z}, G_1 = G_r^{\mu_1}, \ldots, G_L = G_r^{\mu_L}, H_1 = H_r^{\nu_1}, \ldots, H_L = H_r^{\nu_L}, A = e(G_r, g^{\alpha_a}), B = e(H_r, g^{\alpha_b})$. Output the public key as $pk = (\mathcal{G}, \mathcal{T}, p, e, g, G_r, H_r, G_z, H_z, G_1, \ldots, G_L, H_1, \ldots, H_L, A, B)$, and the secret key as $sk = (\alpha_a, \alpha_b, \mu_z, \nu_z, \mu_1, \ldots, \mu_L, \nu_1, \ldots, \nu_L)$.

AHOSign: Given a vector of messages $M_1, \ldots, M_L$ together with sk, choose $\beta, \epsilon, \eta, \iota, \kappa \in_R Z_p$, and compute $\theta_1 = g^\beta$, and $\theta_2 = g^{\epsilon - \mu_z \beta} \prod_{i=1}^L M_i^{-\mu_i}$, $\theta_3 = G_r^\eta$, $\theta_4 = g^{(\alpha_a - \epsilon)/\eta}, \theta_5 = g^{\iota - \nu_z \beta} \prod_{i=1}^L M_i^{-\nu_i}$, $\theta_6 = H_r^\kappa$, $\theta_7 = g^{(\alpha_b - \iota)/\kappa}$. Output the signature $\sigma = (\theta_1, \ldots, \theta_7)$.

AHOVerify: Given the message M and the signature $\sigma = (\theta_1, \ldots, \theta_7)$, accept these if
$$A = e(G_z, \theta_1) \cdot e(G_r, \theta_2) \cdot e(\theta_3, \theta_4) \cdot \prod_{i=1}^L e(G_i, M_i), \quad B = e(H_z, \theta_1) \cdot e(H_r, \theta_5) \cdot e(\theta_6, \theta_7) \cdot \prod_{i=1}^L e(H_i, M_i).$$

This signature is existentially unforgeable against chosen-message attacks under the q-SFP assumption [2]. Using the re-randomization algorithm in [2], this signature can be publicly randomized to obtain another signature $(\theta'_1, \ldots, \theta'_7)$ on the same messages. As a result, $(\theta'_i)_{i=3,4,6,7}$ can be safely revealed, while $(\theta'_i)_{i=1,2,5}$ have to be committed.

2.4 BB Signatures

We utilize Boneh-Boyen (BB) signature scheme [6].

BBKeyGen: Select bilinear groups $\mathcal{G}, \mathcal{T}$ with a prime order p and a bilinear map e. Select $g \in_R \mathcal{G}$. Select $\epsilon \in_R Z_p$ and compute $Y = g^\epsilon$. The secret key is ϵ and the public key is $(p, \mathcal{G}, \mathcal{T}, e, g, Y)$.

BBSign: Given message $m \in Z_p$, compute $A = g^{1/(X+m)}$. The signature is A.

BBVerify: Given message m and the signature A, check $e(A, Y g^m) = e(g, g)$.

BB signatures are existentially unforgeable against *weak* chosen message attack under the q-SDH assumption [6]. In this attack, the adversary must choose messages queried for the oracle, before the public key is given.

2.5 Accumulators

Let U, V be subsets of $\{1, \ldots, n\}$ for some non-negative integer n. Using the accumulators in [13], a verifier can check $U \subset V$ with a pairing relation.

AccSetup: This is the algorithm to output the public parameters. Select bilinear groups $\mathcal{G}, \mathcal{T}$ with a prime order p and a bilinear map e. Select $g \in_R \mathcal{G}$. Select $\gamma \in_R Z_p$ and compute and publish $p, \mathcal{G}, \mathcal{T}, e, g, g_1 = g^{\gamma^1}, \ldots, g_n = g^{\gamma^n}, g_{n+2} = g^{\gamma^{n+2}}, \ldots, g_{2n} = g^{\gamma^{2n}}$ as the public parameters.

AccGen: This is the algorithm to compute the accumulator using the public parameters. The accumulator acc_V of V is computed as $acc_V = \prod_{i \in V} g_{n+1-i}$.

AccWitGen: This is the algorithm to compute the witness of $U \subset V$ using the public parameters. Given U, V and the accumulator acc_V, the witness is computed as $W = \prod_{j \in U} \prod_{j \in V}^{i \neq j} g_{n+1-i+j}$.

AccVerify: This is the algorithm to verify $U \subset V$, using the witness and the public parameters. Given acc_V, U, and W, accept if

$$\frac{e(\prod_{i \in U} g_i, acc_V)}{e(g, W)} = e(g_1, g_n)^{|U|}.$$

The security, i.e., it is infeasible to compute W that **AccVerify** accepts when $U \not\subset V$, is proved under the n-DHE assumption [13].

2.6 Proving Relations on Representations

We adopt zero-knowledge proofs of knowledge (PKs) on representations, which are the generalization of the Schnorr identification protocol [8]. Concretely we utilize a PK proving the knowledge of a representation of $C \in \mathcal{G}$ to the bases $g_1, g_2, \ldots, g_t \in \mathcal{G}$, i.e., $x_1, \ldots, x_t$ s.t. $C = g_1^{x_1} \cdots g_t^{x_t}$. This can be also constructed on group $\mathcal{T}$. The PK can be extended to proving multiple representations with equal parts.

3 System Model for Anonymous Reputation Systems

3.1 Participants and Targets

We consider an interaction system among users, where a user anonymously interacts to another user. The typical example is a marketplace such as eBay, where a seller offers an item and a buyer buys the item. In this paper, we target such a type of service. Before the interaction between the users, the anonymous seller shows his accumulated reputation with the offered item. Based on the reputation, the buyer chooses the item and interacts with the offering seller. After the interaction, the buyer rates the behavior of the seller. In our reputation system, in addition to the users and the service provider (SP) providing the interaction system, another entity Reputation Manager (RM) is introduced. We assume that RM is *honest-but-curious*, that is, it follows the protocol description correctly, as in the previous systems [3,11]. For simplicity of description, we assume that the same party is both of the SP and RM, since the separation is easy.

In this paper, we suppose that both users of sellers and buyers anonymously participate in the system, using some anonymous authentication scheme, such as anonymous credentials, and the anonymous buyer just submits his rating for the seller to RM, independently from his other ratings. Thus, since the anonymity of the buyer is easily satisfied, we omit the process related to the buyer from the following definition of reputation system, and focus on the seller side anonymously accumulating the obtained ratings.

The definitions of syntax and security requirements are shown in Appendix A.

4   Proposed System

4.1   Construction Idea

In the proposed system, instead of the bank maintaining the database of reputations, the certificate certifying the reputation rep and the number of ratings num is issued by RM to a user. By each **Update** protocol, the certificate is updated such that rep is added by the new rating and num is incremented. In the updating process, rep and num have to be secret for RM, and thus we utilize the commitments to rep and num. Using the homomorphic property of the commitments, RM updates the secret rep and num. The commitments are signed by an AHO signature as the certificate. The reason why we adopt the AHO signature is to sign the multiple group elements of commitments. To achieve the anonymity, the correctness of the certificate and the updated rep and num in the commitments is ensured by the zero-knowledge proofs. In **Show** protocol, we employ the range proof technique in [7]: In advance, RM issues the BB signatures for all values in each range. In **Show** protocol, the user proves the knowledge of a BB signature for the proved value (i.e., rep or num). Since only signatures for values in the range are issued, the verifier can confirm that the proved value lies in the range.

Next, we show the idea to check the certified reputation reflects all ratings including negative ratings. Since each **Show** protocol is assigned to an item ID, RM can check whether each item is rated and whether the corresponding certificate is updated via the ID. Namely, RM forces the seller to send the IDs such that the item is rated but the corresponding certificate is not updated. The set of IDs has to be secret to achieve the anonymity, but the set is embedded into the certificate to achieve the unforgeability. Let the set of IDs of rated but non-updated items for all users, which are recorded in RM, be $\tilde{\mathcal{L}}_{RM}$. Let the set of IDs of non-updated items for the seller U be $\mathcal{L}_U$. The check is $\mathcal{L}_U \not\subset \tilde{\mathcal{L}}_{RM}$. To obtain the constant efficiency w.r.t. the set size, we consider the use of accumulator in Sect. 2.5. Since the accumulator gives us only the proof of the subset relation $\subset$, we modify the server's set into $\mathcal{L}_{RM}$ that is the set of non-rated (also non-updated) IDs for all users. In this case, the relation $\mathcal{L}_U \subset \mathcal{L}_{RM}$ means that all the IDs in $\mathcal{L}_U$ have not been rated yet, that is, the seller does not need to update the certificate for IDs in $\mathcal{L}_U$. On the other hand, when an item with ID in $\mathcal{L}_U$ is rated, the ID is deleted from $\mathcal{L}_{RM}$, and thus the seller cannot prove $\mathcal{L}_U \subset \mathcal{L}_{RM}$ unless the ID is deleted from $\mathcal{L}_U$ in **Update** protocol for the ID. Thus, the seller cannot execute **Show** protocol unless the certificate is updated for all the rated items of him.

The accumulator verification is $e(P, acc)/e(g, W) = e(g_1, g_n)^{|\mathcal{L}_U|}$, where $P = \prod_{i \in \mathcal{L}_U} g_i$ and $acc = \prod_{i \in \mathcal{L}_{RM}} g_{n+1-i}$. The commitment to the value P for $\mathcal{L}_U$ is embedded in the certificate. Since P is a group element, instead of the ordinary Pedersen commitment, we adopt the commitment of two components: $C_P = P \cdot \hat{g}^R, C_R = g^R \hat{g}^r$ for randoms r, R. In the accumulator verification, $|\mathcal{L}_U|$ also has to be secret, but the value is not fixed, depending on $\mathcal{L}_U$. This is why we consider that the commitment to $N = |\mathcal{L}_U|$ is also embedded into the certificate, where N is secretly incremented (resp, decremented) in **Show** (resp, **Update**) protocol.

For the consistency of the user, the committed user's secret x is embedded in the certificate. To protect the re-use of the past certificate, the committed tag S of the certificate is also embedded in the certificate. By putting all together, the certificate is

$$Sig(C_x, C_S, C_{rep}, C_{num}, C_N, C_P, C_R),$$

where Sig is the AHO signing, $C_x, C_S, C_{rep}, C_{num}, C_N$ are the commitments to x, S, rep, num, N, and (C_P, C_R) is the commitment to P.

4.2 Proposed Construction

Setup: In this algorithm, Reputation Manager (RM) sets up his keys.

1. Select bilinear groups $\mathcal{G}, \mathcal{T}$ with the same order $p > 2^l$ and the bilinear map e, and $g, \hat{g} \in_R \mathcal{G}$.
2. Generate public parameters of the accumulator: Select $\gamma \in_R Z_p$, and compute

$$pk_{acc} = (g_1 = g^{\gamma^1}, \ldots, g_n = g^{\gamma^n}, g_{n+2} = g^{\gamma^{n+2}}, \ldots, g_{2n} = g^{\gamma^{2n}}).$$

3. Generate a key pair for the AHO signature:

$$pk_{AHO} = (G_r, H_r, G_z, H_z, G_1, \ldots, G_7, H_1, \ldots, H_7, A, B),$$
$$sk_{AHO} = (\alpha_a, \alpha_b, \mu_z, \nu_z, \mu_1, \ldots, \mu_7, \nu_1, \ldots, \nu_7).$$

4. Generate key pairs for BB signatures: Select $\epsilon_1, \ldots, \epsilon_L, \tilde{\epsilon}_1, \ldots, \tilde{\epsilon}_{\tilde{L}} \in_R Z_p$, and compute $Y_1 = g^{\epsilon_1}, \ldots, Y_L = g^{\epsilon_L}, \tilde{Y}_1 = g^{\tilde{\epsilon}_1}, \ldots, \tilde{Y}_{\tilde{L}} = g^{\tilde{\epsilon}_L}$. Define $pk_{BB} = (\{Y_i\}_{i=1,\ldots,L}, \{\tilde{Y}_i\}_{i=1,\ldots,\tilde{L}})$.
5. For the range proof, compute sets of BB signatures: $F_{\ell,i} = g^{1/(\epsilon_\ell + i)}$ for $1 \leq \ell \leq L$ and $2^{\ell-1} \leq i \leq 2^\ell - 1$, and $\tilde{F}_{\ell,i} = g^{1/(\tilde{\epsilon}_\ell + i)}$ for $1 \leq \ell \leq \tilde{L}$ and $2^{\ell-1} \leq i \leq 2^\ell - 1$.
6. Initialize sets $\mathcal{L}_{RM}, \mathcal{P}$ and $\mathcal{S}$ as empty. Output RM's public key

$$rpk = (p, \mathcal{G}, \mathcal{T}, e, g, pk_{acc}, pk_{AHO}, pk_{BB}, \{F_{\ell,i}\}_{1 \leq \ell \leq L, 2^{\ell-1} \leq i \leq 2^\ell - 1},$$
$$\{\tilde{F}_{\ell,i}\}_{1 \leq \ell \leq \tilde{L}, 2^{\ell-1} \leq i \leq 2^\ell - 1}),$$

and RM's secret key $rsk = sk_{AHO}$.

Register: In this protocol, U obtains an initial certificate from RM.

1. [U] Select $x, S_0, r_{x,0}, r_{S_0} \in_R Z_p$, and compute commitments $C_{x,0} = g^x \hat{g}^{r_{x,0}}$, $C_{S_0} = g^{S_0} \hat{g}^{r_{S_0}}$.
2. [U] Send $(C_{x,0}, C_{s_0})$ to RM, and conduct

$$PK\{(x, S_0, r_{x,0}, r_{S_0}) : C_{x,0} = g^x \hat{g}^{r_{x,0}}, C_{S_0} = g^{S_0} \hat{g}^{r_{S_0}}\}.$$

3. [RM] Set $rep_0 = 0, num_0 = 0, N_0 = 0, P_0 = 1, R_0 = 0, r_{rep_0} = r_{num_0} = r_{N_0} = r_{P_0} = r_{R_0} = 0$, and compute initial commitments $C_{rep_0} = g^{rep_0} \hat{g}^{r_{rep_0}}$, $C_{num_0} = g^{num_0} \hat{g}^{r_{num_0}}$, $C_{N_0} = g^{N_0} \hat{g}^{r_{N_0}}$, $C_{P_0} = P_0 \hat{g}^{r_{P_0}}$, $C_{R_0} = g^{R_0} \hat{g}^{r_{R_0}}$. Compute an AHO signature $\sigma_0 = (\theta_{01}, \ldots, \theta_{07})$ on messages $(C_{x,0}, C_{S_0}, C_{rep_0}, C_{num_0}, C_{N_0}, C_{P_0}, C_{R_0})$, and send σ_0 to U.

4. [U] Initialize $\mathcal{L}_U$ as the empty set. Set $rep_0 = 0, num_0 = 0, N_0 = 0, P_0 = 1, R_0 = 0, r_{rep_0} = r_{num_0} = r_{N_0} = r_{P_0} = r_{R_0} = 0$, and compute initial commitments $C_{rep_0} = g^{rep_0} \hat{g}^{r_{rep_0}}$, $C_{num_0} = g^{num_0} \hat{g}^{r_{num_0}}$, $C_{N_0} = g^{N_0} \hat{g}^{r_{N_0}}$, $C_{P_0} = P_0 \hat{g}^{r_{P_0}}$, $C_{R_0} = g^{R_0} \hat{g}^{r_{R_0}}$. Verify the AHO signature σ_0. If it is incorrect, abort. Output rep_0, num_0 and the initial certificate $cert_0 = (\mathcal{L}_U, S_0, N_0, P_0, R_0, C_{x,0}, C_{S_0}, C_{rep_0}, C_{num_0}, C_{N_0}, C_{P_0}, C_{R_0}, r_{x,0}, r_{S_0}, r_{rep_0}, r_{num_0}, r_{N_0}, r_{R_0}, \sigma_0)$ and $sec = x$.

Show: In this protocol, U shows that his/her accumulated reputation and number of ratings lie in integer ranges, after RM checks that all the ratings including negative ones are accumulated in the reputation. Then, RM issues the user an updated certificate.

The inputs of U are $rep_{t-1}, num_{t-1}, sec = x, cert_{t-1} = (\mathcal{L}_U, S_{t-1}, N_{t-1}, P_{t-1}, R_{t-1}, C_{x,t-1}, C_{S_{t-1}}, C_{rep_{t-1}}, C_{num_{t-1}}, C_{N_{t-1}}, C_{P_{t-1}}, C_{R_{t-1}}, r_{x,t-1}, r_{S_{t-1}}, r_{rep_{t-1}}, r_{num_{t-1}}, r_{N_{t-1}}, r_{R_{t-1}}, \sigma_{t-1})$. σ_{t-1} is an AHO signature on commitments $(C_{x,t-1}, C_{S_{t-1}}, C_{rep_{t-1}}, C_{num_{t-1}}, C_{N_{t-1}}, C_{P_{t-1}}, C_{R_{t-1}})$, where

$$C_{x,t-1} = g^x \hat{g}^{r_{x,t-1}}, \quad C_{S_{t-1}} = g^{S_{t-1}} \hat{g}^{r_{S_{t-1}}}, \quad C_{rep_{t-1}} = g^{rep_{t-1}} \hat{g}^{r_{rep_{t-1}}},$$

$$C_{num_{t-1}} = g^{num_{t-1}} \hat{g}^{r_{num_{t-1}}}, \quad C_{N_{t-1}} = g^{N_{t-1}} \hat{g}^{r_{N_{t-1}}}, \quad C_{P_{t-1}} = P_{t-1} \hat{g}^{R_{t-1}},$$

$$C_{R_{t-1}} = g^{R_{t-1}} \hat{g}^{r_{R_{t-1}}}.$$

RM's input $\mathcal{L}_{RM}$ includes ID numbers of items which are offered by all sellers but have not been rated yet. U's input $\mathcal{L}_U$ includes ID numbers of items which are offered by U but have not been updated in his/her certificate yet.

1. [RM] Send $\mathcal{L}_{RM}$ to U.
2. [U] Re-randomize the commitments: Select $r'_{x,t-1}, r'_{S_{t-1}}, r'_{rep_{t-1}}, r'_{num_{t-1}}, R'_{t-1}, r'_{N_{t-1}}, r'_{R_{t-1}} \in_R Z_p$, set $r''_{x,t-1} = r_{x,t-1} + r'_{x,t-1}, r''_{S_{t-1}} = r_{S_{t-1}} + r'_{S_{t-1}}, r''_{rep_{t-1}} = r_{rep_{t-1}} + r'_{rep_{t-1}}, r''_{num_{t-1}} = r_{num_{t-1}} + r'_{num_{t-1}}, r''_{N_{t-1}} = r_{N_{t-1}} + r'_{N_{t-1}}, R''_{t-1} = R_{t-1} + R'_{t-1}, r''_{R_{t-1}} = r_{R_{t-1}} + r'_{R_{t-1}}$, and compute

$$C'_{x,t-1} = C_{x,t-1} \hat{g}^{r'_{x,t-1}} = g^x \hat{g}^{r''_{x,t-1}}, \quad C'_{S_{t-1}} = C_{S_{t-1}} \hat{g}^{r'_{S_{t-1}}} = g^{S_{t-1}} \hat{g}^{r''_{S_{t-1}}},$$

$$C'_{rep_{t-1}} = C_{rep_{t-1}} \hat{g}^{r'_{rep_{t-1}}} = g^{rep_{t-1}} \hat{g}^{r''_{rep_{t-1}}},$$

$$C'_{num_{t-1}} = C_{num_{t-1}} \hat{g}^{r'_{num_{t-1}}} = g^{num_{t-1}} \hat{g}^{r''_{S_{t-1}}},$$

$$C'_{N_{t-1}} = C_{N_{t-1}} \hat{g}^{r'_{N_{t-1}}} = g^{N_{t-1}} \hat{g}^{r''_{S_{t-1}}}, \quad C'_{P_{t-1}} = C_{P_{t-1}} \hat{g}^{R'_{t-1}} = P_{t-1} \hat{g}^{R''_{t-1}},$$

$$C'_{R_{t-1}} = C_{R_{t-1}} \hat{g}^{r'_{R_{t-1}}} = g^{R_{t-1}} \hat{g}^{r''_{R_{t-1}}}.$$

Set $\mathbf{com}_1 = (C'_{x,t-1}, C'_{S_{t-1}}, C'_{rep_{t-1}}, C'_{num_{t-1}}, C'_{N_{t-1}}, C'_{P_{t-1}}, C'_{R_{t-1}})$.

3. [U] Re-randomize the AHO signature σ_{t-1} to obtain $\sigma'_{t-1} = \{\theta'_1, \ldots, \theta'_7\}$, and the commitments $\{C_{\theta'_i}\}_{i \in \{1,2,5\}}$ to $\{\theta'_i\}_{i \in \{1,2,5\}}$ by $C_{\theta'_i} = \theta'_i \hat{g}^{r_{\theta'_i}}$ for randomly chosen $r_{\theta'_i} \in_R Z_p$. Set $\mathbf{com}_{\text{AHO}} = (\{\theta'_i\}_{i=3,4,6,7}, \{C_{\theta'_i}\}_{i=1,2,5})$.

4. [U] To check the list, set $acc = \prod_{i \in \mathcal{L}_{\text{RM}}} g_{n+1-i}$ and $W = \prod_{j \in \mathcal{L}_U} \prod_{i \in \mathcal{L}_{\text{RM}}}^{i \neq j} g_{n+1-i+j}$. Select $r_W \in_R Z_p$, and compute the commitment C_W to W by $C_W = W\hat{g}^{r_W}$. Select $\tilde{r}_N$, and compute the commitment $\tilde{C}_N = g_n^{N_{t-1}} \hat{g}^{\tilde{r}_N}$. Set $\mathbf{com}_{\text{acc}} = (C_W, \tilde{C}_N)$.

5. [U] For the range proof of $2^{\ell-1} \leq rep_{t-1} < 2^\ell$, select BB signature $F_{\ell,rep_{t-1}}$ on rep_{t-1} s.t. $2^{\ell-1} \leq rep_{t-1} < 2^\ell$. Select $r_F \in_R Z_p$, and compute the commitment $C_F = F_{\ell,rep_{t-1}} \hat{g}^{r_F}$. Set $\xi = r_F \cdot rep_{t-1}$. Furthermore, select $r_{r_F}, r_\xi \in_R Z_p$, and compute the auxiliary commitments $C_{r_F} = g^{r_F} \hat{g}^{r_{r_F}}$ and $C_\xi = g^\xi \hat{g}^{r_\xi}$. Set $\zeta = r_\xi - r_{r_F} \cdot rep_{t-1}$. Set $\mathbf{com}_{\text{R1}} = (C_F, C_{r_F}, C_\xi)$.

6. [U] For the range proof of $2^{\tilde{\ell}-1} \leq num_{t-1} < 2^{\tilde{\ell}}$, select BB signature $\tilde{F}_{\tilde{\ell},num_{t-1}}$ on num_{t-1} s.t. $2^{\tilde{\ell}-1} \leq num_{t-1} < 2^{\tilde{\ell}}$. Select $r_{\tilde{F}} \in_R Z_p$, and compute the commitment $C_{\tilde{F}} = \tilde{F}_{\tilde{\ell},num_{t-1}} \hat{g}^{r_{\tilde{F}}}$. Set $\tilde{\xi} = r_{\tilde{F}} \cdot num_{t-1}$. Furthermore, select $r_{r_{\tilde{F}}}, r_{\tilde{\xi}} \in_R Z_p$, and compute the auxiliary commitments $C_{r_{\tilde{F}}} = g^{r_{\tilde{F}}} \hat{g}^{r_{r_{\tilde{F}}}}$ and $C_{\tilde{\xi}} = g^{\tilde{\xi}} \hat{g}^{r_{\tilde{\xi}}}$. Set $\tilde{\zeta} = r_{\tilde{\xi}} - r_{r_{\tilde{F}}} \cdot num_{t-1}$. Set $\mathbf{com}_{\text{R2}} = (C_{\tilde{F}}, C_{r_{\tilde{F}}}, C_{\tilde{\xi}})$.

7. [U] Set $R_t = R''_{t-1} = R_{t-1} + R'_{t-1}$, select $r_{R_t} \in_R Z_p$, and compute commitment $C_{R_t} = g^{R_t} \hat{g}^{r_{R_t}}$. Select $S_t, r_{S_t} \in_R Z_p$, and compute commitment $C_{S_t} = g^{S_t} \hat{g}^{r_{S_t}}$. Set $\mathbf{com}_2 = (C_{R_t}, C_{S_t})$.

8. [U] Send RM the commitments ($\mathbf{com}_1, \mathbf{com}_{\text{AHO}}, \mathbf{com}_{\text{acc}}, \mathbf{com}_{\text{R1}}, \mathbf{com}_{\text{R2}}, \mathbf{com}_2$) and the tag S_{t-1} of this certificate.

9. [RM] For the verification of the accumulator, generate $acc = \prod_{i \in \mathcal{L}_{\text{RM}}} g_{n+1-i}$.

10. [U] Conduct the following PK with RM:

$$PK\{(x, S_{t-1}, rep_{t-1}, num_{t-1}, N_{t-1}, R_{t-1}, r''_{x,t-1}, r''_{S_{t-1}}, r''_{rep_{t-1}}, r''_{num_{t-1}}, r''_{N_{t-1}},$$
$$r''_{R_{t-1}}, r_{R_t}, r'_{x,t-1}, r'_{S_{t-1}}, r'_{rep_{t-1}}, r'_{num_{t-1}}, r'_{N_{t-1}}, R'_{t-1}, r'_{R_{t-1}}, r_{\theta'_1}, r_{\theta'_2}, r_{\theta'_5}, \tilde{r}_N,$$
$$r_W, r_F, \xi, r_{r_F}, r_\xi, \zeta, r_{\tilde{F}}, \tilde{\xi}, r_{r_{\tilde{F}}}, r_{\tilde{\xi}}, \tilde{\zeta}) :$$

$$C'_{x,t-1} = g^x \hat{g}^{r''_{x,t-1}} \wedge C'_{S_{t-1}} g^{-S_{t-1}} = \hat{g}^{r''_{S_{t-1}}} \wedge C'_{rep_{t-1}} = g^{rep_{t-1}} \hat{g}^{r''_{rep_{t-1}}} \quad (1)$$

$$\wedge C'_{num_{t-1}} = g^{num_{t-1}} \hat{g}^{r''_{num_{t-1}}} \wedge C'_{N_{t-1}} = g^{N_{t-1}} \hat{g}^{r''_{N_{t-1}}} \quad (2)$$

$$\wedge C'_{R_{t-1}} = g^{R_{t-1}} \hat{g}^{r''_{R_{t-1}}} \wedge C_{R_t} = g^{R_{t-1}+R'_{t-1}} \hat{g}^{r_{R_t}} \wedge \tilde{C}_N = g_n^{N_{t-1}} \hat{g}^{\tilde{r}_N} \quad (3)$$

$$\wedge A^{-1} \cdot e(G_z, C_{\theta'_1}) \cdot e(G_r, C_{\theta'_2}) \cdot e(\theta'_3, \theta'_4) \cdot e(G_1, C'_{x,t-1}) \cdot e(G_2, C'_{S_{t-1}})$$
$$\cdot e(G_3, C'_{rep_{t-1}}) \cdot e(G_4, C'_{num_{t-1}}) \cdot e(G_5, C'_{N_{t-1}}) \cdot e(G_6, C'_{P_{t-1}}) \cdot e(G_7, C'_{R_{t-1}})$$
$$= e(G_z, \hat{g})^{r_{\theta'_1}} \cdot e(G_r, \hat{g})^{r_{\theta'_2}} \cdot e(G_1, \hat{g})^{r'_{x,t-1}} \cdot e(G_2, \hat{g})^{r'_{S_{t-1}}} \cdot e(G_3, \hat{g})^{r'_{rep_{t-1}}}$$
$$\cdot e(G_4, \hat{g})^{r'_{num_{t-1}}} \cdot e(G_5, \hat{g})^{r'_{N_{t-1}}} \cdot e(G_6, \hat{g})^{R'_{t-1}} \cdot e(G_7, \hat{g})^{r'_{R_{t-1}}} \quad (4)$$

$$\wedge B^{-1} \cdot e(H_z, C'_{\theta'_1}) \cdot e(H_r, C'_{\theta'_2}) \cdot e(\theta'_6, \theta'_7) \cdot e(H_1, C'_{x,t-1}) \cdot e(H_2, C'_{S_{t-1}})$$

$$\cdot e(H_3, C'_{rep_{t-1}}) \cdot e(H_4, C'_{num_{t-1}}) \cdot e(H_5, C'_{N_{t-1}}) \cdot e(H_6, C'_{P_{t-1}}) \cdot e(H_7, C'_{R_{t-1}})$$

$$= e(H_z, \hat{g})^{r_{\theta'_1}} \cdot e(H_r, \hat{g})^{r_{\theta'_5}} \cdot e(H_1, \hat{g})^{r'_{x,t-1}} \cdot e(H_2, \hat{g})^{r'_{S_{t-1}}} \cdot e(H_3, \hat{g})^{r'_{rep_{t-1}}}$$

$$\cdot e(H_4, \hat{g})^{r_{num_{t-1}}} \cdot e(H_5, \hat{g})^{r_{N_{t-1}}} \cdot e(H_6, \hat{g})^{R'_{t-1}} \cdot e(H_7, \hat{g})^{r_{R_{t-1}}} \tag{5}$$

$$\wedge e(C'_{P_{t-1}}, acc) \cdot e(g_1, \tilde{C}_N)^{-1} \cdot e(g, C_W)^{-1}$$

$$= e(\hat{g}, acc)^{-R_{t-1} - R'_{t-1}} \cdot e(g_1, \hat{g})^{-\tilde{r}_N} \cdot e(g, \hat{g})^{-r_W} \tag{6}$$

$$\wedge e(C_F, Y_\ell) \cdot e(g, g)^{-1} = e(\hat{g}, Y_\ell)^{r_F} \cdot e(C_F, g)^{-rep_{t-1}} \cdot e(\hat{g}, g)^\xi \tag{7}$$

$$\wedge C_{r_F} = g^{r_F} \hat{g}^{r_{r_F}} \wedge C_\xi = g^\xi \hat{g}^{r_\xi} \wedge C_\xi = C_{r_F}^{rep_{t-1}} \hat{g}^\zeta \tag{8}$$

$$\wedge e(C_{\tilde{F}}, Y_{\hat{\ell}}) \cdot e(g, g)^{-1} = e(\hat{g}, Y_{\tilde{\ell}})^{r_{\tilde{F}}} \cdot e(C_{\tilde{F}}, g)^{-num_{t-1}} \cdot e(\hat{g}, g)^{\tilde{\xi}} \tag{9}$$

$$\wedge C_{r_{\tilde{F}}} = g^{r_{\tilde{F}}} \hat{g}^{r_{r_{\tilde{F}}}} \wedge C_{\tilde{\xi}} = g^{\tilde{\xi}} \hat{g}^{r_{\tilde{\xi}}} \wedge C_{\tilde{\xi}} = C_{r_{\tilde{F}}}^{num_{t-1}} \hat{g}^{\tilde{\zeta}} \} \tag{10}$$

In this PK, Eqs. (1)–(3) prove the correctness of the commitments, Eqs. (4) and (5) prove an AHO signature on the commitments, Eq. (6) proves the accumulator verification of $\mathcal{L}_U \subset \mathcal{L}_{RM}$, and Eqs. (7)–(10) prove BB signatures on rep_{t-1}, num_{t-1}.

11. [RM] Check if the tag S_{t-1} has been used in past protocols to search it in set $\mathcal{S}$. If it has been used, abort. Otherwise, add S_{t-1} to $\mathcal{S}$.
12. [RM] Pick up an integer i from $[1, n] \backslash \mathcal{L}_{RM}$, and add i to $\mathcal{L}_{RM}$. Compute $C_{P_t} = C'_{P_{t-1}} \cdot g_i$, where $C_{P_t} = P_t \hat{g}^{R''_{t-1}}$ for $P_t = P_{t-1} \cdot g_i$. Compute $C_{N_t} = C'_{N_{t-1}} \cdot g$, where $C_{N_t} = g^{N_t} \hat{g}^{r''_{N_{t-1}}}$ for $N_t = N_{t-1} + 1$.
13. [RM] Compute an AHO signature σ_t on $(C_{x,t}, C_{S_t}, C_{rep_t}, C_{num_t}, C_{N_t}, C_{P_t}, C_{R_t})$, where $C_{x,t} = C'_{x,t-1}$, $C_{rep_t} = C'_{rep_{t-1}}$ and $C_{num_t} = C'_{num_{t-1}}$. Send (σ_t, i) to the user. Output i and $\mathcal{L}_{RM}$.
14. [U] Add i to $\mathcal{L}_U$, and compute $P_t = P_{t-1} \cdot g_i$, where it holds that $P_t = \prod_{i \in \mathcal{L}_U} g_i$.
15. [U] Output i, rep_t, num_t, $cert_t = (\mathcal{L}_U, S_t, N_t, P_t, R_t, C_{x,t}, C_{S_t}, C_{rep_t}, C_{num_t}, C_{N_t}, C_{P_t}, C_{R_t}, r_{x,t}, r_{S_t}, r_{rep_t}, r_{num_t}, r_{N_t}, r_{R_t}, \sigma_t)$, where $r_{rep_t} = r''_{rep_{t-1}}$, $r_{num_t} = r''_{num_{t-1}}, r_{N_t} = r''_{N_{t-1}}, r_{R_t} = r''_{R_{t-1}}$.

Update: In this protocol, RM issues U an updated certificate such that the accumulated reputation is added by the new rating and the number of ratings is incremented.

As in **Show** protocol, the inputs of U are rep_{t-1}, num_{t-1}, $sec = x$, $cert_{t-1} = (\mathcal{L}_U, S_{t-1}, N_{t-1}, P_{t-1}, R_{t-1}, C_{x,t-1}, C_{S_{t-1}}, C_{rep_{t-1}}, C_{num_{t-1}}, C_{N_{t-1}}, C_{P_{t-1}}, C_{R_{t-1}}, r_{x,t-1}, r_{S_{t-1}}, r_{rep_{t-1}}, r_{num_{t-1}}, r_{N_{t-1}}, r_{R_{t-1}}, \sigma_{t-1})$. σ_{t-1} is an AHO signature on commitments $(C_{x,t-1}, C_{S_{t-1}}, C_{rep_{t-1}}, C_{num_{t-1}}, C_{N_{t-1}}, C_{P_{t-1}}, C_{R_{t-1}})$.

1. [U] Send (i, Δ_{rep}) to RM.
2. [RM] Check if (i, Δ_{rep}) exists in $\mathcal{P}$. If it does not exist, abort.
3. [U] Re-randomize the commitments: Select $r'_{x,t-1}, r'_{S_{t-1}}, r'_{rep_{t-1}}, r'_{num_{t-1}}, R'_{t-1}, r'_{N_{t-1}}, r'_{R_{t-1}} \in_R Z_p$, set $r''_{x,t-1} = r_{x,t-1} + r'_{x,t-1}, r''_{S_{t-1}} = r_{S_{t-1}} + r'_{S_{t-1}},$

$r''_{rep_{t-1}} = r_{rep_{t-1}} + r'_{rep_{t-1}}, r''_{num_{t-1}} = r_{num_{t-1}} + r'_{num_{t-1}}, r''_{N_{t-1}} = r_{N_{t-1}} +$
$r'_{N_{t-1}}, R''_{t-1} = R_{t-1} + R'_{t-1}, r''_{R_{t-1}} = r_{R_{t-1}} + r'_{R_{t-1}},$ and compute

$$C'_{x,t-1} = C_{x,t-1}\hat{g}^{r'_{x,t-1}} = g^x\hat{g}^{r''_{x,t-1}}, \quad C'_{S_{t-1}} = C_{S_{t-1}}\hat{g}^{r'_{S_{t-1}}} = g^{S_{t-1}}\hat{g}^{r''_{S_{t-1}}},$$

$$C'_{rep_{t-1}} = C_{rep_{t-1}}\hat{g}^{r'_{rep_{t-1}}} = g^{rep_{t-1}}\hat{g}^{r''_{rep_{t-1}}},$$

$$C'_{num_{t-1}} = C_{num_{t-1}}\hat{g}^{r'_{num_{t-1}}} = g^{num_{t-1}}\hat{g}^{r''_{S_{t-1}}},$$

$$C'_{N_{t-1}} = C_{N_{t-1}}\hat{g}^{r'_{N_{t-1}}} = g^{N_{t-1}}\hat{g}^{r''_{S_{t-1}}}, \quad C'_{P_{t-1}} = C_{P_{t-1}}\hat{g}^{R'_{t-1}} = P_{t-1}\hat{g}^{R''_{t-1}},$$

$$C'_{R_{t-1}} = C_{R_{t-1}}\hat{g}^{r'_{R_{t-1}}} = g^{R_{t-1}}\hat{g}^{r''_{R_{t-1}}}.$$

Set $\mathbf{com}_1 = (C'_{x,t-1}, C'_{S_{t-1}}, C'_{rep_{t-1}}, C'_{num_{t-1}}, C'_{N_{t-1}}, C'_{P_{t-1}}, C'_{R_{t-1}})$.

4. [U] Re-randomize the AHO signature σ_{t-1} to obtain $\sigma'_{t-1} = \{\theta'_1, \ldots, \theta'_7\}$, and the commitments $\{C_{\theta'_i}\}_{i\in\{1,2,5\}}$ to $\{\theta'_i\}_{i\in\{1,2,5\}}$ by $C_{\theta'_i} = \theta'_i\hat{g}^{r_{\theta'_i}}$ for randomly chosen $r_{\theta'_i} \in_R Z_p$. Set $\mathbf{com}_{AHO} = (\{\theta'_i\}_{i=3,4,6,7}, \{C_{\theta'_i}\}_{i=1,2,5})$.
5. [U] Set $\tilde{R}_t = R''_{t-1} = R_{t-1} + R'_{t-1}$, select $r_{R_t} \in_R Z_p$, and compute commitment $C_{R_t} = g^{\tilde{R}_t}\hat{g}^{r_{R_t}}$. Select $S_t, r_{S_t} \in_R Z_p$, and compute commitment $C_{S_t} = g^{S_t}\hat{g}^{r_{S_t}}$. Set $\mathbf{com}_2 = (C_{R_t}, C_{S_t})$.
6. [U] Send RM the commitments $(\mathbf{com}_1, \mathbf{com}_{AHO}, \mathbf{com}_2)$ and the tag S_{t-1} of this certificate.
7. [U] Conduct the following PK with RM:

$$PK\{(x, S_{t-1}, rep_{t-1}, num_{t-1}, N_{t-1}, R_{t-1}, r''_{x,t-1}, r''_{S_{t-1}}, r''_{rep_{t-1}}, r''_{num_{t-1}}, r''_{N_{t-1}},$$

$$r''_{R_{t-1}}, r_{R_t}, r'_{x,t-1}, r'_{S_{t-1}}, r'_{rep_{t-1}}, r'_{num_{t-1}}, r'_{N_{t-1}}, R'_{t-1}, r'_{R_{t-1}}, r_{\theta'_1}, r_{\theta'_2}, r_{\theta'_5}):$$

$$C'_{x,t-1} = g^x\hat{g}^{r''_{x,t-1}} \wedge C'_{S_{t-1}}g^{-S_{t-1}} = \hat{g}^{r''_{S_{t-1}}} \wedge C'_{rep_{t-1}} = g^{rep_{t-1}}\hat{g}^{r''_{rep_{t-1}}}$$

$$\wedge C'_{num_{t-1}} = g^{num_{t-1}}\hat{g}^{r''_{num_{t-1}}} \wedge C'_{N_{t-1}} = g^{N_{t-1}}\hat{g}^{r''_{N_{t-1}}} \wedge C'_{R_{t-1}} = g^{R_{t-1}}\hat{g}^{r''_{R_{t-1}}}$$

$$\wedge C_{R_t} = g^{R_{t-1}+R'_{t-1}}\hat{g}^{r_{R_t}}$$

$$\wedge A^{-1} \cdot e(G_z, C_{\theta'_1}) \cdot e(G_r, C_{\theta'_2}) \cdot e(\theta'_3, \theta'_4) \cdot e(G_1, C'_{x,t-1}) \cdot e(G_2, C'_{S_{t-1}})$$

$$\cdot e(G_3, C'_{rep_{t-1}}) \cdot e(G_4, C'_{num_{t-1}}) \cdot e(G_5, C'_{N_{t-1}}) \cdot e(G_6, C'_{P_{t-1}}) \cdot e(G_7, C'_{R_{t-1}})$$

$$= e(G_z, \hat{g})^{r_{\theta'_1}} \cdot e(G_r, \hat{g})^{r_{\theta'_2}} \cdot e(G_1, \hat{g})^{r_{x,t-1}} \cdot e(G_2, \hat{g})^{r'_{S_{t-1}}} \cdot e(G_3, \hat{g})^{r'_{rep_{t-1}}}$$

$$\cdot e(G_4, \hat{g})^{r'_{num_{t-1}}} \cdot e(G_5, \hat{g})^{r'_{N_{t-1}}} \cdot e(G_6, \hat{g})^{R'_{t-1}} \cdot e(G_7, \hat{g})^{r'_{R_{t-1}}}$$

$$\wedge B^{-1} \cdot e(H_z, C_{\theta'_1}) \cdot e(H_r, C_{\theta'_5}) \cdot e(\theta'_6, \theta'_7) \cdot e(H_1, C'_{x,t-1}) \cdot e(H_2, C'_{S_{t-1}})$$

$$\cdot e(H_3, C'_{rep_{t-1}}) \cdot e(H_4, C'_{num_{t-1}}) \cdot e(H_5, C'_{N_{t-1}}) \cdot e(H_6, C'_{P_{t-1}}) \cdot e(H_7, C'_{R_{t-1}})$$

$$= e(H_z, \hat{g})^{r_{\theta'_1}} \cdot e(H_r, \hat{g})^{r_{\theta'_5}} \cdot e(H_1, \hat{g})^{r_{x,t-1}} \cdot e(H_2, \hat{g})^{r'_{S_{t-1}}} \cdot e(H_3, \hat{g})^{r'_{rep_{t-1}}}$$

$$\cdot e(H_4, \hat{g})^{r'_{num_{t-1}}} \cdot e(H_5, \hat{g})^{r'_{N_{t-1}}} \cdot e(H_6, \hat{g})^{R'_{t-1}} \cdot e(H_7, \hat{g})^{r'_{R_{t-1}}}\}$$

8. [RM] Check if the tag S_{t-1} has been used in past protocols to search it in set $\mathcal{S}$. If it has been used, abort. Otherwise, add S_{t-1} to $\mathcal{S}$.
9. [RM] Compute $C_{P_t} = C'_{P_{t-1}} \cdot g_i^{-1}$, where $C_{P_t} = P_t\hat{g}^{R''_{t-1}}$ for $P_t = P_{t-1} \cdot g_i^{-1}$.
   Compute $C_{N_t} = C'_{N_{t-1}} \cdot g^{-1}$, where $C_{N_t} = g^{N_t}\hat{g}^{r''_{N_{t-1}}}$ for $N_t = N_{t-1} -$
   1. Compute $C_{rep_t} = C'_{rep_{t-1}}g^{\Delta_{rep}}$, where $C_{rep_t} = g^{rep_t}g^{r''_{rep_{t-1}}}$ for $rep_t =$

$rep_{t-1} + \Delta_{rep}$. Compute $C_{num_t} = C'_{num_{t-1}}g$, where $C_{num_t} = g^{num_t}g^{r''_{num_{t-1}}}$ for $num_t = num_{t-1} + 1$.

10. [RM] Compute an AHO signature σ_t on $(C_{x,t}, C_{S_t}, C_{rep_t}, C_{num_t}, C_{N_t}, C_{P_t}, C_{R_t})$, where $C_{x,t} = C'_{x,t-1}$. Send σ_t to the user. Delete (i, Δ_{rep}) from $\mathcal{P}$.

11. [U] Delete i from $\mathcal{L}_U$, and compute $P_t = P_{t-1} \cdot g_i^{-1}$, where it holds that $P_t = \prod_{i \in \mathcal{L}_U} g_i$.

12. [U] Output $rep_t, num_t, cert_t = (\mathcal{L}_U, S_t, N_t, P_t, R_t, C_{x,t}, C_{S_t}, C_{rep_t}, C_{num_t}, C_{N_t}, C_{P_t}, C_{R_t}, r_{x,t}, r_{S_t}, r_{rep_t}, r_{num_t}, r_{N_t}, r_{R_t}, \sigma_t)$, where $r_{rep_t} = r''_{rep_{t-1}}$, $r_{num_t} = r''_{num_{t-1}}, r_{N_t} = r''_{N_{t-1}}, r_{R_t} = r''_{R_{t-1}}$.

5   Security

The proofs of the following lemmas and theorems are shown in the full paper.

Lemma 1. *The PK in* **Show** *protocol proves the knowledge of*

- *an AHO signature σ_{t-1} on $C_{x,t-1}, C_{S_{t-1}}, C_{rep_{t-1}}, C_{num_{t-1}}, C_{N_{t-1}}, C_{P_{t-1}}, C_{R_{t-1}}$, where*

$$C_{x,t-1} = g^x \hat{g}^{r_{x,t-1}}, C_{S_{t-1}} = g^{S_{t-1}} \hat{g}^{r_{S_{t-1}}}, C_{rep_{t-1}} = g^{rep_{t-1}} \hat{g}^{r_{rep_{t-1}}},$$
$$C_{num_{t-1}} = g^{num_{t-1}} \hat{g}^{r_{num_{t-1}}}, C_{N_{t-1}} = g^{N_{t-1}} \hat{g}^{r_{N_{t-1}}}, C_{P_{t-1}} = P_{t-1} \hat{g}^{R_{t-1}},$$
$$C_{R_{t-1}} = g^{R_{t-1}} \hat{g}^{r_{R_{t-1}}},$$

- *accumulator witness W s.t. $e(P_{t-1}, acc)/e(g, W) = e(g_1, g_n)^{N_{t-1}}$ for the above P_{t-1}, N_{t-1} and accumulator acc known to* RM,
- *a BB signature $F_{\ell, rep_{t-1}}$ on above rep_{t-1} w.r.t. public key Y_ℓ,*
- *a BB signature $\tilde{F}_{\tilde{\ell}, num_{t-1}}$ on above num_{t-1} w.r.t. public key $Y_{\tilde{\ell}}$.*

Lemma 2. *The PK in* **Update** *protocol proves the knowledge of an AHO signature σ_{t-1} on $C_{x,t-1}, C_{S_{t-1}}, C_{rep_{t-1}}, C_{num_{t-1}}, C_{N_{t-1}}, C_{P_{t-1}}, C_{R_{t-1}}$, where*

$$C_{x,t-1} = g^x \hat{g}^{r_{x,t-1}}, C_{S_{t-1}} = g^{S_{t-1}} \hat{g}^{r_{S_{t-1}}}, C_{rep_{t-1}} = g^{rep_{t-1}} \hat{g}^{r_{rep_{t-1}}},$$
$$C_{num_{t-1}} = g^{num_{t-1}} \hat{g}^{r_{num_{t-1}}}, C_{N_{t-1}} = g^{N_{t-1}} \hat{g}^{r_{N_{t-1}}}, C_{P_{t-1}} = P_{t-1} \hat{g}^{R_{t-1}},$$
$$C_{R_{t-1}} = g^{R_{t-1}} \hat{g}^{r_{R_{t-1}}}.$$

Theorem 1. *The proposed system is* reputation unforgeable.

Theorem 2. *The proposed system is* seller anonymous.

6   Conclusion

In this paper, we have proposed an anonymous reputation system with the secrecy of the reputations for even the reputation manager. In our system, a ratee cannot discard the negative ratings.

In our system, the reputation manager cannot check if the reputation of a user is accumulated from a few (colluding) ratees. Our future work is the extension to the system where the number of raters can be checked. The implementation of our system and the evaluations are also our future works.

A   Syntax and Security Requirements

A.1   Syntax

The algorithms and protocol of the anonymous reputation system are as follows.

Setup$(I, n, L, \tilde{L})$: This is the key setup algorithm for RM. In the inputs, I is the security parameter, n is the maximum number of items which are offered by sellers but have not been rated yet, and L is the number of ranges used in proving for the accumulated reputation. $\tilde{L}$ is the number of ranges used in proving for the number of ratings. This algorithm outputs RM's public key rpk, RM's secret key rsk, and initialize sets $\mathcal{L}_{RM}$, $\mathcal{P}$ and $\mathcal{S}$ as empty.

Register: This is an interactive protocol between a joining user U and RM for the registration of U. The common input is rpk. The input of RM is rsk. The outputs of U are U's unique secret sec and an initial one-time certificate $cert_0$ indicating accumulated reputation $rep_0 = 0$ and the number of ratings $num_0 = 0$.

Show: This is an interactive protocol between a seller (registered user) U and RM, where U proves that his/her current reputation rep_{t-1} lies in range $[2^{\ell-1}, 2^\ell - 1]$, and proves that the number of ratings num_{t-1} lies in range $[2^{\tilde{\ell}-1}, 2^{\tilde{\ell}} - 1]$. The common input is rpk. The inputs of U are rep_{t-1}, num_{t-1}, the user's secret sec, and the certificate $cert_{t-1}$. The inputs of RM are rsk, $\mathcal{L}_{RM}$, and $\mathcal{S}$. The outputs of U are item ID number i and an updated one-time certificate $cert_t$ for i, and $rep_t = rep_{t-1}$, $num_t = num_{t-1}$. The outputs of RM are updated $\mathcal{L}_{RM}$, and $\mathcal{S}$. The set $\mathcal{L}_{RM} \subset [1, n]$ consists of ID numbers of items which are offered by sellers but have not been rated yet. The set $\mathcal{S}$ consists of tags which are included in certificates, to detect the double use of the certificates. If the certificate $cert_{t-1}$ has been used in a past protocol, this protocol is aborted.

Rate: This is the algorithm of RM that, on inputs item ID number i, the rating value Δ_{rep}, the pending database $\mathcal{P}$ and $\mathcal{L}_{RM}$, deletes i from $\mathcal{L}_{RM}$ and adds (i, Δ_{rep}) to $\mathcal{P}$. The set $\mathcal{P}$ consists of (i, Δ_{rep}) such that the rating Δ_{rep} has not been accumulated to the corresponding certificate yet.

Update: This is an interactive protocol between a seller U and RM to accumulate the rating in the certificate. The common inputs are rpk, the target item ID number i, and the rating Δ_{rep}. The inputs of U are rep_{t-1}, num_{t-1}, the user's secret sec, and the certificate $cert_{t-1}$. The inputs of RM are rsk, $\mathcal{P}$, $\mathcal{L}_{RM}$, and $\mathcal{S}$. The outputs of U are $rep_t = rep_{t-1} + \Delta_{rep}$, $num_t = num_{t-1} + 1$, and the one-time certificate $cert_t$. RM deletes (i, Δ_{rep}) from $\mathcal{P}$. If the certificate $cert_{t-1}$ has been used in a past protocol, this protocol is aborted.

Using the above algorithms and protocols, the system flow is as follows. First of all, RM initializes the system using **Setup**, where the public key rpk is published. When a user wants to participate in this system, the user registers with RM to obtain initial data. When a user wants to offer an item, the user registers his item and conducts **Show** protocol with RM. RM publishes the item with the ranges of rep_{t-1}, num_{t-1} of the seller, where buyers can check the reliability of the seller. After a buyer has an interaction with the seller, the buyer sends his rating to RM. RM forwards the rating to the seller, who conducts **Update** protocol with RM.

A.2   Security Requirements

As the security, we consider the *reputation unforgeability* and the *seller anonymity*.

Reputation Unforgeability. Consider the following reputation unforgeability game. As the proof in [4], in order to identify the user from the **Update** or **Show** protocol transcript, we need a special algorithm, **Extract**.

Reputation unforgeability game: The challenger runs **Setup**, and obtains rpk and rsk. He provides $\mathcal{A}$ with rpk, and run $\mathcal{A}$. He initializes the database $\mathcal{D}$ with entries $(x_i, \mathsf{sum}_{i,rep}, \mathsf{sum}_{i,num})$. In the run, $\mathcal{A}$ can query the challenger about the following queries:

C-Register: To $\mathcal{A}$'s request, the challenger as RM executes **Register** protocol with $\mathcal{A}$ as a user.

C-Show: To $\mathcal{A}$'s request as the seller, the challenger as RM executes **Show** protocol with $\mathcal{A}$.

C-Update: To $\mathcal{A}$'s request for the item ID i and the rating Δ_{rep}, using **Rate**, the challenger updates $\mathcal{P}$ and $\mathcal{L}_{RM}$. Then, the challenger as RM executes **Show** protocol on input (i, Δ_{rep}) with $\mathcal{A}$ as the seller. From the protocol transcript, using **Extract**, the challenger extracts the identity x_i of the user. In the database $\mathcal{D}$, the challenger renews $\mathsf{sum}_{i,rep} = \mathsf{sum}_{i,rep} + \Delta_{rep}$, and $\mathsf{sum}_{i,num} = \mathsf{sum}_{i,num} + 1$ in the entry $(x_i, \mathsf{sum}_{i,rep}, \mathsf{sum}_{i,num})$.

Finally, the challenger as RM executes **Show** protocol with $\mathcal{A}$ as a seller.
Then, $\mathcal{A}$ wins if

1. The final **Show** protocol succeeds for $rep^*_{t-1} \in [2^{\ell-1}, 2^\ell - 1]$ and $num^*_{t-1} \in [2^{\tilde{\ell}-1}, 2^{\tilde{\ell}} - 1]$ for some $\ell, \tilde{\ell}$.
2. For x_{i^*} extracted by **Extract** from the final **Show** protocol, it holds that $\mathsf{sum}_{i^*,rep} \notin [2^{\ell-1}, 2^\ell-1]$ or $\mathsf{sum}_{i^*,num} \notin [2^{\tilde{\ell}-1}, 2^{\tilde{\ell}}-1]$ in the entry $(x_{i^*}, \mathsf{sum}_{i^*,rep}, \mathsf{sum}_{i^*,num})$ in $\mathcal{D}$.

Definition 4. *A reputation system is* reputation unforgeable *if, for any PPT adversary $\mathcal{A}$ involved in the reputation unforgeability game, the probability that $\mathcal{A}$ wins the game is negligible for security parameter l.*

Seller Anonymity. As the syntax shows, the pair of **Show** protocol and **Update** protocol for the same item ID are linkable and the rating Δ_{rep} is revealed. Furthermore, each **Show** protocol reveals the ranges which rep and num lie in. The seller anonymity means that any adversary can obtain no information on the user beyond these. Since the adversary can corrupt RM, the system with the seller anonymity satisfies the reputation secrecy for even the manager. In the similar way to the anonymity definition of an anonymous credential system [4], the seller anonymity is defined as follows: The interaction of the adversary (corrupting RM) with honest users is indistinguishable from some ideal game where **Show** and **Update** protocol transcripts are independent of the user's identity. Consider the simulators, **SimShow, SimUpdate** for **Show, Update**.

Definition 5. *A reputation system is* seller anonymous *if the following properties hold:*

- *No adversary can tell if it is interacting with an honest user with rep_{t-1}, $num_{t-1}, sec, cert_{t-1}$ in* **Show** *protocol, or with* **SimShow** *which is not given $rep_{t-1}, num_{t-1}, sec, cert_{t-1}$.*
- *No adversary can tell if it is interacting with an honest user with rep_{t-1}, $num_{t-1}, sec, cert_{t-1}$ in* **Update** *protocol, or with* **SimUpdate** *which is not given $rep_{t-1}, num_{t-1}, sec, cert_{t-1}$.*

References

1. Abe, M., Fuchsbauer, G., Groth, J., Haralambiev, K., Ohkubo, M.: Structure-preserving signatures and commitments to group elements. In: Rabin, T. (ed.) CRYPTO 2010. LNCS, vol. 6223, pp. 209–236. Springer, Heidelberg (2010)
2. Abe, M., Haralambiev, K., Ohkubo, M.: Signing on elements in bilinear groups for modular protocol design. Cryptology ePrint Archive, Report 2010/133 (2010). http://eprint.iacr.org/
3. Androulaki, E., Choi, S.G., Bellovin, S.M., Malkin, T.: Reputation systems for anonymous networks. In: Borisov, N., Goldberg, I. (eds.) PETS 2008. LNCS, vol. 5134, pp. 202–218. Springer, Heidelberg (2008)
4. Belenkiy, M., Camenisch, J., Chase, M., Kohlweiss, M., Lysyanskaya, A., Shacham, H.: Randomizable proofs and delegatable anonymous credentials. In: Halevi, S. (ed.) CRYPTO 2009. LNCS, vol. 5677, pp. 108–125. Springer, Heidelberg (2009)
5. Bethencourt, J., Shi, E., Song, D.: Signatures of reputation. In: Sion, R. (ed.) FC 2010. LNCS, vol. 6052, pp. 400–407. Springer, Heidelberg (2010)
6. Boneh, D., Boyen, X.: Short signatures without random oracles. In: Cachin, C., Camenisch, J.L. (eds.) EUROCRYPT 2004. LNCS, vol. 3027, pp. 56–73. Springer, Heidelberg (2004)
7. Camenisch, J.L., Chaabouni, R., Shelat, A.: Efficient protocols for set membership and range proofs. In: Pieprzyk, J. (ed.) ASIACRYPT 2008. LNCS, vol. 5350, pp. 234–252. Springer, Heidelberg (2008)
8. Camenisch, J., Kiayias, A., Yung, M.: On the portability of generalized schnorr proofs. In: Joux, A. (ed.) EUROCRYPT 2009. LNCS, vol. 5479, pp. 425–442. Springer, Heidelberg (2009)
9. Camenisch, J., Kohlweiss, M., Soriente, C.: An accumulator based on bilinear maps and efficient revocation for anonymous credentials. In: Jarecki, S., Tsudik, G. (eds.) PKC 2009. LNCS, vol. 5443, pp. 481–500. Springer, Heidelberg (2009)
10. Chaum, D.: The dining cryptographers problem: unconditional sender and recipient untraceability. J. Cryptol. 1(1), 65–75 (1988)

11. Schiffner, S., Clauß, S., Steinbrecher, S.: Privacy and liveliness for reputation systems. In: Martinelli, F., Preneel, B. (eds.) EuroPKI 2009. LNCS, vol. 6391, pp. 209–224. Springer, Heidelberg (2010)
12. Schiffner, S., Clauß, S., Steinbrecher, S.: Privacy, liveliness and fairness for reputation. In: Černá, I., Gyimóthy, T., Hromkovič, J., Jefferey, K., Králović, R., Vukolić, M., Wolf, S. (eds.) SOFSEM 2011. LNCS, vol. 6543, pp. 506–519. Springer, Heidelberg (2011)
13. Sudarsono, A., Nakanishi, T., Funabiki, N.: Efficient proofs of attributes in pairing-based anonymous credential system. In: Fischer-Hübner, S., Hopper, N. (eds.) PETS 2011. LNCS, vol. 6794, pp. 246–263. Springer, Heidelberg (2011)

Security Protocol

Database Outsourcing with Hierarchical Authenticated Data Structures

Mohammad Etemad$^{(\boxtimes)}$ and Alptekin Küpçü

Koç University, İstanbul, Turkey
{metemad,akupcu}@ku.edu.tr

Abstract. In an outsourced database scheme, the data owner delegates the data management tasks to a remote service provider. At a later time, the remote service is supposed to answer any query on the database. The essential requirements are ensuring the data integrity and authenticity with efficient mechanisms. Current approaches employ authenticated data structures to store security information, generated by the client and used by the server, to compute proofs that show the answers to the queries are authentic. The existing solutions have shortcomings with multi-clause queries and duplicate values in a column.

We propose a hierarchical authenticated data structure for storing security information, which alleviates the mentioned problems. We provide a unified formal definition of a secure outsourced database scheme, and prove that our proposed scheme is secure according to this definition, which captures previously separate properties such as correctness, completeness, and freshness. The performance evaluation based on our prototype implementation confirms the efficiency of the proposed outsourced database scheme, showing more than 50 % decrease in proof size and proof generation time compared to previous work, and about 1–20 % communication overhead compared to the query result size.

1 Introduction

Huge amount of data is being produced everyday due to the widespread use of computer systems in organizations and companies. Data needs protection, and most of companies lack enough resources to provide it. By outsourcing data storage and management, they free themselves from data protection difficulties, and concentrate on their own proficiency.

An important problem is that by data outsourcing, the owner loses the direct control over her data and should rely on answers coming from the remote service provider (who is not fully trusted). Therefore, there should be mechanisms giving the data owner the ability for checking the integrity of the outsourced data. To make sure that the server operates correctly, the client should verify the query answers coming from the servers [8]. The server sends to the client a *verification object* (*vo*) along with the query answer (the *result set*). The *vo* enables the client to verify the authenticity of the answer. Since the client may be a portable device with limited processing power, the *vo* should be small, and efficiently verifiable. The client uses the *vo* to verify that the response is [8,9,15,24,25]:

© Springer International Publishing Switzerland 2014
H.-S. Lee and D.-G. Han (Eds.): ICISC 2013, LNCS 8565, pp. 381–399, 2014.
DOI: 10.1007/978-3-319-12160-4_23

- *complete:* the result set sent to the client is exactly the set of records that are the output of executing the query, i.e., no record is added or removed.
- *correct:* the result set sent to the client is provided by the client already, i.e., no unauthorized modification.
- *fresh:* the result set sent to the client is provided using the most recent data on the server, and does not belong to old versions, i.e., no replay attacks.

We want to perform authentic queries on all *searchable* columns (the columns that can be used to build clauses) of a table. All existing methods have a common problem with duplicate values in non-PK searchable columns [10,14,18]. The general method is to sort a table by each searchable column, and build an Authenticated Data Structure (ADS) on the result. In other words, a total ordering on the values of searchable columns is required, which together with the fact that the duplicate values belong to different records, make building the ADS using those values problematic.

We introduce the *hierarchical ADS* (HADS) for solving this problem. HADS is also advantageous in proof generation for multi-dimensional (multi-clause) queries. The HADS can be stored in the same database [2], or separately. Storing it separately breaks the tie to a specific database and brings more flexibility. This way, the outsourced data can be changed without affecting the proof system.

The rationale behind this work is to relate everything to the PKs. Since PKs are unique identifiers of records in a database, we can compare and combine the results of different queries and check the correctness and completeness at the same time (freshness is provided by storing a constant-size metadata locally at the client). We also support dynamic databases where the data owner may apply modification queries (Insert, Delete, Update), in a provable manner.

1.1   Related Work

Elementary approaches. A simple way for verifying the authenticity of an answer to an outsourced database query is to sign each table and store the signature locally [4,25]. This method requires sending the whole table to the client for verification, and hence, does not scale up. Another method is to compute and store with each record, a signature that verifies the contents of the record [4]. The problems are that computing a signature (for each record) is an expensive operation, and this method does not provide completeness.

Approaches based on Verifiable B-tree. Pang and Tan [19] propose using one or more *verifiable* B-trees (VB-tree) for each table. The VB-tree is an extension of B-tree using the Merkle hash tree [12]. The records are sorted by a column before constructing the VB-tree, and for each table we need VB-trees in the number of searchable columns. It does not support completeness, and found insecure for the insecurity of the function used to compute the signatures [14].

A variant of this method, named MB-tree, is used intensively in the literature [3,13,15,25]. MB-tree is similar to VB-tree except that a light hash function is used instead of expensive signatures. The client stores locally the root's digest, or signs and stores it on the server.

Approaches based on authenticated skip list. Another line of work is using an authenticated skip list to store the required information for the verification [16,24]. Skip list is suitable and efficient enough for this purpose, especially when we consider dynamic scenarios [24]. Wang and Du [24] prove that skip-list-based ADS provides soundness and completeness for one-dimensional range queries, and multiple ADSs are required for multi-dimensional range queries.

Palazzi [16,17] constructs one skip list for each searchable column in each table. An important problem with this scheme is that for multi-dimensional queries, only the result of one skip list (determined by the First Column Returned approach [16], or the fastest one [17]) is used. The result set is sent to the client who will apply the other clauses. Therefore, the result set contains a larger set than the real result set of the query, and hence, is not efficient.

Authenticated range query is the method used to prove completeness (i.e., no extra records and no missing ones) [3,9,14,25]. The server (1) finds the *contiguous* records as the result set, and the *boundary* records (one immediately before the first record, the *before* record, and one immediately after the last record, the *after* record), (2) selects the values needed for the ordered ADS membership proof of the boundary records, and (3) puts all these values into the verification object and sends it to the client. The set {*before record, result set, after record*} is guaranteed by the ordered ADS to be a sorted and contiguous set of records, with no extra or missing record between them [11,24].

A common **problem** with all these methods [3,8,9,13–19,25] is the duplicate values in non-PK columns that make building the ADSs problematic since distinct values are required. Pang *et al.* [18] and Li *et al.* [10] propose applying the standard geometric perturbation method, guaranteeing a total ordering. Although this solution works for static data, it is not suitable for a dynamic case, since perturbing a duplicate value may result again in duplicate values. Narasimha and Tsudik [14] propose appending a value, i.e., the record ID, to solve the problem; but then searching on the column will be problematic, i.e., we cannot search by only the real values of the column. Palazzi *et al.* [17] appends to each value, hash of the record the value belongs to, and builds the ADSs using these values. In our performance results, we show that these solutions that keep all duplicate values in the same ADS result in significantly slower systems.

2 Preliminaries

Notation: We use N to denote the number of records of a table, $|C_i|$ to denote the number of distinct values in column i, and t to denote the number of records in the result set. The '|' denotes the concatenation, and PPT denotes probabilistic polynomial time. 'PK' denotes 'primary key' in a database table, and 'pk' stands for 'public key'. A function $\nu(k) : Z^+ \rightarrow [0,1]$ is called *negligible* if $\forall$ *polynomials* p, $\exists$ *constant* k_0 s.t. $\forall$ $k > k_0$, $\nu(k) < |1/p(k)|$. Overwhelming probability is greater than or equal to $1 - \nu(k)$ for some negligible function $\nu(k)$.

A **one-way accumulator** is defined as a family of *one-way, quasi-commutative* hash functions. A function $f : X \times Y \rightarrow X$ is *quasi-commutative* if $\forall x \in X, y_1,$

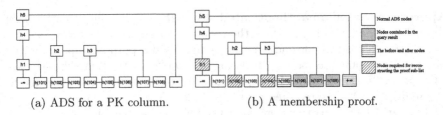

(a) ADS for a PK column.   (b) A membership proof.

Fig. 1. (a) A regular (non-hierarchical) ADS storing the PK column of the Student table, and (b) the membership proof for a query whose result set is {106, 107, 108}.

$y_2 \in Y : f(f(x, y_1), y_2) = f(f(x, y_2), y_1)$. Benaloh and de Mare [1] propose a one-way accumulator based on an RSA modulus and prove its security.

An **authenticated data structure (ADS)** is a scheme for data authentication, where untrusted responders answer queries on the data structure and provide extra information used to produce a cryptographic proof that the answers are valid [20,22,23]. The client uses the proof to reconstruct the ADS locally and verify correctness of the answer [20]. Each node of the ADS is assigned a value that is computed as a function of some neighboring nodes in the structure. We provide a formal definition in Appendix A.

Authenticated skip list is an ADS constructed using a collision resistant hash function. Labels from the queried node to the root make a proof of membership [6]. Figure 1a and b present an authenticated skip list storing a PK column, and the membership proof for the result set {106, 107, 108}, respectively.

Papamanthou *et al.* [21] introduce the **authenticated hash table**, that is a hierarchy of one-way accumulators in a way that provides constant proof size and verification time. It also keeps either query or update time constant while providing the other with sub-linear complexity.

3 Hierarchical Authenticated Data Structures

Hierarchical ADS (HADS) is an ADS consisting of multiple levels of ADSs. Each ADS at level i is constructed on top of a number of ADSs at level $i + 1$. Each element of an ADS at level i stores the digest of and a link to an ADS at level $i+1$. Therefore, multiple ADSs with different underlying structure can be linked together to form a hierarchical ADS with multiple levels. The only restriction is that all ADSs at level i must be of the same underlying structure to have consistent proofs.[1] The elements of last level ADSs contain data items (without links to other ADSs). The client stores the digest of the first level ADS as metadata. Figure 2a presents a two-level HADS instantiation using authenticated skip list at the first, and Merkle hash tree at the second level, and Fig. 2b shows a general four-level HADS architecture (the ADSs are represented like trees for simplicity of presentation, but they can be of any type).

---

[1] We can handle the heterogeneous case as well, but it complicates the presentation.

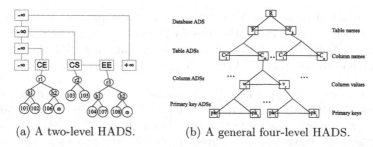

(a) A two-level HADS.   (b) A general four-level HADS.

Fig. 2. (a) A two-level HADS using authenticated skip list and Merkle hash tree, and (b) a general construction of a four-level HADS for storing the whole database.

An **HADS scheme** is an ADS scheme defined with three PPT algorithms *(HKeyGen, HCertify, HVerify)* for the sake of distinguishing them from non-hierarchical versions. All definitions for the ADS (the Appendix A), using HADS algorithm names, directly provide a formal framework for HADS schemes.

3.1 HADS Construction

We construct HADS using (possibly different) ADSs at multiple levels in a hierarchical structure. The modification or proof generation is a recursive operation that needs to traverse the ADSs in a top-down manner. We provide the input as a series of $(key, value)$ pairs in such a way that the pairs needed for the upper levels appear first. The command execution will begin on the first-level ADS, and be directed by the data provided in the form of $(key, value)$ pairs, which are parsed to proper sub-ADSs at each level. For a query command, only the keys will be used, but for the modifications, both key and value will be used.

The *HKeyGen* algorithm generates a public and private key pair for each level, combines all public keys into pk, and all private keys into sk, and outputs the result as the private and public key pair of the HADS (Algorithm 3.1).

Algorithm 3.1. HKeyGen, run by the client.

Input: security parameter k, number of levels n, and type of each level.
Output: the private and public keys of the HADS

1 $sk_{HADS} = \{\}$; //private key of the HADS.
2 $pk_{HADS} = \{\}$; //public key of the HADS.
3 **for** $i = 1$ to n **do**
4      $(sk, pk) = ADS_i.KeyGen(1^k)$; //Ask the level i ADS to produce its keys.
5      $sk_{HADS} = sk_{HADS} \cup sk$;
6      $pk_{HADS} = pk_{HADS} \cup pk$;
7 **return** (sk_{HADS}, pk_{HADS});

The modification and proof generation on HADS are recursive operations, starting at the root ADS, and repeating on all affected ADSs in the hierarchy. Each level's ADS generates its own proof. The ADSs are tied to each other in a way that each leaf node of an ADS at level i stores the digest of and a link to an ADS at level $i + 1$, thus the HADS proof will combine all required ADS proofs (Algorithm 3.2). To simplify this operation, we use another PPT algorithm as a helper method to find the sub-ADSs of a given ADS:

Find(key, value) $\rightarrow$ $(\{(\mathbf{ADS'}, \{(\mathbf{key'}, \mathbf{value'})\})\})$: This algorithm is used (inside the HCertify) to interpret the input data and find the corresponding part for each level, as we traverse the levels. It first finds the ADS at the next level by traversing the current ADS with the provided *key*. Then, it extracts the data inside the *value* as a set of $\{(key', value')\}$ pairs. Finally, it outputs the set of next ADSs and their associated $\{(key', value')\}$ pairs. An example showing this process is given in Sect. 4.1.

Algorithm 3.2. HCertify, run by the server.

Input: the public key pk, the command cmd, the data given as a *(key, value)* pair.
Output: the generated proof

1    $P_{own} = \{\}$; // Proof of the current ADS.
2    $P_{child} = \{\}$; // Proof of all children combined together.
3    $\{(ADS', \{(key', value')\})\} = Find(key, value)$; // Null for the last level.
4   **for** *each element in* $\{(ADS', (key', value')\}$) **do**
5      $\quad P = element.ADS'.HCertify(pk, cmd, element.(key', value'))$; //Ask each child to compute its proof.
6      $\quad P_{child} = P_{child}|P$; // Combine the proofs.
7    $P_{own} = Certify(pk, OP, (key, value))$; // Current ADS proof (not hierarchical).
8   **return** $P_{child}|P_{own}$;

The verification is also a recursive process. The client reconstructs the required parts of the HADS in a bottom-up manner, i.e., she verifies the last level, then uses its digest and the next level proof to verify the above level, and so forth. Finally, when the client reaches the upper-most level and obtains a single digest, she compares it with the local metadata for verification.

4   Outsourced Database Scheme

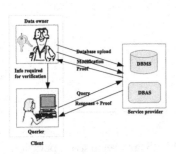

Fig. 3. The ODB model.

Model. The outsourced database (ODB) model, as depicted in Fig. 3, is composed of three parties: the *data owner*, the *querier*, and the *service provider*. The data owner performs required pre-computations, uploads the database, and gives the querier(s) the security information she needs for verification. The data owner then may perform modifications (insertion, deletion, or update) on the outsourced database. The service provider (or simply, the *server*) has the required equipment (software, hardware, and network resources) for storing and maintaining the database in a provable manner. The internal structure of the server is transparent to the outside, i.e., the server may use some levels of replication and distribution to increase the performance and availability. The *querier* (or the *user*) issues a query (either select or modification) to the server, who executes the query, collects the result set, computes the corresponding proof, and sends all back to the querier. The querier then verifies the answer using the security information given by the data owner. It is possible to have multiple queriers or data owners, and data owners can also act as queriers. For simplicity, we will refer to them simply as the *client*. This paper considers only single-client case.

We decouple the real data from the authentication information on the server. The *DBMS* is a regular database management system responsible for storing and updating the data, and executing queries and giving back the answers. The *DBAS* (Database Authentication System) stores the authentication information about the data, and generates the proofs to be sent to the client. Thus, a DBAS can be used together with any DBMS to constitute an ODB. The focus of this work is to construct an efficient and secure DBAS.

Adversarial Model. We assume that the remote server is not fully trusted: he can either act maliciously, or subverted by attackers to do so, or may suffer failures. He may cheat by attacking the integrity of the data (modifying the records) and giving fake responses to the client's queries (executing the query processing algorithm incorrectly, or modifying the query results), or by performing unauthorized modifications on the data, while trying to be undetected.

4.1   Generic ODB Construction

A generic way to construct an ODB is to employ a regular DBMS, together with a DBAS based on an ADS. The HADS can be used to construct the DBAS, solving the problem of duplicate values. If the query has a clause on a non-PK column, say col_i, containing duplicate values, the result set of the query includes all records with the specified value(s) in col_i. The way we can identify these records and compare them with the result set of the other clauses is to relate each record to its corresponding (unique) PK. For each *distinct* value in a non-PK column, we define a *PK set* as:

Definition 1. PK Set. *For each value v_i in a non-PK column, the set of all PK values corresponding to v_i in all records of a table T is called the PK set of v_i, and represented as $PK(v_i)$, i.e., $PK(v_i) = \{k_j \in PK(T) : \exists \, record \, R \in T \, s.t. \, k_j \in R \wedge v_i \in R\}$.*

Note that the PK set includes only the PK values, not the whole records. Any membership scheme can be used for assigning the PK set to a non-PK value, regarding the client and server processing power, and communication requirements of the application under construction. The only difference is the type of corresponding proof that is generated by the server and verified by the client. This brings the flexibility to support multiple membership schemes, and select one based on the state of the system at that time. We will discuss applicable membership schemes in detail, and compare their efficiency in Appendix B.

We use a two-level HADS for implementing an OBD scheme. To store a non-PK column, the distinct values are located in the first level (i.e., each duplicate value will be stored once), and the PK set of each value is located in the second level. The (membership) proof for this scheme consists of two parts: one for proving the existence (or non-existence) of the value in the non-PK column, and one for proving the association of the corresponding PK set with that value.

In our scheme, the client constructs a separate HADS for each searchable column. A one-level HADS (a regular ADS) will be used to store the PK column, similar to the ones presented in the previous work [16,24]. An example ADS for storing a PK column using an authenticated skip list is presented in Fig. 1a. For non-PK columns, a two-level HADS will be used. A sample HADS for storing the column major is illustrated in Fig. 2a. It uses an authenticated skip list at the first level, and a Merkle hash tree at the second level. Each modification on the column leads to an update in both ADSs in the hierarchy.

The client stores security information of each searchable column of each table in a separate HADS, keeps the digests of these HADSs locally as metadata. Later, she checks the authenticity of server's answers against these digests. These values also guarantee the freshness of the answer. If there are s searchable columns in the database, this method requires the client to store s digests. As an alternative design, the client can put the digests of each searchable column in another ADS (the table ADS), and on top of them make another ADS consisting of ADSs for each table in the database (the database ADS). Then, she needs storing only the digest of this new (four-level) HADS as metadata. One may further extend this idea to multiple databases a user owns, and then multiple users in a group, and so forth. By increasing the number of levels of the HADS, it is possible to always make sure the client stores a single digest. This presents a nice trade-off between the client storage and the proof-verification performance. For the sake of simple presentation, we will employ two-level HADS constructions.

Using the authenticated range query for proof generation ensures completeness. To provide correctness, we store along with each record, the hash of that record, $h(record)$. In flat ADSs like the accumulator, the hash values are tied to the elements, while in tree-structured ADSs the hash values are stored at leaves. (The computation of the values of the intermediate nodes, if there exists any, depends on the underlying structure of the ADS in use.) For a PK column, we store $h(record)$, and for non-PK searchable column, we store $h(h(v_i)|h(record)|h(digest\ of\ the\ corresponding\ PK\ set))$, where v_i values are the distinct values of that column. Storing these hashes together with the elements, binds each PK set to the corresponding value in the column, and to the record.

Upon receipt of a result set (and proof), the client verifies it using the information provided in the proof and hashes of received records. If all records are used and the computed digests are equal to the stored ones, then the client accepts the answer.

Therefore, our construction provides the three properties required for a secure ODB scheme: freshness (by storing digests of the HADSs locally as metadata), correctness, and completeness (guaranteed by the HADSs, as discussed). We prove this formally in Appendix A.

Proof Generation. This section provides details on how the DBAS generates proofs. We consider different cases where the query has only one clause, or multiple clauses. For each case we discuss how the proof is generated, and what is included in the proof.

One-dimensional queries: contain one clause. There are two possible cases:

- **The clause is on the PK column:** For example, the query is SELECT * FROM Student WHERE stdID > 105. This case presents a simple range query. The server asks the PK HADS of the Student table to compute and return his proof, and sends it back to the client. The proof includes the *before* and *after* records, and all intermediate nodes' values required for reconstructing the proof sub-list by the client. (Note that we need to employ an ADS which supports efficient range query.) Figure 1b depicts an example, using authenticated skip list as the underlying ADS, where the result set is (106, 107, 108), and the boundary records are 105 and $+\infty$.

- **The clause is on a non-PK column:** A sample query is SELECT * FROM Student WHERE major = 'CE'. The server finds the PK set of the value 'CE' using the HADS storing the *major* column, and adds it to the verification object followed by the proof of membership of the 'CE' itself (in the first level ADS of the *major* column). The client verifies the HADS using the values in the verification object and the answer (the query result set).

Multi-clause queries. For each clause, the server asks the corresponding HADS to give its proof, collects them into the verification object *vo*, and sends the resulting *vo* to the client. Upon receipt, the client verifies all proofs one-by-one, and accepts if all are verified. If the clauses were connected by 'OR', then each proof verifies a subset of the received records, and the answer should be the union of all these verified records. For 'AND' connectors, each proof verifies a superset of records in the result set. To prevent leakage of records not in the result set, the server sends their hashes to enable the client to verify the proofs. Possible scenarios for the two-clause case are:

- **One clause on the PK, the other on a non-PK column:** For example, the query is SELECT * FROM Student WHERE StdID > 105 AND major = 'CE'. Since the order in which the clauses are applied is not important for the proof, we can consider the non-PK clause first, then apply the PK clause on the results of the first step. Therefore, the server first applies the non-PK clause on the first level ADS of the non-PK column's HADS. Then, he applies the PK clause on second level ADSs of the results of the first step. Finally, he adds them both to the *vo*, and sends it to the client.

- **Both clauses on non-PK columns:** A sample query is SELECT * FROM Student WHERE BCity = 'Istanbul' AND major = 'CE'. In this case, the server generates two proofs (one for each clause), each containing the first level ADS proof for the value itself and the corresponding PK set, puts them into the *vo*, and sends the resulting *vo* to the client. If the clauses were connected by 'AND', he also puts the hash of missing records into the *vo*. Missing records in this context are the ones that contain either BCity = 'Istanbul' or major = 'CE' but not both. Note that, we only add hashes of the missing records to the *vo*, but the answer sent by the DBMS does not contain those records and is thus optimal.

Queries with more than two clauses can be handled using a similar logic, depending on whether one of the columns is a PK column or none of them are. Note that in all our proofs, *we do not require any additional records to be sent to the client on top of the result set of the original query.*

An Illustrative Example. To better understand our construction, we provide a simple example. Assume the we use a four-level HADS using the authenticated skip lists to store a database. The first level ADS is the *database ADS* that stores the table names. Each leaf node of this ADS is connected to a *table ADS* at the second level. A table ADS stores the names of a table's searchable columns. Each leaf of a table ADS is connected to a *column ADS* at the third level storing distinct values of that column. Each leaf of the column ADS is linked to a *PK ADS* at fourth level, storing the PK set. This is illustrated in Fig. 2b.

The SQL query SELECT * FROM Student WHERE major in ('CE', 'CS') and BCity = 'Istanbul' is converted into: (Student, {(major, {CE, CS}), (BCity, {Istanbul})}), by the DBAS. With the help of the *Find* algorithm of the HADS that decomposes key-value pairs into the proper parts, the *HCertify* algorithm works as follows: First, it looks for the leaf node at the database ADS storing the Student table. That node contains a link to the table ADS storing list of its columns. The algorithm, then, investigates this Student table ADS with the input {(major, {CE, CS}), (BCity, {Istanbul})}. Now, it should find the leaf nodes storing the values major and BCity. Using the column ADSs for the major and BCity columns (one by one), it goes forward to search for values CE and CS in the ADS of major, and Istanbul in the ADS of BCity. Finally, each column ADS asks all his found PK ADSs (the last level ADSs storing the PK set) to give their proofs. In our example, the major column ADS asks to retrieve the PK sets of CE and CS, and the BCity column ADS asks to retrieve the PK set of Istanbul. The column ADSs then compute their own membership proofs, concatenate them with the PK sets, and return the result to the table (upper level) ADS who performs the same recursive operations. This is repeated until the top level ADS (the database ADS) is reached, resulting in the full proof to be sent to the client. Verification works similarly, in a bottom-up manner, by verifying the PK set proofs first, followed by the column ADS proofs, then table ADS proof, and finally the database ADS proof. If all proofs verify employing all records in the answer, the client accepts the answer as authentic.

Efficient ODB Construction. In Appendix B, we compare the existing ADSs and investigate their eligibility to be used in each level for a two-level construction. It shows that using an authenticated skip list in both levels is the efficient choice. Other alternatives can be chosen regarding the requirements of applications, such as the database being static or dynamic.

5   Performance Analysis

Setup. To evaluate our proposed ODB scheme, we implemented a prototype with the efficient HADS construction which uses a two-level HADS with authenticated skip list at both levels. All experiments were performed on a 2.5 GHz machine with 4 cores (but running on a single core), with 4 GB RAM and Ubuntu 11.10 operating system. The performance numbers are averages of 50 runs.

We use a database containing three tables: $\mathtt{Student}$ and $\mathtt{Course}$ tables, each with 10^5 randomly-generated records, and $\mathtt{S2C}$ table storing the courses taken by students, with 10^6 randomly-generated records. There are two scenarios: each registered student has taken 10 courses in the first scenario, and 100 courses in the second scenario, on average. (Not all students are taking courses since we have 10^6 $\mathtt{S2C}$ records in total.) Each distinct $\mathtt{StdId}$ is used as a foreign key in $\mathtt{S2C}$ 10 times in the first scenario, and 100 times in the second scenario, on average.

We observe the system behavior (proof generation time and proof size) in multiple cases. Since in our scheme proofs are generated using only hashes of values of the column(s) forming the clause (not the whole records), **the proof size is independent of the record size.** Our scheme enhances the efficiency by reducing the computation and proof size, confirmed by experimental results.

One-clause queries. There is only one clause that is on the PK column, or a non-PK column. Since the number of distinct values in the non-PK column is less than that of the PK column, the first level ADS of the non-PK column is smaller than the ADS of the PK column. (We do not count the second level ADSs in the one-clause case, since they are included in whole, without any computation to find and select some). The proof generation time and proof size for a non-PK clause is thus smaller compared to the PK clause, as depicted in Fig. 4a and b. The figures show that the required time and proof size increase very slightly with the result size, for both PK and non-PK columns, if range queries are used.

Two-clause queries. We treat the case with one PK and one non-PK clauses separately from the case with two non-PK clauses. In the first case, we can apply both clauses on the HADS of the non-PK column, by applying the non-PK clause on the first level ADS and the PK clause on the second level ADSs. This is equivalent to applying the non-PK clause first, then applying the PK clause on the results of the first step.

In the second case where both clauses are on non-PK columns, all values of the second level ADSs are included in the result (without further computation), therefore, the dominant factors are the proof generation time and proof size of the first level ADSs. We apply each non-PK clauses on its own HADS and generate two proofs to put in the verification object. Figure 5a and b show the proof generation time and proof size for both cases.

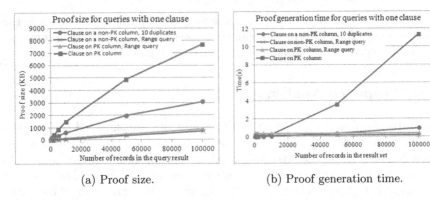

(a) Proof size.   (b) Proof generation time.

Fig. 4. Proof generation time and proof size for queries with one clause.

Comparison to previous work. Several solutions [10,14,17,18] proposed to make the duplicate values unique, so they can be stored in a regular ADS. Following these solutions, the ADSs of non-PK columns will have the same size, and hence, very close operation costs, as the PK column, since they store the same number of records. Comparing the costs in Fig. 4a and b, confirms the advantages of the HADS. For one-clause queries, the proof size is reduced about 10 %, even with range queries, and the proof generation time is dropped about 50 % when HADS is used. Comparing two-clause queries in Fig. 5a and b for the case with one PK and one non-PK clauses, we observe about 25 % reduction in proof size and 40 % decrease in proof generation time, and for the case with two non-PK clauses, we observe about 40 % reduction in proof size and 65 % decrease in proof generation time, when HADS is used.

Multi-clause queries. There are more than two clauses in this case, and the two-clause case is a special case of this one. Again, we can separate this case into two cases depending on whether one of the clauses is on the PK column or none of them are. The server asks each HADS sequentially to give its first-level proof. The total proof generation time and proof size of the server is summation of the corresponding values taken by all HADSs.

Communication overhead. Another important factor is the overhead of our scheme on the communication, i.e., how much does the proof increase the traffic. As the proof size is independent from the record size, for tables with small record size ($<1/2KB$) the overhead is close to the query result size. But, for tables with reasonable record size ($\geq 1/2KB$), the proof size falls down (about 1–20 %) compared to the result size, and gets smaller as the record size increases.

Boolean combination of clauses. Our ODB construction can provably handle selection queries with one or multiple clauses connected by 'OR' or 'AND' connectors. Besides, with reduced use of boundary records, we can easily support clauses formed using the SQL 'IN' operator. This allows us to present proofs for a wide range of database queries.

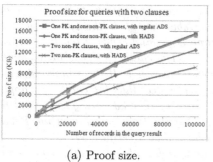

(a) Proof size.

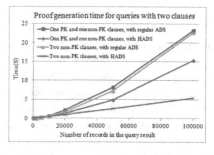

(b) Proof generation time.

Fig. 5. Proof generation time and proof size for queries with two clauses.

Acknowledgements. The authors would like to acknowledge the support of TÜBİTAK, the Scientific and Technological Research Council of Turkey, under project numbers 111E019 and 112E115, as well as European Union COST Action IC1206. We also thank Ertem Esiner, Adilet Kachkeev, and Ozan Okumuşoğlu for their contributions during performance evaluation.

A   ADS Definitions and Security Analysis

Definition 2. *ADS scheme consists of three polynomial-time algorithms [20]:*

KeyGen(1^k) → **(sk, pk):** *is a probabilistic algorithm executed by the client to generate a private and public key pair (sk, pk) given the security parameter k. The client then shares the public key pk with the server.*

Certify(pk, cmd) → **(ans, π):** *is run by the server to respond to a command issued by the client. The public key pk and the command cmd is given as input. If cmd is a query command, it outputs a verification proof π that enables the client to verify the validity of the answer ans. If cmd is a modification command (insertion, update, or deletion), then the ans is null, and π is a consistency proof enabling the client to update her local metadata.*

Verify(sk, pk, cmd, ans, π, st) → **({accept, reject}, st'):** *is run by the client upon receipt of a response to verify it. The public and private keys (pk, sk), the answer ans, the proof π, and the client's current metadata st are given as input. It outputs an accept or reject based on the result of the verification. Moreover, if the command was a modification command and the proof is accepted, then the client updates her metadata accordingly (to st').*

Definition 3. *ADS correctness: For all valid proofs π and answers ans returned by the server in response to a command issued by the client, the verify algorithm accepts with overwhelming probability.*

Definition 4. *The ADS security game: Played between the challenger who acts as the client and the adversary who plays the role of the server.*

Key generation: *The challenger runs KeyGen(1^k) to generate the private and public key pair (sk, pk), and sends the public key pk to the adversary.*

Setup: *The adversary specifies a command cmd, and sends it together with an answer ans and proof π to the challenger. The challenger runs the algorithm Verify, and notifies the adversary about the result. If the command was a modification command, and the proof is accepted, then the challenger applies the changes on her local metadata accordingly. The adversary can repeat this interaction polynomially-many times. Call the latest version of the HADS, constructed using all the commands whose proofs verified, D.*

Challenge: *The adversary specifies a command cmd, an answer ans', and a proof π', and sends them all to the challenger. The adversary wins if the answer ans' is different from the result set of running cmd on D, and cmd, ans', π' are verified as accepted by the challenger.*

Definition 5. *Security of ADS:* *We say that the ADS is secure if no PPT adversary can win the ADS security game with non-negligible probability.*

Definition 6. *An **outsourced database scheme (ODB)** consists of three probabilistic polynomial-time algorithms (OKeyGen, OCertify, OVerify) where:*

OKeyGen(1^k) $\rightarrow$ **(sk, pk):** *is a probabilistic algorithm run by the client to generate a pair of secret and public keys (sk, pk) given the security parameter k. She keeps both keys, and shares only the public key with the server.*

OCertify(pk, cmd) $\rightarrow$ **(ans, π):** *is run by the server to respond to a command cmd issued by the client. It produces an answer ans and a proof π proving the authenticity of the answer. If the command is a modification command, the answer is empty, and the proof proves that the modification is done properly.*

OVerify(pk, sk, cmd, ans, π, st) $\rightarrow$ **({accept, reject}, st'):** *is run by the client upon receipt of the answer ans and proof π, to be verified using the public and private key pair. It outputs an 'accept' or 'reject' notification. If the command was a modification command and the verification result is 'accept', then, the client updates her local metadata (to st'), according to the proof.*

Definition 7. *ODB security game:* *This game is similar to the ADS game (Definition 4), except that proper algorithm names (from ODB scheme) is used.*

Definition 8. *ODB Security:* *We say that an ODB scheme is secure if no PPT adversary can win the ODB security game with non-negligible probability.*

Since the algorithm *OCertify* is used to execute both query and modification commands, the server utilizes it to generate and update the authentication information. It starts with an empty structure, and updates it according to the received modification commands (e.g., the SQL 'Insert' command).

Note that *the ODB security game covers all previously separate guarantees: correctness, completeness, and freshness.* This is simply due to the fact that the game requires that no adversary can return a query answer together with a valid proof such that the returned answer is different from the answer that would have been produced by the actual database. If any one of the freshness, completeness, or correctness guarantees were to be invaded, the adversary would have won the game. Looking ahead, in our proofs, the challenger keeps a local copy of the database, and can detect whether or not the adversary succeeded. If he succeeds, our reduction shows that we break some underlying security assumption.

Theorem 1. *The ADS scheme is secure according to Definition 5.*

Proof. It is proved for different schemes separately by different researchers. Papamanthou et al. [21] proved the security of the authenticated hash tables, Goodrich et al. [7] proved the security of the RSA one-way accumulator [1] based ADS, and Papamanthou and Tamassia [20] proved the security of the ADSs constructed using authenticated skip list or red black tree.

Theorem 2. *Our HADS construction is secure according to Definition 5 (employing HADS algorithm names) if the underlying ADSs are secure.*

Proof. We reduce security of the HADS scheme to the security of the underlying ADSs. If a PPT adversary $\mathcal{A}$ wins the HADS security game with non-negligible probability, we can use it to construct a PPT algorithm $\mathcal{B}$ who breaks the security of at least one of the ADS schemes used, with non-negligible probability. $\mathcal{B}$ acts as the server in the ADS game played with the ADS challenger $\mathcal{C}$, and simultaneously, $\mathcal{B}$ plays the role of the challenger in the HADS game with the adversary $\mathcal{A}$. He receives the public key of an ADS from $\mathcal{C}$, and himself produces $n-1$ pairs of ADS public and private keys. Then, he puts the received key in i^{th} position, and puts the n public keys as a public key of an n-level HADS, and sends it to $\mathcal{A}$. During the setup phase, $\mathcal{B}$ builds a local copy of the HADS for herself. Note that this is invisible to the adversary $\mathcal{A}$, and thus will not affect his behavior. After the setup phase, $\mathcal{A}$ selects a command, generates the answer and proof for the command, and sends them to $\mathcal{B}$. For the adversary to win, the answer must be different from the real answer in at least one location, with its verifying sub-proof π_{i_j}. $\mathcal{B}$ can find it since she maintains a local copy. When $\mathcal{B}$ receives them, she selects the related command, answer and proof parts for the ith position, and forwards them to $\mathcal{C}$. If the guess of i was correct, then $\mathcal{B}$ would succeed. If $\mathcal{A}$ passes the verification with non-negligible probability p, then $\mathcal{B}$ passes the ADS verification with probability greater than or equal to p/n.

Since we employ secure ADSs, p/n must be negligible, which implies that p is negligible, and hence, $\mathcal{A}$ has negligible probability of winning the HADS game. Therefore, if the underlying ADSs are secure, then the HADS scheme is secure.

Theorem 3. *Our ODB scheme is secure according to Definition 8, provided that the underlying HADS scheme is secure.*

Proof. We reduce security of the ODB scheme to the security of underlying HADSs. If a PPT adversary $\mathcal{A}$ wins the ODB security game with non-negligible probability, we can use it to construct a PPT algorithm $\mathcal{B}$ who breaks the security of HADS scheme with non-negligible probability. $\mathcal{B}$ acts as the server in the HADS game played with the HADS challenger $\mathcal{C}$, and simultaneously, $\mathcal{B}$ plays the role of the challenger in the ODB game with the adversary $\mathcal{A}$. He receives the public key of an HADS from $\mathcal{C}$, and relays it to $\mathcal{A}$ (note that all HADSs built for each searchable column will use the same key). During the setup phase, $\mathcal{B}$ builds a local database for herself (which does not change the adversary's view). After the setup phase, $\mathcal{A}$ selects a query, generates the answer and proof for the query, and sends them to $\mathcal{B}$. For the adversary to win, the adversary's answer must be different from the real answer on at least one location, but with a verifying proof. On receipt, $\mathcal{B}$ selects the related command, answer and proof parts for the answer that differs from the real answer (she can find it since she maintains a local copy), and forwards them to $\mathcal{C}$. If $\mathcal{A}$ passes the ODB verification with non-negligible probability p, then $\mathcal{B}$ can also pass the HADS verification (i.e., break HADS security) with non-negligible probability p.

Since we employ a secure HADS, p must be negligible, which implies that the adversary has negligible probability of breaking ODB. Therefore, our ODB scheme is secure (and provides correctness, completeness, and freshness), if the underlying HADS is secure.

B   Efficient ODB Construction

For each level in an HADS, an ADS can be chosen subject to the requirements of that level and the application. Our construction is a two-level HADS, each level having a special role and posing special considerations. We compare the existing ADSs and investigate their eligibility to be used in each level. We consider three classes of ADSs: *logarithmic* (e.g., authenticated skip list [5,6]), *sublinear* (e.g., authenticated hash tables [21]), and *linear* (e.g., one-way accumulator [1]).

First level: This level stores the distinct values of a column, and generates the first part of the proof to be sent to the client. Proof generation is based on the authenticated range queries, which implies that this level should use an ADS who preserves the order of values it stores. One-way accumulator and hash tables does not support this property efficiently, and cannot be used for this level.

Therefore, we choose the authenticated skip list (alternatively, the Merkle hash tree) to be used in the first level. It requires $O(\log(|C_i|))$ and $O(\log(|C_i|) + |t|)$ time/size for the update and query proofs, respectively. There are $|C_i|$ distinct values, on average, in the first level ADS (stored at leaves), therefore, the storage complexity is $2|C_i|$, which is $O(|C_i|)$.

Second level: This level stores the PK set of values in the first level, where the order of PKs is not a matter of importance (although it can be useful for comparing the PK sets of multiple clauses connected with AND). Thus, any ADS can be used with time/space trade-offs discussed below.

Accumulator: For each distinct value in the first level ADS, an accumulated value is computed using all values in its PK set, and is stored together with the value itself. For each PK value, a witness is computed which proves that it belongs to the specified PK set. If we need to select all PK values, it suffices to have only the accumulated value (not the witnesses) to check the integrity. But, if want to select a subset of the PK values, then their witnesses are also required.

For each distinct value in the first level ADS, $N/|C_i|$ PK values and witnesses should be computed and stored, on average, where N is the total number of records in the table. In total, $2|C_i| + |C_i| * N/|C_i| = 2|C_i| + N$ (which is $O(|C_i| + N)$) storage is required (including the $2|C_i|$ space for the first level ADS).

A proof for each value is made up of two parts, one for the first level ADS (e.g., for authenticated skip list, a path from the leaf up to the root, which is $O(\log|C_i|)$), and the other is the accumulated value along with all the values in the PK set, which is $N/|C_i|$ (the accumulated value is already included in the hash value stored at the corresponding leaf of the first level ADS). The client herself can check the validity of the PK set against the accumulated value. Therefore, for a result set of size t, the asymptotic size of the verification object will be $(O(\log|C_i|) + (t|C_i|/N)(1 + N/|C_i|)) \simeq O(\log|C_i| + t)$.

The main problem with the accumulator is the cost of update: with each update, all witnesses should be updated, which is expensive.

Authenticated hash table: This is a sublinear membership scheme with constant query and verification time, making it an interesting scheme for clients with resource-constrained devices. It is a good choice if the data is static. For a leaf node storing v_i, we put the PK set of v_i in an authenticated hash table, and store its root at the leaf node itself.

On average, $N/|C_i|$ PK values linked to each leaf node, therefore, we require $O(|C_i| + (1+\epsilon)N/|C_i| * |C_i|) = O(|C_i| + (1+\epsilon)N)) \approx O(|C_i| + N)$ storage in total (including the $O(|C_i|)$ space for the first level). Here $0 < \epsilon < 1$ is a constant.

The first level ADS proof is the same, but the authenticated hash table requires only constant proof size ϵ [20], reaching $(O(\log|C_i|)+1))$ for one record, and $(O(\log|C_i|) + t)$ for t records in the result set. Moreover, hash operations are much faster than accumulator operations using modular exponentiation.

Authenticated Skip list: This is a membership scheme with logarithmic height and proof size. The way the second-level membership schemes are modified, or the proofs are generated, are the same as for the first-level ADS.

Table 1. A comparison of membership schemes for the second level where the first level is a logarithmic ADS. Proof size and verification time is given for one-dimensional queries. The s, t, t_1, and t_2 denote the number of searchable columns in a table, size of the result set, and number of records in the first and second level ADSs, respectively.

	Accumulator	Authenticated hash table
Storage	$2N + (s-1)(2|C_i| + 2N)$	$2N + (s-1)(2|C_i| + N)$
Proof size	$2\log|C_i| + t + t * N/|C_i|$	$2\log|C_i| + t + t * N/|C_i|$
Verification	$t(\log|C_i| + N/|C_i| + 1)$	$t(\log|C_i| + N/|C_i|)$
Update	$(\log N + (s-1)(\log|C_i| + N/|C_i|))$	$(\log N + (s-1)(\log|C_i| + N/|C_i|))$

	Authenticated skip list	
Storage	$2N + (s-1)(2|C_i| + 2N)$	
Proof size	$2\log|C_i| + t_1 + t_1(2\log|N/C_i| + t_2)$	
Verification	$t_1(\log|C_i| + t_2(\log N/|C_i|))$	
Update	$(\log N + (s-1)(\log|C_i| + \log N/|C_i|)) \approx s\log N$	

Each node requires $\approx 2(N/|C_i|)$ storage to store the PK set, therefore, $2|C_i| + 2|C_i| * N/|C_i| = 2(|C_i| + N) = O(|C_i| + N)$ storage is required to store a column (including the $2|C_i|$ space for the first level ADS). The proof size and time for one value are both $O(\log|C_i| + \log(N/|C_i|)) = O(\log N)$, and for t values are $O(\log|C_i| + t\log(N/|C_i|))$ and $O(\log|C_i| + t)$, respectively.

A comparison of these schemes is given in Table 1, where the first level is a logarithmic ADS and the second levels are shown in the table. The s, t, t_1, and t_2 denote the number of searchable columns in a table, size of the result set, and number of records in the first and second level ADSs, respectively. Note however that unit operations in the accumulator are more costly than those in the others.

References

1. Benaloh, J., de Mare, M.: One-way accumulators: a decentralized alternative to digital signatures. In: Helleseth, T. (ed.) EUROCRYPT 1993. LNCS, vol. 765, pp. 274–285. Springer, Heidelberg (1994)
2. Celko, J.: Joe Celko's Trees and Hierarchies in SQL for Smarties. Morgan Kaufmann, Washington (2004)
3. Devanbu, P., Gertz, M., Martel, C., Stubblebine, S.: Authentic third-party data publication. In: Thuraisingham, B., van de Riet, R., Dittrich, K.R., Tari, Z. (eds.) Data and Application Security. IFIP, vol. 73, pp. 101–112. Springer, Heidelberg (2001)
4. Di Battista, G., Palazzi, B.: Authenticated relational tables and authenticated skip lists. In: Barker, S., Ahn, G.-J. (eds.) Data and Applications Security 2007. LNCS, vol. 4602, pp. 31–46. Springer, Heidelberg (2007)
5. Erway, C., Küpçü, A., Papamanthou, C., Tamassia, R.: Dynamic provable data possession. In: CCS'09, pp. 213–222. ACM (2009)
6. Goodrich, M., Tamassia, R.: Efficient authenticated dictionaries with skip lists and commutative hashing. US Patent App, 10(416,015) (2000)
7. Goodrich, M.T., Tamassia, R., Hasić, J.: An efficient dynamic and distributed cryptographic accumulator. In: Chan, A.H., Gligor, V.D. (eds.) ISC 2002. LNCS, vol. 2433, pp. 372–388. Springer, Heidelberg (2002)
8. Goodrich, M.T., Tamassia, R., Triandopoulos, N.: Super-efficient verification of dynamic outsourced databases. In: Malkin, T. (ed.) CT-RSA 2008. LNCS, vol. 4964, pp. 407–424. Springer, Heidelberg (2008)
9. Li, F., Hadjieleftheriou, M., Kollios, G., Reyzin, L.: Dynamic authenticated index structures for outsourced databases. In: ACM SIGMOD, pp. 121–132 (2006)
10. Li, F., Hadjieleftheriou, M., Kollios, G., Reyzin, L.: Authenticated index structures for aggregation queries. TISSEC 13(4), 32 (2010)
11. Martel, C., Nuckolls, G., Devanbu, P., Gertz, M., Kwong, A., Stubblebine, S.: A general model for authenticated data structures. Algorithmica 39(1), 21–41 (2004)
12. Merkle, R.C.: A certified digital signature. In: Brassard, G. (ed.) CRYPTO 1989. LNCS, vol. 435, pp. 218–238. Springer, Heidelberg (1990)
13. Mykletun, E., Narasimha, M., Tsudik, G.: Providing authentication and integrity in outsourced databases using merkle hash trees. UCI-SCONCE Technical report (2003)
14. Narasimha, M., Tsudik, G.: Authentication of outsourced databases using signature aggregation and chaining. In: Li Lee, M., Tan, K.-L., Wuwongse, V. (eds.) DASFAA 2006. LNCS, vol. 3882, pp. 420–436. Springer, Heidelberg (2006)

15. Nuckolls, G.: Verified query results from hybrid authentication trees. In: Jajodia, S., Wijesekera, D. (eds.) Data and Applications Security 2005. LNCS, vol. 3654, pp. 84–98. Springer, Heidelberg (2005)

16. Palazzi, B.: Outsourced Storage Services: Authentication and Security Visualization. Ph.D. thesis, Roma Tre University (2009)

17. Palazzi, B., Pizzonia, M., Pucacco, S.: Query racing: fast completeness certification of query results. In: Foresti, S., Jajodia, S. (eds.) Data and Applications Security and Privacy XXIV. LNCS, vol. 6166, pp. 177–192. Springer, Heidelberg (2010)

18. Pang, H., Jain, A., Ramamritham, K., Tan, K.: Verifying completeness of relational query results in data publishing. In: ACM SIGMOD, pp. 407–418 (2005)

19. Pang, H., Tan, K.: Authenticating query results in edge computing. In: International Conference on Data Engineering, pp. 560–571. IEEE (2004)

20. Papamanthou, C., Tamassia, R.: Time and space efficient algorithms for two-party authenticated data structures. In: Qing, S., Imai, H., Wang, G. (eds.) ICICS 2007. LNCS, vol. 4861, pp. 1–15. Springer, Heidelberg (2007)

21. Papamanthou, C., Tamassia, R., Triandopoulos, N.: Authenticated hash tables. In: CCS'08, pp. 437–448. ACM (2008)

22. Tamassia, R.: Authenticated data structures. In: Di Battista, G., Zwick, U. (eds.) ESA 2003. LNCS, vol. 2832, pp. 2–5. Springer, Heidelberg (2003)

23. Tamassia, R., Triandopoulos, N.: On the cost of authenticated data structures. Technical report, Center for Geometric Computing, Brown University (2003)

24. Wang, J., Du, X.: Skip list based authenticated data structure in das paradigm. In: GCC'09, pp. 69–75. IEEE (2009)

25. Yang, Y., Papadias, D., Papadopoulos, S., Kalnis, P.: Authenticated join processing in outsourced databases. In: ACM SIGMOD, pp. 5–18. ACM (2009)

Information-Theoretically Secure Entity Authentication in the Multi-user Setting

Shogo Hajime, Yohei Watanabe[✉], and Junji Shikata

Graduate School of Environment and Information Sciences,
Yokohama National University, Yokohama, Japan
{hajime-shogo-vm,watanabe-yohei-xs}@ynu.jp,
shikata@ynu.ac.jp

Abstract. In this paper, we study unilateral entity authentication protocols and mutual entity authentication protocols with information-theoretic security in the multi-user setting. To the best of our knowledge, only one paper by Kurosawa studied an entity authentication protocol with information-theoretic security, and an unilateral entity authentication protocol in the two-user setting was considered in his paper. In this paper, we extend the two-user unilateral entity authentication protocol to the multi-user one. In addition, we formally study an information-theoretically secure mutual entity authentication protocol in the multi-user setting for the first time. Specifically, we formalize a model and security definition, and derive tight lower bounds on size of users' secret-keys, and we show an optimal direct construction.

1 Introduction

1.1 Background

The security of current major cryptographic protocols is based on the assumption of difficulty of computationally hard problems such as the integer factoring problem or the discrete logarithm problem. In this case, it is assumed that an adversary has polynomial-time computational powers. This kind of security is often called *computational security*. On the other hand, *information-theoretic security* (a.k.a. unconditional security) is based on information theory or probability theory, and it is assumed that an adversary has unlimited computational powers in this kind of security. From a viewpoint of the recent development of algorithms and computer technologies, cryptographic protocols with computational security might not maintain sufficient long-term security, since some computationally hard problems are getting more feasible (e.g., recently, the world record of integer factoring is periodically updated) and some new computational mechanism more powerful than the current one may appear (e.g., quantum computers). Therefore, it is interesting and important to further develop the study of cryptographic protocols with information-theoretic security.

The entity authentication schemes are fundamental protocols to confirm the identity of a communication partner, and can be classified into two types: *unilateral* entity authentication schemes and *mutual* entity authentication schemes.

H.-S. Lee and D.-G. Han (Eds.): ICISC 2013, LNCS 8565, pp. 400–417, 2014.
DOI: 10.1007/978-3-319-12160-4_24

In unilateral entity authentication schemes, a user (called a *prover*) can prove himself to another user (called a *verifier*). In mutual entity authentication schemes, the purpose of two users having communication is to prove and verify the identities of themselves each other, and the user who starts the protocol is called an *initiator* and the other one is called a *responder*. Therefore, we consider the roles of the prover and the verifier in unilateral entity authentication protocols, and the roles of the initiator and the responder in mutual entity authentication protocols.

In this paper, we study both unilateral and mutual entity authentication protocols with information-theoretic security. In cryptographic protocols with information-theoretic security, it is usual that each entity of the protocols needs to have some secret key (i.e., secret information). Therefore, for each of unilateral and mutual entity authentication protocols, we consider two types of protocols depending on that the roles are determined or not before secret keys are distributed to users: we call the entity authentication protocols *role-invariable*, if the roles are determined in advance before secret keys are distributed to users; we call the entity authentication protocols *role-variable*, if the roles can be flexibly determined even after secret keys are distributed to users. In this paper, we study role-variable entity authentication protocols: in the unilateral entity authentication protocols, any user can become a prover and a verifier after secret keys are distributed; and in the mutual entity authentication protocols, any user can become an initiator and a responder after secret keys are distributed.

Up to date, there have been many research papers about entity authentication (or identification) protocols with computational security, where there are three kinds of setting: the zero-knowledge setting, the public-key setting, and the symmetric-key setting. In the first line of research (i.e., the zero-knowledge setting), by using the mechanism of zero-knowledge interactive proof systems, several zero-knowledge-based identification schemes are provided. In particular, Fiat and Shamir [5] provided an identification scheme whose security is based on the difficulty of solving the integer factoring problem (other such protocols include Feige-Fiat-Shamir identification protocol [4], Schnorr identification protocol [10], and GQ identification protocol [6]). In the second line of research (i.e., the public-key setting), to realize entity authentication protocols, public-key encryption and/or digital signatures are used as building blocks (e.g., see [3]). In the third line of research (i.e., the symmetric-key setting), symmetric-key encryption and/or MAC are used as primitives for constructing entity authentication protocols. In particular, Bird et al. [2] introduced parallel session attacks and interleaving attacks, and provided the mutual entity authentication protocol which was secure against these attacks. After that, Bellare et al. [1] gave the first formal definition of entity authentication, and provided the first provably secure mutual entity authentication protocol.

To the best of our knowledge, until now, only the paper [7] studies an entity authentication protocol with information-theoretic security, and in [7] an unilateral entity authentication protocol in the two-user setting was considered. In this paper, we extend the two-user unilateral entity authentication protocol to the multi-user one. In addition, we formally study a mutual entity authentication protocol in the multi-user setting for the first time, since merely combining unilateral entity authentication protocols twice does not always imply a mutual one, as demonstrated in [2].

1.2   Our Contribution

In the real-world, authentication protocols including entity authentication are actually used by many users through the Internet. Therefore, it is desirable to realize entity authentication protocols in the multi-user setting. Hence, in this paper we first propose two kinds of authentication protocols in the multi-user setting: unilateral and mutual authentication protocols. In the multi-user setting, we newly need to consider the insider security (i.e., security against an adversary who corrupts several users). Therefore, it should be noted that, technically, our entity authentication protocols in the multi-user setting are not merely the trivial combination of protocols in the two-user setting. Specifically, our contribution is as follows.

- We propose an information-theoretically secure, role-variable, unilateral entity authentication (UEA for short) protocol in the multi-user setting. Specifically, we define a model and formalize security of UEA. We also derive tight lower bounds on size of user's secret-keys and responses required for UEA, and we propose an optimal direct construction of UEA. In addition, we show that our protocol is regarded as an extension of Kurosawa's one [7].
- We propose an information-theoretically secure, role-variable, mutual entity authentication (MEA for short) protocol in the multi-user setting for the first time. Specifically, we define a model and formalize security of MEA. We also derive tight lower bounds on size of user's secret-keys and responses required for MEA, and propose an optimal direct construction of MEA.

Throughout this paper, we use the following notations. For any finite set $\mathcal{Z}$, let $\mathcal{P}(\mathcal{Z}) := \{Z \subset \mathcal{Z}\}$ be the family of all subsets of $\mathcal{Z}$ (i.e. $\mathcal{P}(\mathcal{Z}) = 2^{\mathcal{Z}}$). Also, for any finite set $\mathcal{Z}$ and any non-negative integer z, let $\mathcal{P}(\mathcal{Z}, z) := \{Z \subset \mathcal{Z} \mid |Z| \leq z\}$ be the family of all subsets of $\mathcal{Z}$ whose cardinality is less than or equal to z. And, in order to formally define security, we use the notion of matching conversations in [1].

2   UEA: Unilateral Entity Authentication

2.1   The Model

We show a model of unilateral entity authentication (UEA for short) protocols. For simplicity, we assume that there is a trusted authority (or a trusted initializer) TA whose role is to generate and to distribute secret-keys of entities. We call this model the *trusted initializer model* as in [8]. In UEA, there are $n + 1$ entities, n users $U_1, U_2, \ldots, U_n$ and a trusted authority TA, where n is a positive integer with $n \geq 2$. In this paper, we assume that the identity of each user U_i is also denoted by U_i. In our model, any user U_i can prove "I am U_i" to any user U_j so that U_j is convinced of it by interactive communications with U_i. And, in this scenario, we call the role of U_i a *prover* and the role of U_j a *verifier*.

Informally, UEA is executed as follows. First, TA generates secret-keys of all users and sends them their corresponding keys individually via secure channels. Then, TA deletes them from his own storage. Any user can be either a prover or a verifier. Suppose that U_i is a prover and U_j is a verifier. Our model of UEA requires only two-move communications, namely a verifier U_j sends a transcript, called a *challenge*, to U_i in the first transmission, and U_i next replies a transcript, called a *response*, to U_j in the second transmission. Finally, the verifier U_j verifies whether U_i is a supposed user or not by using information which U_j has.

Formally, we give a definition of UEA as follows.

Definition 1 (UEA). *A unilateral entity authentication (UEA) protocol Π in the multi-user setting involves $n + 1$ entities, TA, $U_1, U_2, \ldots, U_n$ and consists of a four-tuple of algorithms (Gen, Chal, Res, Vrfy) with three finite spaces, $\mathcal{K}$, $\mathcal{X}$ and $\mathcal{Y}$, where Res and Vrfy are deterministic. In addition, Π is executed with four phases as follows.*

- **Notation**
    - *Entities: TA is a trusted authority, U_i ($1 \leq i \leq n$) is a user. Let $\mathcal{U} = \{U_1, U_2, \ldots, U_n\}$ be a set of all users.*
    - *Spaces: $\mathcal{K}_i$ is a finite set of possible U_i's secret-keys. For simplicity, we assume $\mathcal{K} := \mathcal{K}_i$ for every i. $\mathcal{X}$ is a finite set of possible challenges. $\mathcal{Y}$ is a finite set of possible responses.*
    - *Algorithms: Gen is a key generation algorithm which takes a security parameter 1^λ as input and outputs users' secret-keys. Chal is a challenge generation algorithm: it takes two identities as input and outputs a random challenge. Res is a response generation algorithm: it takes a prover's secret-key, a challenge and the verifier's identity as input, and then outputs a response. Vrfy is a verification algorithm: it takes as input a verifier's secret-key, challenges and a response, and the prover's identity, and then it outputs 1 (meaning "accept") or 0 (meaning "reject").*

(1) **Key Generation and Distribution.** *TA generates $K_i \in \mathcal{K}$ for each user U_i ($1 \leq i \leq n$) by using Gen, and he distributes them to corresponding users, respectively, via secure channels.*

(2) **Challenge Generation.** *Suppose that U_i is a prover and U_j is a verifier. Then, U_j generates a challenge $X = Chal(U_j, U_i) \in \mathcal{X}$ by using the identities U_j and U_i, and sends $M_1 := (U_j, U_i, X)$ to U_i.*

(3) **Response Generation.** *Suppose that U_i has received $M_1 = (U_j, U_i, X)$ from U_j. U_i generates a response $Y = Res(U_j, K_i, X) \in \mathcal{Y}$ and sends $M_2 := (U_i, U_j, X, Y)$ to U_j.*

(4) **Response Verification.** *Suppose that U_j has received $M_2 = (U_i, U_j, X', Y')$ from U_i. U_j checks the validity of Y' and X': If $Vrfy(U_i, K_j, X, X', Y') = 1$, then U_j accepts U_i as a prover; If $Vrfy(U_i, K_j, X, X', Y') = 0$, then U_j rejects U_i.*

In the above definition, for a predefined positive integer $t > 0$, we assume that the number of execution of the protocol Π is at most t. Namely, in the protocol Π, we assume that $t \geq \#M_1 \geq \#M_2$. In addition, if $t \geq 2$ and the protocol is executed by U_i and U_j more than once, we assume that challenges sent from U_j to U_i (and from U_i to U_j) are all different (see Remark 1 for details).

2.2 Security Definition

We formalize a security definition for UEA. Let $W \in \mathcal{P}(\mathcal{U}, \omega)$ be a set of dishonest users such that W's cardinality is at most $\omega \leq n - 2$. And, for $W = \{U_{l_1}, U_{l_2}, \ldots, U_{l_j}\} \in \mathcal{P}(\mathcal{U}, \omega)$, $\mathcal{K}_W := \mathcal{K}_{l_1} \times \mathcal{K}_{l_2} \times \cdots \times \mathcal{K}_{l_j}(= \mathcal{K}^j)$ denotes the set of possible secret-keys held by W. If $W = \emptyset$, we understand that there is an adversary outside the group of n users. The goal of W is, for some $U_i, U_j \notin W$, to impersonate U_i and to succeed in that U_j finally accepts it.

Remark 1. If $t \geq 2$ and the protocol is executed by U_i and U_j more than once, we assume that challenges sent from U_j to U_i (and from U_i to U_j) are all different. In the following, we explain why this assumption is necessary and reasonable: First, consider the case that a verifier U_j sends a challenge $X_{j,i}$ to a prover U_i and U_i sends a response $Y_{i,j}$ to U_j. Next, in contrast, let's consider the case that a verifier U_i sends a challenge $X_{i,j}$ to a prover U_j and U_j sends a response $Y_{j,i}$ to U_i. In order to consider role-variable UEA, it is sufficient to realize the mechanism such that $Y_{i,j} = Y_{j,i}$ if $X_{j,i} = X_{i,j}$, and this is a simple approach to realize role-variable UEA. On the other hand, role-invariable UEA is sufficient to realize that mechanism such that $Y_{i,j} \neq Y_{j,i}$ if $X_{j,i} = X_{i,j}$. However, in this mechanism, it is necessary to assume that challenges sent from U_j to U_i (and from U_i to U_j) are all different, since it is trivial to succeed in impersonation attack by sending the same response which the adversary already obtained if the challenges are the same, and such an attack is unavoidable.

And, we give a formal security definition as follows.

Definition 2. *A UEA protocol Π with n users is said to be (ϵ, t, ω, n)-secure, if the success probability of impersonation attacks P satisfies $P \leq \epsilon$, where P is defined as follows. First, for any $W \in \mathcal{P}(\mathcal{U}, \omega)$ and any $U_i, U_j \notin W$, we define a random variable $Z(W, U_i, U_j)$ and an event $\mathsf{Cheat}(W, U_i, U_j)$ by*

1. *$Z(W, U_i, U_j)$: W behaves as the verifier U_j and communicates with U_i in which W sends M_1 of W's arbitrary choice to U_i and then U_i sends M_2 to W. As a result, W obtains a pair of challenges and responses $Z(W, U_i, U_j) := (M_1, M_2)$.*
2. *$\mathsf{Cheat}(W, U_i, U_j)$: W behaves as the prover U_i and communicates with U_j. Finally, U_j accepts it.*

Note that, by the condition $t \geq \#M_1 \geq \#M_2$, W can obtain $Z(W, U_i, U_j)$ at most $t - 1$ times, and we denote

$$Z(W, U_i, U_j)^{t-1} := (Z_1(W, U_i, U_j), Z_2(W, U_i, U_j), \ldots, Z_{t-1}(W, U_i, U_j)),$$

where $Z_k(W, U_i, U_j) = (M_1^{(k)}, M_2^{(k)})$ is the k-th pair of challenges and responses. In this case, we also note that $M_1^{(k)} \neq M_1^{(l)}$ if $k \neq l$ by the assumption (see Remark 1). Then, the success probability of impersonation attacks P is given by

$$P := \max_W \max_{U_i, U_j \notin W} \max_{K_W} \max_{Z(W, U_i, U_j)^{t-1}} \Pr(\textit{Cheat}(W, U_i, U_j) \mid k_W, Z(W, U_i, U_j)^{t-1}),$$

where the maximum is taken over all $W \in \mathcal{P}(\mathcal{U}, \omega)$, $U_i, U_j \notin W$, K_W, and $Z(W, U_i, U_j)^{t-1}$.

Remark 2. In addition to $Z(W, U_i, U_j)$ above, one might consider the following attacking model that W is allowed to perform:

(1-1) For any user $U_j \notin W$, W behaves as a *prover* U_j and communicates with any user $U_i \notin W$.
(1-2) W intercepts the valid communications between any (not corrupted) two users, say U_i and U_j.

However, we do not need to consider the above two attacking models (1-1) and (1-2), since these are not more powerful attacks than $Z(W, U_i, U_j)$: In (1-1), W only obtains M_1 which is independent of U_i's secret-key, For (1-2), communication information by intercepting can be obtained in $Z(W, U_i, U_j)$ where W behaves as a verifier U_j by communicating with U_i.

2.3 Lower Bounds

We show tight lower bounds on size of users' secret-keys and responses. In the following, $Y_i^{(r)}$ denotes a random variable which takes values of the r-th response generated by a prover U_i, and $X_j^{(r)}$ denotes a random variable which takes values of the r-th challenge generated by a verifier U_j.

First, we show a lower bound on the success probability of impersonation attacks. We can prove it in a similar way as Theorem 3.1 in [9], and we omit it here. The proof will be given in the full version of this paper.

Theorem 1. *For any (ϵ, t, ω, n)-secure UEA protocol Π, the success probability of impersonation attacks P satisfies the following inequality. For any adversary $W \in \mathcal{P}(\mathcal{U}, \omega)$, any users $U_i, U_j \notin W$, and any positive integer $r(\leq t)$, it holds that*

$$P \geq 2^{-I(Y_i^{(r)}; K_j \mid K_W, Y_i^{(1)}, \dots, Y_i^{(r-1)}, X_j^{(1)}, \dots, X_j^{(r)})},$$

Next, we show lower bounds on size of users' secret-keys and responses, and its proof is given in Appendix A.

Theorem 2. *For any (ϵ, t, ω, n)-secure UEA protocol Π, we have*

$$\log |\mathcal{K}| \geq t(\omega + 1) \log \epsilon^{-1}, \quad \log |\mathcal{Y}| \geq \log \epsilon^{-1}.$$

As we will see, our construction for the UEA in Sect. 2.4 satisfies all the above lower bounds with equalities. Therefore, the above lower bounds are tight. In addition, we define optimality of constructions for the UEA as follows.

Definition 3. *A construction for an (ϵ, t, ω, n)-secure UEA protocol is optimal, if it satisfies every lower bound in Theorem 2 with equality.*

2.4   Construction

In this section, we provide an optimal construction for (ϵ, t, ω, n)-secure UEA. The detail of the construction is given as follows.

1. *Gen. Gen* picks a λ-bit prime power q, where $q > \max(n, t)$, and constructs the finite field $\mathbb{F}_q$ with q elements. We assume that the identity of each user U_i is encoded as $U_i \in \mathbb{F}_q \backslash \{0\}$. And, *Gen* chooses uniformly at random a polynomial over $\mathbb{F}_q$:

$$f(x, y, z) = \sum_{h=0}^{\omega} \sum_{i=0}^{\omega} \sum_{j=0}^{t-1} a_{h,i,j} x^h y^i z^j,$$

   where $a_{h,i,j} \in \mathbb{F}_q$ such that $a_{h,i,j} = a_{i,h,j}$ for all h, i, j. Then, *Gen* outputs secret-keys $K_i := f(U_i, y, z)$ for U_i $(1 \leq i \leq n)$.
2. *Chal.* It takes identities U_i and U_j as input, and then chooses $X \in \mathbb{F}_q$ uniformly at random and outputs it.
3. *Res.* It takes X from M_1, verifier's identity U_j and a secret-key of the prover U_i, $K_i = f(U_i, y, z)$, as input, and then outputs $Y := f(U_i, y, z)|_{y=U_j, z=X}$.
4. *Vrfy.* It takes (X', Y') from M_2, X, the prover's identity U_i, and a secret-key of the verifier U_j, $K_j = f(U_j, y, z)$, as input, and then, it outputs 1 if and only if $X' = X$ and $Y' = f(U_j, y, z)|_{y=U_i, z=X}$.

The security and optimality of the above construction are stated as follows, and its proof is given in Appendix B.

Theorem 3. *The resulting UEA protocol Π by the above construction is $(1/q, t, \omega, n)$-secure and optimal.*

2.5   Comparison of Our Result with Kurosawa's One

To the best of our knowledge, until now, only the paper [7] studies an entity authentication protocol with information-theoretic security, and it is the role-variable UEA in the two-users setting. Although we have studied the UEA protocol in the multi-users setting, we can compare our UEA with Kurosawa's one in [7] by setting $n = 2$ in our model. As a result, we can see that our protocol UEA is regarded as an extension of Kurosawa's one. For the detailed discussion about similarity and difference between ours and Kurosawa's one, see Appendix C.

3   MEA: Mutual Entity Authentication

3.1   The Model

We show a model of mutual entity authentication (MEA for short) protocols. As in Definition 1 for UEA, in our model of MEA there are $n + 1$ entities, n users $U_1, U_2, \ldots, U_n$ and a trusted authority TA, where $n \geq 2$.

The purpose of MEA is that two users *mutually* prove their identities each other by their communications. Therefore, each user takes the roles of both a prover and a verifier. For any two users who authenticate each other, we call a user who starts communications an *initiator* and the other a *responder* in our model.

Informally, MEA is executed as follows. First, an initiator sends a responder some information (called the first challenge) in the first transmission. Next, the responder sends a response to the first challenge (called the first response) back and some information (called the second challenge) to the initiator in the second transmission. After that, the initiator checks the validity of the first response, and if it is accepted, then he sends a response to the second challenge (called the second response) back to the responder in the final transmission. Finally, the responder checks the validity of the second response.

Formally, we give a definition of MEA as follows.

Definition 4 (MEA). *A mutual entity authentication (MEA) protocol Θ in the multi-user setting involves $n + 1$ entities, TA, $U_1, U_2, \ldots, U_n$ and consists of a seven-tuple of algorithms (Gen, $Chal_1$, $Chal_2$, Res_1, Res_2, $Vrfy_1$, $Vrfy_2$) with three finite spaces, $\mathcal{K}$, $\mathcal{X}$, $\mathcal{Y}$ where Res_1, Res_2, $Vrfy_1$, and $Vrfy_2$ are deterministic. In addition, Θ is executed with five phases as follows.*

- Notation
- *Entities*: TA and $U_i (1 \leq i \leq n)$ are the same as those in Definition 1.
- *Spaces*: $\mathcal{K}$, $\mathcal{X}$, and $\mathcal{Y}$ are the same as those in Definition 1.
- *Algorithms*: Gen is a key generation algorithm which takes a security parameter 1^λ as input and outputs each user's secret-keys. $Chal_1$ and $Chal_2$ are probabilistic algorithms for generating challenges: each of them takes two identities as input and outputs a random challenge. Res_1 and Res_2 are deterministic algorithms for generating responses: Res_1 (resp., Res_2) takes a user's secret-key, the first (resp., second) challenge, and another's identity as input, and then outputs the first (resp., second) response. $Vrfy_1$ (resp., $Vrfy_2$) is a verification algorithm: $Vrfy_1$ (resp., $Vrfy_2$) takes a user's secret-key, a pair of the first challenges and responses (resp., the second challenges and responses), and another's identity as input, and then it outputs 1 (meaning "accept") or 0 (meaning "reject").

(1) **Key Generation and Distribution.** TA generates $K_i \in \mathcal{K}$ for each user U_i $(1 \leq i \leq n)$ by using Gen, and he distributes them to corresponding users via secure channels, respectively.

(2) **Generation for the 1st Challenge.** Suppose that U_j is an initiator and U_i is a responder. Then, U_j generates the first challenge $X_1 = Chal_1(U_j, U_i) \in \mathcal{X}$ by using the identities U_j and U_i, and sends $M_1 := (U_j, U_i, X_1)$ to U_i.

(3) **Generation for the 1st Response and 2nd Challenge.** Suppose that U_i has received $M_1 := (U_j, U_i, X_1)$ from U_j. U_i generates the first response $Y_1 = Res_1(U_j, K_i, X_1) \in \mathcal{Y}$ and the second challenge $X_2 = Chal_2(U_i, U_j) \in \mathcal{X}$. Then, U_i sends $M_2 := (U_i, U_j, X_1, Y_1, X_2)$ to U_j.

(4) **Verification for the 1st Response and Generation for the 2nd Response.** Suppose that U_j has received $M_2 = (U_i, U_j, X_1', Y_1', X_2)$ from U_i. U_j checks the validity of Y_1' and X_1': if $Vrfy_1(U_i, K_j, X_1', Y_1', X_1) = 0$, U_j rejects U_i and aborts the protocol; if $Vrfy_1(U_i, K_j, X_1', Y_1', X_1) = 1$, U_j accepts U_i as the supposed responder, then generates the second response $Y_2 = Res_2(U_i, K_j, X_2) \in \mathcal{Y}$, and then sends $M_3 := (U_j, U_i, X_2, Y_2)$ to U_i.

(5) **Verification for 2nd Response.** Suppose that U_i has received $M_3 = (U_j, U_i, X_2', Y_2')$ from U_j. U_i checks the validity of Y_2' and X_2' as follows. If $Vrfy_2(U_j, K_i, X_2', Y_2', X_2) = 1$, U_i accepts U_j as the supposed initiator. If $Vrfy_2(U_j, K_i, X_2', Y_2', X_2) = 0$, U_i rejects U_j.

In the above definition, for a predefined positive integer $t > 0$, we assume that the number of execution of the protocol Θ is at most t. Namely, in the protocol Θ, we assume that $t \geq \#M_1 \geq \#M_2 \geq \#M_3$. In addition, if $t \geq 2$ and the protocol is executed by U_j and U_i more than once, we assume that: the first challenges sent from U_j to U_i (and from U_i to U_j) are all different; and the second challenges sent from U_i to U_j (and from U_j to U_i) are all different. For details, see Remark 3.

3.2   Security Definition

We formalize a security definition for MEA. We consider the following reasonable attacking scenario. When W ($\in \mathcal{P}(\mathcal{U}, \omega)$) wants to impersonate U_i, W tries to get some information which is related to U_i's secret-key. Specifically, we can consider two situations: first, W behaves as the initiator U_j and sends M_1 of W's arbitrary choice to U_i, and then, W gets M_2 corresponding M_1 from U_i and aborts the protocol; secondly, W intercepts the communication between the initiator U_i and the responder U_j, and then W gets transmissions between them, (M_1, M_2, M_3). Note that we do not consider the case that W intercepts the communication between the initiator U_j and the responder U_i (see Remarks 4 and 5) Finally, by using the information which W has obtained, W impersonates U_i and communicates with U_j hoping that U_j would accept W as U_i.

Remark 3. Suppose that an initiator U_j sends the first challenge $X_{j,i,1}$ to a responder U_i and U_i sends the first response $Y_{i,j,1}$ to U_j. Next, suppose that the responder U_i sends the second challenge $X_{i,j,2}$ to the initiator U_j and U_j sends the second response $Y_{i,j,2}$ to U_i. In order to simply realize role-variable MEA, it is sufficient to realize the mechanism such that (i): $Y_{i,j,1} = Y_{j,i,1}$ if $X_{j,i,1} = X_{i,j,1}$; and (ii) $Y_{i,j,2} = Y_{j,i,2}$ if $X_{j,i,2} = X_{i,j,2}$. As we explained in Remark 1, this mechanism is also a simple approach to realize role-variable MEA, and it is reasonable by the same reason in Remark 1.

Based on the above consideration, our formal security definition is stated as follows.

Definition 5. *An MEA protocol Θ with n users is said to be (ϵ, t, ω, n)-secure, if it holds that*

$$\max(\Pr(\textit{Cheat}_1), \Pr(\textit{Cheat}_2)) \leq \epsilon,$$

where $\Pr(\textit{Cheat}_1)$ and $\Pr(\textit{Cheat}_2)$ are defined as follows.

Information gathering phase: *For any $W \in \mathcal{P}(\mathcal{U}, \omega)$ and any $U_i, U_j \notin W$, we define random variables $Z^{Ses}(W, U_i, U_j)$ and $Z^{Int}(W, U_i, U_j)$ by*

1. $Z^{Ses}(W, U_i, U_j)$: *W behaves as the initiator U_j and communicates with the responder U_i; W sends M_1 of W's arbitrary choice to U_i, and then U_i sends M_2 to W; and W aborts the protocol. As a result, W obtains information $Z^{Ses}(W, U_i, U_j) := (M_1, M_2)$.*

2. $Z^{Int}(W, U_i, U_j)$: *W intercepts transmissions between the initiator U_i and the responder U_j; U_i sends M_1 to U_j, then U_j sends M_2 to U_i, and then U_i sends M_3 to U_j. As a result, W obtains information $Z^{Int}(W, U_i, U_j) := (M_1, M_2, M_3)$.*

Impersonation phase: *For any $W \in \mathcal{P}(\mathcal{U}, \omega)$ and any $U_i, U_j \notin W$, we define two events $\textit{Cheat}_1(W, U_i, U_j)$ and $\textit{Cheat}_2(W, U_i, U_j)$ by*

3. $\textit{Cheat}_1(W, U_i, U_j)$: *$W$ behaves as the responder U_i and communicates with the initiator U_j. Then, U_j accepts the first response.*

4. $\textit{Cheat}_2(W, U_i, U_j)$: *$W$ behaves as the initiator U_i and communicates with the responder U_j. Finally, U_j accepts the second response.*

Note that, by the condition $t \geq \#M_1 \geq \#M_2 \geq \#M_3$, W can obtain $Z^{Ses}(W, U_i, U_j)$ t_1 times and $Z^{Int}(W, U_i, U_j)$ t_2 times such that $t_1 + t_2 = t - 1$, and we denote

$$Z^{Ses}(W, U_i, U_j)^{t_1} := (Z_1^{Ses}(W, U_i, U_j), Z_2^{Ses}(W, U_i, U_j), \ldots, Z_{t_1}^{Ses}(W, U_i, U_j)),$$

$$Z^{Int}(W, U_i, U_j)^{t_2} := (Z_1^{Int}(W, U_i, U_j), Z_2^{Int}(W, U_i, U_j), \ldots, Z_{t_2}^{Int}(W, U_i, U_j)),$$

where $Z_k^{Ses}(W, U_i, U_j) = (M_1^{(k)}, M_2^{(k)})$ is the k-th random variable $Z^{Ses}(W, U_i, U_j)$, $Z_k^{Int}(W, U_i, U_j) = (M_1^{(k)}, M_2^{(k)}, M_3^{(k)})$ is the k-th random variable $Z^{Int}(W, U_i, U_j)$. In these cases, we also note that $M_1^{(k)} \neq M_1^{(l)}$ if $k \neq l$ by the assumption. Then, $\Pr(\textit{Cheat}_1)$ and $\Pr(\textit{Cheat}_2)$ are given as follows.

(i) Cheat against the initiator U_j. $\Pr(\textit{Cheat}_1)$ is defined by

$$\Pr(\textit{Cheat}_1) := \max_W \max_{U_i, U_j \notin W} \max_{k_W} \max_{Z^{Ses}(W,U_i,U_j)^{t-1}}$$
$$\Pr(\textit{Cheat}_1(W, U_i, U_j) \mid k_W, Z^{Ses}(W, U_i, U_j)^{t-1}),$$

where the maximum is taken over all possible $W \in \mathcal{P}(\mathcal{U}, \omega)$, $U_i, U_j \notin W$, k_W, and $Z^{Ses}(W, U_i, U_j)^{t-1}$ (see Remark 4 for details).

(ii) Cheat against the responder U_j. $\Pr(\text{Cheat}_2)$ is defined by

$$\Pr(\text{Cheat}_2) := \max_{W} \max_{U_i, U_j \notin W} \max_{k_W} \max_{Z^{Int}(W, U_i, U_j)^{t-1}}$$

$$\Pr(\text{Cheat}_2(W, U_i, U_j) \mid k_W, Z^{Int}(W, U_i, U_j)^{t-1}),$$

where the maximum is taken over all $W \in \mathcal{P}(\mathcal{U}, \omega)$, $U_i, U_j \notin W$, k_W, and $Z^{Int}(W, U_i, U_j)^{t-1}$ (see Remark 5 for details).

Remark 4. In *Cheat against the initiator U_j*, we do not have to consider the case that W intercepts the communication between the initiator U_j and the responder U_i by the following reason: the information obtained by performing $Z^{Int}(W, U_i, U_j)$ is not more than the information obtained by performing $Z^{Ses}(W, U_i, U_j)$ in which W can arbitrarily choose challenges.

Remark 5. In *Cheat against the responder U_j*, we do not need to consider the case that W behaves the responder U_j and performs $Z^{Ses}(W, U_i, U_j)$, since in this case W only obtains M_1 which is independent of U_i's secret-key unless the initiator U_i accepts the first response generated by W (i.e., unless W succeeds in the impersonation attack against the initiator U_i).

3.3 Lower Bounds

We show tight lower bounds on size of user's secret-keys and responses. In the following, $Y_{i,\alpha}^{(r)}$ means: a random variable which takes values of the r-th first (resp., second) response generated by U_i, if $\alpha = 1$ (resp., $\alpha = 2$). And, $X_{j,\alpha}^{(r)}$ means: a random variable which takes values of the r-th first (resp., second) challenge generated by U_j, if $\alpha = 1$ (resp., $\alpha = 2$). In addition, for a positive integer r and $\alpha \in \{1, 2\}$, we define $X_{j,\alpha}^{[r]} := (X_{j,\alpha}^{(1)}, X_{j,\alpha}^{(2)}, \ldots, X_{j,\alpha}^{(r)})$ and $Y_{i,\alpha}^{[r]} := (Y_{i,\alpha}^{(1)}, Y_{i,\alpha}^{(2)}, \ldots, Y_{i,\alpha}^{(r)})$.

First, we show lower bounds on the success probabilities of impersonation attacks, and the proof is given in a similar way as in Theorem 1.

Theorem 4. *For any (ϵ, t, ω, n)-secure MEA protocol Θ, the success probabilities of impersonation attacks $\Pr(\text{Cheat}_1)$ and $\Pr(\text{Cheat}_2)$ satisfy the following inequalities. For any adversary $W \in \mathcal{P}(\mathcal{U}, \omega)$, any users $U_i, U_j \notin W$, and any positive integer $r (\leq t)$, it holds that*

$$\Pr(\text{Cheat}_1) \geq 2^{-I(Y_{i,1}^{(r)}; K_j \mid K_W, \, Y_{i,1}^{[r-1]}, \, X_{j,1}^{[r]})},$$

$$\Pr(\text{Cheat}_2) \geq 2^{-I(Y_{i,2}^{(r)}; K_j \mid K_W, \, Y_{j,1}^{[r]}, \, X_{i,1}^{[r]}, \, Y_{i,2}^{[r-1]}, \, X_{j,2}^{[r]})}.$$

Next, we show lower bounds on size of secret-keys and responses, and its proof is given in Appendix D.

Theorem 5. *For any (ϵ, t, ω, n)-secure MEA protocol Θ, we have*

$$\log |\mathcal{K}| \geq 2t(\omega + 1) \log \epsilon^{-1}, \quad \log |\mathcal{Y}| \geq \log \epsilon^{-1}.$$

As we will see, our construction for MEA in Sect. 3.4 satisfies all the lower bounds in Theorem 5 with equalities. Therefore, the lower bounds in Theorem 5 are tight. In addition, we define optimality of constructions for MEA as follows.

Definition 6. *A construction for an (ϵ, t, ω, n)-secure MEA protocol is optimal, if it satisfies every lower bound in Theorem 5 with equality.*

3.4 Construction

In this section, we propose an optimal construction for an (ϵ, t, ω, n)-secure MEA protocol. The detail of the construction is given as follows.

1. *Gen.* It picks a λ-bit prime power q, where $q > \max(n, t)$, and constructs the finite field $\mathbb{F}_q$ with q elements. We assume that the identity of each user U_i is encoded as $U_i \in \mathbb{F}_q \backslash \{0\}$. And, *Gen* chooses uniformly at random two polynomials over $\mathbb{F}_q$:

$$f(x, y, z) = \sum_{h=0}^{\omega} \sum_{i=0}^{\omega} \sum_{j=0}^{t-1} a_{h,i,j} x^h y^i z^j, \quad g(x, y, z) = \sum_{h=0}^{\omega} \sum_{i=0}^{\omega} \sum_{j=0}^{t-1} b_{h,i,j} x^h y^i z^j,$$

where $a_{h,i,j}, b_{h,i,j} \in \mathbb{F}_q$ such that $a_{h,i,j} = a_{i,h,j}$ and $b_{h,i,j} = b_{i,h,j}$ for all h, i, j. *Gen* outputs secret-keys $K_i := (f(U_i, y, z), g(U_i, y, z))$ for $U_i (1 \leq i \leq n)$.
2. *Chal$_1$.* It chooses $X_1 \in \mathbb{F}_q$ uniformly at random and outputs it.
3. *Res$_1$.* It takes X_1 from M_1, the initiator's identity U_j, and a secret-key of the responder U_i, $K_i := (f(U_i, y, z), g(U_i, y, z))$, as input, and then outputs $Y_1 = f(U_i, y, z)|_{y=U_j, z=X_1}$.
4. *Chal$_2$.* It chooses $X_2 \in \mathbb{F}_q$ uniformly at random and outputs it.
5. *Vrfy$_1$.* It takes (X_1', Y_1') from M_2, X_1, the responder's identity U_i, and a secret-key of the initiator U_j, $K_j := (f(U_j, y, z), g(U_j, y, z))$, as input, and then, it outputs 1 if and only if $X_1' = X_1$ and $Y_1' = f(U_j, y, z)|_{y=U_i, z=X_1}$.
6. *Res$_2$.* It takes X_2 from M_2, the responder's identity U_i, and a secret-key of the initiator U_j, $K_j := (f(U_j, y, z), g(U_j, y, z))$, as input, and then outputs $Y_2 = g(U_j, y, z)|_{y=U_i, z=X_2}$.
7. *Vrfy$_2$.* It takes (X_2', Y_2') from M_3, X_2, the initiator's identity U_j, and a secret-key of the responder U_i, $K_i := (f(U_i, y, z), g(U_i, y, z))$, as input, and then, it outputs 1 if and only if $X_2' = X_2$ and $Y_2' = g(U_i, y, z)|_{y=U_j, z=X_2}$.

The security and optimality of the above construction are stated as follows, and its proof is given in Appendix E.

Theorem 6. *The resulting MEA protocol Θ by the above construction is $(1/q, t, \omega, n)$-secure and optimal.*

Acknowledgements. We would like to thank anonymous reviewers for their valuable comments.

A   Proof of Theorem 2

First, we show the second inequality. By Theorem 1, we have $H(Y_i^{(r)}) \geq \log \epsilon^{-1}$ for any $i \in \{1, 2, \dots, n\}$ and $r \in \{1, 2, \dots, t\}$. Thus, it follows that $\log |\mathcal{Y}| \geq \log \epsilon^{-1}$.

Next, we show the first inequality. Without loss of generality, we suppose that $V := \{U_1, \dots, U_{\omega+1}\}$ and $U_i, U_j \notin V$. Then, we obtain

$$
\begin{aligned}
H(K_j) \geq & I(K_1, \dots, K_{\omega+1}; K_j \mid X_j^{(1)}, \dots, X_j^{(t)}) \\
= & H(K_1, \dots, K_{\omega+1} \mid X_j^{(1)}, \dots, X_j^{(t)}) \\
& - H(K_1, \dots, K_{\omega+1} | K_j, X_j^{(1)}, \dots, X_j^{(t)}).
\end{aligned} \tag{1}
$$

Now, we have the following inequalities.

$$
\begin{aligned}
& H(K_1, \dots, K_{\omega+1} | X_j^{(1)}, \dots, X_j^{(t)}) \\
= & \sum_{s=1}^{\omega+1} H(K_s | K_1, \dots, K_{s-1}, X_j^{(1)}, \dots, X_j^{(t)}) \\
= & \sum_{s=1}^{\omega+1} \{ I(Y_s^{(1)}, \dots, Y_s^{(t)}; K_s | K_1, \dots, K_{s-1}, X_j^{(1)}, \dots, X_j^{(t)}) \\
& \quad + H(K_s | Y_s^{(1)}, \dots, Y_s^{(t)}, K_1, \dots, K_{s-1}, X_j^{(1)}, \dots, X_j^{(t)}) \} \\
= & \sum_{s=1}^{\omega+1} \{ H(Y_s^{(1)}, \dots, Y_s^{(t)} | K_1, \dots, K_{s-1}, X_j^{(1)}, \dots, X_j^{(t)}) \\
& \quad - H(Y_s^{(1)}, \dots, Y_s^{(t)} | K_1, \dots, K_s, X_j^{(1)}, \dots, X_j^{(t)}) \\
& \quad + H(K_s | Y_s^{(1)}, \dots, Y_s^{(t)}, K_1, \dots, K_{s-1}, K_j, X_j^{(1)}, \dots, X_j^{(t)}) \} \\
= & \sum_{s=1}^{\omega+1} \{ H(Y_s^{(1)}, \dots, Y_s^{(t)} | K_1, \dots, K_{s-1}, X_j^{(1)}, \dots, X_j^{(t)}) \\
& \quad + H(K_s | Y_s^{(1)}, \dots, Y_s^{(t)}, K_1, \dots, K_{s-1}, K_j, X_j^{(1)}, \dots, X_j^{(t)}) \} \\
= & \sum_{r=1}^{t} \sum_{s=1}^{\omega+1} H(Y_s^{(r)} | K_1, \dots, K_{s-1}, X_j^{(1)}, \dots, X_j^{(t)}, Y_s^{(1)}, \dots, Y_s^{(r-1)}) \\
& \quad + \sum_{s=1}^{\omega+1} H(K_s | Y_s^{(1)}, \dots, Y_s^{(t)}, K_1, \dots, K_{s-1}, K_j, X_j^{(1)}, \dots, X_j^{(t)}). \tag{2}
\end{aligned}
$$

On the other hand, we get

$$
\begin{aligned}
& H(K_1, \dots, K_{\omega+1} | K_j, X_j^{(1)}, \dots, X_j^{(t)}) \\
= & \sum_{s=1}^{\omega+1} H(K_s | K_j, K_1, \dots, K_{s-1}, X_j^{(1)}, \dots, X_j^{(t)})
\end{aligned}
$$

$$= \sum_{s=1}^{\omega+1} \{ I(Y_s^{(1)}, \ldots, Y_s^{(t)}; K_s | K_1, \ldots, K_{s-1}, K_j, X_j^{(1)}, \ldots, X_j^{(t)})$$

$$+ H(K_s | Y_s^{(1)}, \ldots, Y_s^{(t)}, K_1, \ldots, K_{s-1}, K_j, X_j^{(1)}, \ldots, X_j^{(t)}) \}$$

$$= \sum_{s=1}^{\omega+1} \{ H(Y_s^{(1)}, \ldots, Y_s^{(t)} | K_1, \ldots, K_{s-1}, K_j, X_j^{(1)}, \ldots, X_j^{(t)})$$

$$- H(Y_s^{(1)}, \ldots, Y_s^{(t)} | K_1, \ldots, K_s, K_j, X_j^{(1)}, \ldots, X_j^{(t)})$$

$$+ H(K_s | Y_s^{(1)}, \ldots, Y_s^{(t)}, K_1, \ldots, K_{s-1}, K_j, X_j^{(1)}, \ldots, X_j^{(t)}) \}$$

$$= \sum_{s=1}^{\omega+1} \{ H(Y_s^{(1)}, \ldots, Y_s^{(t)} | K_1, \ldots, K_{s-1}, K_j, X_j^{(1)}, \ldots, X_j^{(t)})$$

$$+ H(K_s | Y_s^{(1)}, \ldots, Y_s^{(t)}, K_1, \ldots, K_{s-1}, K_j, X_j^{(1)}, \ldots, X_j^{(t)}) \}$$

$$= \sum_{r=1}^{t} \sum_{s=1}^{\omega+1} H(Y_s^{(r)} | K_1, \ldots, K_{s-1}, K_j, X_j^{(1)}, \ldots, X_j^{(t)}, Y_s^{(1)}, \ldots, Y_s^{(r-1)})$$

$$+ \sum_{s=1}^{\omega+1} H(K_s | Y_s^{(1)}, \ldots, Y_s^{(t)}, K_1, \ldots, K_{s-1}, K_j, X_j^{(1)}, \ldots, X_j^{(t)}). \tag{3}$$

Then, from (1), (2) and (3), we have

$$H(K_j) = H(K_1, \ldots, K_{\omega+1} \mid X_j^{(1)}, \ldots, X_j^{(t)}) - H(K_1, \ldots, K_{\omega+1} | K_j, X_j^{(1)}, \ldots, X_j^{(t)})$$

$$= \sum_{r=1}^{t} \sum_{s=1}^{\omega+1} H(Y_s^{(r)} | K_1, \ldots, K_{s-1}, X_j^{(1)}, \ldots, X_j^{(t)}, Y_s^{(1)}, \ldots, Y_s^{(r-1)})$$

$$+ \sum_{s=1}^{\omega+1} H(K_s | Y_s^{(1)}, \ldots, Y_s^{(t)}, K_1, \ldots, K_{s-1}, K_j, X_j^{(1)}, \ldots, X_j^{(t)})$$

$$- \sum_{r=1}^{t} \sum_{s=1}^{\omega+1} H(Y_s^{(r)} | K_1, \ldots, K_{s-1}, K_j, X_j^{(1)}, \ldots, X_j^{(t)}, Y_s^{(1)}, \ldots, Y_s^{(r-1)})$$

$$- \sum_{s=1}^{\omega+1} H(K_s | Y_s^{(1)}, \ldots, Y_s^{(t)}, K_1, \ldots, K_{s-1}, K_j, X_j^{(1)}, \ldots, X_j^{(t)})$$

$$= \sum_{r=1}^{t} \sum_{s=1}^{\omega+1} I(Y_s^{(r)}; K_j | K_1, \ldots, K_{s-1}, X_j^{(1)}, \ldots, X_j^{(t)}, Y_s^{(1)}, \ldots, Y_s^{(r-1)})$$

$$\geq t(\omega + 1) \log \epsilon^{-1},$$

where the last inequality follows from Theorem 1. $\qquad\square$

B   Proof of Theorem 3

For simplicity, we describe the outline of the proof of $P \leq 1/q$. The full proof will appear in the full version of this paper. Without loss of generality, we suppose that $W = \{U_1, \ldots, U_\omega\}$ and $U_i, U_j \notin W$. To succeed in the impersonation attack such that U_i is a prover and U_j is a verifier, the adversary W will generate a fraudulent response $Y \in \mathbb{F}_q$ for a given challenge X under the following conditions: the adversary has ω secret-keys, and at most $t - 1$ pairs of challenges and responses $Z(W, U_i, U_j)^{t-1}$. However, the degrees of $f(x, y, z)$ with respect to variables x, y, and z is at most ω, ω, and $t - 1$, respectively, the adversary cannot guess at least one coefficient of $f(x, y, z)$ with probability larger than $1/q$. Therefore, W cannot guess the response which U_j will accept with probability more than $1/q$. Hence, we have $P \leq 1/q$.

Finally, it is straightforward to see that the construction satisfies all the lower bounds in Theorem 2 with equalities.   □

C   Comparison to Previous Results

We compare our UEA in the two-users setting (i.e., the special case of $n = 2$) with Kurosawa's one in [7] in details, and we show that our protocol is regarded as an extension of Kurosawa's one. In the following discussion, let $n = 2, \omega = 0$ and $t = N + 1$ in our model. Then, we can consider similarity and difference between ours and Kurosawa's one as follows.

Similarity

(1) Models: The two models are essentially the same except for the differences (3) and (4) below.
(2) Constructions: Our construction and Kurosawa's one are the same.

Difference

(3) Secret-keys in the models: Two users' secret-keys in our model may be different (i.e., asymmetric), while in [7] they are the same (i.e., symmetric). Thus, our model is more general than the one in [7].
(4) The way of counting M_1 and M_2 in the protocols: The following difference exists in adversarial models. The adversary is allowed to attack only once after performing $Z(W, U_i, U_j)$ $t - 1$ times in our security definition, whereas the adversary is allowed to attack t times after performing $Z(W, U_i, U_j)$ $t - 1$ times in the security definition in [7].

   In [7], the maximum number of protocol execution is defined by the number up to which *each* user can execute, and each user needs to count the number of having generated M_1 and M_2. On the other hand, in our model, the maximum number of protocol execution is defined by the number up to which *all* users can execute, and it is necessary that it counts the total number of having generated M_1 and M_2 in the protocol.
(5) Security definitions: When U_i wants to prove his identification to U_j more than once, the possibility that challenges sent from U_j to U_i are the same is considered and evaluated in [7]. On the other hand, we have assumed that challenges sent from U_j to U_i are all different (see also Remark 1), since we would like to consider the worst case (i.e., the adversary will take the best strategy).

Moreover, we have formalized the success probability of *Cheat* when the adversary obtains best information to succeed in the attack by performing $Z(W, U_i, U_j) \, t-1$ times. On the other hand, in [7] the case is not considered, namely, by gathering $t-1$ responses for randomly chosen $t-1$ challenges, the adversary randomly repeats the impersonation attack t times, and the success probability is defined by that at least one of the attacks is successful. Therefore, from the above aspects, our security definition is stronger than the one in [7].

(6) Lower bounds. Since our security definition is different from the one in [7], it is natural that our lower bound on the success probability of attacks is different from the one in [7]. Technically, our lower bound on secret-keys has been derived from that of the success probability of attacks, while in [7] his lower bound was derived from the number of responses, and these two proof techniques are different. However, the construction of ours and his (note that constructions are the same) meets both lower bounds with equalities.

From the above discussion, we can consider that our protocol is an extension of Kurosawa's one [7] for the multi-user setting.

D Proof of Theorem 5

First, we prove the second inequality. From Theorem 4, we have $H(Y_{i,\alpha}^{(t)}) \geq \log \epsilon^{-1}$. Thus, it follows that $\log |\mathcal{Y}| \geq \log \epsilon^{-1}$.

Next, we show the first inequality. Without loss of generality, we suppose that $V := \{U_1, \ldots, U_{\omega+1}\}$ and $U_i, U_j \notin V$. Let $K_{[s]} = (K_1 \ldots K_s)$, $X_{j,1}^{[t]} = (X_{j,1}^{(1)}, \ldots, X_{j,1}^{(t)})$, and $Y_{i,1}^{[t]} = (Y_{i,1}^{(1)}, \ldots, Y_{i,1}^{(t)})$.

$$H(K_j)$$

$$\geq I(K_{[\omega+1]}; K_j | X_{j,1}^{[t]})$$

$$= \sum_{s=1}^{\omega+1} I(K_s; K_j | K_{[s-1]}, X_{j,1}^{[t]})$$

$$= \sum_{s=1}^{\omega+1} H(K_j | K_{[s-1]}, X_{j,1}^{[t]}) - \sum_{s=1}^{\omega+1} H(K_j | K_{[s]}, X_{j,1}^{[t]})$$

$$= \sum_{s=1}^{\omega+1} I(Y_{s,1}^{[t]}; K_j | K_{[s-1]}, X_{j,1}^{[t]}) + \sum_{s=1}^{\omega+1} H(K_j | K_{[s-1]}, X_{j,1}^{[t]} Y_{s,1}^{[t]}) - \sum_{s=1}^{\omega+1} H(K_j | K_{[s]}, X_{j,1}^{[t]})$$

$$\geq \sum_{s=1}^{\omega+1} \sum_{r=1}^{t} I(Y_{s,1}^{(r)}; K_j | K_{[s-1]}, X_{j,1}^{[t]}, Y_{s1}^{[r-1]}) + \sum_{s=1}^{\omega+1} H(K_j | K_{[s-1]}, X_{j,1}^{[t]}, X_{j,2}^{[t]}, Y_{s,1}^{[t]})$$

$$- \sum_{s=1}^{\omega+1} H(K_j | K_{[s]}, X_{j,1}^{[t]})$$

$$= \sum_{s=1}^{\omega+1} \sum_{r=1}^{t} I(Y_{s,1}^{(r)}; K_j | K_{[s-1]}, X_{j,1}^{[t]}, Y_{s,1}^{[r-1]}) + \sum_{s=1}^{\omega+1} I(Y_{s,2}^{[t]}; K_j | K_{[s-1]}, X_{j,1}^{[t]}, X_{j,2}^{[t]}, Y_{s,1}^{[t]})$$

$$+ \sum_{s=1}^{\omega+1} H(K_j | K_{[s-1]}, X_{j,1}^{[t]}, X_{j,2}^{[t]}, Y_{s,1}^{[t]}, Y_{s,2}^{[t]}) - \sum_{s=1}^{\omega+1} H(K_j | K_{[s]}, X_{j,1}^{[t]})$$

$$= \sum_{s=1}^{\omega+1} \sum_{r=1}^{t} I(Y_{s,1}^{(r)}; K_j | K_{[s-1]}, X_{j,1}^{[t]}, Y_{s,1}^{[r-1]})$$

$$+ \sum_{s=1}^{\omega+1} \sum_{r=1}^{t} I(Y_{s,2}^{(r)}; K_j | K_{[s-1]}, X_{j,1}^{[t]}, X_{j,2}^{[t]}, Y_{s,1}^{[t]}, Y_{s,2}^{[r-1]})$$

$$+ \sum_{s=1}^{\omega+1} \{ H(K_j | K_{[s-1]}, X_{j,1}^{[t]}, X_{j,2}^{[t]}, Y_{s,1}^{[t]}, Y_{s,2}^{[t]}) - H(K_j | K_{[s]}, X_{j,1}^{[t]}) \}$$

$$\geq \sum_{s=1}^{\omega+1} \sum_{r=1}^{t} I(Y_{s,1}^{(r)}; K_j | K_{[s-1]}, X_{j,1}^{[t]}, Y_{s,1}^{[r-1]})$$

$$+ \sum_{s=1}^{\omega+1} \sum_{r=1}^{t} I(Y_{s,2}^{(r)}; K_j | K_{[s-1]}, X_{j,1}^{[t]}, X_{j,2}^{[t]}, Y_{s,1}^{[t]}, Y_{s,2}^{[r-1]})$$

$$\geq 2t(\omega + 1) \log \epsilon^{-1}, \tag{4}$$

where (4) follows from that K_j is independent from $(K_{[s]}, X_{j,1}^{[t]}, X_{j,2}^{[t]}, Y_{s,1}^{[t]}, Y_{s,2}^{[t]})$ and the last inequality follows from Theorem 4. □

E   Proof of Theorem 6

For simplicity, we describe the outline of the proof of $\max(\Pr(\mathsf{Cheat}_1), \Pr(\mathsf{Cheat}_2)) \leq 1/q$. The full proof will appear in the full version of this paper. Without loss of generality, we suppose that $W = \{U_1, \ldots, U_\omega\}$ and $U_i, U_j \notin W$.

1. We show $\Pr(\mathsf{Cheat}_1) \leq 1/q$. To succeed in the impersonation attack such that U_i is a responder and U_j is an initiator, the adversary W will generate a fraudulent response $Y_1 \in \mathbb{F}_q$ for a given challenge X_1 under the following conditions: the adversary W has ω secret-keys, and obtains $Z^{\mathsf{Ses}}(W, U_i, U_j)^{t-1}$, namely, $t - 1$ pairs of M_1 and M_2. However, the degrees of $f(x, y, z)$ with respect to variables x, y and z is at most ω, ω and $t - 1$, respectively, and W cannot guess at least one coefficient of $f(x, y, z)$ with probability larger than $1/q$.

2. We show $\Pr(\mathsf{Cheat}_2) \leq 1/q$. To succeed in the impersonation attack such that U_i is an initiator and U_j is a responder, the adversary W will generate a fraudulent response $Y_2 \in \mathbb{F}_q$ for a given challenge X_2 under the following conditions: the adversary W has ω secret-keys, and obtains $Z^{\mathsf{Int}}(W, U_i, U_j)^{t-1}$, namely, $t - 1$ (M_1, M_2, M_3). However, the degree of $g(x, y, z)$ with respect to variables x, y and z is at most ω, ω and $t - 1$, respectively, and W cannot guess at least one coefficient of $g(x, y, z)$ with probability larger than $1/q$.

Therefore, we have $\max(\Pr(\mathsf{Cheat}_1), \Pr(\mathsf{Cheat}_2)) \leq 1/q$.

Finally, it is straightforward to see that the construction satisfies all the lower bounds in Theorem 5 with equalities. □

References

1. Bellare, M., Rogaway, P.: Entity authentication and key distribution. In: Stinson, D.R. (ed.) CRYPTO 1993. LNCS, vol. 773, pp. 232–249. Springer, Heidelberg (1994)
2. Bird, R.S., Gopal, I., Herzberg, A., Janson, P., Kutten, S., Molva, R., Yung, M.: Systematic design of two-party authentication protocols. In: Feigenbaum, J. (ed.) CRYPTO 1991. LNCS, vol. 576, pp. 44–61. Springer, Heidelberg (1992)
3. Diffie, W., Van Oorschot, P., Wiener, M.: Authentication and authenticated key exchanges. Des. Codes Cryptogr. 2(2), 107–125 (1992)
4. Feige, U., Fiat, A., Shamir, A.: Zero-knowledge proofs of identity. J. Cryptol. 1(2), 77–94 (1988)
5. Fiat, A., Shamir, A.: How to prove yourself: practical solutions to identification and signature problems. In: Odlyzko, A.M. (ed.) CRYPTO 1986. LNCS, vol. 263, pp. 186–194. Springer, Heidelberg (1987)
6. Guillou, L.C., Quisquater, J.-J.: A "Paradoxical" identity-based signature scheme resulting from zero-knowledge. In: Goldwasser, S. (ed.) CRYPTO 1988. LNCS, vol. 403, pp. 216–231. Springer, Heidelberg (1990)
7. Kurosawa, K.: Unconditionally secure entity authentication. In: 1998 IEEE International Symposium on Information Theory, Proceedings, p. 298, Aug 1998
8. Rivest, R.L.: Unconditionally secure commitment and oblivious transfer schemes using private channels and a trusted initializer (1999)
9. Safavi-Naini, R., Wang, H.: Multireceiver authentication codes: models, bounds, constructions and extensions. Inf. Comput. 151, 148–172 (1998)
10. Schnorr, C.-P.: Efficient identification and signatures for smart cards. In: Quisquater, J.-J., Vandewalle, J. (eds.) EUROCRYPT 1989. LNCS, vol. 434, pp. 688–689. Springer, Heidelberg (1990)

Practical Receipt-Free Sealed-Bid Auction in the Coercive Environment

Jaydeep Howlader[✉], Sanjit Kumar Roy, and Ashis Kumar Mal

National Institute of Technology, Durgapur, India
jaydeep.howlader@it.nitdgp.ac.in, sanjit_it@yahoo.co.in,
ashis.mal@ece.nitdgp.ac.in

Abstract. Sealed-Bid auction is an efficient and rational method to establish the price in open market. However sealed-bid auctions are subject to bid-rigging attack. Receipt-free mechanisms were proposed to prevent bid-rigging. The prior receipt-free mechanisms are based on two assumptions; firstly, existence of untappable channel between bidders and auction authorities. Secondly, mechanisms assume the authorities to be honest (not colluding). Moreover the bandwidth required to communicate the receipt-free bids is huge. This paper presents a sealed-bid auction mechanism to resist bid-rigging. The proposed method does not assume untappable channel nor consider the authorities to be necessarily honest. The proposed mechanism also manages the bandwidth efficiently, and improves the performance of the system.

1 Introduction

Sealed-bid is a form of auction mechanism where bids are submitted in sealed-envelop. The bids are remained sealed until the schedule time of *opening*. No bids are accepted after the schedule time of *opening*. During *opening* the sealed-bids are opened and the winning price and/or winner(s) are determined. It is rather delicate to implement a sealed-bid auction in the electronic media as there are various essential security requirements to be realized. Moreover, the adversarial behavior of the entities (*insider* or *outsider*) may lead to the failure of a naively implemented system. Unlike the *outsiders'* threat, the adversarial behavior of the *insiders* are often difficult to counter. For example:

- Auctioneer (*insider*) opens the bid prior to the schedule *opening* and conveys the bid-values to the adversary [4,14]. Thus fails to meet the *confidentiality of bid* property.
- Auctioneer allows certain bidder(s) to withdraw or submit unlawfully. Thus fails to meet the *fairness* property.
- Auctioneer deliberately suppresses some of the valid bids to make a certain bidder to be the winner. Thus fails to meet the *correctness* property.
- Auctioneer discloses all the bidding prices and the identity of the corresponding bidders after the *opening*. Thus fails to meet the *privacy of the bidder* [29] property.

© Springer International Publishing Switzerland 2014
H.-S. Lee and D.-G. Han (Eds.): ICISC 2013, LNCS 8565, pp. 418–434, 2014.
DOI: 10.1007/978-3-319-12160-4_25

– Coercer (*insider* entity) used to corrupt the authorities to retrieve critical information which may yield to bid-rigging [18]. Thus fails to meet the *uncoercibility* property.

During the last couple of decades sealed-bid auction mechanisms were studied and analyzed in various literatures. In spite of satisfying various security requirements (confidentiality, privacy, fairness, correctness etc.), sealed-bid auction mechanisms are subject to bid-rigging attack. Bid-rigging is a form of coercing where the powerful adversary (e.g. mafia) commands the other bidders to bid as per his choice so that he could win the auction by bidding unreasonably low value. Though the bids are submitted securely, coercer used to enforce the bidders to disclose all the private parameters (e.g. secret randomness, keys etc.) correspond to their secret bids. Thus coercer verifies whether the bidders obey his command. The coercer may corrupt some of the authorities and retrieves vital information that would indulge coercing.

1.1 Related Work

There have been substantive research works on sealed-bid auction. Franklin and Reiter [14] first proposed a protocol for secure electronic auction. Kikuchi *et al.* [16] proposed the multi-round auction protocol for tie-breaking. Naor *et al.* [20] proposed a two-server auction mechanism that protected the privacy of the bidders. In the sequel we include the recent works as [3,6,9,27]. However, those mechanisms have no protection to reveal the private inputs if the bidder is willing to do so. In spite of satisfying variety of security requirements, the prior mechanisms are unable to provide bid-rigging.

Abe and Suzuki [18] first introduced the receipt-free mechanism to counter bid-rigging problem. The mechanism was based on *threshold encryption* [1], with n number of auctioneers. Chen *et al.* [28] argued that Abe and Suzuki's mechanism [18] could not provide receipt-freeness to the winning bidder. Moreover, the mechanism failed to provide receipt-freeness in the presence of colluding auctioneer(s). Chen *et al.* proposed another receipt-free auction mechanism [28]. In their mechanism, seller along with the bidder jointly constructed the receipt-free bid. They argued that, seller would not be colluded due to *benefit collision*. Her *et al.* countered their argument and showed that seller could also be colluded when she tried to make a special bidder to be the winner. Her *et al.* further proposed another receipt-free auction mechanism [29] based on anonymous channel and pseudo ID. The mechanism required prior bidders' registration. Nevertheless, their mechanism failed to provide receipt-freeness if the registrar was dishonest. Huang *et al.* [30] proposed some improvement of Abe and Suzuki's mechanism [18] while reducing the bandwidth of bids, but could not overcome the problem related to dishonest auctioneer(s). Later on Howlader *et al.* [10] attempted another receipt-free mechanism based on multi-party computation. However the mechanism failed to provide receipt-freeness as the bidders' verification process carried the receipt of the bid.

Table 1. The physical constrains and assumptions made in various sealed-bid auction mechanisms. l denotes the length of the price list, n denotes the number of auctioneers and c denotes constant

Constraints & Assumptions	Abe and Suzuki [18]	Chen et al. [28]	Her et al. [29]	Huang et al. [30]	Howlader et al. [10]	Gao et al. [8]
Untappable channel	One way	Both way	One way	One way	One way	Not specified
Anonymity	×	×	√	×		×
Honest authority	All honest auctioneer	Honest seller	Honest registrar	All honest auctioneer	At least one honest sealer	Honest auctioneer
Bandwidth	$O(l \times n)$	$O(l)$	$O(c)$	$O(log\ l \times n)$	$O(l)$	$O(c)$

Some Impractical Assumptions: The above mechanisms are based on the two assumptions:

Firstly, the availability of untappable channel[1] between bidders and authorities (auctioneers, seller, sealer etc.). However, untappable channel is often impractical and difficult to deploy. However, some techniques based on deniable encryption [12,21] ware proposed in [13,24] to relax the untappable channel. The notion of deniability allows the bidders to plausibly evade the coercer. However, those techniques fail in the presence of colluding authorities [11]. Later on Howleder *et al.* introduced *'Coercing Resistant Mix (CRM)'* [11] which integrated deniability with anonymity to transients the physical requirement of untappable channel.

Secondly, the prior receipt-free mechanisms consider the authorities to be honest. More specifically, the authorities not only execute the protocol honestly, but also avoid any such conspiracy that may leak certain information to the coercer.

1.2   Our Contribution

We withdraw the untappable channel, henceforth coercer can intercept the public transcripts at any extend. Furthermore, we consider a broader notion of coerciveness rather than only receipt-freeness. Coercer may collude some of the authorities who execute the protocol correctly but reveal certain information to the coercer in order to indulge coercing. We replace the untappable channel with CRM [11]. CRM allows the adversary to intercept the public transcripts, but provides the bidders to formulate *'fake bids'* such that, adversary could not able to distinguish between the *fakes* and the *trues*. On the other hand, untraceable delivery of messages restricts the recipient (authority) to link 'who-bids-what'. Though the recipient receives decrypted messages, but unable to determine 'who-bids-what'.

Based on the cryptographic techniques, the receipt-free auction mechanisms are categorized in two classes. The mechanisms [18,30] are based on threshold

---

[1] A channel that provides perfect security in an information-theoretic sense. Even encryption does not provide an untappable channel.

secret sharing which outputs committed transcripts. However, those mechanisms fail to provide receipt-freeness if any one of the authority reveals his share. Whereas the mechanisms [28, 29] are based on designated-verifiability of re-encryption proof [2], where bidder and authority (either seller, auctioneer) collaboratively form the receipt-free bids. Nevertheless, those schemes also fail if the entities are not trustworthy.

The proposed mechanism is based on secure multi-party computation [5,25]. The sealing operation is done with respect to a private key which is distributed among a set of qualifying sealers. A quorum of qualifying sealers performs the sealing operation form the sealed-bids. Unlike the prior mechanisms the proposed scheme guarantees receipt-freeness even at least one of the authority remain honest (not colluded).

2 Preliminaries

Three main building blocks are used in the proposed receipt-free mechanism. They are Deniable Encryption, Coercer Resistant MIX and Distributed Key Generation.

A Plan-Ahead Deniable Encryption (PDE) [12,21] outputs the cipher c_d such that, the encryption of the fake and the true messages look alike. The PDE consists of three algorithms $PDE(Enc, Dec, \varphi)$. The encryption (Enc) is defined as $Enc^-(m_t, pk, r_t)$, where m_t is the true message, pk is the public key and r_t is the true randomness, and outputs a cipher c. However, Enc produces deniable cipher c_d when executed with another parameter called fake message m_f, as $Enc^{m_f}(m_t, pk, r_t)$. PDE allows the sender to evade coercion by producing m_f instead of m_t. The decryption (Dec) is defined as $Dec(c$ or $c_d, sk)$, where sk is the private key and outputs the plaintext m_t with negligible decryption error. The faking algorithm(φ) is defined as $\varphi(c_d, m_t, m_f)$ and outputs the fake randomness r_f such that $Enc^-(m_t, pk, r_t)$ and $Enc^-(m_f, pk, r_f)$ look alike.

MIX (MIX-cascade) is a system consists of a finite number of nodes and provides anonymous communication [15,17,19]. MIX takes a list of ciphertexts as input and outputs a random permutation of the plaintexts. Every node performs a cryptographic transformation and a random permutation, and forwards the list to the next node. We denote MIX operation as $MIX(Enc_{pk}[m_1, \ldots, m_N]) \rightarrow \prod[m_1, \ldots, m_N]$ where pk is the public key of the MIX and $\prod$ denotes a random permutation of the list. Unlike the general MIXes those take non-probabilistic ciphers [25,26][2] as input, CRM takes deniable ciphers as input. Deniability allows the sender to plausibly deny the true message while anonymity restricts the dishonest recipients to retrace the senders of individual messages.

Distributed Key Generation (DKG) allows a set of n entities to generate jointly a pair of public-private key according to the distribution defined by

---

[2] Probabilistic encryption uses randomness in encryption so that, when encrypting the same message several times it will, in general yield different ciphertexts.

the underlying cryptosystem. The public key is output in the clear, the private key is secretly shared among the n entities via a threshold encryption scheme. A robust and efficient DKG protocol is proposed by Gennaro et al. [23] to share the secret x amongst a set of qualifying entities and the makes $y = g^x$ public. The protocol is able to identify the malicious entities and computes the public-private values with the inputs of the qualifying entities. DKG is denoted as $DKG_P(s_1, \ldots, s_n) \rightarrow (h, x, \mathcal{P})$, where P is the set of n entities, s_i is the random secret initiated by the entity $P_i \in P$, $h = g^x$ is the public value, $x = f_{s_i \in \mathcal{P}}(s_i)$ is the secret shared amongst the entities $P_i \in \mathcal{P}$ and $\mathcal{P}$ is the set of qualifying entities.

3   Receipt-Free Sealed-Bid Auction

The receipt-freeness is proposed to prevent bid-rigging in sealed-bid auction. Following are the entities of the proposed receipt-free auction:

3.1   Entities

- There is a finite set of bidders denoted as $B = \{B_1, B_2, \ldots, B_m\}$.
- There is a finite set of sealers denoted as $S = \{S_1, S_2, \ldots, S_k\}$. Sealer is an authority who executes sealing operation and forms the receipt-free bid.
- There is a single auctioneer. The auctioneer is responsible to open the bids (with the cooperation of sealers) and determines the winning price and winner.
- Coercer is an adversary who indulges bid-rigging. Coercer is able to impel the bidders to reveal all their private data (keys and randomnesses). Furthermore the coercer is allowed to intercept the public transcripts and also corrupts some of the sealers to retrieve critical information that may yield coercing.
- We use a **Bulletin Board** ($\mathcal{BB}$). This is a publicly accessible memory with read and appendive-write access.
- We integrate CRM in place of untappable channel.

3.2   System Setting

Let p, q be large primes such that q divides $p - 1$, G_q be the unique subgroup of $\mathbb{Z}_p^*$ of order q, and $g \in \mathbb{Z}_p^*$ is an element of order q. Following we define the keys of different entities. The operations are closure to the multiplicative group $\mathbb{Z}_p^*$.

- Bidder B_i's private key be $x_{B_i} \in \mathbb{Z}_p^*$ and public key be $h_{B_i} = g^{x_{B_i}}$.
- Auctioneer's private key be $x_A \in \mathbb{Z}_p^*$ and public key be $h_A = g^{x_A}$.
- The sealers execute the Distributed Key Generation (DKG) protocol [22,23] that outputs a set of qualifying sealers denoted as $QUAL$ (of k sealers) with the public key h_S. Each member $S_i \in QUAL$ has his private key as x_i such that any quorum of $t > k/2$ sealers denoted as $QRM \subseteq QUAL$ are able to seal the bidders' encrypted bid-vectors. Without loss of generality, we

---

Algorithm 1. Bidder B_i bidding operation

---

begin
    for $k = d - 1$ *to* 0 **do**
        for $j = 9$ *to* 0 **do**
            B_i randomly selects $r_{i,(k,j)}, \hat{r}_{i,(k,j)} \in_R \mathbb{Z}_p^*$ and computes $\left(X_{i,(k,j)}, Y_{i,(k,j)}\right)$

$$X_{i,(k,j)} = g^{r_{i,(k,j)}}$$

$$Y_{i,(k,j)} = \begin{cases} (h_A.h_S)^{r_{i,(k,j)}}.G_{i,(k,j)} & \text{if } j = \delta_k \\ (h_A.h_S)^{r_{i,(k,j)}} & \text{otherwise} \end{cases}$$

            // where $G_{i,(k,j)} = \hat{r}_{i,(k,j)} G_i^{r_{i,(k,j)}}$ represents the *Yes* mark, $G_i = g_y^{x_{B_i}}$
    B_i outputs the encrypted bid-vector $\langle \mathcal{X}_i, \mathcal{Y}_i \rangle$ corresponds to the price list $\mathcal{P}$

---

assume that $QRM = \{S_1, S_2, \ldots, S_t\}$. Sealer $S_i \in QRM$ configures his sealing key as $x_{S_i} = f_i(0)$ where $f_i(x) = \lambda_{ij} x_i$ is a polynomial of degree t. $\lambda_{ij}{}^3$ is the Lagrange interpolation coefficient for the sealer S_i.

- After configuring the QRM each sealer $S_i \in QRM$ publishes his public key for sealing as $h_{S_i} = g^{x_{S_i}}$. We denote $h_{S/S_1,S_2,\ldots,S_r} = h_S(h_{S_1}h_{S_2}\ldots h_{S_r})^{-1}$. Intuitively $h_{S/S_1,\ldots,S_t} = 1$.
- $g_y \in \mathbb{Z}_p^*$ be an element of order q indicates the *YES Mark*.
- Let the maximum estimated price of the item is lesser the 10^d. Auctioneer publishes the price list $\mathcal{P}$ consisting of d ordered vectors. We denote $\mathcal{P} := \mathcal{P}_{d-1}, \mathcal{P}_{d-2}, \ldots, \mathcal{P}_0$ where every $\mathcal{P}_i$ consists of 10 elements and denoted as $\mathcal{P}_i := P_{i9}, P_{i8}, \ldots, P_{i0}$. The element P_{ij} represents the value $j \times 10^i$. Thus the decimal value of $\delta_{d-1}\delta_{d-2}\ldots\delta_0$ has an equivalent representation as $\sum_{i=0}^{d-1} P_{i\delta_i}$. Figure 1 describes the bid-vector representation of the decimal value (bid value).

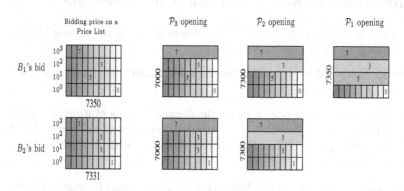

Fig. 1. Opening of two bid-vectors $B_1 : 7350$ and $B_2 : 7331$. During the opening of $\mathcal{P}_1$ the bid-vector B_1 is extracted while B_2 is excluded as $P_{1,5}$ appears before $P_{1,3}$.

---

^{3} Lagrange interpolation coefficient for the ith sealer is $\lambda_{ij} = \prod\limits_{\substack{i \neq j \\ 1 \leq j \leq t}} \frac{x-j}{i-j}$.

Algorithm 2. Sealing operation

---

begin

  if *($S_{l=1}$ is the first Sealer $\in QRM$)* **then**

    S_l receives $\langle \mathcal{X}_i, \mathcal{Y}_i \rangle$ and computes $\langle \mathcal{X}_{S_l i}, \mathcal{Y}_{S_l i} \rangle$ as follows

    for $k = d - 1$ *to* 0 **do**

      for $j = 9$ *to* 0 **do**

        S_l randomly selects $r_{S_l i,(k,j)}, \hat{r}_{S_l i,(k,j)} \in_R \mathbb{Z}_p$ and computes

$$
\begin{aligned}
X_{S_l i,(k,j)} &= g^{r_{S_l i,(k,j)}} X_{i,(k,j)} \\
Y_{S_l i,(k,j)} &= \hat{r}_{S_l i,(k,j)} . h_A^{r_{S_l i,(k,j)}} . h_{S/S_l}^{r_{S_l i,(k,j)}} . (X_{i,(k,d)})^{-x_{S_l}} . Y_{i,(k,d)}
\end{aligned} \tag{1}
$$

    // We denote $G_{\square} = \begin{cases} G_{i,(k,j)} & \text{if } B_i \text{ has marked } P_{(k,j)} \text{ with YES} \\ 1 & \text{otherwise} \end{cases}$

    $S_{l=1}$ forwards the partially sealed bid-vector $\langle \mathcal{X}_{S_l i}, \mathcal{Y}_{S_l i} \rangle$ corresponds to $\langle \mathcal{X}_i, \mathcal{Y}_i \rangle$

    to the next Sealer

  else if *($S_{l \neq 1}$ is the intermediate Sealer $\in QRM$)* **then**

    S_l receives the partially sealed bid-vector from S_{l-1} as $\langle \mathcal{X}_{S_{l-1} i}, \mathcal{Y}_{S_{l-1} i} \rangle$ and

    computes $\langle \mathcal{X}_{S_l i}, \mathcal{Y}_{S_l i} \rangle$ as follows

    for $k = d - 1$ *to* 0 **do**

      for $j = 9$ *to* 0 **do**

$$
\begin{aligned}
X_{S_l i,(k,j)} &= g^{r_{S_l i,(k,j)}} . X_{S_{l-1} i,(k,j)} \\
Y_{S_l i,(k,j)} &= \hat{r}_{S_l i,(k,j)} . h_A^{r_{S_l i,(k,j)}} . (h_{S/S_1,\ldots,S_l})^{r_{S_l i,(k,j)}} . \\
&\quad (X_{S_{l-1} i,(k,d)})^{-x_{S_l}} . Y_{S_{l-1} i,(k,d)}
\end{aligned} \tag{2}
$$

    if *($S_{l=t}$ is the last sealer $\in QRM$)* **then**

      $S_{l=t}$ publishes the sealed bid-vector $\langle \mathcal{X}_{S_l i}, \mathcal{Y}_{S_l i} \rangle$ on the $\mathcal{BB}$

    else

      S_l forwards the partially sealed bid-vector to the next sealer

---

4   Receipt-Free Sealed-Bid Auction Mechanism

The receipt-free sealed-bid auction mechanism is consisting of four phases: *bidding*, *sealing*, *opening* and *trading*.

Bidding: Every bidder $B_i \in B$ determines his bidding price and constructs the encrypted bid-vector as follows:

- Let $\delta_{d-1}\delta_{d-2} \ldots \delta_0$ $(0 \leq \delta_i \leq 9)$ be the decimal representation of the bidding price. B_i executes Algorithm 1 to output the encrypted bid-vector $\langle \mathcal{X}_i, \mathcal{Y}_i \rangle$.
- B_i marks the price indices $P_{k\delta_k}$ $(0 \leq k \leq d - 1)$ with *Yes* while encrypting the price list $\mathcal{P}$.

B_i constructs a fake encrypted bid-vector as $\langle \bar{\mathcal{X}}_i, \bar{\mathcal{Y}}_i \rangle$ and forwards the deniable cipher $Enc^{\langle \bar{\mathcal{X}}_i, \bar{\mathcal{Y}}_i \rangle}(\langle \mathcal{X}_i, \mathcal{Y}_i \rangle, pk_{CRM}, r_t)$ to the CRM. CRM accumulates a batch of deniable ciphers and anonymously delivers the batch to the $QUAL$.

Sealing: A quorum of sealers (denoted as $QRM \subset QUAL$), possessing the public key as h_S, performs the sealing operation. The encrypted bid-vectors are processed by at least $t > k/2$ sealers from the QRM. Every sealer $S_l \in QRM$

executes the Algorithm 2 and outputs the partially sealed bid-vector. During *sealing*, every sealer S_l engraves his secret randomness, $r_{S_li,(k,j)}$ & $\hat{r}_{S_li,(k,j)}$ and nullifies his key component, h_{S_l} (in Algorithm 2, Eqs. 1 and 2) from the partially sealed bid-vector. After t sealing operation sealer S_t publishes the sealed-bid on the $\mathcal{BB}$.

Bid Verification (BV): The inherent property of receipt-freeness is the inability to prove to anyone how a bidder has bid. However, receipt-freeness allows the bidder to verify the correctness of the sealing operation. Algorithm 3 describes the BV mechanism. The BV does not reveal the secret value i.e., even the coercer observes the process of BV, bidder can execute the BV correctly without revealing any partial information related to his secret. BV is done with respect to the cumulative response $\mathcal{R}_{S_tik}$ computed by every sealers.

Opening: At the schedule *Opening*, bids are opened. Bids are opened in decreasing order (starting from the highest price). We define two subprocesses: Evaluating *Yes Mark* (EYM) for the price vector $\mathcal{P}_k$ and Extracting Bids having *Yes Mark* (EBY) on price index $P_{k,j}$.

- EYM: Auctioneer and sealers jointly execute the process. EYM takes input a price vector $\mathcal{P}_k$ and output the highest price index $P_{k,j}$ that contains some *Yes Marks*. Algorithm 4 describes the process.
- EBY: After EYM outputs an index $P_{k,j}$, EBY extracts and outputs a list of bids (sealed-bids) that contains the sealed-bids having *Yes Marks* on the $P_{k,j}$ index.

The *opening* phase is initiated with the construction of the list L containing all the sealed bids followed by invoking the subprocess $EYM(L, \mathcal{P}_{d-1})$. EYM will output the price index $P_{d-1,w_{d-1}}$ and the list L_{d-1} containing those sealed bids which possess *Yes Mark* on the index $P_{d-1,w_{d-1}}$. Auctioneer sets the winning price as $w = w_{d-1}xxx$. Auctioneer subsequently iterates the subprocess $EYM(L_k, \mathcal{P}_k)$ (for $k = d-2, \ldots 0$) and finally the winning price $w = w_{d-1} \ldots w_0$ and the list of winning bids L_0 is determined.

Trading: The auction mechanism determines the winning bids, but not the winner. The winning bidder claims his winning and executes a zero-knowledge (ZK) protocol with the auctioneer to substantiate his winning. Let B_i be the winning bidder and $w = w_{d-1} \ldots w_0$ be the winning price. Bidder B_i proves G_i and h_{B_i} have common exponent over g_y and g respectively.

For $k = d - 1, \ldots 0$, B_i discloses all $\hat{r}_{i,(k,w_k)}$ and proves that $X_{i,(k,w_k)}$ and $G_{i,(k.w_k)} \cdot (\hat{r}_{i,(k,w_k)})^{-1}$ have common exponents over g and G_i respectively. The details of the ZK protocol is presented in the Appendix.

5 Security Analysis

In this section we present the security properties of the proposed scheme:

Receipt-Freeness: If A is an auction protocol and simulated as

$$A \overset{\triangle}{=} Bid(\forall i B_i, b_i, r_{B_i}) | Seal(\forall t S_t, r_{S_t}, \hat{r}_{S_t}) | out(sb_i) |$$
$$Rev(B_c, r_{B_c}) |! Rev(\exists h S_h, r_{S_h}, \hat{r}_{B_h}) | Rev(\forall t S_t, r_{S_t}, \hat{r}_{S_t})$$

Algorithm 3. Bid Verification

---

begin

  for $\forall S_l \in QRM$ do

    if ($S_{l=1}$ is the first Sealer $\in QRM$) then

      $S_{l=1}$ computes the response-vector $\mathcal{R}_{S_l i,k}$ as follows

      for $k = d - 1$ to 0 do

$$\mathcal{R}_{S_l i,k} = \left(\prod_{j=0}^{9} \hat{r}_{S_l i, (k,j)} \right)$$

      $S_{l=1}$ appends the response-vector with the partially sealed bid-vector as $\langle \mathcal{X}_{S_l i, (k,-)}, \mathcal{Y}_{S_l i, (k,-)} \rangle \mathcal{R}_{S_l i,k}$ (for $0 \leq k \leq d - 1$) and forwards.

    else if ($S_{l \neq 1}$ is the intermediate Sealer $\in QRM$ then

      S_l receives $\langle \mathcal{X}_{S_{l-1} i, (k,-)}, \mathcal{Y}_{S_{l-1} i, (k,-)} \rangle \mathcal{R}_{S_{l-1} i,k}$ and computes his response-vector $\mathcal{R}_{S_l ik}$ as follows

      for $k = d - 1$ to 0 do

$$\mathcal{R}_{S_l i,k} = \left(\prod_{j=0}^{9} \hat{r}_{S_l i, (k,j)} \right) . \mathcal{R}_{S_{l-1} i,k} = \left(\prod_{j=0}^{9} \prod_{t=1}^{l} \hat{r}_{S_t i, (k,j)} \right)$$

      S_l overwrites the preceding response-vector $\mathcal{R}_{S_{l-1} i,k}$ with his response-vector as $\langle \mathcal{X}_{S_l i, (k,-)}, \mathcal{Y}_{S_l i, (k,-)} \rangle \mathcal{R}_{S_l i,k}$ (for $0 \leq k \leq d - 1$) and forwards.

    if $S_{l=t}$ is the final sealer $\in QRM$ then

      S_t publishes $\langle \mathcal{X}_{S_t i, (k,-)}, \mathcal{Y}_{S_t i, (k,-)} \rangle \mathcal{R}_{S_t i,k}$ on $\mathcal{BB}$

  // After all sealers compute their responses, Auctioneer blindly signs the response as follows

  for $\forall i$ sealed-bid vectors $\langle \mathcal{X}_{S_t i, (k,-)}, \mathcal{Y}_{S_t i, (k,-)} \rangle \mathcal{R}_{S_t i,k}$ Auctioneer computes do

    for $k = d - 1$ to 0 do

$$\mathbb{X}_{i,k} = \left(\prod_{j=0}^{9} X_{S_t i, (k,j)} \right)^{x_A} = h_A^{\sum_{j=0}^{9} \left(r_{i,(k,j)} + \sum_{l=1}^{t} r_{S_l i, (k,j)} \right)}$$

    Auctioneer appends the blind signature with the sealed bid-vectors as $\langle \mathcal{X}_{S_t i, (k,-)}, \mathcal{Y}_{S_t i, (k,-)} \rangle \mathcal{R}_{S_t i,k}, \mathbb{X}_{i,k}$ (for $0 \leq k \leq d - 1$) and publishes on $\mathcal{BB}$.

  // After Auctioneer publishes the blind signatures, Bidder B_i verifies his sealed bid as follows

  for $l = 1$ to m do

    Bidder B_i set $VEFY = TRUE$

    for $k = d - 1$ to 0 do

      if $\left(\prod_{j=0}^{9} Y_{S_t l(k,j)}! = \mathcal{R}_{S_t lk} . \mathbb{X}_{lk} . \prod_{j=0}^{9} G_{i,(k,j)} \right)$ then

        $VEFY = VEFY \cap FALSE$

    if ($VEFY == TRUE$) then

      B_i verifies and RETURN

  if $VEFY == FALSE$ then

    B_i raises a complain

ProcS$(L, S_l, P_{k,j})$
S_l computes $V_{S_l(k,j)} = \prod_{(x_i,y_i) \in L} \hat{r}_{S_l i,(k,j)}$
Sealer S_l outputs $V_{S_l(k,j)}$ on the $\mathcal{BB}$

ProcA$(L, P_{k,j})$

Auctioneer computes $V_{(k,j)} = \prod_{1}^{t} V_{S_l(k,j)}$

$$= \left(\prod_{i=1}^{m} \prod_{1}^{t} \hat{r}_{S_l i,(k,j)} \right).$$

Furthermore auctioneer computes

$$\mathbb{Y}_{(k,j)} = \prod_{b_i \in L} Y_{S_t i,(k,j)} X_{S_t i,(k,j)}^{-x_A}$$

$$= \left(\prod_{b_i \in L} \prod_{l=1}^{t} \hat{r}_{S_l i,(k,j)} \right)$$

$$= g^{\sum_{b_i \in L} \sum_{l=1}^{t} r_{S_l i,(k,j)}} \cdot \prod_{b_i \in L} G_{\Box i,(k,j)}$$

Auctioneer evaluates and outputs
$\mathbb{G}_{(k,j)} = \mathbb{Y}_{(k,j)} \cdot V_{(k,j)}^{-1}$
Auctioneer outputs $V_{(k,j)}, \mathbb{Y}_{(k,j)}$ on $\mathcal{BB}$

```
1  ProcSwap(L = {b1, b2}, Lvoid = {v1, v2})
   // L:  list having Yes mark
   // Lvoid:  void list
2  Construct L̄ = {b1, v2} & L̿ = {v1, b2}
3  for l = 1 to t do
4      ProcS(L̄, Sl, Pk,j)
5      ProcS(L̿, Sl, Pk,j)
6  end
7  if ProcA(L̄, Pk,j) ≠ 1 then
8      b1 has Yes Mark and included
9      in the output list
10 end
11 if ProcA(L̿, Pk,j) ≠ 1 then
12     b2 has Yes Mark and included
13     in the output list
14 end
```

Algorithm 4: EYM$(L, \mathcal{P}_k)$

Input: $L = \{b_i\}$ be stack of sealed bids
```
for j = 9 to 0 do
    // Every Sealer St ∈ QRM
    // executes ProcS()
    for l = 1 to t do
        ProcS(L, Sl, Pk,j)
    // Auctioneer executes ProcA()
    ProcA(L, Pk,j) → G
    if (G ≠ 1) then
        EBY(L, Pk,j)
```

Algorithm 5: EBY$(L, P_{k,j})$

List L is divided in two
halves $L1$ & $L2$
```
// Every sealer Sl ∈ QRM
// executes ProcS() for L1 & L2
for l = 1 to t do
    ProcS(L1, Pk,j); ProcS(L2, Pk,j);
// Auctioneer executes ProcA()
// for the two halves
ProcA(L1, Pk,j) → G1
ProcA(L2, Pk,j) → G2
if (G1 ≠ 1) then
    if (|L1| ≥ 2) then
        EBY(L1, Pk,j)
    else
        ProcSwap(L1, Lvoid)

if (G2 ≠ 1) then
    if (|L2| ≥ 2) then
        EBY(L2, Pk,j)
    else
        ProcSwap(L2, Lvoid)
```

where every bidder B_i encrypts his bid b_i with the randomness r_{B_i}, every sealer S_t seals the bids with randomness $r_{S_i}, \hat{r}_{S_i}$ and produces the sealed bids sb_i, thereafter, the coerced bidder B_c and all sealers except the honest sealer S_h reveal their secrets. The protocol still conceals the private values. We show that, adversary who may compute buy could not resolve the secret as the private values are

$$Y_{S_t c,(k,j)} \cdot \left(\prod_{l=1 l \neq h}^{t} \hat{r}_{S_l c,(k.j)} \cdot h_A^{\left(r_{c,(k,j)} + \sum_{l=1 l \neq h}^{t} r_{S_l c,(k,j)} \right)} \right)^{-1} = \hat{r}_{S_h c,(k,j)} \cdot G_\Box$$

blinded with the honest bidder's randomness $(\hat{r}_{S_hc(k,j)})$. Similarly, bidder B_c could flip the *Yes-to-No* and vice-versa. The proposed mechanism ensures receipt-freeness as adversary could not distinguish between a situation where B_c reveals his true secret and the situation where he produces fake secret.

Correctness: The auction mechanism declares the winning price and keeps all the loosing bids secret. The *correctness* defines the ability to verify the outcome of the auction by any entity. Let auctioneer declared $w = w_{d-1}w_{d-2}\dots w_0$ as the winning price. Therefore during *opening* the subprocesses **ProcS()** and **ProcA()** have published all $V_{S_i(k,j)}$ and $\mathbb{V}_{(k,j)}$ & $\mathbb{Y}_{(k,j)}$ $(0 \le k \le d-1, 9 \ge j \ge w_k)$ on $\mathcal{BB}$ on the $\mathcal{BB}$. Anyone who wants to verify the correctness of the auction result can examine the result with the information published on the $\mathcal{BB}$.

Nonrepudiation: We assume that bidder bids honestly. The *opening* of bids only determines the winning price and the list of winning bids, but winner is not determined. Bidder executes the ZK protocol to substantiate his winning. However, the odd may happen, when the winning bidder does not respond. We present the mechanism to identify the winning bidder while he has not responded. Let $w = w_{d-1}w_{d-2}\dots w_0$ be the winning price and L_0 be the list of sealed-bids extracted as the winning bid(s). Let $\langle \mathcal{X}_{S_t i}, \mathcal{Y}_{S_t i} \rangle \in L_0$ be an winning bid. In the *opening* phase, procedure **ProcSwap()** computes the *Yes Mark* on every P_{k,w_k} of the winning bid. Let $\mathcal{G} = \{G_{i(k,w_k)} \mid 0 \le k \le d-1\}$ be the set of *Yes Marks* computed by **ProcSwap()** during *opening*. Now auctioneer has to identify the bidder(s) who had bid with the above set of *Yes Marks*. Auctioneer initiates the following:

- Auctioneer asks all sealer $S_l \in QRM$ to publish the initial encrypted price-vectors on $\mathcal{BB}$. Thus all $\langle \mathcal{X}_i, \mathcal{Y}_i \rangle$ (for $i = 1, 2, \dots m$) appears on the $\mathcal{BB}$.
- Auctioneer asks the bidders to substantiate their encrypted bids for every P_{k,w_k} indices. That is, all the losing bidder B_i will show that:
  1. he knows the discrete logarithm of $X_{i(k,w_k)}$ (say $r_{i(k,w_k)}$) and
  2. shows that $Y_{i(k,w_k)} = (h_S h_A)^{r_{i(k,w_k)}}$.
  However, the winning bidder B_w will fail to establish the second as he had computed $Y_{w(k,w_k)} = (h_S h_A)^{r_{w(k,w_k)}}.G_{w(k,w_k)}$.

6   Performance

The proposed scheme improves the performance by reducing the bandwidth of the receipt-free bids. The existing receipt-free auction mechanisms e.g. [10,18,28] require huge bandwidth to communicate the encrypted bids. Table 1 presents the bandwidth requirement for various auction mechanisms. In this section we analyze the bandwidth requirement, communication overhead and computational complexity of the proposed mechanism. Let L, n and m represent the number of bidding price, number of auctioneer/sealer and number of bidder respectively.

Table 2. Number of message exchanges in various auction mechanisms

No. of Rounds	Abe & Suzuki [18]	Huang et al. [30]	proposed mechanism
During Bidding	nmL	$nm(log\ L)$	$m(log_{10}\ L)$
During Opening	$t \geq n/2$	$t \geq n/2$	worst case $10d$ and dm

No. of rounds)	Chen et al. [28]	Her et al. [29]
During Bidding	at least mnL	at least mn
During Opening	at most L	at most L

Table 3. Time latency for *Bidding* and *Sealing* operation

Key size (bits)	Howlader et al. [10]				Proposed mechanism			
	Bidding time in sec.		Sealing time in sec.		Bidding time in sec.		Sealing time in sec.	
	Price list length		Price list length		Price list length		Price list length	
	5,000	10,000	5,000	10,000	5,000	10,000	5,000	10,000
512	14	29	37	75	0.22	0.22	0.48	0.48
1024	98	195	248	495	1.48	1.48	2.76	2.76
1536	308	615	766	1515	4.63	8.45	5.69	10.24

We represent the price list as a d-tuples of constant length ordered-vectors. A price list of d vectors is capable to represent the value up to 10^d. Reduction in the size of price list decreases the bandwidth requirement and computational overhead. We estimate bandwidth of every receipt-free bid is $O(log_{10}\ L)$.

Moreover, The proposed mechanism defines less number of message exchange between the entities. Table 2 presents the number of message exchanges required to execute the *proofs & verification*. We also present the average time latency of bidding and sealing operation with varying key size and number of bidding price. Table 3 shows the comparison of time latency between to mechanisms.

7   Conclusion

The proposed auction scheme attempts to solve two existing problems; firstly, it provides receipt-freeness without any untappable channel and secondly, it ensures uncoerciveness even in the presence of colluding authorities. The mechanism guarantees uncoerciveness even all the sealer except one are dishonest. No prior registration of bidder is required. So any one who possesses the required key may participate in the auction. Bidders are not necessarily be present during *opening* i.e. ensures 'bid-and-go' concept. The proposed mechanism improves the performance and efficiency by reducing the bandwidth and communication round.

Appendix

Proof of Sealing

Sealer S_l receives the partially sealed bid-vector $\langle \mathcal{X}_{S_{l-1}i}, \mathcal{Y}_{S_{l-1}i} \rangle$ from the preceding sealer S_{l-1}, selects $\hat{r}_{Sli,(k,j)}, r_{Sli,(k,j)} \in_R \mathbb{Z}_p$ randomly, performs the sealing operation and forwards the partially sealed bid-vector to the next sealer S_{l+1}. Figure 2 describes the process. The sealing operation of the S_l is as follows:

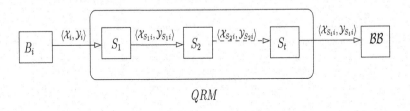

$$QRM$$

Fig. 2. Sequence of sealing operation

$$X_{Sli,(k,j)} = g^{r_{Sli,(k,j)}}.X_{S_{l-1}i,(k.j)}$$

$$= g^{r_{Sli,(k,j)}}.g^{\left(r_{i,(k,j)}+\sum\limits_{t=1}^{l-1} r_{Sti,(k,j)}\right)}$$

$$= g^{\left(r_{i,(k,j)}+\sum\limits_{t=1}^{l} r_{Sti,(k,j)}\right)}$$

$$Y_{Sli,(k,j)} = \hat{r}_{Sli,(k,j)}.h_A^{r_{Sli,(k,j)}}.(h_{S/S_1,\ldots S_l})^{r_{Sli,(k,j)}}.\left(X_{S_{l-1}i,(k,j)}\right)^{-x_{S_l}}.Y_{S_{l-1}i,(k,j)}$$

$$= \hat{r}_{Sli,(k,j)}.h_A^{r_{Sli,(k,j)}}.(h_{S/S_1,\ldots S_l})^{r_{Sli,(k,j)}}.$$

$$\prod_{t=1}^{l-1}\hat{r}_{Sti,(k,j)}.h_A^{\left(r_{i,(k,j)}+\sum\limits_{t=1}^{l-1} r_{Sti,(k,j)}\right)}.(h_{S/S_1\ldots S_l})^{\left(r_{i,(k,j)}+\sum\limits_{t=1}^{l-1} r_{Sti,(k,j)}\right)}.G_\square$$

$$= \prod_{t=1}^{l}\hat{r}_{Sti,(k,j)}.h_A^{\left(r_{i,(k,j)}+\sum\limits_{t=1}^{l} r_{Sti,(k,j)}\right)}.(h_{S/S_1\ldots S_l})^{\left(r_{i,(k,j)}+\sum\limits_{t=1}^{l} r_{Sti,(k,j)}\right)}.G_\square$$

After t sealing operation the bid-vector is reduced to

$$X_{Sti,(k,j)} = g^{\left(r_{i,(k,j)}+\sum\limits_{l=1}^{t} r_{Sli,(k,j)}\right)}$$

$$Y_{Sti,(k,j)} = \prod_{l=1}^{t}\hat{r}_{Sli,(k,j)}.h_A^{\left(r_{i,(k,j)}+\sum\limits_{l=1}^{t} r_{Sli,(k,j)}\right)}.(h_{S/S_1\ldots S_t})^{\left(r_{i,(k,j)}+\sum\limits_{l=1}^{t} r_{Sli,(k,j)}\right)}.G_\square$$

$$= \prod_{l=1}^{t}\hat{r}_{Sli,(k,j)}.h_A^{\left(r_{i,(k,j)}+\sum\limits_{l=1}^{t} r_{Sli,(k,j)}\right)}.G_\square$$

Algorithm 6. $ZK1(B_i, G_i, g_y, h_{B_i}, g)$

---

begin

    Bidder B_i selects $a, b \in_R \mathbb{Z}_p$ and computes $\alpha = g^a$, $\beta = g_y^b$. Bidder B_i sends α and β to the auctioneer

    Auctioneer selects $c \in_R \mathbb{Z}_p$ and sends to B_i

    Bidder B_i computes $r = a + cx_{B_i}$ and sends to the auctioneer

    Auctioneer verifies

$$g^r \stackrel{?}{=} \alpha.h_{B_i}^c \tag{3}$$

$$g_y^r \stackrel{?}{=} \beta.G_i^c \tag{4}$$

    if *(relation 3 &4 are TRUE)* **then**

        Returns TRUE

Algorithm 7. $ZK2(B_i, QUAL, w)$

---

begin

    Bidder B_i compute $\hat{R}_i = \prod_{k=0}^{d-1} \hat{r}_{i,(k,w_k)}$ and sends to the auctioneer

    All sealer $S_l \in QRM$ computes $\hat{R}_{S_l} = \prod_{k=0}^{d-1} \hat{r}_{S_l i,(k,w_k)}$ and $R_{S_l} = \sum_k^{d-1} r_{S_l i,(k,w_k)}$ and

    sends to the auctioneer

    Auctioneer computes

$$\mathbb{X}_i = \prod_{k=0}^{d-1} X_{S_l i,(k,w_k)} \cdot \left(g^{\sum_{l=1}^{t} R_{S_l}} \right)^{-1} = g^{\sum_{k=0}^{d-1} r_{i,(k,w_k)}}$$

$$\mathbb{G} = \prod_{k=0}^{d-1} G_{i,(k,w_k)} \cdot \left(\hat{R}_i \right)^{-1} = G_i^{\sum_{k=0}^{d-1} r_{i,(k,w_k)}}$$

    Bidder B_i and auctioneer execute $ZK1(B_i, \mathbb{G}, G_i, \mathbb{X}_i, g)$

ZK Protocol

Zero-Knowledge (ZK) protocol [7] is a tool by which the prover can prove to another party (the verifier) that a function has been correctly computed, without revealing the secret parameters of the computation. The auction mechanism uses the ZK protocol to determine the winning bidder. Let $w = w_{d-1} \ldots w_0$ be the winning price and B_i responds as the winner. The bidder B_i have to prove the following:

- B_i publishes $G_i = g_y^{x_{B_i}}$ and proves that G_i and h_{B_i} having common exponent (x_{B_i}) over g_y and g respectively, without disclosing the secret x_{B_i}. Algorithm 6 describes the proof.
- For $k = 0, 1, \ldots d-1$, B_i publishes the product of all $\hat{r}_{i,(k,w_k)}$ and proves that he knows the common exponents over $X_{i,(k,w_k)}$s and $G_{i,(k,w_k)}$s. The proof would not be carried on individual items but exercised on the product of all $X_{i,(k,w_k)}$ (for $k = 0, 1, \ldots d-1$). The Algorithm 7 describes the proof.

Does ProcSwap() vulnerable

The subprocess $EBY()$ is a recursive process that partitions the list L into two halves and invokes the **ProcSwap()**. Figure 3 shows the process of partitioning ans swapping operation. $EBY()$ divides the list into some stacks of sealed bids. Every stack contains only two sealed bids where at least one of them must contains the *Yes Mark* on the P_{k,w_k} index. However, **ProcSwap()** procedure takes a stack (size 2) and demands additional information to determine the bid containing the *Yes Mark*. We claim that the additional information that is published in order to execute **ProcSwap()** does not compromise the receipt-freeness property.

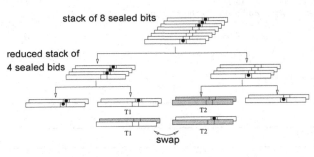

Fig. 3. Process of $EBY()$

Lemma 1. *Let a, b, c & $d \in \mathbb{Z}_p$ such that;*

$$a.b = k_1 \qquad c.d = k_2$$
$$a.c = k_3 \qquad b.d = k_4$$

Though the values of k_1, k_2, k_3 & k_4 are known, it is computationally infeasible to find the unique solution of a, b, c & d.

Proof. In the above set of equation, any one of the equation is derivable from the other three equations. Let $a.b = k_1$, $c.d = k_2$ and $a.c = k_3$ are given, the fourth equation can be derivable from the given three equations, that is, $b.d = (a.b).(c.d).(a.c)^{-1} = k_1.k_2.k_3^{-1}$. Therefore the above system is effectively consists of three equations with four unknown variables. Henceforth infeasible to determine the unique solution of the a, b, c & b. If p is sufficiently big any random search is inefficient to get the solution of $a, b, c,$ & d $\qquad \square$.

Let $T1$ be a stack containing two bids B_1 and B_2. Also let $T2$ be another stack containing two void bids V_1 and V_2. Therefore the $\mathcal{BB}$ already contains the values

$$k_1 = \hat{r}_{S_1 B_1,(k,j)}.\hat{r}_{S_1 B_2,(k,j)}$$

$$k_2 = \hat{r}_{S_1 V_1,(k,j)}.\hat{r}_{S_1 V_2,(k,j)}$$

(The procedure **ProcS**$(T1, S_1, P_{k,j})$ and **ProcS**$(T2, S_1, P_{k,j})$ publish the values). The call to the procedure **ProcSwap(T1,T2)** demands

$$k_3 = \hat{r}_{S_1 B_1,(k,j)}.\hat{r}_{S_1 V_2,(k,j)}$$

$$k_4 = \hat{r}_{S_2 V_1,(k,j)}.\hat{r}_{S_1 V_2,(k,j)}$$

Knowing the values k_1, k_2, k_3 & k_4 adversary would not able to resolve the secrets $\hat{r}_{S_1 B_1,(k,j)}$ and $\hat{r}_{S_1 B_2,(k,j)}$ without better than any random guess.

References

1. Shamir, A.: How to share a secret. Commun. ACM **22**(11), 612–613 (1979)
2. Lee, B., Kim, K.: Receipt-free electronic voting scheme with a tamper-resistant randomizer. In: Lee, P.J., Lim, C.H. (eds.) ICISC 2002. LNCS, vol. 2587, pp. 389–406. Springer, Heidelberg (2003)
3. Bárász, M., Ligeti, P., Mérai, L., Nagy, D.A.: Anonymous sealed bid auction protocol based on a variant of the dining cryptographers' protocol. Periodica Math. Hung. **65**(2), 167–176 (2012)
4. Boyd, C., Mao, W.: Security issues for electronic auctions. HP Laboratories Technical report, Hewlett-Packard Laboratories (2000)
5. Yao, A.C.: Protocols for secure computations. In: 23rd Annual Symposium on Foundations of Computer Science, SFCS '82, pp. 160–164. IEEE Computer Society (1982)
6. Wu, C.-C., Chang, C.-C., Lin, I.-C.: New sealed-bid electronic auction with fairness, security and efficiency. J. Comput. Sci. Technol. **23**(2), 253–264 (2008)
7. Chaum, D., Pedersen, T.P.: Wallet databases with observers. In: Brickell, E.F. (ed.) CRYPTO 1992. LNCS, vol. 740, pp. 89–105. Springer, Heidelberg (1993)
8. Gao, C., an Yao, Z., Xie, D., Wei, B.: Electronic sealed-bid auction with incoercinility. In: Wan, X. (ed.) Electronic Power Systems and Computers. LNEE, vol. 99, pp. 47–54. Springer, Heidelberg (2011)
9. Xiong, H., Qin, Z., Zhang, F., Yang, Y., Zhao, Y.: A sealed-bid electronic auction protocol based on ring signature. In: ICCCAS, pp. 480–483. IEEE (2007)
10. Howlader, J., Ghosh, A., Pal, T.D.R.: Secure receipt-free sealed-bid electronic auction. In: Ranka, S., Aluru, S., Buyya, R., Chung, Y.-C., Dua, S., Grama, A., Gupta, S.K.S., Kumar, R., Phoha, V.V. (eds.) IC3 2009. CCIS, vol. 40, pp. 228–239. Springer, Heidelberg (2009)
11. Howlader, J., Kar, J., Mal, A.K.: Coercion resistant MIX for electronic auction. In: Venkatakrishnan, V., Goswami, D. (eds.) ICISS 2012. LNCS, vol. 7671, pp. 238–248. Springer, Heidelberg (2012)
12. Howlader, J., Basu, S.: Sender-side public key deniable encryption scheme. In: ARTCom, pp. 9–13. IEEE Computer Society (2009)
13. Howlader, J., Nair, V., Basu, S., Mal, A.K.: Uncoercibility in e-voting and e-auctioning mechanisms using deniable encryption. IJNSA **3**(2), 97–109 (2011)
14. Franklin, M.K., Reiter, M.K.: The design and implementation of a secure auction service. IEEE Trans. Softw. Eng. **22**(5), 302–312 (1996)
15. Sako, K., Kilian, J.: Receipt-free mix-type voting scheme. In: Guillou, L.C., Quisquater, J.-J. (eds.) EUROCRYPT 1995. LNCS, vol. 921, pp. 393–403. Springer, Heidelberg (1995)
16. Kikuchi, H., Hakavy, M., Tygar, D.: Multi-round anonymous auction protocols. Inst. Electron. Inf. Commun. Eng. Trans. Inf. Syst. E82-D(4), 769–777 (1999)
17. Chaum, D.L.: Untraceable electronic mail, return addresses, and digital pseudonyms. Commun. ACM **24**(2), 84–90 (1981)
18. Abe, M., Suzuki, K.: Receipt-free sealed-bid auction. In: Chan, A.H., Gligor, V.D. (eds.) ISC 2002. LNCS, vol. 2433, pp. 191–199. Springer, Heidelberg (2002)
19. Jakobsson, M.: A practical mix. In: Nyberg, K. (ed.) EUROCRYPT 1998. LNCS, vol. 1403, pp. 448–461. Springer, Heidelberg (1998)
20. Noar, M., Pinkas, B., Sumner, R.: Privacy preserving auction and mechanism design. In: ACM Conference on Electronic Commerce, pp. 129–139. ACM (1999)

21. Canetti, R., Dwork, C., Naor, M., Ostrovsky, R.: Deniable encryption. In: Kaliski Jr., B.S. (ed.) CRYPTO 1997. LNCS, vol. 1294, pp. 90–104. Springer, Heidelberg (1997)
22. Gennaro, R., Jarecki, S., Krawczyk, H., Rabin, T.: Secure distributed key generation for discrete-log based cryptosystems. In: Stern, J. (ed.) EUROCRYPT 1999. LNCS, vol. 1592, pp. 295–310. Springer, Heidelberg (1999)
23. Gennaro, R., Jarecki, S., Krawczyk, H., Rabin, T.: Secure distributed key generation for discrete-log based cryptosystems. J. Cryptol. 20(1), 51–83 (2007)
24. Rjašková, Z.: Electronic voting schemes. Master's thesis, Department of Computer Science Faculty of Mathematics, Physics and Informatics Comenius University, Bratislava (2002)
25. Goldwasser, S., Micali, S.: How to play any mental game or a completeness theorem for protocols with honest majority. In: 19th Annual ACM Symposium on Theory of Computing, pp. 365–377. ACM (1982)
26. Goldwasser, S., Micali, S.: Probabilistic encryption. J. Comput. Syst. Sci. 28(2), 270–299 (1984)
27. Ham, W., Kim, K., Imai, H.: Yet another strong sealed-bid auctions. In: SCIS, pp. 11–16 (2003)
28. Chen, X., Lee, B., Kim, K.: Receipt-free electronic auction schemes using homomorphic encryption. In: Lim, J.-I., Lee, D.-H. (eds.) ICISC 2003. LNCS, vol. 2971, pp. 259–273. Springer, Heidelberg (2004)
29. Her, Y.-S., Imamoto, K., Sakurai, K.: Receipt-free sealed-bid auction based on mix-net and pseudo ID (2004)
30. Huang, Z., Qiu, W., Guan, H., Chen, K.: Efficient receipt-free electronic auction protocol. In: SITIS, pp. 1023–1028. IEEE Computer Society (2007)

Revocable Group Signatures with Compact Revocation List Using Accumulators

Toru Nakanishi$^{(\boxtimes)}$ and Nobuo Funabiki

Department of Communication Network Engineering, Okayama University,
Okayama City, Japan
{nakanisi,funabiki}@cne.okayama-u.ac.jp

Abstract. Group signatures allow a group member to anonymously sign a message on behalf of the group. One of the important issues is the revocation, and lots of revocable schemes have been proposed so far. The scheme recently proposed by Libert et al. achieves that $O(1)$ or $O(\log N)$ efficiency except for the revocation list size (also the revocation cost), for the total number of members N and the number of revoked members R. However, since a signature is required for each subset in the used subset difference method, the size is about $900R$ Bytes in the 128-bit security. In the case of $R = 100,000$, it amounts to about 80 MB. In this paper, we extend the scheme to reduce the revocation list (also the revocation cost). In the proposed scheme, an extended accumulator accumulates T subsets, which is signed for the revocation list. The revocation list size is reduced by $1/T$, although the public key size, membership certificate size and the cost of a witness computation needed for signing increase related to T.

Keywords: Anonymity · Group signatures · Revocations · Accumulators

1 Introduction

The *group signature scheme* [13] allows a group member to anonymously sign a message on behalf of the group. In the group signature scheme, two types of trusted parties participate: A *group manager* (*GM*) has the authority to add a user to the own group. An *opener* can identify the signer from a signature. One of important issues in the group signature schemes is a *revocation* that the signing capability of a user is revoked. The revocation may happen, when the user leaves the group voluntarily or the account is banned due to the illegal usage, etc.

Lots of revocable group signature schemes have been proposed (e.g., [6–8,10–12,16,17,19,20]). Hereafter, let N be the total number of group members, and R be the number of revoked members. In the early scheme [7], the signature size is $O(R)$ (also, the costs of signing and verification). Then, the accumulator-based scheme has been proposed in [12], which is followed in [11], to achieve

This work was supported by JSPS KAKENHI Grant Number 25330153.

H.-S. Lee and D.-G. Han (Eds.): ICISC 2013, LNCS 8565, pp. 435–451, 2014.
DOI: 10.1007/978-3-319-12160-4_26

the constant-size signature with the constant verification costs. However, each member has to update a secret key (a witness for the accumulator) using the revocation data, which implies that signing costs is $O(R)$ in the worst case.

In [19], revocable schemes with the costs of constant signing and verification have been proposed. The demerit of the schemes is the long public key size. The basic scheme needs $O(N)$ size, and the extended one needs $O(\sqrt{N})$ in exchange for the extra signing cost. Recently, in [17], Libert et al. proposed an elegant scalable scheme using Naor et al.'s broadcast encryption framework [21]. This scheme achieves the constant verification cost, and the polylogarithmic public and secret key sizes. Finally, the same authors proposed the extended version with $O(1)$ secret key size [16], as achieving $O(1)$ signature size, $O(1)$ signing/verification costs and $O(\log N)$ public key size.

In this paper, we consider reducing the revocation list size. In [16], to indicate the revoked members, $O(R)$ size is needed for the revocation list. Furthermore, in the list, a signature is required for each subset in the used subset difference (SD) method, and the number of the signatures is bounded by $2R - 1$. The signature is an AHO signature [2], which needs 7 elements of a bilinear group. Assuming 128-bit security, the signature size is 448 Bytes. Thus, the revocation list size is about $900R$ Bytes or more. In an example of $R = 10,000$, the size amounts to 8 MB or more, and in case of $R = 100,000$, it becomes 80 MB or more. Note that the signer has to fetch all data of the latest revocation list every revocation epoch, as noted in [3]. This is because fetching a part of the list can reveal the information to trace the signer. Therefore, the large data may cause a delay in mobile environments.

In this paper, we propose a revocable group signature scheme with a compact revocation list as the extension of the state-of-the-art scheme [16]. In our scheme, using an extended accumulator based on [4], GM accumulates T subsets in the SD method, and signs the accumulated value. This is why the number of signatures is reduced by $1/T$. The revocation cost is similar. In case of $R = 100,000$, the size of the signature data including the accumulated value is reduced to 1,000 KB if $T = 100$. The compensation is increasing the public key size, the membership certificate size, and the cost of a witness computation needed for signing. Nevertheless, in case of $T = 100$, the public key size is 2,500 KB and the membership certificate size is 13 KB. In real applications, the public key and the certificate are not often distributed. On the other hand, the revocation list has to be distributed every revocation epoch. Thus, we consider that it is sufficiently practical to decrease the revocation list size while increasing the public key and the membership certificate sizes. The witness computation cost is about 120 exponentiations in case of $T = 100$. This cost is comparable to the computation cost of commitments in the original signing. This computation is needed only once every revocation epoch. As shown in Sect. 5, we can reduce the cost by computing only the modified parts from the previous epoch. Therefore, we consider that the extra costs are not a serious issue.

Due to the page limitation, the preliminary section reviewing the bilinear map and utilized primitives is in Appendix A.

2 Extended Accumulator

In [11], an efficient pairing-based accumulator is proposed. The accumulator is generated from a set of values, and we can verify that a single value is included in the set. In [22], the extended version is proposed, where we can verify that multiple values are included in the specified set, all at once. In [4], another extension is proposed, where we can verify that, for a set U, for all multiple sets $V_1, \ldots, V_T$, a value from U is included in each V_t, i.e., $U \cap V_t \neq \emptyset$, all at once. This is applied to the verification for CNF formulas on attributes in the anonymous credential system of [4]. For a CNF formula $(\mathsf{a}_1 \in U \vee \cdots \vee \mathsf{a}_{L'} \in U) \wedge (\mathsf{b}_1 \in U \vee \cdots \vee \mathsf{b}_L \in U) \cdots$, setting $V_1 = \{\mathsf{a}_1, \ldots, \}, V_2 = \{\mathsf{b}_1, \ldots\}, \ldots$, we can verify the formula by checking $U \cap V_t \neq \emptyset$ for all t.

This paper furthermore extends the accumulator in [4], since our group signature scheme also needs the CNF-type verification. The scheme requires the verification of the logical formula as $(\mathsf{a}_{t1} \in U \wedge \cdots \wedge \mathsf{a}_{tL_t} \in U) \wedge (\mathsf{b}_{t1} \in U \vee \cdots \vee \mathsf{b}_{tL} \in U)$ for some t, given $V_t = \{\mathsf{a}_{t1}, \ldots, \mathsf{a}_{tL_t}\}, \tilde{V}_t = \{\mathsf{b}_{t1}, \ldots, \mathsf{b}_{tL}\}$ for all $1 \leq t \leq T$. The length of the AND relation is variable, but the length of the matched AND relation has to be hidden in the group signature scheme. Thus, we introduce a dummy parameter SP. The other point of extension is to unbind the limitation of the number of given sets $(V_1, \tilde{V}_1), \ldots, (V_T, \tilde{V}_T)$, i.e., $2T$. In the previous accumulator, the number is bounded by the order p of the bilinear groups. In our construction, for any K, D s.t. $T = K \cdot D$, the target sets are divided to $((V_{1,1}, \tilde{V}_{1,1}), \ldots, (V_{1,D}, \tilde{V}_{1,D})), \ldots, ((V_{K,1}, \tilde{V}_{K,1}), \ldots, (V_{K,D}, \tilde{V}_{K,D}))$. Using randomized public parameters $(g_{k,1}, \ldots)$ for each $1 \leq k \leq K$, although D is bounded by p, $T = K \cdot D$ becomes unbounded.

2.1 Proposed Construction

For all $1 \leq k \leq K$ and all $1 \leq d \leq D$, define $V_{k,d}$ and $\tilde{V}_{k,d}$ as subsets of $\{1, \ldots, n\}$. Define $\mathcal{V} = \{(V_{k,d}, \tilde{V}_{k,d})\}_{k=1,\ldots,K,d=1,\ldots,D}$. Let U be a subset of $\{1, \ldots, n\}$ satisfying $U \cap V_{\tilde{k},\tilde{d}} = V_{\tilde{k},\tilde{d}}$ and $U \cap \tilde{V}_{\tilde{k},\tilde{d}} \neq \emptyset$ for some $1 \leq \tilde{d} \leq D$ and some $1 \leq \tilde{k} \leq K$. In this construction, we assume that the maximum of $|V_{k,d}|$ and $|\tilde{V}_{k,d}|$ is ζ for all $1 \leq k \leq K$ and all $1 \leq d \leq D$. In addition, we assume $(U \cap V_{k,d}) = (U \cap \tilde{V}_{k,d}) = \emptyset$ for all $1 \leq k \leq K$ and all $1 \leq d \leq D$ except some k' and d'. If $U \cap V_{\tilde{k},\tilde{d}} = V_{\tilde{k},\tilde{d}}$ and $U \cap \tilde{V}_{\tilde{k},\tilde{d}} \neq \emptyset$, then it implies $k' = \tilde{k}$ and $d' = \tilde{d}$. These assumptions hold in our application to the revocable group signatures. We introduce mutually different special elements $\mathsf{SP}_{k,d} \in \mathcal{N}$ for all k, d such that $\mathsf{SP}_{k,d} \notin V_{k',d'}$ for all k', d'. We assume that $\mathsf{SP}_{\tilde{k},\tilde{d}} \in U$ but $\mathsf{SP}_{k,d} \notin U$ for any $k \neq \tilde{k}, d \neq \tilde{d}$.

AccSetup: This is the algorithm to output the public parameters. The inputs are the security parameter l and $n, K, D, \{\mathsf{SP}_{k,d}\}_{1 \leq k \leq K, 1 \leq d \leq K}, \zeta$. Select bilinear groups $\mathcal{G}, \mathcal{T}$ with a prime order $p > 2^l$ and a bilinear map e. Select

$g \in_R \mathcal{G}$. Select $\gamma, \eta_1, \ldots, \eta_K \in_R Z_p$, and compute $g_1 = g^{\gamma^1}, \ldots, g_n = g^{\gamma^n}, g_{n+2} = g^{\gamma^{n+2}}, \ldots, g_{2n} = g^{\gamma^{2n}}$, and $g_{k,1} = g_1^{\eta_k}, \ldots, g_{k,n} = g_n^{\eta_k}, g_{k,n+2} = g_{n+2}^{\eta_k}, \ldots, g_{k,2n} = g_{2n}^{\eta_k} z_k = e(g,g)^{\eta_k \gamma^{n+1}}$ for all $1 \le k \le K$. For all $1 \le d \le D$, compute $c_d = (\zeta+1)^{2d-2}, \tilde{c}_d = (\zeta+1)^{2d-1}$ and set $\mathcal{C} = ((c_1, \tilde{c}_1), \ldots, (c_D, \tilde{c}_D))$. We assume that $(\zeta+1)c_D < p$. Publish $n, K, D, \{SP_{k,d}\}_{1 \le k \le K, 1 \le d \le K}, \zeta, \mathcal{C}, p,$
$\mathcal{G}, \mathcal{T}, e, g, (g_1, \ldots, g_n, g_{n+2}, \ldots, g_{2n}), \{g_{k,1}, \ldots, g_{k,n}, g_{k,n+2}, \ldots, g_{k,2n}, z_k\}_{k=1}^K$
as the public parameters.

AccGen: This is the algorithm to compute the accumulator using the public parameters. The accumulator $acc_{\mathcal{V}}$ of $\mathcal{V}$ is computed as

$$acc_{\mathcal{V}} = \prod_{1 \le k \le K} \prod_{1 \le d \le D} \left(\left(\prod_{j \in V_{k,d}} g_{k,n+1-j} \right)^{c_d} \cdot \left(\prod_{j=1}^{\zeta - |V_{k,d}|} g_{k,n+1-SP_{k,d}} \right)^{c_d} \cdot \left(\prod_{j \in \tilde{V}_{k,d}} g_{k,n+1-j} \right)^{\tilde{c}_d} \right).$$

AccWitGen: This is the algorithm to compute the witness that $U \cap V_{\tilde{k},\tilde{d}} = V_{\tilde{k},\tilde{d}}$ and $U \cap \tilde{V}_{\tilde{k},\tilde{d}} \ne \emptyset$ for some $1 \le \tilde{d} \le D$ and some $1 \le \tilde{k} \le K$, using the public parameters. Given U, $\mathcal{V}$, and the accumulator $acc_{\mathcal{V}}$, the witness is computed as

$$W = \prod_{i \in U} \prod_{1 \le k \le K} \prod_{1 \le d \le D} \left(\left(\prod_{\substack{j \in V_{k,d} \\ j \ne i}} g_{k,n+1-j+i} \right)^{c_d} \cdot \left(\prod_{j=1}^{\zeta - |V_{k,d}|, i \ne SP_{k,d}} g_{k,n+1-SP_{k,d}+i} \right)^{c_d} \cdot \right.$$
$$\left. \left(\prod_{\substack{j \in \tilde{V}_{k,d} \\ j \ne i}} g_{k,n+1-j+i} \right)^{\tilde{c}_d} \right).$$

Furthermore, the auxiliary parameters are set as $\tilde{k}, \tilde{d}, \delta_{\tilde{k},\tilde{d}} = |U \cap \tilde{V}_{\tilde{k},\tilde{d}}|$.

AccVerify: This is the algorithm to verify that $U \cap V_{\tilde{k},\tilde{d}} = V_{\tilde{k},\tilde{d}}$ and $U \cap \tilde{V}_{\tilde{k},\tilde{d}} \ne \emptyset$ for some $1 \le \tilde{d} \le D$ and some $1 \le \tilde{k} \le K$, using the witness, the auxiliary parameters, and the public parameters. Given $acc_{\mathcal{V}}, U, W, \tilde{k}, \tilde{d}$ and $\delta_{\tilde{k},\tilde{d}}$, accept if

$$\frac{e(\prod_{i \in U} g_i, acc_{\mathcal{V}})}{e(g, W)} = z_{\tilde{k}}^{\zeta c_{\tilde{d}} + \delta_{\tilde{k},\tilde{d}} \tilde{c}_{\tilde{d}}}, \qquad 1 \le \delta_{\tilde{k},\tilde{d}} \le \zeta. \qquad (1)$$

2.2   Security

We can show the correctness and the security. The proofs are shown in the full paper.

Theorem 1. *Assume that* **AccSetup**, **AccGen**, **AccWitGen** *correctly compute all parameters. Then,* **AccVerify** *accepts* $U, acc_{\mathcal{V}}, W, \tilde{k}, \tilde{d}$ *and* $\delta_{\tilde{k},\tilde{d}}$ *that they outputs.*

Theorem 2. *Under the n-DHE assumption, any adversary cannot output* $(U, \mathcal{V}, W, \tilde{k}, \tilde{d}, \delta_{\tilde{k},\tilde{d}})$, *on inputs* $n, K, D, \{SP_{k,d}\}_{1 \le k \le K, 1 \le d \le K}, \zeta, \mathcal{C}, p, \mathcal{G}, \mathcal{T}, e, g, (g_1, \ldots, g_n, g_{n+2}, \ldots, g_{2n}), \{g_{k,1}, \ldots, g_{k,n}, g_{k,n+2}, \ldots, g_{k,2n}, z_k\}_{k=1}^K$ *s.t.* **AccVerify** *accepts* $U, acc_{\mathcal{V}}, W, \tilde{k}, \tilde{d}, \delta_{\tilde{k},\tilde{d}}$ *but* $U \cap V_{k',d'} \ne V_{k',d'}$ *or* $U \cap \tilde{V}_{k',d'} = \emptyset$ *for some k', d', assuming the following preconditions.*

1. $(U \cap V_{k,d}) = (U \cap \tilde{V}_{k,d}) = \emptyset$ for all $1 \leq k \leq K$ and all $1 \leq d \leq D$ except $k = k'$ and $d = d'$,
2. only $SP_{k',d'}$ is included in U (other $SP_{k,d}$ is not included).

3 Syntax and Security of Revocable Group Signatures

3.1 Syntax

Setup(l, N, K, D): Given the security parameter $l \in \mathbb{N}$, the maximum number of group members $N \in \mathbb{N}$, and the efficiency parameters $K, D \in \mathbb{N}$, this algorithm outputs a group public key gpk, a GM's secret key gsk, and an opener's secret key osk. This algorithm initializes a public state St comprising a set data structure $St_{users} = \emptyset$ and a string data structure $St_{trans} = \epsilon$.

Join: This is an interactive protocol between the group manager GM and a joining user $\mathcal{U}_i$. The interactive Turing machines are denoted as J_{GM} and $J_{\mathcal{U}_i}$, respectively. After the protocol $[J_{GM}(l, St, gpk, gsk), J_{\mathcal{U}_i}(l, gpk)]$ is executed, $J_{\mathcal{U}_i}$ outputs a membership secret sec_i and a membership certificate $cert_i$. The protocol is successful, J_{GM} updates St by setting $St_{user} = St_{user} \cup \{i\}$ and $St_{trans} = St_{trans} \| \langle i, \mathsf{transcript}_i \rangle$.

Revoke($gpk, gsk, \tau, \mathcal{R}_\tau$): Given gpk, gsk, epoch τ and $\mathcal{R}_\tau \subset \{1, \ldots, N\}$ that is the identities of revoked members at the epoch τ, this algorithm outputs the revocation list RL_τ.

Sign($gpk, \tau, RL_\tau, cert_i, sec_i, M$): Given gpk, τ, RL_τ, the signing member's $cert_i$, sec_i, and the message M to be signed, this algorithm outputs $\perp$ if $i \in \mathcal{R}_t$ or the signature σ otherwise.

Verify($gpk, \tau, RL_\tau, \sigma, M$): Given gpk, τ, RL_τ, the signature σ and message M, this algorithm outputs 1 if the signature is valid and not revoked for the revocation list RL_τ, or 0 otherwise.

Open($gpk, \tau, RL_\tau, \sigma, M, St, osk$): Given $gpk, \tau, RL_\tau, \sigma, M$ as in **Verify**, the state St in **Join**, and the opener's secret key osk, this algorithm outputs $i \in St_{users} \cup \{\perp\}$ which means the identity of the signer of σ or a symbol of an opening failure.

3.2 Security Model

The security of the revocable group signature scheme consists of *security against misidentification attacks*, *security against framing attacks*, and *anonymity*. The security against misidentification attacks requires that the adversary cannot forge a signature that is identified to one outside the set of corrupted and non-revoked members. The security against framing attacks requires that a signature of an honest member cannot be computed by other members and even GM. The anonymity captures the anonymity and the unlinkability of signatures. The formal definitions are described in the full paper.

4 A Revocable Group Signature with Compact Revocation List and Constant Verification Time

4.1 Construction Idea

The proposed scheme is based on the previous scheme [16]. The approach of the previous scheme is as follows. The subset cover framework with the SD method is used. To each member, a leaf node v in the binary tree with the height L for $N = 2^L$ is assigned. Every node in the tree is assigned to a unique number. In **Join**, to the member, a membership certificate is issued, which is an AHO signature on a public key and an accumulated data for the node numbers on the path from the root to v, $\mathsf{ID}_1, \ldots, \mathsf{ID}_L$. For the accumulation, they adopt a vector commitment [18] that is similar to the accumulators. In **Revoke**, GM publishes the revocation list, where each entry consists of accumulated values for primary and secondary nodes in each S_i in the SD method, and the AHO signature on them and the current time epoch τ. In the group signature, to show that the signer is not a revoked member, she proves

1. an AHO signature binds between τ and the primary node with number $\tilde{\mathsf{ID}}_{i,\phi_i}$ of level ϕ_i and the secondary node $\tilde{\mathsf{ID}}_{i,\psi_i}$ of level ψ_i in an S_i,
2. for ID_{ϕ_i} with level ϕ_i and ID_{ψ_i} with level ψ_i in the membership certificate, it holds that $\mathsf{ID}_{\phi_i} = \tilde{\mathsf{ID}}_{i,\phi_i}$ and $\mathsf{ID}_{\psi_i} \neq \tilde{\mathsf{ID}}_{i,\psi_i}$.

The second relation means that the primary node $\tilde{\mathsf{ID}}_{i,\phi_i}$ is an ancestor of v and the secondary node $\tilde{\mathsf{ID}}_{i,\psi_i}$ is not, i.e., the subset S_i includes v, which implies that the member is not revoked due to the subset cover framework. In this approach, an AHO signature is needed for each subset S_i. Each signature needs long data (448 Bytes in 128-bit security), and thus the revocation list becomes long as R increases.

In our approach, to accumulate the revocation list, we adopt the extended accumulator in Sect. 2. Although the same tree structure in the subset cover framework is used, a different coding is used. In the tree, for the edge to the left (resp., right) child in the depth j, use index $(j, 0)$ (resp, $(j, 1)$). Then, for the leaf v assigned to the member, let $(1, x_1), \ldots, (L, x_L)$ be the path from the root to the leaf v, where $x_\ell \in \{0, 1\}$. Similarly, for the subset S_i, let $(1, s_{i,1}), \ldots, (\phi_i, s_{i,\phi_i})$ denote the path from the root to the primary root and let $(1, s_{i,1}), \ldots, (\psi_i, s_{i,\psi_i})$ denote the path to the secondary root, where $\phi_i, \psi_i \in \{1, \ldots, L\}$ and $s_{i,j} \in \{0, 1\}$. To prove the non-revocation, the signer prove that $((1, x_1) = (1, s_{i_1})) \wedge \cdots \wedge ((\phi_i, x_{\phi_i}) = (\phi_i, s_{\phi_i}))$ (i.e., the primary node is an ancestor v) and $((\phi_i + 1, x_{\phi_i+1}) \neq (\phi_i+1, s_{\phi_i+1})) \vee \cdots \vee ((\psi_i, x_{\psi_i}) \neq (\psi_i, s_{\psi_i}))$ (i.e., the secondary node is not an ancestor of v). The latter relation can be rewritten as $((\phi_i+1, x_{\phi_i+1}) = (\phi_i + 1, \overline{s_{\phi_i+1}})) \vee \cdots \vee ((\psi_i, x_{\psi_i}) = (\psi_i, \overline{s_{\psi_i}}))$.

Using the accumulator, we can prove the relations. Let T be the number of accumulated S_i. For T, given K, D such that $T = K \cdot D$. For all $1 \leq t \leq T$, consider function I_t mapping $\{(\ell, b)\}_{1 \leq \ell \leq L, b \in \{0,1\}}$ to $\{T + 1, \ldots, n\}$ such that $\{I_t(\ell, b)\}_{1 \leq \ell \leq L, b \in \{0,1\}} \cap \{I_{t'}(\ell, b)\}_{1 \leq \ell \leq L, b \in \{0,1\}} = \emptyset$ for any pair $1 \leq t, t' \leq T$.

Set $\mathsf{SP}_{k,d} = D \cdot (k-1) + d$ for all $1 \le k \le K$ and $1 \le d \le D$. Note that $\mathsf{SP}_{k,d} \in \{1, \ldots, T\}$. The relation is required to satisfy the precondition of the accumulator. Define $U_t = \{I_t(1, x_1), \ldots, I_t(L, x_L), \mathsf{SP}_{k,d}\}$ for all $1 \le t \le T$, where $k = \lceil t/D \rceil$ and $d = t \bmod D$. The accumulated $P_t = \prod_{i \in U_t} g_i$ is embedded into a membership certificate for all t. As for the revocation list, for $w = \lceil m/T \rceil$, divide $S_1, \ldots, S_m$ into w sequences:

$$\mathcal{S}_1 = (S_1, \ldots, S_T), \mathcal{S}_2 = (S_{T+1}, \ldots, S_{2T}), \ldots, \mathcal{S}_w = (S_{(w-1)T+1}, \ldots, S_m),$$

where $\mathcal{S}_1, \ldots, \mathcal{S}_{w-1}$ contain T elements and $\mathcal{S}_w$ contains T or less elements. Here, we can connect any S_i to the corresponding sequence $\mathcal{S}_w$ by the relation $\omega = \lceil i/T \rceil$. For each $\mathcal{S}_w$, do the following. Compute $t = i \bmod T$ to determine the position of S_i in $\mathcal{S}_w$. Transform t to the corresponding (k, d) in the accumulator, by $k = \lceil t/D \rceil$ and $d = t \bmod D$. For all (k, d) correspondent $1 \le t \le T$ in $\mathcal{S}_w$ (i.e., $(\omega - 1)T + 1 \le i \le \omega T$), set $V_{k,d} = \{I_t(1, s_{i,1}), \ldots, I_t(\phi_i, s_{i,\phi_i})\}$ and $\tilde{V}_{k,d} = \{I_t(\phi_i + 1, \overline{s_{i,\phi_i+1}}), \ldots, I_t(\psi_i, \overline{s_{i,\psi_i}})\}$. As the revocation list, GM publishes the accumulator $acc_\mathcal{V}$ for $\mathcal{V} = \{(V_{k,d}, \tilde{V}_{k,d})\}_{k=1,\ldots,K, d=1,\ldots,D}$ together with the AHO signature. By accumulating S_i's into $\mathcal{S}_w$, the number of published signatures is reduced by $1/T$.

In the group signature, for some $\tilde{t}$, the signer proves that $U_{\tilde{t}} \cap V_{\tilde{k},\tilde{d}} = V_{\tilde{k},\tilde{d}}$ and $U_{\tilde{t}} \cap \tilde{V}_{\tilde{k},\tilde{d}} \ne \emptyset$ for some $1 \le \tilde{d} \le D$ and some $1 \le \tilde{k} \le K$, using the accumulator verification. The former relation means the AND relation $((1, x_1) = (1, s_{i_1})) \wedge \cdots$ and the latter means that OR relation $((\phi_i + 1, x_{\phi_i+1}) = (\phi_i + 1, \overline{s_{\phi_i+1}})) \vee \cdots$. In the verification relations (1) of the accumulator, the right hand reveals the indexes $\tilde{k}, \tilde{d}$ via $z_{\tilde{k}}, c_{\tilde{d}}, \tilde{c}_{\tilde{d}}$. To hide the indexes, we utilize the technique of membership proof using signatures [9]. Also, we utilize the technique to prove $1 \le \delta_{\tilde{k},\tilde{d}} \le \zeta$ in the accumulator.

4.2 Proposed Construction

Setup. The inputs are the security parameter l, the maximum number of group members N, and the efficiency parameters K, D.

1. Select bilinear groups $\mathcal{G}, \mathcal{T}$ with the same order $p > 2^l$ and the bilinear map e, and $g \in_R \mathcal{G}$.
2. Set parameter $T = K \cdot D$.
3. Generate public parameters of the extended accumulator: Set $\zeta = L$. Set $\mathsf{SP}_{k,d} = D \cdot (k-1) + d$ for all $1 \le k \le K$ and $1 \le d \le D$. Note that $\mathsf{SP}_{k,d} \in \{1, \ldots, T\}$. Select $\gamma, \eta_1, \ldots, \eta_K \in_R Z_p$, and compute $g_1 = g^{\gamma^1}, \ldots, g_n = g^{\gamma^n}, g_{n+2} = g^{\gamma^{n+2}}, \ldots, g_{2n} = g^{\gamma^{2n}}$, and $g_{k,1} = g_1^{\eta_k}, \ldots, g_{k,n} = g_n^{\eta_k}, g_{k,n+2} = g_{n+2}^{\eta_k}, \ldots, g_{k,2n} = g_{2n}^{\eta_k}$ $z_k = e(g,g)^{\eta_k \gamma^{n+1}}$ for all $1 \le k \le K$. For all $1 \le d \le D$, compute $c_d = (\zeta + 1)^{2d-2}$, $\tilde{c}_d = (\zeta + 1)^{2d-1}$ and set $\mathcal{C} = ((c_1, \tilde{c}_1), \ldots, (c_D, \tilde{c}_D))$. Set

$$pk_{acc} = (\{\mathsf{SP}_{k,d}\}_{1 \le k \le K, 1 \le d \le D}, \zeta, \mathcal{C}, (g_1, \ldots, g_n, g_{n+2}, \ldots, g_{2n}),$$
$$\{g_{k,1}, \ldots, g_{k,n}, g_{k,n+2}, \ldots, g_{k,2n}, z_k\}_{k=1}^K).$$

4. Define $n_1 = n_3 = n_4 = 2, n_2 = 1$. Generate four key pairs for the AHO signature:

$$pk_{\mathrm{AHO}}^{(d)} = (G_r^{(d)}, H_r^{(d)}, G_z^{(d)}, H_z^{(d)}, \{G_i^{(d)}, H_i^{(d)}\}_{i=1}^{n_d}, A^{(d)}, B^{(d)}),$$
$$sk_{\mathrm{AHO}}^{(d)} = (\alpha_a^{(d)}, \alpha_b^{(d)}, \mu_z^{(d)}, \nu_z^{(d)}, \mu, \nu),$$

where $d \in \{1, 2, 3, 4\}$.

5. Generate a CRS for the GS NIWI proof: select $\boldsymbol{f} = (\boldsymbol{f}_1, \boldsymbol{f}_2, \boldsymbol{f}_3)$, where $\boldsymbol{f}_1 = (f_1, 1, g)$, $\boldsymbol{f}_2 = (1, f_2, g)$, $\boldsymbol{f}_3 = \boldsymbol{f}_1^{\xi_1} \cdot \boldsymbol{f}_2^{\xi_2}$ for $\xi_1, \xi_2, y_1, y_2 \in_R Z_p^*$ and $f_1 = g^{y_1}, f_2 = g^{y_2}$. Set $\tilde{\boldsymbol{f}} = \boldsymbol{f}_3 \cdot (1, 1, g)$.

6. Define set $\Phi = \{(g_{k,1}^{c_d}, g_{k,1}^{\tilde{c}_d}) | 1 \le k \le K, 1 \le d \le D\}$, where $|\Phi| = K \cdot D = T$. For every $(g_{k,1}^{c_d}, g_{k,1}^{\tilde{c}_d}) \in \Phi$, generate the AHO signature on two messages $(g_{k,1}^{c_d}, g_{k,1}^{\tilde{c}_d})$, using $sk_{\mathrm{AHO}}^{(1)}$. The signature is denoted as $\tilde{\sigma}_t = (\tilde{\theta}_{t1}, \ldots, \tilde{\theta}_{t7})$, where $t = D \cdot (k - 1) + d$.

7. For every $1 \le \delta \le \zeta$, generate the AHO signature on message g_n^δ, using $sk_{\mathrm{AHO}}^{(2)}$. The signature is denoted as $\hat{\sigma}_\delta = (\hat{\theta}_{\delta 1}, \ldots, \hat{\theta}_{\delta 7})$.

8. Select $\mathcal{U}, \mathcal{V} \in_R \mathcal{G}$ for a pubic encryption.

9. Select a strongly unforgeable one-time signature $\Sigma_{\mathrm{OTS}} = (\mathbf{Setup}_{\mathrm{OTS}}, \mathbf{Sign}_{\mathrm{OTS}}, \mathbf{Verify}_{\mathrm{OTS}})$.

10. Output the group public key $gpk = (K, D, p, \mathcal{G}, \mathcal{T}, e, g, pk_{\mathrm{acc}}, \{pk_{\mathrm{AHO}}^{(i)}\}_{i=1,2,3,4}, \boldsymbol{f}, \tilde{\boldsymbol{f}}, \{\tilde{\sigma}_t\}_{t \in \Phi}, \{\hat{\sigma}_\delta\}_{1 \le \delta \le \zeta}, (\mathcal{U}, \mathcal{V}), \Sigma_{\mathrm{OTS}})$, the GM's secret key $gsk = (\{sk_{\mathrm{AHO}}^{(i)}\}_{i=1,2,3,4})$ and the opener's secret key $osk = (y_1, y_2)$.

Join. The common inputs of J_{GM} and $\mathsf{J}_{\mathcal{U}_i}$ are I, gpk. The additional inputs of J_{GM} are St, gsk.

1. $\mathsf{J}_{\mathcal{U}_i}$ selects $x \in_R \mathcal{G}$, computes $X = g^x$ and send X to J_{GM}. If X is already registered in database St_{trans}, J_{GM} halts and returns $\perp$ to $\mathsf{J}_{\mathcal{U}_i}$.

2. J_{GM} assigns to the user a leaf v in the tree. Let $(1, x_1), \ldots, (L, x_L)$ be the path from the root to the leaf v. Define $U_t = \{I_t(1, x_1), \ldots, I_t(L, x_L), \mathsf{SP}_{k,d}\}$ for all $1 \le t \le T$, where $k = \lceil t/D \rceil$ and $d = t \bmod D$. J_{GM} computes $P_t = \prod_{i \in U_t} g_i$ for all $1 \le t \le T$.

3. J_{GM} generates an AHO signature $\sigma_t = (\theta_{t,1}, \ldots, \theta_{t,7})$ on (X, P_t) for all $1 \le t \le T$, using $sk_{\mathrm{AHO}}^{(3)}$.

4. J_{GM} sends $v, \{P_t\}_{1 \le t \le T}$ to $\mathsf{J}_{\mathcal{U}_i}$. $\mathsf{J}_{\mathcal{U}_i}$ checks the correctness of P_t's. If these are incorrect, $\mathsf{J}_{\mathcal{U}_i}$ aborts. Otherwise, $\mathsf{J}_{\mathcal{U}_i}$ sends J_{GM} the ordinary digital signature sig_i on (X, v).

5. J_{GM} verifies sig. If it is incorrect, J_{GM} aborts. Otherwise, J_{GM} sends the AHO signature σ_t to $\mathsf{J}_{\mathcal{U}_i}$, and stores $\langle i, \mathsf{transcript}_i = (v, X, \{P_t, \sigma_t\}_{1 \le t \le T}, sig_i)\rangle$ in the database St_{trans}.

6. $\mathsf{J}_{\mathcal{U}_i}$ outputs the membership certificate $cert_i = (v, X, \{U_t, P_t, \sigma_t\}_{1 \le t \le T})$ and the membership secret $sec_i = x$.

Revoke. The inputs are gpk, gsk, the epoch τ and the revocation members $\mathcal{R}_\tau$.

1. By the subset covering of the SD scheme, find a cover of the unrevoked users, $S_1, \ldots, S_m$. Set $w = \lceil m/T \rceil$. Divide $S_1, \ldots, S_m$ into w sequences:

$$\mathcal{S}_1 = (S_1, \ldots, S_T), \mathcal{S}_2 = (S_{T+1}, \ldots, S_{2T}), \ldots, \mathcal{S}_w = (S_{(w-1)T+1}, \ldots, S_m),$$

where $\mathcal{S}_1, \ldots, \mathcal{S}_{w-1}$ contain T elements and $\mathcal{S}_w$ contains T or less elements. Here, we can connect any S_i to the corresponding sequence $\mathcal{S}_\omega$ by the relation $\omega = \lceil i/T \rceil$. For the sub-tree S_i, let $(1, s_{i,1}), \ldots, (\phi_i, s_{i,\phi_i})$ denote the path from the root to the primary root and let $(1, s_{i,1}), \ldots, (\psi_i, s_{i,\psi_i})$ denote the path to the secondary root, where $\phi_i, \psi_i \in \{1, \ldots, L\}$ and each $s_{i,j} \in \{0, 1\}$.

2. For $\mathcal{S}_\omega$ with all $1 \leq \omega \leq w$, do the following.
   (a) To determine the position of S_i in $\mathcal{S}_\omega$, compute $t = i \bmod T$. Transform t to the corresponding (k, d) in the accumulator, by $k = \lceil t/D \rceil$ and $d = t \bmod D$. For all (k, d) correspondent $1 \leq t \leq T$ in $\mathcal{S}_\omega$ (i.e., $(\omega-1)T+1 \leq i \leq \omega T$), set $V_{k,d} = \{I_t(1, s_{i,1}), \ldots, I_t(\phi_i, s_{i,\phi_i})\}$ and $\tilde{V}_{k,d} = \{I_t(\phi_i + 1, \overline{s_{i,\phi_i+1}}), \ldots, I_t(\psi_i, s_{i,\psi_i})\}$, where $\overline{s_{i,\ell}}$ is the negation of $s_{i,\ell}$.
   (b) Compute $acc_\omega = \prod_{1 \leq k \leq K} \prod_{1 \leq d \leq D} ((\prod_{j \in V_{k,d}} g_{k,n+1-j})^{c_d} \cdot (\prod_{j=1}^{\zeta-|V_{k,d}|} g_{k,n+1-\mathsf{SP}_{k,d}})^{c_d} \cdot (\prod_{j \in \tilde{V}_{k,d}} g_{k,n+1-j})^{\tilde{c}_d})$.

3. For all $1 \leq \omega \leq w$, compute the AHO signature on pair (g^τ, acc_ω): $\Theta_\omega = (\Theta_{\omega,1}, \ldots, \Theta_{\omega,7})$, using $sk_{\mathsf{AHO}}^{(4)}$.

4. Output the revocation list: $RL_\tau = (\tau, \mathcal{R}_\tau, \{S_i\}_{i=1}^m, \{acc_\omega, \Theta_\omega\}_{\omega=1}^w)$.

Sign. The inputs are $gpk, \tau, RL_\tau, cert_i, sec_i$ and the message M.

1. Using $\mathbf{Setup_{OTS}}$, generate a key pair $(\mathsf{SK}, \mathsf{VK})$ of the one-time signature.

2. Using RL_τ, find the set $S_{\tilde{i}}$ including the signing user. For the subset $S_{\tilde{i}}$, let $(1, s_{\tilde{i},1}), \ldots, (\phi_{\tilde{i}}, s_{\tilde{i},\phi_{\tilde{i}}})$ denote the path from the root to the primary root and let $(1, s_{\tilde{i},1}), \ldots, (\psi_{\tilde{i}}, s_{\tilde{i},\psi_{\tilde{i}}})$ denote the path to the secondary root. Then, find $\mathcal{S}_{\tilde{\omega}}$ including $S_{\tilde{i}}$ by $\tilde{\omega} = \lceil \tilde{i}/T \rceil$. To determine the position of $S_{\tilde{i}}$ in $\mathcal{S}_{\tilde{\omega}}$, compute $\tilde{t} = \tilde{i} \bmod T$. Furthermore, find the corresponding $(\tilde{k}, \tilde{d})$ by $\tilde{k} = \lceil \tilde{t}/D \rceil$ and $\tilde{d} = \tilde{t} \bmod D$ satisfying $\tilde{t} = D \cdot (\tilde{k} - 1) + \tilde{d} - 1$.

3. Pick up $acc_{\tilde{\omega}}, \Theta_{\tilde{\omega}} = (\Theta_{\tilde{\omega},1}, \ldots, \Theta_{\tilde{\omega},7})$ from RL_τ, and $U_{\tilde{i}}, P_{\tilde{i}}, \sigma_{\tilde{i}} = (\theta_{\tilde{i},1}, \ldots, \theta_{\tilde{i},7})$ from $cert_i$. For $\tilde{t}, \tilde{k}, \tilde{d}$, pick up the AHO signature on $(J_{\tilde{i}1}, J_{\tilde{i}2}) = (g_{\tilde{k},1}^{c_{\tilde{d}}}, g_{\tilde{k},1}^{\tilde{c}_{\tilde{d}}})$, i.e., $\tilde{\sigma}_{\tilde{t}} = (\tilde{\theta}_{\tilde{t}1}, \ldots, \tilde{\theta}_{\tilde{t}7})$ from gpk. In the same way to **Revoke**, set $V_{k,d}$ and $\tilde{V}_{k,d}$ for all (k, d) in $\mathcal{S}_{\tilde{\omega}}$. Compute $\delta_{\tilde{k},\tilde{d}} = |U_{\tilde{i}} \cap \tilde{V}_{\tilde{k},\tilde{d}}|$. Pick up the AHO signature on $Q_{\delta_{\tilde{k},\tilde{d}}} = g_n^{\delta_{\tilde{k},\tilde{d}}}$, i.e., $\hat{\sigma}_{\delta_{\tilde{k},\tilde{d}}} = (\hat{\theta}_{\delta_{\tilde{k},\tilde{d}}1}, \ldots, \hat{\theta}_{\delta_{\tilde{k},\tilde{d}}7})$ from gpk.

4. Compute the witness of $U_{\tilde{i}} \cap V_{\tilde{k},\tilde{d}} = V_{\tilde{k},\tilde{d}}$ and $U_{\tilde{i}} \cap \tilde{V}_{\tilde{k},\tilde{d}} \neq \emptyset$, as follows.
   $W = \prod_{i \in U} \prod_{1 \leq k \leq K} \prod_{1 \leq d \leq D} ((\prod_{j \in V_{k,d}}^{j \neq i} g_{k,n+1-j+i})^{c_d} \cdot (\prod_{j=1}^{\zeta-|V_{k,d}|, i \neq \mathsf{SP}_{k,d}} g_{k,n+1-\mathsf{SP}_{k,d}+i})^{c_d} \cdot (\prod_{j \in \tilde{V}_{k,d}}^{j \neq i} g_{k,n+1-j+i})^{\tilde{c}_d})$.

5. Compute GS commitments $com_{P_{\tilde{i}}}, com_{acc_{\tilde{\omega}}}, com_W, com_{J_{\tilde{i}1}}, com_{J_{\tilde{i}2}}, com_{Q_{\delta_{\tilde{k},\tilde{d}}}}, com_X$ to $P_{\tilde{i}}, acc_{\tilde{\omega}}, W, J_{\tilde{i}1}, J_{\tilde{i}2}, Q_{\delta_{\tilde{k},\tilde{d}}}, X$. Then, re-randomize the AHO signatures $\sigma_{\tilde{i}}, \tilde{\sigma}_{\tilde{i}}, \hat{\sigma}_{\delta_{\tilde{k},\tilde{d}}}, \Theta_{\tilde{\omega}}$ to obtain $\sigma'_{\tilde{t}} = \{\theta'_1, \ldots, \theta'_7\}, \tilde{\sigma}'_{\tilde{t}} = \{\tilde{\theta}'_1, \ldots, \tilde{\theta}'_7\}, \hat{\sigma}'_{\delta_{\tilde{k},\tilde{d}}} =$

$\{\hat{\theta}'_1, \ldots, \hat{\theta}'_7\}$, $\Theta'_{\tilde{\omega}} = \{\Theta'_1, \ldots, \Theta'_7\}$, and compute GS commitments $\{com_{\theta'_i}\}_{i \in \{1,2,5\}}$, $\{com_{\tilde{\theta}'_i}\}_{i \in \{1,2,5\}}$, $\{com_{\hat{\theta}'_i}\}_{i \in \{1,2,5\}}$, $\{com_{\Theta'_i}\}_{i \in \{1,2,5\}}$ to $\{\theta'_i\}_{i \in \{1,2,5\}}$, $\{\tilde{\theta}'_i\}_{i \in \{1,2,5\}}$, $\{\hat{\theta}'_i\}_{i \in \{1,2,5\}}$, $\{\Theta'_i\}_{i \in \{1,2,5\}}$.

6. Generate $\{\pi_i\}_{i=1}^9$ s.t.

$$1_T = e(P_{\tilde{t}}, acc_{\tilde{\omega}}) \cdot e(g, W)^{-1} \cdot e(J_{\tilde{t}1}, g_n^\varsigma)^{-1} \cdot e(J_{\tilde{t}2}, Q_{\delta_{\tilde{k}, \tilde{d}}})^{-1}, \tag{2}$$

$$A^{(1)} \cdot e(\tilde{\theta}'_3, \tilde{\theta}'_4)^{-1} = e(G_z^{(1)}, \tilde{\theta}'_1) \cdot e(G_r^{(1)}, \tilde{\theta}'_2) \cdot e(G_1^{(1)}, J_{\tilde{t}1}) \cdot e(G_2^{(1)}, J_{\tilde{t}2}), \tag{3}$$

$$B^{(1)} \cdot e(\tilde{\theta}'_6, \tilde{\theta}'_7)^{-1} = e(H_z^{(1)}, \tilde{\theta}'_1) \cdot e(H_r^{(1)}, \tilde{\theta}'_5) \cdot e(H_1^{(1)}, J_{\tilde{t}1}) \cdot e(H_2^{(1)}, J_{\tilde{t}2}), \tag{4}$$

$$A^{(2)} \cdot e(\hat{\theta}'_3, \hat{\theta}'_4)^{-1} = e(G_z^{(2)}, \hat{\theta}'_1) \cdot e(G_r^{(2)}, \hat{\theta}'_2) \cdot e(G_1^{(2)}, Q_{\delta_{\tilde{k}, \tilde{d}}}), \tag{5}$$

$$B^{(2)} \cdot e(\hat{\theta}'_6, \hat{\theta}'_7)^{-1} = e(H_z^{(2)}, \hat{\theta}'_1) \cdot e(H_r^{(2)}, \hat{\theta}'_5) \cdot e(H_1^{(2)}, Q_{\delta_{\tilde{k}, \tilde{d}}}), \tag{6}$$

$$A^{(3)} \cdot e(\theta'_3, \theta'_4)^{-1} = e(G_z^{(3)}, \theta'_1) \cdot e(G_r^{(3)}, \theta'_2) \cdot e(G_1^{(3)}, X) \cdot e(G_2^{(3)}, P_{\tilde{t}}), \tag{7}$$

$$B^{(3)} \cdot e(\theta'_6, \theta'_7)^{-1} = e(H_z^{(3)}, \theta'_1) \cdot e(H_r^{(3)}, \theta'_5) \cdot e(H_1^{(3)}, X) \cdot e(H_2^{(3)}, P_{\tilde{t}}), \tag{8}$$

$$A^{(4)} \cdot e(\Theta'_3, \Theta'_4)^{-1} \cdot e(G_1^{(4)}, g^\tau)^{-1} = e(G_z^{(4)}, \Theta'_1) \cdot e(G_r^{(4)}, \Theta'_2) \cdot e(G_2^{(4)}, acc_{\tilde{\omega}}), \tag{9}$$

$$B^{(4)} \cdot e(\Theta'_6, \Theta'_7)^{-1} \cdot e(H_1^{(4)}, g^\tau)^{-1} = e(H_z^{(4)}, \Theta'_1) \cdot e(H_r^{(4)}, \Theta'_5) \cdot e(H_2^{(4)}, acc_{\tilde{\omega}}). \tag{10}$$

In the GS proofs, the Eq. (2) shows the accumulator verification, the Eqs. (3), (4) shows the AHO signature verification on $(J_{\tilde{t}1}, J_{\tilde{t}2})$, the Eqs. (5), (6) shows the AHO signature verification on $Q_{\delta_{\tilde{k}, \tilde{d}}}$, the Eqs. (7), (8) shows the AHO signature verification on $(X, P_{\tilde{t}})$, and the Eqs. (9), (10) shows the AHO signature verification on $(g^\tau, acc_{\tilde{\omega}})$.

7. The remaining process is as the same as in [16]. Using VK as a tag, compute a tag-based encryption [15] of X. Namely, select $z_1, z_2 \in Z_p$, and compute

$$(\Gamma_1, \Gamma_2, \Gamma_3, \Gamma_4, \Gamma_5) = (f_1^{z_1}, f_2^{z_2}, X \cdot g^{z_1+z_2}, (g^{\mathsf{VK}} \cdot \mathcal{U})^{z_1}, (g^{\mathsf{VK}} \cdot \mathcal{V})^{z_2}).$$

8. Generate NIZK proofs that $com_X = (1, 1, X) \cdot \boldsymbol{f}_1^{r_{X,1}} \cdot \boldsymbol{f}_2^{r_{X,2}} \cdot \boldsymbol{f}_3^{r_{X,3}}$ and $(\Gamma_1, \Gamma_2, \Gamma_3)$ is a BBS ciphertext of X, as in [16]. For $\boldsymbol{f}_3 = (f_{3,1}, f_{3,2}, f_{3,3})$, we can write $com_X = (f_1^{r_{X,1}} \cdot f_{3,1}^{r_{X,3}}, f_2^{r_{X,2}} \cdot f_{3,2}^{r_{X,3}}, X \cdot g^{r_{X,1}+r_{X,2}} \cdot f_{3,3}^{r_{X,3}})$. Thus, we have

$$com_X \cdot (\Gamma_1, \Gamma_2, \Gamma_3)^{-1} = (f_1^{\chi_1} \cdot f_{3,1}^{\chi_3}, f_2^{\chi_2} \cdot f_{3,2}^{\chi_3}, g^{\chi_1+\chi_2} \cdot f_{3,3}^{\chi_3}), \tag{11}$$

where $\chi_1 = r_{X,1} - z_1, \chi_2 = r_{X,2} - z_2, \chi_3 = r_{X,3}$. Compute GS commitments com_{χ_i} to the exponent χ_i for $i = 1, 2, 3$ using $\tilde{\boldsymbol{f}}$, and generate the NIZK proofs $\pi_{10}, \pi_{11}, \pi_{12}$ satisfying the three linear relations (11).

9. Compute a weakly secure BB signature $\sigma_{\mathsf{VK}} = g^{1/(x+\mathsf{VK})}$ on VK and the commitment $com_{\sigma_{\mathsf{VK}}}$ to σ_{VK}. Next, generate the NIZK proof π_{13} satisfying $e(\sigma_{\mathsf{VK}}, X \cdot g^{\mathsf{VK}}) = e(g, g)$.

10. Compute a one-time signature

$$\sigma_{\mathsf{OTS}} = \mathbf{Sign}_{\mathsf{OTS}}(\mathsf{SK}, (M, RL_\tau, \{\Gamma_i\}_{i=1}^5, \{\theta'_i, \tilde{\theta}'_i, \hat{\theta}'_i, \Theta'_i\}_{i=3,4,6,7}, \mathbf{com}, \boldsymbol{\Pi})),$$

where $\mathbf{com} = (com_{P_{\tilde{t}}}, com_{acc_{\tilde{\omega}}}, com_W, com_{J_{\tilde{t}1}}, com_{J_{\tilde{t}2}}, com_{Q_{\delta_{\tilde{k}, \tilde{d}}}}, com_X,$ $\{com_{\chi_i}\}_{i=1}^3, \qquad \{com_{\theta'_i}\}_{i \in \{1,2,5\}}, \{com_{\tilde{\theta}'_i}\}_{i \in \{1,2,5\}}, \{com_{\hat{\theta}'_i}\}_{i \in \{1,2,5\}},$

$\{com_{\Theta'_i}\}_{i\in\{1,2,5\}}, com_{\sigma_{VK}}), \ \Pi \ = \ \{\pi_i\}_{i=1}^{13}$. Output the signature $\sigma \ = \ (VK, \{\Gamma_i\}_{i=1}^5, \{\theta'_i, \tilde{\theta}'_i, \hat{\theta}'_i, \Theta'_i\}_{i=3,4,6,7}, \textbf{com}, \boldsymbol{\Pi}, \sigma_{OTS})$.

Verify. The input are $gpk, \tau, RL_\tau, \sigma, M$. If

$$\textbf{Verify}_{OTS}(VK, (M, RL_\tau, \{\Gamma_i\}_{i=1}^5, \{\theta'_i, \tilde{\theta}'_i, \hat{\theta}'_i, \Theta'_i\}_{i=3,4,6,7}, \textbf{com}, \boldsymbol{\Pi})) = 0$$

or $\{\Gamma_i\}_{i=1}^5$ is not a valid tag-based encryption, output 0. Then, output 1 if all proofs are accepted. Otherwise, output 0.

Open. The inputs are $gpk, \tau, RL_\tau, \sigma, M, St, osk$. If **Verify** on σ and M outputs 0, output $\perp$. Otherwise, using $osk = (y_1, y_2)$, decrypt $\tilde{X} = \Gamma_3 \cdot \Gamma_1^{-1/y_1} \cdot \Gamma_2^{-1/y_2}$. Search the database St_{trans} to find a record $\langle i, (\text{transcript}_i, v, X, \{P_t, \sigma_t\}_{1\le t\le T}, sig_i)\rangle$ with $X = \tilde{X}$. If the search fails, output $\perp$. Otherwise, output i.

4.3 Security

The proofs of the security are in the full paper.

5 Efficiency

We compare the efficiency of our scheme to the previous scheme [16]. In addition to parameters N, R, the efficiency of our system depends on n, T, K, D, where $T = K \cdot D$, and $n \approx T \log N$. Here, as in [16], we consider the 128-bit security level, and we assume that the element in $\mathcal{G}$ can be represented by 512 bits.

We compare the constant signature size. The signature in the previous scheme needs 144 $\mathcal{G}$-elements and the size is 9 KB. In our scheme, the signature needs 143 $\mathcal{G}$-elements, whose size is also 9 KB.

In the proposed scheme, we have the trade-off: Decreasing the revocation list size leads to increasing the sizes of public key and membership certificate. Consider the revocation list size. The revocation list consists of a non-cryptographic part related to IDs of revoked members (i.e., $\mathcal{R}_\tau, \{S_i\}_{i=1}^m$) and a cryptographic part of accumulators and the signatures (i.e., $\{acc_\omega, \Theta_\omega\}_{\omega=1}^w$). The non-cryptographic part is bounded by $5 \cdot \log N \cdot R$ bits. The cryptographic part in our scheme is bounded by $512 \cdot 8\lceil(2R-1)/T\rceil$ bits, while the part needs at most $512 \cdot 7\lceil(2R-1)\rceil$ bits in [16]. Thus, by increasing T, this part is greatly reduced. However, the other efficiency becomes worse as follows. The public key size of our scheme is approximately $2K \cdot T \cdot \log N \cdot 512$ bits. The membership certificate size is approximately $8 \cdot 512 \cdot T$ bits.

Next, we compare the signing costs. The computational cost of signing is comparable except for the computation of W. As discussed in Appendix B, T exponentiations (and $2D$ exponentiations) are the extra cost compared to [16]. However, note that the computation of W is required once every revocation epoch in practice. Namely, after W is computed in an epoch, the following signing does not need the extra cost during the same epoch. Furthermore, we can reduce the computation of W by using W in the previous epoch. Thus, we consider that the extra costs are not a serious issue.

Now we consider concrete examples. We assume $N/R = 10$. To balance K and D, we set $K = D \approx \sqrt{T}$. Table 1 shows the comparisons of the revocation list size between the previous scheme [16] and the proposed scheme using $T = 49, T = 100$, in cases of $N = 10,000, N = 100,000, N = 1,000,000$. As for the cryptographic part ($\{acc_\omega, \Theta_\omega\}_{\omega=1}^{w}$), the size is greatly reduced, as T is increased. Since the non-cryptographic part cannot be reduced, we ignore cases of $T > 100$. Similarly, for $N \gg 1,000,000$, due to the huge data of the non-cryptographic part, any revocable group signatures are essentially impractical.

Table 1. Comparisons of the revocation list size.

	$\mathcal{R}_\tau, \{S_i\}_{i=1}^{m}$	$\{acc_\omega, \Theta_\omega\}_{\omega=1}^{w}$		
		[16]	Proposed ($T = 49$)	Proposed ($T = 100$)
$N = 10,000(R = 1,000)$	6.8 KB	880 KB	21 KB	10 KB
$N = 100,000(R = 10,000)$	83 KB	8,800 KB	210 KB	100 KB
$N = 1,000,000(R = 100,000)$	980 KB	88,000 KB	2,100 KB	1,000 KB

Table 2 shows the comparisons of the public key size and the membership certificate size, where $N = 1,000,000$ and $R = 100,000$. Since the public key size depends on only $\log N$, the size in cases of the other N, R is similar to this table. The membership certificate size is the same when N, R are changed. Compared to [16], the extra sizes in public key and membership certificate are needed, and are increased when T is increased. In real applications, the public key and the certificate are not often distributed. On the other hand, the revocation list has to be distributed every revocation epoch. Thus, we consider that it is sufficiently practical to decrease the revocation list size while increasing the public key and the membership certificate sizes.

As for the signing cost, in our scheme, the extra cost of about 120 exponentiations is required in case of $T = 100$. The extra cost is comparable to the computations of commitments **com** with about 140 exponentiations. As shown above, the cost can be reduced in the implementation.

Table 2. Public key size and membership certificate size for T ($N = 1,000,000, R = 100,000$).

	[16]	Proposed ($T = 49$)	Proposed ($T = 100$)
Public key size ($g_{k,j}$'s)	2.6 KB	860 KB	2,500 KB
Membership certificate size	0.20 KB	25 KB	50 KB

A   Preliminaries

A.1   Bilinear Groups

Our scheme utilizes the following bilinear groups:

1. $\mathcal{G}$ and $\mathcal{T}$ are multiplicative cyclic groups of prime order p,
2. g is a randomly chosen generator of $\mathcal{G}$,
3. e is an efficiently computable bilinear map: $\mathcal{G} \times \mathcal{G} \to \mathcal{T}$, i.e., (1) for all $u, v \in \mathcal{G}$ and $a, b \in Z$, $e(u^a, v^b) = e(u, v)^{ab}$, and (2) $e(g, g) \neq 1_{\mathcal{T}}$.

A.2   Assumptions

As in the underlying scheme [16], the security of our system is based on the DLIN (Decision LINear) assumption [6], the SDH (Strong DH) assumption [5], and the q-SFP (Simultaneous Flexible Pairing) assumption [2]. We also adopt n-DHE (DH Exponent) assumption [11] for the accumulator.

Definition 1 (DLIN assumption). *For all PPT algorithm $\mathcal{A}$, the probability*

$$|\Pr[\mathcal{A}(g, g^a, g^b, g^{ac}, g^{bd}, g^{c+d}) = 1] - \Pr[\mathcal{A}(g, g^a, g^b, g^{ac}, g^{bd}, g^z) = 1]|$$

is negligible, where $g \in_R \mathcal{G}$ and $a, b, c, d, z \in_R Z_p$.

Definition 2 (q-SDH assumption). *For all PPT algorithm $\mathcal{A}$, the probability*

$$\Pr[\mathcal{A}(g, g^a, \ldots, g^{a^q}) = (b, g^{1/(a+b)}) \wedge b \in Z_p]$$

is negligible, where $g \in_R \mathcal{G}$ and $a \in_R Z_p$.

Definition 3 (q-SFP assumption). *For all PPT algorithm $\mathcal{A}$, the probability*

$$\Pr[\mathcal{A}(g_z, h_z, g_r, h_r, a, \tilde{a}, b, \tilde{b}, \{(z_j, r_j, s_j, t_j, u_j, v_j, w_j)\}_{j=1}^{q}) = (z^*, r^*, s^*, t^*, u^*, v^*, w^*) \in \mathcal{G}^7$$
$$\wedge e(a, \tilde{a}) = e(g_z, z^*)e(g_r, r^*)e(s^*, t^*) \wedge e(b, \tilde{b}) = e(h_z, z^*)e(h_r, u^*)e(v^*, w^*)$$
$$\wedge z^* \neq 1_{\mathcal{G}} \wedge z^* \neq z_j \text{ for all } 1 \leq j \leq q]$$

is negligible, where $(g_z, h_z, g_r, h_r, a, \tilde{a}, b, \tilde{b}) \in \mathcal{G}^8$ and all tuples $\{(z_j, r_j, s_j, t_j, u_j, v_j, w_j)\}_{j=1}^{q})$ satisfy the above relations.

Definition 4 (n-DHE assumption). *For all PPT algorithm $\mathcal{A}$, the probability*

$$\Pr[\mathcal{A}(g, g^a, \ldots, g^{a^n}, g^{a^{n+2}}, \ldots, g^{a^{2n}}) = g^{a^{n+1}}]$$

is negligible, where $g \in_R \mathcal{G}$ and $a \in_R Z_p$.

A.3   Structure-Preserving Signatures (AHO Signatures)

We utilize the structure-preserving signatures, since the knowledge of the signature can be proved by Groth-Sahai proofs. As in [16], we adopt the AHO signature scheme in [1,2]. Using the AHO scheme, we can sign multiple group elements to obtain a constant-size signature.

AHOKeyGen: Select bilinear groups $\mathcal{G}, \mathcal{T}$ with a prime order p and a bilinear map e. Select $g, G_r, H_r \in_R \mathcal{G}$, and $\mu_z, \nu_z, \mu, \nu, \alpha_a, \alpha_b \in_R Z_p$. Compute $G_z = G_r^{\mu_z}, H_z = H_r^{\nu_z}, G = G_r^{\mu}, H = H_r^{\nu}, A = e(G_r, g^{\alpha_a}), B = e(H_r, g^{\alpha_b})$. Output the public key as $pk = (\mathcal{G}, \mathcal{T}, p, e, g, \ G_r, H_r, G_z, H_z, G, H, A, B)$, and the secret key as $sk = (\alpha_a, \alpha_b, \mu_z, \nu_z, \mu, \nu)$.

AHOSign: Given message M together with sk, choose $\beta, \epsilon, \eta, \iota, \kappa \in_R Z_p$, and compute $\theta_1 = g^{\beta}$, and $\theta_2 = g^{\epsilon - \mu_z \beta} M^{-\mu}$, $\theta_3 = G_r^{\eta}$, $\theta_4 = g^{(\alpha_a - \epsilon)/\eta}, \theta_5 = g^{\iota - \nu_z \beta} M^{-\nu}$, $\theta_6 = H_r^{\kappa}$, $\theta_7 = g^{(\alpha_b - \iota)/\kappa}$. Output the signature $\sigma = (\theta_1, \ldots, \theta_7)$.

AHOVerify: Given the message M and the signature $\sigma = (\theta_1, \ldots, \theta_7)$, accept these if
$$A = e(G_z, \theta_1) \cdot e(G_r, \theta_2) \cdot e(\theta_3, \theta_4) \cdot e(G, M), \quad B = e(H_z, \theta_1) \cdot e(H_r, \theta_5) \cdot e(\theta_6, \theta_7) \cdot e(H, M).$$

This signature is existentially unforgeable against chosen-message attacks under the q-SFP assumption [2]. Using the re-randomization algorithm in [2], this signature can be publicly randomized to obtain another signature $(\theta_1', \ldots, \theta_7')$ on the same message. As a result, in the following Groth-Sahai proof, $(\theta_i')_{i=3,4,6,7}$ can be safely revealed, while $(\theta_i')_{i=1,2,5}$ have to be committed.

A.4   Groth-Sahai (GS) Proofs

To prove the secrets in relations of the bilinear maps, we utilize Groth-Sahai (GS) proofs [14]. As in [16], we adopt the instantiation based on DLIN assumption. For the bilinear groups, the proof system needs a common reference string $(\boldsymbol{f_1}, \boldsymbol{f_2}, \boldsymbol{f_3}) \in \mathcal{G}^3$ for $\boldsymbol{f_1} = (f_1, 1, g), \boldsymbol{f_2} = (1, f_2, g)$ for some $f_1, f_2 \in \mathcal{G}$. The commitment to an element X is computed as $\boldsymbol{C} = (1, 1, X) \cdot \boldsymbol{f_1^r} \cdot \boldsymbol{f_2^s} \cdot \boldsymbol{f_3^t}$ for $r, s, t \in_R Z_p^*$. In case of the CRS setting for perfectly sound proofs, $\boldsymbol{f_3} = \boldsymbol{f_1^{\xi_1}} \cdot \boldsymbol{f_2^{\xi_2}}$ for $\xi_1, \xi_2 \in_R Z_p^*$. Then, the commitment $\boldsymbol{C} = (f_1^{r+\xi_1 t}, f_2^{s+\xi_2 t}, X g^{r+s+t(\xi_1+\xi_2)})$ is the linear encryption in [6]. On the other hand, in the setting of the witness indistinguishability, $\boldsymbol{f_1}, \boldsymbol{f_2}, \boldsymbol{f_3}$ are linearly independent, and thus $\boldsymbol{C}$ is perfectly hiding. The DLIN assumption implies the indistinguishability of the CRS.

The commitment to an exponent $x \in Z_p$ is computed as $\boldsymbol{C} = \tilde{\boldsymbol{f}}^x \cdot \boldsymbol{f_1^r} \cdot \boldsymbol{f_2^s}$ for $r, s \in_R Z_p^*$, for a CRS $\tilde{\boldsymbol{f}}, \boldsymbol{f_1}, \boldsymbol{f_2}$. In the setting of perfectly sound proofs, $\tilde{\boldsymbol{f}}, \boldsymbol{f_1}, \boldsymbol{f_2}$ are linearly independent (As in [16], for example, we can set $\tilde{\boldsymbol{f}} = \boldsymbol{f_3} \cdot (1, 1, g)$ with $\boldsymbol{f_3} = \boldsymbol{f_1^{\xi_1}} \cdot \boldsymbol{f_2^{\xi_2}}$). In the WI setting, $\tilde{\boldsymbol{f}} = \boldsymbol{f_1^{\xi_1}} \cdot \boldsymbol{f_2^{\xi_2}}$ provides a perfectly hiding commitment.

To prove that the committed variables satisfy the pairing relations, the prover prepares the commitments, and replaces the variables in the pairing relations by the commitments. An NIWI (non-interactive witness indistinguishable) proof allows us to prove the set of pairing product equations:

$$\prod_{i=1}^{n} e(A_i, X_i) \cdot \prod_{i=1}^{n} \prod_{j=1}^{n} e(X_i, X_j)^{a_{ij}} = t,$$

for variables $X_1, \ldots, X_n \in \mathcal{G}$ and constants $A_1, \ldots, A_n \in \mathcal{G}, a_{ij} \in Z_p, t \in \mathcal{T}$. NIWI proofs also exist for multi-exponentiation equations:

$$\prod_{i=1}^{m} A_i^{y_i} \cdot \prod_{j=1}^{n} X_j^{b_j} \cdot \prod_{i=1}^{m} \prod_{j=1}^{n} X_j^{y_i \gamma_{ij}} = T,$$

for variables $X_1, \ldots, X_n \in \mathcal{G}, y_1, \ldots, y_m \in Z_p$ and constants $T, A_1, \ldots, A_m \in \mathcal{G}$, $b_1, \ldots, b_n, \gamma_{ij} \in Z_p$. For the multi-exponentiation equations, we can obtain the NIZK (non-interactive zero-knowledge) proofs with no additional cost.

A.5 Subset Cover Framework for Broadcast Encryption

As in [16], we adopt the subset cover framework for broadcast encryption in [21]. In this framework, a binary tree is used, where each leaf is assigned to each receiver (its secret key). Namely, for $N = 2^L$ receivers, the height of the tree is L. Let $\mathcal{N}$ be the universe of users and $\mathcal{R} \subset \mathcal{N}$ be the set of revoked receivers. In this framework, the set of non-revoked users is partitioned into m disjoint subsets $S_1, \ldots, S_m$ such that $\mathcal{N} \backslash \mathcal{R} = S_1 \cup \cdots \cup S_m$.

In the framework, there are mainly the complete subtree (CS) method and the subset difference (SD) method. In the revocable group signature scheme of [16], the SD method is adapted to achieve $O(|\mathcal{R}|)$ revocation list. In this method, the disjoint set S_i is determined by two nodes in the tree, *primary* node v_{i,ϕ_i} and *secondary* node v_{i,ψ_i} that is a descendant node of v_{i,ϕ_i}, and S_i consists of the leaves of the subtree rooted by v_{i,ϕ_i} that are not in the subtree rooted by v_{i,ψ_i}. The number of subsets is bounded by $m = 2 \cdot |\mathcal{R}| - 1$, as proved in [21].

B Evaluation of Witness Computation

In Sect. 5, the efficiency of our scheme is compared to the underlying scheme [16]. Here, we show the detailed efficiency discussion of the witness computation. The computation of W can be replaced:

$$W = \prod_{1 \leq d \leq D} ((\prod_{i \in U} \prod_{1 \leq k \leq K} (\prod_{\substack{j \in V_{k,d} \\ j \neq i}} g_{k,n+1-j+i}) \cdot (\prod_{j=1}^{\zeta - |V_{k,d}|, i \neq SP_{k,d}} g_{k,n+1-SP_{k,d}+i}))^{c_d}$$

$$\cdot (\prod_{i \in U} \prod_{1 \leq k \leq K} \prod_{\substack{j \in \tilde{V}_{k,d} \\ j \neq i}} g_{k,n+1-j+i})^{\tilde{c}_d}).$$

Then, the number of exponentiations by $c_d, \tilde{c}_d$ is $2D$. The number of multiplications is $T \cdot \log^2 N$. As discussed in [16], $\log^2 N$ multiplications is bounded by the cost of a single exponentiation. This is why T exponentiations (and $2D$ exponentiations) are the extra cost compared to [16].

As mentioned in Sect. 5, the witness computation can be reduced by using W in the previous epoch. In the case that the modification to the revocation list does not influence $\mathcal{S}_{\tilde{\omega}}$ including $S_{\tilde{i}}$ (i.e., revocations happens in the other covers), the signer does not need to compute W. In the other cases, we can also reduce the cost: For only modified covers S_i correspondent (k, d), divide W by the old terms for (k, d) and multiply it by the new terms. Thus, we consider that the extra costs are not a serious issue.

References

1. Abe, M., Fuchsbauer, G., Groth, J., Haralambiev, K., Ohkubo, M.: Structure-preserving signatures and commitments to group elements. In: Rabin, T. (ed.) CRYPTO 2010. LNCS, vol. 6223, pp. 209–236. Springer, Heidelberg (2010)
2. Abe, M., Haralambiev, K., Ohkubo, M.: Signing on elements in bilinear groups for modular protocol design. Cryptology ePrint Archive, Report 2010/133 (2010). http://eprint.iacr.org/
3. Ateniese, G., Song, D., Tsudik, G.: Quasi-efficient revocation of group signatures. In: Blaze, M. (ed.) FC 2002. LNCS, vol. 2357, pp. 183–197. Springer, Heidelberg (2003)
4. Begum, N., Nakanishi, T., Funabiki, N.: Efficient proofs for CNF formulas on attributes in pairing-based anonymous credential system. In: Kwon, T., Lee, M.-K., Kwon, D. (eds.) ICISC 2012. LNCS, vol. 7839, pp. 495–509. Springer, Heidelberg (2013)
5. Boneh, D., Boyen, X.: Short signatures without random oracles. In: Cachin, C., Camenisch, J.L. (eds.) EUROCRYPT 2004. LNCS, vol. 3027, pp. 56–73. Springer, Heidelberg (2004)
6. Boneh, D., Boyen, X., Shacham, H.: Short group signatures. In: Franklin, M. (ed.) CRYPTO 2004. LNCS, vol. 3152, pp. 41–55. Springer, Heidelberg (2004)
7. Boneh, D., Shacham, H.: Group signatures with verifier-local revocation. In: Proceedings of the 11th ACM Conference on Computer and Communications Security (ACM-CCS '04), pp. 168–177 (2004)
8. Bresson, E., Stern, J.: Group signature scheme with efficient revocation. In: Kim, K. (ed.) PKC 2001. LNCS, vol. 1992, pp. 190–206. Springer, Heidelberg (2001)
9. Camenisch, J.L., Chaabouni, R., Shelat, A.: Efficient protocols for set membership and range proofs. In: Pieprzyk, J. (ed.) ASIACRYPT 2008. LNCS, vol. 5350, pp. 234–252. Springer, Heidelberg (2008)
10. Camenisch, J.L., Groth, J.: Group signatures: better efficiency and new theoretical aspects. In: Blundo, C., Cimato, S. (eds.) SCN 2004. LNCS, vol. 3352, pp. 120–133. Springer, Heidelberg (2005)
11. Camenisch, J., Kohlweiss, M., Soriente, C.: An accumulator based on bilinear maps and efficient revocation for anonymous credentials. In: Jarecki, S., Tsudik, G. (eds.) PKC 2009. LNCS, vol. 5443, pp. 481–500. Springer, Heidelberg (2009)
12. Camenisch, J.L., Lysyanskaya, A.: Dynamic accumulators and application to efficient revocation of anonymous credentials. In: Yung, M. (ed.) CRYPTO 2002. LNCS, vol. 2442, pp. 61–76. Springer, Heidelberg (2002)
13. Chaum, D., van Heyst, E.: Group signatures. In: Davies, D.W. (ed.) EUROCRYPT 1991. LNCS, vol. 547, pp. 257–265. Springer, Heidelberg (1991)
14. Groth, J., Sahai, A.: Efficient non-interactive proof systems for bilinear groups. In: Smart, N.P. (ed.) EUROCRYPT 2008. LNCS, vol. 4965, pp. 415–432. Springer, Heidelberg (2008)

15. Kiltz, E.: Chosen-ciphertext security from tag-based encryption. In: Halevi, S., Rabin, T. (eds.) TCC 2006. LNCS, vol. 3876, pp. 581–600. Springer, Heidelberg (2006)

16. Libert, B., Peters, T., Yung, M.: Group signatures with almost-for-free revocation. In: Safavi-Naini, R., Canetti, R. (eds.) CRYPTO 2012. LNCS, vol. 7417, pp. 571–589. Springer, Heidelberg (2012)

17. Libert, B., Peters, T., Yung, M.: Scalable group signatures with revocation. In: Pointcheval, D., Johansson, T. (eds.) EUROCRYPT 2012. LNCS, vol. 7237, pp. 609–627. Springer, Heidelberg (2012)

18. Libert, B., Yung, M.: Concise mercurial vector commitments and independent zero-knowledge sets with short proofs. In: Micciancio, D. (ed.) TCC 2010. LNCS, vol. 5978, pp. 499–517. Springer, Heidelberg (2010)

19. Nakanishi, T., Fujii, H., Hira, Y., Funabiki, N.: Revocable group signature schemes with constant costs for signing and verifying. In: Jarecki, S., Tsudik, G. (eds.) PKC 2009. LNCS, vol. 5443, pp. 463–480. Springer, Heidelberg (2009)

20. Nakanishi, T., Funabiki, N.: Verifier-local revocation group signature schemes with backward unlinkability from bilinear maps. In: Roy, B. (ed.) ASIACRYPT 2005. LNCS, vol. 3788, pp. 533–548. Springer, Heidelberg (2005)

21. Naor, D., Naor, M., Lotspiech, J.: Revocation and tracing schemes for stateless receivers. In: Kilian, J. (ed.) CRYPTO 2001. LNCS, vol. 2139, pp. 41–62. Springer, Heidelberg (2001)

22. Sudarsono, A., Nakanishi, T., Funabiki, N.: Efficient proofs of attributes in pairing-based anonymous credential system. In: Fischer-Hübner, S., Hopper, N. (eds.) PETS 2011. LNCS, vol. 6794, pp. 246–263. Springer, Heidelberg (2011)

Cyber Security

Semantic Feature Selection for Text with Application to Phishing Email Detection

Rakesh Verma$^{(\boxtimes)}$ and Nabil Hossain

Department of Computer Science, University of Houston,
4800 Calhoun Road, Houston, TX, USA
rmverma@cs.uh.edu, nabilhossain@gmail.com

Abstract. In a phishing attack, an unsuspecting victim is lured, typically via an email, to a web site designed to steal sensitive information such as bank/credit card account numbers, login information for accounts, etc. Each year Internet users lose billions of dollars to this scourge. In this paper, we present a general semantic feature selection method for text problems based on the statistical t-test and WordNet, and we show its effectiveness on phishing email detection by designing classifiers that combine semantics and statistics in analyzing the text in the email. Our feature selection method is general and useful for other applications involving text-based analysis as well. Our email *body-text-only* classifier achieves more than 95 % accuracy on detecting phishing emails with a false positive rate of 2.24 %. Due to its use of semantics, our feature selection method is robust against adaptive attacks and avoids the problem of frequent retraining needed by machine learning classifiers.

Keywords: Security · Phishing · Natural language detection · Semantic classification · Feature selection for text

1 Introduction

Phishing is an attack in which an unsuspecting victim is lured to a web site designed to steal sensitive information (e.g., login names, passwords and financial information). Every year money, time and productivity are lost by Internet users and businesses to this plague. Hence, phishing is a serious threat to societies and economies based on the Internet. Several communication channels are available to phishers for initiating attacks, but since email is the most popular medium, we focus on detecting phishing attacks launched through emails.

As [1] observed, detecting phishing email messages automatically is a non-trivial task since phishing emails are designed cleverly to look legitimate. Besides attachments, an email can be decomposed into three main components: a header, a text body, and links. While the header and links have been well studied by

Research supported in part by NSF grants DUE 1241772 and CNS 1319212.

© Springer International Publishing Switzerland 2014
H.-S. Lee and D.-G. Han (Eds.): ICISC 2013, LNCS 8565, pp. 455–468, 2014.
DOI: 10.1007/978-3-319-12160-4_27

phishing detection methods previously, unsupervised natural language processing (NLP) techniques for text analysis of phishing emails have been tried by only a few researchers. In [2], rudimentary analysis of the anchor text was used to enhance detection. In [3], hand-crafted patterns and some scoring functions for verbs in the email were designed using trial and error.

In contrast to the unsupervised techniques mentioned above, several machine learning approaches have been tried previously. The latest attempt to use machine learning techniques is [4], which uses probabilistic latent dirichlet allocation, ensemble methods such as Adaboost and cotraining. The last two methods mentioned above differ in the use of *unsupervised* NLP technique in [3] versus the use of machine learning requiring labeled data in [4], which is somewhat alleviated by cotraining. Besides the need for labeled training data, supervised machine learning methods have two additional disadvantages: the problem of overtraining and the need for retraining due to model mismatch with the new data over even short periods of time. For instance, some researchers retrain their logistic regression scheme for identifying phishing web-sites *every day*.

1.1 Feature Selection

A well-known problem in text classification is the extremely high dimensional feature space, which sometimes makes learning algorithms intractable [5]. A popular method, called feature selection, to deal with this intractability reduces the dimensionality of the feature space. Many feature selection methods have been studied earlier including document frequency, information gain, mutual information, chi-square test, Bi-Normal Separation, and weighted log-likelihood ratio [6–8]. The problem with comparing these methods is that they are typically based on different assumptions or measurements of the data sets. For example, mutual information and information gain are based on information theory, while chi-square is based on statistical independence assumption. Empirical studies that compare these methods are heavily affected by the datasets.

Moreover, as [5] states, in real applications, choosing an appropriate feature selection method remains hard for a new task because too many methods exist. In an early survey paper [9], eight methods are mentioned for dealing with different text classification tasks, but none is shown to be robust across different classification applications. Therefore, [5] proposed a framework for theoretical comparison of six popular feature selection methods for text classification.

In contrast to [5], we show a semantic feature selection method based on the statistical t-test that is simple, robust, and effective. The t-test is a well-known statistical hypothesis test. Using it, we determine whether a feature's variance between two corpora is of a *statistically significant* degree. We use a two-tailed, two samples of unequal variances t-test since usually the corpora are not even of the same size let alone same variance. Instead of a purely syntactic feature selection method, we use semantics based on WordNet. We apply our semantic feature selection technique to phishing email detection and show that our classifiers significantly outperform the best previous comparable method.

As explained below, due to our use of semantics, our classifiers are robust against adaptive attacks, and they avoid the need for frequent retraining.

1.2 Our Contributions and Results

Our primary contributions include: a careful study of the t-test method for feature extraction, a comparison with the previous method of [3] on the *same*, public phishing email database, and more extensive testing of our approach on *public* good databases of 3,000 Enron inbox emails[1] and 4,000 Enron sent emails as opposed to the *private* database of 1,000 good emails used in [3]. Note that we keep the good databases separate in order to use the Enron sent emails only for testing purposes to evaluate how our classifier adapts to a different domain. This is the first detailed comparison of human-intuition based and statistical NLP based methods for phishing detection. We can also develop a comprehensive and effective NLP based phishing detection method by combining the link and header analysis as suggested in [3] and in [10].

Specifically, our statistical email text-only classifier, achieves detection rates above 95 % for phishing emails with an accuracy higher than 97 % on the non-phishing emails. This is an increase in effectiveness of over 20 % versus the best previous work [3] on phishing emails on the same dataset, and of over 10 % on two larger non-phishing public email datasets.

Besides beating the text-based classification method of [3], our method, when combined with header and link analysis, gives comparable performance to the *best* machine learning methods in the literature, such as [4], *without the problem of retraining frequently*, since our methods are not purely statistical, but they use semantics as well. In addition, our semantic feature selection method has the advantage of robustness against adaptive attacks.

The adaptive phisher may try to defeat our method by varying the email's syntax, e.g. by using different words that have similar meanings to those used in previous attacks, or by varying sentence structures, while keeping the same sense of urgency in driving the recipient to precipitate action in clicking a link. However, since we combine semantics with statistics, this will be a very difficult exercise to carry out since it would require deep examination of WordNet and a thesaurus that is richer than WordNet to come up with such an email. The effort involved would rise significantly in the process and the payoff may be little since the resulting email will sound artificial, pedantic and stilted to the reader. The overall effect will be to reduce the return on the phisher's investment drastically since phishing websites typically last only a few days before they are shut down.

The rest of this paper is organized as follows: the next section introduces necessary natural language preliminaries. Section 3 outlines our hypotheses, goals, and gives a preview of our classifiers. Section 4 presents four different classifiers with varying use of semantics to give an idea of the performance gain due to semantics. The subsequent section presents our results and analysis. Section 6 presents relevant related work on phishing detection, and Sect. 7 concludes.

---

[1] http://www.cs.cmu.edu/~enron/

2   Natural Language Preliminaries

Some of our classifiers apply the following NLP techniques on the email text:

(i) **lexical analysis:** to break the email text into sentences and to further split these sentences into words

(ii) **part-of-speech tagging:** to tag each word with its part-of-speech using the Stanford POS tagger

(iii) **named entity recognition:** to identify the named entities, which include proper nouns such as names of organizations, people, or locations

(iv) **normalization:** conversion of words to lower case

(v) **stemming:** to convert each word to its stem using the Porter Stemmer [11] (e.g. reducing the verb "watching" to "watch")

(vi) **stopword removal:** to remove frequently occurring words such as 'a', 'an', etc., using a list of stopwords.

As opposed to purely syntactic or statistical techniques based on feature counting, some of our classifiers also make use of semantic NLP techniques by incorporating the WordNet lexical database and word-sense disambiguation. The latter is used to derive the appropriate *sense* or meaning of a word based on the context in which the word occurs. For example, the word "bank" might exhibit the *sense* of a financial institution in one context and a shore in another.

2.1   WordNet

WordNet is a lexical database, which exhibits properties of both a dictionary and a thesaurus [12]. In WordNet, all the words that exhibit the same concept are grouped into a *synset*, in other words a set of synonyms. The synsets can be considered as WordNet's building blocks, forming the fundamental semantic relation in the lexical database through synonymy. The *hyponymy* relation between synsets is the semantic relation that inter-connects and organizes all the nouns into a hierarchy, building a graph of nouns. The hypernymy and hyponymy relations are viewed as the relations of subordination, in other words subsumption or class inclusion, defined as follows: A is a *hypernym* of B if the meaning of A encompasses the meaning of B, which is called the *hyponym* of A. For instance, "red" is a hyponym of "color" since red is a type of color. Here, "color" is the *hypernym* of "red", since "color" broadly captures or generalizes the meaning of "red". Nouns usually have a single hypernym [12], and the WordNet noun hierarchy graph is acyclic, having a tree-like structure. All WordNet nouns are encompassed by the word *entity*, which is the root of this tree. The more we proceed down this tree, the more specific the nouns become. For instance, the hyponym set of *entity* is {*physical entity, thing, abstract entity*}, and the hyponym set of *physical entity* include *object, substance, etc.* However, the hypernymy structure for verbs is not acyclic [13]. Although the hypernym relation for verbs is captured in a similar hierarchical structure, this structure is "forest-like." Note that it is not really a forest as it contains cycles.

As mentioned earlier, a word can exhibit different meanings or senses in different contexts. Because each synset is designed to capture a unique concept, the proper sense of a word must be used to obtain its appropriate synset from WordNet. Hence, we perform word sense disambiguation using SenseLearner [14] prior to invoking any WordNet inquiry.

3   Our Hypotheses, Goals and Preview of Classifiers

As mentioned in [3], NLP by computers is well-recognized to be a very challenging task because of the inherent ambiguity and rich structure of natural languages. This could explain why only a few researchers have used NLP techniques for phishing email detection. In this paper, we investigate two basic questions:

(i) Can statistical techniques applied to the text of an email differentiate phishing emails from benign emails?
(ii) Do NLP techniques such as part-of-speech (POS) tagging and the use of semantics help improve the statistical methods, and if so, by how much?

We explore methods for feature extraction based on statistical tests performed on the email's text with and without the use of semantics, and our results demonstrate that statistical methods based on semantics can achieve a somewhat surprisingly high degree of accuracy in detecting phishing emails. We show that NLP techniques such as part-of-speech tagging and the use of semantics through WordNet enhance the performance of the classifier, but there is not much room for improvement left after applying the statistical methods alone for these techniques to make a huge difference in performance. However, these methods are still important since they give our classifier a robustness against attacks, for instance, attacks by the active phisher mentioned earlier.

Our methods for statistical analysis focus on the key differences between a phishing and a legitimate email. First, a phishing email is designed to motivate the reader to take some action. The action typically requires the reader to visit a malicious site created with the goal of stealing personal sensitive information. Second, since phishing web sites are on the Internet for a week or two typically before they are discovered and either blacklisted or removed, the phisher must convey a sense of urgency or give a short deadline to the target in taking the action. In a previous paper [3], we also tried to take advantage of this combination of action and urgency to detect phishing emails. However, there an intuition-based NLP component was used, which could not reach detection rates better than 70 % with accuracy of no more than 80 % on non-phishing emails. The statistical methods presented here significantly outperform the previous detector on tests involving two larger, public databases of emails from Enron.

4   Phishing Classifiers

In this section, we discuss our dataset and describe four classifiers for phishing email detection, with particular emphasis on the feature selection criteria.

Dataset: Our dataset comprised of 4,550 public phishing emails from [15] and 10,000 legitimate emails from the public Enron inbox email database. We randomly selected 70 % of both the phishing and the legitimate emails for statistical analysis, hereafter called the analysis sets, and the remaining 30 % for testing purposes. We also used a set of 4,000 non-phishing emails obtained from the "sent mails" section of the Enron email database as a different domain to test our classifiers. We now describe the four classifiers we designed.

4.1   Classifier 1: Pattern Matching (PM) Only

This is the most basic classifier, which relies only on simple pattern matching. Here we design two subclassifiers: *Action-detector* and *Nonsensical-detector.*

Action-detector: We analyzed random emails from our analysis sets and observed that phishing emails had a tendency to focus on the recipient. One observation was the frequent use of the possessive adjective "your" in phishing emails. In the analysis sets, 84.7 % of the phishing emails had the word "your", as opposed to 34.7 % of the legitimate emails. This trend occurred because in order to raise concern, phishers often talk about the breach in security of properties in the user's possession, such as a bank account owned by the user.

Next we performed a statistical analysis of the unigrams next to all the occurrences of "your." Our goal here was to detect those properties belonging to the recipient that the phisher often declares as compromised, e.g. "amazon" (indicating the amazon.com account of an online shopper). However, many of the unigrams were adjectives describing the property, defeating our purpose. Hence we chose to analyze bigrams following "your" instead. Bigrams allowed us to detect patterns such as "your credit card," where we are more interested in the word 'card,' which indicates a secure property owned by the user.

Feature selection and justification: We constructed frequency data for all bigrams following "your" for both phishing and legitimate databases. Based on a 2-tailed t-test and an α value of 0.01 (the probability of a Type I error), we chose a bigram as a possible feature if the t-value for the bigram exceeded the critical value based on α and the degrees of freedom of the word. Then we calculated weights for each bigram b, denoted $w(b)$, using the formula:

$$\mathbf{w}(b) = \frac{p_b - l_b}{p_b}, \text{where}$$

- p_b = percentage of phishing emails that contain b
- l_b = percentage of legitimate emails that contain b.

Features that had weights less than 0 were discarded (and also features that appear in less than 5 % of the emails) as these features were significant for legitimate emails. Observe that the remaining features have weights in the interval [0,1], where features with higher weights allow better detection rate per phishing email encountered. Note that the denominator in the **weight formula** prioritizes a feature that is present in 20 % phishing and 1 % legitimate emails over a feature that is present in 80 % phishing and 61 % legitimate emails. Next, we computed a frequency distribution of the selected bigrams using their weights and then selected those bigrams that had weights greater than $m - s$, where m is the mean bigram weight, and s is the standard deviation of the distribution. We call this set *PROPERTY* as it lists the possible set of user's properties, which the phisher tends to declare as compromised. Note that from now on, the term *t-selection* will refer to the same statistical feature selection used to filter features for *PROPERTY*.

So far, we have designed a feature selection method for detecting the property which the phisher falsely claims to have been compromised. The next task is to detect the pattern that calls for an action to restore security of this property. For this purpose, we checked the email for the presence of words that indicated the user to click on the links. First, we computed statistics of all the words in sentences having a hyperlink or any word from the set { "url", "link", "website"}. Here we performed the same *t-selection*, as mentioned above, to choose the features. We call the resulting set of words *ACTION*, which represents the intent of the phisher to elicit an action from the user.

At this point, we are set to design the *Action-detector* subclassifier: for each email encountered, we mark the email as phishing if it has:

(i) the word "your" followed by a bigram belonging to *PROPERTY* (e.g. "your paypal account"), and

(ii) a word from *ACTION* in a sentence containing a hyperlink or any word from { "url", "link", "website"} (e.g. "click the link"),

Nonsensical-detector. If *Action-detector* fails to mark any email as phishing, control passes to the *Nonsensical-detector*. After analyzing some phishing emails incorrectly classified by *Action-detector*, we discovered that many of these phishing emails involved dumping words and links into the text, making the text totally irrelevant to the email's subject. This observation motivated the *Nonsensical-detector* subclassifier whose purpose is to detect emails where:

(i) the body text is not *similar* to the subject, and

(ii) the email has at least one link.

Definition 1. *An email body text is* **similar** *to its subject if all of the words in the subject (excluding stopwords) are present in the email's text.*

First, we removed stopwords from the subject and selected features from the subject using t-test on the remaining words. The goal here is to filter words that imply an awareness, action or urgency, which are common in subjects of phishing emails. We call this set *PH-SUB*. The *Nonsensical-detector* subclassifier is then designed as follows: for each email encountered, if the email subject has at least: a named-entity, or a word from *PH-SUB*, then we mark the email as phishing if:

(i) it contains at least one link, and

(ii) its text is **not similar** to the subject,

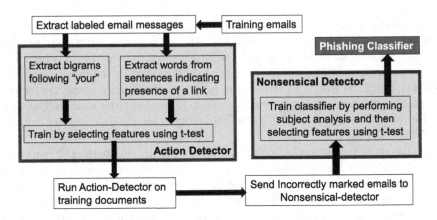

Fig. 1. Flowchart showing how the classifier is trained.

This detector requires a named-entity in the subject since the body of the email is completely tangential and irrelevant. Thus the phisher is relying on the subject of the email to scare the user into taking action with respect to some property of the user, which implies the presence of a named entity in the subject. In emails of this nature with irrelevant information in the email's body, we assume the named-entity in the subject to be the property of the user under threat (e.g. "KeyBank", when the subject reads: "KeyBank security"). A flowchart for building the classifier is shown in Fig. 1.

4.2   Classifier 2: PM + POS Tagging

This classifier builds on Classifier 1. Here we make use of part-of-speech tags in an attempt to reduce the error in classification that occurs when simple pattern matching techniques are used. When the bigrams following the word "your" are extracted, we perform the additional check to discard bigrams that do not contain a noun or a named-entity since the user's property, that the phisher tends to focus on, has to be a noun. When we perform statistical analysis on the words in sentences having a link, we discard words that are not verbs. Recall that the word we are looking for indicates the user to click on the link, and this word has to be a verb as it represents the action from the user's part. For the *Nonsensical-detector*, we impose the restriction of detecting named-entities, nouns, verbs, adverbs and adjectives only when selecting features for *PH-SUB*. Furthermore, for the similarity check, we select only named-entities and nouns from the subject and look for the absence of corresponding nouns and named entities in the email's text. We expect that the use of appropriate POS tags in Classifier 2 will improve accuracy over Classifier 1. For instance, among the patterns "press the link below" and "here is the website of the printing press," we are only interested in the presence of the word "press" in the former, but Classifier 1 sees both the occurrences of "press" as belonging to *ACTION*.

4.3   Classifier 3: PM + POS + Word Senses

We extend Classifier 2 by extracting the senses of words using SenseLearner [14] and taking advantage of these senses to improve classification. The goal is to reduce errors that result from ambiguity in the meaning of polysemous keywords. For instance, when "your account" appears, we are only interested in financial accounts and not in someone's account of an event. Toward this end, we performed statistical analysis on words with their POS tags and senses to train the classifier. Then we designed this classifier to look for patterns that match selected features up to their senses whenever the classifier analyzed an email.

4.4   Classifier 4: PM + POS + Word Senses + WordNet

So far our analysis has selected a certain set of features biased to the analysis dataset. This is very similar to the way training works in machine learning based classifiers. A better way to extend the features and improve the robustness and generalization capability of our feature selection method is to find words closely associated with them so that similar patterns can be obtained. To this end, we incorporate WordNet in this classifier.

In Classifier 4, we extend the sets *PROPERTY, ACTION* and *PH-SUB* into *ext-PROPERTY, ext-ACTION* and *ext-PH-SUB* respectively by computing first the synonyms and then direct hyponyms of all synonyms of each selected feature (with its POS tag and sense), expanding the corresponding sets. Note that *PROPERTY* contains bigrams and we only extract the nouns and add their synonyms and the direct hyponyms of all the synonyms to the set. In addition, we modify the classifier as follows:

(i)   When we look for properties, we check to see whether the bigram that follows the word "your" includes a noun that belongs to *ext-PROPERTY*, instead of looking for the occurrence of the whole bigram in *ext-PROPERTY*.

(ii) In order to detect actions, we check each sentence, that indicates the presence of a link, for the occurrence of a verb from *ext-ACTION*.

(iii) When we check for *similarity*, for each noun in the email's subject, we look in the email's text for the presence of a hyponym or a synonym of the noun.

5   Analysis and Results

In this section, we present the results obtained using each of the classifiers. We also compare our classifiers to existing phishing email filters, and we present insights into the nature of our datasets.

As shown in Table 1,[2] the results demonstrate that Classifier 4 performs the best among all the classifiers in marking both phishing and legitimate emails accurately. We used the same phishing corpus as PhishNet-NLP [3], and we

---

[2] The 'Other' category is explained in Table 2.

Table 1. Results of using the classifiers on the test set.

Classifier	P	I	S
Classifier 1	**92.88**	**4.96**	**4.17**
Action-Detector	73.6	1.92	1.96
Nonsensical-Detector	12.84	2.87	2.21
Other	6.44	0.17	0
Classifier 2	**92.01**	**4.88**	**3.9**
Action-Detector	72.23	1.4	1.76
Nonsensical-Detector	13.34	3.31	2.14
Other	6.44	0.17	0
Classifier 3	**94.8**	**2.16**	**2.37**
Action-Detector	75.1	0.5	0.72
Nonsensical-Detector	13.3	1.49	1.65
Other	6.44	0.17	0
Classifier 4	**95.02**	**2.23**	**2.42**
Action-Detector	75.82	0.57	0.77
Nonsensical-Detector	12.74	1.5	1.65
Other	6.44	0.17	0

$P = \%$ phishing detected on 1365 phishing emails
$I = \%$ false positives on 3000 non-phishing Enron Inbox emails
$S = \%$ false positives on 4000 non-phishing Enron Sent emails

tested our classifiers on 1365 phishing emails. Classifier 4 has 95.02 % phishing email detection as opposed to 77.1 % by the text analysis classifier of PhishNet-NLP. Of the 3000 legitimate emails tested, Classifier 4 marked 97.76 % of the emails as legitimate compared to 85.1 % for the text analysis classifier of PhishNet-NLP. We tested on the public Enron email database whereas the legitimate email database of PhishNet-NLP was not revealed. Furthermore, on the database of 4,000 non-phishing emails from Enron's sent mails section used only for testing, Classifier 4 obtains an accuracy of 97.58 %, exhibiting potential for adaptation to a new domain. Its performance also justifies the use of semantics in classification in addition to the robustness as explained above.

PILFER [16], based on machine learning, correctly marked 92 % of the 860 phishing emails and 99.9 % of the 6950 non-phishing emails it was tested on. Using probabilistic Latent Dirichlet Allocation, ensemble machine learning methods and cotraining, [4] claimed an F-score of 1. All these methods use features from the *entire* email, i.e., the header, the body text and the links in the email whereas our classifiers relied on the text in the body of the email only.

5.1   Performance Analysis

Dataset Characteristics. After filtering the phishing emails from the analysis set using *Action-detector* and *Nonsensical-detector*, we analyzed the emails that were not detected by both of these subclassifiers. We sorted most of these emails into the following categories and took measures to correctly label them:

- **Spam Flagged:** Detected by checking if the Spam-Flag field of the email header reads YES.
- **Emails in Foreign Language:** In these emails, the text cannot be analyzed in English. So we looked for frequent occurrences of the foreign language translations of any of the words from {of, the, for, a, an} that are not present in the English vocabulary. If this check is successful, then successful detection involves finding a link.
- **Emails containing only links:** These emails do not have sufficient text for processing. We chose not to create a subclassifier that checks for validity of links as it defeats our purpose of creating an independent NLP classifier. We marked these emails as phishing, which gave rise to some false positives.
- **Emails with no subject, no text, no link and no attachment:** Here, we checked whether both the subject line and the text were missing.

Evaluation. Table 2 shows frequency of emails triggering each subclassifier of Classifier 4 on both the legitimate and phishing email test sets.

6   Related Research on Phishing

Phishing has attracted significant research interest as a social engineering threat. Solutions to this problem have included angles such as: education or training,

Table 2. Analyzing performance of Classifier 4 on test set.

Subclassifier	P	L
Action-detector	1035	17
Nonsensical-detector	174	45
Other	88	5
Spam-flagged	42	0
Foreign emails	20	1
Emails with only links	18	4
No subject and no text	8	0
Total	1297	67

P - # Phishing emails detected in 1365 phishing email dataset
L - # Legitimate emails misclassified in 3000 Enron inbox email database.

server-side and browser-side techniques, evaluation of anti-phishing tools, detection methods, and studies that focus on the reasons for the success of phishing attacks. Since [3,4] represent the best unsupervised and supervised techniques, we refer to them for related work on these approaches for phishing email detection. Some existing works making use of these approaches include [2,16–24]. Since discussing the vast literature on phishing is not feasible, we focus on prior research directly related to our work.

We can identify two ways of classifying phishing detection methods. The first classification considers the information used for detection. Here, there are two kinds of methods: those that rely on analyzing the content of the target web pages (targets of the links in the email) and methods that are based on the content of the emails. The second classification is based on the domain of the technique employed for detecting phishing attacks (emails and web pages). Here, there are detection methods based on: information retrieval, machine learning, and string/pattern/visual matching.

Applications of machine learning known as content-based filtering methods, on a feature set, are designed to highlight user-targeted deception in electronic communication [16,19–23]. These methods, deployed in much phishing email detection research, involve training a classifier on a set of features extracted from the email structure and content within the training data. When training is completed, the resulting classifier is then applied to the email stream to filter phishing emails. The key differences in content-based filtering strategies are the number of features selected for training, and the types of these features.

Incorporating NLP and machine learning, [4] uses a 3-layered approach to phishing email detection. A topic model is built using Probabilistic Latent Semantic Analysis in the first layer, then Adaboost and Co-training are used to develop a robust classifier, which achieves an F-score of 1 on the test set, raising the possibility of overfitting the data. Machine learning phishing detection methods have to be updated regularly to adapt to new directions taken by phishers, making the maintenance process expensive. See [24] for a comparison of machine learning methods for detecting phishing. A non-machine learning based classifier is PhishCatch [2], which uses heuristics to analyze emails through simple header and link analyses, and a rudimentary text analysis that looks for the presence of some text filters. In [3], the authors create three independent classifiers: using NLP and WordNet to detect user actions upon receiving emails, building on the header analysis of [2], and a link analysis classifier that checks whether links in the email are fraudulent. The evolution of phishing emails is analyzed by [1], the authors classify phishing email messages into two categories: *flash* and *non-flash* attacks, and phishing features into *transitory* and *pervasive*.

In [25], a stateless rule-based phishing filter called Phishwish is proposed, which uses a small set of rules and does not need training. Although Phishwish obtains a high detection accuracy with low false positives, it is tested only on a small data set of 117 emails (81 phishing and 36 valid). For more details on phishing, please see the books by [26–28]. Turner and Housley [29] present a detailed treatment of email operational details and security.

7 Conclusions

We presented a robust and effective semantic feature selection method for text data that is based on the t-test and generally applicable to text classification. This method was applied to automatic classification of phishing emails. We created four classifiers of increasing sophistication starting with simple pattern-matching classifiers and then designing more sophisticated ones by combining statistical methods with part-of-speech tagging, word sense, and the WordNet lexical database. Our classifiers perform significantly better than the best previous body text-based phishing classifier. When combined with header and link information it is comparable in performance with the best and most sophisticated machine learning methods that also use all the information in the email. This demonstrates the efficacy and robustness of our feature selection method. Cross-validation of results is left for the future.

References

1. Irani, D., Webb, S., Giffin, J., Pu, C.: Evolutionary study of phishing. In: 3rd Anti-Phishing Working Group eCrime Researchers Summit (2008)
2. Yu, W., Nargundkar, S., Tiruthani, N.: Phishcatch - a phishing detection tool. In: 33rd IEEE International Computer Software and Applications Conference, pp. 451–456 (2009)
3. Verma, R., Shashidhar, N., Hossain, N.: Detecting phishing emails the natural language way. In: Foresti, S., Yung, M., Martinelli, F. (eds.) ESORICS 2012. LNCS, vol. 7459, pp. 824–841. Springer, Heidelberg (2012)
4. Ramanathan, V., Wechsler, H.: Phishgillnet - phishing detection using probabilistic latent semantic analysis. EURASIP J. Inf. Secur. **2012**, 1 (2012)
5. Li, S., Xia, R., Zong, C., Huang, C.R.: A framework of feature selection methods for text categorization. In: ACL/AFNLP, pp. 692–700 (2009)
6. Yang, Y., Pedersen, J.O.: A comparative study on feature selection in text categorization. In: ICML, pp. 412–420 (1997)
7. Nigam, K., McCallum, A., Thrun, S., Mitchell, T.M.: Text classification from labeled and unlabeled documents using EM. Mach. Learn. **39**(2/3), 103–134 (2000)
8. Forman, G.: An extensive empirical study of feature selection metrics for text classification. J. Mach. Learn. Res. **3**, 1289–1305 (2003)
9. Sebastiani, F.: Machine learning in automated text categorization. ACM Comput. Surv. **34**(1), 1–47 (2002)
10. Herzberg, A.: Combining authentication, reputation and classification to make phishing unprofitable. In: Gritzalis, D., Lopez, J. (eds.) SEC 2009. IFIP AICT, vol. 297, pp. 13–24. Springer, Heidelberg (2009)
11. Porter, M.: An algorithm for suffix stripping. Program **14**(3), 130–137 (1980)
12. Fellbaum, C. (ed.): WordNet an Electronic Lexical Database. MIT Press, Cambridge (1998)
13. Richens, T.: Anomalies in the WordNet verb hierarchy. In: COLING, pp. 729–736 (2008)
14. Mihalcea, R., Csomai, A.: Senselearner: word sense disambiguation for all words in unrestricted text. In: ACL (2005)

15. Nazario, J.: The online phishing corpus (2004). http://monkey.org/~jose/wiki/doku.php

16. Fette, I., Sadeh, N., Tomasic, A.: Learning to detect phishing emails. In: Proceedings of the 16th International Conference on World Wide Web, ACM, pp. 649–656 (2007)

17. Ludl, C., McAllister, S., Kirda, E., Kruegel, C.: On the effectiveness of techniques to detect phishing sites. In: Hämmerli, B.M., Sommer, R. (eds.) DIMVA 2007. LNCS, vol. 4579, pp. 20–39. Springer, Heidelberg (2007)

18. Sheng, S., Wardman, B., Warner, G., Cranor, L., Hong, J., Zhang, C.: An empirical analysis of phishing blacklists. In: Proceedings of the 6th Conference on Email and Anti-Spam (2009)

19. Chandrasekaran, M., Narayanan, K., Upadhyaya, S.: Phishing email detection based on structural properties. In: NYS CyberSecurity Conference (2006)

20. Bergholz, A., Chang, J., Paaß, G., Reichartz, F., Strobel, S.: Improved phishing detection using model-based features. In: Proceedings of the Conference on Email and Anti-Spam (CEAS) (2008)

21. Basnet, R., Mukkamala, S., Sung, A.: Detection of phishing attacks: a machine learning approach. In: Prasad, B. (ed.) Soft Computing Applications in Industry. Studies in Fuzziness and Soft Computing, vol. 226, pp. 373–383. Springer, Heidelberg (2008)

22. Bergholz, A., Beer, J.D., Glahn, S., Moens, M.F., Paaß, G., Strobel, S.: New filtering approaches for phishing email. J. Comput. Secur. 18(1), 7–35 (2010)

23. Gansterer, W.N., Pölz, D.: E-mail classification for phishing defense. In: Boughanem, M., Berrut, C., Mothe, J., Soule-Dupuy, C. (eds.) ECIR 2009. LNCS, vol. 5478, pp. 449–460. Springer, Heidelberg (2009)

24. Abu-Nimeh, S., Nappa, D., Wang, X., Nair, S.: A comparison of machine learning techniques for phishing detection. In: Proceedings of the Anti-Phishing Working Group's 2nd Annual eCrime Researchers Summit, ACM, pp. 60–69 (2007)

25. Cook, D.L., Gurbani, V.K., Daniluk, M.: Phishwish: a simple and stateless phishing filter. Secur. Commun. Netw. 2(1), 29–43 (2009)

26. Jakobsson, M., Myers, S.: Phishing and Countermeasures: Understanding the Increasing Problem of Electronic Identity Theft. Wiley-Interscience, Hoboken (2006)

27. James, L.: Phishing Exposed. Syngress Publishing, Rockland (2005)

28. Ollmann, G.: The phishing guide. Next Generation Security Software Ltd. (2004)

29. Turner, S., Housley, R.: Implementing Email and Security Tokens: Current Standards, Tools, and Practices. Wiley, Hoboken (2008)

Who Is Sending a Spam Email: Clustering and Characterizing Spamming Hosts

Jiyoung Woo, Hyun Jae Kang, Ah Reum Kang, Hyukmin Kwon, and Huy Kang Kim[✉]

Graduate School of Information Security, Korea University, Seoul, Korea
{jywoo, trifle19, armk, hack, cenda}@korea.ac.kr

Abstract. In this work, we propose a spam analyzing system that clusters the spamming hosts, characterizes and visualizes the spammers' behaviors, and detects malicious clusters. The proposed system integrates behavior profiling in IP address level, IP address based clustering, characterizing spammer clusters, examining the maliciousness of embedded URLs, and deriving visual signatures for future detection of malicious spammers. We classify spamming hosts into botnet, worm, or individual spammers and derive their characteristics. We then design a clustering scheme to automatically classify the host IP addresses and to identify malicious groups according to known characteristics of each type of host. For rapid decision making in identifying botnets, we derive visual signatures using a parallel coordinates. We validate the proposed system using these spam email data collected by the spam trap system operated by the Korea Internet and Security Agency.

Keywords: Spam email · Spamming host · Botnet · Clustering · Visualization

1 Introduction

In 2012, unsolicited email messages, generally called "spam", comprised 69 % of all email traffic, according to the Symantec 2013 Internet Security Threat Report [16]. The proportion of spam email sent from botnets was 77 % of all spam. A botnet is a network of compromised computers, called bots, which are commanded and controlled by a botnet owner from a command-control server. When infected, they are driven to connect to malicious websites that embed malicious code through download forms or to send emails with malicious code attached. Bots are used for various kinds of cyber attacks by spreading malicious code to steal passwords, log keystrokes, and act as a proxy server to conceal the attacker's identity or by performing distributed denial-of-service (DDoS) attacks. The largest botnets were taken down by US government for several years; however, the total spam rate and the proportion attributed to botnets are still high. Because botnets are typically used to perform DDoS attacks, we can extract useful information about botnets from these attacks. However, evaluating network traffic during a DDoS attack is passive, because the botnet attacks after its size has expanded significantly. In addition, network traffic data is difficult to obtain, because DDoS attacks do not occur often. On the other hand, detecting botnets through email spam is proactive and more efficient than through other types of attacks, because daily

© Springer International Publishing Switzerland 2014
H.-S. Lee and D.-G. Han (Eds.): ICISC 2013, LNCS 8565, pp. 469–482, 2014.
DOI: 10.1007/978-3-319-12160-4_28

data regarding botnet activity is easier to obtain, and the botnet could be detected before it expands significantly. Thorough analysis of spam email enables us to detect messages sent by bots in botnets and to identify the bots that belong to the same botnet.

Against spam email, current IP address-based blacklisting or content-based filtering expose many limitations. Spammers evade the text-based filter using image spam and obfuscating the words and they also evade IP blacklisting by changing the sender's IP addresses in a low cost. To overcome these shortcomings, we need a behavior-based method, which is difficult for spammers to evade. Furthermore, it is impossible to respond all incoming spams, so if we can group spam email and distinguish it from botnets, we can make more flexible incident response policy and react some spam email need with priority. In this study, we propose a framework that performs clustering spam email and identifies malicious groups. The proposed system integrates behavior profiling in IP address level, IP address based clustering, characterizing spammer clusters, examining maliciousness of embedded URLs, and deriving visual signatures by visualizing behavior profiles using a parallel coordinate diagram.

2 Literature Review

Recent research studies on botnet detection focused on inspecting network traffics for anomalous patterns during a DDoS attack. We reviewed the studies that used visualization to detect the botnet. The visualization of traffic flow exposes anomalous events, such as unusual high traffic volume or drastic changes in traffic volume within a time period. To detect malicious activities, these studies mainly adopted a visual layout that illustrates the traffic volume among hosts, ports, and protocols and highlights the changes in network attributes.

The parallel coordinate diagram is widely used, which can represent a multi-dimensional dataset and can display the coverage of a variable and the frequency of its attributes. In Tricaud's work [1], the network flow variables that were selected as axes are the timeline, source IP address, destination IP address, source port, and destination port; in Choi's work [2], the source IP address, destination IP address, port, and packet; in Itoh's [3] hierarchical display, the agent, IP address, URL, and request; in Yin's work [4], the internal sender domain, internal host, and external receiving domain within a time period; and in Conti's work [5], the internal/external IP address and port. These studies explored variable selection and variable layouts to find the best coordinates to detect anomalies in network traffic using visual patterns.

Recent studies examined the spam email as a data source for botnet detection. We reviewed the key papers from these studies according to the data source, metric, and technique. The data feed to the detection system was prepared at the message level or the user level. The contents of spam email including URLs, attached files, and message contents are used as features for clustering and classification. The network traffics are also used as features to measure pollution level of messages and similarity between messages. Previous studies used classification method to detect malicious groups when they are able to build ground truth. In the lack of ground truth, the scoring or clustering methods are generally applied. Similar to the approaches for detecting email spam, the

Table 1. Key papers based on data sources, metrics, and techniques

Data sources			Metrics	Techniques	Key papers
Message level	Content	URL, attachment, message content	Obfuscation, similarity, pollution level	Clustering, classification	[6, 7, 13]
	Network traffic	Protocol, IP address, port	Similarity, pollution level	Clustering, classification, scoring	[6–8]
User level	User behaviors	Sending/receiving, login/logout, membership	Burstiness, distribution, similarity	Clustering, classification, anomaly detection	[8–12]
	Coordination	IP address, user	Similarity	Graph theory	[10]

message content can be measured in terms of the degree of obfuscation and pollution level to search for messages from a botnet (Table 1).

Through a systematic literature review on botnet detection, we identified the following research gaps: (1) Most of the previous studies on botnet utilized network traffic to isolate DDoS attacks that were performed primarily by botnets. (2) Studies that used spam as a data source mainly used the clustering and classification methods excluding visualization as techniques. (3) The features used in user behavior analysis are limited and temporal features and ratio features are excluded. (4) Previous works on the spamming botnet do not characterize other spamming sources. In this study, we will extend the previous studies by enriching the features of user behaviors to detect malicious spamming groups and providing systematic behavior profiles of malicious groups. The behavior profiling makes spammers have more difficulties in evading the detection method than text-based methods. We will also apply a visualization method on the user behavior profile to detect malicious groups. The lightweight clustering and visualization method for spammer detection will enable instant reaction to spammers through a fast and efficient analysis.

3 Analyzing Spam Mail Data

3.1 Spamming Group Characteristics

Spam by botnet: In a botnet, bots become the hosts that send malicious URLs inside spam emails to others. The aim of the botnet is to control bots, so the bots remains in contact with victims. These programmed bots exhibit regular patterns in terms of the frequency of spam bursts, and bots that belong to a same botnet have similar delivery behaviors.

Spam by worms: The major characteristics of the worm are self-propagating and spreading malicious codes. Because of self-propagating nature of the worm, emails sent by the worm often include malicious attached files. The victims (sender) send spam containing malicious codes to collect email accounts (receivers). While bots in the botnet exhibit similar behaviors, the computers infected by a worm have individual and independent behaviors. The worm makes one-time interactions with victims. After a host infects other victims, it does not need to maintain contact with them; therefore, the worm's behavior is less regular.

Spam by individual spammer: Individual spammers send various unsolicited bulk emails to many unspecified receivers; they hold different email accounts to avoid detection and blocking. While the botnet and the worm aim to infect others with malicious code, the individual spammers send messages that contain advertisement URLs.

3.2   System Design

We designed a visual spam analyzing system that builds spammers' behavior profiles, clusters the spammers, characterizes and visualizes their behaviors, and detects malicious clusters. The spam trap is a honey pot system designed to collect spam emails. The proposed system extracts the data from collected spam, organizes them by IP address, and derives the delivery behaviors from the data. To build spammers' behavior profiles, we designed systematic features in terms of volume, diversity, and regularity. IP addresses are clustered based on the similarity of sending behaviors. We designed a clustering module to group spammers into the most homogeneous groups in sending spam emails. We then analyze the behavior patterns of the cluster and judge the cluster's maliciousness based on the spamming group characteristics. The system also evaluates the clustering results based on behavior profiles by checking the maliciousness of IP addresses. An IP address is identified as malicious when it sends spam emails that link malicious URLs. Finally, the representative IP addresses from each cluster are feed to the visualization module. The visualizer displays the behavior profile

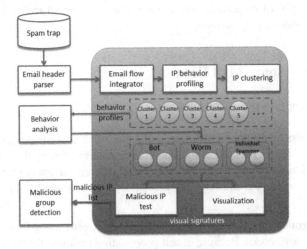

Fig. 1. System design

using a parallel coordinate diagram. The statistics and the visual signatures help the decision maker to classify the spammer into botnets, worms or individual spammers (Fig. 1).

User Behavior Profiling. We consider the following characteristics in deriving user behavior profiles.

Number of sender accounts vs. number of receiver accounts: The bot and the worm use a limited number of sender accounts and fewer receiver accounts. The individual spammer uses a large number of sender accounts; the receiver accounts are fewer than sender accounts but still many.

Characteristics of URLs in the messages: The bot and the worm have few embedded URLs in their messages, whereas the individual spammer embeds diverse URLs in messages.

Time diversity: The worm and the individual spammer have irregular patterns in sending spam emails, but the bot is programmed to send out messages regularly.

We designed the clustering scheme to use the IP address as the identity of the host because a host controls many sender accounts. To represent the email-delivery behaviors of hosts, we extracted the following metadata from the email headers and performed clustering based on the extracted information:

Email metadata = (sender IP address, sender account, receiver account, title, embedded URL, attached file, time)

The email metadata were accumulated during a specific time period and sorted into tuples according to the IP address. A tuple consists of the following: number of sender accounts, number of receiver accounts, number of email titles, number of embedded URLs in spam messages for the time interval Δ, and time ratio.

(IP_i, Δ) = (# of sent messages, # of sender accounts, # of receiver accounts, # of titles, # of URLs, time_ratio)

Bots/worms/individual spammers are classified in terms of volume, diversity and regularity. The spamming botnet sends the significant volume of messages, which embed limited URLs, from limited accounts to limited accounts regularly. The volume is measured as the number of sending frequency. The diversity is measured as the number of sender accounts, the number of receiver accounts, the number of URLs, and the number of titles. The temporal regularity is calculated with the following proposed light comparison ratio, which shows the changes in the sending frequency within sequential time intervals.

$$R(time\_ratio) = \frac{sending\ frequency\ at\ time\ t}{sending\ frequency\ at\ time\ t - 1}$$

Additionally, we use a ratio tuple by dividing the original tuple by sending frequency. The number of sending messages, accounts, titles, and URLs are highly correlated with sending frequency. The ratio over sending frequency shows normalized sending patterns. Finally, we diversify the clustering features by adding following ratios: the ratio of sender accounts over receiver accounts, and the ratio of the number of URLs over the number of subjects.

$$(IP_i, \Delta) / Freq = \left(\frac{\# \text{ of sent messages}}{\text{sending frequency}}, \frac{\# \text{ of sender accounts}}{\text{sending frequency}}, \frac{\# \text{ of receiver accounts}}{\text{sending frequency}}, \frac{\# \text{ of titles}}{\text{sending frequency}}, \frac{\# \text{ of URLs}}{\text{sending frequency}} \right)$$

Clustering the Spam Email Data and Detecting Malicious Groups. From previous research and domain expert's knowledge, we found that bots, worms, and individual spammers have different spam-delivery patterns. To identify suspected malicious groups from the spam emails collected in the spam trap system, we design the clustering scheme. This clustering scheme reduces the processing time compared to manual examination of individual IP addresses. Moreover, because bots in different botnets have different spam-delivery patterns, and the different groups can be separated through clustering based on the significant differentiators. Each email flow is transformed to a high-dimensional feature space through the predefined feature set. We then measure the similarity of behaviors of IP addresses. Since the feature set consists of numeric data derived from the email flow, the similarity between IP addresses is calculated easily by measuring the Euclidean distance between tuples. The k-means algorithm, one of representative of clustering methods, divides data set into k clusters based on distance between a data point and typical k points, named centroid. Repeating the process of searching new centroids that minimizes the sum of squares of errors (SSE) between the points and the centroids, the method finds optimal k different clusters [17]. We use k-means algorithm to cluster the IP addresses to enable the decision maker to set the number of clusters. After the clusters are formed, we examine the clusters' behavior profiles considering the characteristics of spammer groups as described in 3.1. Our study should be ideally validated by comparing detected malicious groups against botnet hosts and worm hosts. In the absence of such ground truth for spammer groups, botnet/worm/individual spammer, the maliciousness test of URLs in email data will provide an objective validation. To check whether suspected clusters are malicious, we calculate ratios of malicious IP addresses in each cluster. Malicious URLs induce receivers to download malicious code. URL also can be determined malicious when the URL is on a spam blacklist. We conclude an IP address is malicious, when corresponding IP address sends messages including any malicious URLs.

Visualization. To derive visual signatures for future botnet detection, we implement the visualization system. We employ the parallel coordinate diagram to develop visual signatures. The parallel coordinate diagram can express multi-dimensional variables into two-dimensional space, and it shows the flow pattern by representing the coordinates of attributes of variables in adjacent lines. We use the email flow as a unit of visualization for easy and instant detection of malicious groups. We set the IP address as the first coordinates because we aim to detect the IP addresses of bots. To get an intuitive illustration of the email flow, we set the sequence of parallel lines as follows: sender account (from_email), receiver account (to_email), subject, URL, and time ratio.

4 Experiments

4.1 Clustering with K-means Algorithm

The KISA is the Korean national organization in charge of Internet security. The organization developed a honeypot spam trap that stores the email header data, including sender IP address, sender account, sender domain, sender mailer, receiver account, email title, embedded URL, attached file, and time. We analyzed the spam email data collected on December 6th, 2011. Following is an overview on spam traffics of the day. There are total 1,097,936 spam emails collected by the spam trap, that were sent from 135,552 distinct accounts using 21,085 different IP addresses to 53,117 distinct recipient accounts with 6,682 unique email titles and 30,137 different embedded URLs. 93.01 % of spam emails embedded URLs in their messages and 1 % of the spam emails attached files.

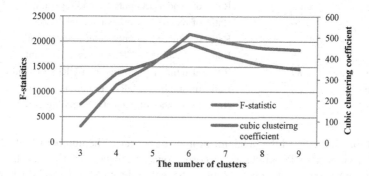

Fig. 2. F statistic and cubic clustering coefficient values

Figure 2 shows pseudo-F statistic and cubic clustering coefficient values when the number of clusters varies. The pseudo-F statistic describes the ratio of between cluster variance to within cluster variance [14]. The clusters are more separated with other clusters and more closely concentrated in each clusters, when Pseudo-F statistic increases. The cubic clustering coefficient (CCC) is also used to estimate the number of clusters to minimize the within-cluster sum of squares [15]. It is based on the assumption that data was obtained from a uniform distribution. If CCC gets larger value, clusters differ from a uniform distribution (no clusters).

After deciding the number of clusters as 6 and performing the IP address clustering, we performed the impact analysis of each feature in the categorization of clusters. Table 2 represents the importance ratio of corresponding attribute name, and explanations of attributes in detail. As shown in the table, attributes in ratio tuple primarily acts on our clustering process. We can see the ratio attributes which are not influenced by sending frequency, have significant effects on clustering groups based on sending patterns. The importance value indicates a relative role of a variable in splitting clusters and measures how much the error reduces when the variable is used as a main splitting rule. After the clustering is performed, the tree rules composed of variables are generated to classify the data according to cluster results. It is the sum of square of the product of the variable's agreement in a rule and the reduction of the sum of square of error from the clusters generated by the rule. As the importance value of a variable increases, the variable is considered more importantly in generating clusters.

Table 2. The importance values of features for clustering

Name	Importance	Detail
Freq	0	Sending count
Sub	0	Number of subjects (titles)
From	0	Number of sender accounts
To	0	Number of receiver accounts
Attached	0	Number of email with attached files
URL	0.22	Number of URLs
URL_YN	0	Number of email embedding URLs
From/Freq	0.67	Ratio of sender accounts to sending count
To/Freq	0.26	Ratio of receiver accounts to sending count
From/To	0	Ratio of sender accounts to receiver accounts
URL/Freq	0.76	Ratio of email with URLs to sending count
URL_YN/Freq	0.89	Ratio of number of emails with URLs to sending count
URL/Sub	0	Ratio of number of URLs to number of subjects
Sub/Freq	1	Ratio of number of subjects to sending count

On Table 3, we listed the behavior profiles of clusters. The number of IP addresses means the number of IP addresses in corresponding cluster. Attached is the ratio of messages containing attached files. Ratio is the mean of each IP adderess' R (time_ratio) value explained in chapter 3. Other attributes are average values of the features in Table 2. Based on the characteristics of each cluster, we identified malicious groups as follows.

Table 3. The behavior characteristics of clusters

Cluster	# IP addresses	Freq	Sub	From	To	Attached	URL	URL_YN	Time ratio
1	5729	5.67	4.77	5.06	5.06	0.00	4.88	5.66	1.08
2	2165	32.46	1.73	5.25	14.79	0.55	0.12	0.68	2.09
3	2670	2.41	1.55	1.81	2.14	0.19	0.02	0.03	1.11
4	6451	60.90	8.57	16.02	24.06	0.02	7.83	60.50	2.74
5	3890	92.64	46.46	53.07	52.31	0.00	52.87	92.60	4.51
6	181	1301.34	381.24	663.86	594.27	0.00	664.90	99.9	13.95

Cluster	From/ Freq	To/ Freq	From/ To	URL/ Freq	URL_YN /Freq	URL/ Sub	Sub/ Freq	Category
1	0.97	0.98	0.99	0.93	1.00	0.99	0.95	Bot
2	0.32	0.52	0.71	0.01	0.03	0.05	0.17	Worm
3	0.88	0.98	0.91	0.00	0.01	0.01	0.85	Normal user
4	0.30	0.59	0.69	0.17	0.98	0.76	0.23	Bot
5	0.60	0.64	0.98	0.55	1.00	1.05	0.54	Bot
6	0.52	0.48	1.10	0.52	1.00	1.68	0.32	Spammer

First, we analyzed sending patterns of cluster 3, cluster 6, and cluster 2. Most of the messages sent by the IP addresses in cluster 3 do not include URLs or attached files, and the number of the messages was low. If it is a botnet group, the number of the messages will be more sizable and the messages will contain URLs or files. Cluster 3 seems to be a normal user group with low rates of embedded URLs and files. Cluster 6 holds many interesting attributes. It includes only 181 IP addresses but they sent a large number of messages. Also the sender accounts and the receiver accounts were excessively diverse. We guess that cluster 6 is a professional individual spammer group, since the botnet or the worm uses limited number of sender accounts and receiver accounts. Cluster 2 had some different characteristics. The messages sent by IP addresses in cluster 2 mostly contained attached files, while other clusters have low attachment rates. Since emailing worms usually attach malicious code, we guessed cluster 2 as a worm group. Cluster 1, 4, and 5 had similar sending patterns. They have limited number of sender accounts, subjects, receiver accounts, and URLs. The ratio of sender accounts, receiver accounts, and subjects over sending count are lower than 1. This indicates that the messages in those clusters were sent from same accounts and with subjects in limited range.

We validated our judgment based on the distance between clusters. We performed the multidimensional scaling to derive two principal dimensions formed by combinations of variables and measured the distances between clusters. The first principal dimension is derived so that it explains the variance of data maximally, and the second principal dimension is selected as the vertical axis against the first dimension. Figure 3 displays the clusters centers on the two principal dimensions. We found that botnet clusters locate within a close distance and the worm is close to the botnets.

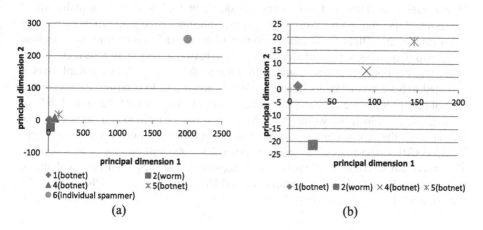

Fig. 3. The proximity map of clusters.

4.2   The Ratio of Malicious IP Addresses

As an alternative validation to confirm the reputation of the IP addresses, we used "VirusTotal (http://www.virustotal.com)" to inquire the maliciousness history of the IP addresses. VirusTotal is a world-largest free online service that analyzes files, URLs and IP addresses enabling the identification of viruses, worms, Trojans and other kinds of malicious contents detected by antivirus engines and website scanners. We checked the 30,137 URLs by performing submission to VirusTotal, and retrieved URL scan reports. We collected whole reports of 19,620 URLs, and 4,713 URLs were diagnosed malicious. The time gap between when the spam email is collected and when the embedded URLs are tested makes the number of tested URLs less than the number of feed URLs. However, the current lists are sufficient to compare how different the clusters are. We got 6,582 malicious IP addresses among 21,085 different IP addresses. Table 4 summarized the evaluation results.

Table 4. The test results of maliciousness of IP addresses in each cluster

Cluster	# of IP address	# of malicious IP address	Percentage (%)	Cluster category
1	5729	1927	33.6	Bot
2	2165	26	1.2	Worm
3	2670	17	0.6	Normal user
4	6451	1948	30.2	Bot
5	3890	2483	63.8	Bot
6	181	181	100	Individual spammer

Comparing the percentages of malicious IP addresses, the results indicated that there are substantial differences between each cluster, especially when considering with cluster categories. Three botnet clusters include about 30.2 ∼ 63.8 % of malicious IP addresses. Bots send spam emails to infect other machines or to gain profits by running spam campaigns. Thus, spam emails from botnets naturally contain many malicious URLs and IP addresses. Considering the time gap between the testing time and the data collecting, the botnet clusters' results were meaningful. The cluster of normal users is expected to have no malicious IP addresses. It is acceptable to determine cluster 3 as a normal user group since cluster 3 shows nearly zero malicious URL rate with 0.6 % of error. Cluster 2, which is a worm group, have a low rate of malicious IP addresses. The messages of the worm cluster contained many attachments but only few messages included URLs. The individual spammer group has 100 % of malicious IP addresses. The individual spammers are professional spammers, and they send large volume of spam emails. Even they do not contain infected URLs, the embedded URLs are on the spam blacklist.

4.3   Visual Signatures

We visualized the email flow of top sender accounts or IP addresses in terms of sending volume. The representative cases are displayed to derive visual signatures for future botnet/worm/professional spammer detection. We plotted parallel coordinate diagrams with choosing 5 sender accounts in each botnet group and a worm group, and choosing

5 IP addresses in the individual spammer group. To get ratio, we put t = 12 h in R (time_ratio). The diagram of worm is similar to the diagram of botnet except the diagram of worm has less URLs and diverse time ratio for an IP address. The bots in a botnet have similar and regular sending patterns, so botnet diagrams have the fixed time ratio. On the contrary to this, those values in worm diagrams vary. To represent the individual spammer diagram, we plotted it by choosing top five IP addresses to emphasize the complexity of sending behavior. The diagram showed a large volume of messages, numerous sender accounts/receiver accounts/URLs, and diverse ratios. With the visualization system plotting parallel coordinate diagrams, and simply choosing appropriate elements to plot, they can be used as visual signatures to decide botnet/ worm/individual spammer group (Fig. 4).

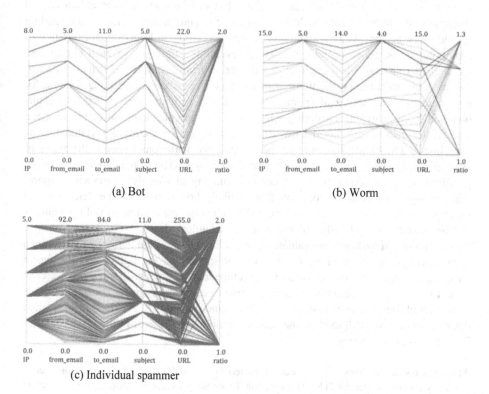

Fig. 4. Parallel coordinate diagrams of malicious groups

4.4 Behavior Profiling

So far, we validated our judgment on malicious groups. We then built profiles of botnet/worm/individual spammer for future detection of botnet. The important features derived from clustering are examined to derive discriminators of malicious group species. We derived one standard deviation range of important features and derive the botnet profiles with features that have no overlapped ranges with normal user, worm, and individual spammer (see Appendix Table 5). The botnet profiles are derived as follows.

Botnet profiles: 0.44<URL<378, From/Freq<0.61, 0.75<To/Freq<0.89, 0.94<URL_YN/Freq<1

5 Conclusion

In this study, we proposed spam analyzing system that clusters the spammers, characterizes and visualizes the spammers' behaviors, and detects malicious clusters. We classified the sending hosts into botnet, worm, or individual spammers, and used a wide range of characteristics to map out the behavior of botnets, worms and individual spammers. We then designed a clustering scheme to automatically classify the sending IP addresses and to identify malicious groups according to known characteristics of spamming hosts. Since pseudo F-statistics reveals the tightness of each cluster and cubic clustering coefficient captures the deviation from a uniform distribution, combining both to determine the number of clusters gives a good clustering scheme for huge datasets such as email spams. We used two validations steps for the results obtained from analyzing clustering which reaffirm the categorization of the clusters. The cluster also reveals normal user traffic which acts as a control variable for the experiment. The visual signature further reveals the variations between the types of spammers i.e. botnets, worms and individual spammers. The visual signatures using a parallel coordinate enable the rapid decision making in identifying malicious spamming groups. The issue of common fate of likely honest users in the detection and group mechanism when the infrastructure (IP addresses) are used as part of the features can be solved when white-list IP addresses are maintained.

The proposed system was evaluated using a large-scale spam dataset collected by a spam trap system operated by KISA. We confirmed that the botnet and the worm cluster have high rates of malicious URLs embedded in emails. In addition, we confirmed that the visual patterns of representative cases of each cluster are differentiable from each cluster. In the next stage, we will expand our study to use the one-year spam dataset. Second, we will explore the diverse combination of axes in the visual chart to improve visual signatures.

Acknowledgement. This research was supported by the MKE (The Ministry of Knowledge Economy), Korea, under the ITRC (Information Technology Research Center) support program (NIPA-2013-H0301-13-1003) supervised by the NIPA (National IT Industry Promotion Agency). This research was supported by Korean Ministry of Environment as the Eco-Innovation project (Global Top project). (GT-SWS-11-02-007-3).

Appendix

Table 5. Statistics of important features according to host species

Feature	Botnet		Worm		Normal user		Individual spammer	
	$\mu - \sigma$	$\mu + \sigma$	$\mu - \sigma$	$\mu + \sigma$	$\mu - \sigma$	$\mu + \sigma$	$\mu - \sigma$	$\mu + \sigma$
URL	0	64.73	0	0.44	0	0.17	378.04	951.75
From/Freq	0.29	0.94	0.18	0.45	0.68	1.09	0.44	0.61
To/Freq	0.46	1.02	0.29	0.75	0.89	1.06	0.40	0.56
URL/Freq	0.17	0.89	0	0.03	0	0.04	0.44	0.61
URL_YN/ Freq	0.94	1.05	0	0.11	0	0.05	1.00	1.00
Sub/Freq	0.22	0.90	0.03	0.32	0.60	1.10	0.25	0.40

References

1. Tricaud, S., Saadé, P.: Applied parallel coordinates for logs and network traffic attack analysis. J. Comput. Virol. **6**, 1–29 (2010)
2. Choi, H., Lee, H., Kim, H.: Fast detection and visualization of network attacks on parallel coordinates. Comput. Secur. **28**, 276–288 (2009)
3. Itoh, T., Takakura, H., Sawada, A., Koyamada, K.: Hierarchical visualization of network intrusion detection data. Comput. Graph. Appl. IEEE **26**, 40–47 (2006)
4. Yin, X., Yurcik, W., Treaster, M., Li, Y., Lakkaraju, K.: VisFlowConnect: netflow visualizations of link relationships for security situational awareness. In: Proceedings of the 2004 ACM Workshop on Visualization and Data Mining for Computer Security, pp. 26–34 (2004)
5. Conti, G., Abdullah, K.: Passive visual fingerprinting of network attack tools. In: Proceedings of the 2004 ACM Workshop on Visualization and Data Mining for Computer Security, pp. 45–54 (2004)
6. Xie, Y., Yu, F., Achan, K., Panigrahy, R., Hulten, G., Osipkov, I.: Spamming botnets: signatures and characteristics. ACM SIGCOMM Comput. Commun. Rev. **38**, 171–182 (2008)
7. John, J.P., Moshchuk, A., Gribble, S.D., Krishnamurthy, A.: Studying spamming botnets using botlab. In: NSDI'09 Proceedings of the 6th USENIX Symposium on Netwoked Systems Design and Implementation, vol. 9, pp. 291–306 (2009)
8. Li, F., Hsieh, M.-h.: An empirical study of clustering behavior of spammers and groupbased anti-spam strategies. In: CEAS 2006 Third Conference on Email and AntiSpam (2006)
9. Zhuang, L., Dunagan, J., Simon, D.R., Wang, H.J., Tygar, J.: Characterizing botnets from email spam records. In: Proceedings of the 1st Usenix Workshop on Large-Scale Exploits and Emergent Threats (2008)
10. Zhao, Y., Xie, Y., Yu, F., Ke, Q., Yu, Y., Chen, Y., Gillum, E.: BotGraph: large scale spamming botnet detection. In: NSDI'09 Proceedings of the 6th USENIX Symposium on Netwoked Systems Design and Implementation, vol. 9, pp. 321–334 (2009)
11. Sroufe, P., Phithakkitnukoon, S., Dantu, R., Cangussu, J.: Email shape analysis for spam botnet detection. In: Proceedings of IEEE Consumer Communications and Networking Conference, 2009 (2009)

12. Pathak, A., Qian, F., Hu, Y.C., Mao, Z.M., Ranjan, S.: Botnet spam campaigns can be long lasting: evidence, implications, and analysis. In: Proceedings of the Eleventh International Joint Conference on Measurement and Modeling of Computer Systems, pp. 13–24 (2009)
13. Jeong, H., Kim, H.K., Lee, S., Kim, E.: Detection of Zombie PCs based on email spam analysis. KSII Trans. Internet Inf. Syst. (TIIS) **6**, 1445–1462 (2012)
14. Calinski, T., Harabasz, J.: A dendrite method for cluster analysis. Commun. Stat.-Theor. Methods **3**, 1–27 (1974)
15. Sarle, W.: SAS Technical Report A-108 (1983)
16. Symantec Corporation: Internet Security Threat Report 2013, vol. 18 (2013)
17. Berkhin, P.: A survey of clustering data mining techniques. In: Kogan, J., Nicholas, C., Teboulle, M. (eds.) Grouping Multidimensional Data, pp. 25–71. Springer, Heidelberg (2006)

Dark Side of the Shader: Mobile GPU-Aided Malware Delivery

Janis Danisevskis[✉], Marta Piekarska, and Jean-Pierre Seifert

Security in Telecommunications, Technische Universität Berlin, Berlin, Germany
{janis,marta,jpseifert}@sec.t-labs.tu-berlin.de

Abstract. Mobile phones are the most intimate computing devices of our time. We use them for private and business purposes. At the same time lax update habits of manufacturers make them accumulate disclosed vulnerabilities. That is why smartphones have become very attractive targets for attackers. Until today Graphics Processing Units (GPU) were not considered an interesting mean of payload delivery in mobile devices. However, in this paper, we present how the Direct Memory Access (DMA) capabilities of a mobile GPU can be abused for a privilege escalation attack. We describe a successful and real-world GPU-based attack, discuss problems that the GPU's different programming model poses, and techniques that lead to a successful attack. We also show a proof-of-concept exploit against a very popular smartphone line. We conclude that DMA-based malware is a serious threat to mobile devices.

Keywords: DMA · GPU · Mobile malware · Privilege escalation

1 Introduction

One of the key pillars of today's smartphones is their stunning graphics performance, which is improved with every new mobile generation. Compared to early cellular phones, which offered only text capabilities, their animated graphics along with their shiny displays allows for a huge zoo of different applications, including valuable and sensitive applications. Since the underlying graphics hardware and software is very complex, it comes as no surprise that the underlying GPU technology raises some obvious security questions due to their heavy DMA usage. Examples like [5,15] support those security concerns. For this reason we consider the risk of modern GPUs as a new attack vector for smartphones. Towards this, the presented paper makes the following contributions for a better understanding of the security of modern GPUs:

- **Mobile GPU Malware.** We show, to the best of our knowledge, the first GPU malware running on a mobile device.
- **Attack Vector.** We design an innovative attack vector that allows to abuse the DMA of a GPU for copying user-chosen data.
- **Exploit.** We present a real life exploit that effects millions of devices.

For its novelty claims we now consider the related work on GPU or DMA-assisted malware research.

© Springer International Publishing Switzerland 2014
H.-S. Lee and D.-G. Han (Eds.): ICISC 2013, LNCS 8565, pp. 483–495, 2014.
DOI: 10.1007/978-3-319-12160-4_29

GPU-Assisted Malware. Until now little research has been done on the topic of GPU-assisted malware. Vasiliadis et al. [16] demonstrate how the general purpose computing facilities of modern GPUs can be used to increase malware robustness against detection. With their method polymorphic code versions are generated on the GPU, but the malicious payload is still executed on the CPU. Their work not only shows that GPU-assisted malware is a feasible concept, but also how big the potential of using a GPU in general purpose computing is, as well as in malicious code spreading. Moreover the authors anticipate the possible attack vectors that can accrue from unrestricted access to the frame-buffer.

Carlson [3] examines the potential of using coprocessors, such as the GPU, for both defensive and offensive purpose on mobile devices in particular. He shows techniques for using the mobile GPU for signature verifications, encryption and decryption, memory tracking and dynamic disassembly.

In their work Ladakis et al. [7] describe a GPU-based keylogger. The authors monitor the systems' keyboard buffer directly from the GPU, making use of its DMA capabilities. They used a CPU process to control the execution of their malware. However, unlike our method, their prototype implementation requires root privileges to initialize the environment.

DMA Attacks. We have seen various DMA based memory acquisition techniques through peripheral buses such as FireWire, PCI [4] and Thunderbolt [14]. In 2004 Dornseif [5] showed the first Firewire-based DMA attack. The author used an iPod with modified firmware to obtain unrestricted access to the main memory of a PC. Boileau [1] extended the attack to Windows XP in 2006. The concept was further turned into a tool [10]. Breuk and Spruyt [2] presented multiphase attacks with direct access to the machine.

The first paper to introduce the term *DMA malware* was written by Stewin and Bystrov [15]. They present a keylogger, which abuses the DMA engine of dedicated hardware to launch undetectable attacks against the host.

The Rest of the Paper is structured as follows. In the next section we will give the background and terminology, describe some aspects of the SoC (system on chip) architecture, have a brief look on what direct memory access is, and discuss a typical GPU pipeline. In Sect. 3, we present the design of our attack vector, and what threat model we assumed. In Sect. 4, we reveal the details of the proof-of-concept exploit. We conclude with Sects. 5 and 6, where we give insight into the research we would like to conduct in the future, and summarize our findings.

2   Background

In this section we describe the background and the terminology which is important to understand the rest of the paper. We explain some essentials of contemporary smartphone systems on chip (SoC), followed by a short glance on direct memory access (DMA). Last, in this section, we cover the basics of GPU programming.

2.1   SoC Architecture

A typical smartphone SoC combines multiple building blocks on a single silicon substrate. This consolidation of integrated circuits is very efficient, both in terms of manufacturing cost and in terms of integration size. In Fig. 1 we show a very simplified sketch of an SoC, with focus on the communication between the building blocks. The system bus connects all the building blocks, and the main memory which is usually not part of the SoC itself. On a real SoC the system bus is usually divided, and comprises many physical interfaces and protocols. Everything that is connected to the system bus including each byte of the main memory is addressable through a unique physical address. An entity that can put addresses on the bus, and then read from, or write to the addressed resource is called a bus master. On one hand the distinguishing feature that makes a smartphone the versatile gadget it is, is the capability to run third party applications. These applications, however, can be buggy or intentionally malevolent, and must be considered untrustworthy. The CPU, which executes them, is, on the other hand, the most prominent bus master in the SoC. To confine potentially misbehaving entities, the operating system provides each application with a virtual address space by means of a memory management unit (MMU). The operating system of a smartphone carefully abstracts from the peripherals in the system. There is one building block, however, which can be programmed by user applications, and act as bus master at the same time: the graphics processing unit (GPU). As depicted in Fig. 1 the GPU also deploys an MMU to restrict access to the system bus, thus confining user jobs. The GPU's MMU must be very tightly controlled by the operating system so as to not jeopardize the integrity of the system.

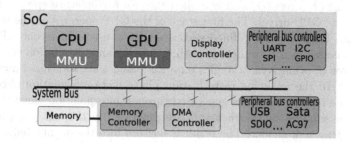

Fig. 1. Sketch of a typical system on chip (SoC) that can be found in a smartphone.

2.2   DMA

The technique of letting certain devices access the main memory directly is very commonly used to offload high-bandwidth memory transfers by these devices off the CPU. In Sect. 1 we have presented resources that show how this powerful feature was used for debugging, forensics and as an attack vector. With the advent of virtualization technologies we have seen the introduction of input/output memory management units (IOMMUs). They allow to both restrict the memory regions a device can access and partition the memory flexibly. This development can now also be witnessed in the embedded domain. From a security perspective IOMMUs as well as their CPU-bound counterparts must be tightly controlled by the device's operating system.

2.3   Graphics Processing Unit

GPUs are used to offload computationally intensive graphics rendering tasks off the CPU. They are designed to process large amounts of data with low entropy. This allows massive parallelism and long pipelines, thus trading latency for bandwidth. Giesen [6] and Luebke and Humphreys [9] give good insight into the workings of contemporary GPUs.

The programmer uses a high level API such as OpenGL or Direct3D to program the GPU. The primitives that comprise an OpenGL program are riddled with terms stemming from the field of computer graphics. Figure 2 shows a typical graphics processing pipeline (GPP). The input to the GPP is a set of *attributes, uniforms* and *textures*. Attributes are user-defined and hold per vertex meta-information. Vertices are three dimensional vectors that denote endpoints of lines or corners of polygons. The set of vertices represents the geometry of the scene to be rendered. Uniforms hold per scene meta-information provided by the user such as for example a rotational matrix. Textures are used to increase the level of detail by mapping images on to the geometry's surface. Recent versions of the graphics programming APIs allow the use of *shaders*, user provided programs that are loaded into the programmable stages of the GPP. Shaders are written in an extension specific language (e.g. GLSL in case of OpenGL [12] or HLSL in case of Direct3D) and compiled into an architecture specific instruction set by the GPU driver. The first stage of the GPP operates on the geometry of the scene. Here the user-defined vertex-shader is used. On recent GPUs this might be accompanied by either, or both, geometry and tessellation shaders. As a result a set of primitives, triangles on a 2D plane with additional meta-data, is produced. In the following rasterization phase meta-information about each sample of the rendered scene is generated through interpolation along the primitives. These samples-called *fragments*-are processed in the last programmable stage—the fragment-shader. The result is written into the output buffer.

3   The Attack Vector

The scheme of our attack is based on the idea that an attacker gains control over the memory protection mechanism of the GPU and misuses it to read from or write to otherwise inaccessible locations of the main memory of the system.

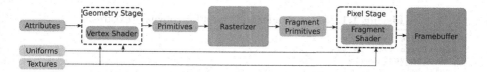

Fig. 2. A typical graphics processing pipeline.

We thought it conceivable that, if OpenGL can be used to render an image onto the screen without any transformation, the same mechanism could be used to make an exact copy of binary data. We will now discuss how this *identical scene* can be rendered using OpenGL and under which circumstances this would mimic the C-library function `memcpy`.

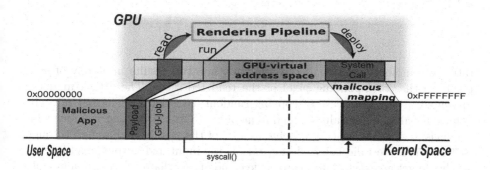

Fig. 3. The attack vector.

3.1 Identical Scene Rendering

From an OpenGL programmer's perspective, the geometry of the identical scene is a flat square that fills the whole viewport[1]. So we compose a single square using a set of four vertices. There is no need to alter the geometry in the vertex processing phase of the GPP, thus, in the vertex shader, we just pass the vertex' position on to the next stage, as can be seen in Line 6 of Listing 1.1. In order to add the details to the scene which comprise the actual data that shall be copied, we interpret the input as a texture and map it onto the square. To fit it into the correct position we pass the texture coordinates to the GPP as attributes. Line 7 of Listing 1.1 shows how this coordinate is assigned to the varying[2] `texture_coord` in the vertex shader. This coordinate is then used to sample the texture using the sampling function `texture2D` in the fragment shader (Listing 1.2, Line 6). Given that the output area has the same aspect

---

[1] The visible part of a scene.

[2] Varyings carry meta-information from the geometry phase to the fragment phase of the GPP, and are subject to interpolation in the rasterization phase.

Listing 1.1. Vertex Shader code used for copying Textures.

```
1   attribute vec4 in_vertex;
2   attribute vec2 in_texture_coord;
3   varying vec2 texture_coord;
4   void main()
5   {
6       gl_Position = in_vertex;
7       texture_coord = in_texture_coord;
8   }
```

Listing 1.2. Fragment Shader code used for copying Textures.

```
1   precision highp float;
2   varying vec2 texture_coord;
3   uniform sampler2D in_texture;
4   void main()
5   {
6       gl_FragColor = texture2D(in_texture, texture_coord);
7   }
```

ratio and number of pixels as the input texture, this results in a copy of each texel[3] to the corresponding pixel of the rendered scene. The attack model is presented in Fig. 3. In case of copying random data the pixel format must be defined for all possible values stored in memory. RGBA8888 comprises four 8 bit channels: red, green, blue and alpha, and all of the possible values 0x0 through 0xFFFF FFFF are valid colors. Using this as the input and output pixel format, we should get an exact binary copy. One could argue, that the GPU renders into the frame buffer, thus this copy mechanism is of no use for our purpose. But as for the SoC architecture of Sect. 2.1 the frame buffer is just another region in main memory. Thus the output of the GPU can be redirected anywhere in the main memory as we will show in Sect. 4.

3.2   The Threat Model

We will now discuss the threat model of the attack. On a very high level we want to evade the memory isolation with all well-known consequences. We assume an Android smartphone with its integrity and memory isolation mechanisms intact. The goal of the attacker shall be arbitrary code execution in privileged mode on the CPU. The entry point to the device shall be that of a trojan. That is, the attacker tricks the unsuspecting user to install an application. Moreover, this application shall not raise suspicion by requesting unreasonable access rights. In fact the application shall not need any access right that can—on Android—only be granted if specified in the application's manifest.

---

[3] Texture pixel.

Listing 1.3. The payload.

```
 0:    0xe52de004 |  push    {lr}                ; (str lr, [sp, #-4]!)
 4:    0xe3a00000 |  mov     r0, #0
 8:    0xe59f1010 |  ldr     r1, [pc, #16]   ; 20 <.text+0x20>
 c:    0xe12fff31 |  blx     r1
10:    0xe59f100c |  ldr     r1, [pc, #12]   ; 24 <.text+0x24>
14:    0xe12fff31 |  blx     r1
18:    0xe3a00000 |  mov     r0, #0
1c:    0xe49df004 |  pop     {pc}                ; (ldr pc, [sp], #4)
20:    0xc038dc44 |  placeholder for prepare_kernel_cred
24:    0xc038ddd8 |  placeholder for commit_cred
```

4   The Proof-of-Concept Attack

In Sect. 3 we described how we planed to gain read and write access to arbitrary main memory locations. We will now explain the detail of our exploit.

The exploit was targeted at a very popular smartphone model running Android, which employs an ARM Mali MP 400 GPU. We found that several firmware versions were vulnerable to our attack. Even more, the successor of the targeted model was vulnerable as well. The goal of our proof-of-concept exploit was to elevate the privileges of a normal user-space application by means of patching the kernel's text section. Once write access to the kernel memory is established this is fairly straightforward and has been described before [8,13].

In this section we will briefly describe the payload that we delivered using the GPU. Then, we will introduce the bug in the kernel that made this exploit possible. Next, we will focus on the delivery of the payload. We conclude this section with a discussion of pitfalls that we encountered during our work.

4.1   Payload

As we wanted to perform privilege escalation by patching a system call we needed a piece of code that changes the caller's user id to 0 or root. We used a well established method as presented by McAllister [11]. The C-code equivalent of the payload was:

<code>commit_creds(prepare_kernel_cred(NULL));</code>

Listing 1.3 shows the compiled assembly as well as the word-wise hexadecimal representation of the payload. Figure 4 shows the payload when interpreted as texture. We leave a detailed inspection of the object code to the reader.

4.2   The Bug

The Mali driver stack is split into a part that resides in the Linux kernel and a set of user-space libraries. The kernel driver exposes its interface to the user through the device node /dev/mali. Access to this device node is not restricted. This is not a problem as the kernel driver provides abstractions that allow, in principle,

Fig. 4. The payload as 4 by 4 texture padded with 6 words of 0 when interpreted as RGBA pixel format.

safe usage by multiple users. Most notably, for our cause, it provides each user session with a private address space that is controlled by means of the GPU's MMUs[4]. The user-space libraries make up the larger part of the driver. They provide common APIs such as the embedded graphics library (EGL) and the open graphics library (OpenGL). The lower end of this part of the driver stack connects to the user-kernel interfaces of the frame buffer and the Mali driver. Their task is to populate the session address space, layout graphics processing jobs in the allocated memory and submit them to the kernel driver. It shall be noted that the values written to the registers of the Mali GPU come directly from the user space. With the above mentioned we can state the following assumption, that must hold for the driver stack to sustain the kernel enforced memory space isolation.

It is not important what the user runs on the GPU as long as the session address space of the GPU does not violate the memory isolation imposed by the kernel.

The Mali kernel driver provides the user with three mechanisms to populate the session address space of the GPU. The user can (1) call `mmap` on the open session, which will allocate physical memory tiles, map them into the caller's address space and, at the same time, into the session address space of the GPU. The Mali driver is accompanied by the universal memory provider (UMP) kernel driver, which allows the user to allocate physical memory buffers. Applying `mmap` on the UMP session the user can have those buffers mapped into her process' address space. As the Mali driver is UMP aware the user can also (2) attach UMP buffers to the session address space. The third mechanism allows the user to (3) supply the kernel driver with physical addresses. This mechanism was introduced to map the frame-buffer memory into the GPU's session address space. As long as the driver performs a range check on the supplied addresses, this is a viable technique. But in the case of the driver we assessed, this range check was misconfigured so as to include all of the physical memory. This allowed any user to map any part of the main memory into the GPU's session address space. Thus the assumption we stated above was violated.[5]

---

[4] The Mali MP 400 GPU has one geometry processor (GP) and up to four pixel presenters (PP). Each of these processing cores has its own MMU.

[5] The OEM was informed about our findings and fixed the bug.

Listing 1.4. ioctl–call to insert arbitrary physical mappings into the GPU's virtual address space.

```
_mali_uk_map_external_mem_s  map = {  0  };

map.phys_addr = sysc_phys & ~0xfff;  // round down by masking the lower 12 bits
map.size = 0x2000;                   // map two contiguous pages
map.mali_address = sysc_mali_virt_page;  // address by which the Mali"sees"
                                         // the mapped memory

// perform the actual operation
ioctl(<filedescriptor /dev/mali>, Mali_IOC_MEM_MAP_EXT, &map);
```

4.3 Exploit

Having the attack vector (Sect. 3) and a bug (Sect. 4.2), we were able to construct an exploit that would elevate the privileges of a process, by patching a system call in the kernel's text section, and then calling said system call. In Sect. 4.1 we described the payload that we wanted to deliver. In this section we first discuss how we determined the physical address of the location to be patched and how, using the above mentioned bug, we attached it to the session address space of the Mali GPU. Next, we show how we configured the GPU to write the output to the desired location. Finally, we explain what was necessary to combine all the details to form a rendering job that could be submitted to the Mali kernel driver.

Finding the Patchable Location. Since we wanted as few side effects on the running system as possible, we decided on patching sys_reboot. Because sys_reboot is only called on power down the only side effect would be that the phone would simply not power off unless the battery was drained or yanked from the device. To determine the physical address we consulted /proc/kallsyms once more but because this pseudo file provides virtual addresses we needed to translate the address using a fixed offset of 0x80000000. We shall call this address sysc_phys for future reference.

Attaching the Patchable Location. This is where we actually used the bug we have just described above. It was as simple as calling an ioctl call on the device node /dev/mali. As mappings can only be created with page granularity, we had to round our physical address down to the nearest page boundary. Because our target system call may cross a page boundary, we decided to always map two contiguous pages. We chose the target address for the mapping as sysc_mali_virt_page.

Configuring the Write-Back-Unit. The write-back-unit of the Mali GPU has an address register that denotes the target buffer where the GPU will output the result of the GPP. Here we specify the address of the syscall to be patched in terms of the Mali-virtual address. That is `sysc_mali_virt_page` plus the information that we lost by rounding earlier: `sysc_phys & 0xfff`.

Devising the GPU Job. To copy our payload into the kernel text section we used the *identical scene* rendering (see Sect. 3). We found that the smallest scene we could render had a size of four by four pixels so we padded our payload with another six words to a total of 16 words and used it as a texture.

Running the GPU Job. The previous steps in themselves are fairly straight-forward. However we were using functionality that is not exposed by the APIs visible to the common graphics programmer such as EGL and OpenGL. To administer the fine grained control over the session address space, as well as the write-back-unit of the GPU, we had to bypass EGL and OpenGL and work with the kernel-user interface of the Mali directly. To trick EGL and OpenGL into generating the desired GPU job would have meant a fair amount of binary patching. Instead we employed the ongoing effort by Verhagen et al.[6] to produce an open source driver for the Mali GPU. The driver—yet far from usable for the casual user—provided all we needed to customize our memory layout of the Mali session and let our job run on the GPU.

4.4   Caveats

We encountered a couple of pitfalls on our way to a working exploit. For once, we found out that for very small output regions, as in our case, the range of memory that was modified by the write-back-unit was larger than the configured output region. 236 bytes beyond the end of the output region where initialized with the configured background color. We did not find out what caused this. It may be that we simply did not configure the GPU correctly. It might also be possible, that such small output regions were simply not anticipated by the GPU designers. This limited our choice of patchable locations to functions that were long enough not to write beyond their end. If the input texture and output buffer where chosen large enough the effect, however, ceased to exist.

To be able to modify arbitrary bits of code in the kernel text section despite the effect we just described, we considered copying large chunks of kernel memory, then modifying them and copying them back. This, however, was jeopardized by another effect we did not anticipate. At certain positions in the output image, certain values were distorted and offset by one. The distortions followed a regular and predictable spacial pattern as depicted in Fig. 5. Each cell represents a single pixel. In the marked pixels, every byte, or every color channel, was distorted in the following way: in case of the pixels marked with diagonal lines, the copied value was increased by one, as long as it belonged to the range—in hexadecimal notation—[F0-F8;D0-D8;B0-B8;90-98;78;68;58;48]. At the positions marked with the vertical lines, bytes from range [E9-EF;C9-CF;A9-AF;89-8F] were decreased

---

[6] http://limadriver.org

by one. It turned out, that our copy was not so exact after all. Simply copying code sections back and forth would have broken the running kernel most certainly. We do not know where these distortions came from. They may have been caused by misconfiguration on our side, a bug, a precision-performance trade-off or some kind of watermarking. But this is pure speculation.

Even though the copying was not as exact as we anticipated the exploit worked flawlessly. In Fig. 5 we show a 16 by 16 texture. Note however that the payload texture we show in Fig. 4 is only 4 by 4 pixels in size. Therefore the distortion rules apply as if it was fit into the top left corner of Fig. 5. Thus only the fourth word would have been subject to distortions, but only if its value were in the effected range, which it is not. If it were, however, we would have incorporated a branch instruction to skip the distorted memory location.

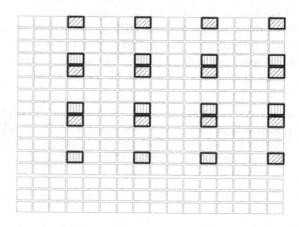

Fig. 5. Pixel distortion during copy.

5   Future Work

We successfully applied the concept of the identical scene to an OpenGL ES 2.0 capable GPU. It would be interesting to see if the same can be done with earlier fixed function GPUs. There is still a big field of research in the domain of GPU malware or GPU-assisted malware. With a better understanding of the GPU we exploited in this work, we might be able to perfect the memory copying capability. As a next step we could apply filters and search for patterns instead of just copying. Finally it should be investigated whether the work of Ladakis et al. [7] can be replicated with GPUs without general purpose computing capabilities. As future work we also plan on investigating methods for secure mapping of DMA memory regions into the user-space such as Linux' direct rendering manager (DRM), UMP and the DMA buffer-sharing API. These techniques were designed to prevent attacks like the one we have just presented. With the gained experience we plan on applying similar techniques to more distributed microkernel based system designs with very strong isolation demands.

6   Conclusion

In this paper we argued that by the concept of the *identical scene* rendering it should be possible to perform a copy operation with a GPU on an embedded device. Using this concept we exploited a bug that we found in a popular Android smartphone's GPU driver. The bug we found allowed us to manipulate the memory protection of the GPU and thus to evade the kernel-imposed memory isolation. We succeeded in patching the running Linux kernel of the device and thus gained superuser privileges starting off with no more privileges than even the simplest Android application has. We also showed once more that keeping large parts of a driver stack closed source is, from a security perspective, no replacement for a thorough kernel-user interface. The considerably high impact of our proof-of-concept exploit arises from the popularity of the targeted smartphones and the low hurdle for it to be applied.

The bug that enables us to abuse the GPU is fairly easy to fix. Also, it is unclear whether our approach can be applied to other smartphones. But given the history of discovered bugs in third party kernel drivers and the fast product cycles of smartphones this notion can not simply be dismissed.

Acknowledgements. We would like to thank Luc Verhagen and his team for their work on the open source Mali GPU driver. We would also like to acknowledge the contribution of Christian Ludwig in the discovery of the bug presented in this paper. This research was partially funded by the BMWF grant 01IS12032.

References

1. Boileau, A.: Hit by a bus: physical access attacks with firewire. Ruxcon (2006)
2. Breuk, R., Spruyt, A.: Integrating DMA attacks in exploitation frameworks (2012). http://staff.science.uva.nl/delaat/rp/2011-2012/p14/report.pdf
3. Carlson, J.: GPUs for mobile malware mitigation and more. Recon (2012)
4. Carrier, B.D., Grand, J.: A hardware-based memory acquisition procedure for digital investigations. Digit. Investig. **1**(1), 50–60 (2004). http://dx.doi.org/10.1016/j.diin.2003.12.001
5. Dornseif, M.: 0wn3d by an iPod: Firewire/1394 issues. In: PacSec (2004)
6. Giesen, F.: A trip through the graphics pipeline (2011). http://fgiesen.wordpress.com/2011/07/09/a-trip-through-the-graphics-pipeline-2011-index/, blog: The ryg blog
7. Ladakis, E., Koromilas, L., Vasiliadis, G., Polychonakis, M., Ioannidis, S.: You can type, but you can't hide: a stealthy GPU-based keylogger. In: Proceedings of the European Workshop on System Security (EuroSec) (2013)
8. Lineberry, A.: Malicious code injection via /dev/mem. In: Proceedings of Blackhat Europe (2009)
9. Luebke, D., Humphreys, G.: How GPUs work. Computer **40**(2), 126–130 (2007)
10. Maartmann-Moe, C.: Ftwautopwn. http://www.breaknenter.org/projects/ftwautopwn/, source code
11. McAllister, K.: Writing kernel exploits (2012). http://ugcs.net/keegan/talks/kernel-exploit/talk.pdf

12. Munshi, A., Ginsburg, D., Shreiner, D.: OpenGL(R) ES 2.0 Programming Guide, 1st edn. Addison-Wesley Professional, Reading (2008)
13. Piegdon, D.R.: Hacking in physically addressable memory - a proof of concept. In: Seminar of Advanced Exploitation Techniques (2006)
14. Sevinsky, R.: Funderbolt. adventures in thunderbolt dma attacks (2013). https://media.blackhat.com/us-13/US-13-Sevinsky-Funderbolt-Adventures-in-Thunderbolt-DMA-Attacks-Slides.pdf
15. Stewin, P., Bystrov, I.: Understanding DMA malware. In: Flegel, U., Markatos, E., Robertson, W. (eds.) DIMVA 2012. LNCS, vol. 7591, pp. 21–41. Springer, Heidelberg (2013)
16. Vasiliadis, G., Polychronakis, M., Ioannidis, S.: GPU-assisted malware. In: Proceedings of the 5th International Conference on Malicious and Unwanted Software (MALWARE) (2010)

Industry-Wide Misunderstandings of HTTPS

Stephen Bono[✉] and Jacob Thompson[✉]

Independent Security Evaluators, Baltimore, USA
`{sbono,jthompson}@securityevaluators.com`

Abstract. In a survey of 30 sites that serve sensitive content over an HTTPS-protected connection, we found that over 70 % of them failed to appropriately prevent disk caching, and left unencrypted sensitive content behind on end-users' machines, at risk for later exposure. Moreover, over half of the sites that failed to prevent disk caching appeared to have attempted to do so using out-dated, non-standard, or erroneous methods, some of which failed entirely, while others were only successful at preventing disk caching in certain browsers, but not all.

In an effort to explain this wide-spread failure, our research has uncovered drastically inconsistent behavior across browsers, inconsistent support of standard and non-standard anti-disk caching directives, and even inconsistent and incorrect recommendations from authoritative sources in the security community. Through this history we show that web developers are not solely to blame, and that web browser developers, web server developers, security professionals and authors of online sources, and perhaps even the standards bodies should share in this failure.

In this paper, we identify the disk caching behaviors of all major browsers, and describe how to reliably prevent disk caching for each of them. We present the results of our site survey, demonstrating wide-spread failures to prevent disk caching of sensitive data. We introduce a tool for Firefox users to reliably prevent disk caching of HTTPS protected content, despite failures by the web application, and we provide an online tool to help web developers identify how to reliably prevent disk caching across multiple browsers. Lastly, we make recommendations to the various parties with a hand in this failure on how to address these issues going forward.

1 Introduction

Users often visit the same web pages more than once. While some of the page contents change, the vast majority of the page and associated resources (such as images) remain static. To re-download this unchanged content on every visit to the page is a waste of time and bandwidth [1]. Consequently, when a user accesses a web page, the web browser caches most content locally on the user's machine. This content can either be saved in temporary memory (RAM), which is lost as soon as the user exits the browser, or on disk, which persists even after the user exits the browser or reboots the computer. When a user visits a page repeatedly, the content is retrieved from cache instead of over the Internet. Memory caches are lost when the browser exits, so the browser uses the disk cache whenever possible.

H.-S. Lee and D.-G. Han (Eds.): ICISC 2013, LNCS 8565, pp. 496–513, 2014.
DOI: 10.1007/978-3-319-12160-4_30

Secure web sites use the HTTPS and SSL/TLS protocols to encrypt information as it travels over the Internet, to prevent an eavesdropper or man-in-the-middle from recovering or modifying the communication. Although there are no technical constraints preventing content sent over an encrypted connection from being decrypted and written to disk, it is logical to presume that if content is too sensitive to be sent over a network without encryption, then it may also be too sensitive to store unprotected on a hard drive [2].

When HTTPS was first introduced, there was no standard, unambiguous way for a web server to mark content as too sensitive to store in cache. As a result, web browser authors created their own mechanisms for a web server to restrict disk caching [2]. Some browser authors chose to, by default, never write content transferred over HTTPS to disk [3], or did not disk cache content unless a server explicitly allowed it ("opt-in") [4], while others chose to write this content to the disk cache, unless a server header explicitly prohibited it ("opt-out") [5].

We surveyed 30 sites that serve sensitive content over HTTPS, and found that 21 of those sites failed to appropriately prevent disk caching across all browsers. Of those 21, over half appear to have attempted to prevent disk caching using outdated, non-standard, or erroneous methods, while the remainder simply made no attempt. The sites surveyed included banks and other financial institutions, insurance companies, and utility companies. The sites served content that we deemed sensitive such as bank account statements, credit reports, check images, pay stubs, health and vehicle insurance information, and prescription names and dosages.

Our research found that despite the existence of reliable methods to prevent disk caching, the diversity and inconsistency across browsers in how disk caching is handled, as well as general misunderstandings within the security community, including respected sources such as OWASP, have led to wide-spread failure of web applications to reliably prevent disk caching of sensitive data. In this paper, we provide a history of inconsistent browser behavior and an understanding of that behavior as evidenced through our own verification and online references. We identify and catalog six different behaviors and techniques that effectively prevent disk caching for various versions of Internet Explorer, Firefox, Chrome, and Safari, as well as obsolete browsers such as Netscape and Mozilla (for reference purposes) – to our knowledge, no such catalog exists. We provide the best recommended actions a web developer can make to most effectively prevent disk caching across all browsers, as well as make recommendations to the security community, browser developers, and standards bodies. Lastly, we introduce a Firefox extension that end-users can install to effectively prevent disk caching, and an online resource for web application developers to test browser behaviors.

2 A Brief History

In 1997[1], the first HTTP/1.1 [6] standard was published, which standardized the header that a server must set to prevent content from being written to a disk cache. By that time, all web browser authors had already adopted either an "opt-in" HTTPS disk caching

---

[1] The current RFC 2616 was published in 1999, but obsoleted this older RFC 2068 which already defined Cache-control: no store.

policy, or an "opt-out" policy with multiple, non-standard ways to opt out. Despite the new standard, web developers could continue to use the old, non-standard methods and they would continue to work only in the browsers that recognized them [2].

Between the release of Netscape Navigator 3.0 in 1996, and 2008, when Google Chrome was released, the only browser with a significant market share that used an "opt-out" HTTPS disk caching policy was Internet Explorer. Internet Explorer has always been very forgiving in determining a web server's intention that a response not be written to the disk cache. We identified four separate ways [2] that a web developer can prevent a response from being cached to disk. Only one of those ways, the header `Cache-Control: no-store`, is actually standard [6].

Encrypted web servers (HTTPS) have higher overhead and lower performance than unencrypted servers due to the need to perform encryption, and in the past this overhead was much more pronounced. For this reason, many web sites used HTTPS only when absolutely necessary, such as for sending a password or credit card information. After the sensitive transaction was completed, the sites would switch back to an unencrypted connection. Two examples are Gmail, which transmitted e-mails over unencrypted connections until 2010 [7], and Facebook, which continued to use unencrypted connections until 2012 [8]. Since HTTPS was reserved for only the most sensitive information, an "opt-in" disk caching policy was a reasonable design.

By 2011, many sites had begun using HTTPS even for non-sensitive content, and Mozilla Corporation recognized [9] that the "opt-in" HTTPS disk caching policy in Firefox was introducing a performance penalty compared to other browsers, including Google Chrome, which uses an "opt-out" policy. As a result, Firefox 4.0 and all later versions use an "opt-out" HTTPS disk caching policy [9]. A Firefox 3.6 user would be unaffected by this issue, even when browsing HTTPS sites that fail to set the necessary header, but would become affected as soon as that user updated to Firefox 4 or later.

Online banking, which is among the most security-sensitive uses of a web browser, exploded in popularity in the early 2000s. At this time, Internet Explorer had over 90 % market share, and Safari and Chrome did not exist. Internet Explorer's only significant competitors at the time (Netscape 3.0 and later, Mozilla, and Firefox) either did not disk cache HTTPS content at all (unless a user manually modified a configuration parameter), or used an "opt-in" policy, and thus required no special treatment to prevent caching of encrypted bank pages. Many of the web sites that we tested responded with sufficient headers to prevent caching in all versions of Internet Explorer, all versions of Safari, and Firefox 3.6 and earlier, but not Firefox 4.0 and later, or any version of Chrome. We believe that ensuring that sensitive content is not cached on disk by the browser was a design goal in these web applications. While this anti-disk cache functionality worked correctly in the past, it no longer works in two of today's most popular browsers: Chrome, and Firefox 4.0 and later. Since this has been an issue in Chrome since its release in 2008, and in Firefox since 2011, the maintainers of HTTPS sites do not appear to perform regression testing for this issue.

Today, Internet Explorer continues to follow the same HTTPS disk caching policy as it always has: enable disk caching by default, but allow four different ways to disable it. Google Chrome and Firefox, in contrast, enable disk caching by default, but allow only one way to prevent it—the one given in the standard, the header `Cache-Control: no-store`.

Google Chrome and Mozilla Firefox, together, now have over a 60 % market share on non-mobile devices [10], but many web sites still use antiquated, non-standard methods to prevent disk caching of sensitive HTTPS content that only function in Internet Explorer.

3 The Evolution of Caching Policies

Prior to HTTP/1.1 being standardized in 1997, there was no unambiguous way for a web server to instruct a client that a response should not be cached to persistent storage. Indeed, the HTTP/1.0 RFC noted [11]:

Some HTTP/1.0 applications use heuristics to describe what is or is not a "cacheable" response, but these rules are not standardized.

The cache controlling mechanisms that did exist, such as the "Expires" header, were intended to prevent a user agent from displaying stale content, and were unrelated to security. It is unnecessary to totally block the client from retaining a copy of sensitive content in memory for later reuse, instead, the objective is only to prevent the information from being written to disk.

When Netscape 1 introduced SSL and HTTPS in 1995, the browser never wrote HTTPS content to the disk cache [3]. A web server could not override this for non-sensitive content, nor could a user alter this behavior in the preferences.

This behavior changed in Netscape 2, which introduced an "opt-out" policy. Whether content was delivered over HTTP or HTTPS no longer factored into the caching decision; instead, the browser introduced a non-standard `Pragma: no-cache` response header allowing a server to prohibit the disk caching of a response. In the standard [11], `Pragma` was originally intended to be a request header, allowing a client to override any cached copies stored on intermediate proxy servers; nonetheless, introducing it as a response header at least created a way to prevent disk storage of sensitive data. However, Netscape also allowed the `Pragma: no-cache` header to be specified as a `meta http-equiv` HTML tag in the document. This was a bad design choice for two reasons: first, caching code must read the response and parse the HTML before the caching decision can be made, lowering performance; second, the tag can only be used in HTML files, and not images, JavaScript files, and so on. This "opt-out" HTTPS caching policy was incorporated by Microsoft into Internet Explorer 3 as well [2].

Possibly recognizing the potential security issue of web developers neglecting to mark sensitive data with the `Pragma` header, Netscape 3 reverted to the previous behavior of never caching HTTPS responses to disk; We verified this behavior by testing Netscape Navigator 3.04 Gold. Disk caching of HTTPS data could be re-enabled by the user in the preferences dialog, but there was still no way for a server to explicitly "opt-in" to caching of non-sensitive HTTPS content. In contrast to Netscape 3, Microsoft continued to use "opt-out" HTTPS caching in later Internet Explorer versions. Thus Netscape 3 marked the beginning of inconsistent HTTPS disk caching policies between browsers, which remains unresolved even today.

In addition to the non-standard `Pragma` header introduced by Netscape, Microsoft added support for new, standardized caching headers to Internet Explorer as they came into existence. Internet Explorer 4 added support for the `Cache-Control: no-store` header introduced in the HTTP/1.1 standard. But it also added new quirks:

- IE 4 through 9 treated the `Cache-Control: no-cache` header, intended to prevent stale responses and not a security measure, identically to the `Cache-Control: no-store` header. In version 10, `Cache-Control: no-cache` no longer prevents disk caching.
- If IE 4 through 8 made a request using HTTP/1.1, and the server responded using HTTP/1.0, any Cache-Control headers in the server's response would be ignored. This was resolved in version 9, where Cache-Control headers are recognized even when sent by an HTTP/1.0 server. Despite the fix, all Windows XP and 2003 systems contain version 8 or earlier of Internet Explorer, and are affected by this issue.
- The above HTTP/1.0 behavior is triggered by a configuration change introduced in Apache mod_ssl in 2000 (version 2.6.5) that forces a downgrade from HTTP/1.1 to HTTP/1.0 whenever the server responds to Internet Explorer over HTTPS. This configuration was intended to work around a bug in IE 5's handling of HTTP/1.1 keep-alive connections. In 2010, long after the Internet Explorer bug was patched in version 6, Apache finally updated the workaround to exclude unaffected releases [12]. However, this configuration change has not yet percolated to all Linux distributions' standard branches of Apache, including the latest version of CentOS[2] as of this writing, 6.4.

Netscape continued with the policy of not disk caching HTTPS content by default throughout versions 3 and 4 of their browser, the last release of which occurred in 2002. Despite this, Netscape retained vestigial support for the `Pragma: no-cache` header introduced in version 2—in case the user modified the preferences to enable persistent HTTPS caching. This support was dropped when the Mozilla project began a browser rewrite in 1998, but with little consequence at the time, since the rewritten browser never cached HTTPS content by default [13].[3]

After these changes in the mid-1990s, browser caching policies, while still inconsistent and only partially following standards, did stabilize. Apple released Safari in 2003, which to this day never writes HTTPS content to the disk cache. The iOS version also follows this policy.

The stability came to an end in 2008, when Google released the Chrome browser. Chrome, and its mobile variant, Android Browser, have the most aggressive HTTPS disk caching policy ever created at the time. Content is always written to the disk cache unless one of two conditions are met: (1) the response includes the header `Cache-Control: no-store`, or (2) the server has an invalid certificate [14]. No support is included for non-standard headers supported by Internet Explorer (i.e., `Pragma:`

---

[2] http://mirror.umd.edu/centos/6.4/updates/i386/Packages/mod_ssl-2.2.15-28.el6.centos.i686.rpm

[3] This page [13] shows that `browser.cache.disk_cache_ssl` was set to false in revision 1.1 when Netscape first released source.

no-cache and Cache-Control: no-cache), which at the time of Chrome's release, was the only other web browser that even cached HTTPS content at all by default.

Concurrent with the release of Chrome, Mozilla began loosening the Firefox HTTPS disk caching policy as well. In Firefox 3, Mozilla introduced a unique caching policy, that in our opinion represented the best trade-off between security and performance. HTTPS continued to be treated as an indicator that content should not be disk cached, but Firefox now allowed servers to explicitly "opt-in" to caching, by including the header Cache-Control: public [3]. While originally intended for multiuser caching proxies, Cache-Control: public is defined as:

Indicates that the response is cacheable by any cache, even if it would normally be non-cacheable or cacheable only within a non-shared cache.

Thus the presence of this header is a good indicator that content is non-sensitive and safe to cache.

Still, Mozilla modified the HTTPS caching policy once again in Firefox 4, this time to cache all HTTPS content unless it is explicitly labeled as sensitive using Cache-Control: no-store, effectively reversing the behavior of Firefox 3. Paradoxically, this meant that the original functionality of the Pragma: no-cache header introduced by Firefox's ancestral Netscape browser was now only supported by Internet Explorer.

All of the different ways we found to control disk caching of HTTPS content are shown in Table 1.

Table 1. Variants of headers or HTML meta tags used to enable or prevent disk caching of HTTPS content, and listings of browsers that support each one.

Header or tag	Supporting browsers
None needed—No HTTPS disk caching by default	Netscape 1, 3 + , Firefox 1-3.5, Safari
Pragma: no-cache header (opt-out)	Netscape 2, IE 3+
Pragma: no-cache meta tag (opt-out)	Netscape 2, IE 3+
Cache-Control: no-cache header (opt-out)	IE 4-9
Cache-Control: no-store header (opt-out)	IE 4 + , Firefox 4 + , Chrome 1+
Cache-Control: public header (opt-in)	Firefox 3-3.5

4   Current Caching Policies by Browser

Disk caching of HTTPS-delivered web pages varies by web browser. Here, we discuss the policies of four browsers that we tested.

Internet Explorer. Microsoft Internet Explorer caches HTTPS-delivered content to disk, unless one or more of the following are present [2]:

- The HTTP header Cache-Control: no-store.
- In version 9 and earlier only, The HTTP header Cache-Control: no-cache.
- The HTTP header Pragma: no-cache.

- The HTML tag `<META HTTP-EQUIV="Pragma" CONTENT="no-cache">`. Microsoft discourages the use of this method; it may not work properly for pages larger than 32 kb [13].

Note that the Cache-Control header cannot be set using an HTML `<META HTTP-EQUIV>` tag. Additionally, Internet Explorer interprets some of these headers differently, depending upon whether the page was delivered using HTTPS or HTTP [2]. We verified that using the 32-bit version of Internet Explorer 10.0.9200.16635 on 64-bit Windows 7, HTTPS content is disk cached unless the server sends the `Pragma: no-cache` header or `Cache-Control: no-store` header, or the document contains the `Pragma: no-cache` header in an HTML `meta http-equiv` tag. We verified that using the 32-bit version of Internet Explorer 9.0.8112.16421, HTTPS content is disk cached unless the server sends the `Cache-Control: no-cache` header, or the response employs either of the two methods described for IE 10.

Firefox. Prior to version 4.0, Mozilla Firefox (and its predecessors, including Mozilla and Netscape) either never cache HTTPS pages to disk at all [3] or cache only pages sent with:

- The HTTP header `Cache-Control: public`.

Firefox contains a hidden browser preference, `browser.cache.disk_cache_ssl`, that when set to `true`, switches Firefox from the previous, cautious policy above, to a new policy that strictly follows the HTTP standard, disk caching all content unless specifically instructed not to do so by the server. In 2011, the default value of this preference was switched from `false` to `true` [9]. As a result, Firefox 4.0 and all later versions cache HTTPS-delivered content to disk, unless the following is present:

- The HTTP header `Cache-Control: no-store`.

We verified that using the 32-bit version of Mozilla Firefox 3.6.28 on 64-bit Windows 7 (and earlier), HTTPS content is not disk cached unless the server sends the `Cache-Control: public` header. We verified that using the 32-bit version of Mozilla Firefox 21.0 on 64-bit Windows 7, Mozilla Firefox 21.0 on Mac OS X 10.7.5, and Mozilla Firefox 21.0 on Android 2.3.6, HTTPS content is disk cached unless the server sends the `Cache-Control: no-store` header.

Chrome. Google Chrome caches HTTPS-delivered content to disk, unless the following is present:

- The HTTP header `Cache-Control: no-store`.

We verified that when using Google Chrome 27.0.1453.94 m on Windows 7, or the Browser app in Android 2.3.6 (which is based on Chrome), HTTPS content is disk cached unless the server sends the `Cache-Control: no-store` header.

Safari. Apple Safari does not cache HTTPS-delivered content to disk, regardless of any headers sent by the server. We tested the mobile version of Safari on an iPad 2, and the HTTPS caching behavior was identical to the desktop version.

We verified that using Safari 6.0 (7536.25) on Mac OS X 10.7.5, and Mobile Safari on iOS 5.1.1, HTTPS content is never disk cached.

A word about private browsing modes. Virtually all web browsers now include a "private browsing" mode, that in addition to preventing browsing history from being retained, disables the disk cache entirely. While sufficient for a user to avoid this issue, we do not consider advising users to use private browsing to be a reasonable solution for several reasons. First, private browsing modes are not the default, and must manually be enabled by a user. Second, other aspects of private browsing, such as not retaining persistent cookies, break useful functionality in web sites, such as remembering usernames or remembering the computer to avoid answering security questions on each login. Third, since private browsing disables the disk cache entirely, it has negative side effects on the performance of the Internet as a whole, since even unencrypted HTTP content must be re-downloaded if the browser has been closed.

5 Reliably Preventing Disk Caching

Due to the historical inconsistency and confusion surrounding HTTPS and disk caching, it is worth briefly mentioning how to most reliably prevent disk caching of an HTTPS response. To do so, the web server should be configured to send the following:

- The response header `Pragma: no-cache`.
- The response header `Cache-Control: no-store`.

The Pragma header covers the special case of HTTP/1.0 servers and Internet Explorer 8. The Cache-Control header, as specified in the HTTP standard, covers all other cases, including standards-compliant browsers that may begin caching HTTPS content in the future (e.g., Safari). As both older Apache servers and IE 8 browsers are decommissioned over time, the Pragma header will no longer be needed.

6 Site Survey

Methodology. We tested thirty secure, password-protected sites that displayed sensitive personal information in a web browser. This involved accessing SSL-protected websites as an authorized user, logging out of the site, and closing the browser. Then, we reopened the browser, placed it in offline mode, and checked the disk cache for entries containing sensitive data.

Initial Results. As of April 25, 2013, twenty-one of the thirty sites tested were not sending the `Cache-Control: no-store` header required by the HTTPS standard to prevent disk caching of sensitive data. Some were not sending any caching-related headers at all, while others were sending caching headers that prevent disk caching only in Internet Explorer, or other headers not relevant to web browser caches.

The sites shown in Table 2 sent sensitive information with both of the headers `Cache-Control: no-cache`, and `Pragma: no-cache`, which together, prevent disk caching in Internet Explorer, but not Firefox or Chrome.

Table 2. Sites sending sensitive data with the headers Pragma: no-cache and Cache-Control: no-cache.

Site	Sensitive data
ADP	Partial SSN, name, address, financial data
BGE	Name, address, account number, account balance
M&T Bank Wealthcare	Name, account number, account balance
Scottrade	Account number, account balance
TreasuryDirect	Partial SSN, name, address, phone number
Verizon Wireless	Call details

The sites shown in Table 3 sent sensitive information with the header `Cache-Control: no-cache` which prevents disk caching in Internet Explorer 9 and earlier, but not Internet Explorer 10, Firefox or Chrome.

Table 3. Sites sending sensitive data with the header Cache-Control: no-cache.

Site	Sensitive data
BB&T	Name, partial account numbers, account balances
Liberty Mutual	Name, policy number, policy limits, account balances
PayPal	Name, address, phone number

The sites shown in Table 4 sent sensitive information with the header `Cache-Control: private`, which has no effect on whether or not a web browser caches the information to disk.

Table 4. Sites sending sensitive data with the header Cache-Control: private.

Site	Sensitive data
Allstate	Auto insurance policies
eBillity	Worker summary reports
eRenterPlan	Name, address, phone number

Lastly, the sites shown in Table 5 sent sensitive information without any cache-related HTTP headers at all.

Figures 1, 2, 3, 4, 5, and 6 in Appendix A show screenshots of some of the sensitive data we recovered from the disk cache.

Table 5. Sites sending sensitive information without cache-related headers.

Site	Sensitive data
Argus Health	Prescription claims
Boscov's Charge Card	Statements, full account numbers
Equifax	Full credit reports
GEICO	Partial SSN, DOB, name, address
MetLife	Name, policy number, policy amount, beneficiaries
PNC Bank	Check images
T. Rowe Price	401(k) balances
Toyota Financial	Name, address, account number, VIN
Trade King	Account number, balance

7   Updates

We notified each company in April, 2013, by email to the security- or phishing-related email address, or when email was not available, using a web-based contact form. The following companies acknowledged our advisories with a non-automated response:

- Argus Health.
- M & T Bank.
- PayPal.

Only BB&T has made any identifiable progress in over four months since notification toward implementing proper cache control behavior. The account summary page is now sending `Cache-Control: no-store`, but check images are still sent with inadequate protections.

8   Observations and Concerns

We believe that the amount of personal data that is currently being written to the disk cache when visiting these sites is alarming. It is important to note the distinction between a user consciously selecting a "save to disk" option, e.g., to save a bank statement, and content silently being written to the disk cache without users' knowledge. Non-technical users likely believe that if, after visiting a site and viewing personal data, they logout and close their browsers, that their data will be purged. Our findings prove this assumption incorrect in 70 % of the cases tested.

Based on the quantity of sites (twelve of twenty-one) that sent at least one cache-related header, even if it was not the one mandated by the standard to prevent disk caching, we do not believe that it is intended by these industries that this content be written to the disk cache. More significantly, the maintainers of these sites may erroneously believe that they have set the required headers to prevent disk caching, based on outdated and incorrect information published on the Internet. One tutorial [14] correctly states the purpose of all of these headers, but does not put them in the proper context with regard to HTTPS, stating "SSL pages are not cached (or decrypted) by proxy caches," which, while true for proxies, does not address the behavior of browsers. An OWASP page [15] incorrectly asserts that "If a web page is delivered over SSL, no content can be cached." When even the security community makes outdated and incorrect assumptions about this issue, it is unrealistic that more generally-focused web developers will do better.

Web browser authors, with the most striking example being Mozilla, seem to dismiss the current reality of servers sending sensitive information without the header needed to prevent it from being cached to disk. A comment on the bug report involving the change to Firefox 4's SSL caching policy by a member of Mozilla Corporation's security team stated [9]:

Among sites that don't use cache-control:no-store, the correlation between "SSL" and "sensitive" is very low.

Our findings show that this assertion does not hold when real-world sites are examined, even two years after the change.

The fact that the unencrypted, disk cached data is only stored on the user's personal machine should not be discounted. The possibilities for this information to be exposed are numerous: malware infections, theft of laptops and mobile devices, theft of physical backup media or compromise of "cloud" backup services, shared machines and user accounts [17], and of course, shared computers in libraries, hotels, and Internet cafes. An Intel-sponsored Ponemon Institute study estimated the cost of recovering from the loss or theft of a single laptop as $49,246 [16], and a Lookout Mobile Security study estimated that lost and stolen phones cost consumers more than $30 billion in 2012 [17].

9   Recommendations

To Web Developers and Web Framework Authors. Developers of web applications and web frameworks should audit all existing code to ensure that sensitive data is labeled with the appropriate caching directives. Professionals in these fields must become more familiar with the fine details of the HTTP standard, and assume that browser software will always make performance vs. security trade-offs against security. Proper security assessments of sites containing sensitive information should be conducted regularly, and an examination of disk cached content across all supported browsers should be part of that assessment process.

To the Security Community. All existing guidance and advice in regard to the HTTPS caching issue should be revised to reflect the reality of the HTTP standard. Security professionals should be cautious in making assertions or recommendations based on working knowledge alone, and be sure to consult the relevant standards and perform testing to back up their beliefs.

To Web Browser Authors. In a time where security threats and identity theft are rampant, all browsers should adopt an "opt-in" only policy for caching sensitive data to disk; and further, users should have an easily accessible option to refuse any or all "opt-in" directives. At the very least, we recommend that browsers with a very strict "opt-out" HTTPS disk caching policy, such as Firefox and Chrome, consider interpreting the

Pragma HTTP header and meta tag supported by Internet Explorer, as well. Internet Explorer has been disk caching HTTPS content for far longer than either of these browsers, so many sites seem to have been developed with IE-centric security assumptions in mind.

To Standards Committees. We recommend that standards bodies incorporate sound security principles, such as secure-by-default, defense-in-depth, and fail safe, into future standards. Traditionally, standards authors have attempted to maintain the layered architecture of Internet standards, and avoid tightly coupling an application-layer protocol like HTTP to the layers below. Indeed, RFC 2616 [put back ref?], the latest version of HTTP/1.1, mentions "SSL" once and does not mention "HTTPS" at all. While avoiding any consideration of whether an encrypted or unencrypted connection is used might make for a cleaner design with fewer special cases, it has practical security consequences. If HTTP/1.1 had simply specified that persistent caching was disabled by default on encrypted connections, and specified a header allowing a server to mark content as non-sensitive, then this entire issue could have been avoided.

To End-Users. Users should make the following configuration changes, depending on each browser, keeping in mind there may be performance trade-offs associated with these actions:

Internet Explorer. Internet Explorer already abides by most web application attempts to prevent disk caching. To further restrict what can be cached, a user can open Internet Options, choose the "Advanced" tab, and under "Security," check "Do not save encrypted pages to disk." This option may have unwanted side effects, such as interfering with file downloads from HTTPS sites. Alternatively, use "InPrivate Browsing" mode.

Firefox. Install our "HTTPS Caching Controller" Firefox add-on,[4] which adds a toolbar button allowing disk caching of SSL content to be disabled or enabled at any time. This add-on works only on the desktop version of Firefox. Manually, or on the mobile version, navigate to `about:config`, locate the preference `browser.cache.disk_cache_ssl`, and set the value to `false`. Alternatively, use "Private Browsing" mode.

Chrome. Google Chrome does not appear to have configurable functionality to limit the disk caching of HTTPS content (without affecting HTTP content) without modifying the source code. A workaround is to use "Incognito" mode, which prevents *all* disk caching.

The mobile Android Browser is similar. Android users can switch to another browser, such as the mobile version of Firefox, or use "Incognito" mode.

Safari. Safari users (both desktop and mobile) need not take any action, since, as of this writing, Safari does not cache any content transferred over HTTPS.

General. In addition to taking these precautions, never log into account-related or other security-sensitive sites from a computer or other device you do not own and control.

---

[4] http://securityevaluators.com/content/case-studies/caching/extension.jsp

10   Conclusions and Future Work

We have shown here, through direct verification and through online investigation, that the history of web browser caching behavior is a complicated one. The inconsistency across browser platforms and even across individual browser versions, has caused security and development communities much confusion, as evidenced by online sources and the alarming results of our study: that over 70 % of HTTPS-protected sites containing highly sensitive data fail to properly prohibit disk caching, and of them over 50 % appear to desire such prohibition.

We have identified the actual disk caching behavior of the four most popular web browsers, and suggest to web developers the most effective ways to prevent disk caching of sensitive content across all browsers.

For end-users, we have provided a Firefox extension that effectively prohibits disk caching of user-chosen sensitive data, rather than relying on the web application itself to make the appropriate decisions.

Moving forward, standards bodies should consider updating the HTTP standard so that the persistent caching of HTTPS data follows an "opt-in" policy, that is, the standard should recommend never caching HTTPS-protected content unless the web application specifically indicates that data is safe to cache.

Our data set consisted of 30 web sites, and additional statistical study could be performed to determine how many sites fail to properly prohibit the disk caching of sensitive data. Furthermore, given the lack of response to our disclosure of this information, it would be interesting to statistically gauge the response time of these organizations.

Appendix A

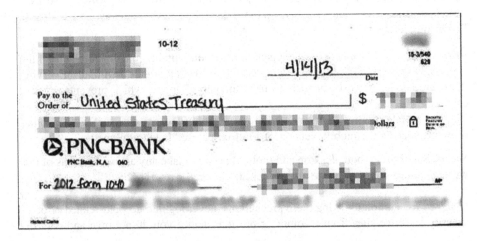

Fig. 1. Check image from PNC.

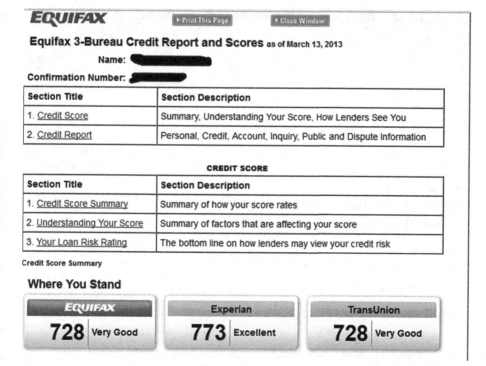

Fig. 2. Full credit report from Equifax.

510   S. Bono and J. Thompson

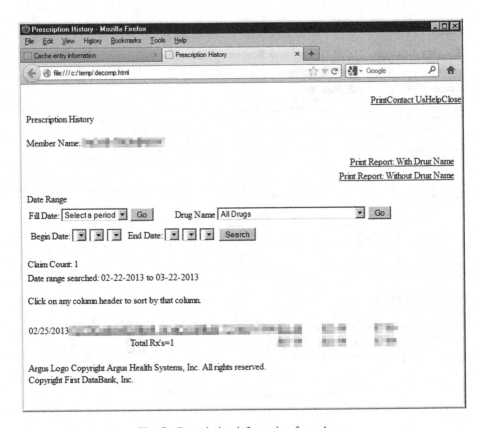

Fig. 3. Prescription information from Argus

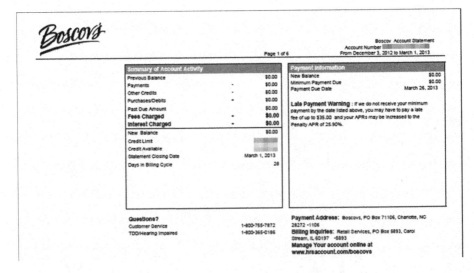

Fig. 4. Credit card account statement from Boscov's

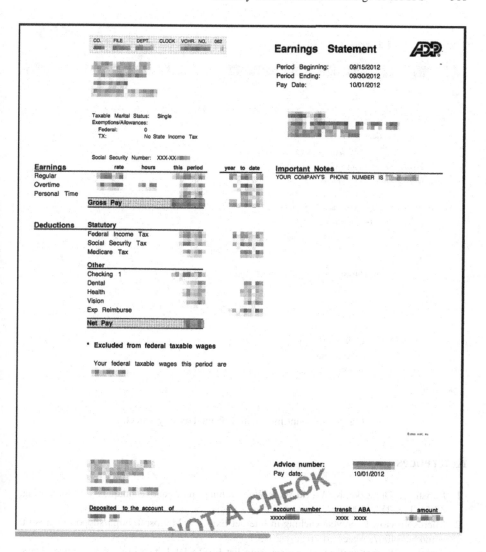

Fig. 5. Paystub from ADP.

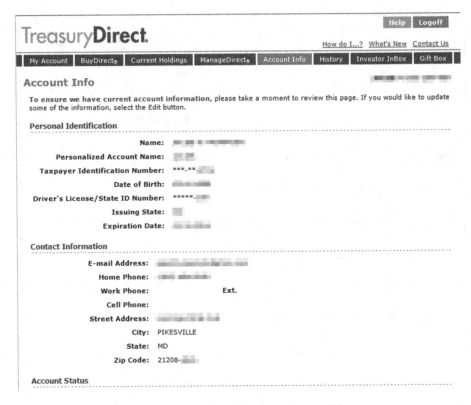

Fig. 6. Account information from Treasury Direct.

References

1. Barish, G., Obraczke, K.: World Wide Web caching: trends and techniques. Commun. Mag. **38**(5), 178–184 (2000)
2. Microsoft: How to prevent caching in Internet Explorer, Microsoft. http://support.microsoft.com/kb/234067. Accessed 26 July 2013
3. Appel, S.: Secure sockets layer discussion list FAQ v1.1.1, faqs.org, 16 November 1998. http://www.faqs.org/faqs/computer-security/ssl-talk-faq/. Accessed 26 July 2013
4. Mozilla: Firefox ignores "Cache-control: public" header on TLS connections, Mozilla, 19 July 2006. https://bugzilla.mozilla.org/show_bug.cgi?id=345181. Accessed 26 July 2013
5. Microsoft: Cannot open files on secure servers, Microsoft. http://support.microsoft.com/kb/254324. Accessed 26 July 2013
6. Fielding, R., Gettys, J., Mogul, J., Frystyk, H., Berners-Lee, T.: Hypertext Transfer Protocol – HTTP/1.1 (RFC 2068), IETF (1997)
7. Schillace, S.: Default https access for Gmail, Google, 12 January 2010. http://gmailblog.blogspot.com/2010/01/default-https-access-for-gmail.html. Accessed 25 July 2013
8. Rice, A.: Keeping users safe, Facebook, 13 May 2011. https://developers.facebook.com/blog/post/499/. Accessed 26 July 2013

9. Mozilla: Should cache SSL content to disk even without Cache-Conrol: public, Mozilla, 30 November 2009. https://bugzilla.mozilla.org/show_bug.cgi?id=531801. Accessed 26 July 2013

10. Everyone: Usage share of web browsers, Wikipedia. http://en.wikipedia.org/wiki/Browser_market_share. Accessed 25 July 2013

11. Berners-Lee, T., Fielding, R., Frystyk, H.: Hypertext transfer protocol - HTTP/1.0 (RFC 1945), IETF (1996)

12. The Apache Software Foundation: Revision 966055, The Apache Software Foundation, 20 July 2010. http://svn.apache.org/viewvc?view=revision&revision=966055. Accessed 26 July 2013

13. Microsoft: "Pragma: No-cache" tag may not prevent page from being cached, Microsoft. http://support.microsoft.com/kb/222064. Accessed 26 July 2013

14. Nottingham, M.: Caching tutorial for web authors and webmasters, 06 May 2013. http://www.mnot.net/cache_docs. Accessed 26 July 2013

15. OWASP: OWASP Application Security FAQ, OWASP, 22 April 2007. https://www.owasp.org/index.php/OWASP_Application_Security_FAQ#Am_I_totally_safe_with_these_directives.3F. Accessed 26 July 2013

16. Ponemon Institute: The billion dollar lost laptop problem, Ponemon Institute, (2010)

17. Lookout: Lookout projects lost and stolen phones could cost U.S. consumers over $30 billion in 2012, 21 March 2012

18. Chromium: Contents of /releases/1.0.154.53/src/net/http/http_cache.cc, Chromium, 26 July 2008. http://src.chromium.org/viewvc/chrome/releases/1.0.154.53/src/net/http/http_cache.cc?revision=14. Accessed 26 July 2013

Public Key Cryptography

Efficient Code Based Hybrid and Deterministic Encryptions in the Standard Model

K. Preetha Mathew[1]($\boxtimes$), Sachin Vasant[2], and C. Pandu Rangan[1]

[1] Theoretical Computer Science Lab, Department of Computer Science and Engineering, Indian Institute of Technology Madras, Chennai, India
{kpreetha,prangan}@cse.iitm.ac.in
[2] Department of Computer Science, Boston University, Boston, USA
sachinv@cs.bu.edu

Abstract. In this paper, we propose an IND-CCA2 secure Key-Encapsulation (KEM) in the standard model using the Niederreiter Encryption scheme. Also, we propose a PRIV-1CCA secure deterministic variant of the Niederreiter encryption scheme in the standard model. The security of these constructions are reduced to the hardness of the *Syndrome Decoding* problem and the *Goppa Code Distinguishability* problem. To the best of our knowledge, the proposed constructions are the first of its kind under coding-based assumption in the standard model that do not use the κ-repetition paradigm initiated by Rosen and Segev at Theory of Cryptography Conference (TCC), 2009.

Keywords: Standard model · Deterministic encryption · KEM-DEM · Neiderreiter cryptosystem · Syndrome decoding · Code indistinguishability

1 Introduction

The notion of code-based cryptography originated with the seminal paper by McEliece [31] in 1977. McEliece proposed an encryption scheme based on the hardness of the bounded decoding problem, which uses the generator matrix of a Goppa code (for which efficient decoding algorithms exist [27]) as the secret key, and the generator matrix blinded with a random non-singular matrix and a permutation matrix is the public key. Niederreiter [17] proposed the dual of the McEliece cryptosystem. The security of the Niederreiter encryption scheme relied on the hardness of syndrome decoding. The currently existing provably secure systems are based on number theoretic assumptions. As per Shor's algorithm [33] the underlying hard problems upon which the systems are built will be broken by the advent of quantum computers. Therefore it is desired to have cryptographic primitives based on different security assumptions other than number theoretic assumptions only, because if one such system fails it is possible to make a shift easily to other assumptions. Hence, code-based cryptography is attaining more significance now a days.

© Springer International Publishing Switzerland 2014
H.-S. Lee and D.-G. Han (Eds.): ICISC 2013, LNCS 8565, pp. 517–535, 2014.
DOI: 10.1007/978-3-319-12160-4_31

Hybrid encryption is concerned with building encryption schemes with the help of both asymmetric cryptosystems and symmetric key cryptosystems. A symmetric encryption scheme is used to overcome the problems associated with encrypting long messages using the pure asymmetric key encryptions. A hybrid encryption can be obtained by generating a random symmetric key using asymmetric encryption. The message is encrypted using symmetric key encryption with symmetric key obtained by decrypting the key encrypted by asymmetric encryption. This is the approach used in a number of schemes like [7,15,20,21] etc. The current approach of hybrid encryption schemes was initiated and developed by Cramer and Shoup [7,34], which is termed as the KEM-DEM model. The KEM-DEM model consists of two components namely a Key Encapsulation Mechanism (KEM) which is an asymmetric encryption and a Data Encapsulation Mechanism (DEM), which uses a symmetric key encryption to encrypt long messages. Cramer and Shoup also showed that a secure KEM, combined with an appropriately secure symmetric-key encryption scheme, yields a hybrid encryption scheme which is IND-CCA2 secure. Kurosawa and Desmedt [20] showed that a key encapsulation mechanism (KEM) does not have to be IND-CCA2 secure in the construction of hybrid encryption schemes. The above method is used in hybrid encryption schemes proposed by Kiltz et al. [19] for coining a new paradigm for hybrid encryption in which they used the technique of randomness extraction in the symmetric key derivation of KEM before the authenticated encryption (DEM). Hofheinz et al. [18] put forward a new paradigm for building hybrid encryption schemes from constrained chosen-ciphertext secure (CCCA) key-encapsulation mechanisms (KEMs) plus authenticated symmetric encryption. CCCA has less demanding security requirements than standard chosen-ciphertext (CCA) security. Hofheinz et al. proved that CCCA KEM along with an one-time authenticated encryption is sufficient for secure hybrid encryption.

Cui et al. [8] presented efficient constructions of deterministic encryption from hybrid encryption based on McEliece assumptions in the random oracle model. An encryption scheme is deterministic, if $Enc(m)$ always maps to the same value, i.e., encryption does not use a random tape. A deterministic encryption can be used for efficiently indexing and searching an encrypted database. Therefore, it serves the purpose of efficiently searchable encryption. Efficiently searchable encryption (ESE) was introduced as a primitive by Bellare et al. [2], for the purpose of securing remote databases. While other primitives for securing remote databases like Encryption-with-keyword search allows searching the database in time linear to the number of records in the database, an ESE allows creation of index structures for encrypted records just like index structures that could be created for an unencrypted database.

It is seen that the notion of indistinguishability cannot be used to define the security of deterministic encryption (or ESEs) [2]. Therefore Bellare et al. [2] proposed a new security models for ESEs, namely, security against a privacy adversary (PRIV security). An ESE is PRIV-secure if given the ciphertext-block c of a message-block, no probabilistic polynomial time (PPT) adversary has a non-negligible advantage on computing some function on the corresponding encrypted message-block **m**. It is to be noted that PRIV security is meaningful only if the distribution of the messages selected from the message space has a high min-entropy. Such an assumption is practical in the sense of securing indexable fields such as the SSN numbers, phone numbers or the primary keys. For a ESE scheme, if any PRIV-adversary having access to a decryption oracle (for polynomially bounded number of decryption queries) has only a negligible advantage in finding the target value in bounded polynomial time, the scheme is said to be PRIV-CCA secure. PRIV-CCA secure systems in the random oracle model were provided in [2,8]. Secure systems and different PRIV notions were presented and analysed in [3,5]. Fuller et al. [16] presented different PRIV notions and provided the first CCA secure deterministic Niederreiter variant in the standard model. Their proposal uses the κ-repetition paradigm initiated by Rosen and Segev [32].

Motivation. A secure and anonymous hybrid encryption was proposed by Edoardo Persichetti using Niederreiter encryption [29] recently. The proposal is in the random oracle model. Cryptosystems proved secure under the assumption of random oracles assume that output of the hash functions follows a uniform distribution. But Canneti et al. [6] revealed that replacing random oracles with existing hash functions may lead to insecure implementation of the scheme. Thus, it is now preferred that the scheme be proven secure without the random oracle assumption (i.e., in the standard model). Also an efficiently searchable encryption is a requirement for construction of a secure and efficient remote database. A deterministic encryption serves the purpose in an efficient manner. The existing detrministic encryption based on McEliece assumption is in random oracle model.

Fuller et al. [16] constructed a q-bounded PRIV-CCA secure Niederreiter variant using the κ-correlation property. In the paper lossy trapdoor functions and its applications [28] the authors presented a black box construction of IND-CCA2 secure encryption scheme based on lossy TDFs and all-but-one trapdoor functions, with a witness recovering decryption algorithm. The decryption first recovers the randomness that was used to create the ciphertext, and then tests the validity of the ciphertext simply by re-encrypting the message under retrieved randomness. The κ-repetition paradigm initiated by Rosen and Segev [32], states that if a function consisting of κ instances of a one-way trapdoor function is an one-way trapdoor function, then it is κ-correlation secure. Dowsley et al. [10] showed that a randomized version of the CPA secure McEliece cryptosystem can be used to construct CCA2 secure scheme in the standard model using κ-repetition paradigm. The construction that adhere more to the construction of Rosen and Segev [32] is given by Persichetti [30]. Freeman et al. [14] showed that the Niederreiter encryption is κ- correlation secure provided the parameters are chosen such that broadcast attack [25] is to be avoided. It can be seen that, for Niederreiter system to remain κ-correlation secure, very large parameters are required. Therefore such schemes might not be practical. A code-based hybrid encryption and also a code based deterministic encryption that is secure in the standard model, without the use of κ-repetition paradigm, has practical significance.

Our Contributions. In this paper, we propose the following:

1. A Key Encapsulation Mechanism using the Niederreiter encryption scheme. The scheme proven to be IND-CCA2 secure in the standard model. The hardness assumptions are based on Syndrome decoding and Goppa-code indistinguishability.
2. A deterministic variant of the Niederreiter encryption scheme. We prove the PRIV-1CCA security in standard model. PRIV-1CCA is a weaker security model than the q-bounded PRIV-CCA model used by Fuller et al. [16]. It is a practical model as shown in [5], as it can be used if the field to be encrypted does not display dependencies between values in different records (for example phone numbers).

The essential idea is the use of two trapdoors, one for the decryption in the scheme and the other to simulate the decryption oracle (in the proof). The use of two trapdoors was employed in the construction of a (H)IBE using lattices by Agrawal et al. [1] and IND-CCA2 Niederreiter variant in the standard model by Mathew et al. [22]. In this paper, the target collision resistant (TCR) hash functions is used as in [5] instead of one time signature as in [22] because TCR hash function can be efficient than one time signature. According to [5] full witness recovery can also be achieved by using TCR hash function.

The proposed scheme use two polynomially computable injective functions that map a commitment in the ciphertext to the space of corresponding matrices and the fact that the product of a parity-check matrix with the corresponding generator matrix is zero, to obtain all-but-one trapdoor (with the ciphertext commitment being used as the branch). The construction is based on the generic construction by Boldyreva et al. in [5] using code-based assumptions. We use witness recovery in our constructs, like in [19,22,28]. It can be noted that the proposed IND-CCA2 KEM along with an authenticated DEM results in an IND-CCA2 secure hybrid encryption.

Organisation of the paper. Section 2 lists the preliminaries which include the security notions and the hardness assumptions used in the paper. Section 3 gives the proposed KEM construction and its proof of security. Section 4 elaborates on the deterministic encryption scheme and formally argues the PRIV-1CCA construction in the standard model (Proof given in appendix). Concluding remarks are offered in Sect. 5.

2 Preliminaries

2.1 Notation

If x is a string, then $|x|$ denotes its length, while $|S|$ represents the cardinality of the set S. $\kappa \in \mathbb{N}$ denotes security parameter. $s \in_R S$ denotes the operation of choosing an element s from a set S uniformly at random. $w \leftarrow \mathcal{A}(x, y, ...)$ represents the running of algorithm $\mathcal{A}$ with inputs $x, y, ...$ and producing output w. We write $w \leftarrow \mathcal{A}^{\mathcal{O}}(x, y, ...)$ for representing an algorithm $\mathcal{A}$ having access to oracle $\mathcal{O}$.

We denote by $\Pr[E]$ the probability that the event E occurs. For a random variable X we denote $Pr_X[x]$ as the probability that the random variable X takes the value x, in other words, Pr_X is the probability distribution of X. $X|E$ denotes the random variable X conditioned on an event E and the distribution is denoted by $Pr_{X|E}$. The statistical distance between two random variables X and Y is denoted by $\Delta(X, Y) = \frac{1}{2}(\sum_x |Pr_X[x] - Pr_Y[x]|)$. *Minimum entropy* for a random variable X refers to the value $H_\infty(X) = -\log_2(\max_x Pr_X[x])$. The *minimum conditional entropy* for X conditioned over Y denotes the value $H_\infty(X|Y) = -\log_2(\max_{x,y} Pr_{X|Y=y}[x])$. The *average min-conditional entropy* is defined by $\tilde{H}_\infty(X|Y) = -\log_2(\sum_y (Pr_Y[y](max_x Pr_{X|Y=y}[x])))$.

For a matrix M, its transpose is represented by M^T and its inverse (if it exists) is represented by M^{-1}. If a and b are two bit strings of same length, we denote their bitwise XOR by $a \oplus b$.

The notations used for coding theory in this paper are as follows. A binary linear-error correcting code of length n and dimension k or a $[n, k]$- code is a k-*dimensional* subspace of $\mathbb{F}_2^n$. The rate of a code can be calculated as $\frac{k}{n}$. A code is high-rate if $\frac{k}{n} \to 1$. If the minimum hamming distance between any two codewords is d, then the code is a $[n, k, d]$ code. The hamming weight of a codeword x, $\mathsf{wt}(x)$, is the number of non-zero bits in the codeword. For $t \leq \lfloor \frac{d-1}{2} \rfloor$, the code is said to be t-error correcting if it detects and corrects errors of weight at most t. Hence, the code can also be represented as a $[n, k, 2t + 1]$ code. The generator matrix $G \in \mathbb{F}_2^{k \times n}$ of a $[n, k]$ linear code C is a matrix of rank k whose rows span the code C. The parity-check matrix $H \in \mathbb{F}_2^{n-k \times n}$ of a $[n, k]$ code C is a matrix satisfying $HG^T = 0$. Hence, code C can be defined as $\{mG : \forall m \in \mathbb{F}_2^k\}$ or $\{c : Hc^T = 0\}$.

2.2 Hybrid Encryption

We adhere to the definitions and notations given in [18, 20].

Key Encapsulation Mechanism. A key-encapsulation mechanism KEM consists of the triple (KEM.Kg, KEM.Enc, KEM.Dec) of algorithms. KEM.Kg is a PPT algorithm that takes the security parameter κ as input to output the tuple (pk, sk), where pk is the public key of the entity and sk is the corresponding secret key. KEM.Enc is a PPT algorithm that takes as input the security parameter κ and pk. It selects the symmetric encryption key uniformly at random and outputs an encapsulation of the key c. KEM.Dec is a deterministic polynomial time algorithm that takes as input the encapsulation c and sk to output the symmetric key K or the rejection symbol $\perp$ in case the encapsulation is invalid.

The IND-CCA2 security of a KEM (with the key-space of the symmetric keys being $\mathcal{K}$) against a PPT adversary $\mathcal{A}^{\mathcal{D}(\cdot)}$ having access to a decapsulation oracle is associated with the following experiment:

$$\mathbf{Exp}_{KEM,\mathcal{A}}^{IND-CCA2}(\kappa)$$
$(\mathsf{pk},\mathsf{sk}) \leftarrow \mathsf{KEM.Kg}(\kappa)$
$K^{\dagger} \in_R \mathcal{K}$
$(K^*, c^*) \leftarrow \mathsf{KEM.Enc}(\kappa, \mathsf{pk})$
$b \in_R \{0, 1\}$
$if\ (b == 1)\ then\ K = K^*$
$else\ K = K^{\dagger}$
$b' \leftarrow \mathcal{A}^{\mathcal{D}(\cdot)}(\mathsf{pk}, K, c^*)$
$if\ (b == b')\ return\ 1$
$else\ return\ 0$

Let $Pr[\mathcal{A}^{\mathcal{D}(\cdot)}]$ be the probability that $\mathcal{A}$ wins the experiment (i.e., 1 is returned). Then the advantage of the adversary is defined by $\mathsf{Adv}_{KEM,\mathcal{A}}^{IND-CCA2}(\kappa) = |Pr[\mathcal{A}^{\mathcal{D}(\cdot)}] - \frac{1}{2}|$. A KEM is IND-CCA2 secure if for all PPT adversaries $\mathcal{A}$ the advantage is negligible with respect to the security parameter κ.

Authenticated Encryption. (Data Encapsulation Mechanism (DEM)) An authenticated encryption scheme AE consists of the tuple $(\mathsf{AE.Enc}, \mathsf{AE.Dec})$ of deterministic polynomial time algorithms. AE.Enc takes as input a message m from the message space and the symmetric key K from the key-space to output a ciphertext χ. AE.Dec takes the ciphertext χ and the key K as input to output the message (in case the ciphertext is valid) or the rejection symbol $\perp$. The decryption algorithm must satisfy the soundness requirement, i.e., the output of $\mathsf{AE.Dec}(K, \mathsf{AE.Enc}(K, m)$ must be m with overwhelming probability for all messages m in the message space.

For any authenticated encryption scheme to be one-time secure, any adversary PPT adversary $\mathcal{B}$ (allowed exactly one query to encryption and the decryption oracle each) must have only a negligible advantage in distinguishing ciphertexts of two messages m_0 and m_1.

Hybrid Encryption. A hybrid encryption scheme can be constructed from a KEM and a DEM as follows: According to the composition theorem in [7] an IND-CCA2 secure Hybrid encryption scheme can be constructed using an IND-CCA2 secure KEM and an one-time authenticated encryption as a DEM.

KeyGen(κ)	Encrypt(pk, m)	Decrypt(sk, $C = (c, \chi)$)
$(\mathsf{pk}, \mathsf{sk}) \leftarrow \mathsf{KEM.Kg}(\kappa)$	$(K, c) \leftarrow \mathsf{KEM.Enc}(\mathsf{pk}, \kappa)$	$(K\ or \perp) \leftarrow \mathsf{KEM.Dec}(\mathsf{sk}, c)$
return $((\mathsf{pk}, \mathsf{sk}))$	$\chi \leftarrow \mathsf{AE.Enc}(K, m)$	$m' = (m\ or \perp) \leftarrow \mathsf{AE.Dec}(K, \chi)$
	return $C = (c, \chi)$	**return** m'

2.3 Deterministic Encryption

The definitions and notations adopted in this paper are based on [5].

A deterministic encryption scheme DET consists of the triple $(\mathsf{DET.Kg}, \mathsf{DET.Enc}, \mathsf{DET.Dec})$ of algorithms. DET.Kg is a PPT algorithm that takes the security parameter κ as input to output the tuple $(\mathsf{pk}, \mathsf{sk})$, where pk is the public key of the entity and sk is the corresponding secret key. DET.Enc is a deterministic polynomial time algorithm that takes as input the message m from the message space $\mathcal{M}$ of large min-entropy and pk and outputs the ciphertext c. KEM.Dec is a deterministic polynomial time algorithm that takes as input the ciphertext c and sk to output the message m' or the rejection symbol $\perp$ in case the encapsulation is invalid.

A DET is PRIV-CCA secure against any PPT adversary $\mathcal{A}^{\mathcal{D}(\cdot)}$ having access to a decryption oracle, any function f and a block M of n messages from a message space $\mathcal{M}$ where the min-entropy that $M[i] = m$ is high, the PRIV advantage defined as follows

$$\mathsf{Adv}_{\mathsf{PKE},\mathcal{A}}^{priv-cca}(\kappa) = |\mathbf{Real}_{\mathcal{A}\mathcal{E}}(\mathcal{A}, M, f) - \mathbf{Ideal}_{\mathcal{A}\mathcal{E}}(\mathcal{A}, M, f)|$$

is negligible with respect to a security parameter κ. Here,

$$\mathbf{Real}_{\mathcal{A}\mathcal{E}}(\mathcal{A}, M, f) = Pr[f(M) \leftarrow \mathcal{A}^{\mathcal{D}(\cdot)}(\mathsf{pk}, \mathsf{DET.Enc}(\mathsf{pk}, M))]$$

and

$$\mathbf{Ideal}_{\mathcal{A}\mathcal{E}}(\mathcal{A}, M, f) = Pr[f(M) \leftarrow \mathcal{A}^{\mathcal{D}(\cdot)}(\mathsf{pk}, \mathsf{DET.Enc}(\mathsf{pk}, M'))]$$

where pk is a public key selected from the public-key space and M, M' are blocks of length n from message space $\mathcal{M}$.

It is shown in [5] that PRIV security for block sources is equivalent to PRIV security for single hard to guess message and is introduced as PRIV1 security. Therefore PRIV-1CCA security is defined for message blocks of size one.

2.4 Hash Functions-Security Notions

Target Collision Resistance [5]. A hash function h is target collision resistant if for every polynomial time adversary, the TCR advantage defined as probability any value x_1, the hashing key K and a value x_2 such that $h(K, x_1) = h(K, x_2)$ is negligible.

$$Adv_{\mathcal{H}}^{\mathsf{TCR}}(A) = Pr[H(K, x_1) = H(K, x_2) : (x_1, st) \leftarrow^R \mathcal{A}, K \leftarrow^R \mathcal{K}, x_2 \leftarrow^R A(K, st)] \quad (1)$$

Generalised Leftover Hash Lemma [9]. The generalised hash lemma states that the output of an universal hash function is statistically close to random provided the entropy of the input space conditioned over any random variable (independent of the distribution defining the key-generation) is large.

Lemma 1. *Let h be an universal hash function using the key-space $\mathcal{K}$ and input domain $\{0,1\}^l$ with range R. Let K be a random variable describing the key generation from $\mathcal{K}$, and U be an uniform distribution over R. Then for any random variable X over the input domain $\{0,1\}^l$ and any random variable Z, both independent of K, satisfying $\tilde{H}_\infty(X|Z) \geq \log|R| + 2\log(1/\epsilon)$, the output of the hash function is statistically close to U, i.e., $\Delta((Z, K, h(K, X)), (Z, K, U)) \leq \epsilon$.*

2.5   Security Assumptions

The following are some of the hard problems on which the security of the proposed cryptosystems are based.

Definition 1 (Syndrome Decoding Problem). *For some parameters* $[n, k, 2t + 1]$ *given an* $a \in \mathbb{F}_2^{n-k}$ *and a matrix* $H \in \mathbb{F}_2^{n-k \times n}$, *find a vector* $e \in \mathbb{F}_2^n$ *with weight* $\mathsf{wt}(e) \leq t$ *such that* $He^T = a$.

The advantage of a PPT algorithm $\mathcal{D}$ of solving the problem is denoted by $\mathsf{Adv}_{\mathcal{D}}^{\mathsf{SD}}(n, k, t)$.

Assumption 1. *For any probabilistic polynomial time algorithm* $\mathcal{F}$, $\mathsf{Adv}_{\mathcal{F}}^{\mathsf{SD}}(C) < \epsilon_1(n, k)$ *where* $\epsilon_1(n, k)$ *is a negligible value with respect to* n *and* k.

For Goppa codes, there is a polynomial time bounded decoding/syndrome decoding algorithm [27]. Thus, there is a preference for most code-based cryptosystems to use the Goppa code as a trapdoor.

Definition 2 (Goppa code-distinguishability). *For parameters* $[n, k, 2t+1]$ *given a matrix* $H \in \mathbb{F}_2^{n-k \times n}$, *output 1 if* H *is a parity check matrix of a Goppa code, 0 if* H *is not a parity check matrix of any Goppa code.*

The advantage of a PPT algorithm $\mathcal{D}$ of solving the problem is denoted by $\mathsf{Adv}_{\mathcal{D}}^{\mathsf{CD}}(n, k)$.

Assumption 2. *For any probabilistic polynomial time distinguisher* $\mathcal{D}$, $\mathsf{Adv}_{\mathcal{D}}^{\mathsf{CD}}$ $(n, k) < \epsilon_2(n, k)$ *where* $\epsilon_2(n, k)$ *is a negligible function if it is not a high rate Goppa code, [11].*

$$|Pr[\mathcal{D}(H) = 1] - Pr[\mathcal{D}(M) = 1]| < \epsilon_2(n, k)$$

where H *is the parity check matrix of the Goppa code and* $M \in_R \mathbb{F}_2^{n-k \times n}$.

3   Hybrid Encryption

3.1   Proposed KEM

System Parameters. Let $D_{(n,t)}$ be the domain of the set of all binary error vectors (of weight $\leq t$) of length n. The system parameters for the security parameter κ are as follows:

- Target Collision Resistant hash functions $h_1 : F_2^{(n-k)} \to \{0, 1\}^{\kappa}$.
- An injective function $f_1 : \{0, 1\}^{\kappa} \to \mathbb{F}_2^{n-k \times n-k}$ which takes binary vectors from a sufficiently large space as input, and outputs the a full-rank matrix H.
- An injective function $f_2 : \{0, 1\}^{\kappa} \to \mathcal{P}_{n \times n}$ which takes binary vectors from a sufficiently large space as input and output a $n \times n$ permutation matrix P, for the Niederreiter cryptosystem.

Table 1. Parameters for proposed hybrid encryption scheme, and its security as per [4].

(n, k, t)	Security factor
$(2^{16}, 1744, 36)$	84.88
$(2^{17}, 2480, 46)$	107.41
$(2^{18}, 3480, 68)$	147.94
$(2^{19}, 4624, 97)$	191.18

The parameters (n, k, t) are listed in Table 1. Note that the parameters are selected in such a way that function f_1, f_2 are injective and h_1 is target collision resistant. One cannot use enumerative coding to find the input to h_1.

Key Generation. For the security parameter 1^κ, the KeyGen is as follows:

- Randomly select two distinct $[n, k, 2t+1]$ Goppa codes with parity check matrices H_1, H_2 respectively.
- Randomly select an invertible matrix $Q_1 \in_R \mathbb{F}_2^{n-k \times n-k}$ and $n \times n$ permutation matrices P_1, P_2.
- Define $\widetilde{H}_1 = Q_1 H_1 P_1$ and $\widetilde{H}_2 = H_2 P_2 \oplus H_1 P_1$.

Thus, we have:

- **Public Keys:** $\widetilde{H}_1$ & $\widetilde{H}_2$
- **Secret Keys:** H_1, H_2, Q_1, P_1, P_2

Key-Encapsulation:

- Generate $r \in_R D_{(n,t)}$ such that $r = r_1 || K$ where r_1 is of length n_1 and K is of length n_2 such that $n = n_1 + n_2$.
- Generate $c_1 \leftarrow h_1(\widetilde{H}_1 r^T)$.
- Compute $H_{c_1} = f_1(c_1)$ and $P_{c_1} = f_2(c_1)$.
- Define $K_1 = \widetilde{H}_1 P_{c_1}$ and $K_2 = H_{c_1} \widetilde{H}_2 P_{c_1}$.
- Define $c_2 = K_1 r^T$, and $c_3 = K_2 r^T$.

The ciphertext that is sent is $c = (c_1, c_2, c_3)$.

Thus, K would be the required information for symmetric key which can be used inside a hard core function.

Key Decapsulation. The decryption on the ciphertext $c = (c_1, c_2, c_3)$ is done as follows:

Compute, $H_{c_1} \leftarrow f_1(c_1)$, $P_{c_1} \leftarrow f_2(c_1)$.

if (Decode$_{H_1}(Q_1^{-1} c_2) \rightarrow \perp$)

    return $\perp$.

else

    $r' \leftarrow P_{c_1}^T P_1^T \text{Decode}_{H_1}(Q_1^{-1} c_2)$

    if$(c_3 \neq H_{c_1} \widetilde{H}_2 P_{c_1} r'^T || c_1 \neq h_1(\widetilde{H}_1 r'^T))$ // Witness Validation

        return $\perp$.

    else
        return K from r.
end

Correctness. For decapsulation of a valid encapsulation, H_{c_1} & P_{c_1} can be computed. c is sent to the receiver. If encapsulation is valid, then c_2 and c_3 are decodable syndromes for the error vector r' for K_1 and K_2 respectively. Thus, as long as the decoding algorithm is correct, the decryption is correct for a valid ciphertext. If the ciphertext is invalid, the ciphertext is either rejected by the decoding algorithm (if c_2 is not a decodable syndrome), the consistency checking mechanism (if c_2 and c_3 are not the syndromes of the same error vector for K_1 and K_2 respectively) or the integrity check mechanism (if the obtained key is not committed in c_1).

3.2 IND-CCA2 Security of KEM

As the scheme uses the semantic secure encryption of Nojima et al. [26] the following theorem is used in proof. Also witness recovery is used for the scheme as in [22]. So the proof follows the same pattern as in [22].

Theorem 1. *[26] If there exists an algorithm $\mathcal{D}$ which runs in time τ, such that*

$$Pr[r \in_R \mathbb{F}_2^n, \ wt(r) = t, \ R \in_R \mathbb{F}_2^{n-k \times n}|\mathcal{D}(Rr^T, R) = 1] - $$
$$Pr[s \in_R \mathbb{F}_2^{n-k}, \ R \in_R \mathbb{F}_2^{n-k \times n}|\mathcal{D}(s, R) = 1] \ \geq \ \delta$$

then one can construct an algorithm $\mathcal{D}'$ running in time $\tau' = O(n^2(\tau + n^2)/\delta^2)$, such that $4\sqrt[3]{n} \cdot \mathsf{Adv}_{\mathcal{D}'}^{\mathsf{SD}}(n, k) \geq \delta$.

Theorem 2. *The proposed KEM is IND-CCA2 secure as long as h_1 is a TCR hash function, and the Goppa-code distinguishability and syndrome decoding of the corresponding parameters are hard to solve.*

Proof: The proof is presented as a sequence of games, Game 0, Game 1 .... While, Game 0 fits the scheme exactly as in the IND-CCA2 game. Subsequent games change the environment, such that the view of the adversary in discriminating between two consecutive games is at best negligible in κ or reduces to the solution of a hard-problem instance. We denote the challenger/simulator as a PPT algorithm $\mathcal{C}$ and the adversary of the system as a PPT algorithm $\mathcal{A}$.

Game 0. $\mathcal{C}$ adapts the proposed KEM directly to the IND-CCA2 game. The system parameters are set as in the proposed scheme, with the security parameter κ. The key-generation oracle and the decapsulation oracle is run using the described scheme. $\mathcal{C}$ computes K^* and $c^* = (c_1^*, c_2^*, c_3^*)$ using $\mathsf{Enc}(\kappa)$. c^* is the encapsulation of the challenge key given to $\mathcal{A}$, i.e., given c^*, $\mathcal{A}$ must identify if the valid key has been encapsulated. $\mathcal{A}$ outputs b', $b' \leftarrow \mathcal{A}^{\mathcal{D}(\cdot)}(c^*)$. $\mathcal{A}$ wins if where $b == b'$.

Let the event that the adversary $\mathcal{A}$ wins the game be quantified by the random variable X_0. Then,

$$\mathsf{Adv}^{cca2}_{\mathsf{KEM},\mathcal{A}}(\kappa) = |Pr[X_0] - \frac{1}{2}| \tag{2}$$

Game 1. Decapsulation Oracle is simulated by $\mathcal{C}$ as follows:

Input: The ciphertext $c = (c_1, c_2, c_3)$

Output: The key K.

if $(c_1 == c_1^*)$

   Return $\perp$

else

   $H_{c_1} \leftarrow f_1(c_1)$, $P_{c_1} \leftarrow f_2(c_1)$

   Compute $c_2' = Q_1^{-1} c_2$

   Compute $c_2'' = H_{c_1} c_2'$

   Compute $y = c_3 \oplus c_2''$

   Compute $Q' = H_{c_1}$

     if $(\mathsf{Decode}_{H_2}(Q'^{-1}y) \to \perp)$ // Invalid encapsulation

       Return $\perp$

     else

       Compute $r' = P_{c_1}^T P_2^T \mathsf{Decode}_{H_2}(Q'^{-1}y)$

       if $(c_2 \neq \tilde{H}_1 P_{c_1} r'^T || c_3 \neq H_{c_1} \tilde{H}_2 P_{c_1} r'^T)$

         Return $\perp$ // Witness inconsistency

       else

         if $(c_1 \neq h_1(\tilde{H}_1 r'^T))$

           Return $\perp$

         else

           Return K from r'

end

Let the event that the adversary $\mathcal{A}$ wins in this game be quantified by the random variable X_1. The difference in the distribution (or view of the adversary) between X_0 and X_1 is the situation in which $\mathcal{C}$ returns $\perp$ if $c_1 = c_1^*$ in this game, during the decapsulation oracle. The simulator returns $\perp$ implying the ciphertext is invalid (as the integrity check will not hold). But, it can be seen that $\mathcal{A}$ may have given a valid ciphertext (that is not the challenge ciphertext), i.e., a ciphertext for some $K' \neq K^*$. Clearly, this would violate the target collision resistance of h_1. Hence,

$$|Pr[X_0] - Pr[X_1]| \leq \mathsf{Adv}^{\mathsf{TCR}}_{\mathcal{A}}(h_1) \tag{3}$$

Game 2. Key Generation: The public key-generation process is altered. $\mathcal{C}$ replaces the Goppa parity-check matrix of H_1 with the parity check matrix R of a random $[n, k, 2t+1]$ code. Thus $H_1 \leftarrow R$. $\mathcal{C}$ computes $c^* = (c_1^*, c_2^*, c_3^*) = \mathsf{Enc}(\kappa^*)$. It can be noted that only in the case that c_1^* is used, the decryption oracle will fail. But this remains consistent with the decryption oracle described in the previous game.

$$|Pr[X_2]| = |Pr[X_1]| \tag{4}$$

Game 3. Key for Challenge text and construct challenge: The Public key generated is again altered. Replace H_2 with parity check of random matrix R_2 so that now $\widetilde{H}_1$ and $\widetilde{H}_2$ are parity-check matrices of random codes.

Thus, for the event that $\mathcal{A}$ wins Game 3, X_3, $\mathcal{C}$ can construct a Goppa-code distinguisher based on the difference in the distributions of X_2 and X_3 is distinguishing Goppa-code with random code. Also $\mathcal{C}$ uses the challenge $K^\dagger$ and computes c^* using the altered public keys. The winning of this game is by syndrome decoding of random code and Code Distinguishability. If the event that $\mathcal{A}$ wins this game be X_3, then by Theorem 1 (application to K_1 and K_2 individually), we have

$$|Pr[X_2] - Pr[X_3]| \leq 4(\sqrt[3]{n \cdot \mathsf{Adv}^{\mathsf{SD}}_{\mathcal{D}'}(n, k, t)}) + \mathsf{Adv}^{\mathsf{CD}}_{\mathcal{C}}(n, k) \qquad (5)$$

Also, it can be noted that no information of $K^\dagger$ is revealed in c^*, therefore, generating a random c_1^* does not affect the validity of the ciphertext.

$$Pr[X_3] = \frac{1}{2} \qquad (6)$$

Hence,

$$\mathsf{Adv}^{IND-CCA2}_{\mathsf{KEM}, \mathcal{A}}(\kappa) = |Pr[X_0] - Pr[X_3]|$$

by repeatedly applying the difference lemma and using the Eqs. (2)–(4), we get,

$$\mathsf{Adv}^{IND-CCA2}_{\mathsf{KEM}, \mathcal{A}}(\kappa) \leq \mathsf{Adv}^{\mathsf{TCR}}_{\mathcal{A}}(h_1) + \mathsf{Adv}^{\mathsf{CD}}_{\mathcal{C}}(n, k) + 4(\sqrt[3]{n \cdot \mathsf{Adv}^{\mathsf{SD}}_{\mathcal{D}'}(n, k, t)})$$

Thus, the advantage of the PPT adversary $\mathcal{A}$ in the IND-CCA2 game is bounded by the target-collision resistance of h_1, the Goppa-distinguishability of H_1 and the hardness of syndrome decoding. Hence, the proposed scheme is IND-CCA2 secure as long as h_1 is a TCR hash function, and the Goppa-code distinguishability and syndrome decoding of the corresponding parameters are hard to solve.   □

Using the IND-CCA2 secure KEM proposed above and any authenticated one-time symmetric encryption, an IND-CCA2 secure Hybrid encryption scheme can be constructed in the standard model (using the composition theorem in [7]).

4   Deterministic Encryption

The deterministic encryption is constructed in a manner similar to the KEM in the previous section. Instead of selecting the key uniformly at random, the security of the scheme is based on the large entropy of the message space. If m has enough min entropy, then, intuitively, the Left Over Hash Lemma (LHL) implies that each of the hashes are close to uniform, independent of the specific distribution of m, bounding $\mathcal{A}'s$ advantage to be small. As per Generalised Left Over Hash Lemma (LHL), TCR smooths out an input distribution (distribution of m in this paper) to nearly uniform on its range, provided that the input distribution has sufficient minimum entropy, since TCR comes under universal one-wayness [24].

4.1 Proposed Scheme

System Parameters. Let $D_{(n,t)}$ be the domain of the set of all binary error vectors (of weight $\leq t$) of length n. The scheme uses the same technique as that of hybrid encryption. The system parameters for the security parameter κ are as follows:

- Target Collision Resistant hash functions $h_1 : F_2^{(n-k)} \to \{0,1\}^\kappa$ and $h_2 : \{0,1\}^n \to D_{(n,t)}$.
- A hard-core function $h : D_{(n,t)} \to \{0,1\}^n$ where $\{0,1\}^n$ is the message space.
- An injective function $f_1 : \{0,1\}^\kappa \to \mathbb{F}_2^{n-k \times n-k}$ which takes binary vectors from a sufficiently large space as input, and outputs a full rank matrix H.
- An injective function $f_2 : \{0,1\}^\kappa \to \mathcal{P}_{n \times n}$ which takes binary vectors from a sufficiently large space as input and output a $n \times n$ permutation matrix P, for the Niederreiter cryptosystem.

Key Generation. For the security parameter 1^κ, the KeyGen is as follows:

- Randomly select two distinct $[n, k, 2t+1]$ Goppa codes with parity check matrices H_1, H_2 respectively.
- Randomly select an invertible matrix $Q_1 \in_R \mathbb{F}_2^{n-k \times n-k}$ and a $n \times n$ permutation matrices P_1, P_2.
- Define $\widetilde{H}_1 = Q_1 H_1 P_1$ and $\widetilde{H}_2 = H_2 P_2 \oplus H_1 P_1$.

Thus, we have:

- **Public Keys:** $\widetilde{H}_1$ & $\widetilde{H}_2$.
- **Secret Keys:** H_1, H_2, Q_1, P_1, P_2.

Encryption: On a message $m \in \mathbb{F}_2^n$ with $wt(m) \leq t$, the following steps constitute the encryption algorithm:

- Generate $c_1 \leftarrow h_1(\widetilde{H}_1 m^T)$ and $r \leftarrow h_2(m)$,
- Compute $H_{c_1} = f_1(c_1)$ and $P_{c_1} = f_2(c_1)$.
- Define $K_1 = \widetilde{H}_1 P_{c_1}$ and $K_2 = H_{c_1} \widetilde{H}_2 P_{c_1}$.
- Define $c_2 = K_1 r^T$, and $c_3 = K_2 r^T$.
- $c_4 = m \oplus h(r)$.

The ciphertext that is sent is $c = (c_1, c_2, c_3, c_4)$.

Decryption. The decryption on the ciphertext $c = (c_1, c_2, c_3, c_4)$ is done as follows:

Compute, $H_{c_1} \leftarrow f_1(c_1)$, $P_{c_1} \leftarrow f_2(c_1)$.

if $(\text{Decode}_{H_1}(Q_1^{-1} c_2) \to \perp)$

    return $\perp$.

else

    $r' \leftarrow P_{c_1}^T P_1^T \text{Decode}_{H_1}(Q_1^{-1} c_1)$

    if$(c_3 \neq H_{c_1} \widetilde{H}_2 P_{c_1} r'^T)$

        return $\perp$.

else

        $m' \leftarrow c_4 \oplus h(r')$

        if$(c_1 \neq h_1(\widetilde{H}_1 m'^T) || r' \neq h_2(m'))$

            return $\bot$.

        else

            return m'.

end

Correctness. For decryption of a valid ciphertext, H_{c_1} & P_{c_1} can be computed as c_1 is sent as the ciphertext. If the ciphertext is valid, then c_2 and c_3 are decodable syndromes for the error vector r' for K_1 and K_2 respectively. The knowledge of r' can be used to obtain m' from c_4 due to the property of the X-OR operation. Thus, as long as the decoding algorithm is correct, the decryption is correct for a valid ciphertext. If the ciphertext is invalid, the ciphertext is either rejected by the decoding algorithm (if c_2 is not a decodable syndrome), the consistency checking mechanism (if c_2 and c_3 are not the syndromes of the same error vector for K_1 and K_2 respectively) or the integrity check mechanism (if the decrypted message is not the message committed in c_1 or the encrypted key r' is not a commitment on m').

4.2   Security of the Scheme

Theorem 3. *The proposed scheme is PRIV-1CCA secure as long as h_1, h_2 are TCR hash functions, and the Goppa-code distinguishability and syndrome decoding of the corresponding parameters are hard to solve.*

The proof is given appendix due to space constraints. The proof is similar to the proof of hybrid encryption.

4.3   Parameters

From the previous sections, we have seen that the selection of parameters is important in defining the negligible advantage an adversary has, in solving the syndrome decoding problem and Goppa indistinguishability problem. Since, the required codes need not have a very high rate, the distinguisher attack [12] does not hold. Also these parameters ensures the target collision resistance of the hash functions. It also ensures that the functions f_1 and f_2 both injective. The parameters shown in Table 1 achieves a security greater than 2^{80}, which is the desired security bound. The schemes proposed by Edoardo Persichetti using Niederreiter encryption [29] and Cui et al. [8] using McEliece assumptions are in the random oracle model. The scheme presented by Fuller et al. [16] constructed a q-bounded PRIV-CCA secure Niederreiter variant in standard model using the κ repetition, which requires the more cipher text components and therefore have communication overhead. Our scheme is efficient as it requires only three cipher text components for hybrid encryption and four components for deterministic encryption. Comparing the schemes with κ repetition the size of cipher text is approximately $\kappa \times (n - k)$ whereas the cipher text size of our scheme is $\kappa + 2 \times (n - k)$.

5   Conclusion

In this paper, we have proposed efficient construction for a KEM and a deterministic encryption. The KEM was shown to be IND-CCA2 secure based on the syndrome decoding and the Goppa-code distinguishability hardness assumptions in the standard model. The deterministic encryption achieves PRIV-1CCA security based on the aforementioned assumption in the standard model. Both schemes avoided the use of κ-repetition paradigm. Hence, such schemes can be instantiated in practice using practical parameters as in [13]. Thus the KEM can be used to obtain a IND-CCA2 secure code-based hybrid encryption in the standard model. Also, the deterministic encryption can be used as an efficiently searchable encryption for securing remote databases. Bounded multi-message security (q bounded PRIV-CCA2) and its instantiation without κ-repetition paradigm using code-based assumptions remains open.

A   Appendix

A.1   Proof of Security for Deterministic Encryption

Proof: The proof is presented as a sequence of games, Game 0, Game 1 .... While, Game 0 fits the scheme exactly as in the PRIV-1CCA game. Subsequent games change the environment, such that the view of the adversary in discriminating between two consecutive games is at best negligible in κ or reduces to the solution of a hard-problem instance. We denote the challenger/simulator as a PPT algorithm $\mathcal{C}$ and the adversary of the system as a PPT algorithm $\mathcal{A}$.

Game 0. $\mathcal{C}$ adapts the proposed scheme directly to the PRIV-1CCA game. The system parameters are set as in the proposed scheme, with the security parameter κ. The key-generation oracle and the decryption oracle is run using the described scheme. Let M be a random variable over the message space with a min-entropy. Let $m^* \xleftarrow{\$} M$ and the function to be computed on m^* be f. $\mathcal{C}$ computes $c^* = (c_1^*, c_2^*, c_3^*, c_4^*) = \mathsf{Enc}(m^*)$. c^* is the "challenge ciphertext" given to $\mathcal{A}$,i.e., given c^*, $\mathcal{A}$ must compute $f(m^*)$. $\mathcal{A}$ outputs t, $t \leftarrow \mathcal{A}^{\mathcal{D}(\cdot)}(M, f, c^*)$. $\mathcal{A}$ wins if where $t == f(m^*)$.

Let the event that the adversary $\mathcal{A}$ wins the game be quantified by the random variable X_0. Then,

$$\mathbf{Real}_{\mathcal{AE}}(\mathcal{A}, M, f) = Pr[X_0] \qquad (7)$$

Game 1. Decryption Oracle is simulated by $\mathcal{C}$ as follows:

Input: The ciphertext $c = (c_1, c_2, c_3, c_4)$

Output: The message m.

if $(c_1 == c_1^*)$

    Return $\perp$

else

    $H_{c_1} \leftarrow f_1(c_1), P_{c_1} \leftarrow f_2(c_1)$

Compute $c_2' = Q_1^{-1} c_2$
Compute $c_2'' = H_{c_1} c_2'$
Compute $y = c_3 \oplus c_2''$
Compute $Q' = H_{c_1}$
   if $(\mathsf{Decode}_{H_2}(Q'^{-1}y) \to \perp)$ // Invalid ciphertext
    Return $\perp$
else
   Compute $r' = P_{c_1}^T P_2^T \mathsf{Decode}_{H_2}(Q'^{-1}y)$
   if $(c_2 \neq \tilde{H}_1 P_{c_1} r'^T$ OR $c_3 \neq H_{c_1} \tilde{H}_2 P_{c_1} r'^T)$
    Return $\perp$ // Ciphertext inconsistent
   else
    $m' \leftarrow c_4 \oplus h(r')$.
    if$(\ c_1 \neq h_1(\tilde{H}_1 m'^T) || r' \neq h_2(m'))$
      Return $\perp$
    else
      Return m'
end

Let the event that the adversary $\mathcal{A}$ wins in this game be quantified by the random variable X_1. The difference in the distribution (or view of the adversary) between X_0 and X_1 is the situation in which $\mathcal{C}$ returns $\perp$ if $c_1 = c_1^*$ in this game, during the decryption oracle. The simulator returns $\perp$ implying the ciphertext is invalid (as the integrity check will not hold). But, it can be seen that $\mathcal{A}$ may have given a valid ciphertext (that is not the challenge ciphertext), i.e., a ciphertext for some $m' \neq m^*$. Clearly, this would violate the target collision resistance of h_1 or of h_2. $\mathcal{H}$ is target collision resistant if for every polynomial time adversary $\mathcal{A}$ the TCR advantage is

$$Adv_{\mathcal{H}}^{\mathsf{TCR}}(A) = Pr[H(K, x_1) = H(K, x_2) : (x_1, st) \leftarrow^R A, K \leftarrow^R \mathcal{K}, x_2 \leftarrow^R A(K, st)] \tag{8}$$

of A against $\mathcal{H}$ is negligible(ϵ). That is in TCR the adversary must commit to an element in collision before seeing the hash key. As per Generalised Left Over Hash Lemma(LHL), TCR smooths out an input distribution (distribution of m in this paper) to nearly uniform on its range, provided that the input distribution has sufficient minimum entropy, since TCR comes under universal one-wayness [5,24]. Let $Adv_{h_1}^{\mathsf{TCR}}(\mathcal{A}) = \epsilon_1, Adv_{h_2}^{\mathsf{TCR}}(\mathcal{A}) = \epsilon_2$. Hence,

$$|Pr[X_0] - Pr[X_1]| \leq \epsilon_1 + \epsilon_2 \tag{9}$$

Game 2. Key Generation: The key-generation process is altered. $\mathcal{C}$ replaces the Goppa parity-check matrix of H_1 with the parity check matrix R of a random $[n, k, 2t + 1]$ code. Thus $H_1 \leftarrow R$. Also, the knowledge of the target message m^* is made use of. $\mathcal{C}$ computes $c^* = (c_1^*, c_2^*, c_3^*, c_4^*) = \mathsf{Enc}(m^*)$. The remainder of the key-generation process remains unchanged.

$$|Pr[X_2] = Pr[X_1]| \tag{10}$$

There is consistency with the decryption oracle described in the previous game. The only difference is the use of a random code instead of a Goppa code for H_1.

Game 3. Key for Challenge text and construct challenge: The Public key generated is again altered. Replace H_2 with parity check of random matrix R_2 so that now $\widetilde{H}_1$ and $\widetilde{H}_2$ are parity-check matrices of random codes. Thus, for the event that $\mathcal{A}$ wins **Game 2**, X_2, $\mathcal{C}$ can construct a Goppa-code distinguisher based on the difference in the distributions of X_2 and X_3 is distinguishing Goppa code with random code. $\mathcal{C}$ uses the challenge $K^\dagger$ and computes c^* using the altered public keys. The winning of this game is only by syndrome decoding of random code Thus, for the event that $\mathcal{A}$ wins Game3, X_3, $\mathcal{C}$ can construct a Goppa-code distinguisher based on the difference in the distributions of X_2 and X_3. Also compute challenge c^* using the new public keys. The winning of this game is solving syndrome decoding.

$$|Pr[X_3] - Pr[X_2]| \leq \mathsf{Adv}_{\mathcal{C}}^{\mathsf{CD}}(n, k) + 4(\sqrt[3]{n \cdot \mathsf{Adv}_{\mathcal{D}'}^{\mathsf{SD}}(n, k)}) \qquad (11)$$

Also, it can be noted that no information of m^* is revealed in c^*. It can be noted that generating a random c_4^* does not affect the validity of the ciphertext. This is due to the us of the Generalised Left-over Hash Lemma on all three functions h_1, h_2 (as the entropy of the message space is large), and the resultant use of the hash lemma on h_3 (the domain of which is the same as the range of h_2). Therefore,

$$\mathbf{Ideal}_{\mathcal{A}\mathcal{E}}(\mathcal{A}, M, f) = Pr[X_3] \qquad (12)$$

Since,

$$\mathsf{Adv}_{\mathsf{PKE},\mathcal{A}}^{priv-1cca}(\kappa) = |\mathbf{Real}_{\mathcal{A}\mathcal{E}}(\mathcal{A}, M, f) - \mathbf{Ideal}_{\mathcal{A}\mathcal{E}}(\mathcal{A}, M, f)|$$

Substituting Eqs. (6) and (10), we have

$$\mathsf{Adv}_{\mathsf{PKE},\mathcal{A}}^{priv-1cca}(\kappa) \leq |Pr[X_0] - Pr[X_3]|$$

By repeatedly applying the difference lemma and using the Eqs. (7)–(9), we get,

$$\mathsf{Adv}_{\mathsf{PKE},\mathcal{A}}^{priv-1cca}(\kappa) \leq \epsilon_1 + \epsilon_2 + \mathsf{Adv}_{\mathcal{C}}^{\mathsf{CD}}(n, k) + 4(\sqrt[3]{n \cdot \mathsf{Adv}_{\mathcal{D}'}^{\mathsf{SD}}(n, k)})$$

Thus, the advantage of the PPT adversary $\mathcal{A}$ in the PRIV-1CCA game is bounded by the target-collision resistance of h_1 and h_2, the Goppa-distinguishability of H_1 and the hardness of syndrome decoding. Thus, the proposed scheme is PRIV-1CCA secure as long as h_1 and h_2 are TCR hash functions, and the Goppa-code distinguishability and syndrome decoding of the corresponding parameters are hard to solve. $\qquad\square$

References

1. Agrawal, S., Boneh, D., Boyen, X.: Efficient lattice (H)IBE in the standard model. In: Gilbert, H. (ed.) EUROCRYPT 2010. LNCS, vol. 6110, pp. 553–572. Springer, Heidelberg (2010)
2. Bellare, M., Boldyreva, A., O'Neill, A.: Deterministic and efficiently searchable encryption. In: Menezes [23], pp. 535–552
3. Bellare, M., Fischlin, M., O'Neill, A., Ristenpart, T.: Deterministic encryption: definitional equivalences and constructions without random oracles. In: Wagner [35], pp. 360–378
4. Bernstein, D.J., Lange, T., Peters, C.: Attacking and defending the McEliece cryptosystem. In: Buchmann, J., Ding, J. (eds.) PQCrypto 2008. LNCS, vol. 5299, pp. 31–46. Springer, Heidelberg (2008)
5. Boldyreva, A., Fehr, S., O'Neill, A.: On notions of security for deterministic encryption, and efficient constructions without random oracles. In: Wagner [35], pp. 335–359
6. Canetti, R., Goldreich, O., Halevi, S.: The random oracle methodology, revisited. J. ACM **51**(4), 557–594 (2004)
7. Cramer, R., Shoup, V.: Design and analysis of practical public-key encryption schemes secure against adaptive chosen ciphertext attack. SIAM J. Comput. **33**, 167–226 (2003)
8. Cui, Y., Morozov, K., Kobara, K., Imai, H.: Efficient constructions of deterministic encryption from hybrid encryption and code-based PKE. In: Bras-Amorós, M., Høholdt, T. (eds.) AAECC-18 2009. LNCS, vol. 5527, pp. 159–168. Springer, Heidelberg (2009)
9. Dodis, Y., Ostrovsky, R., Reyzin, L., Smith, A.: Fuzzy extractors: how to generate strong keys from biometrics and other noisy data. SIAM J. Comput. **38**(1), 97–139 (2008)
10. Dowsley, R., Müller-Quade, J., Nascimento, A.C.A.: A CCA2 secure public key encryption scheme based on the McEliece assumptions in the standard model. In: Fischlin, M. (ed.) CT-RSA 2009. LNCS, vol. 5473, pp. 240–251. Springer, Heidelberg (2009)
11. Faugére, J.-C., Otmani, A., Perret, L., Tillich, J.-P.: Algebraic cryptanalysis of McEliece variants with compact keys - toward a complexity analysis. In: SCC '10: Proceedings of the 2nd International Conference on Symbolic Computation and Cryptography, RHUL, June 2010, pp. 45–55 (2010)
12. Faugère, J.-C., Gauthier, V., Otmani, A., Perret, L., Tillich, J.-P.: A distinguisher for high rate McEliece cryptosystems. In: Information Theory Workshop (ITW). IEEE (2011)
13. Finiasz, M., Sendrier, N.: Security bounds for the design of code-based cryptosystems. In: Matsui, M. (ed.) ASIACRYPT 2009. LNCS, vol. 5912, pp. 88–105. Springer, Heidelberg (2009)
14. Freeman, D.M., Goldreich, O., Kiltz, E., Rosen, A., Segev, G.: More constructions of lossy and correlation-secure trapdoor functions. In: Nguyen, P.Q., Pointcheval, D. (eds.) PKC 2010. LNCS, vol. 6056, pp. 279–295. Springer, Heidelberg (2010)
15. Fujisaki, E., Okamoto, T.: Secure integration of asymmetric and symmetric encryption schemes. In: Wiener, M. (ed.) CRYPTO 1999. LNCS, vol. 1666, pp. 537–554. Springer, Heidelberg (1999)
16. Fuller, B., O'Neill, A., Reyzin, L.: A unified approach to deterministic encryption: new constructions and a connection to computational entropy. In: Cramer, R. (ed.) TCC 2012. LNCS, vol. 7194, pp. 582–599. Springer, Heidelberg (2012)

17. Niederreiter, H.: Knapsack-type cryptosystems and algebraic coding theory. Prob. Contr. Inf. Theor. **15**, 159–166 (1986)
18. Hofheinz, D., Kiltz, E.: Secure hybrid encryption from weakened key encapsulation. In: Menezes [23], pp. 553–571
19. Kiltz, E., Pietrzak, K., Stam, M., Yung, M.: A new randomness extraction paradigm for hybrid encryption. In: Joux, A. (ed.) EUROCRYPT 2009. LNCS, vol. 5479, pp. 590–609. Springer, Heidelberg (2009)
20. Kurosawa, K., Desmedt, Y.G.: A new paradigm of hybrid encryption scheme. In: Franklin, M. (ed.) CRYPTO 2004. LNCS, vol. 3152, pp. 426–442. Springer, Heidelberg (2004)
21. Lucks, S.: A variant of the Cramer-Shoup cryptosystem for groups of unknown order. In: Zheng, Y. (ed.) ASIACRYPT 2002. LNCS, vol. 2501, pp. 27–45. Springer, Heidelberg (2002)
22. Preetha Mathew, K., Vasant, S., Venkatesan, S., Pandu Rangan, C.: An efficient IND-CCA2 secure variant of the Niederreiter encryption scheme in the standard model. In: Susilo, W., Mu, Y., Seberry, J. (eds.) ACISP 2012. LNCS, vol. 7372, pp. 166–179. Springer, Heidelberg (2012)
23. Menezes, A. (ed.): CRYPTO 2007. LNCS, vol. 4622. Springer, Heidelberg (2007)
24. Naor, M., Yung, M.: Universal one-way hash functions and their cryptographic applications. pp. 33–43 (1989)
25. Niebuhr, R., Cayrel, P.-L.: Broadcast attacks against code-based schemes. In: Armknecht, F., Lucks, S. (eds.) WEWoRC 2011. LNCS, vol. 7242, pp. 1–17. Springer, Heidelberg (2012)
26. Nojima, R., Imai, H., Kobara, K., Morozov, K.: Semantic security for the McEliece cryptosystem without random oracles. Des. Codes Cryptogr. **49**(1–3), 289–305 (2008)
27. Patterson, N.: The algebraic decoding of Goppa codes. IEEE Trans. Inf. Theor. **21**(2), 203–207 (1975)
28. Peikert, C., Waters, B.: Lossy trapdoor functions and their applications. In: Dwork, C. (ed.) STOC, pp. 187–196. ACM (2008)
29. Persichetti, E.: Secure and anonymous hybrid encryption from coding theory. In: Gaborit, P. (ed.) PQCrypto 2013. LNCS, vol. 7932, pp. 174–187. Springer, Heidelberg (2013)
30. Persichetti, E.: On a CCA2-secure variant of McEliece in the standard model. In: IACR Cryptology ePrint Archive (2012). http://eprint.iacr.org/2012/268
31. McEliece, R.J.: A public-key cryptosystem based on algebraic coding theory. JPL DSN Progress Report, pp. 114–116 (1978)
32. Rosen, A., Segev, G.: Chosen-ciphertext security via correlated products. In: Reingold, O. (ed.) TCC 2009. LNCS, vol. 5444, pp. 419–436. Springer, Heidelberg (2009)
33. Shor, P.W.: Polynomial time algorithms for discrete logarithms and factoring on a quantum computer. In: ANTS, p. 289 (1994)
34. Shoup, V.: Using hash functions as a hedge against chosen ciphertext attack. In: Preneel, B. (ed.) EUROCRYPT 2000. LNCS, vol. 1807, p. 275. Springer, Heidelberg (2000)
35. Wagner, D. (ed.): CRYPTO 2008. LNCS, vol. 5157. Springer, Heidelberg (2008)

Author Index

Printed in the United States
By Bookmasters